LOVE LETTERS to trump

Gerry Courtney

Printed in the United States of America

ISBN 978-0-692-19920-6

CONTENTS

Introduction

I have been photographing the *"Love Letters"* to trump for the past twenty months. Resisters have attended these marches with all kinds of signs: Some were filled with incredible bitterness, unique art, and penetrating observations.

For the purpose of this book I chose the *"Love Letters"* based upon; humor, creative art, and insightful statements.

As you read the signs, you may be taken back to the issues and words cosigned to a particular time of the trump regime. In this way, *"Love Letters to trump"* serves as a historical document.

I hope you become informed, inspired, as well as find humor during these dangerous times.

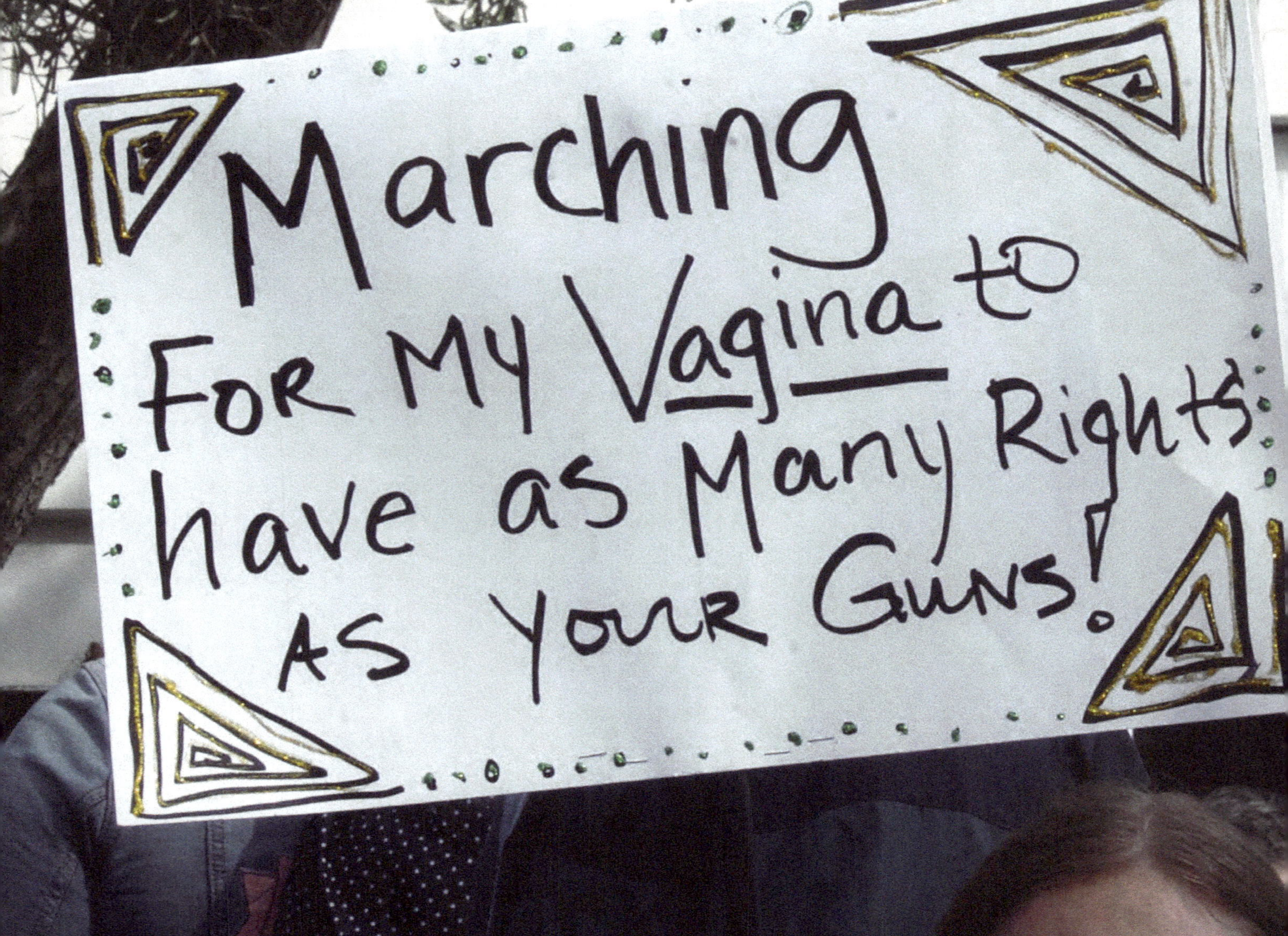

Womens' March 2017

Women's marches 1/21/17

Nearly 100,000 Resisters took to the streets of Oakland and San Francisco to display their love letters to trump.

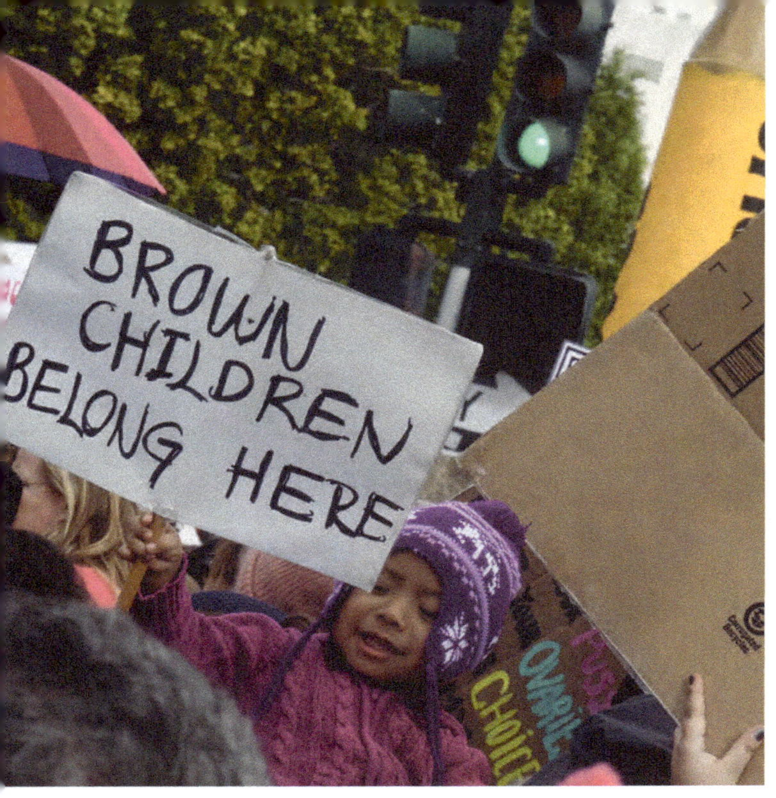
BROWN
CHILDREN
BELONG HERE

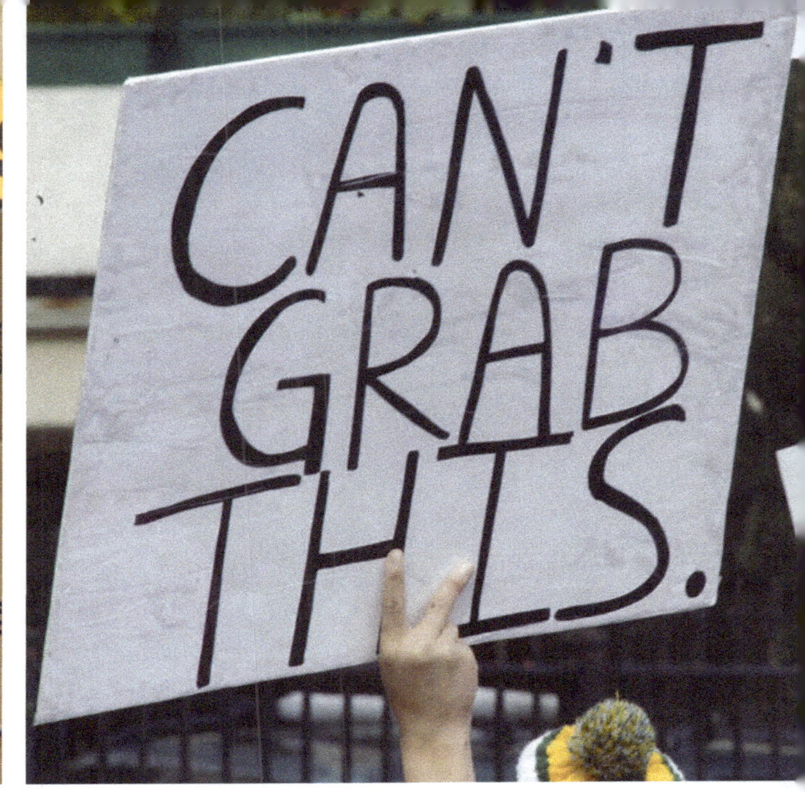
CAN'T
GRAB
THIS.

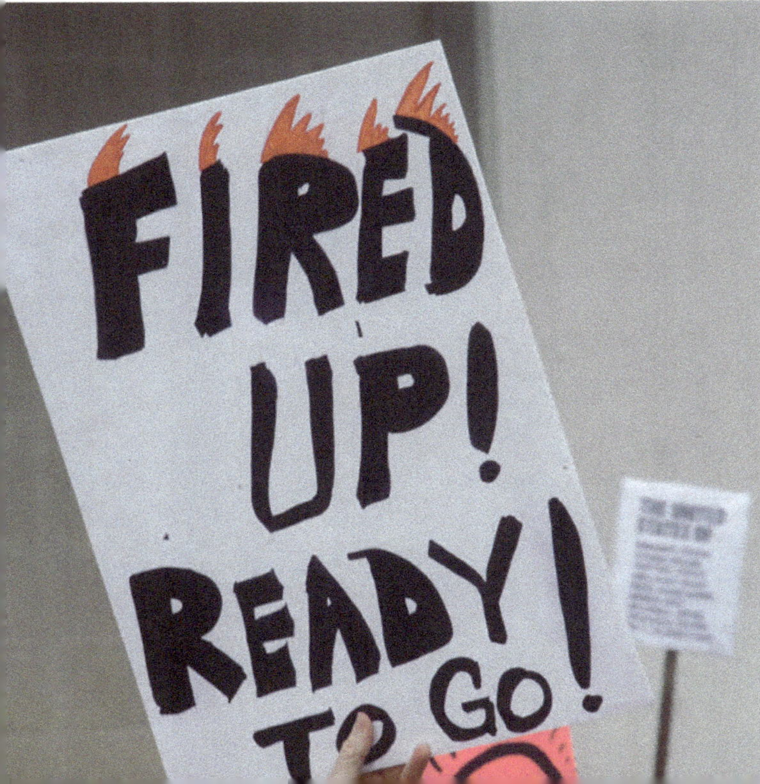
FIRED
UP!
READY !
TO GO !

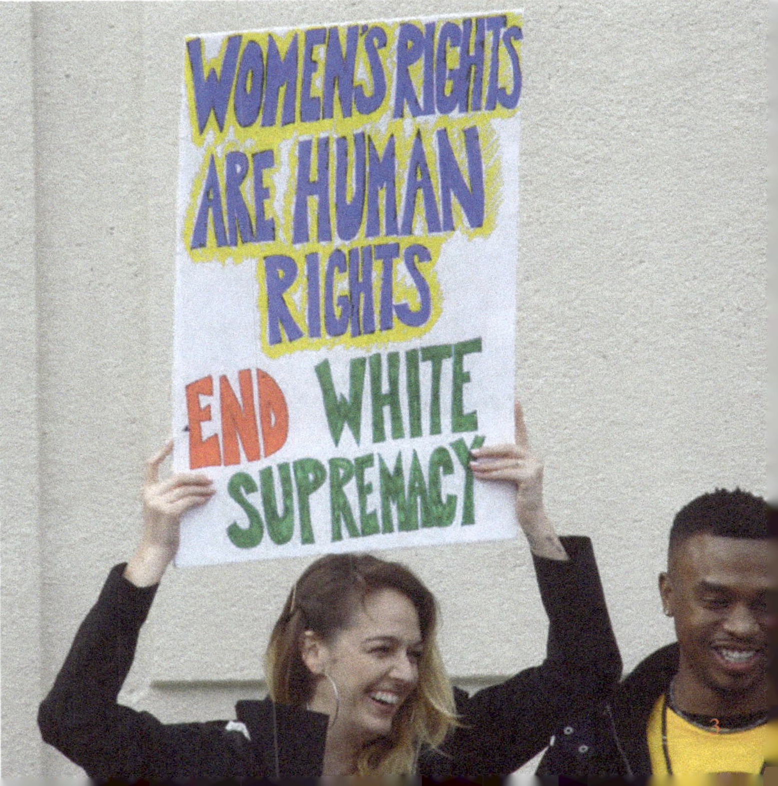
WOMEN'S RIGHTS
ARE HUMAN
RIGHTS
END WHITE
SUPREMACY

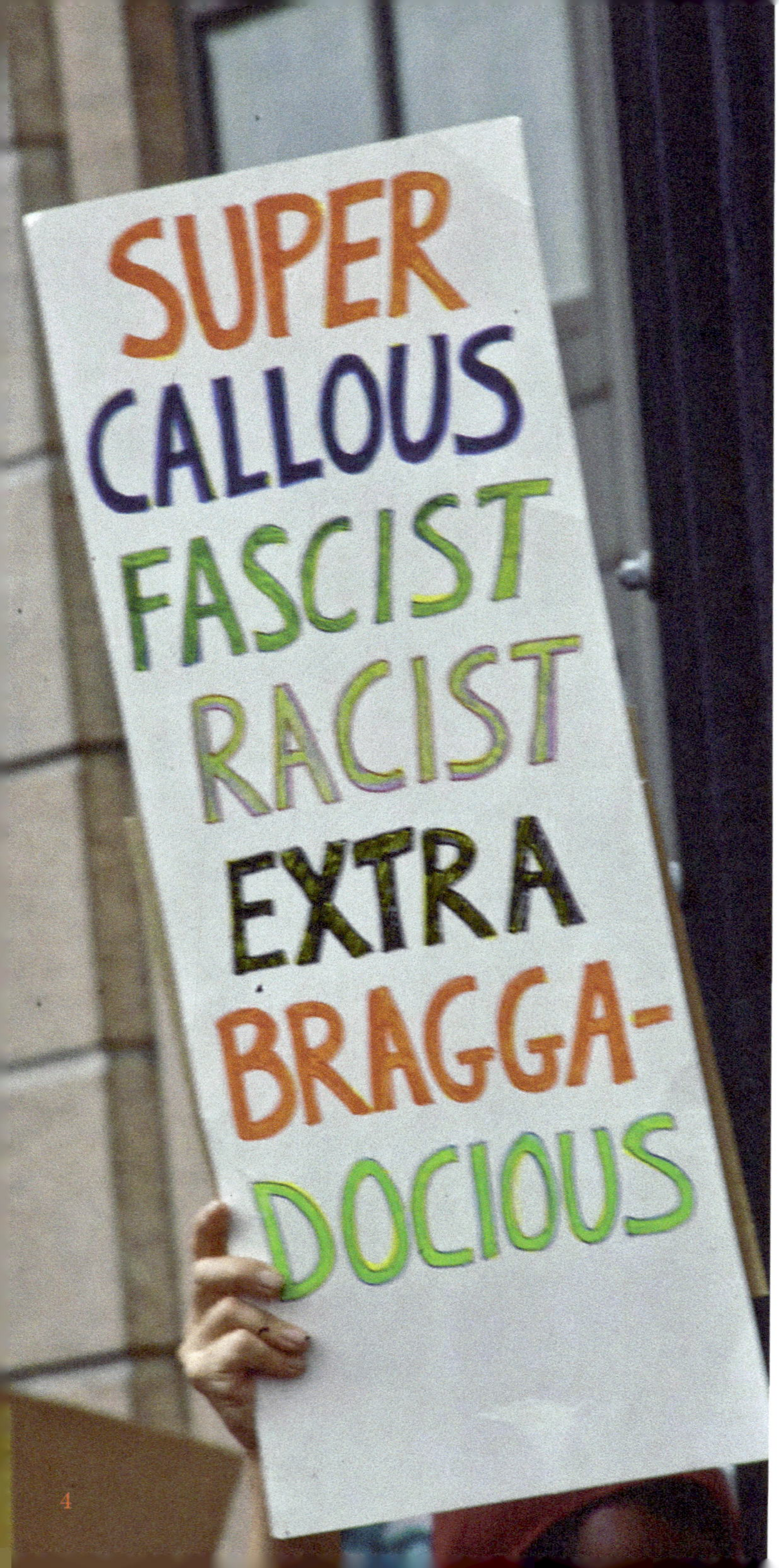

SUPER
CALLOUS
FASCIST
RACIST
EXTRA
BRAGGA-
DOCIOUS

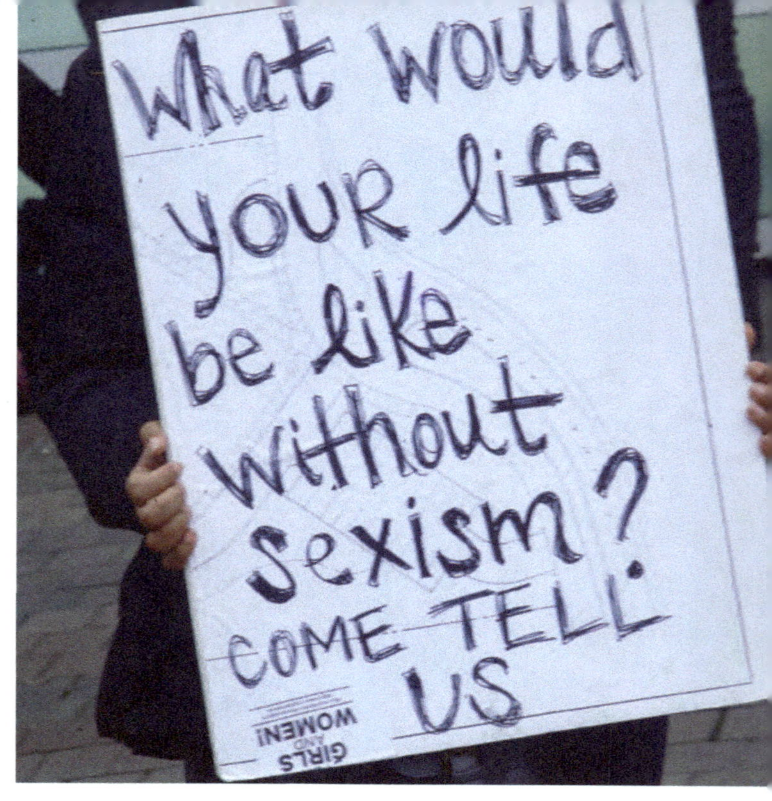

What would
your life
be like
without
sexism?
COME TELL
US
GIRLS AND WOMEN!

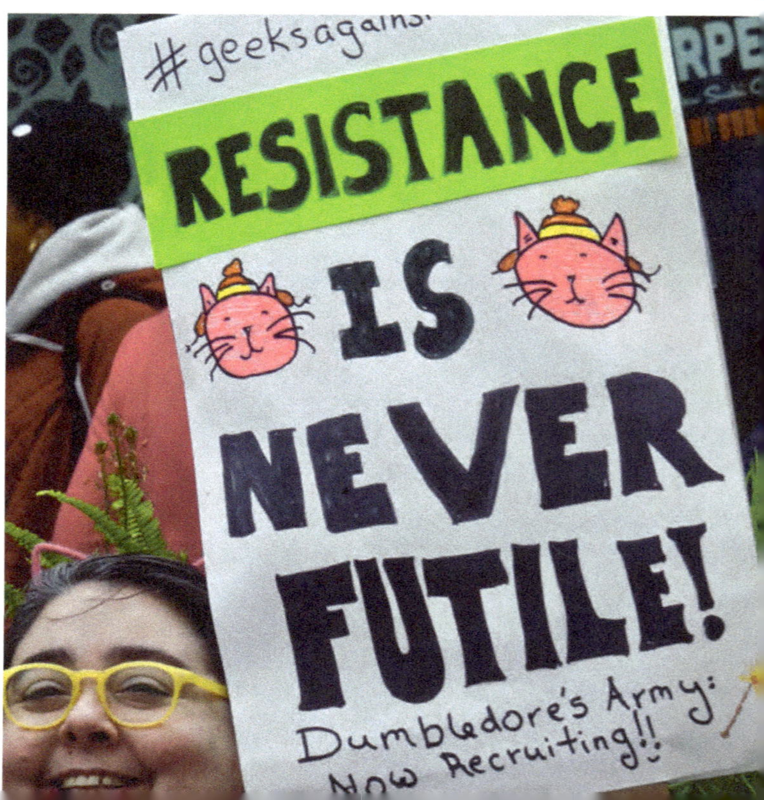

#geeksagainst
RESISTANCE
IS
NEVER
FUTILE!
Dumbledore's Army:
Now Recruiting!!

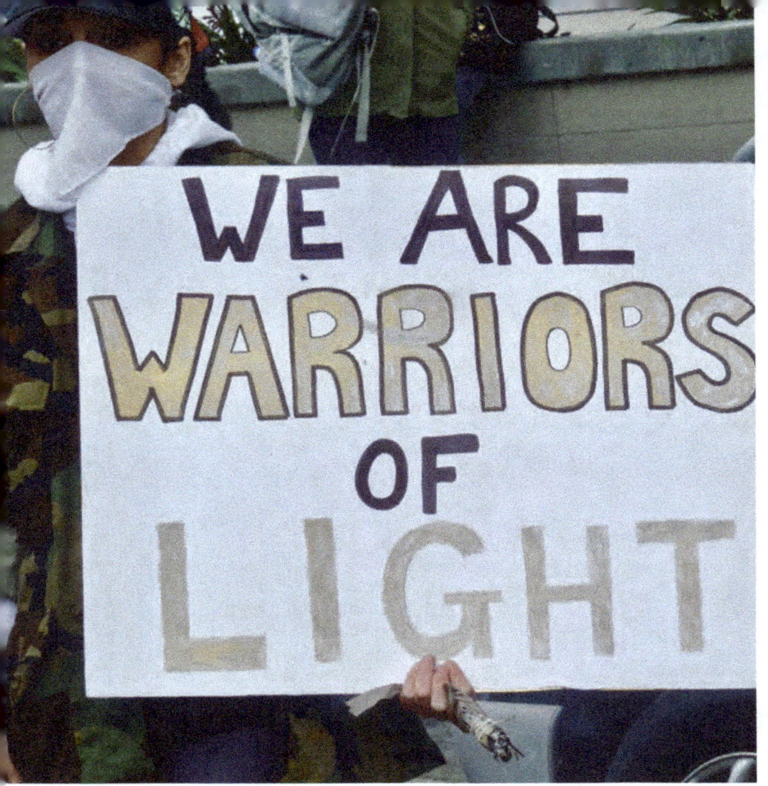

WE ARE
WARRIORS
OF
LIGHT

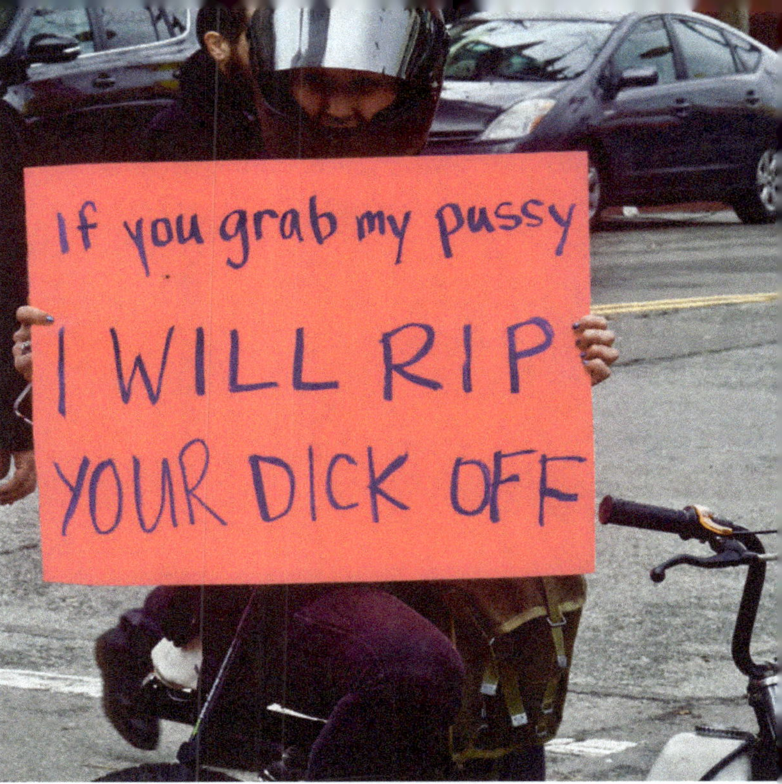

If you grab my pussy
I WILL RIP
YOUR DICK OFF

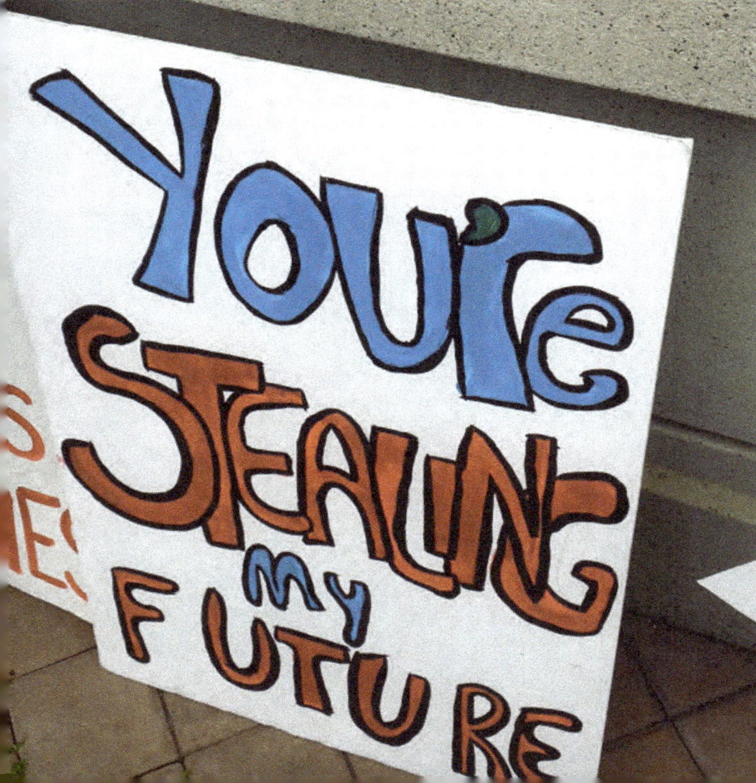

You're
STEALING
MY
FUTURE

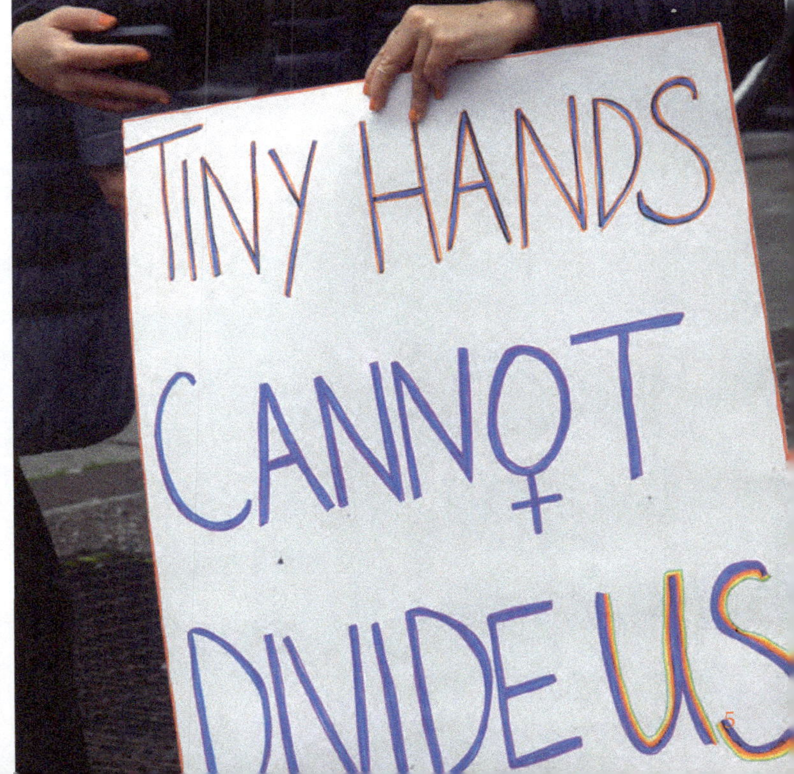

TINY HANDS
CANNOT
DIVIDE US

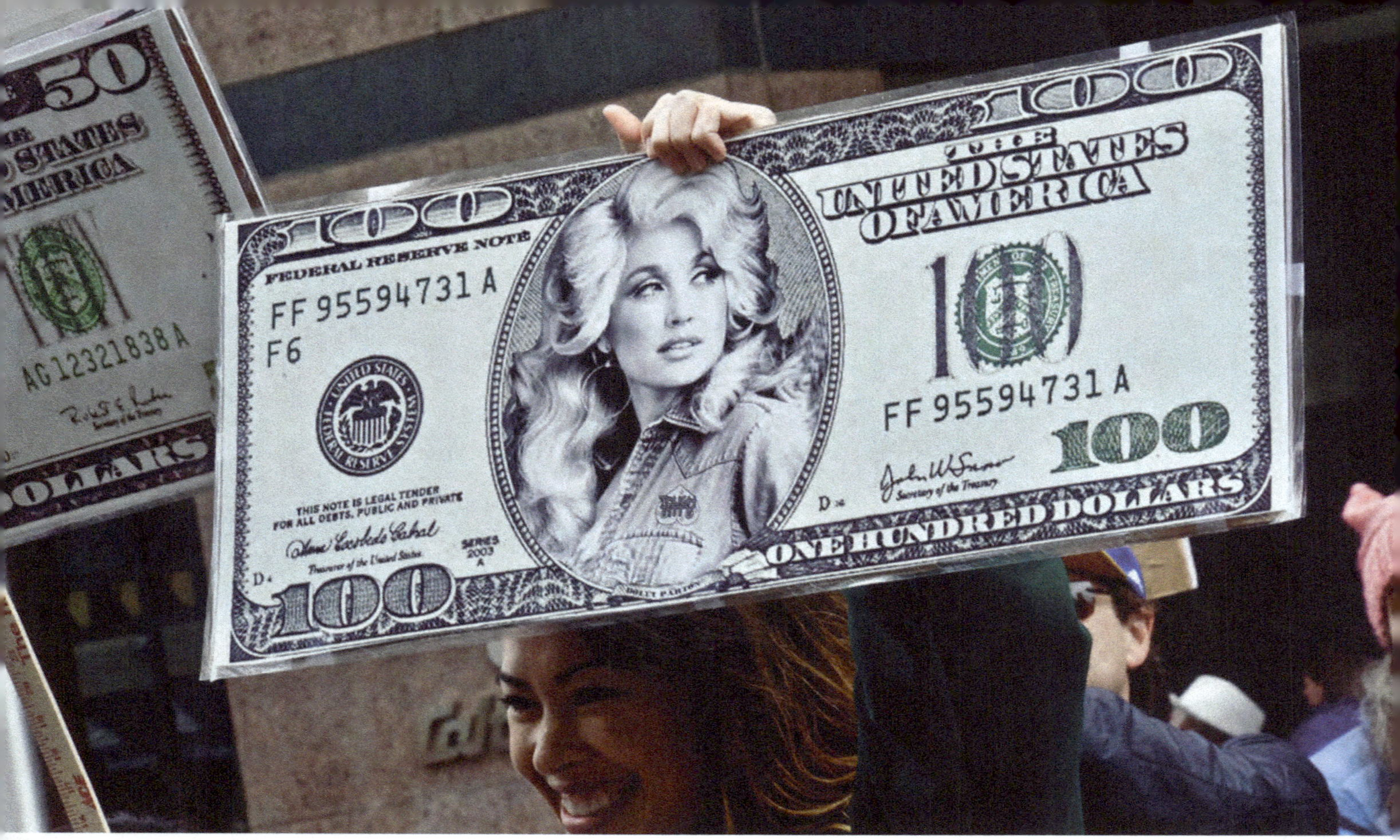

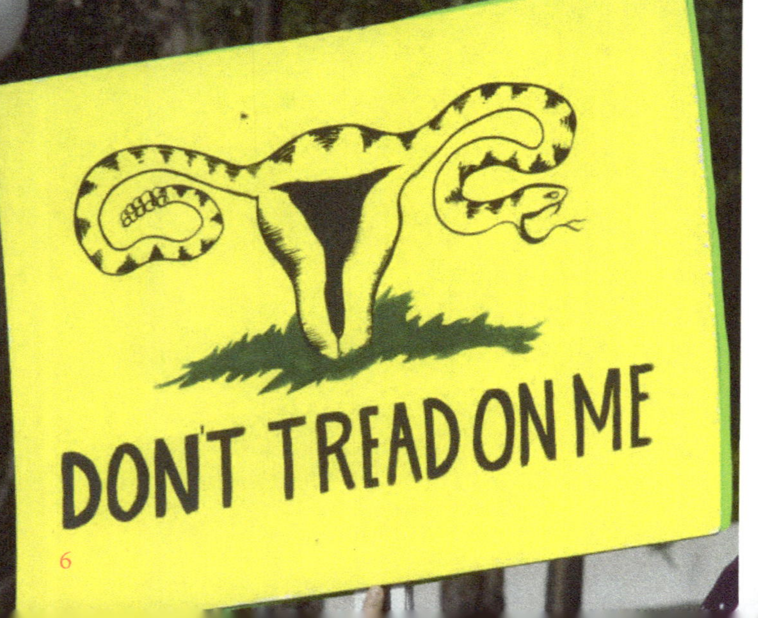
DON'T TREAD ON ME

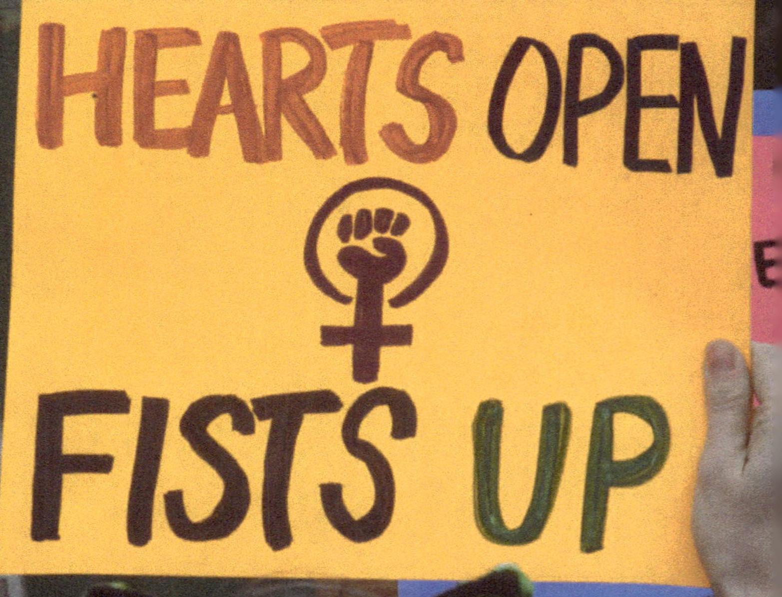
HEARTS OPEN
FISTS UP

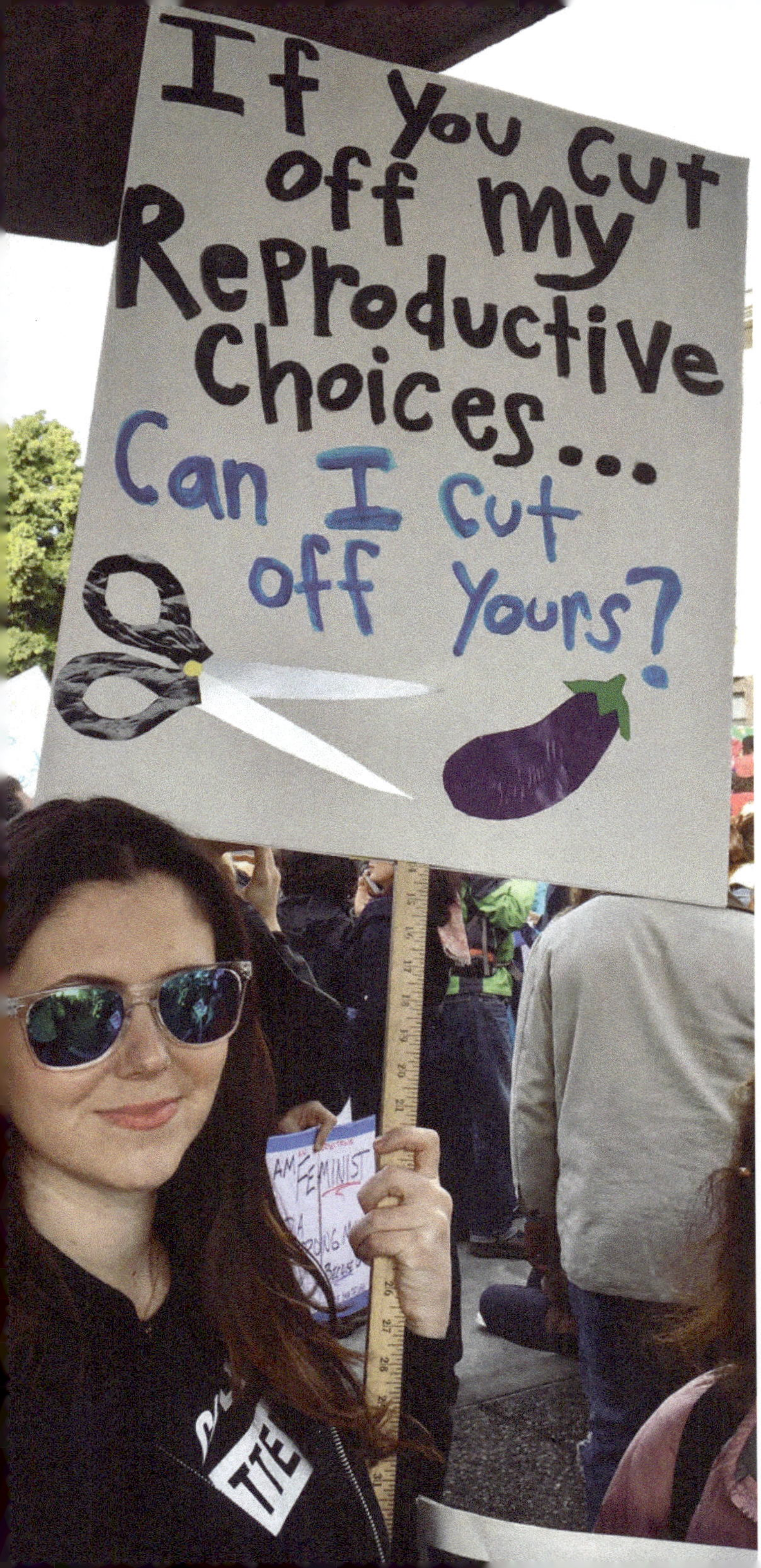

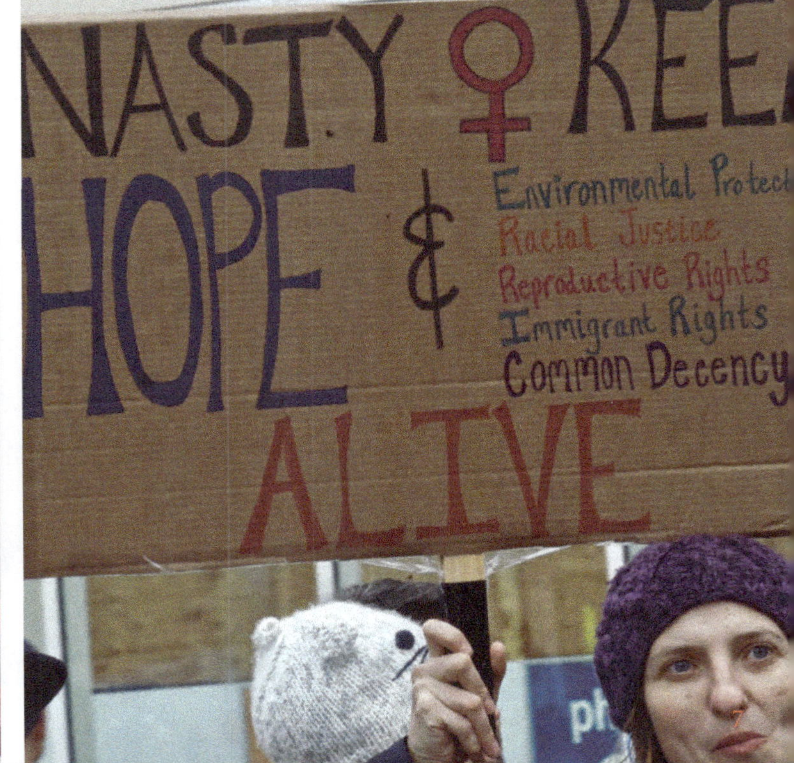
If you cut off my Reproductive Choices...
Can I cut off Yours?
I've been to the future. 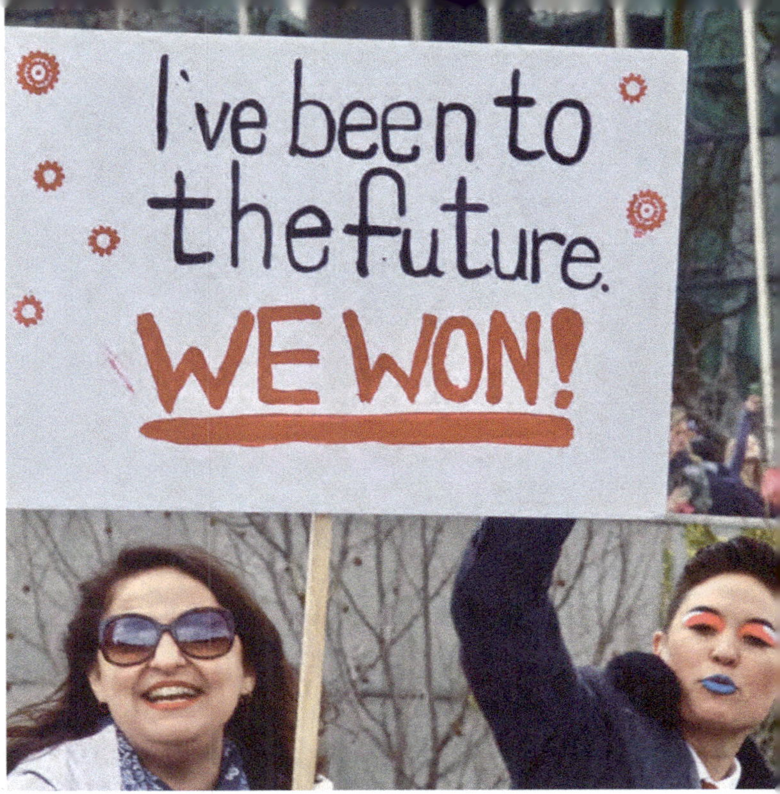
WE WON!
NASTY
KEE
HOPE &
ALIVE
Environmental Protec
Racial Justice
Reproductive Rights
Immigrant Rights
Common Decency

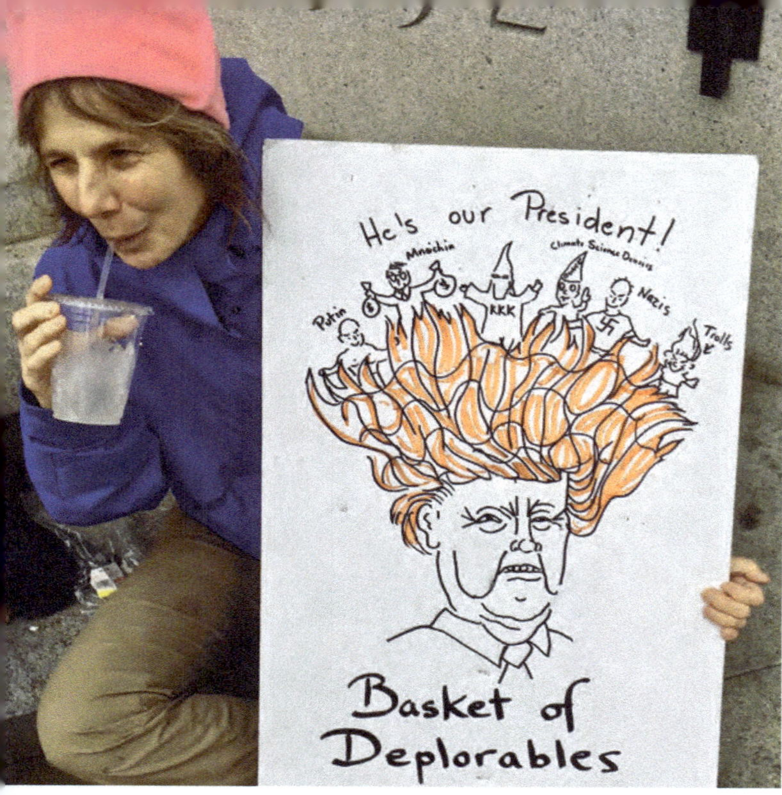
He's our President!
Mnuchin
Climate Science Denier
Putin
RKK
Nazis
Trolls
Basket of
Deplorables

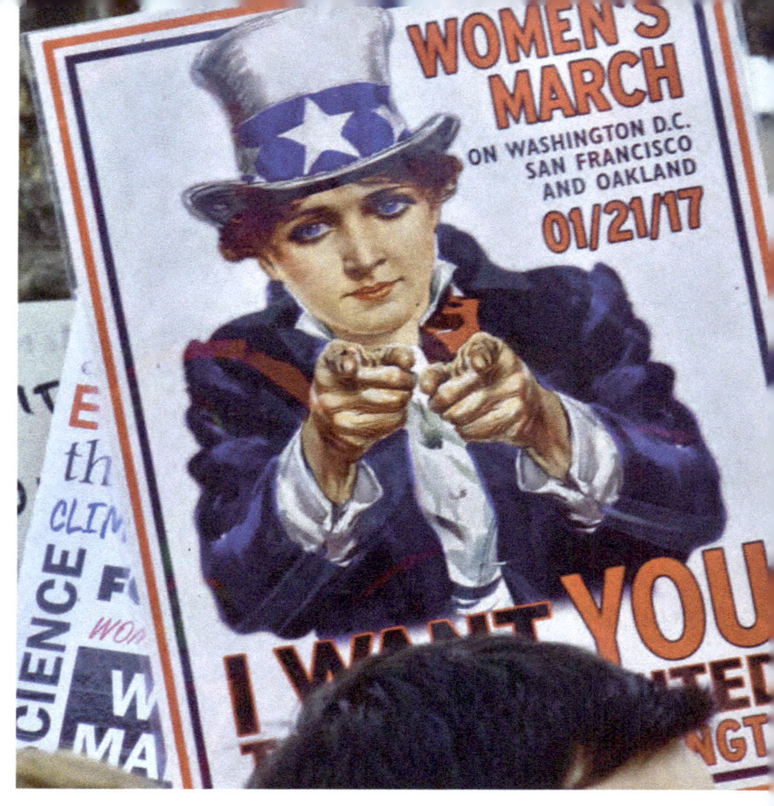
WOMEN'S
MARCH
ON WASHINGTON D.C.
SAN FRANCISCO
AND OAKLAND
01/21/17
I WANT YOU
SCIENCE
CLIM
F
WON
W
MA

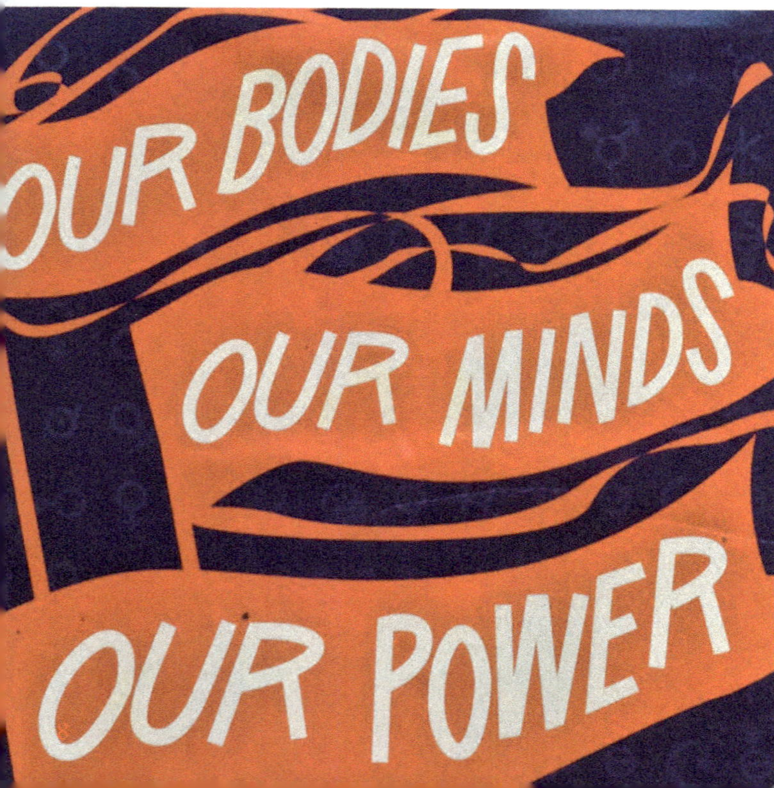
OUR BODIES
OUR MINDS
OUR POWER

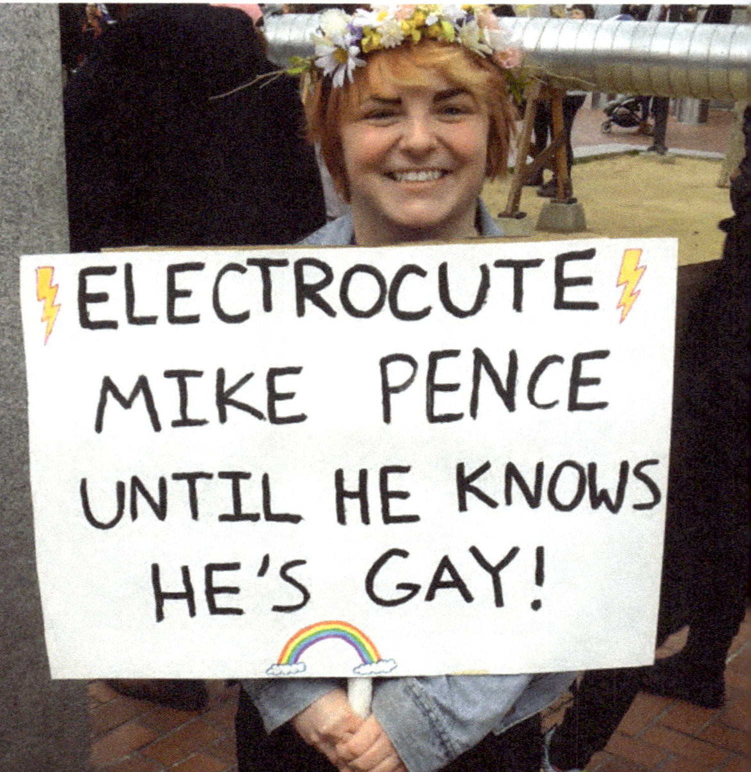
ELECTROCUTE
MIKE PENCE
UNTIL HE KNOWS
HE'S GAY!

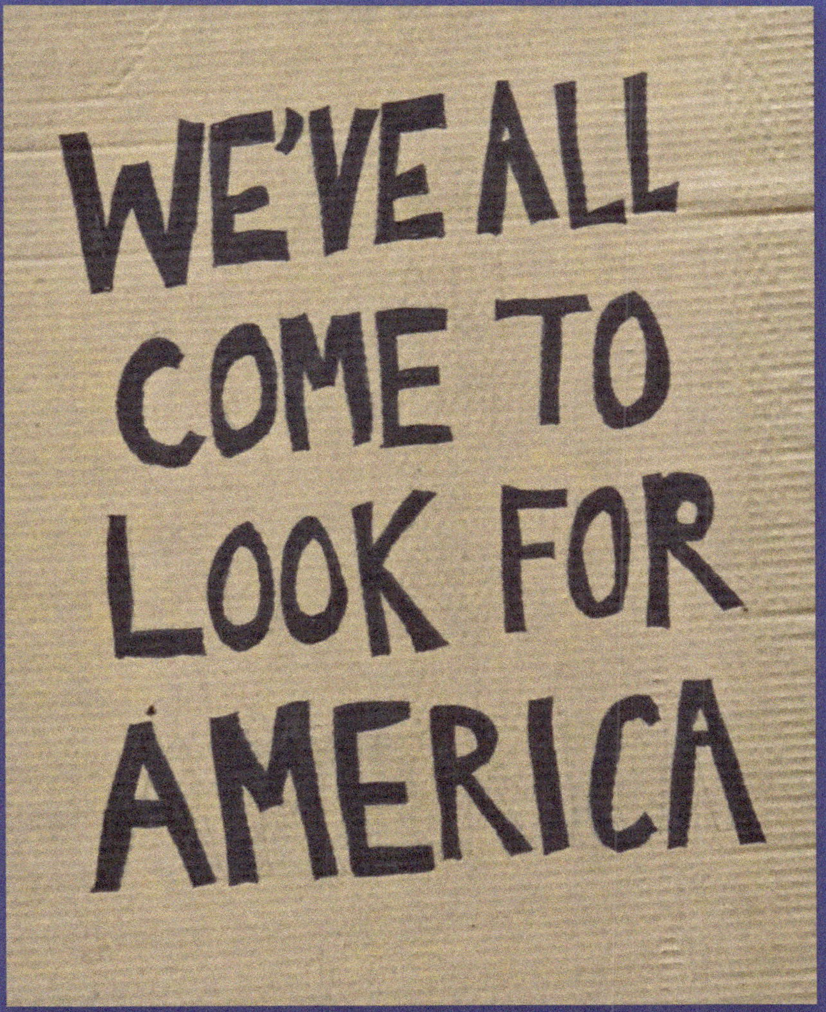

WE'VE ALL
COME TO
LOOK FOR
AMERICA

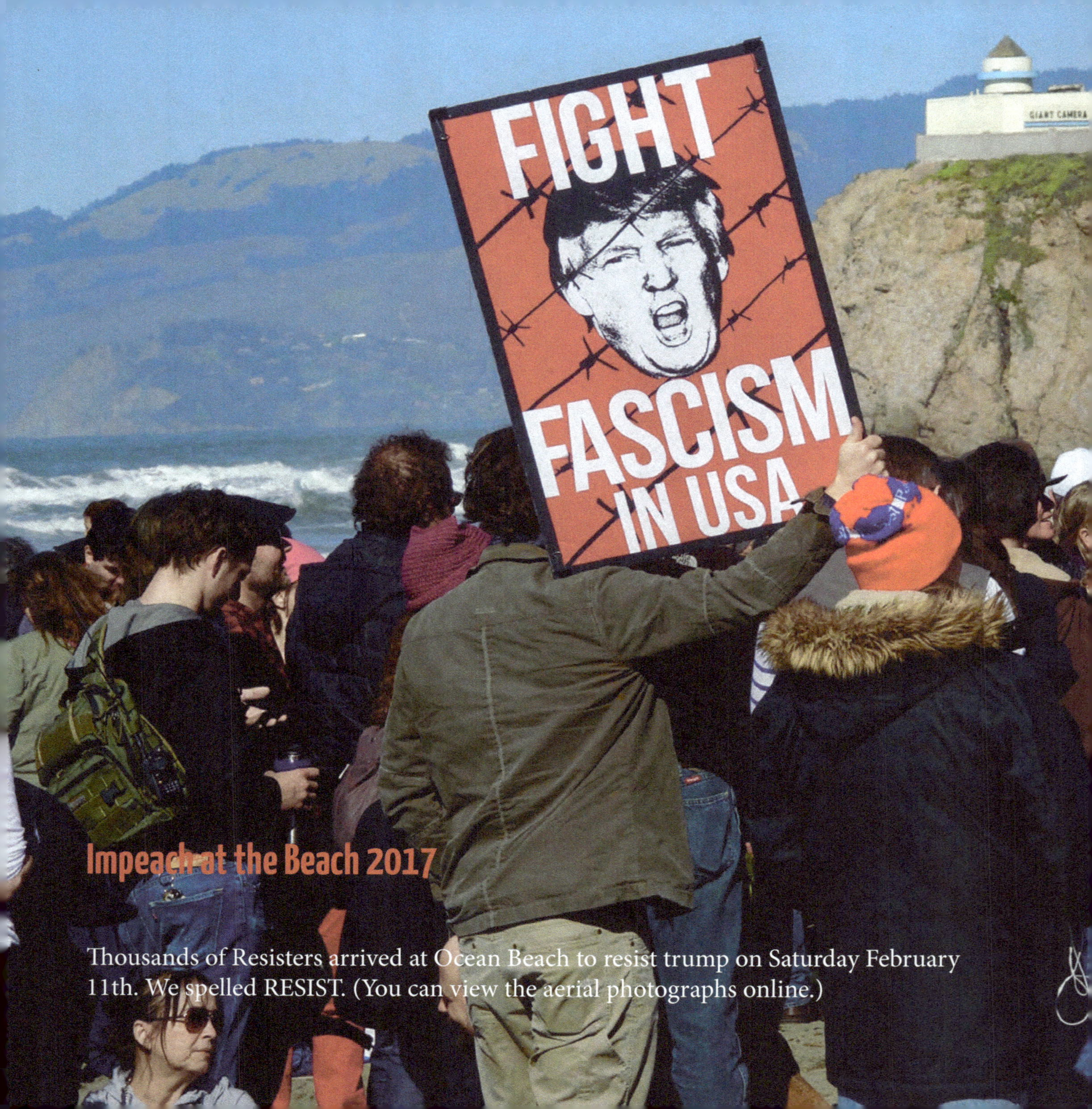

Impeach at the Beach 2017

Thousands of Resisters arrived at Ocean Beach to resist trump on Saturday February 11th. We spelled RESIST. (You can view the aerial photographs online.)

ONCE YOU BUILD IT, THEY WILL COME AND TEAR IT DOWN!

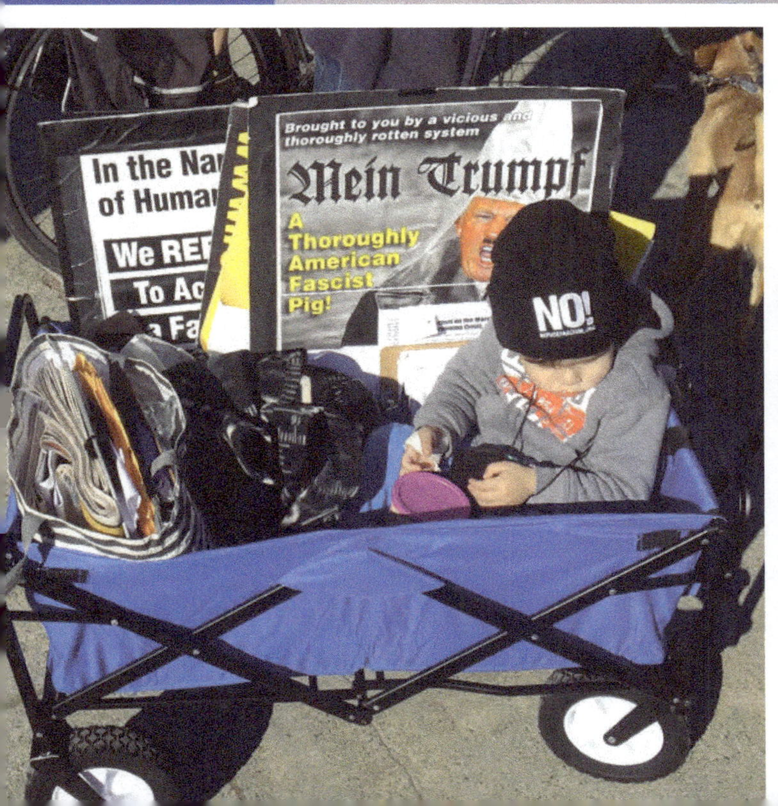

In the Name of Humanity
We REFUSE To Accept a Fascist
Brought to you by a vicious and thoroughly rotten system
Mein Trumpf
A Thoroughly American Fascist Pig!
NO!

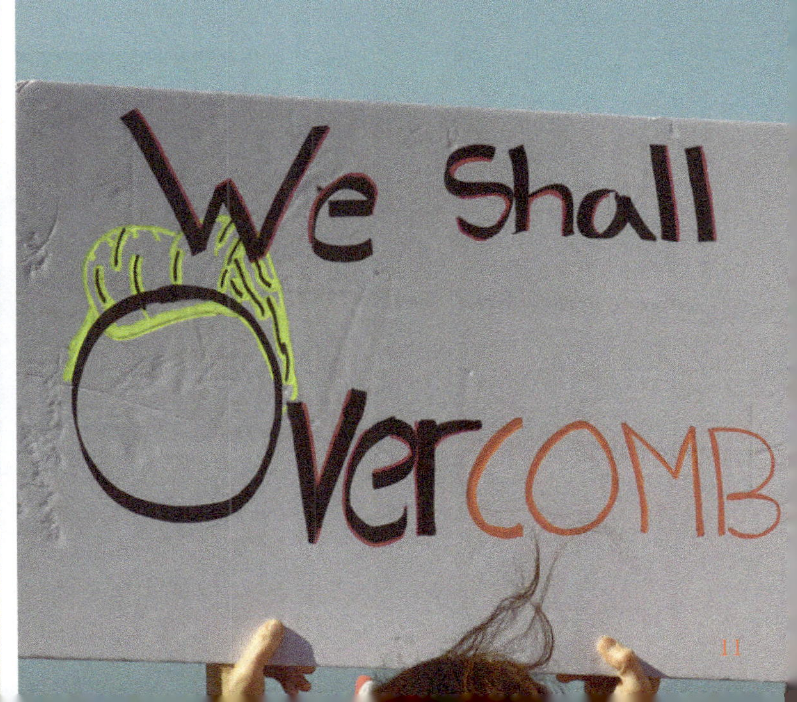

We Shall OverCOMB

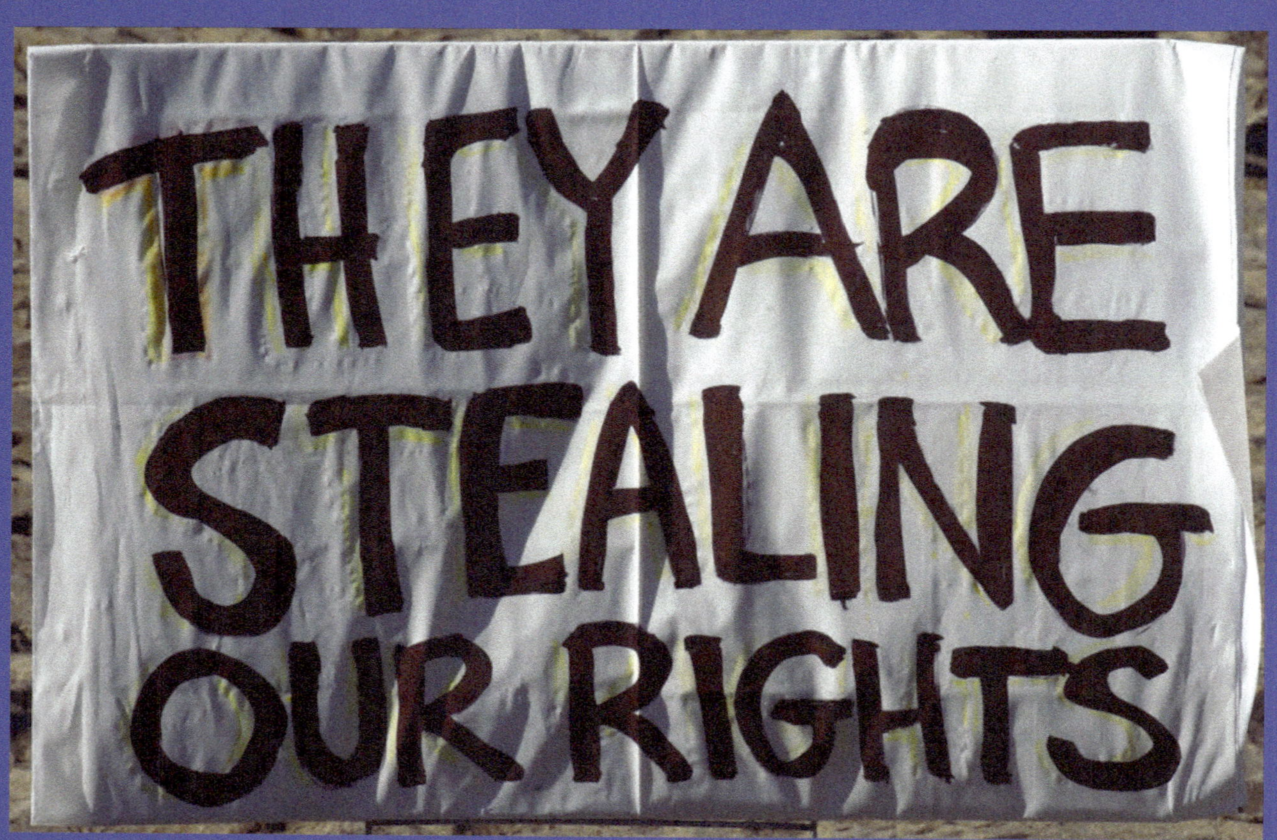

12

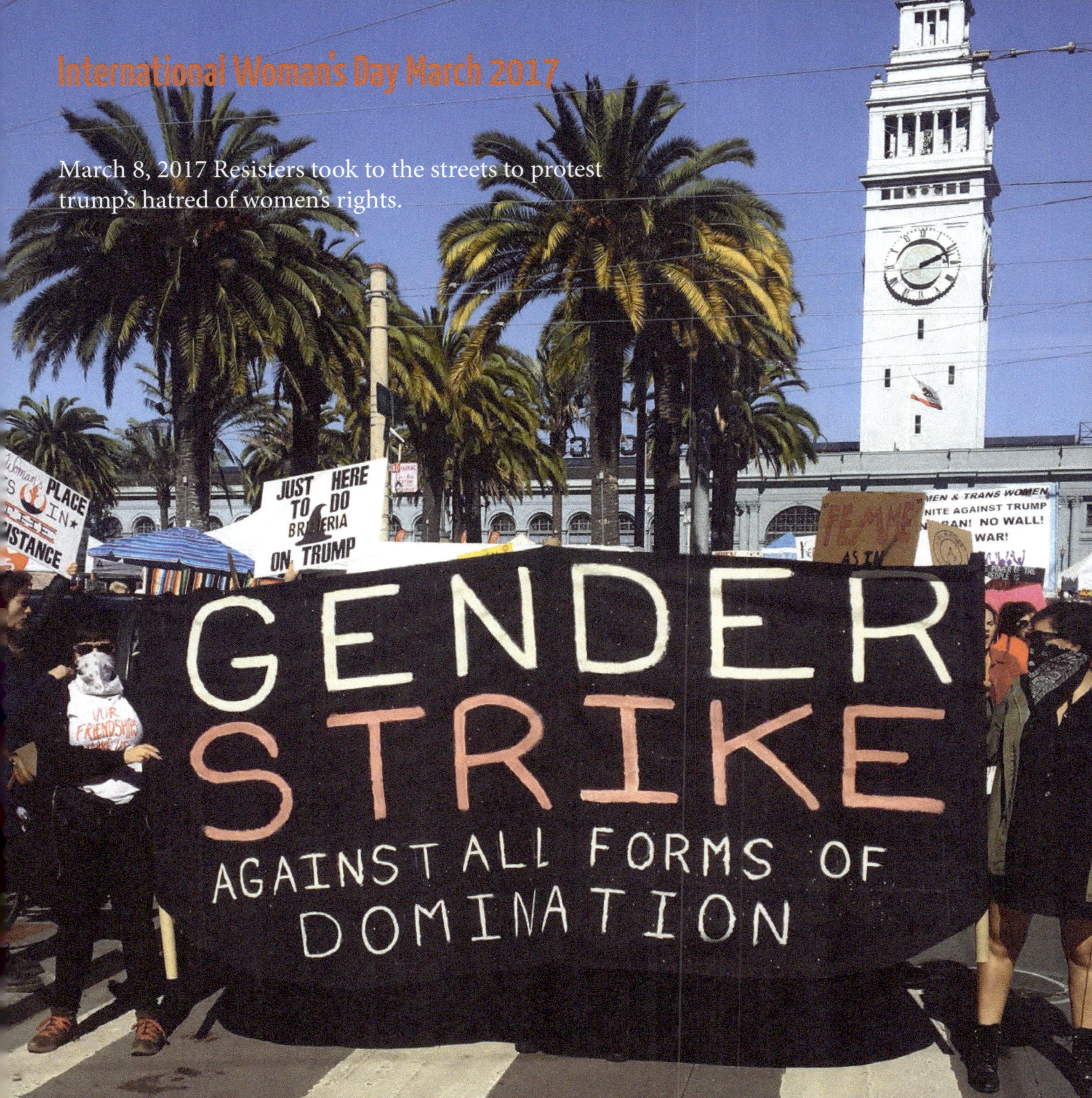

International Woman's Day March 2017
March 8, 2017 Resisters took to the streets to protest trump's hatred of women's rights.
WOMAN'S PLACE IS IN THE RESISTANCE
JUST HERE TO DO BRUJERIA ON TRUMP
FEMME AS IN
MEN & TRANS WOMEN UNITE AGAINST TRUMP NO BAN! NO WALL! NO WAR!
OUR FRIENDSHIP
GENDER STRIKE
AGAINST ALL FORMS OF DOMINATION

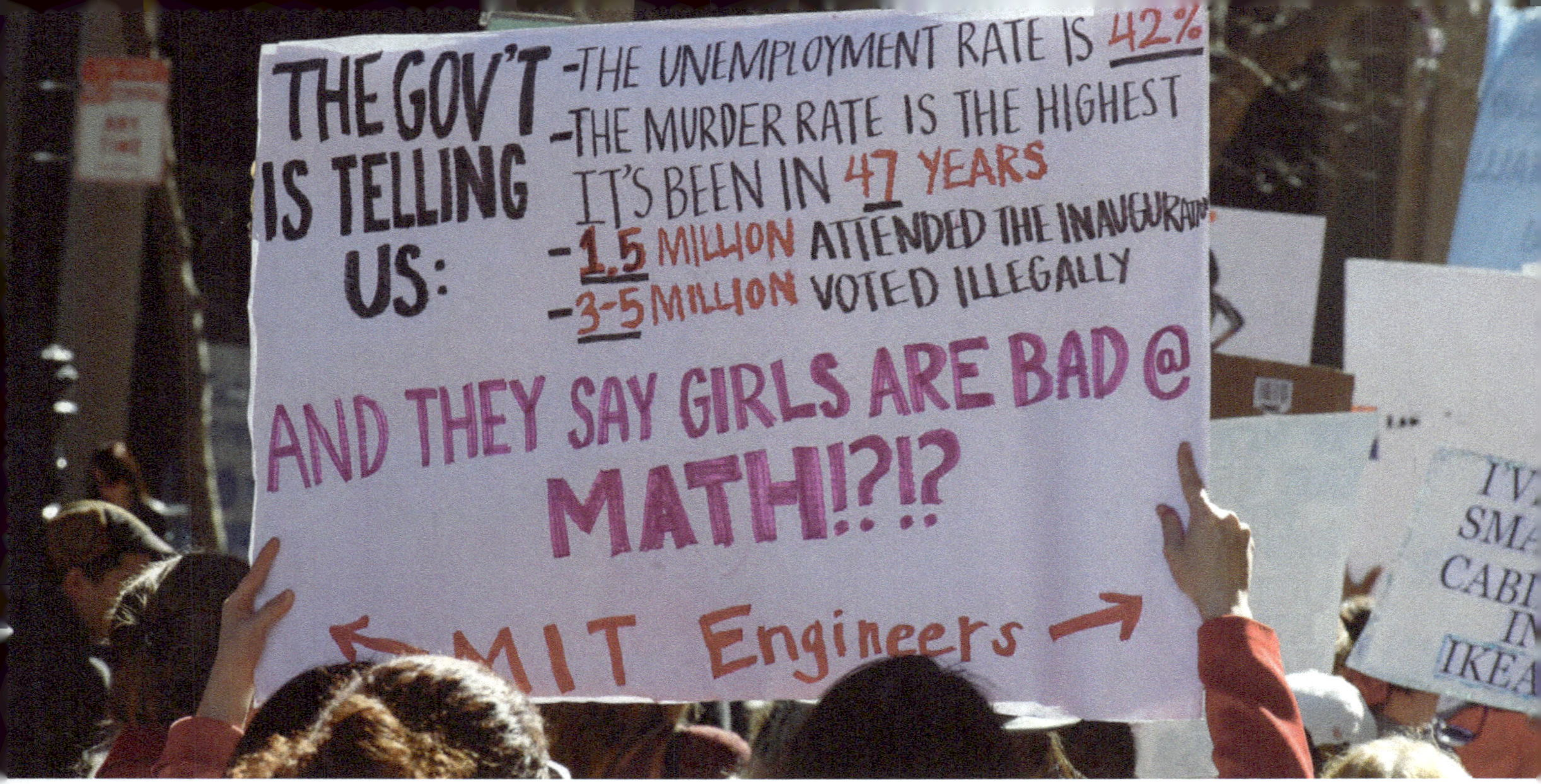

THE GOV'T IS TELLING US:
-THE UNEMPLOYMENT RATE IS 42%
-THE MURDER RATE IS THE HIGHEST IT'S BEEN IN 47 YEARS
-1.5 MILLION ATTENDED THE INAUGURATION
-3-5 MILLION VOTED ILLEGALLY
AND THEY SAY GIRLS ARE BAD @ MATH!?!?
← MIT Engineers →

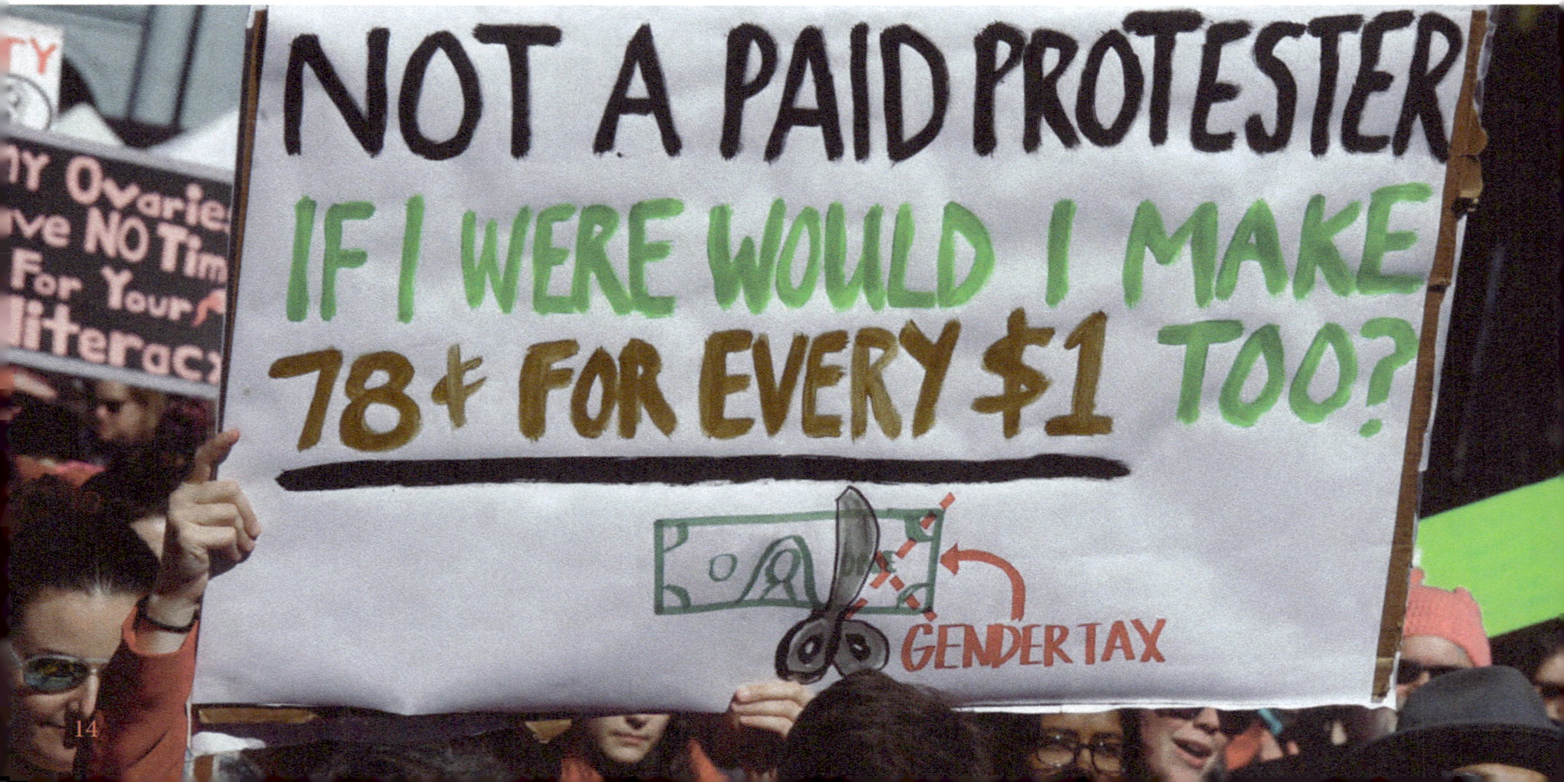

NOT A PAID PROTESTER
IF I WERE WOULD I MAKE 78¢ FOR EVERY $1 TOO?
GENDER TAX

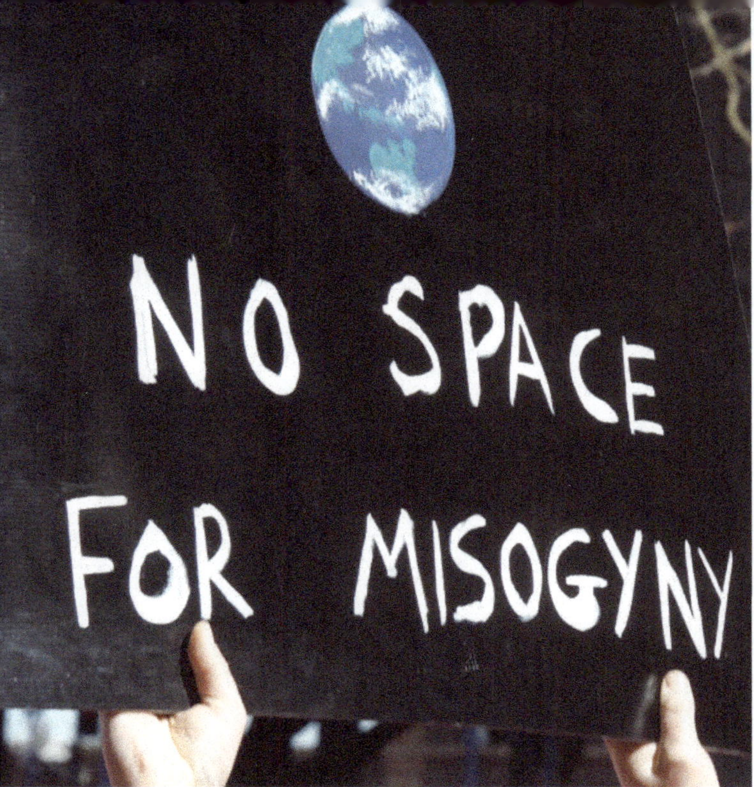

NO SPACE
FOR MISOGYNY

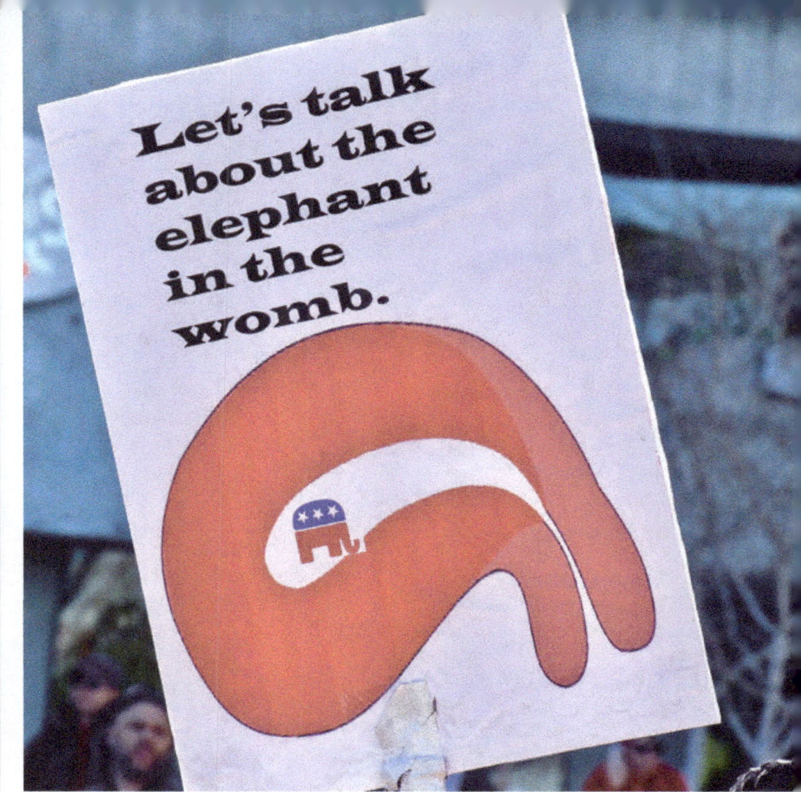

Let's talk
about the
elephant
in the
womb.

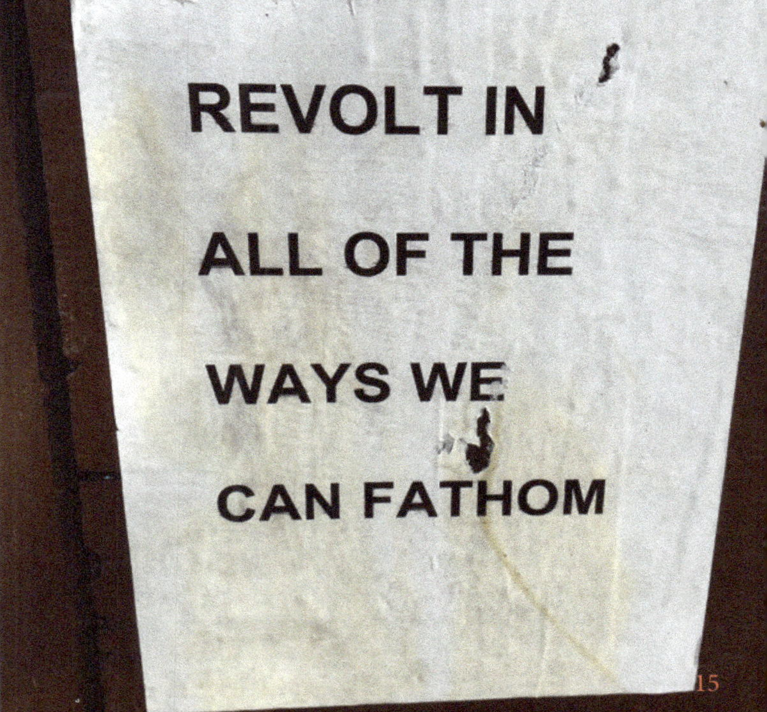

REVOLT IN
ALL OF THE
WAYS WE
CAN FATHOM

WOMEN
ARE
NOT
BITCHES, HO'S,
INCUBATORS,
PUNCHING BAGS,
SEX OBJECTS,
OR BREEDERS!
WOMEN
ARE FULL
HUMAN
BEINGS!

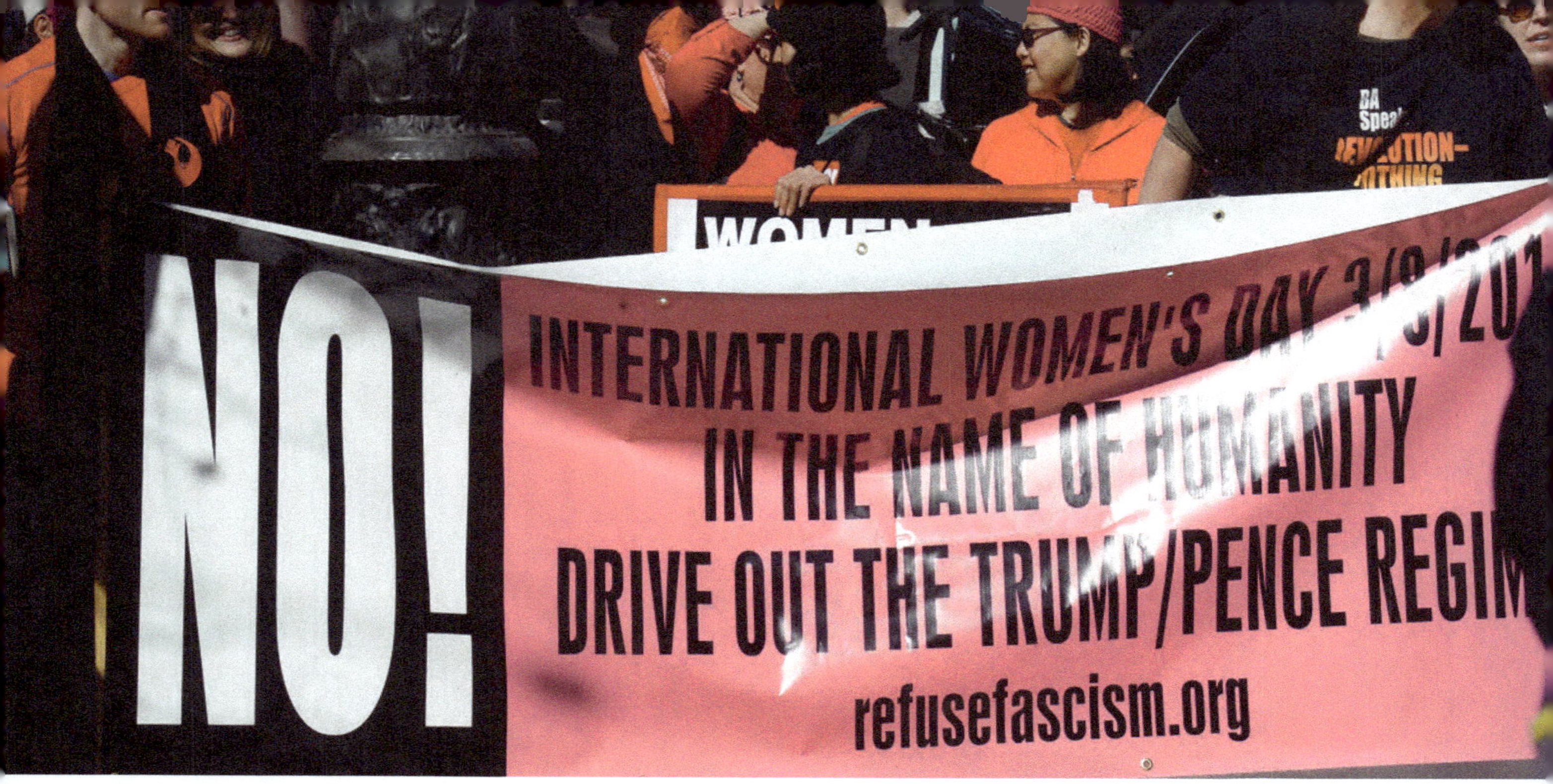

NO!
WOMEN
INTERNATIONAL WOMEN'S DAY 3/8/20
IN THE NAME OF HUMANITY
DRIVE OUT THE TRUMP/PENCE REGIM
refusefascism.org

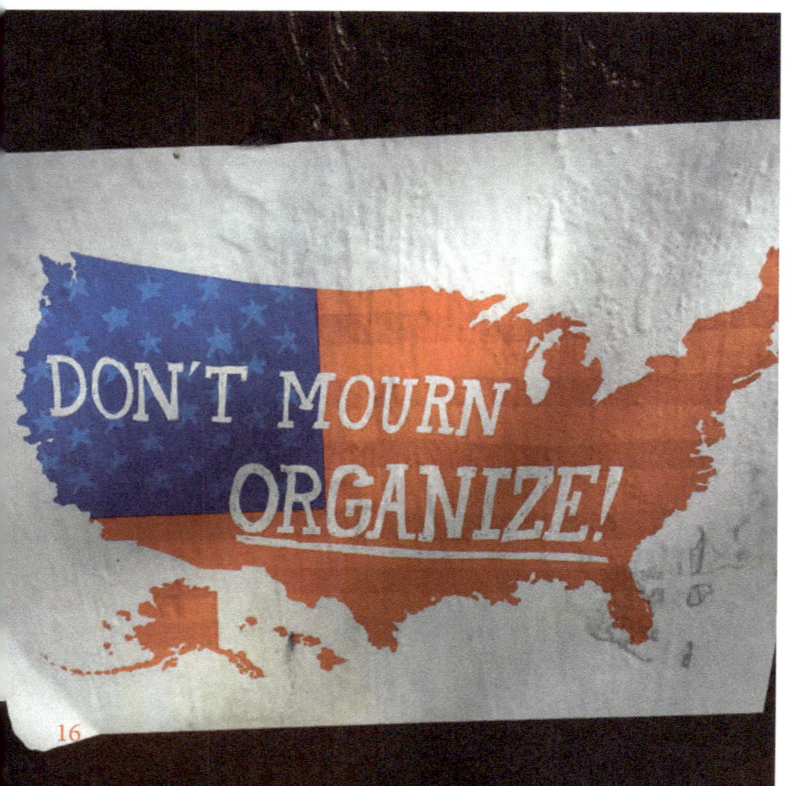

DON'T MOURN
ORGANIZE!

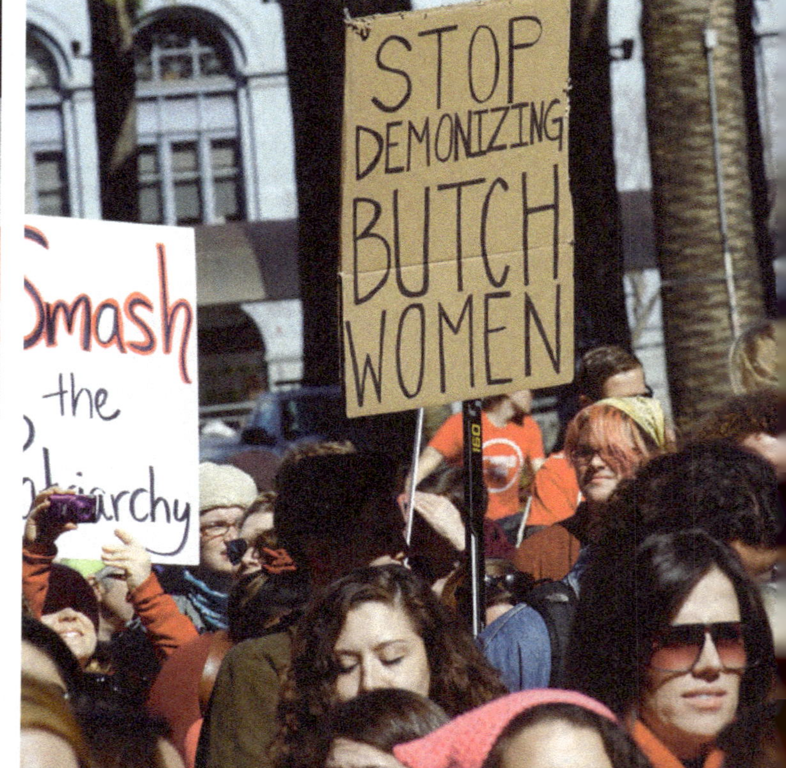

STOP
DEMONIZING
BUTCH
WOMEN
Smash
the
Patriarchy

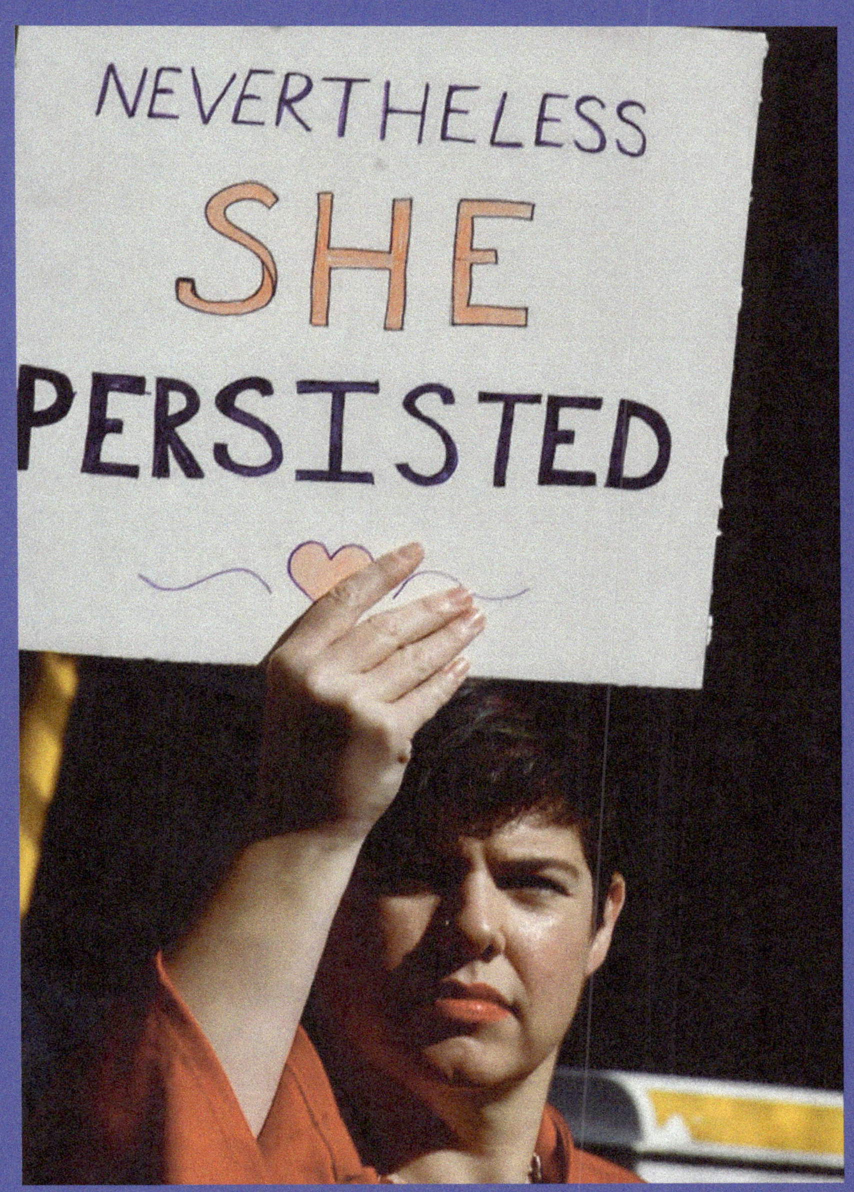

NEVERTHELESS
SHE
PERSISTED

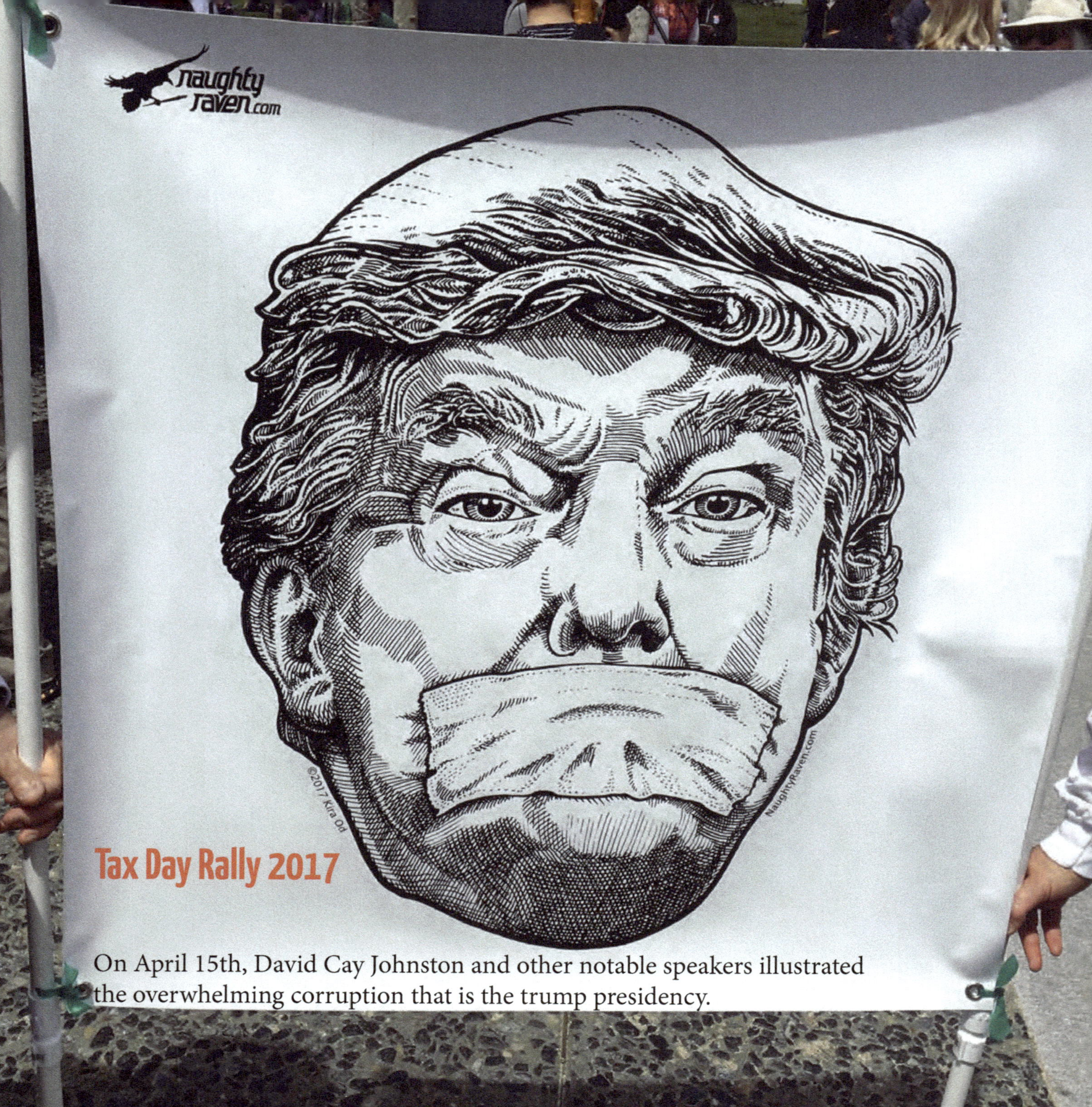

naughty
raven.com
©2017 Kra Od
NaughtyRaven.com
Tax Day Rally 2017
On April 15th, David Cay Johnston and other notable speakers illustrated
the overwhelming corruption that is the trump presidency.

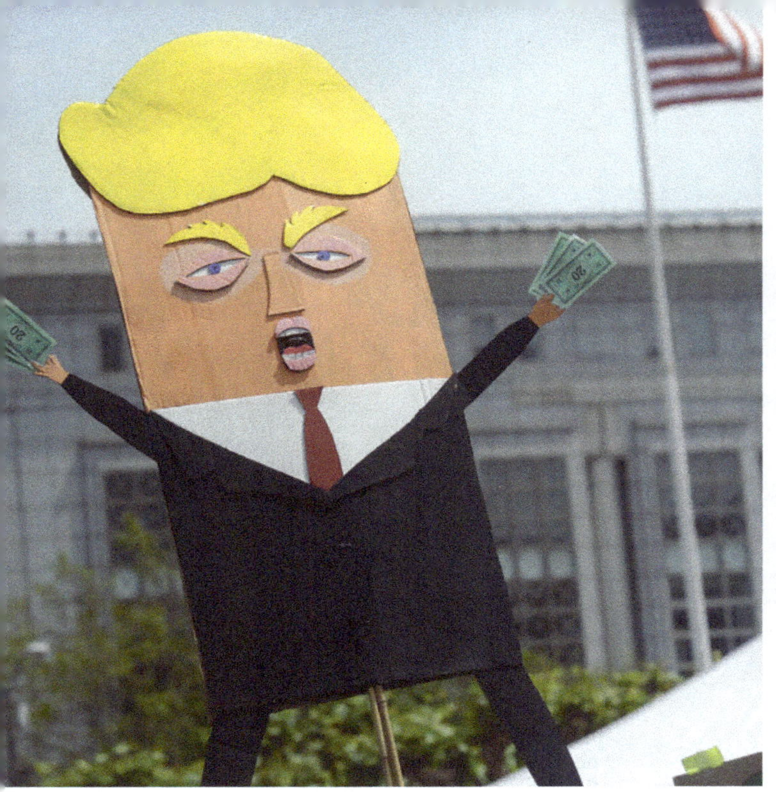

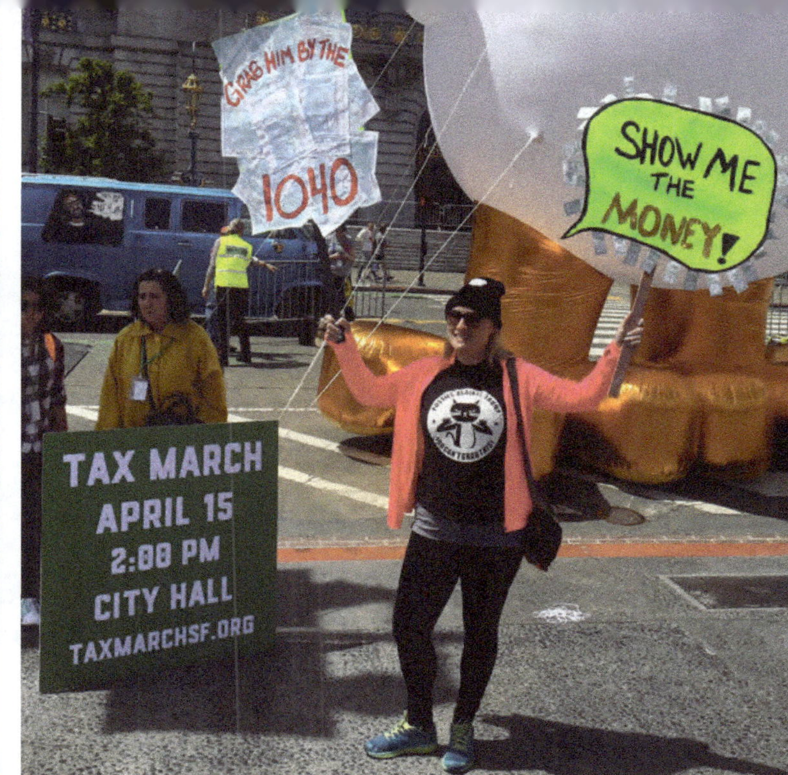
GRAB HIM BY THE
1040
SHOW ME THE MONEY!
TAX MARCH
APRIL 15
2:00 PM
CITY HALL
TAXMARCHSF.ORG

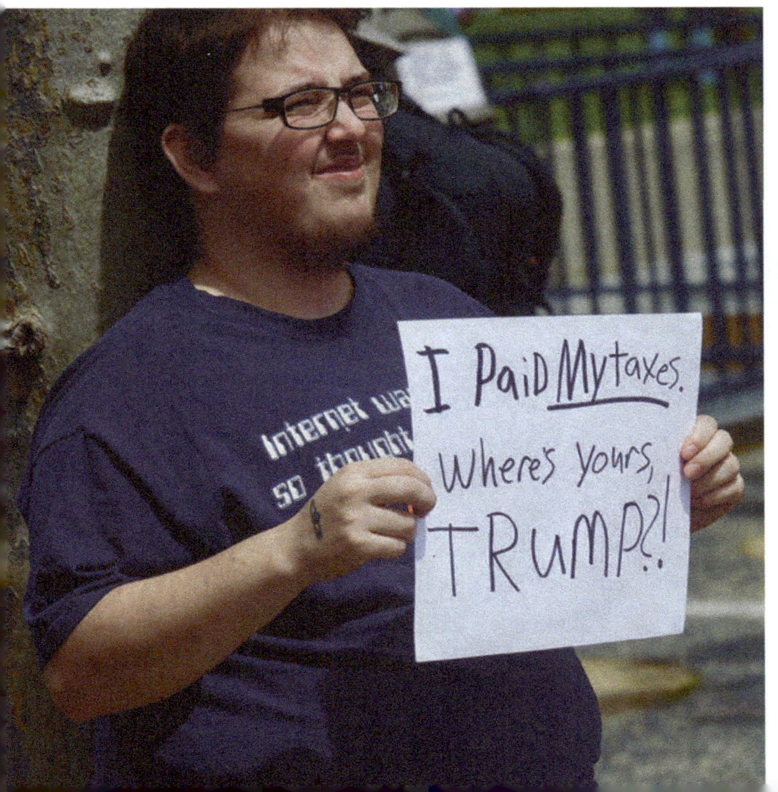
I PaiD My taxes.
Where's yours,
TRUMP?!

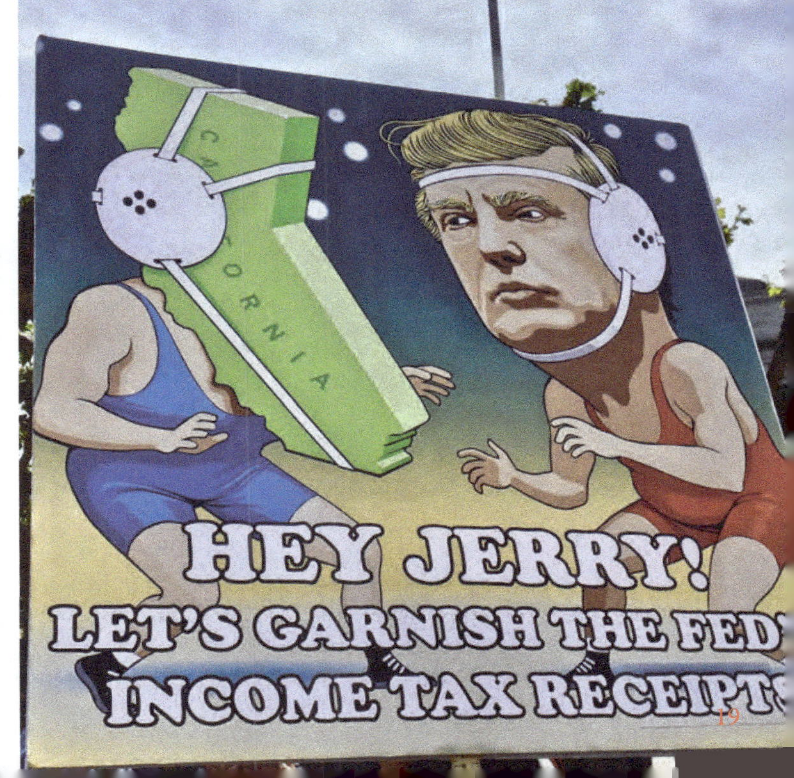
CALIFORNIA
HEY JERRY!
LET'S GARNISH THE FED
INCOME TAX RECEIPT

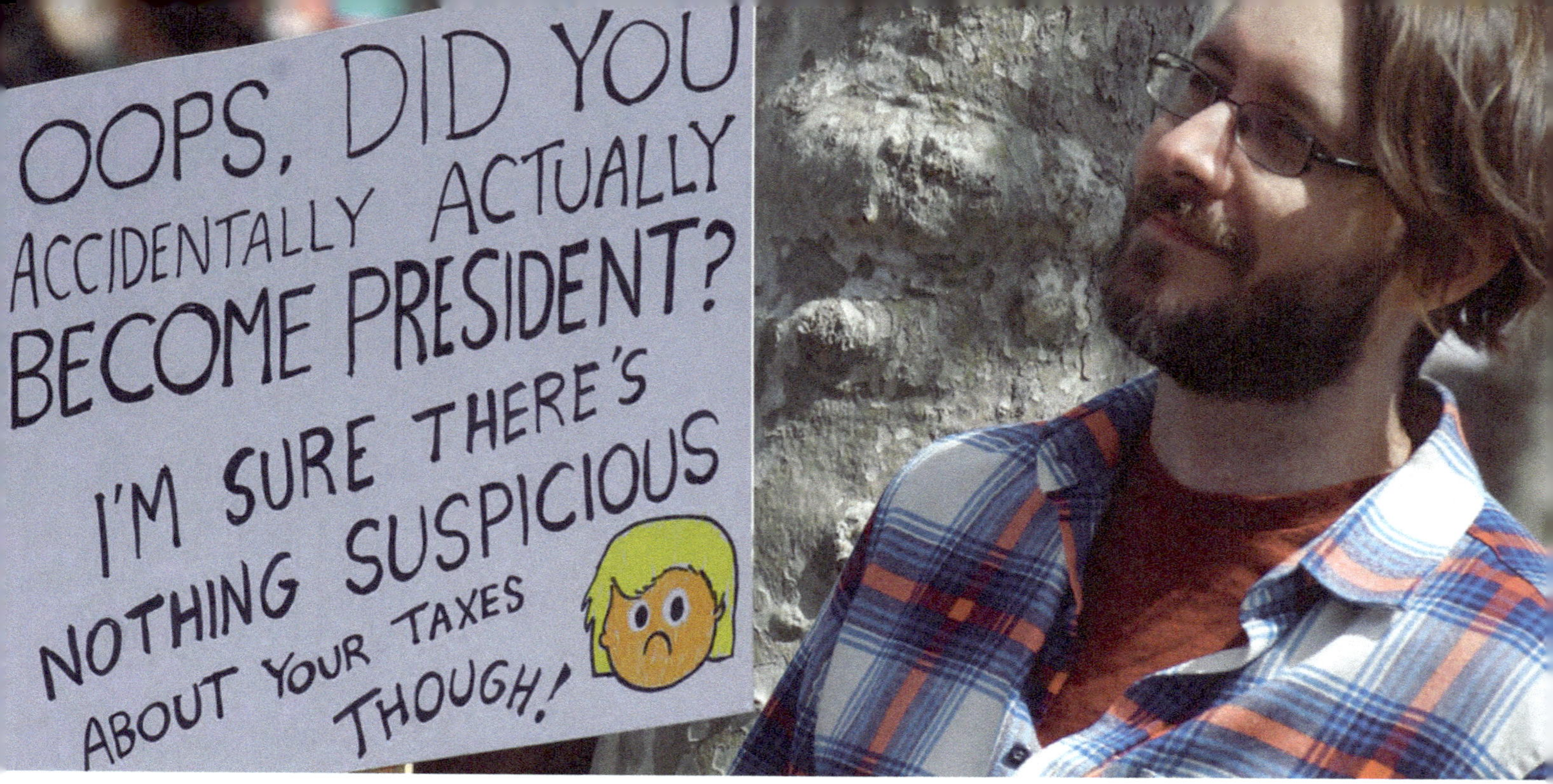

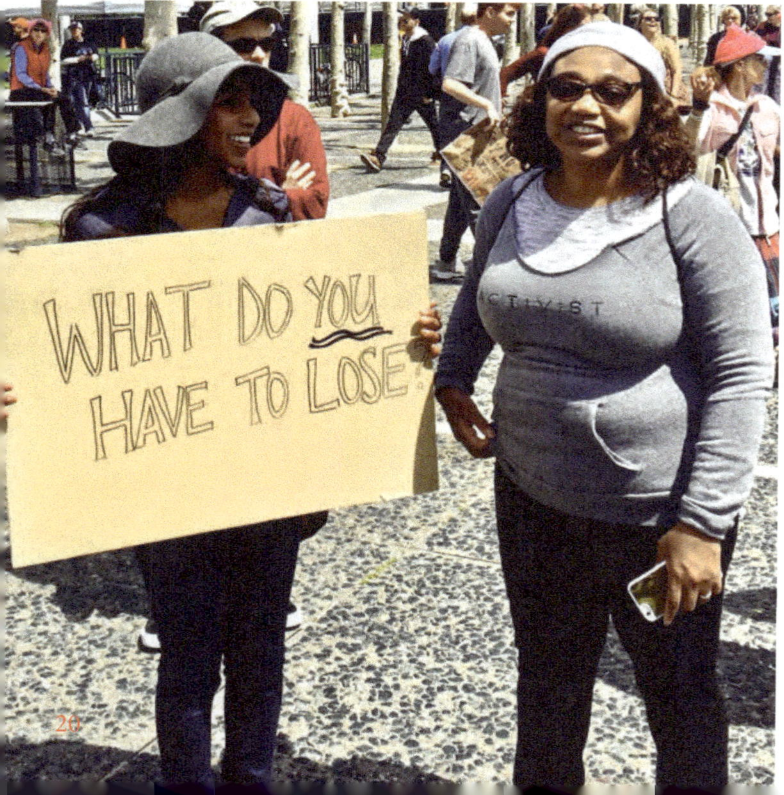

OOPS, DID YOU ACCIDENTALLY ACTUALLY BECOME PRESIDENT?
I'M SURE THERE'S NOTHING SUSPICIOUS ABOUT YOUR TAXES THOUGH!
WHAT DO YOU HAVE TO LOSE
ACTIVIST

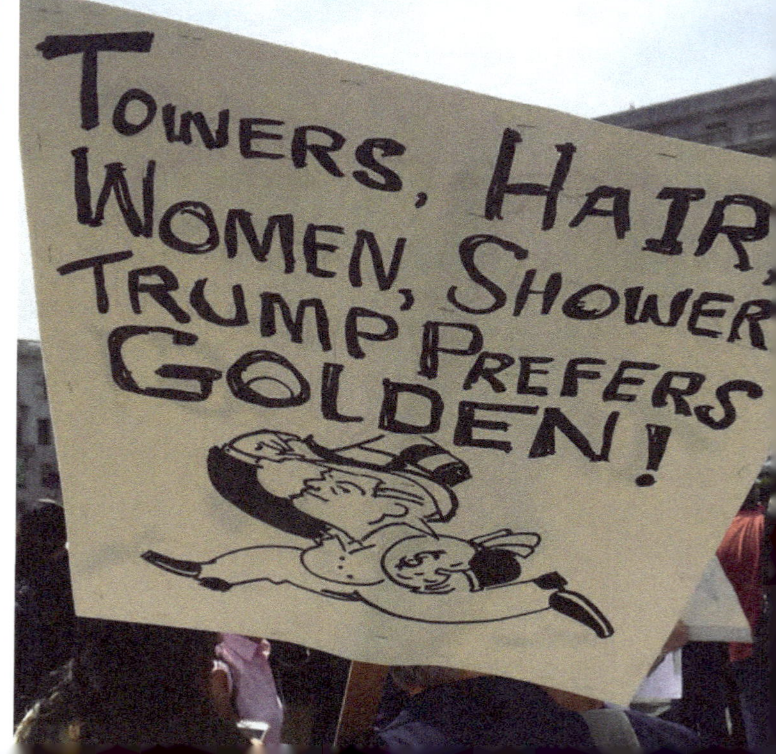

TOWERS, HAIR, WOMEN, SHOWER, TRUMP PREFERS GOLDEN!

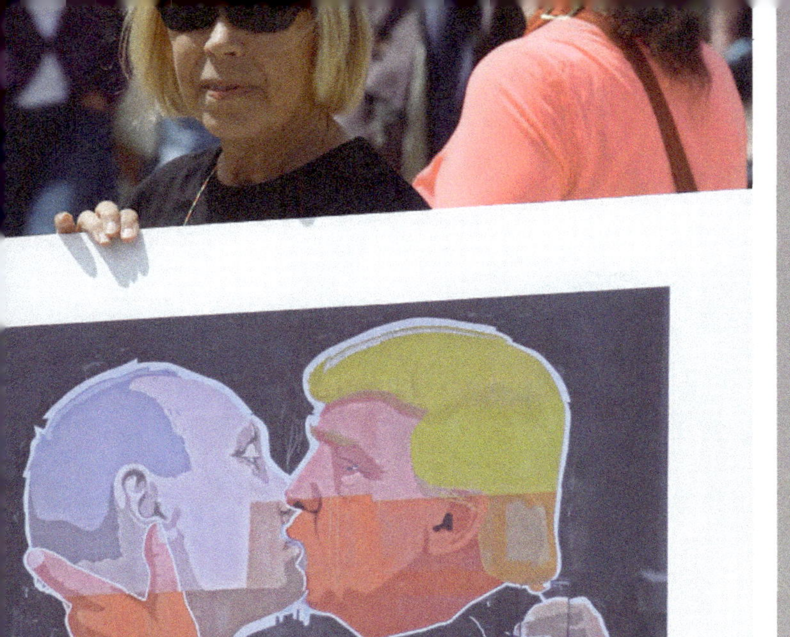
Is this what you're hiding in your tax returns?

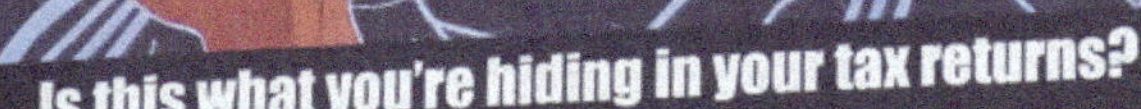

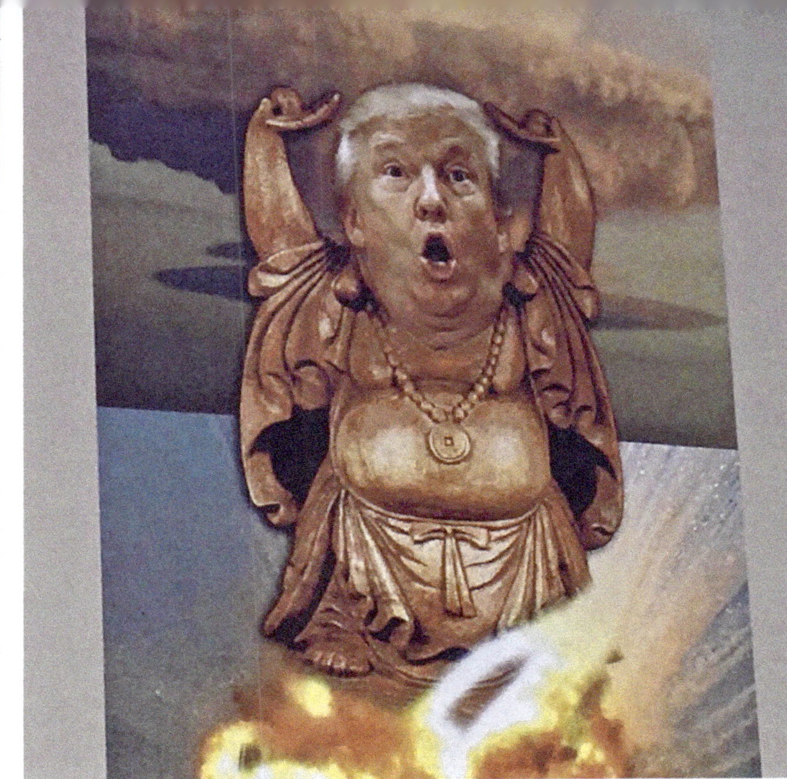

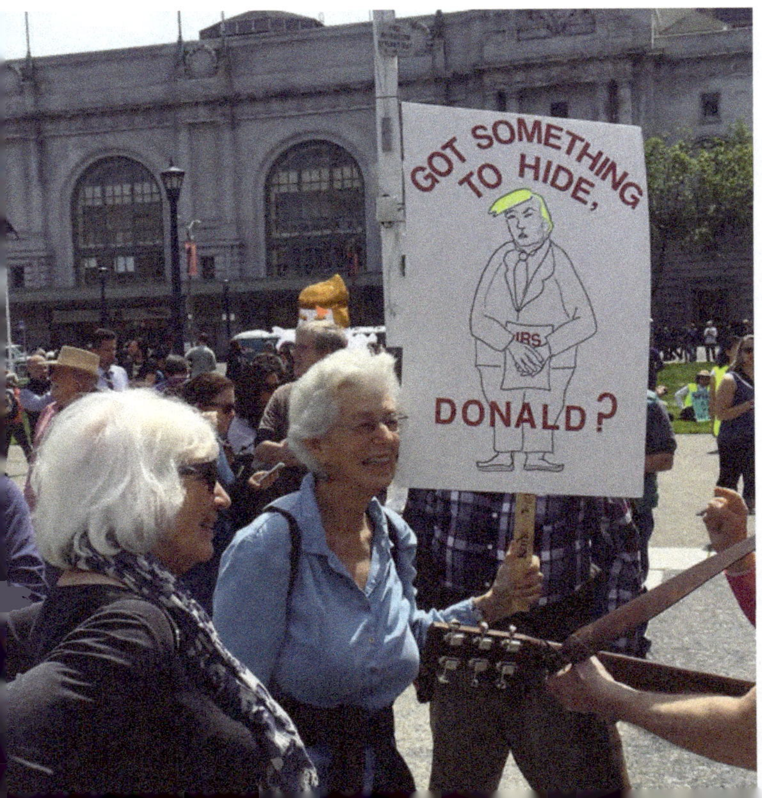
GOT SOMETHING TO HIDE,
DONALD?

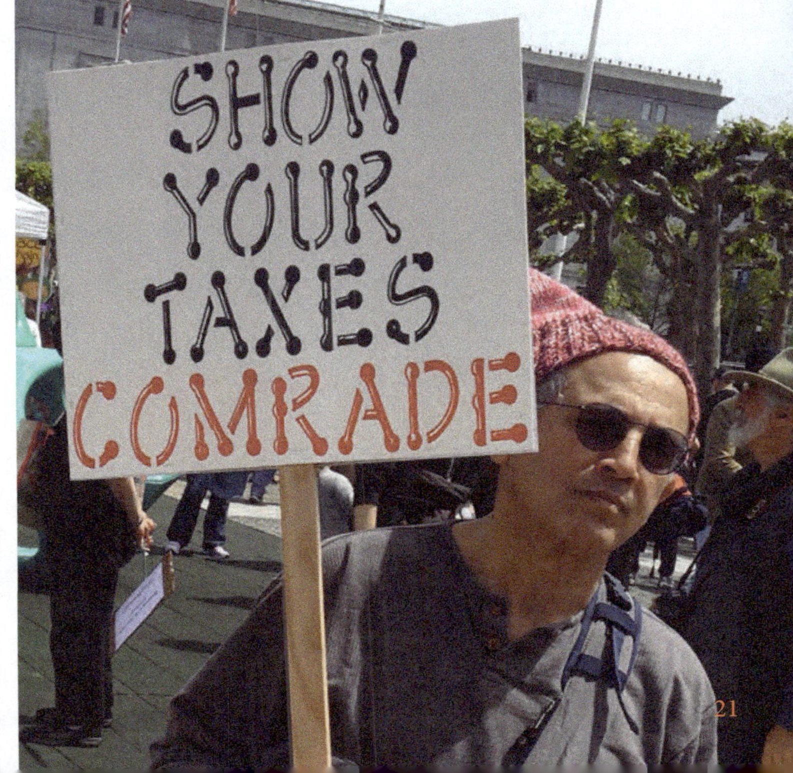
SHOW YOUR TAXES COMRADE

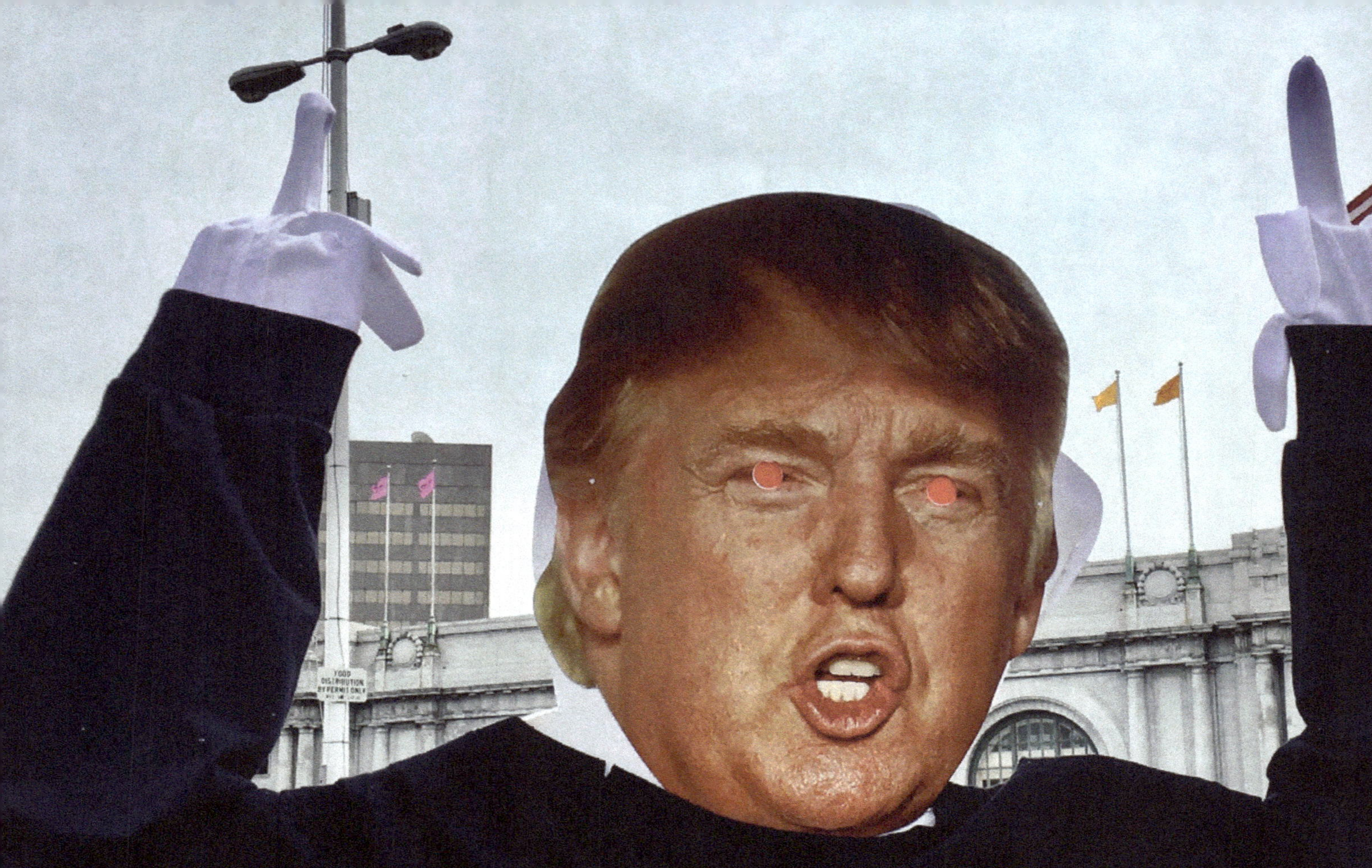

March for Science 2017

On April 22, 2017 the marchers reminded us how science, the earth, medicine, etc. is under attack by the trump regime.

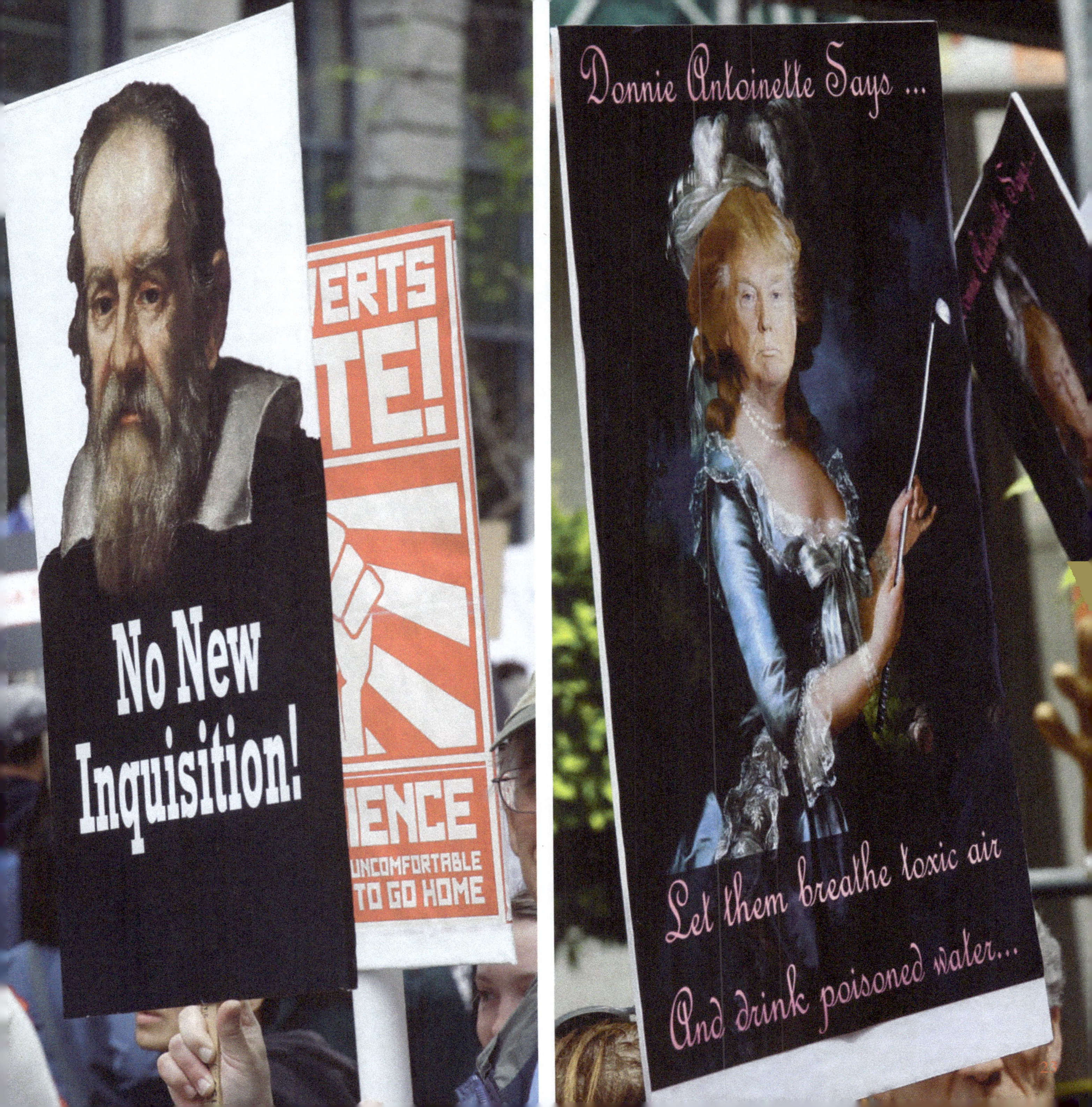
No New
Inquisition!
ERTS
TE!
ENCE
UNCOMFORTABLE
TO GO HOME
Donnie Antoinette Says ...
Let them breathe toxic air
And drink poisoned water...

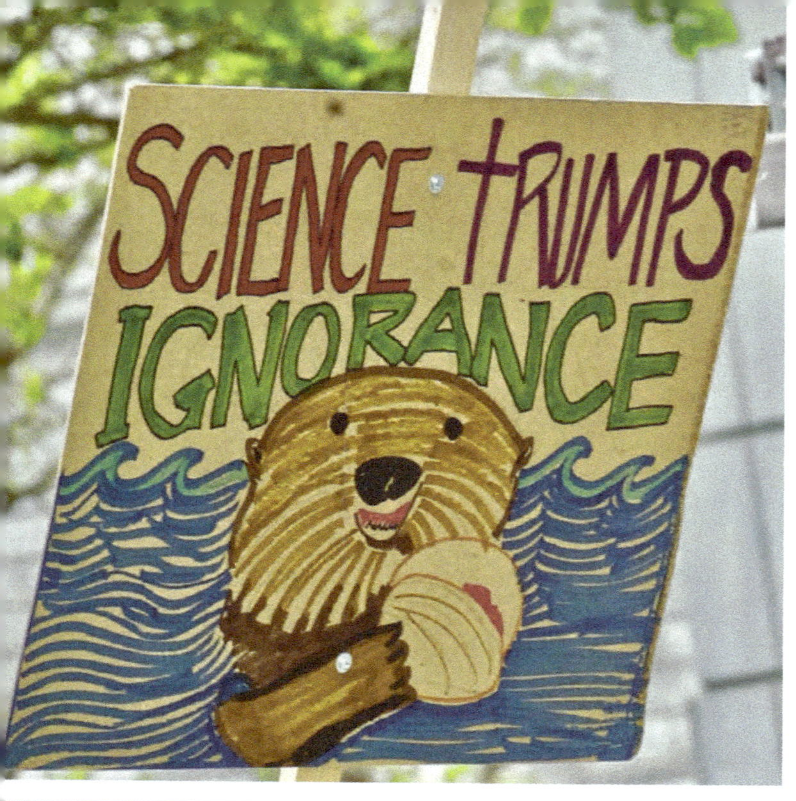

SCIENCE TRUMPS
IGNORANCE

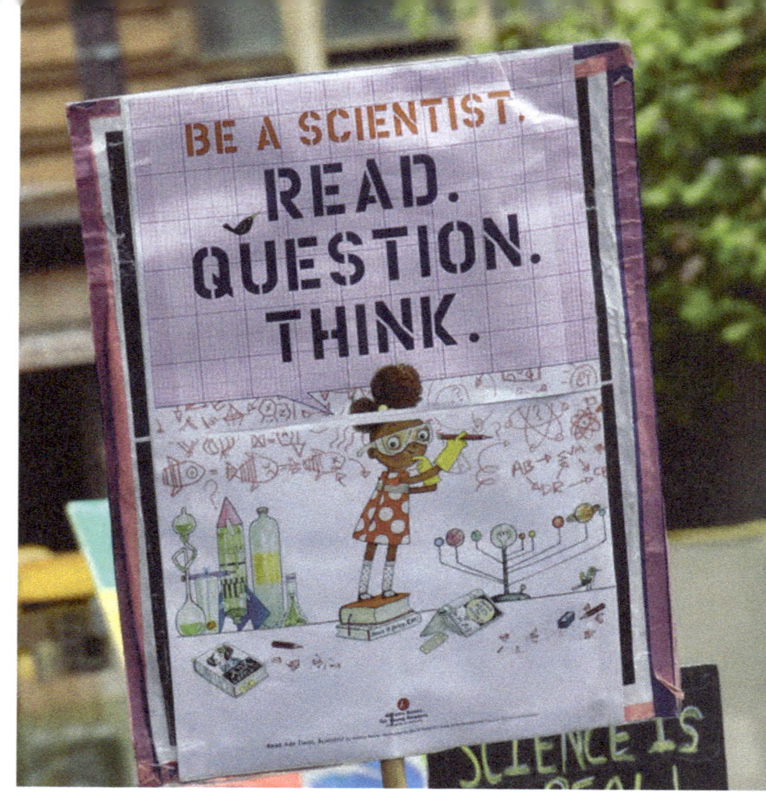

BE A SCIENTIST.
READ.
QUESTION.
THINK.

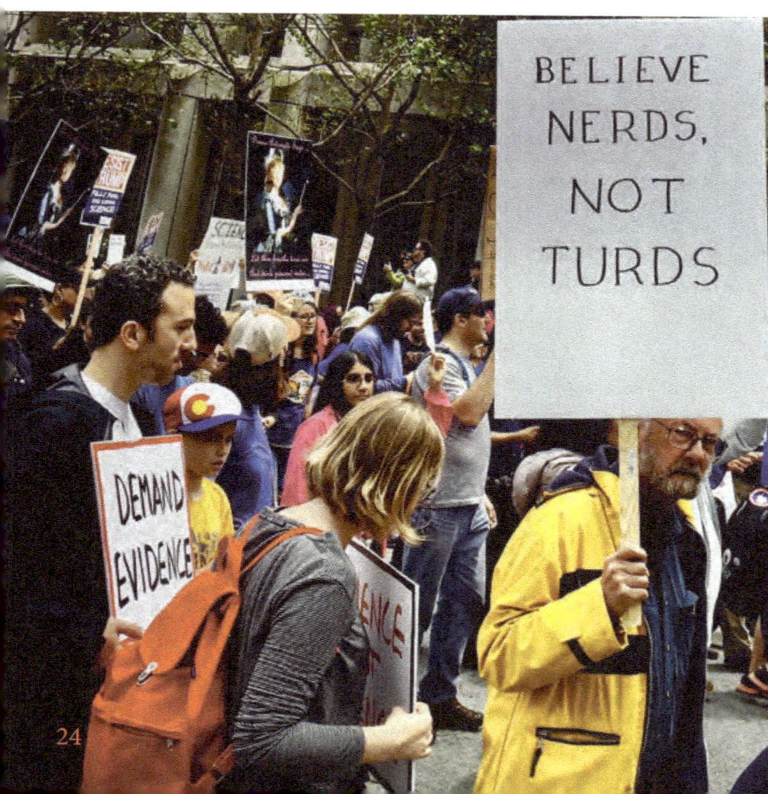

BELIEVE
NERDS,
NOT
TURDS
DEMAND
EVIDENCE

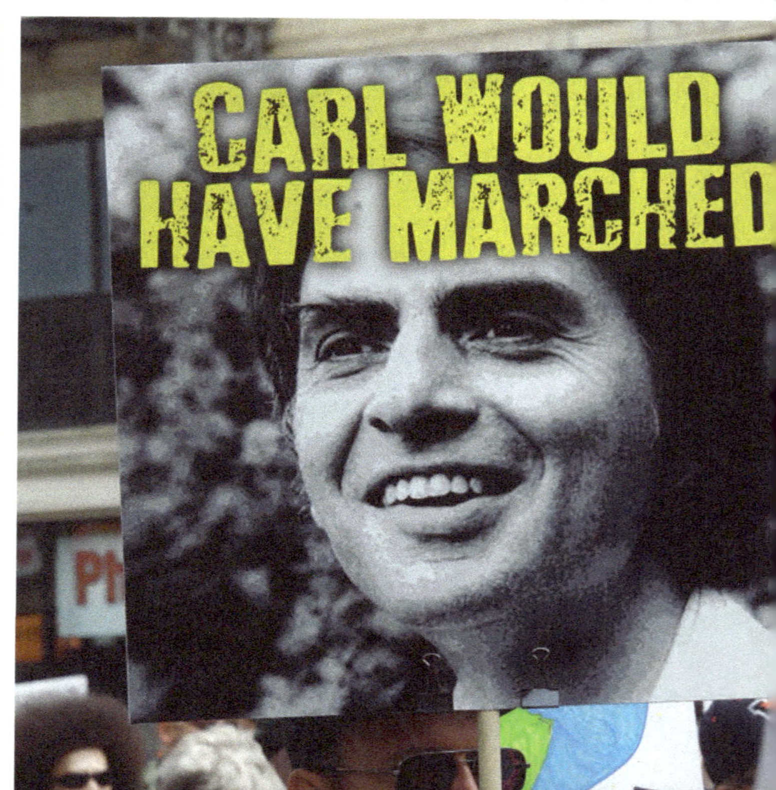

CARL WOULD
HAVE MARCHED

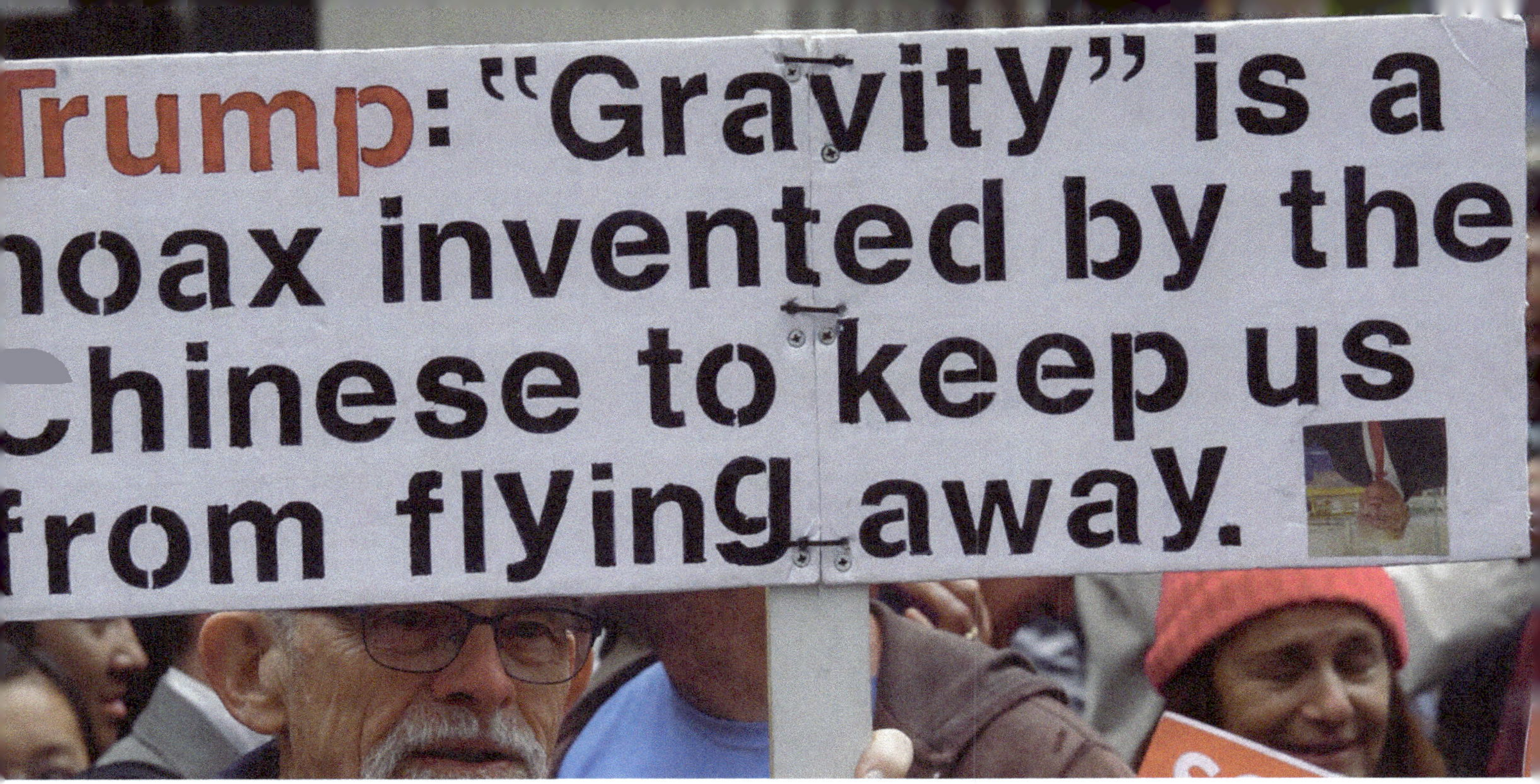

Trump: "Gravity" is a hoax invented by the Chinese to keep us from flying away.

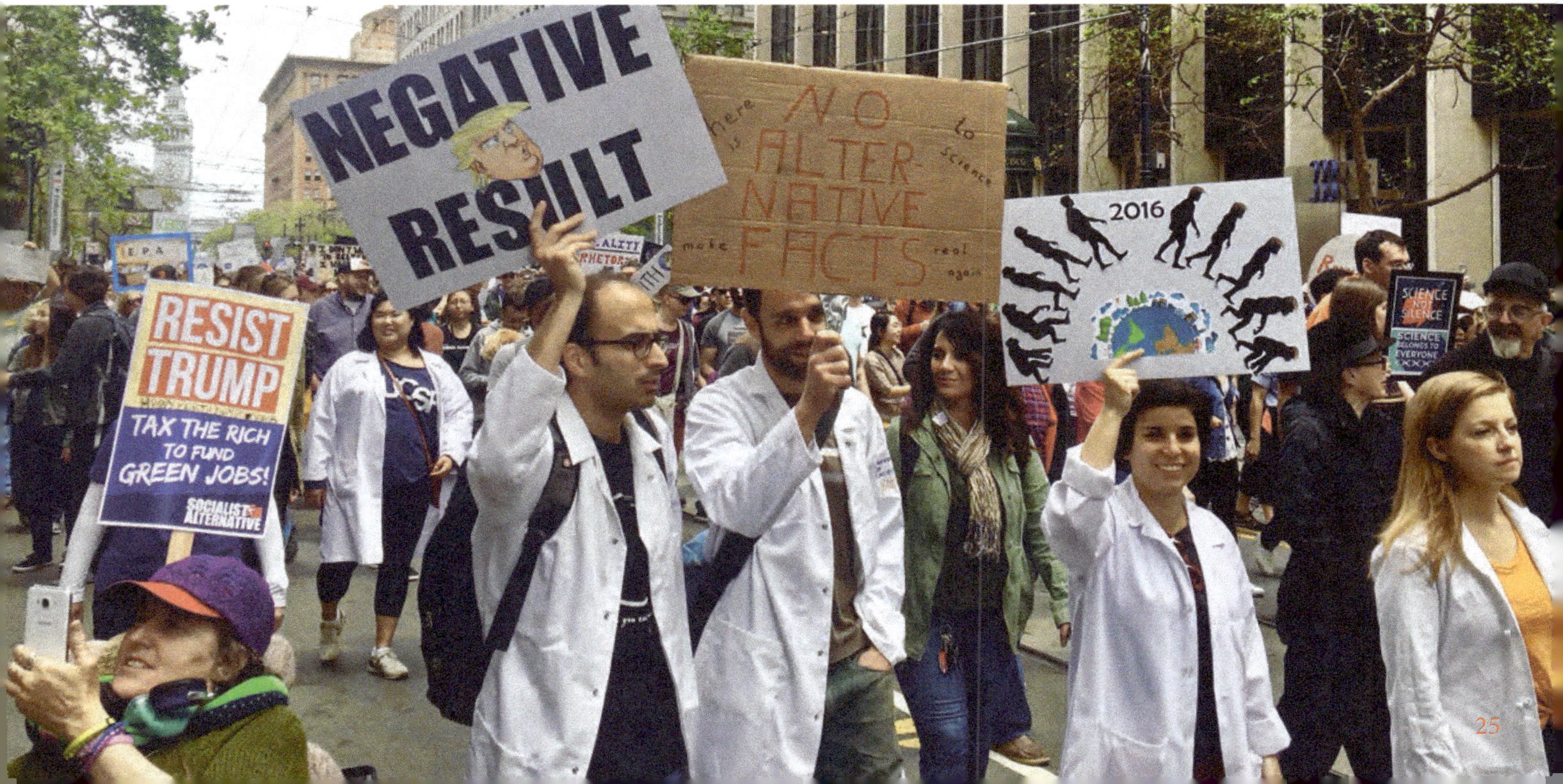

NEGATIVE RESULT
NO ALTER-NATIVE FACTS
here is to science
make real again
RESIST TRUMP
TAX THE RICH TO FUND GREEN JOBS!
SOCIALIST ALTERNATIVE
EPA
2016
SCIENCE NOT SILENCE
SCIENCE BELONGS TO EVERYONE

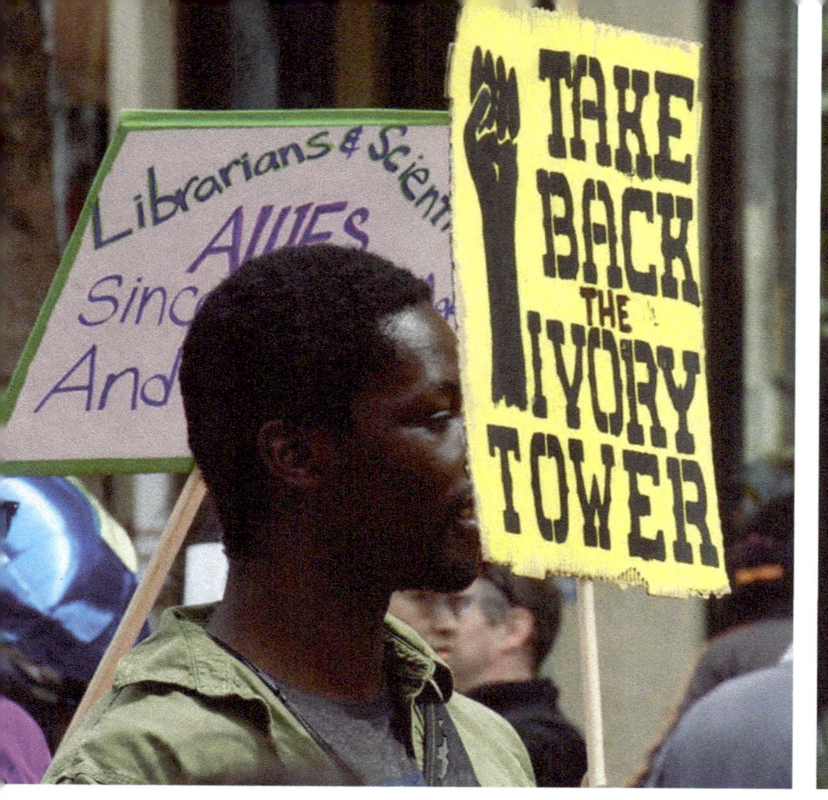

Librarians & Scientists
Allies
Since
And
TAKE BACK THE IVORY TOWER

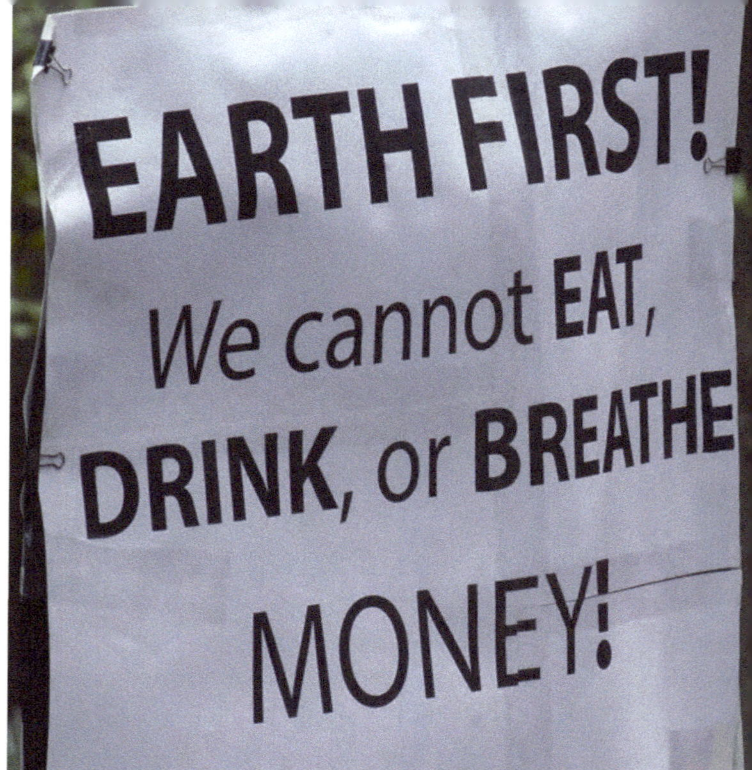

EARTH FIRST!
We cannot EAT,
DRINK, or BREATHE
MONEY!

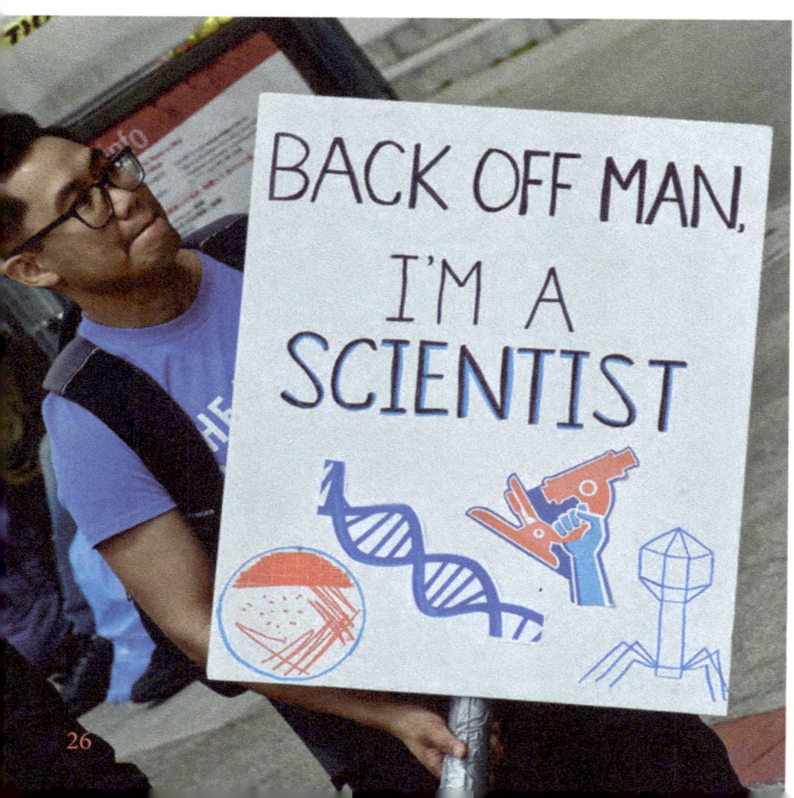

BACK OFF MAN,
I'M A
SCIENTIST

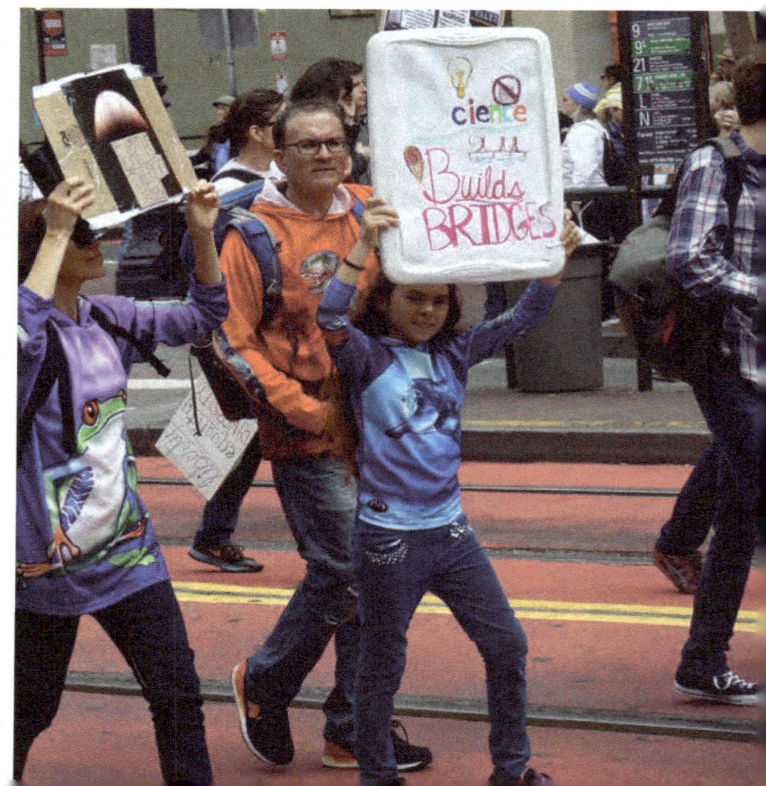

cience
Builds BRIDGES

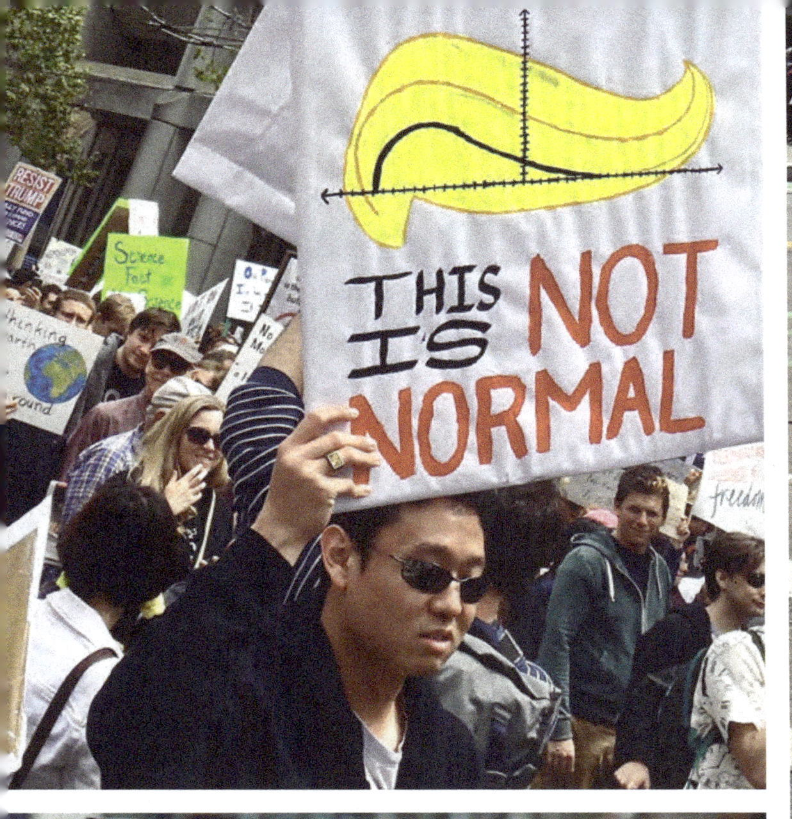
THIS IS NOT NORMAL

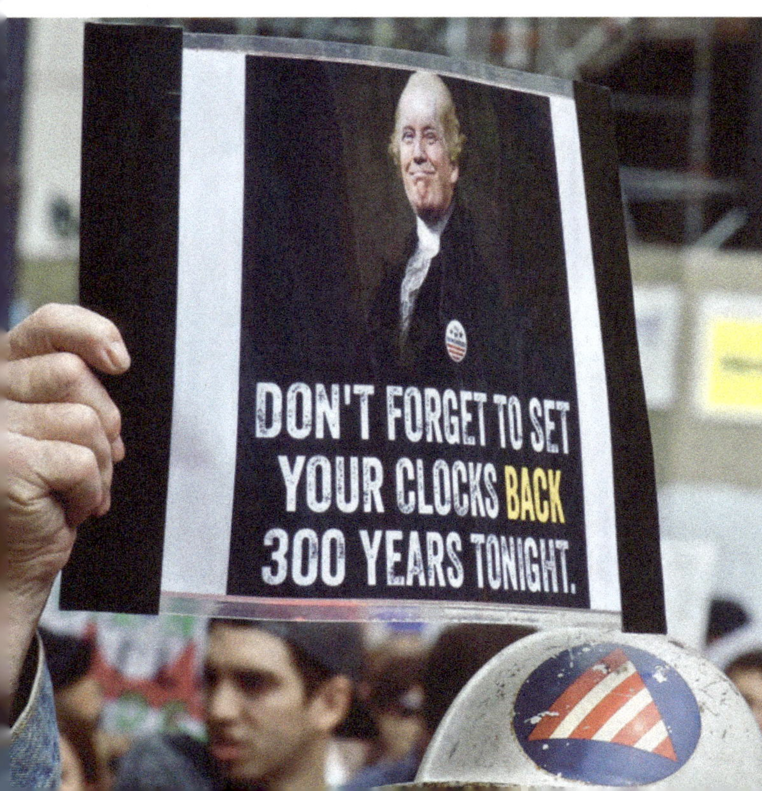
DON'T FORGET TO SET YOUR CLOCKS BACK 300 YEARS TONIGHT.

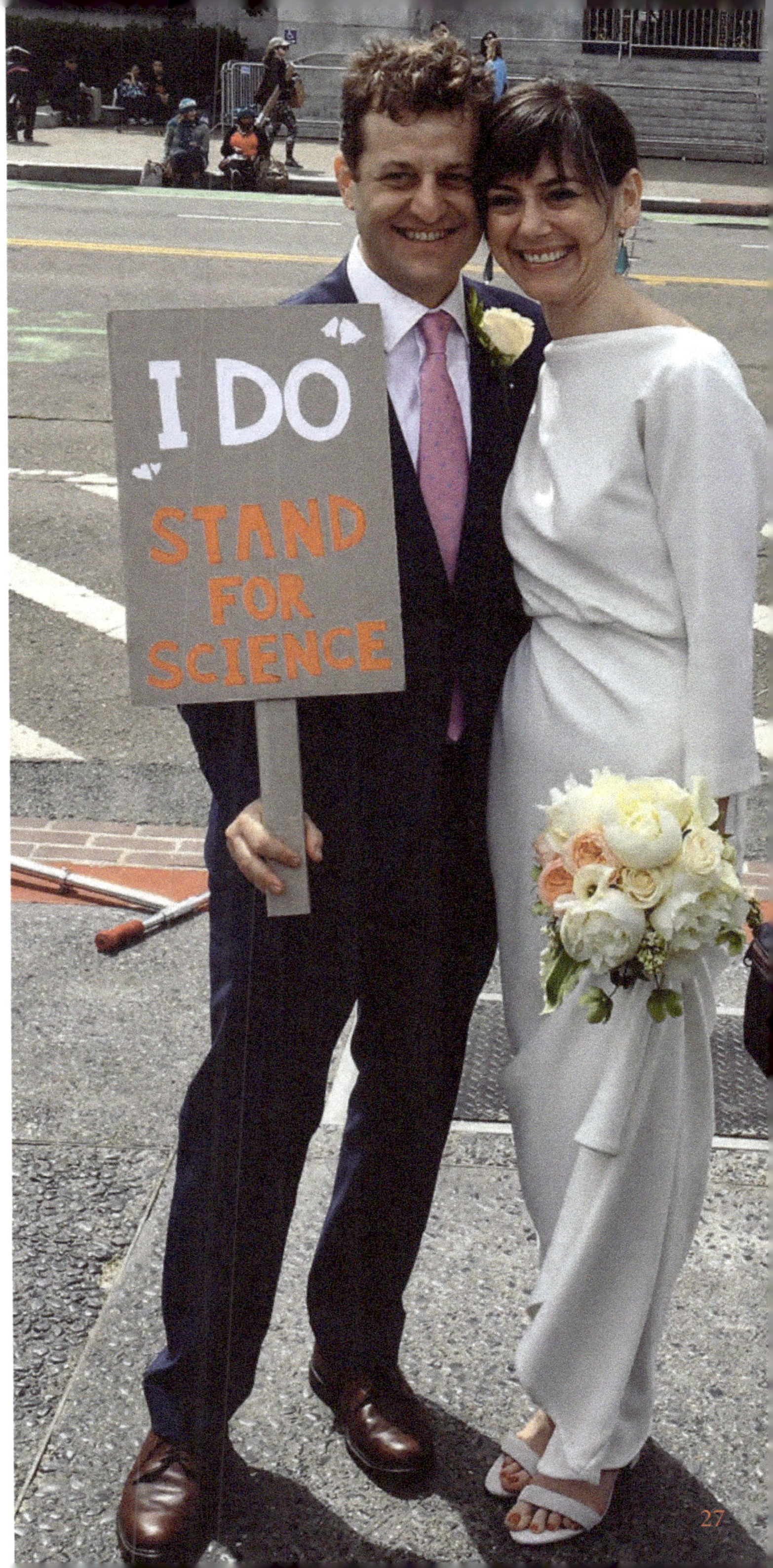

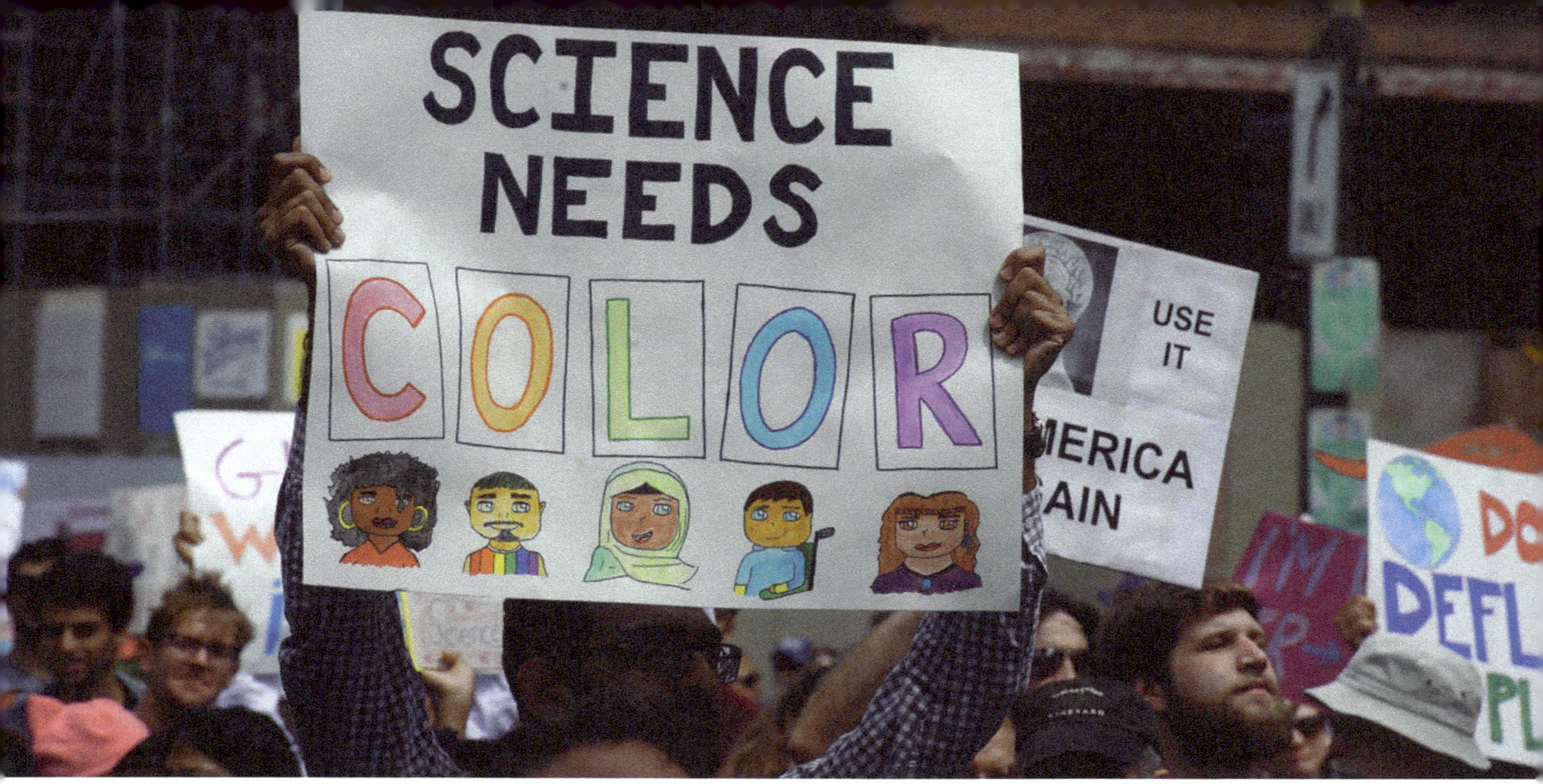

SCIENCE
NEEDS
COLOR
USE
IT
MERICA
AIN

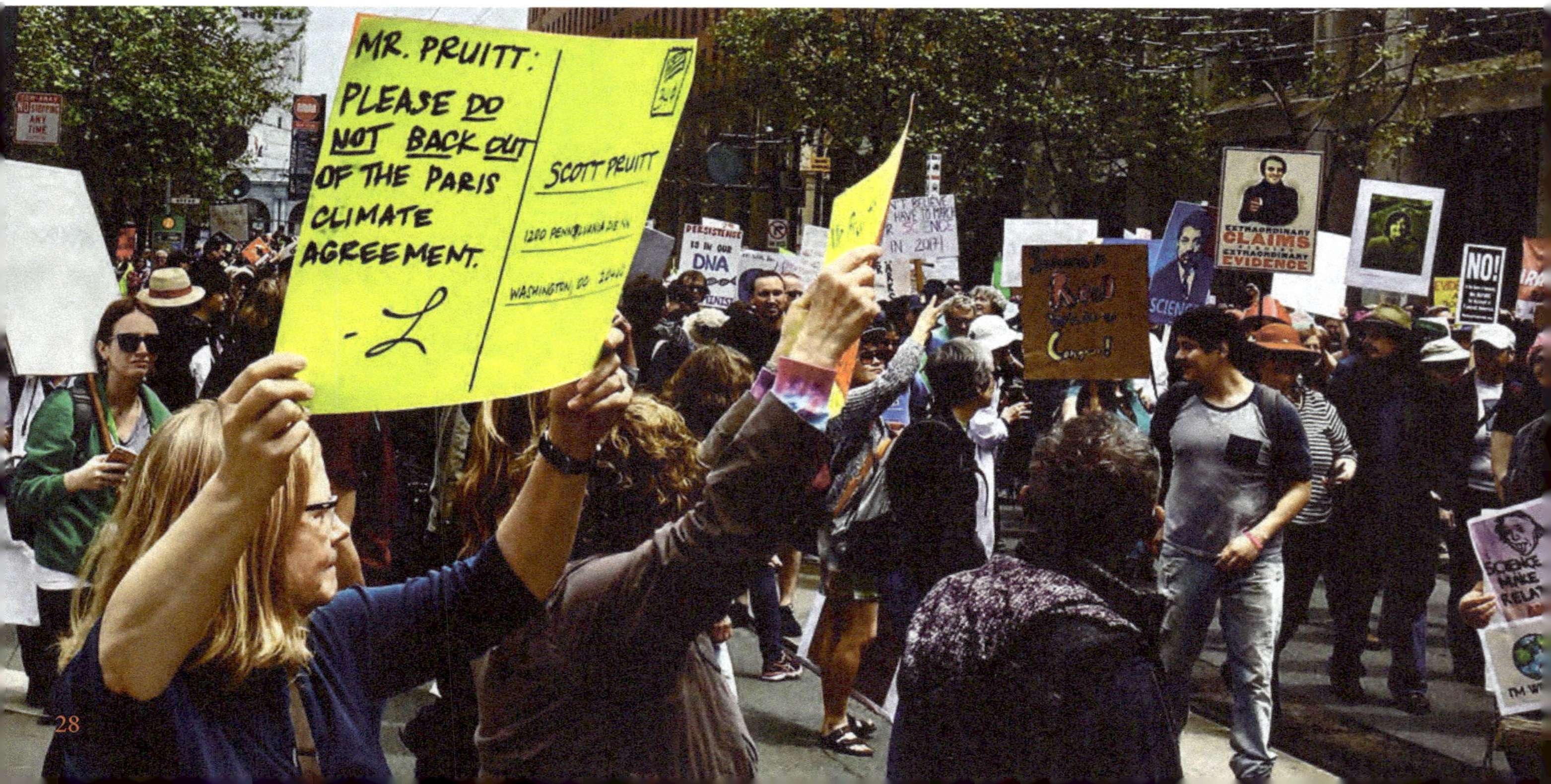

MR. PRUITT:
PLEASE DO
NOT BACK OUT
OF THE PARIS
CLIMATE
AGREEMENT.
- L
SCOTT PRUITT
1200 PENNSYLVANIA AVE NW
WASHINGTON, DC 20460
PERSISTENCE
IS IN OUR
DNA
EXTRAORDINARY
CLAIMS
EXTRAORDINARY
EVIDENCE
NO!
SCIENCE

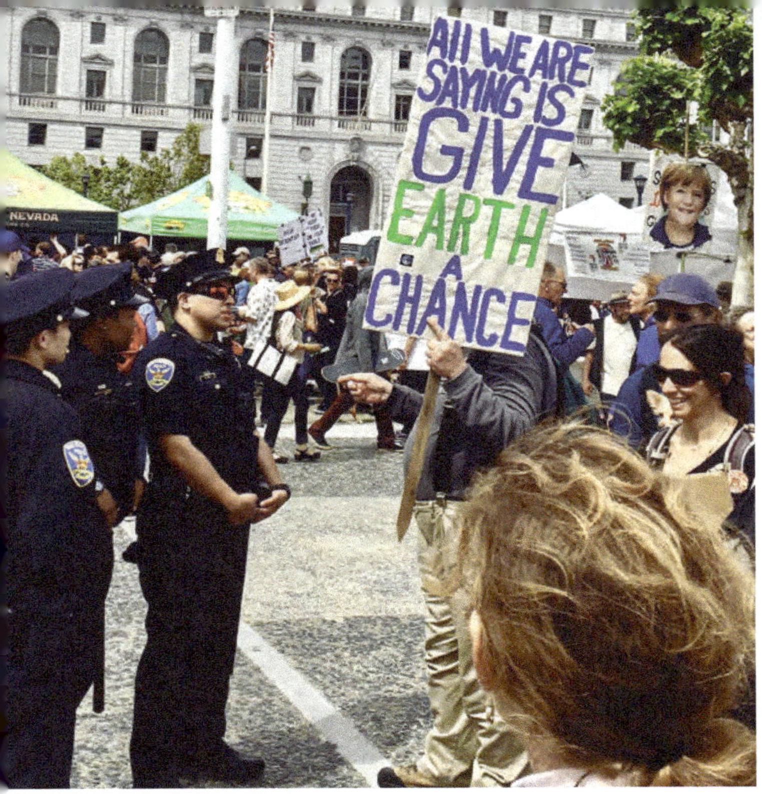
All WE ARE SAYING IS GIVE EARTH A CHANCE

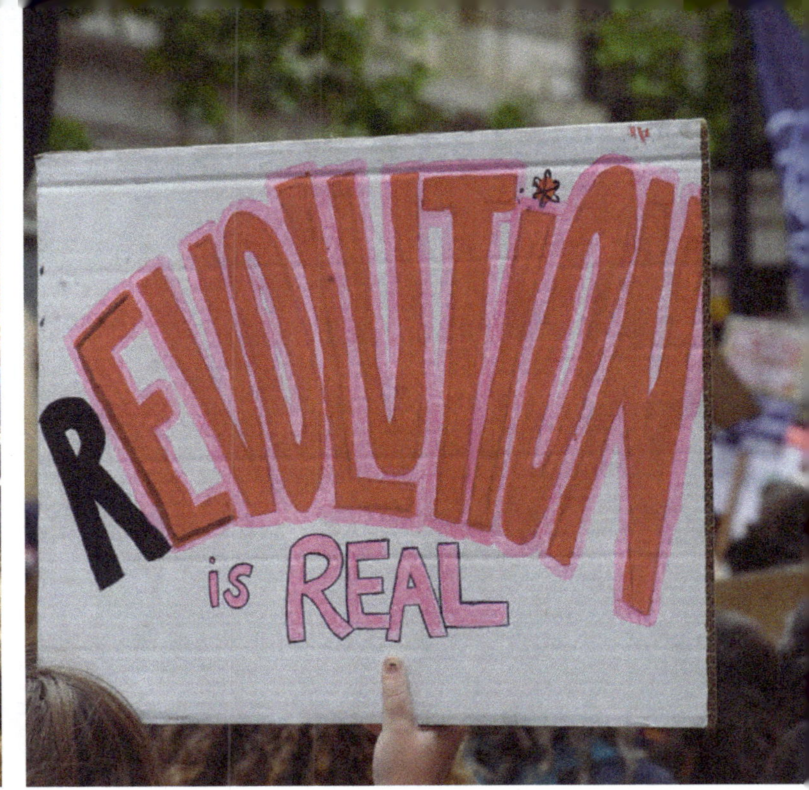
REVOLUTION
is REAL

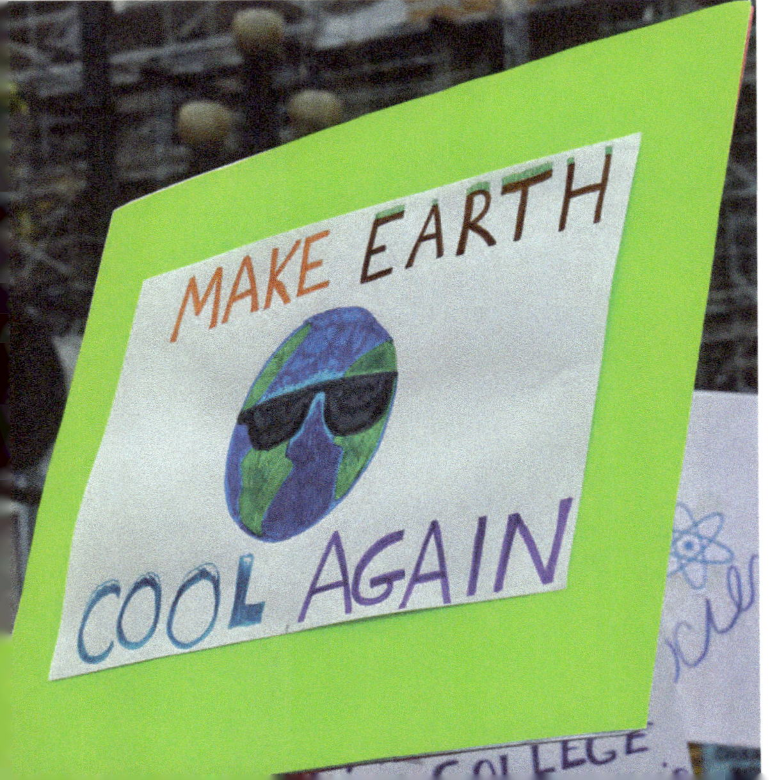
MAKE EARTH COOL AGAIN

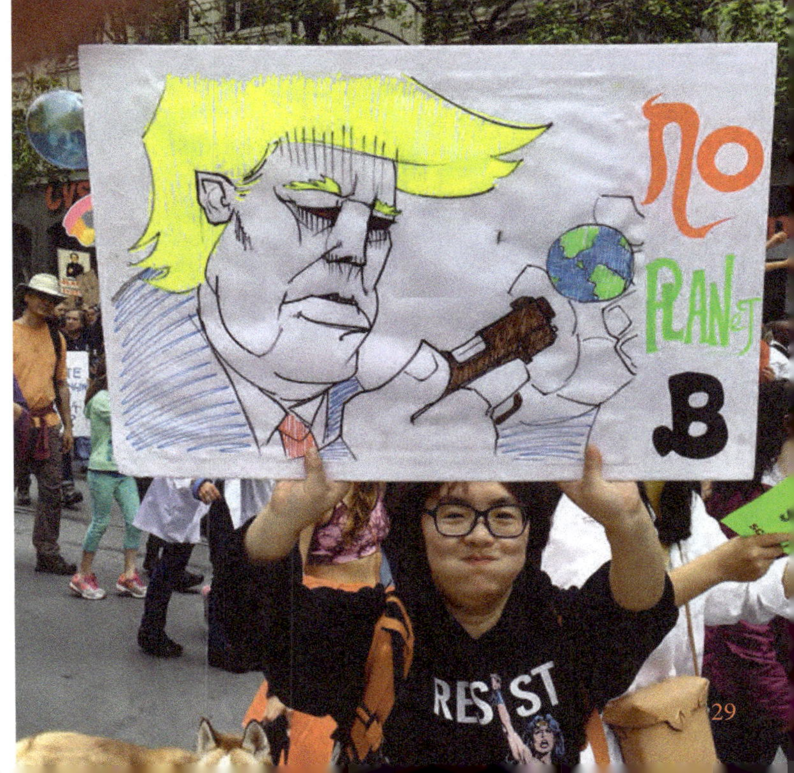
NO PLANET B
RESIST

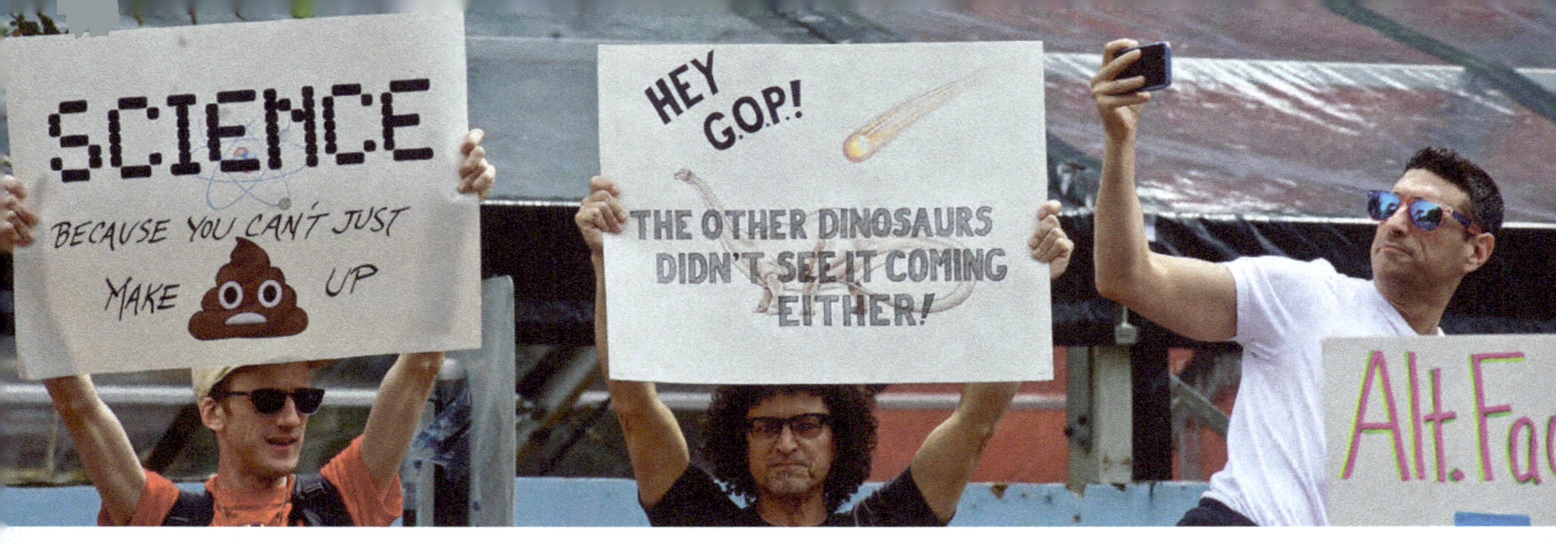

SCIENCE
BECAUSE YOU CAN'T JUST MAKE 💩 UP
HEY G.O.P.!
THE OTHER DINOSAURS DIDN'T SEE IT COMING EITHER!
Alt.Fac

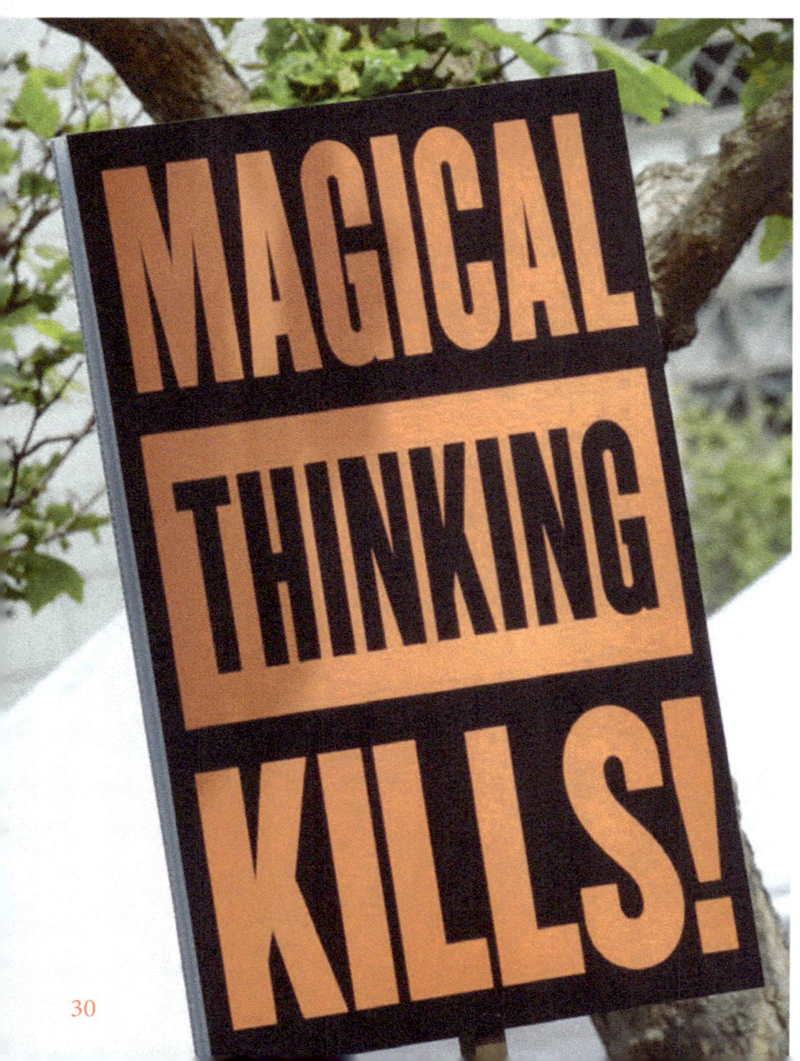

MAGICAL THINKING KILLS!

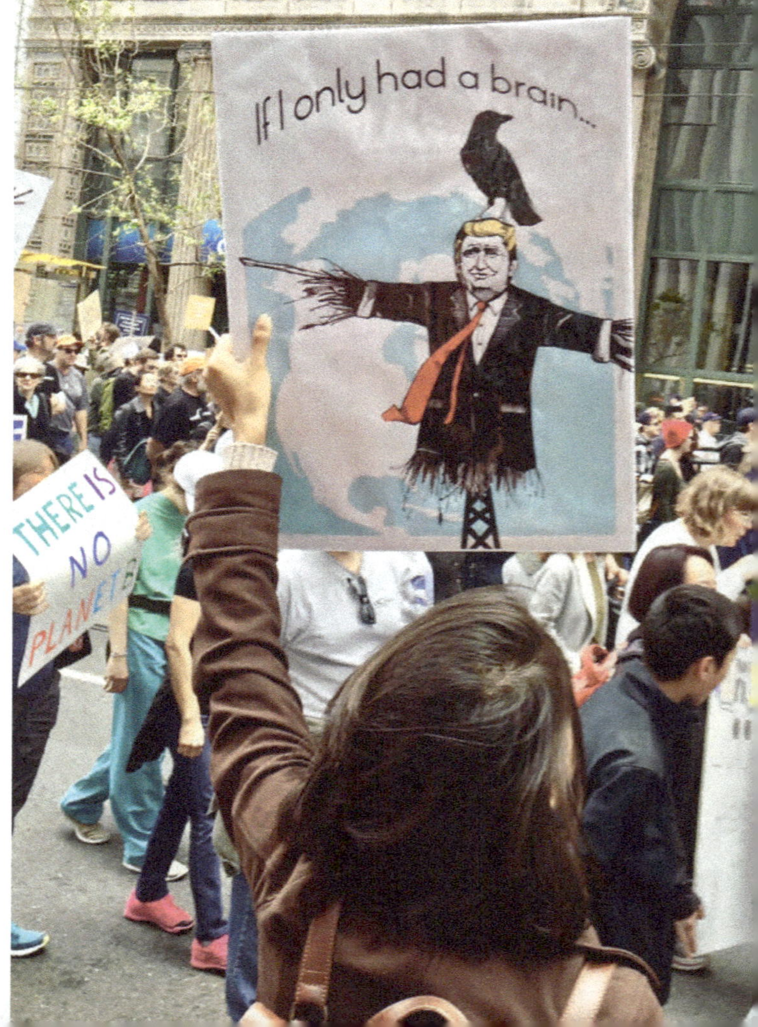

If I only had a brain...
THERE IS NO PLANET

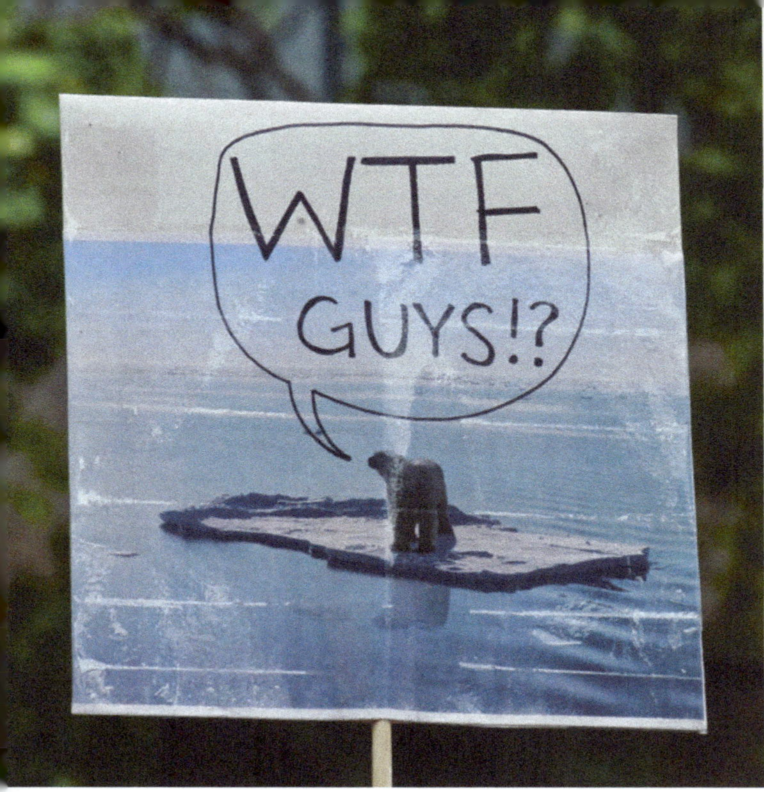

WTF
GUYS!?

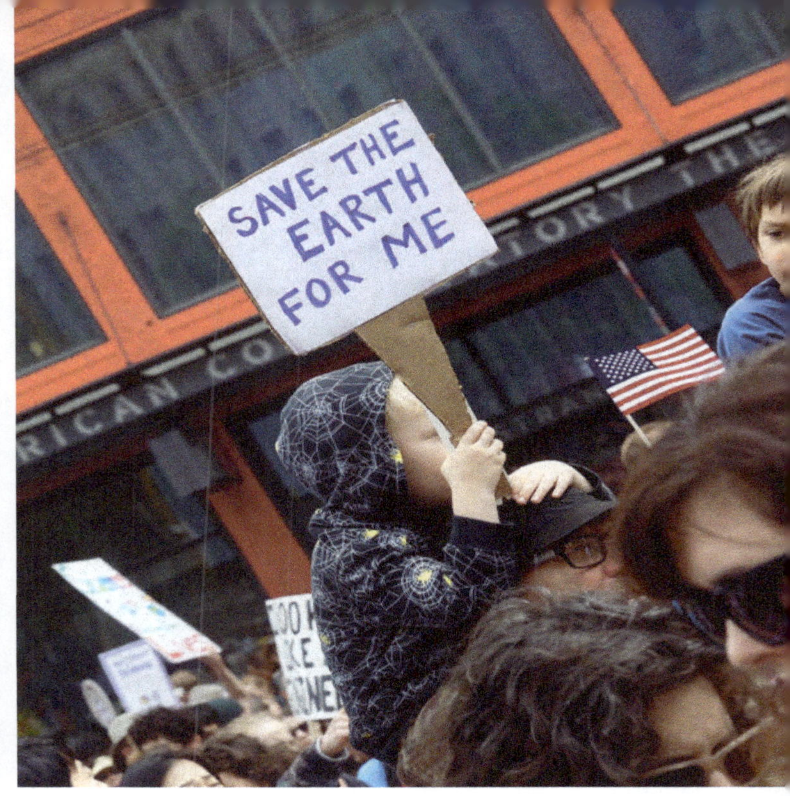

SAVE THE
EARTH
FOR ME

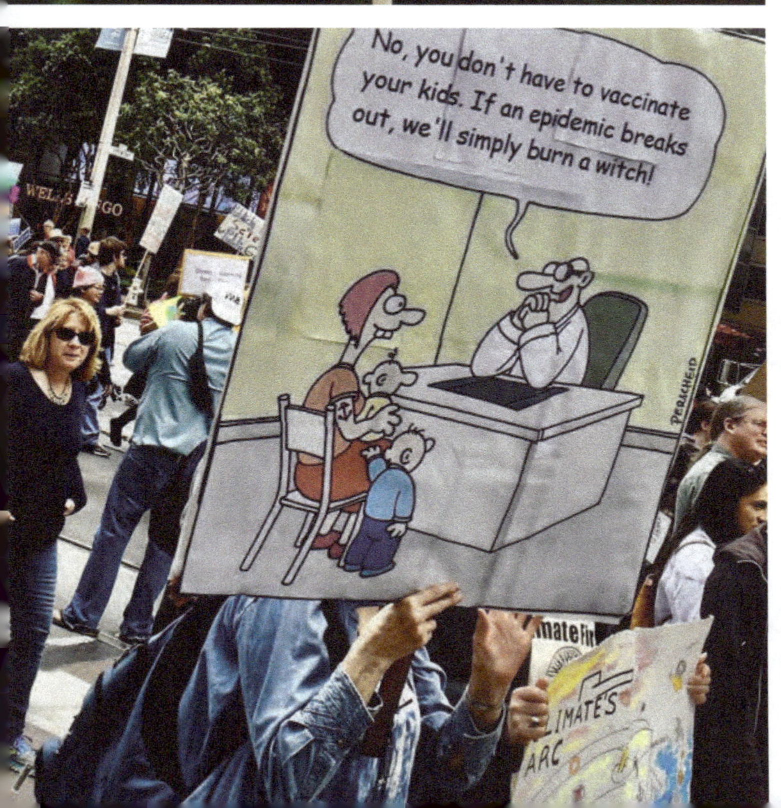

No, you don't have to vaccinate
your kids. If an epidemic breaks
out, we'll simply burn a witch!

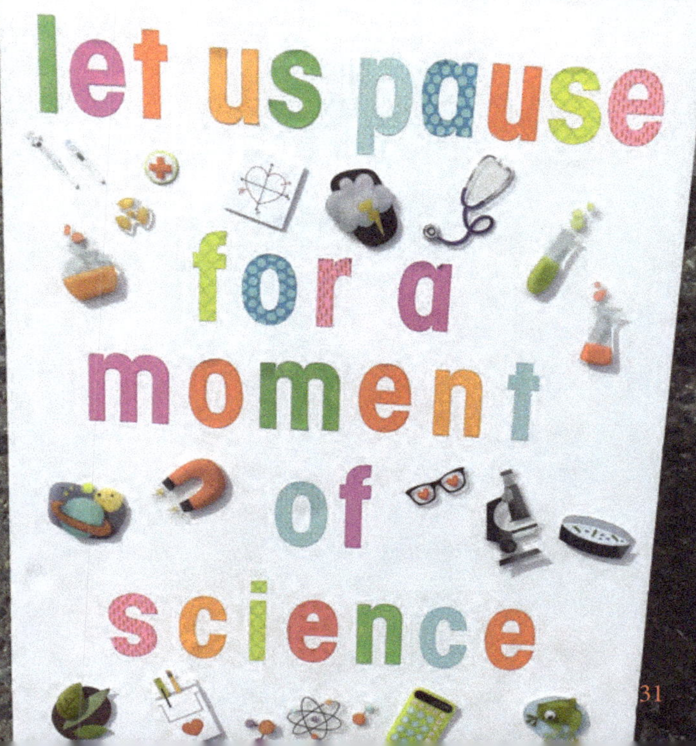

let us pause
for a
moment
of
science

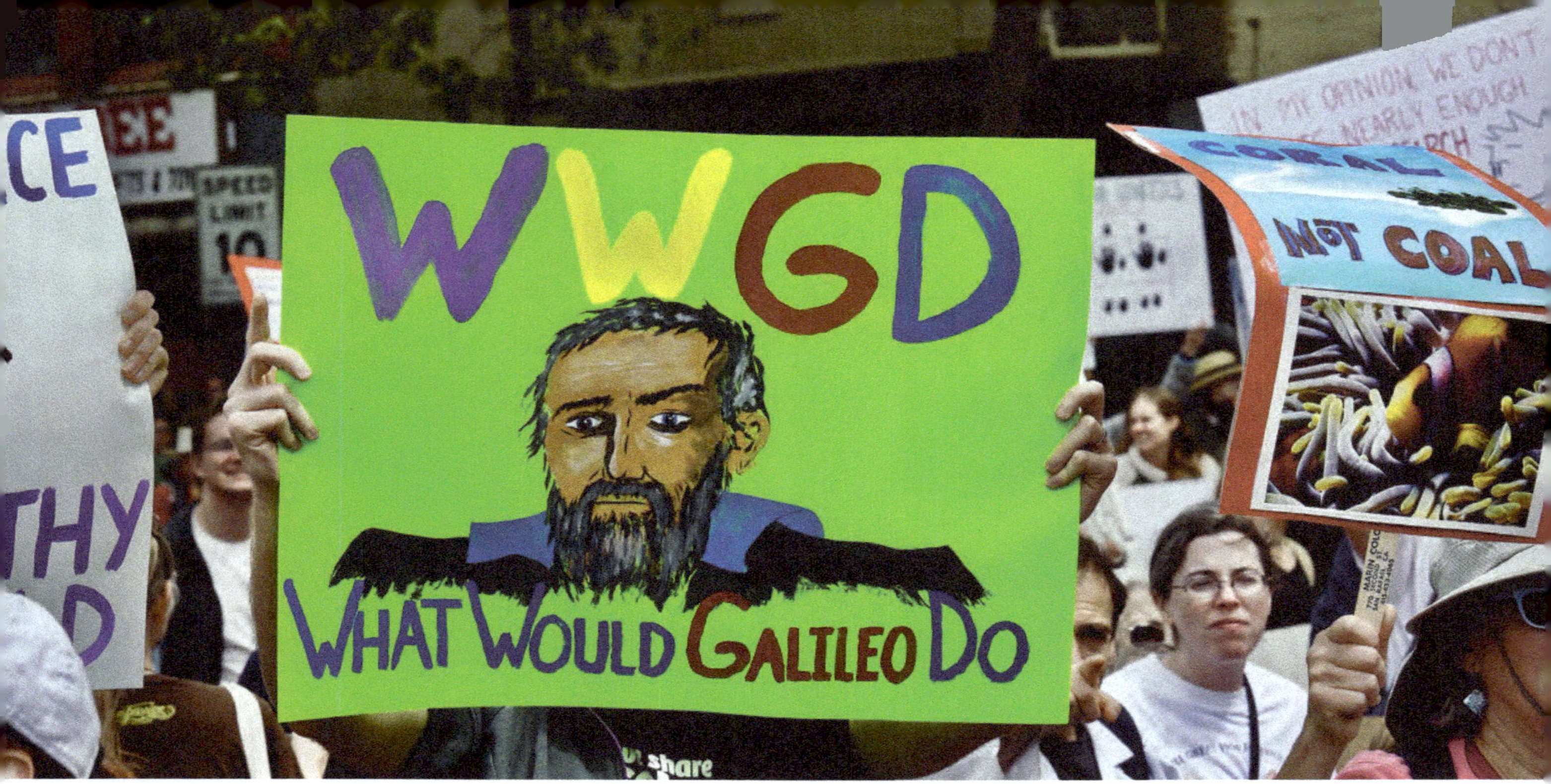

WWGD

WHAT WOULD GALILEO DO

CORAL
NOT COAL

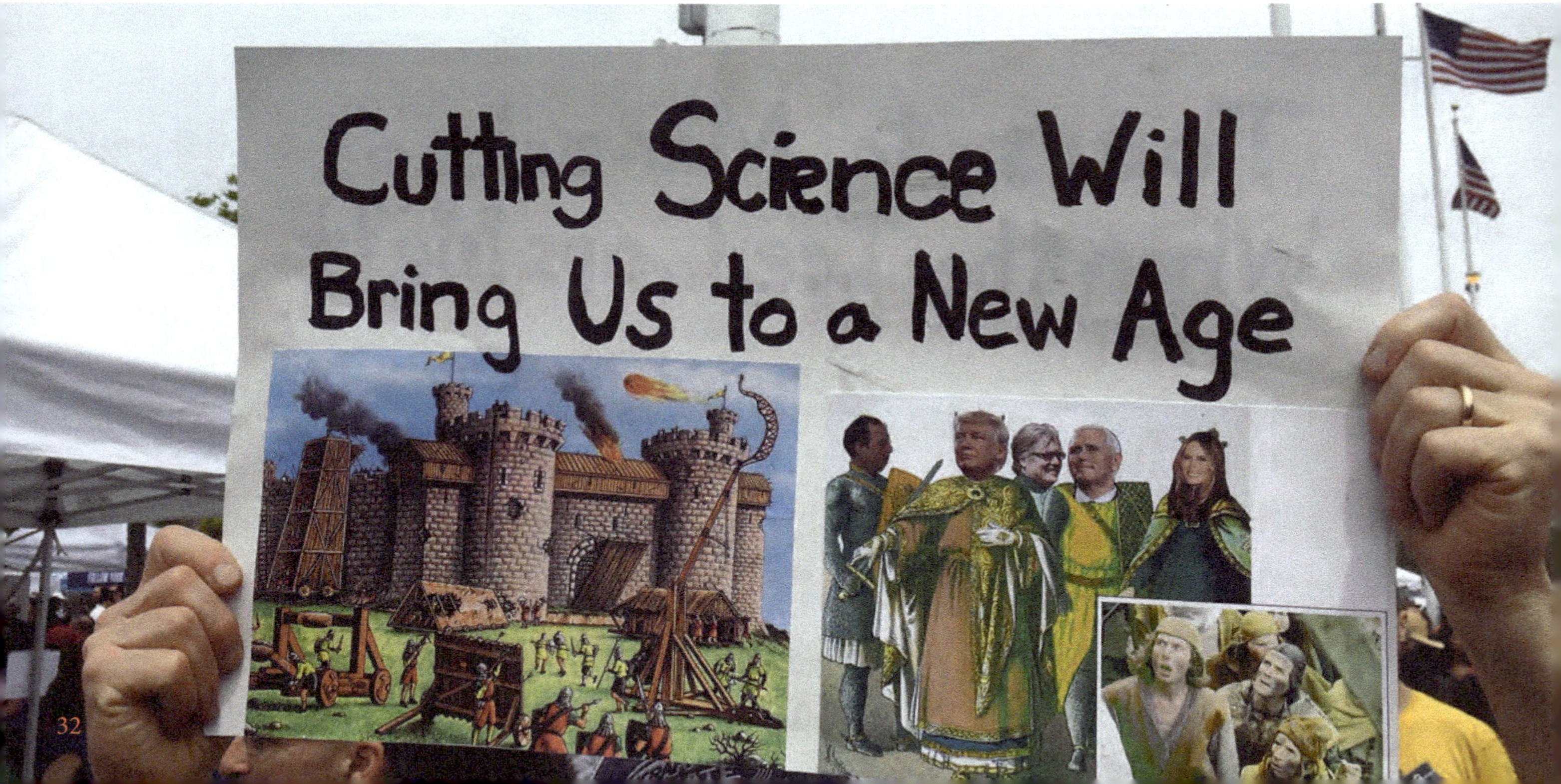

IN MY OPINION WE DON'T
NEARLY ENOUGH

Cutting Science Will
Bring Us to a New Age

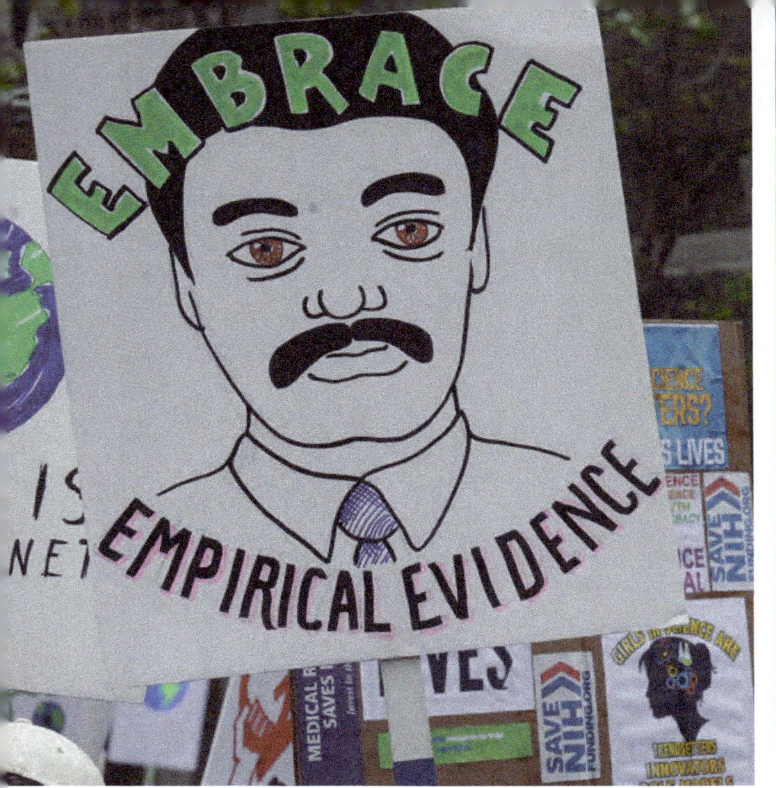
EMBRACE
EMPIRICAL EVIDENCE
IS
NET

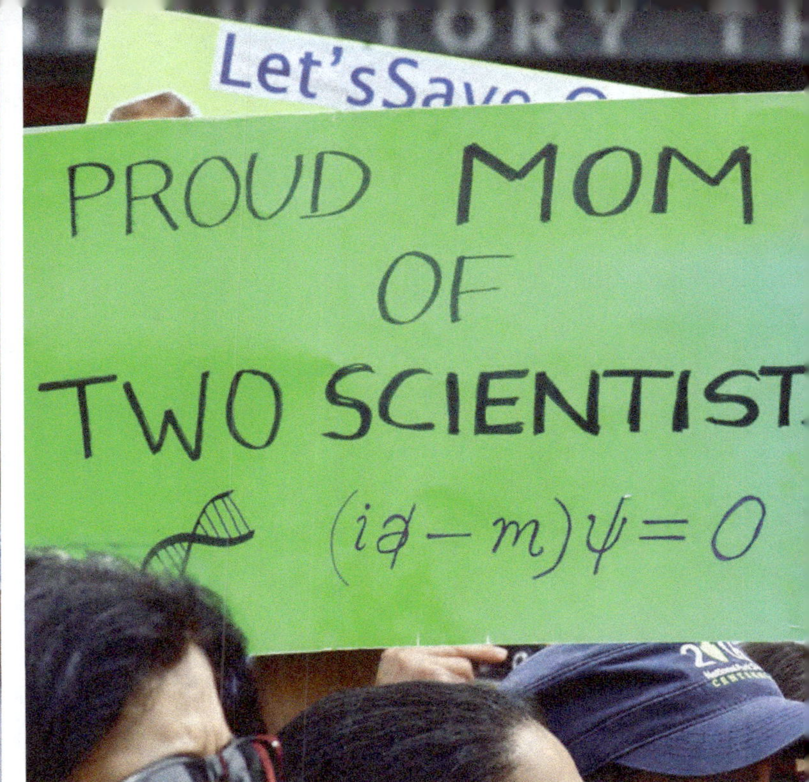
Let's Save
PROUD MOM
OF
TWO SCIENTIST
$(i\partial - m)\psi = 0$

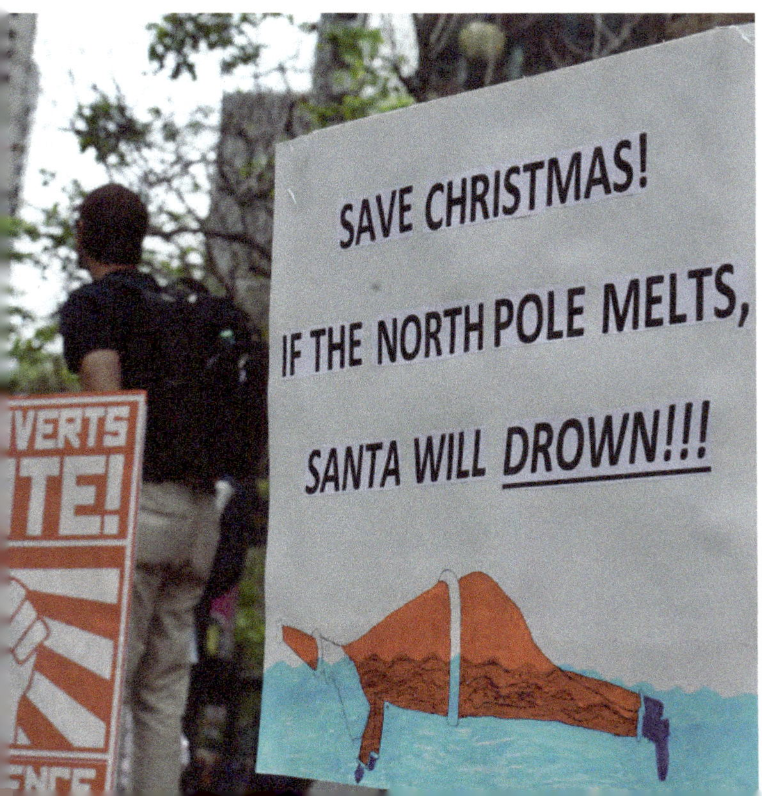
SAVE CHRISTMAS!
IF THE NORTH POLE MELTS,
SANTA WILL DROWN!!!
VERTS
TE!

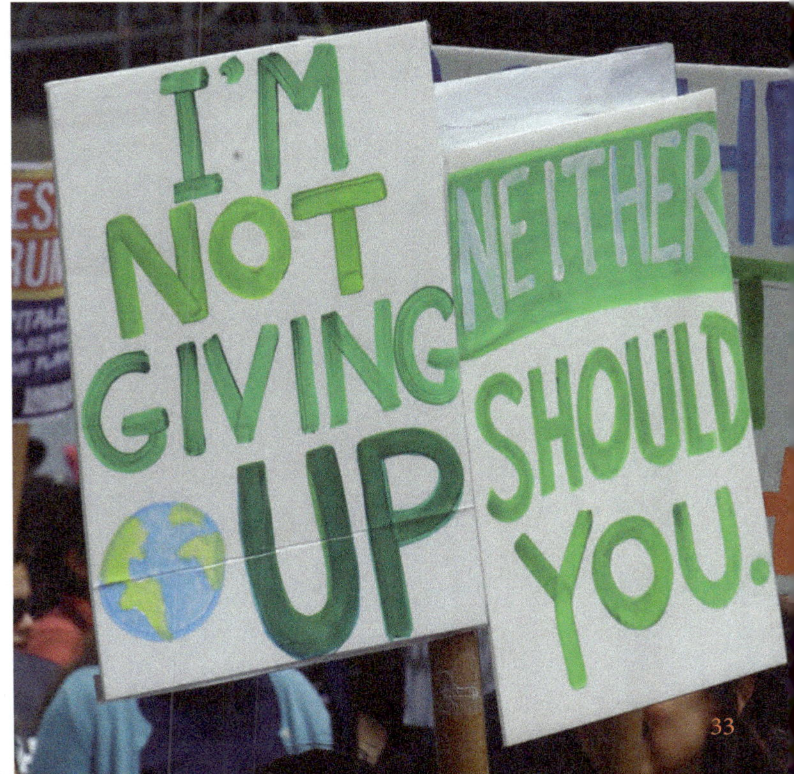
I'M NOT GIVING UP
NEITHER SHOULD YOU.

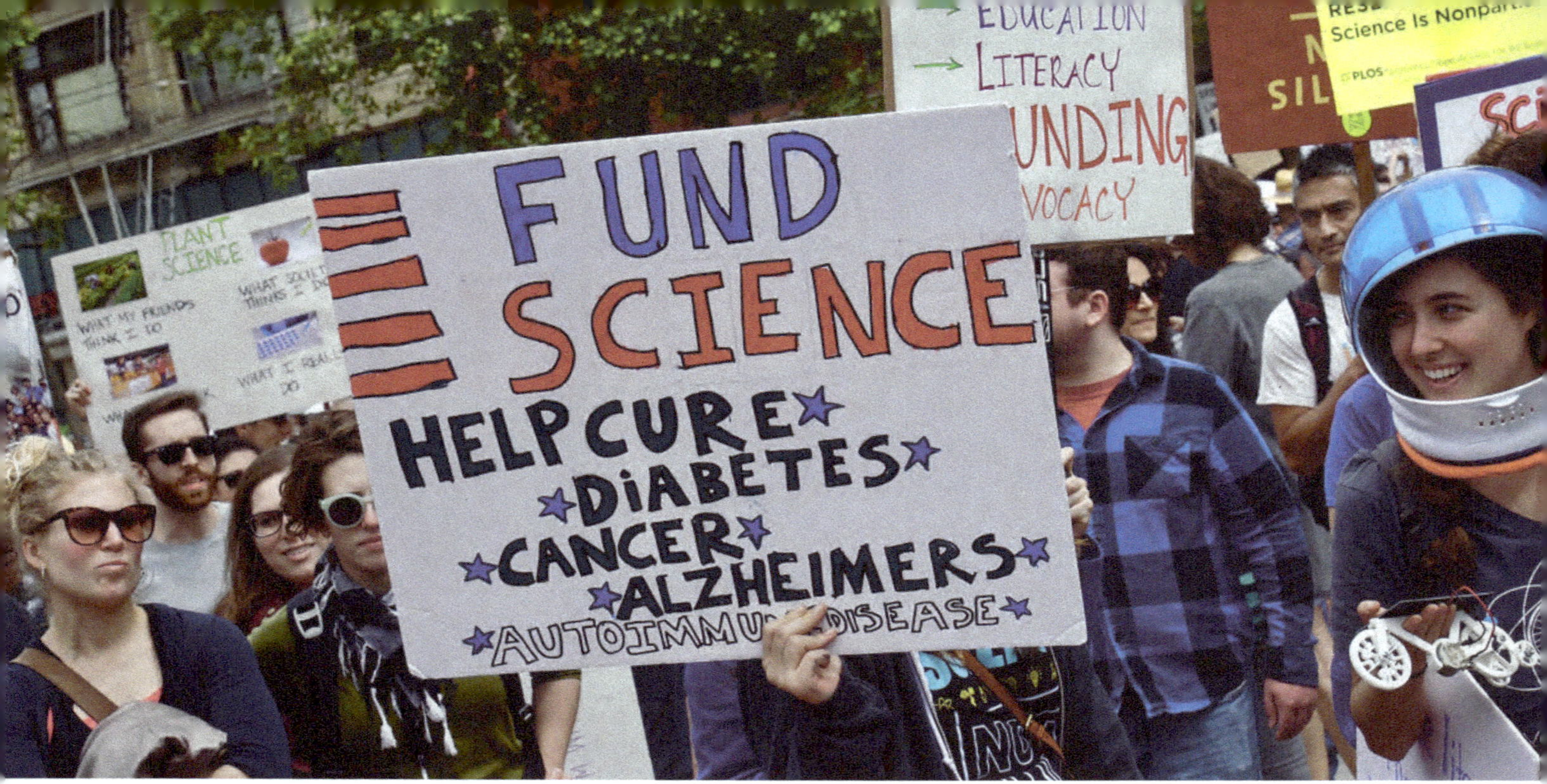

EDUCATION
LITERACY
FUNDING
ADVOCACY
Science Is Nonpartisan
PLOS
PLANT SCIENCE
WHAT MY FRIENDS THINK I DO
WHAT SOCIETY THINKS I DO
WHAT I REALLY DO
FUND SCIENCE
HELP CURE
DIABETES
CANCER
ALZHEIMERS
AUTOIMMUNE DISEASE

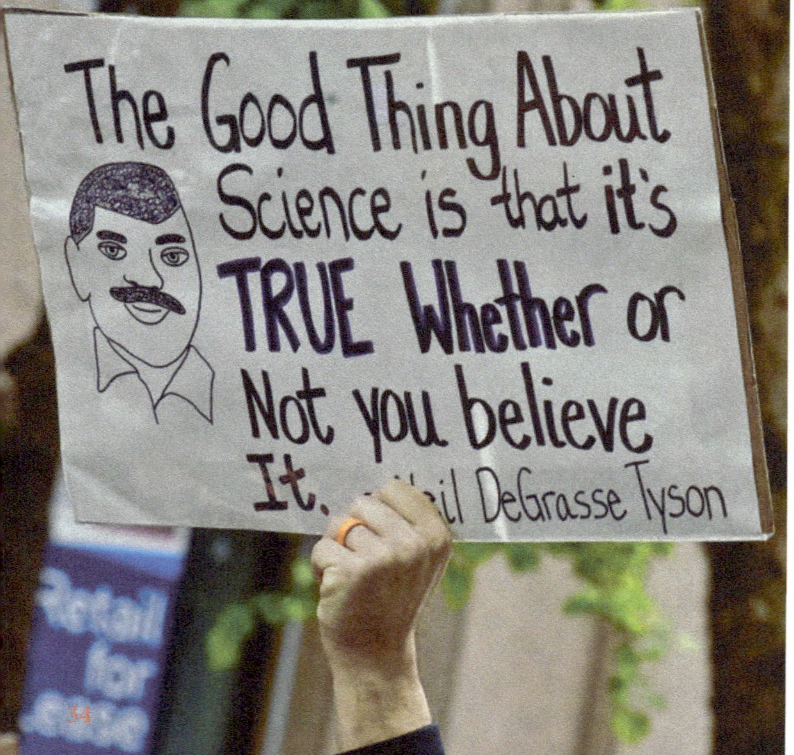
The Good Thing About Science is that it's TRUE Whether or Not you believe It. - Neil DeGrasse Tyson

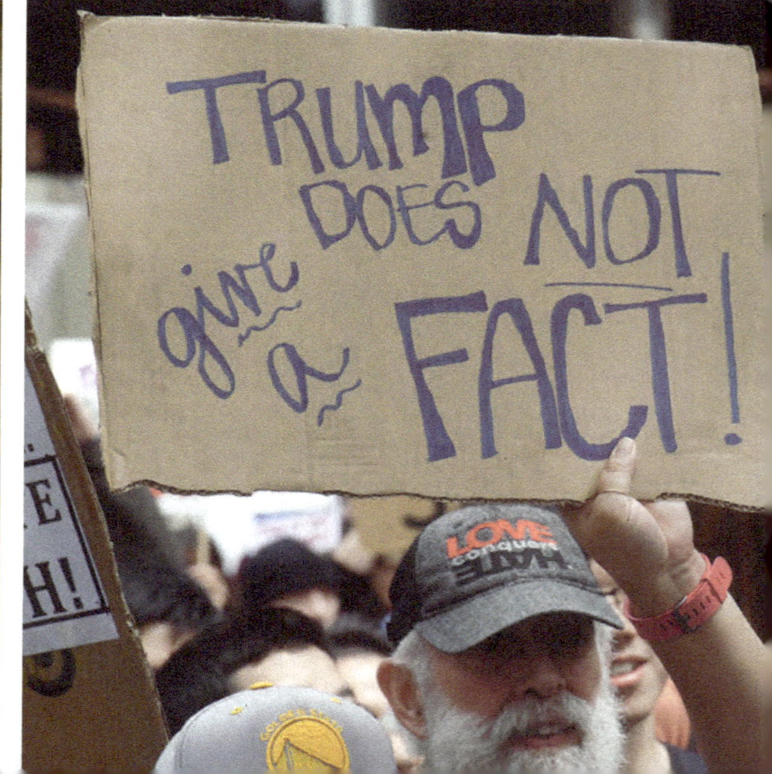
TRUMP DOES NOT give a FACT!

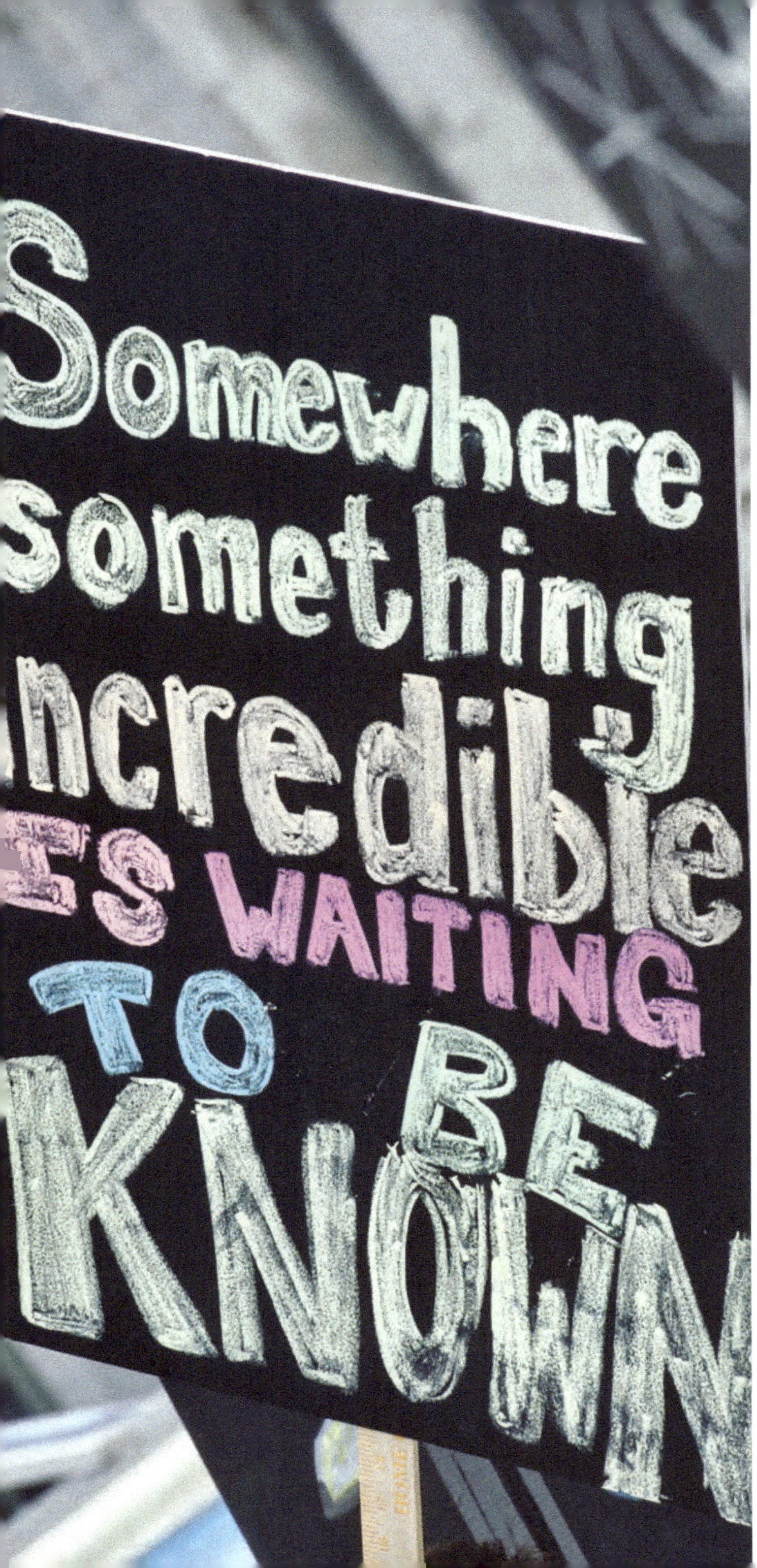

Somewhere
something
incredible
is WAITING
TO BE
KNOWN

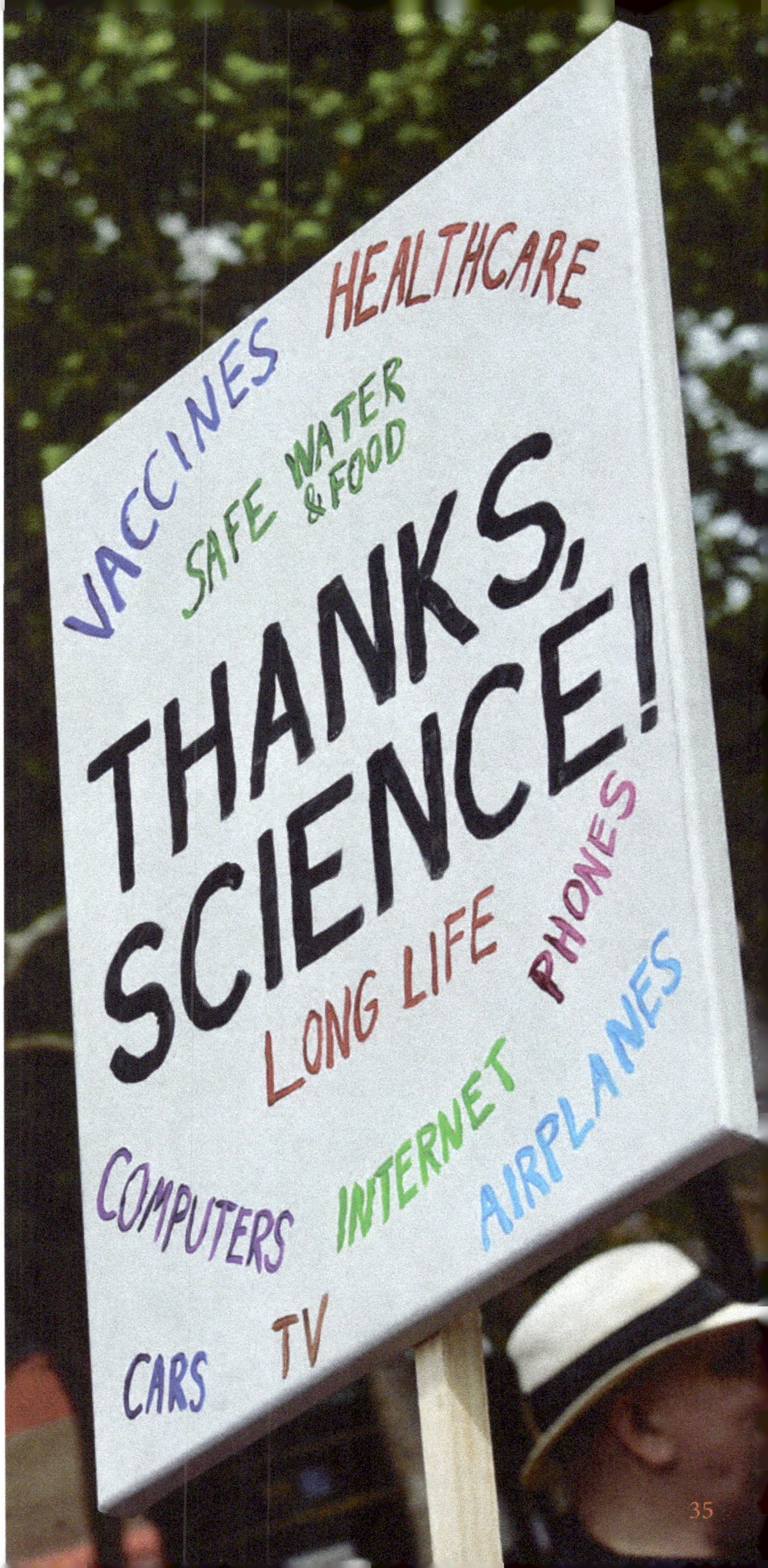

VACCINES
HEALTHCARE
SAFE WATER & FOOD
THANKS, SCIENCE!
LONG LIFE
PHONES
COMPUTERS
INTERNET
AIRPLANES
CARS
TV

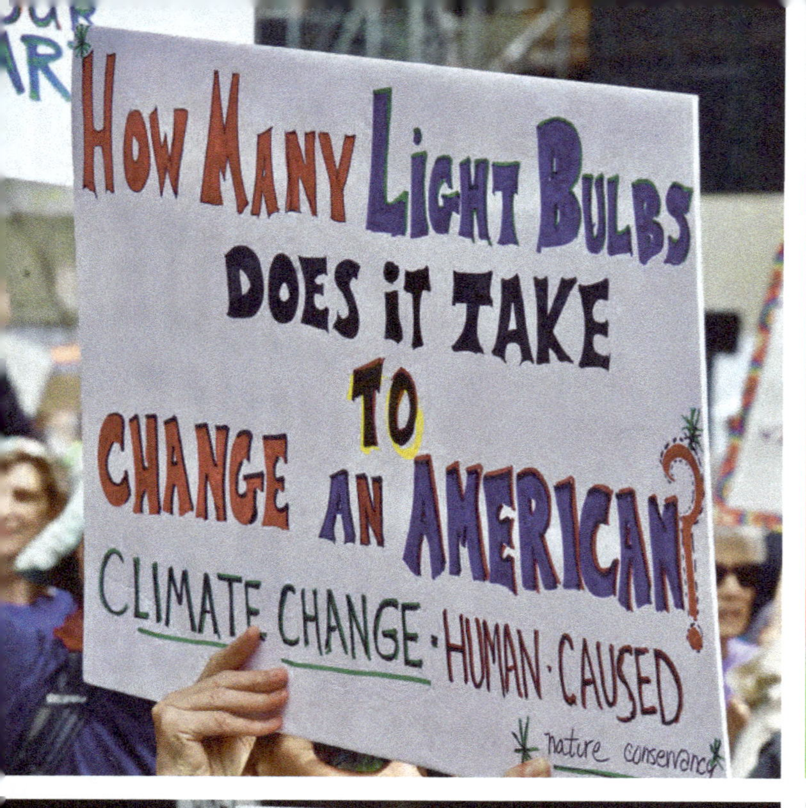
How Many Light Bulbs
Does it Take
to
Change an American?
CLIMATE CHANGE · HUMAN · CAUSED
nature conservancy

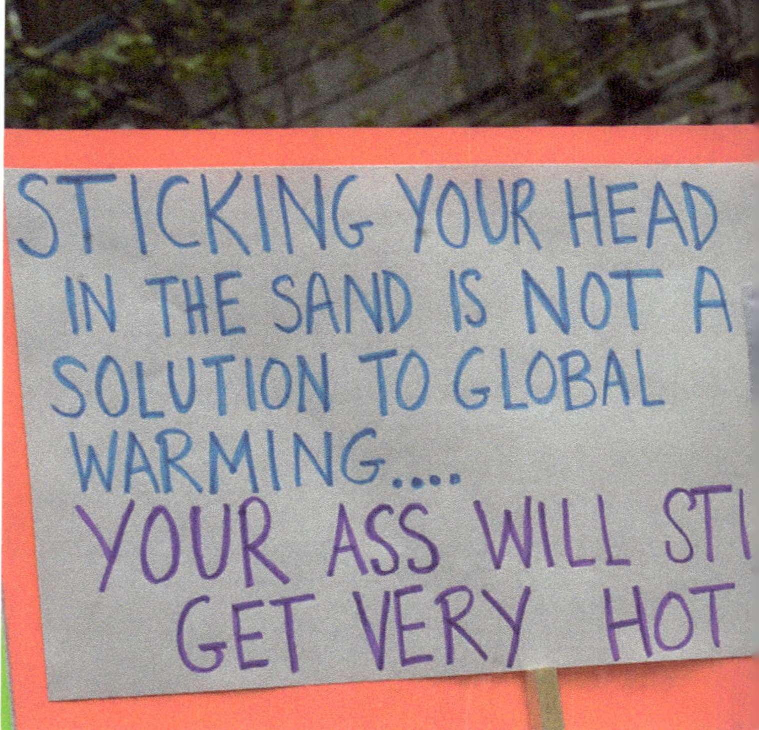
STICKING YOUR HEAD
IN THE SAND IS NOT A
SOLUTION TO GLOBAL
WARMING....
YOUR ASS WILL STI
GET VERY HOT

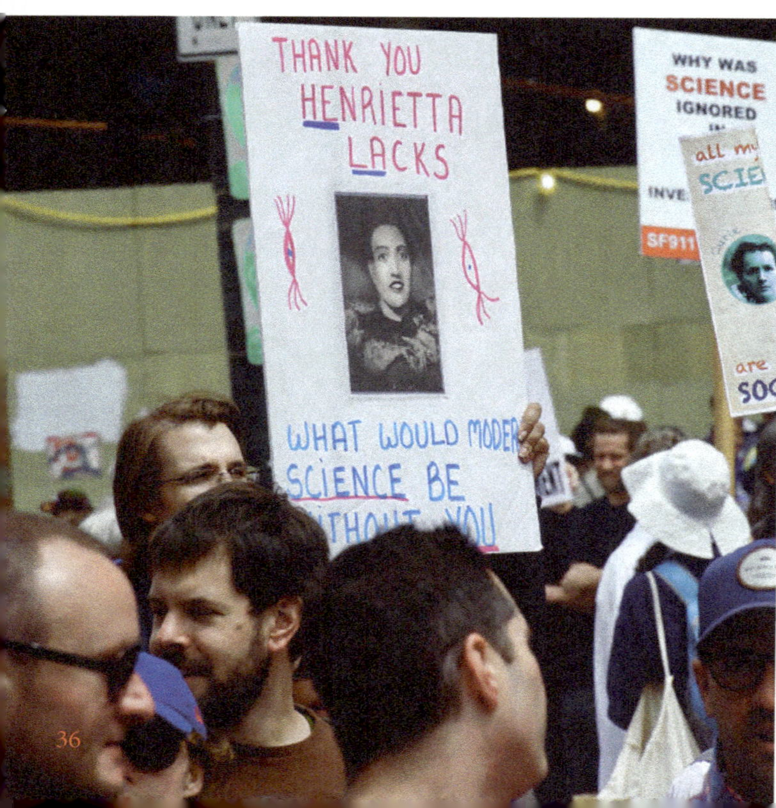
THANK YOU
HENRIETTA
LACKS
WHAT WOULD MODERN
SCIENCE BE
WITHOUT YOU
WHY WAS
SCIENCE
IGNORED
all my
SCIE
INVE
SF911
are
SOO

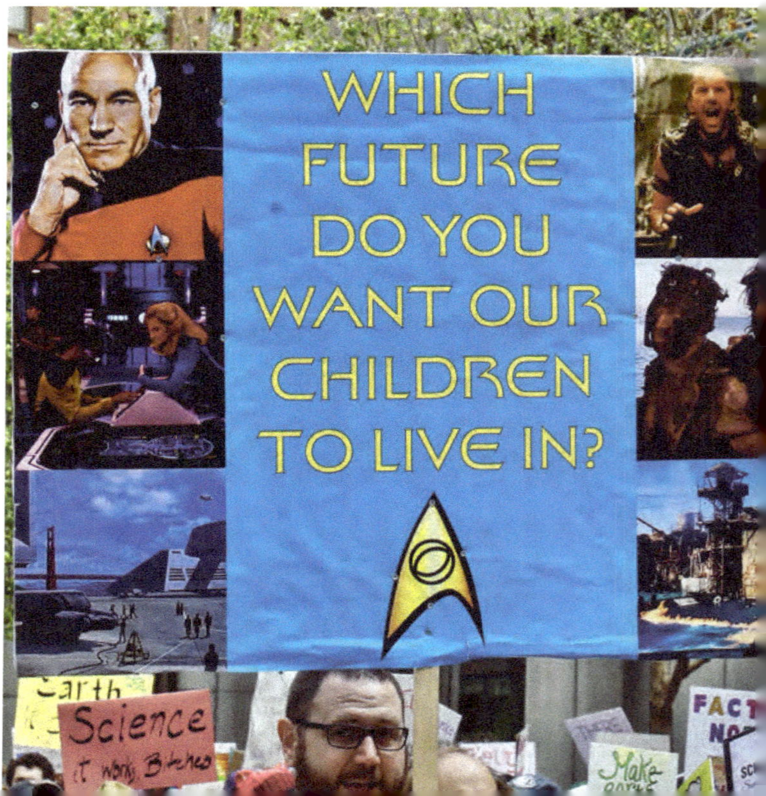
WHICH
FUTURE
DO YOU
WANT OUR
CHILDREN
TO LIVE IN?
arth
Science
it works, B-tches
FACT

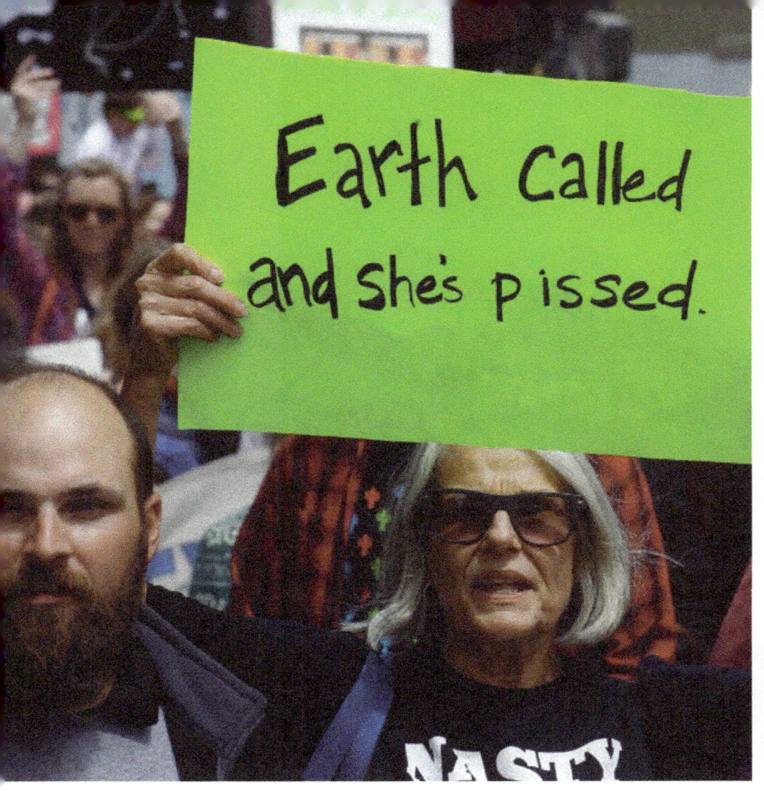

Earth called and she's pissed.
NASTY

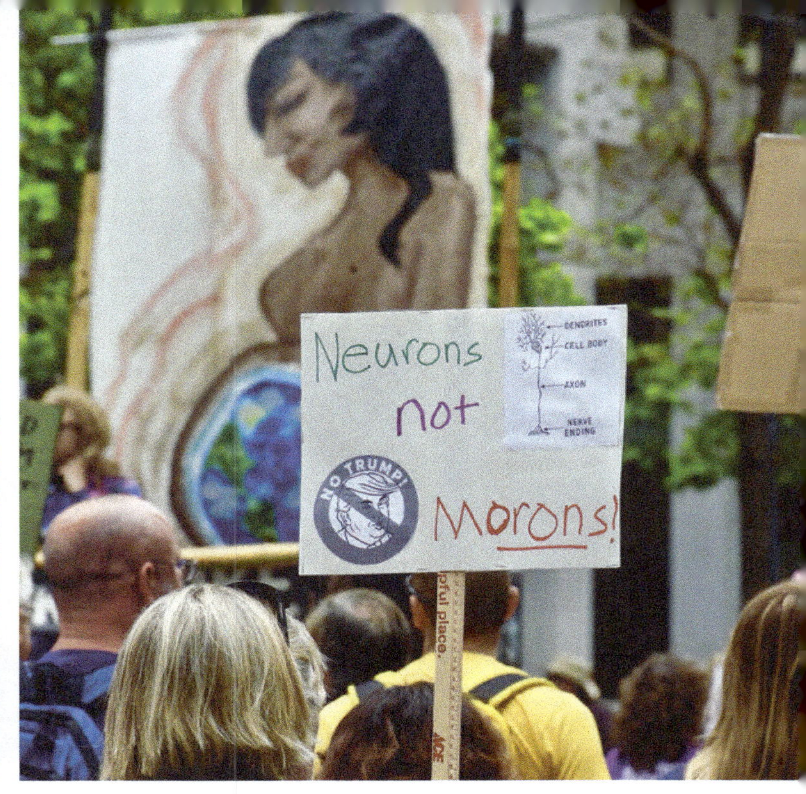

Neurons not Morons!
DENDRITES
CELL BODY
AXON
NERVE ENDING
NO TRUMP!

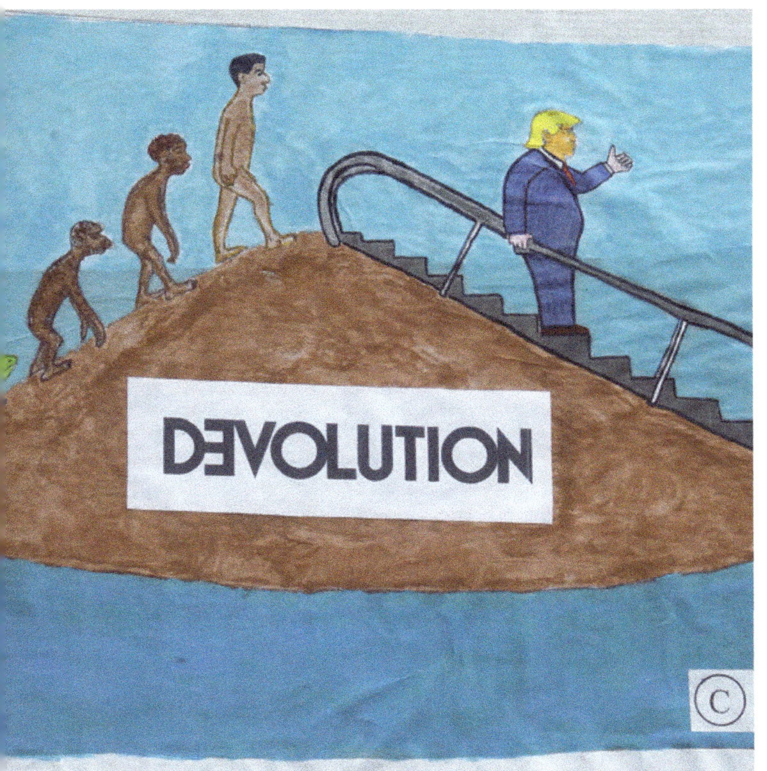

DEVOLUTION

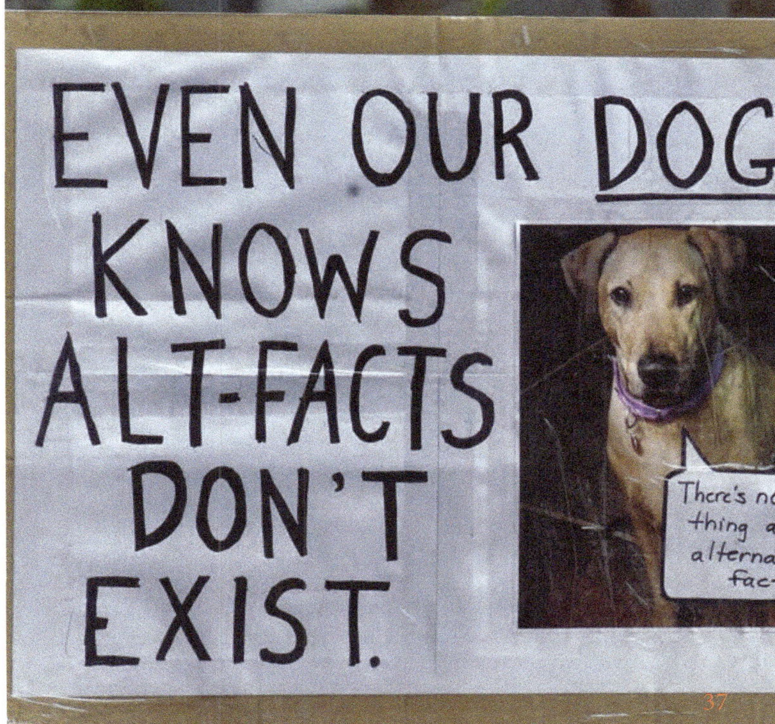

EVEN OUR DOG KNOWS ALT-FACTS DON'T EXIST.
There's no thing a alterna fact

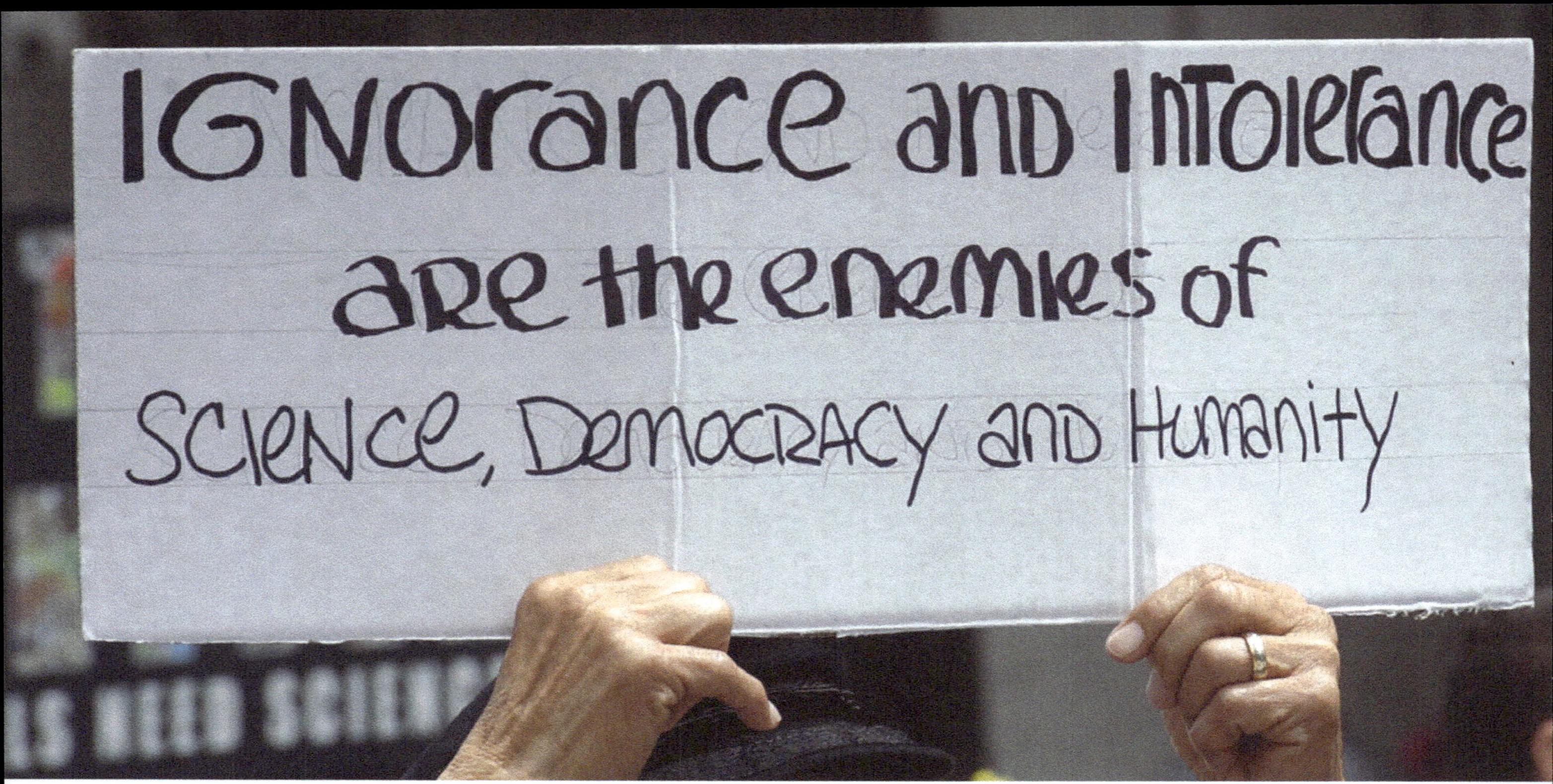

IGNorance and INToIerance
are the enemies of
SCIeNCe, DemocRaCY and HumaNity

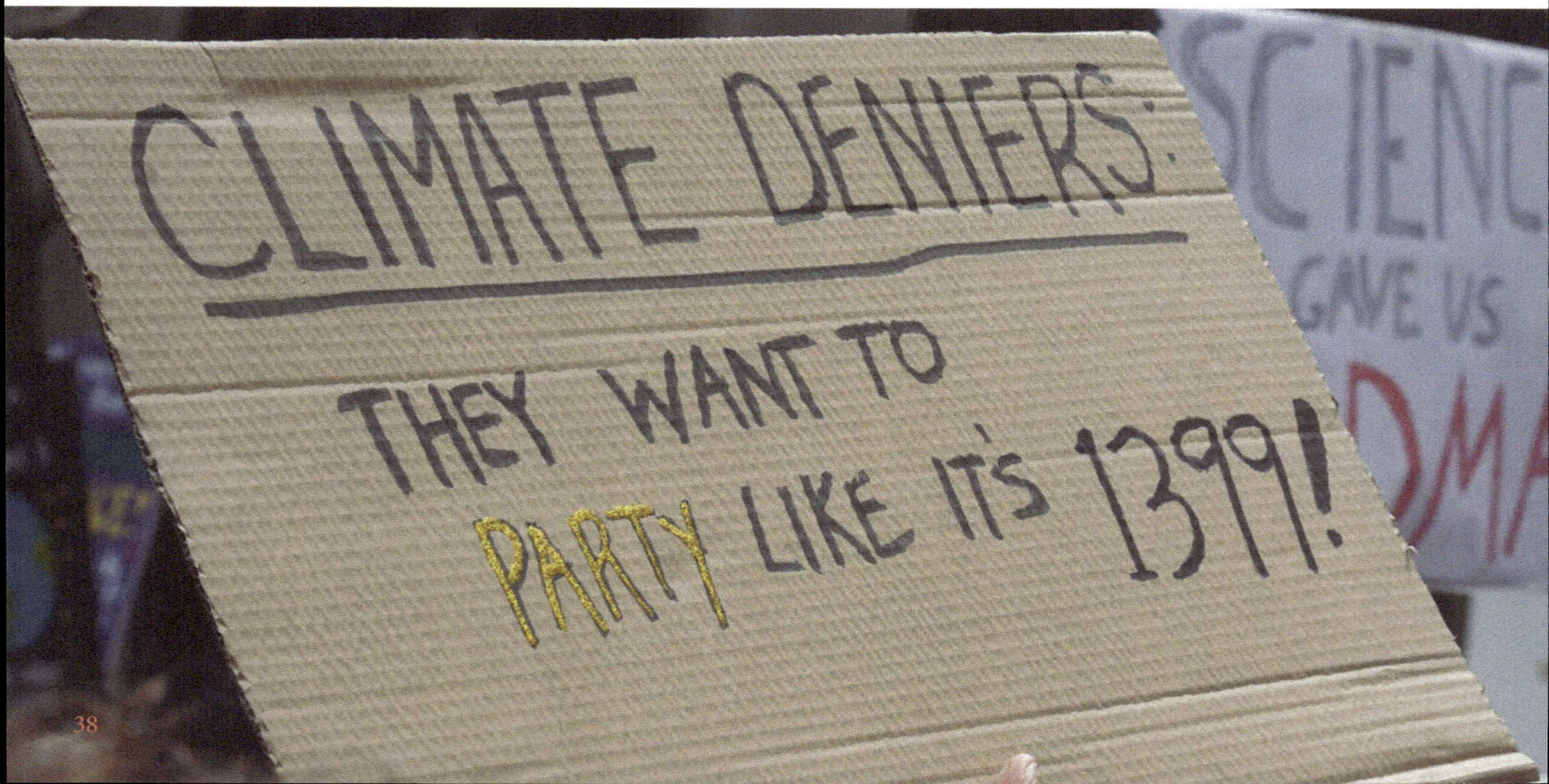

S NEED SCIEN

CLIMATE DENIERS:
THEY WANT TO
PARTY LIKE ITS 1399!

SCIENC
GAVE US
DNA

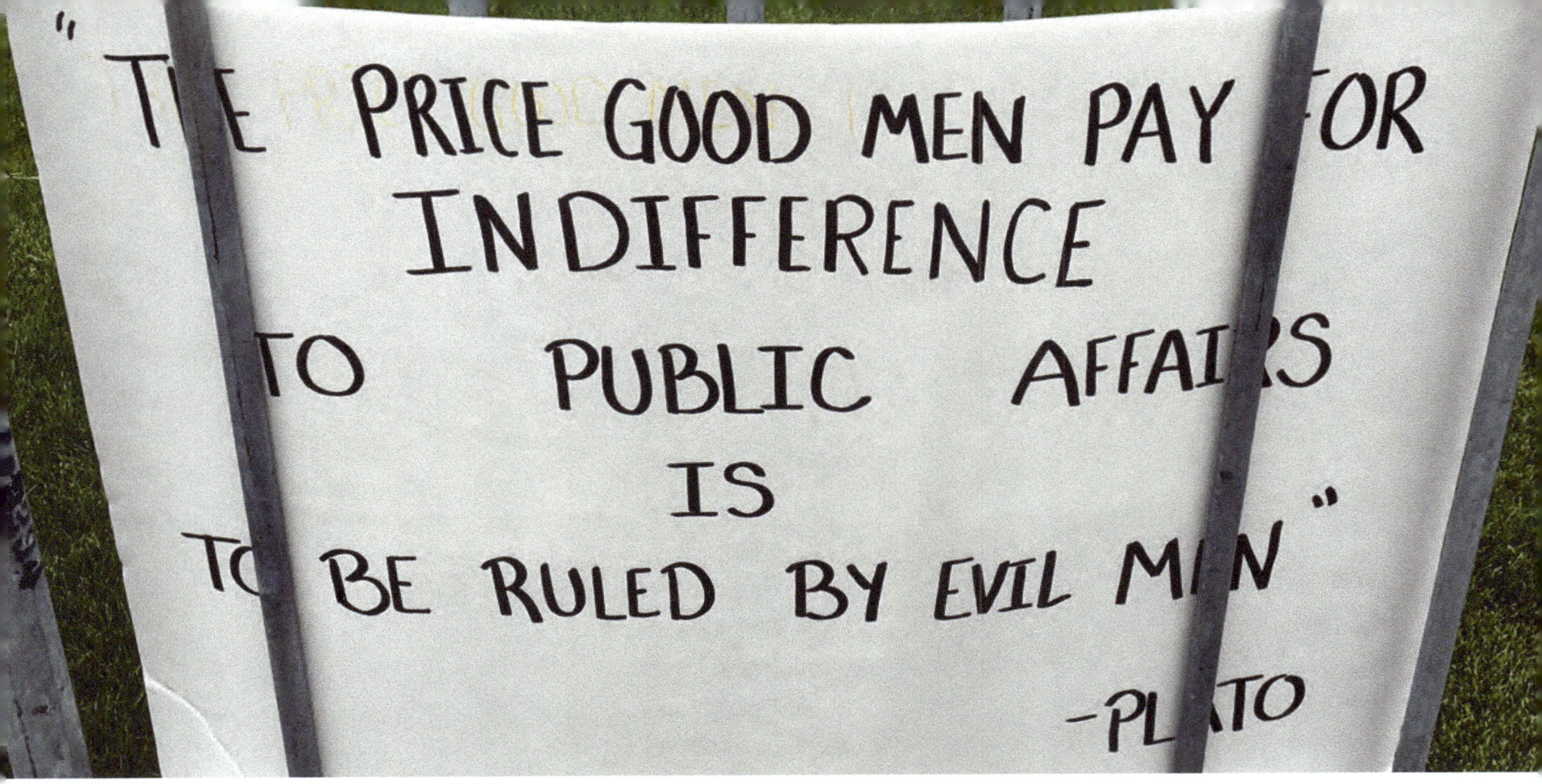

"THE PRICE GOOD MEN PAY FOR
INDIFFERENCE
TO   PUBLIC   AFFAIRS
IS
TO BE RULED BY EVIL MEN "
-PLATO

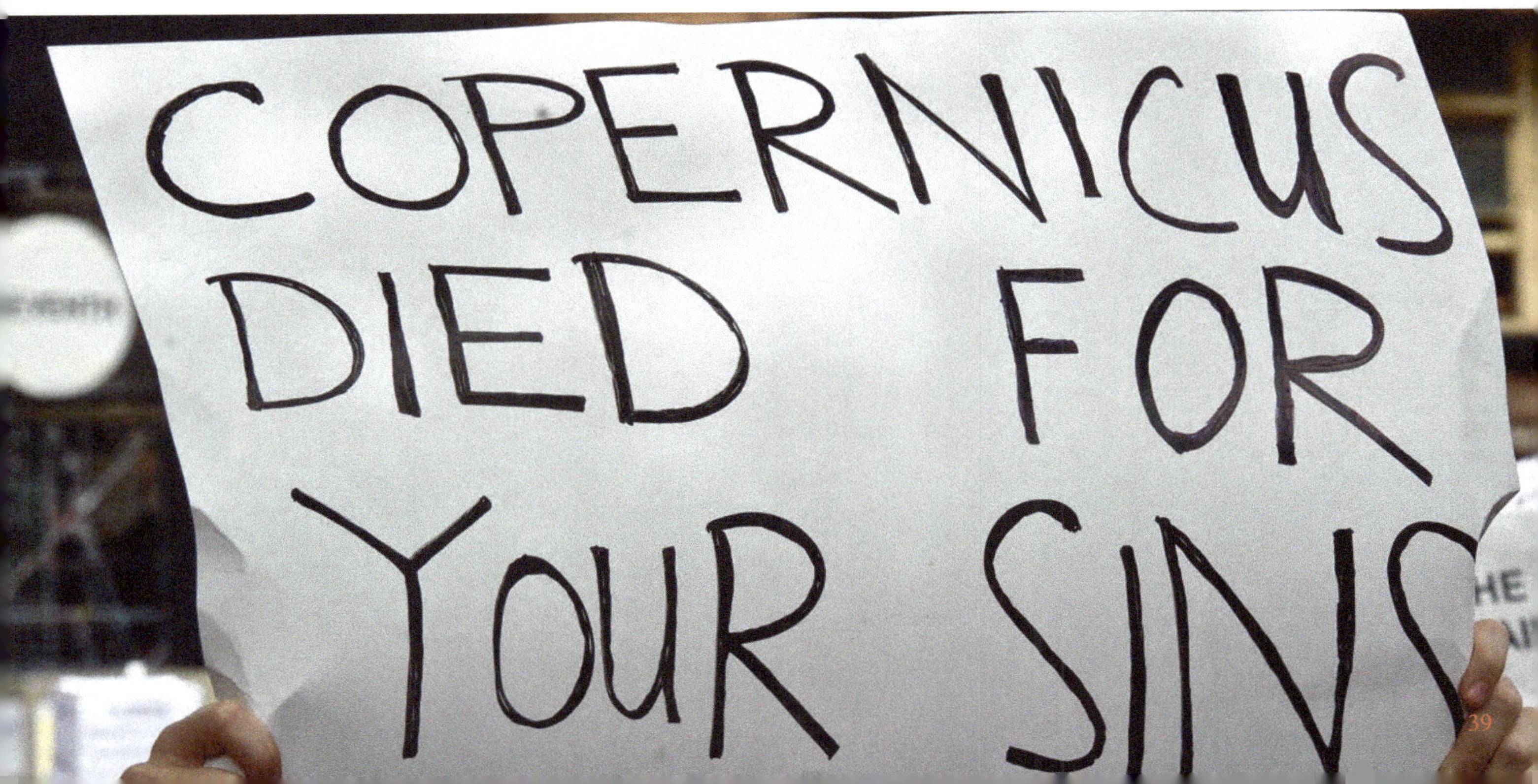

COPERNICUS
DIED   FOR
YOUR SINS

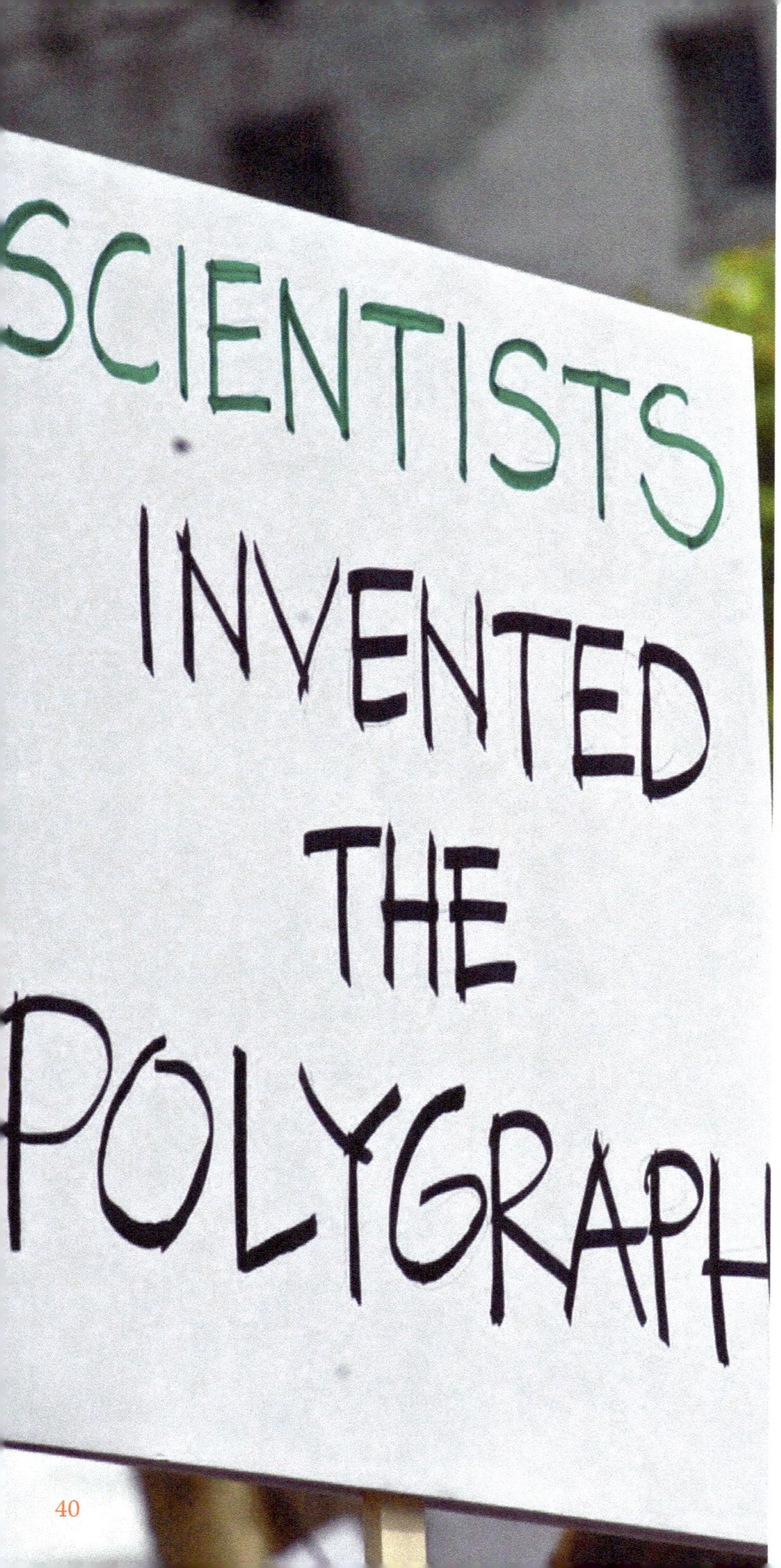

SCIENTISTS INVENTED THE POLYGRAPH

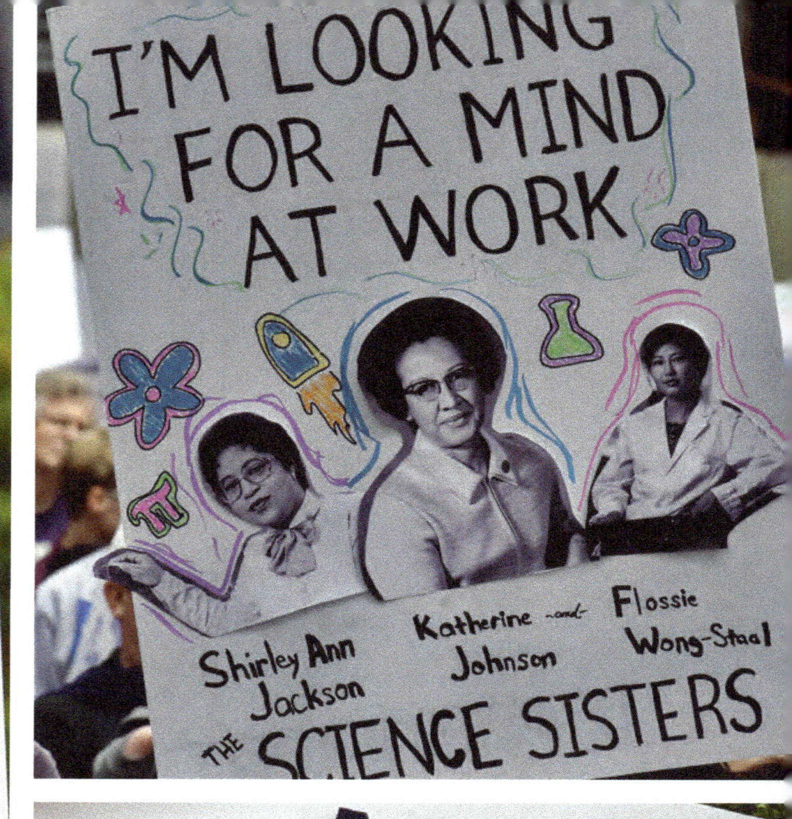

I'M LOOKING FOR A MIND AT WORK
Shirley Ann Jackson
Katherine -and- Johnson
Flossie Wong-Staal
THE SCIENCE SISTERS

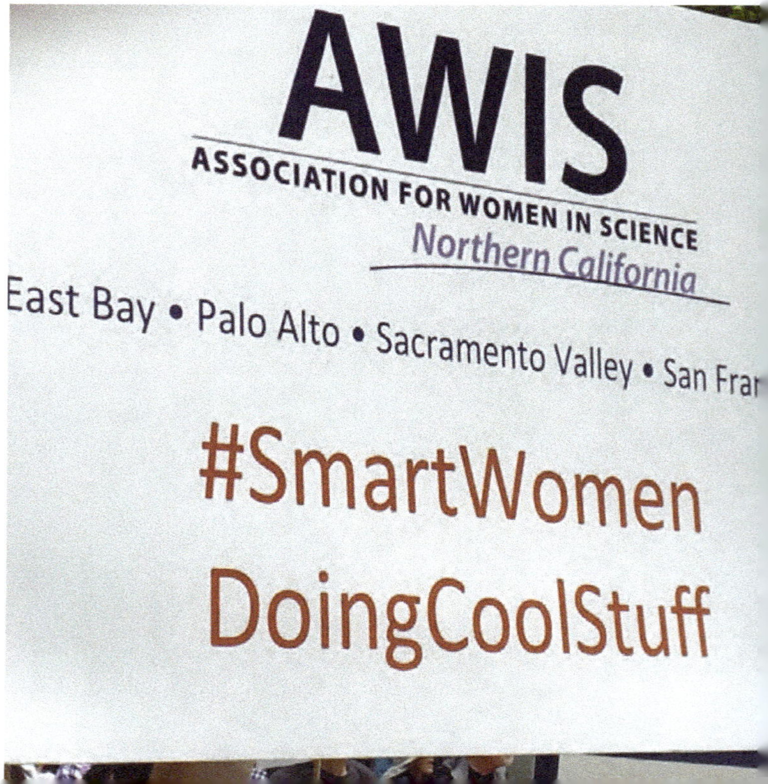

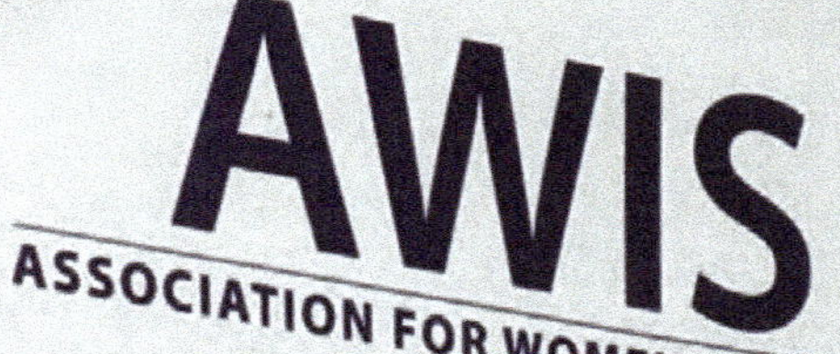

AWIS
ASSOCIATION FOR WOMEN IN SCIENCE
Northern California
East Bay • Palo Alto • Sacramento Valley • San Fran
#SmartWomen
DoingCoolStuff

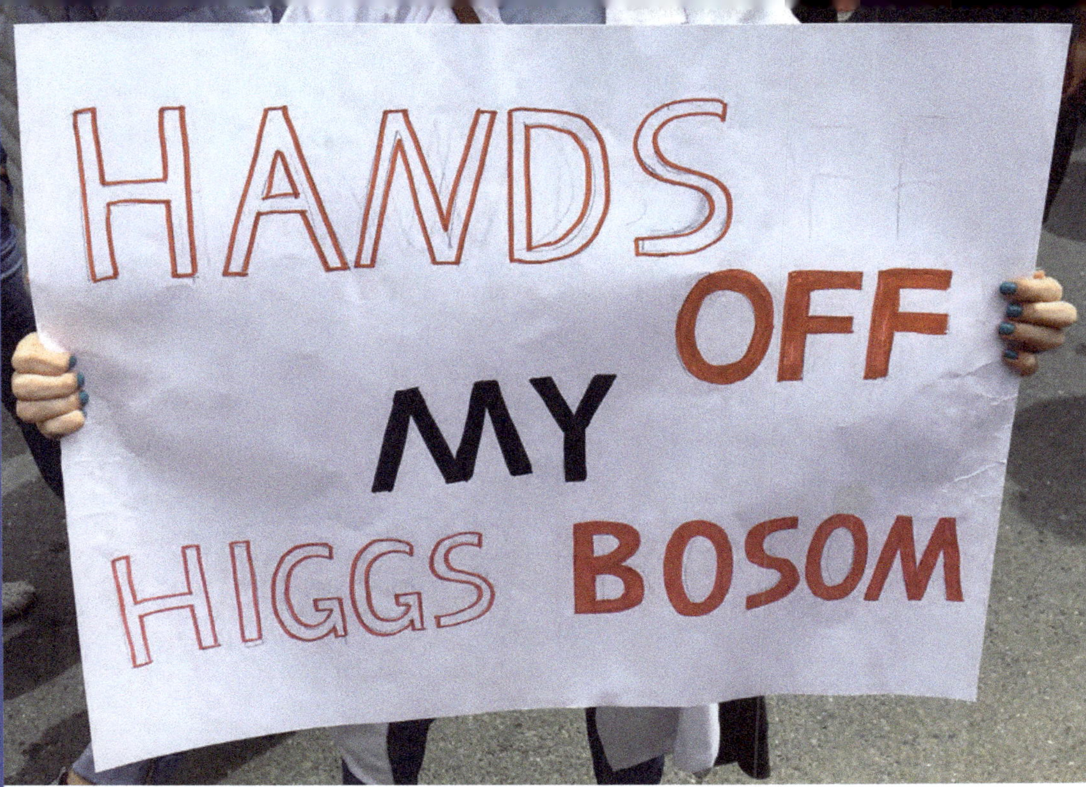

HANDS OFF MY HIGGS BOSOM

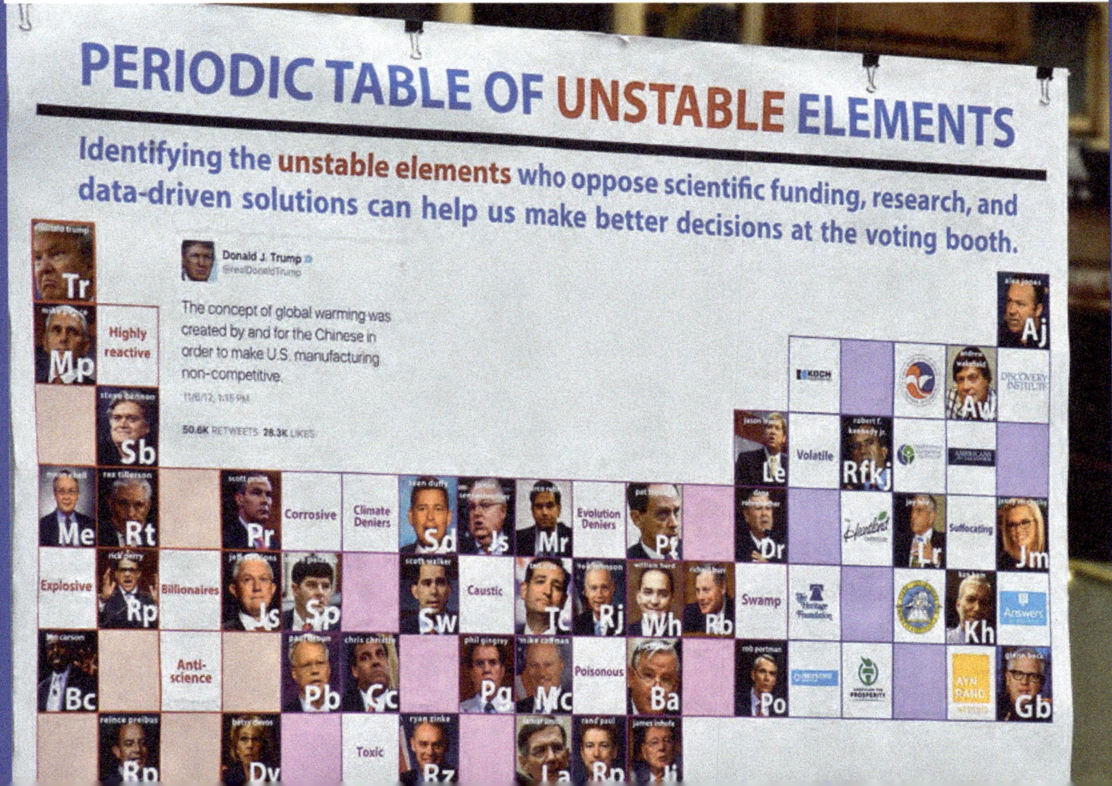

PERIODIC TABLE OF UNSTABLE ELEMENTS
Identifying the unstable elements who oppose scientific funding, research, and data-driven solutions can help us make better decisions at the voting booth.
Donald J. Trump @realDonaldTrump
The concept of global warming was created by and for the Chinese in order to make U.S. manufacturing non-competitive.
11/6/12, 1:15 PM
50.6K RETWEETS 28.3K LIKES
Highly reactive
Corrosive
Climate Deniers
Evolution Deniers
Volatile
Suffocating
Explosive
Billionaires
Caustic
Swamp
Anti-science
Poisonous
Toxic

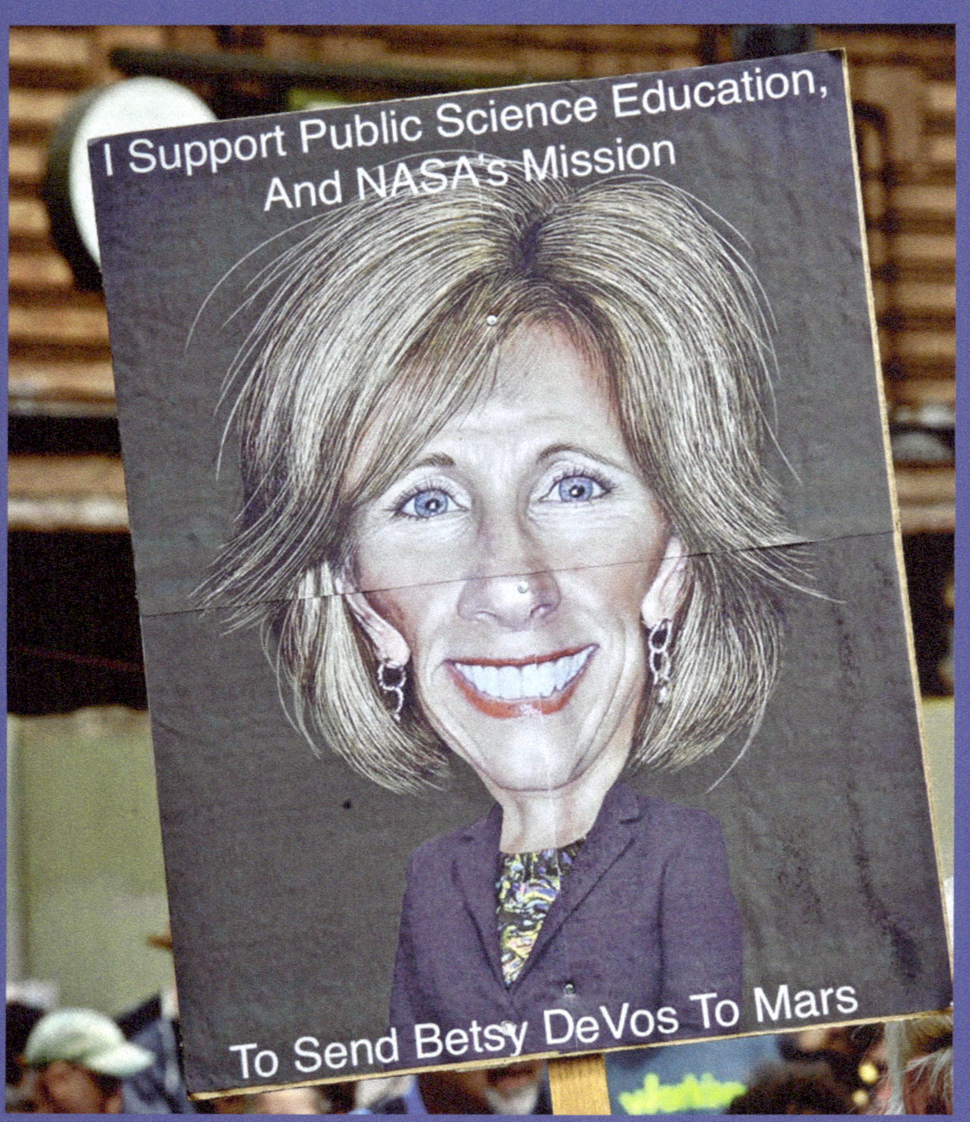

I Support Public Science Education,
And NASA's Mission
To Send Betsy DeVos To Mars

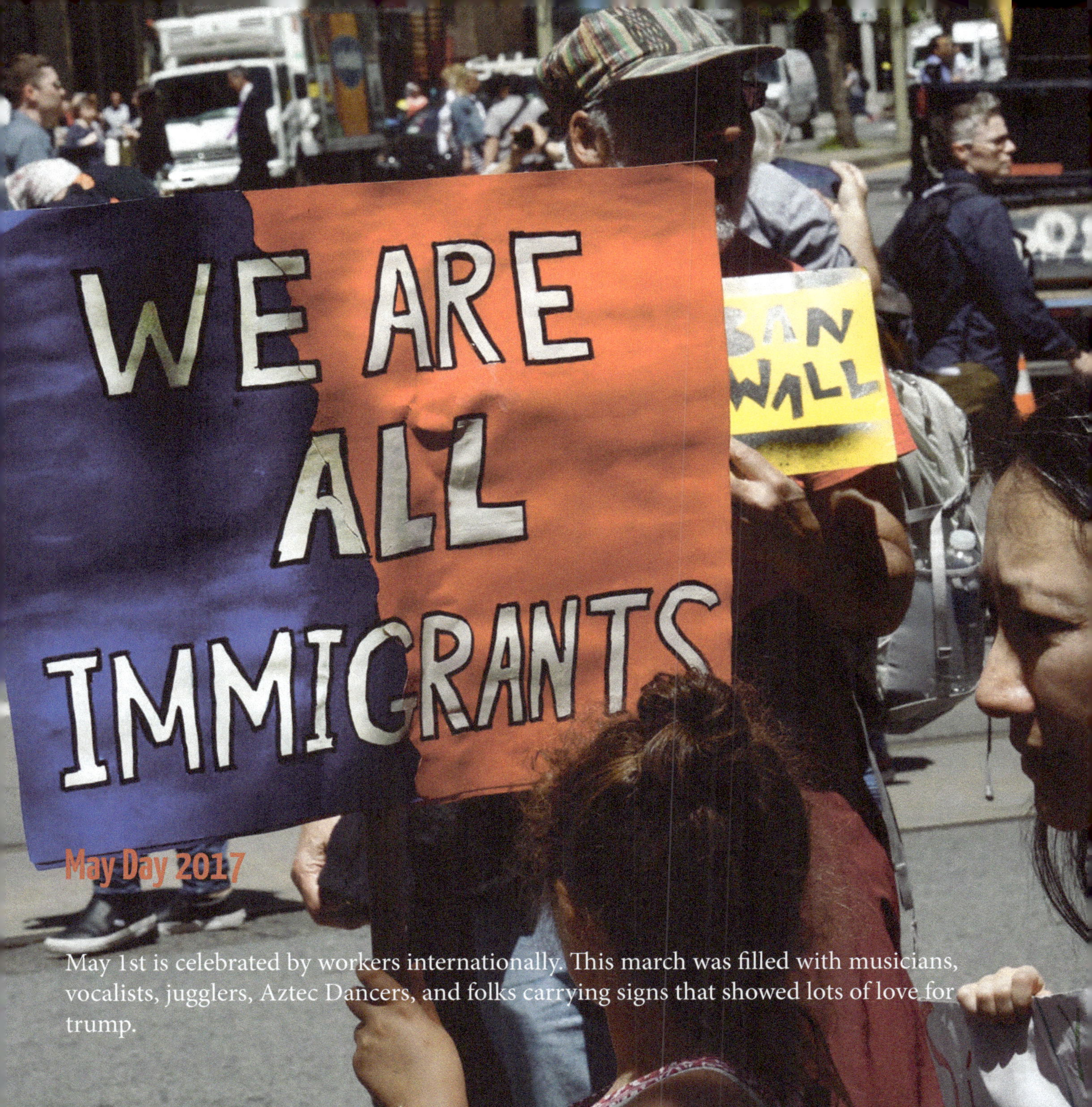

May 1st is celebrated by workers internationally. This march was filled with musicians, vocalists, jugglers, Aztec Dancers, and folks carrying signs that showed lots of love for trump.

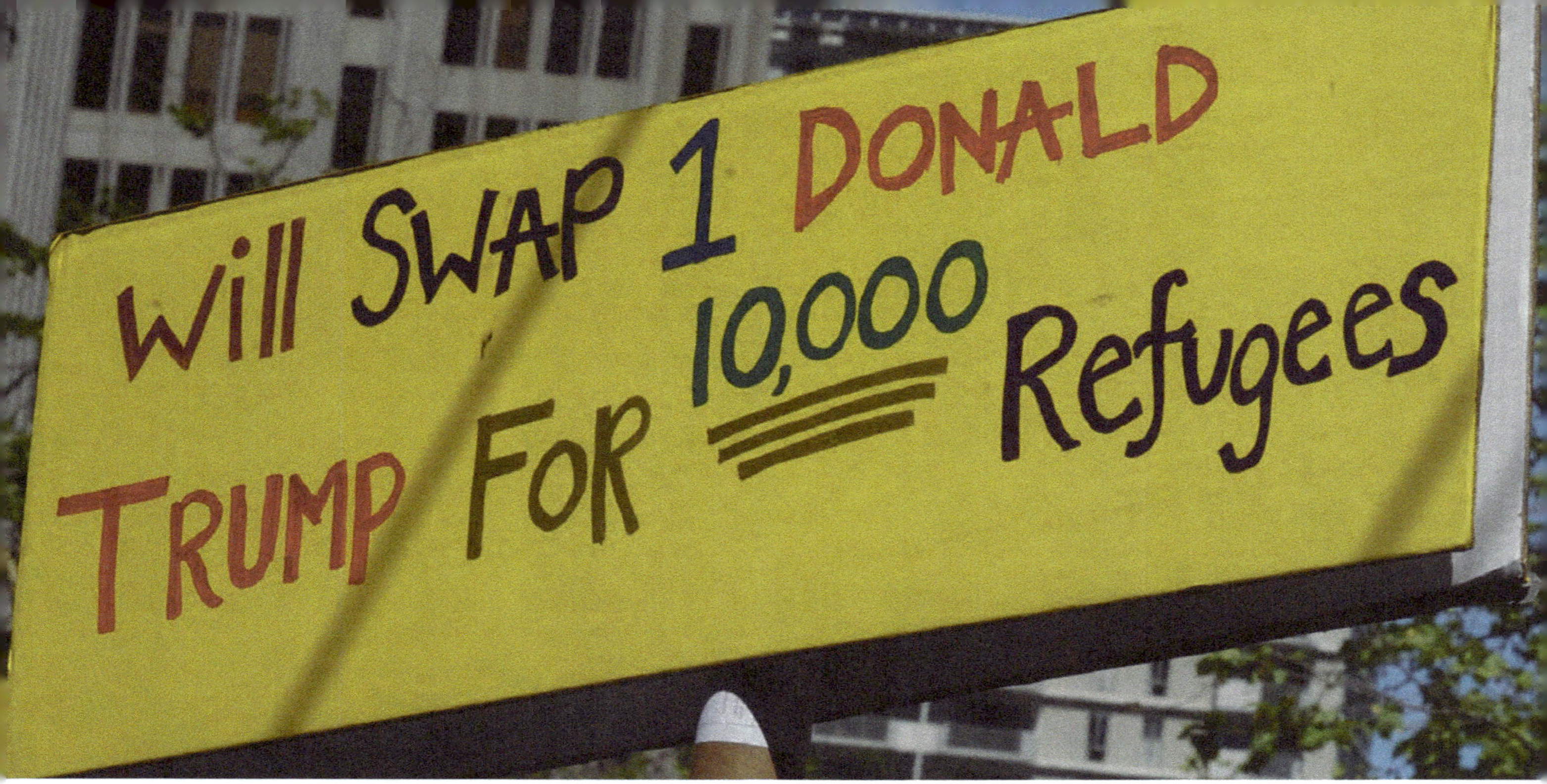

Will SWAP 1 DONALD
TRUMP FOR 10,000 Refugees

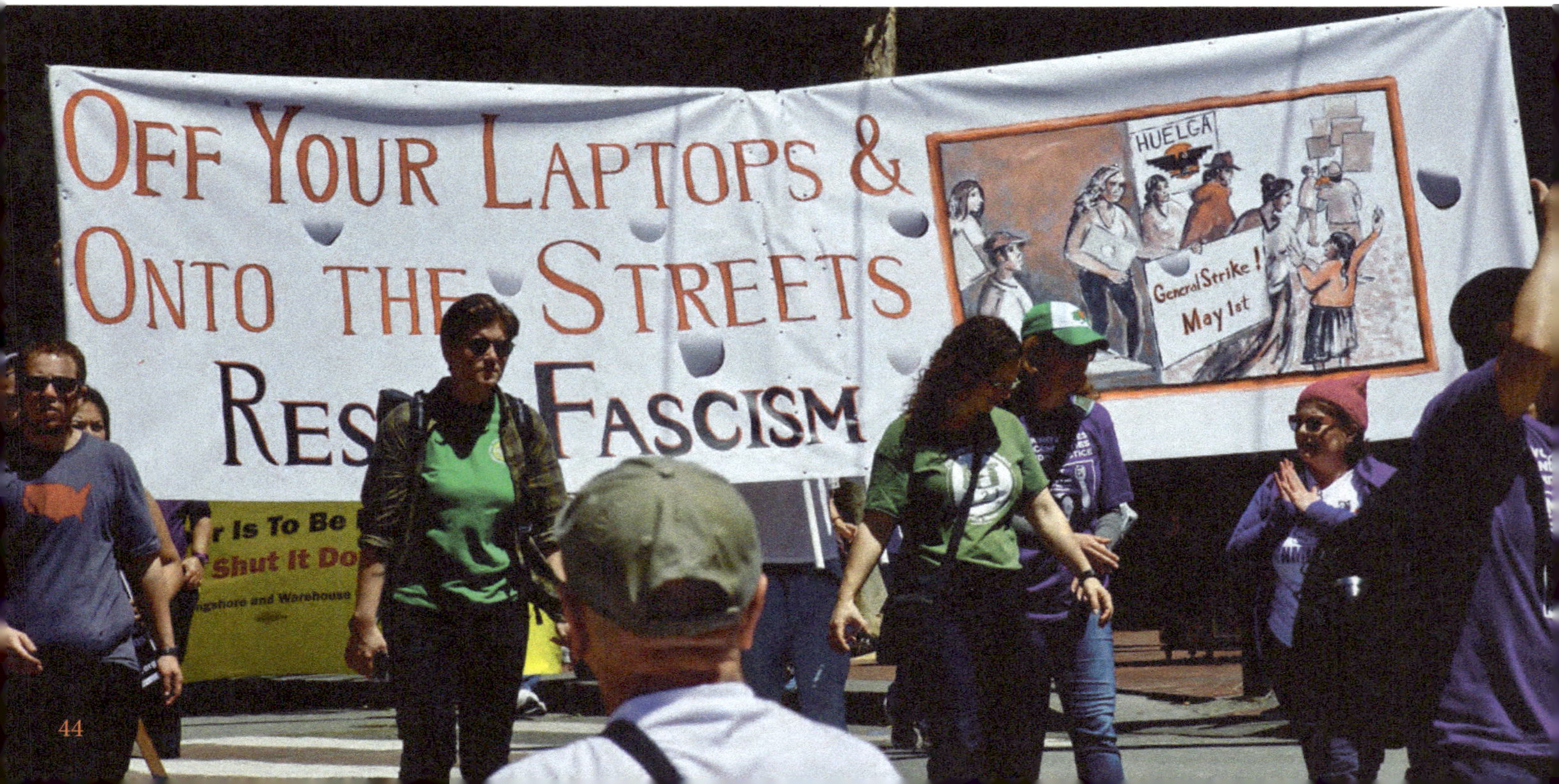

OFF YOUR LAPTOPS &
ONTO THE STREETS
Res Fascism
HUELGA
General Strike!
May 1st
r Is To Be
Shut It Do
ngshore and Warehouse

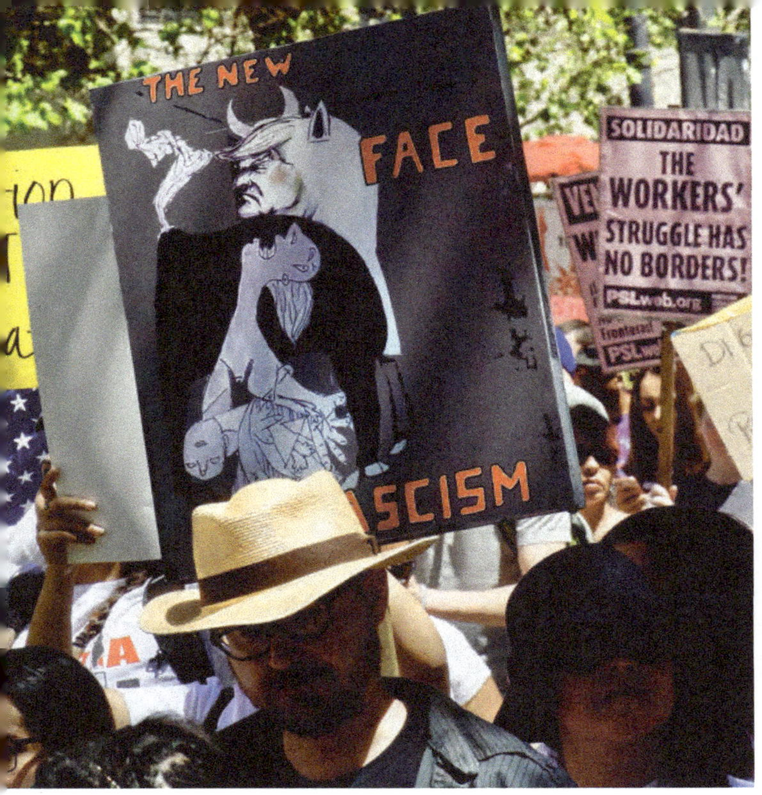

THE NEW
FACE
SOLIDARIDAD
THE WORKERS' STRUGGLE HAS NO BORDERS!
PSLweb.org
FASCISM

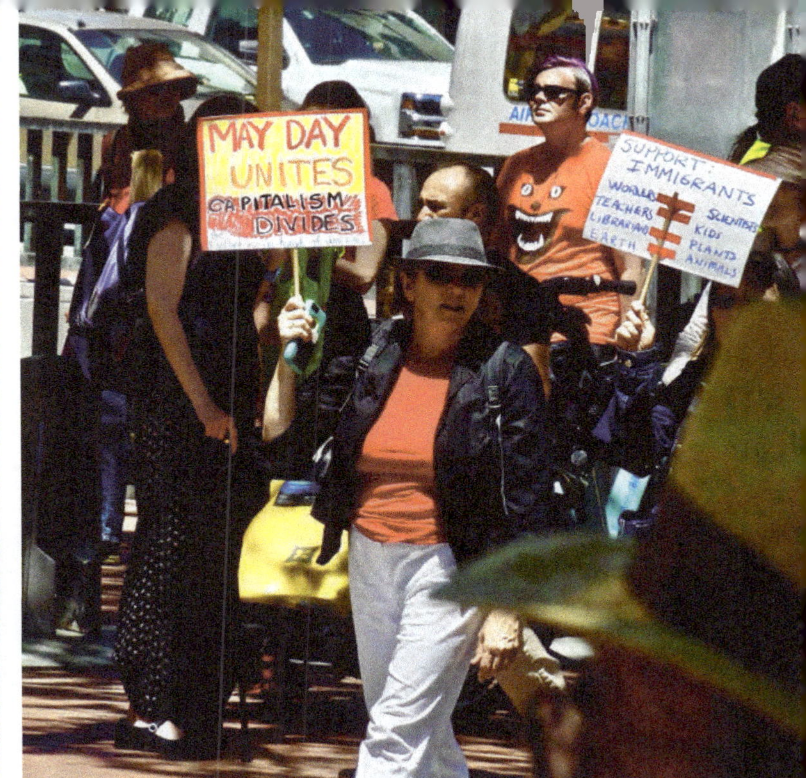

MAY DAY UNITES
CAPITALISM DIVIDES
SUPPORT IMMIGRANTS
WORKERS
TEACHERS
LIBRARIANS
EARTH
SCIENTISTS
KIDS
PLANTS
ANIMALS

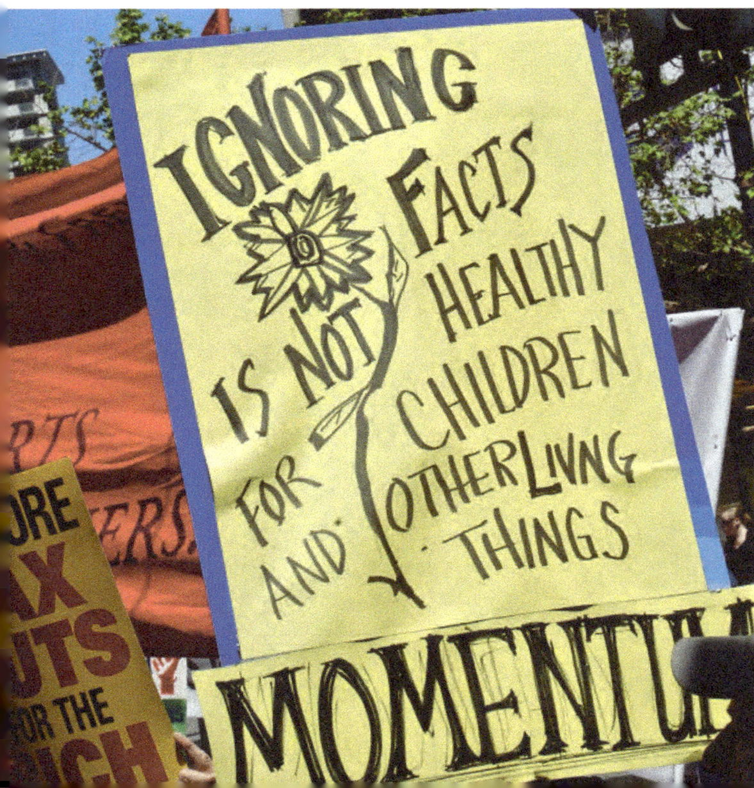

IGNORING FACTS IS NOT HEALTHY FOR CHILDREN AND OTHER LIVING THINGS
MOMENTUM
TAX CUTS FOR THE RICH

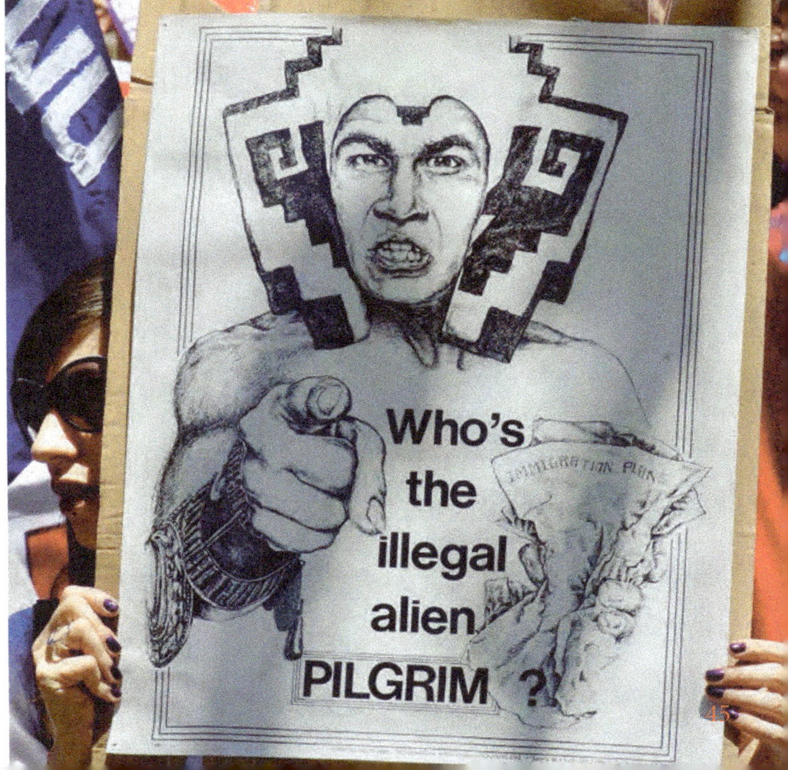

Who's the illegal alien PILGRIM ?
IMMIGRATION PLAN

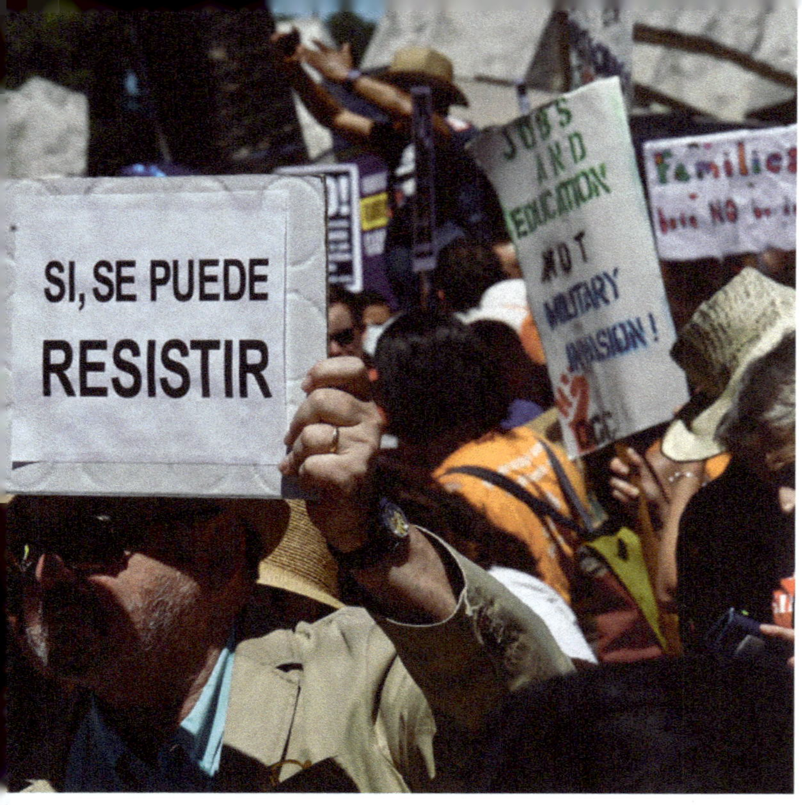
SI, SE PUEDE
RESISTIR
JOBS
AND
EDUCATION
NOT
MILITARY
INVASION !
Families

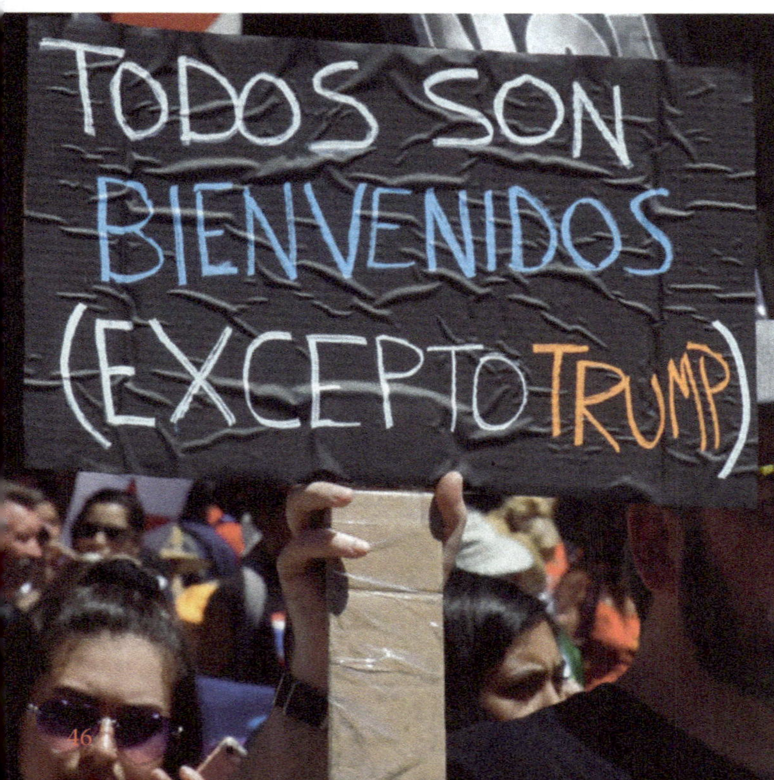
TODOS SON
BIENVENIDOS
(EXCEPTO TRUMP)

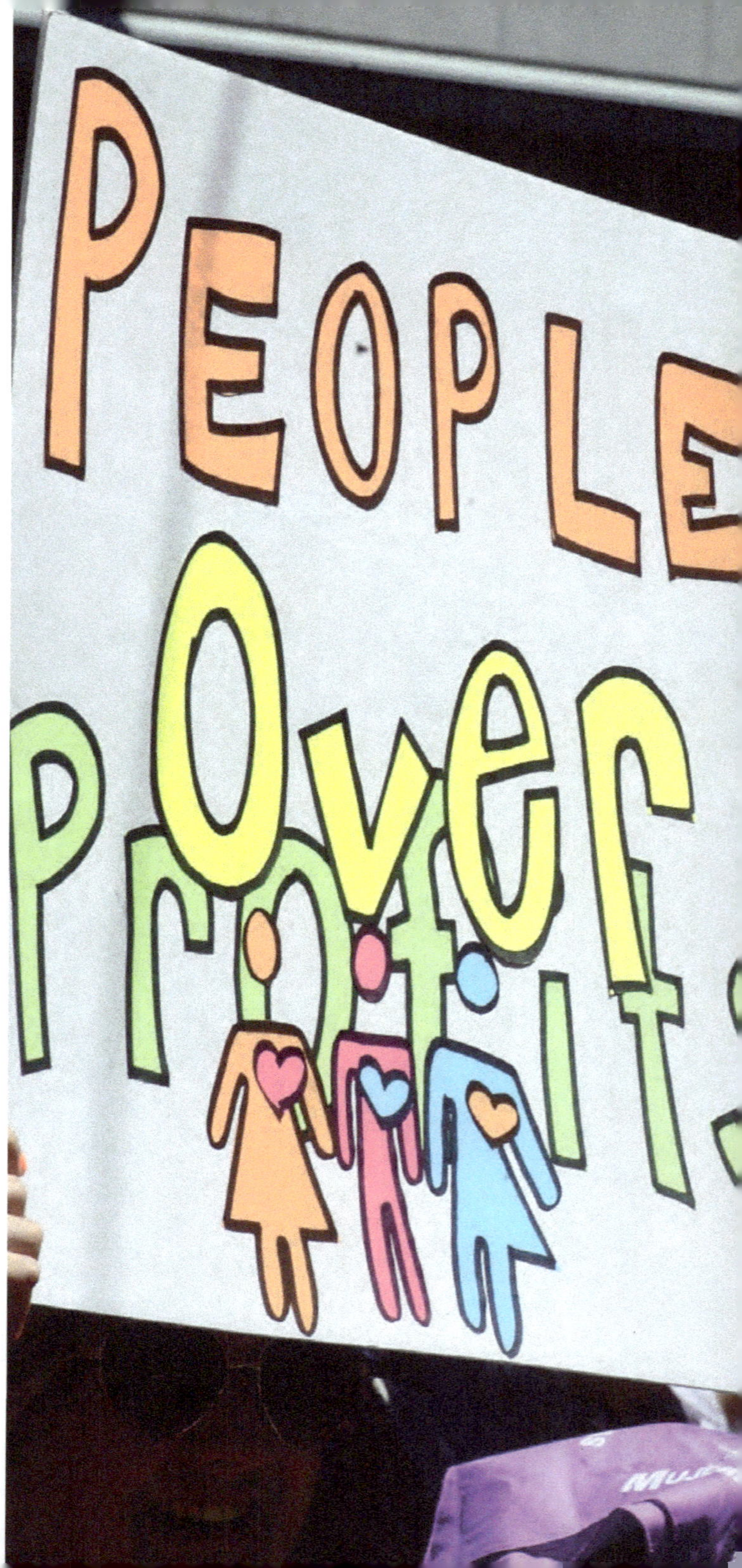

PEOPLE
over
profits

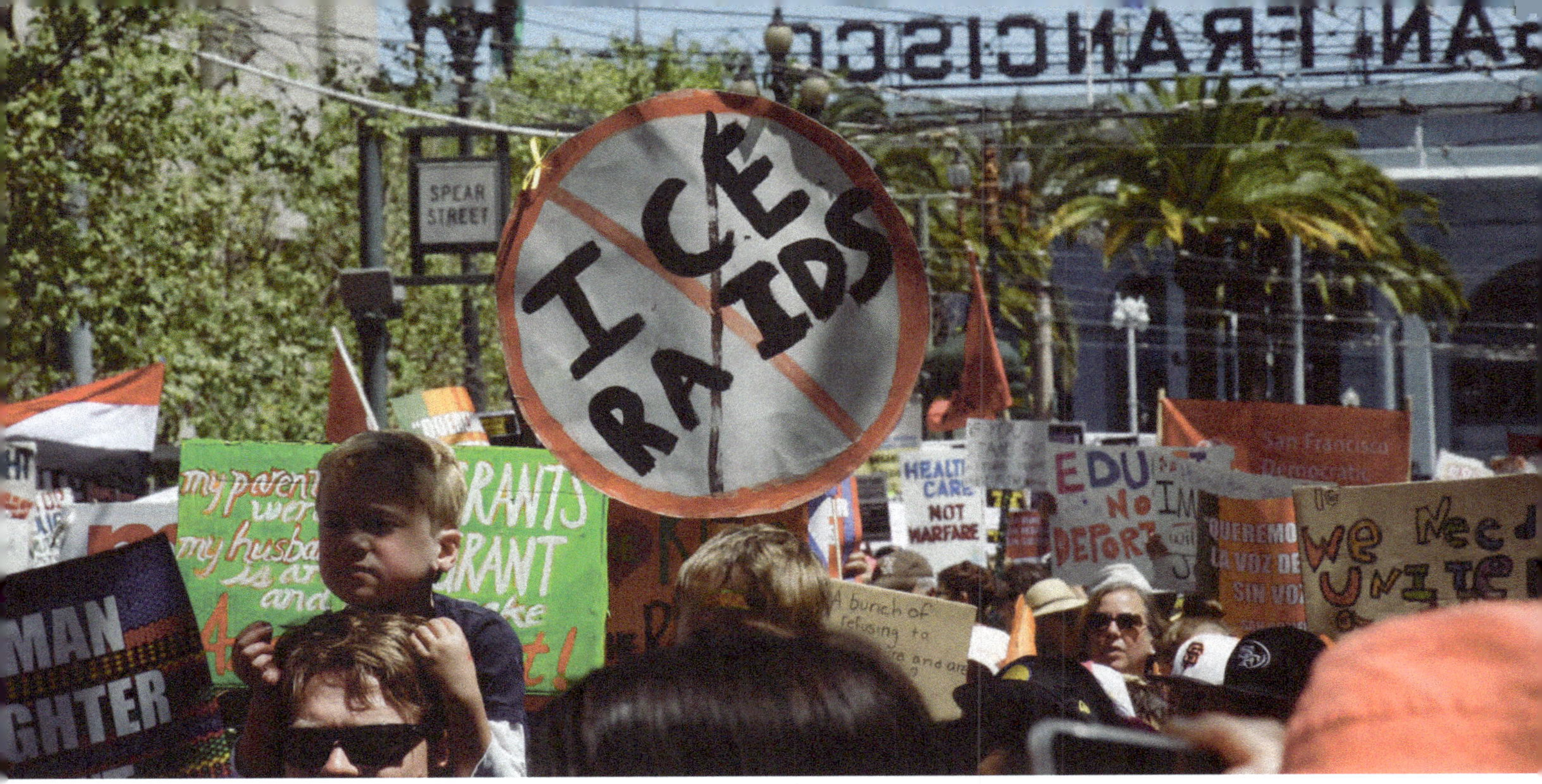

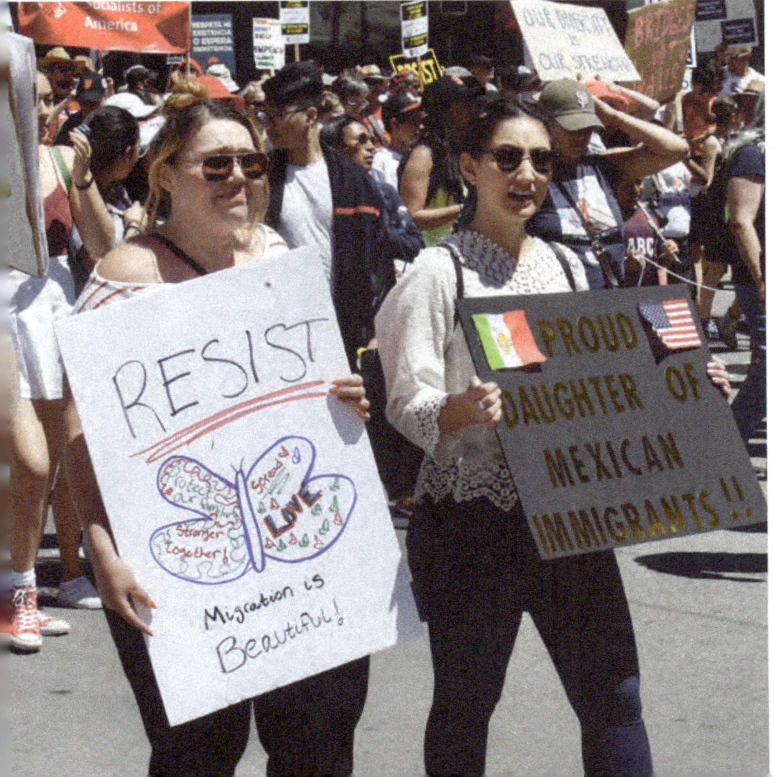
RESIST
LOVE
Stronger Together!
Migration is Beautiful!
PROUD DAUGHTER OF MEXICAN IMMIGRANTS !!

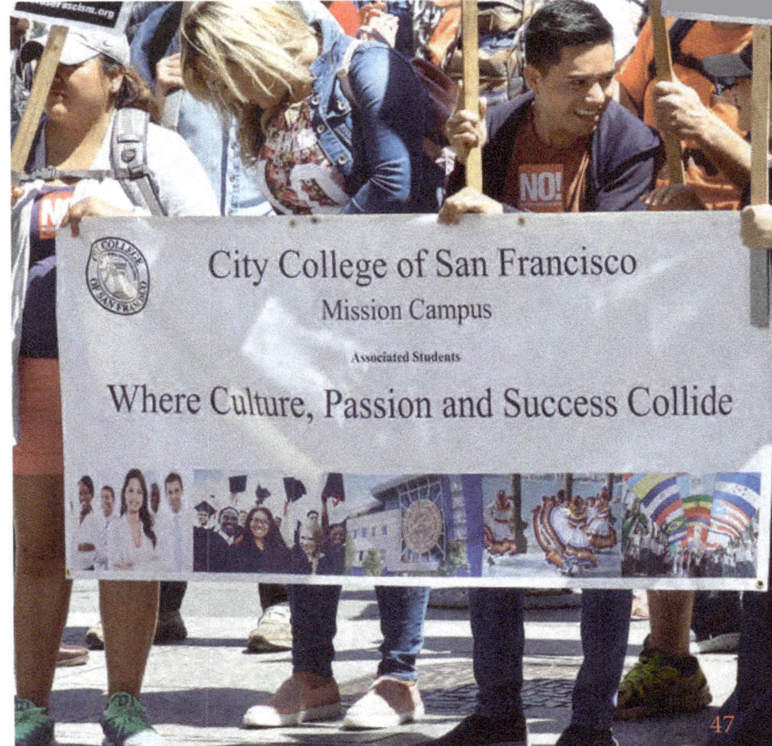
NO!
City College of San Francisco
Mission Campus
Associated Students
Where Culture, Passion and Success Collide

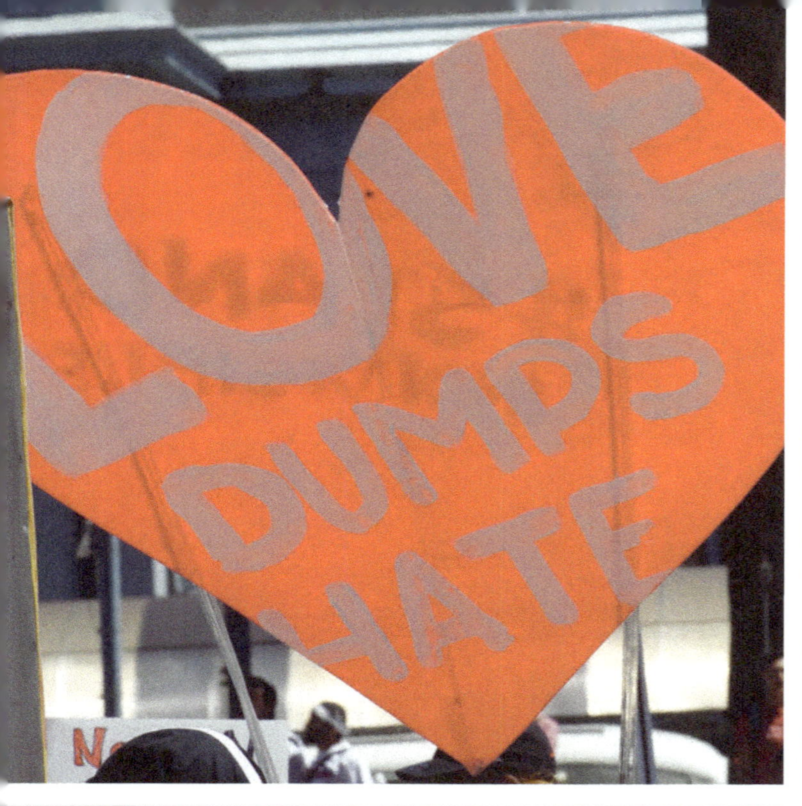
LOVE
DUMPS
HATE

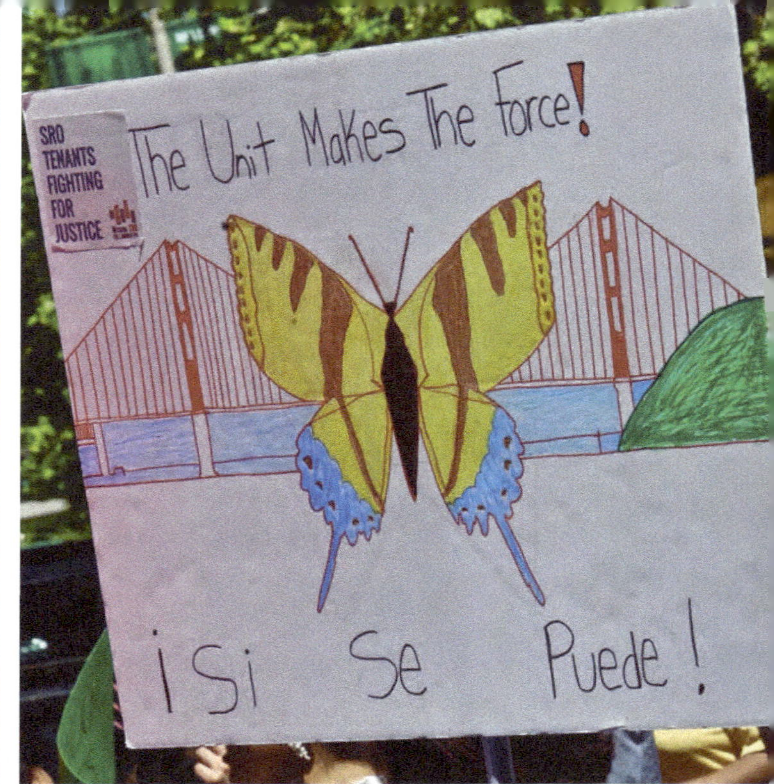
SRO
TENANTS
FIGHTING
FOR
JUSTICE
The Unit Makes The Force!
¡Si Se Puede!

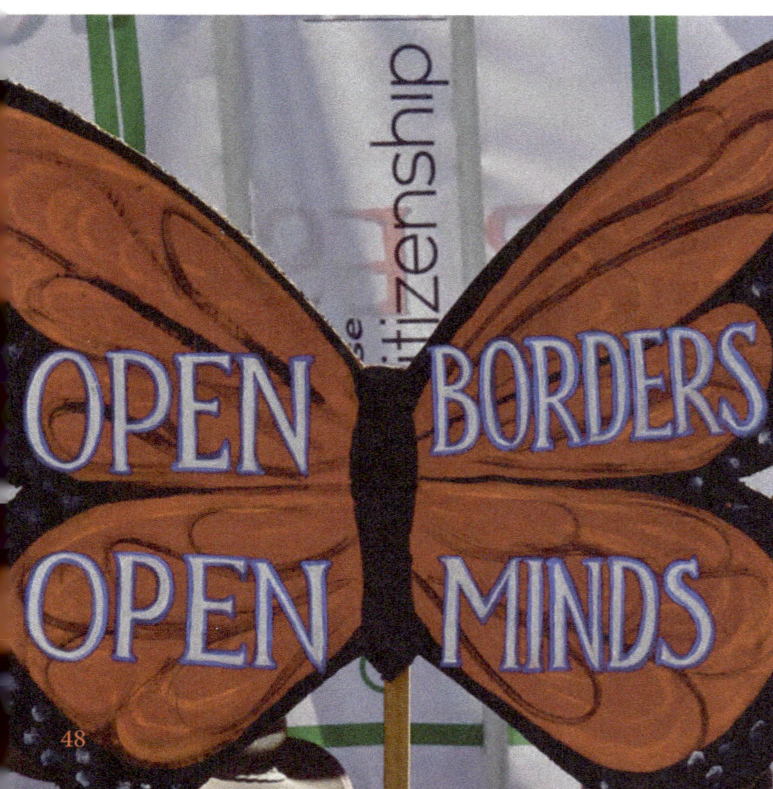
Citizenship
OPEN BORDERS
OPEN MINDS

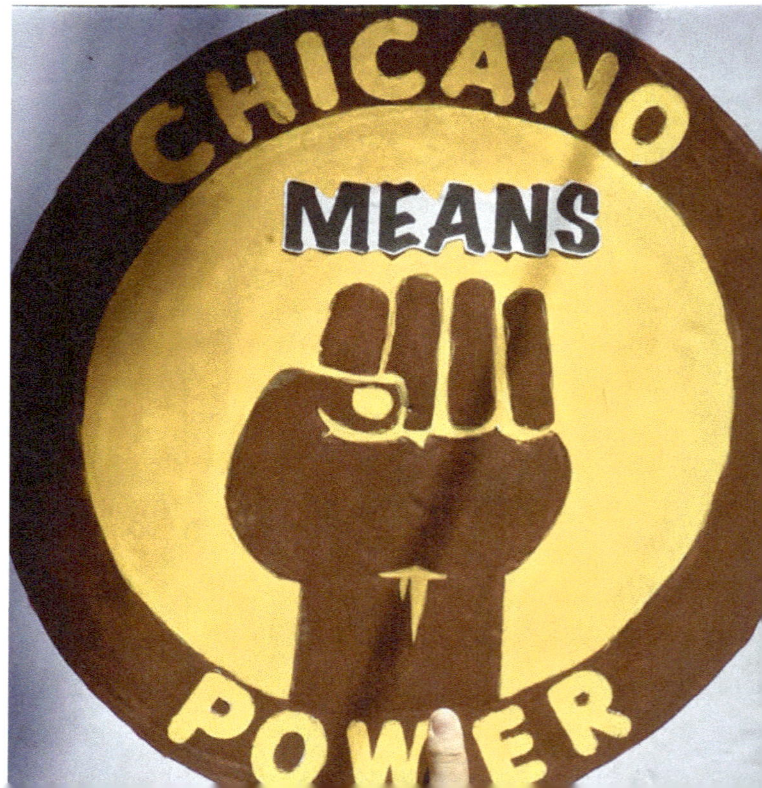
CHICANO
MEANS
POWER

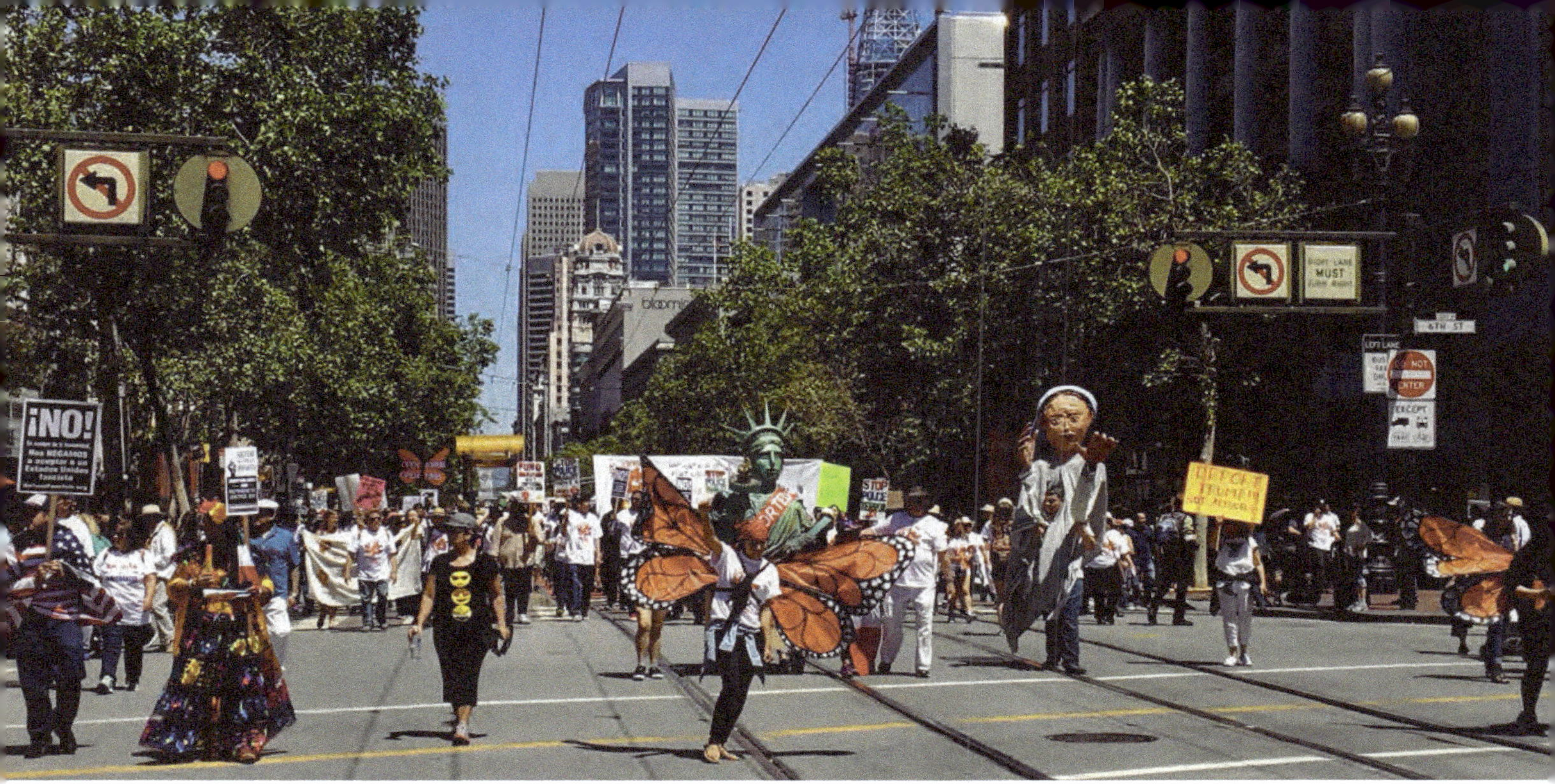

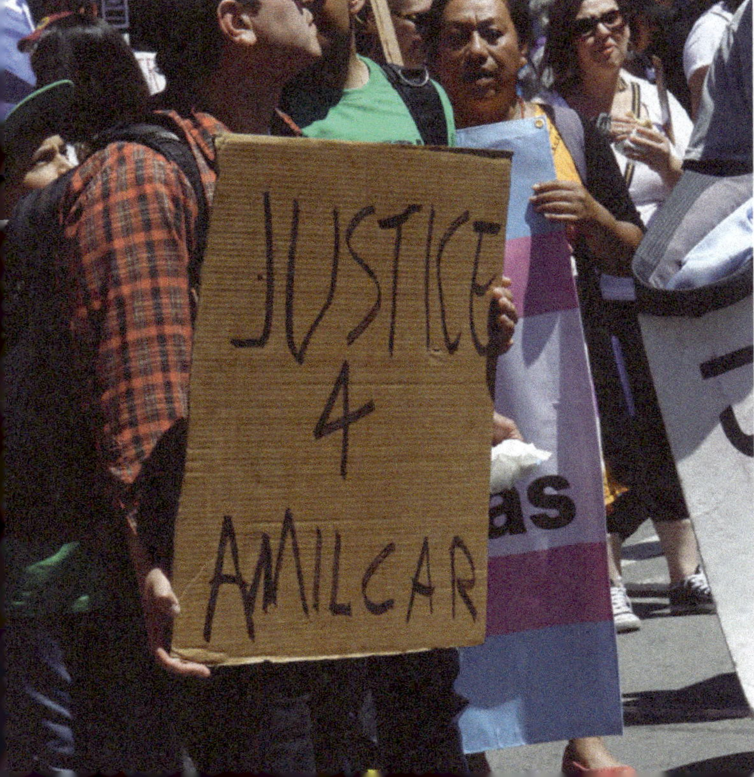

JUSTICE
4
AMILCAR

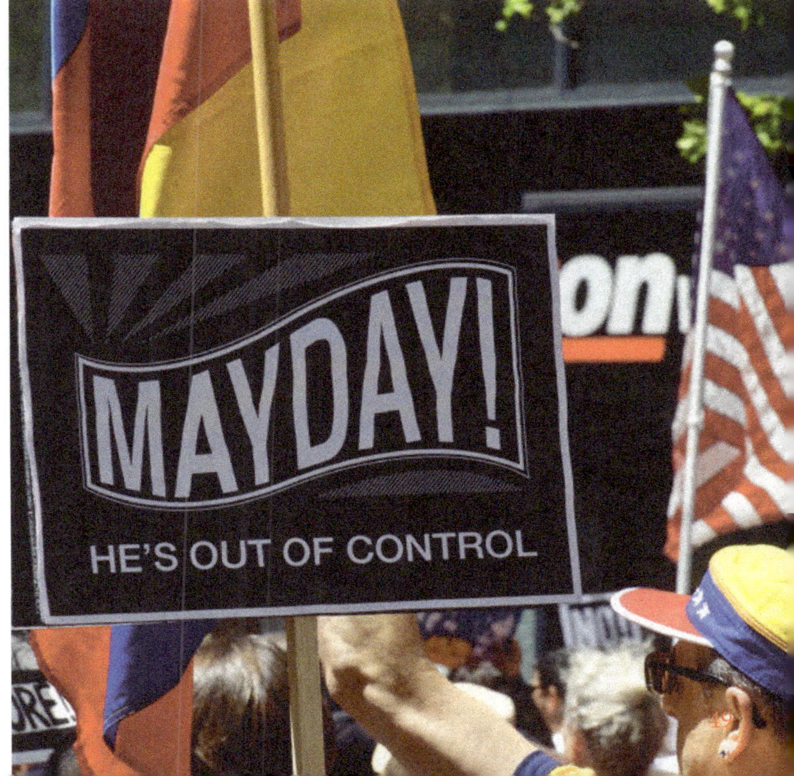

MAYDAY!
HE'S OUT OF CONTROL

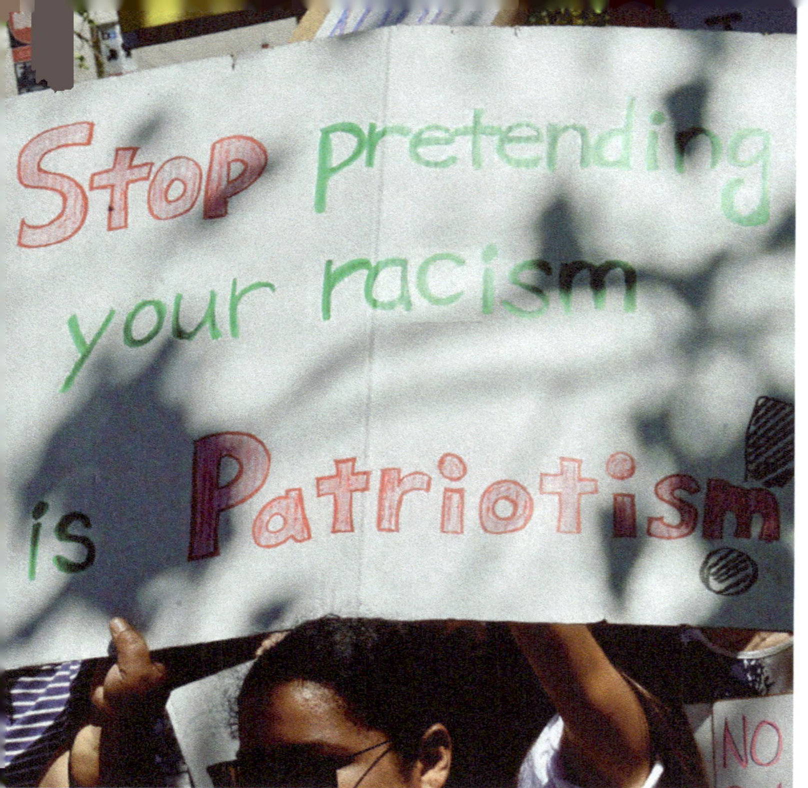

Stop pretending
your racism
is Patriotism

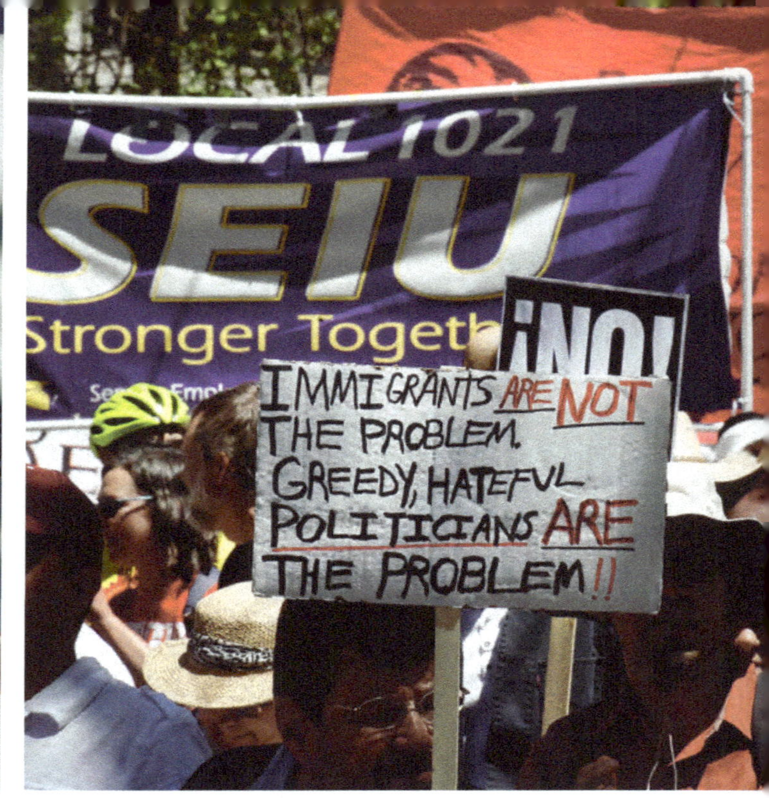

LOCAL 1021
SEIU
Stronger Togeth
¡NO!
IMMIGRANTS ARE NOT
THE PROBLEM.
GREEDY, HATEFUL
POLITICIANS ARE
THE PROBLEM!!

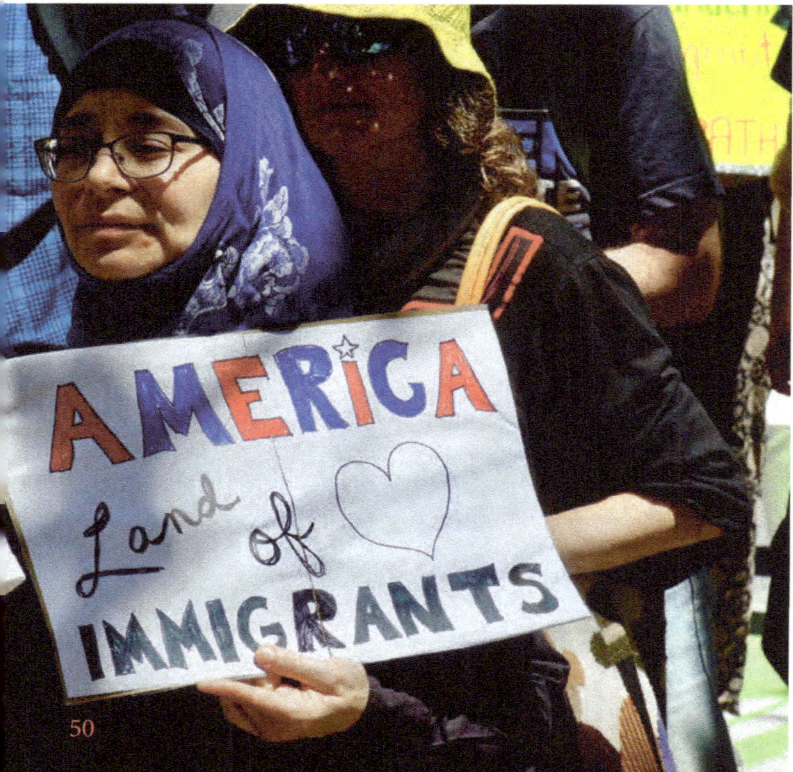

AMERICA
Land of
IMMIGRANTS

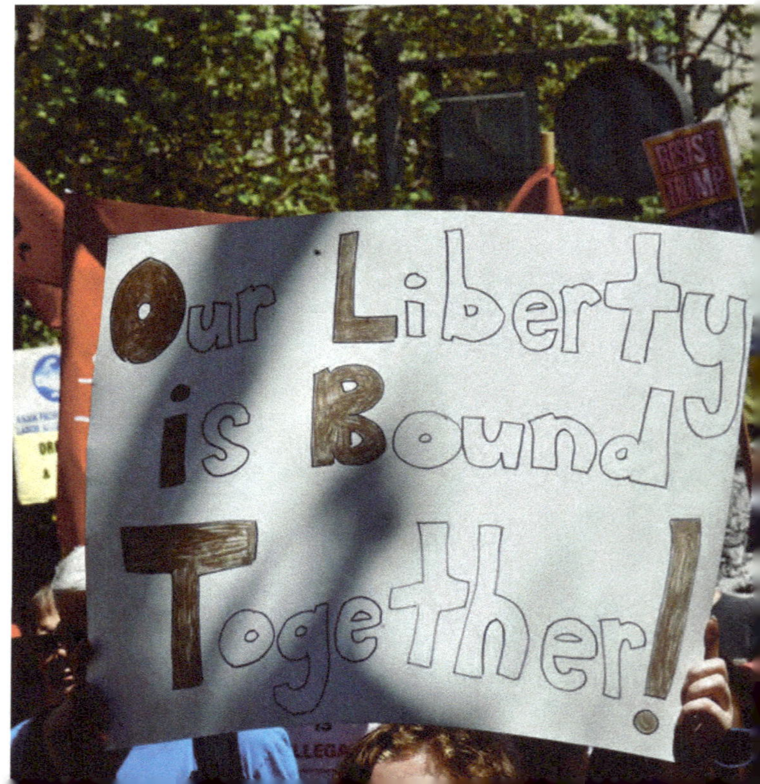

RESIST TRUMP
Our Liberty
is Bound
Together!

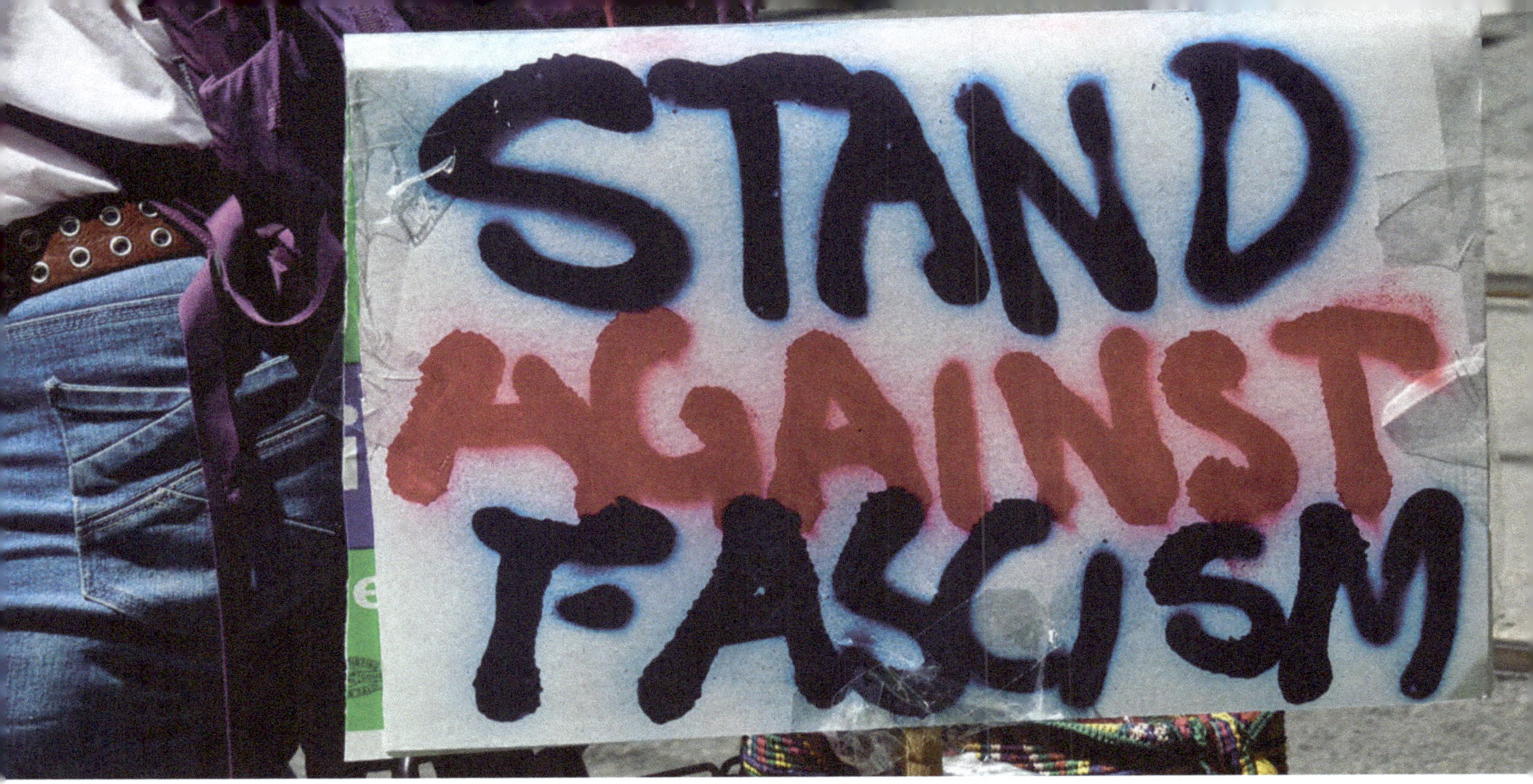

STAND
AGAINST
FASCISM

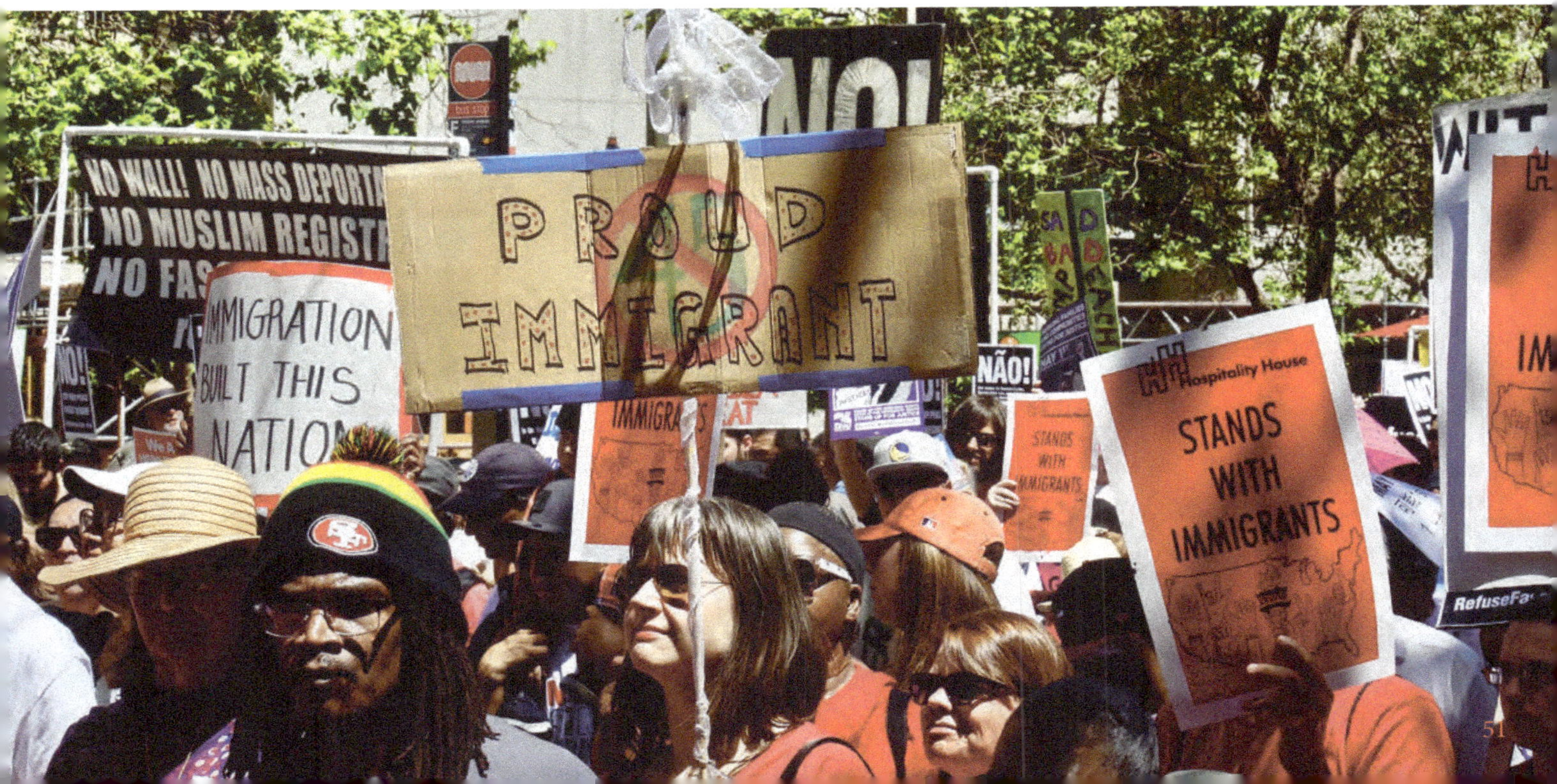

NO!
NO WALL! NO MASS DEPORTA
NO MUSLIM REGISTR
NO FAS
IMMIGRATION
BUILT THIS
NATION
PROUD
IMMIGRANT
NÃO!
STANDS
WITH
IMMIGRANTS
Hospitality House
STANDS
WITH
IMMIGRANTS
RefuseFa
51

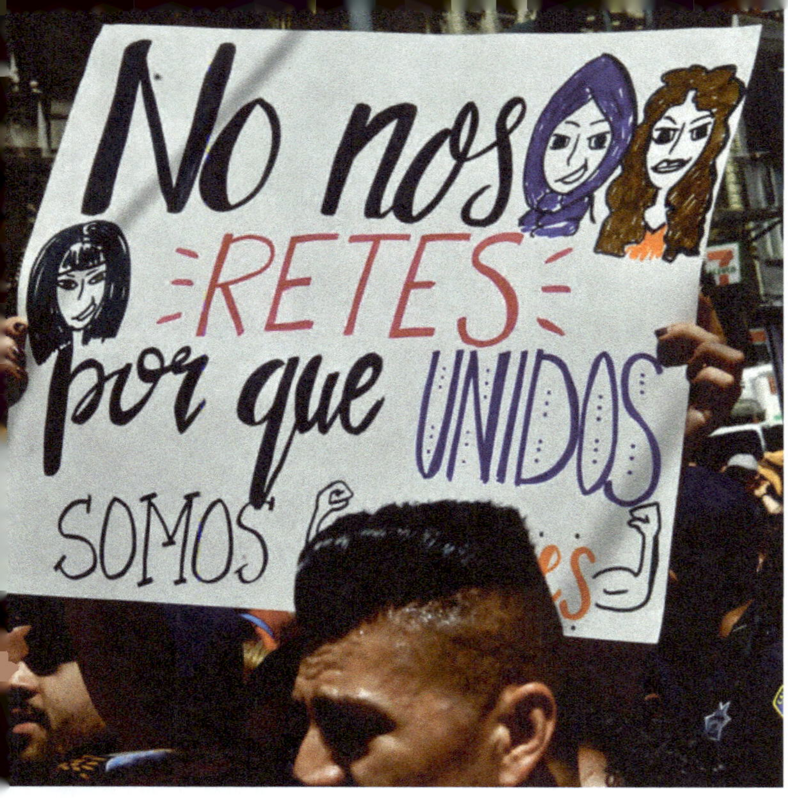

No nos
RETES
por que
SOMOS
UNIDOS

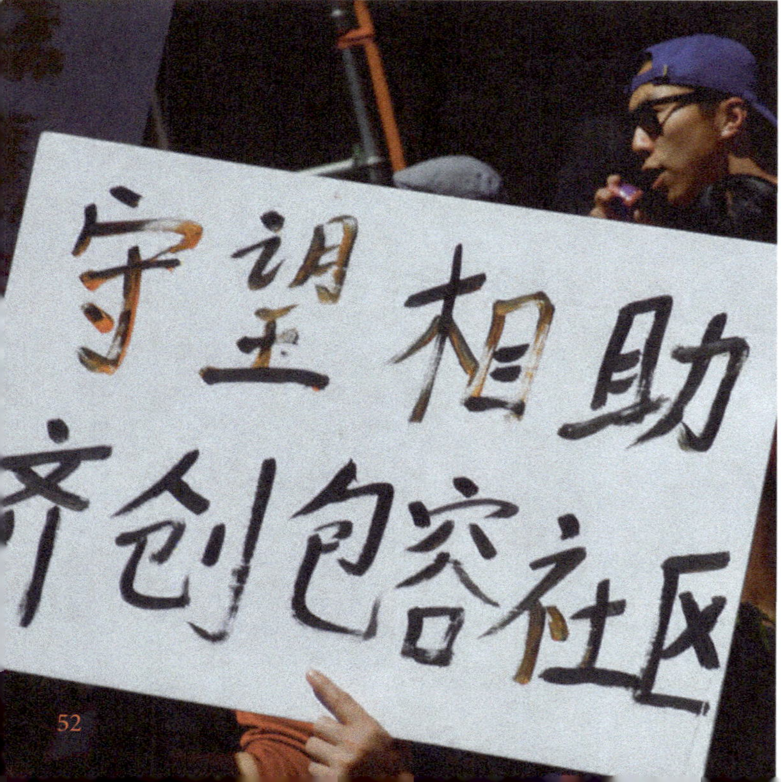

守望相助
齐创包容社区

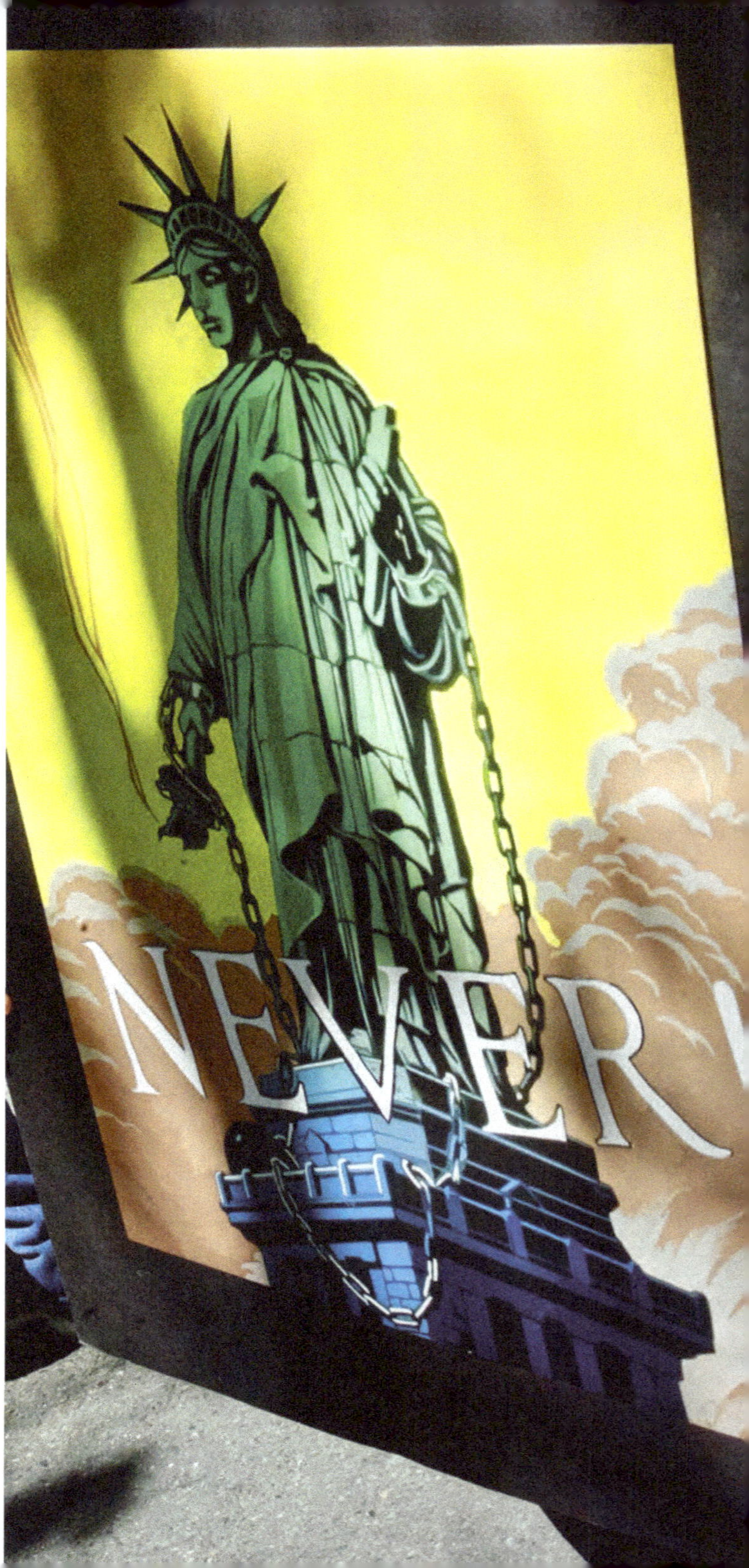

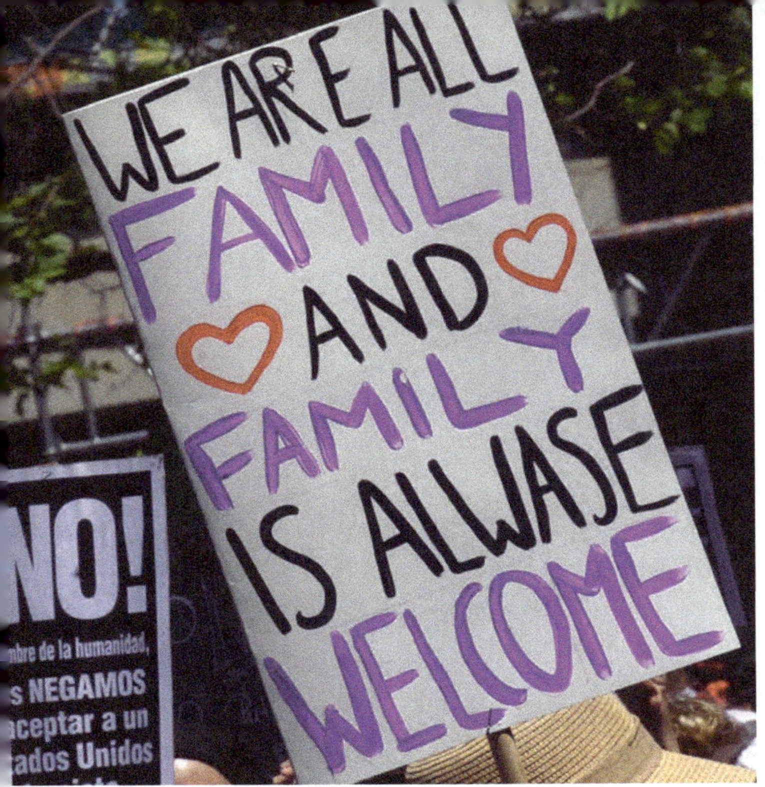

WE ARE ALL
FAMILY
AND
FAMILY
IS ALWASE
WELCOME
NO!
bre de la humanidad,
s NEGAMOS
ceptar a un
ados Unidos

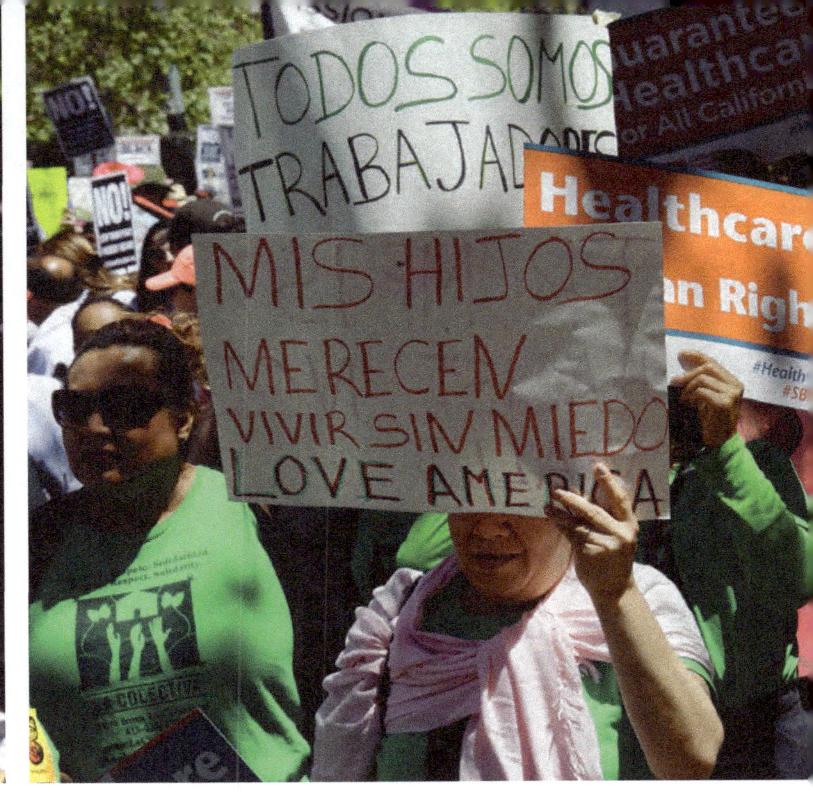

TODOS SOMOS
TRABAJADORES
MIS HIJOS
MERECEN
VIVIR SIN MIEDO
LOVE AMERICA
Guarantee
Healthcare
for All Californ
Healthcare
an Right
#Health
#SB

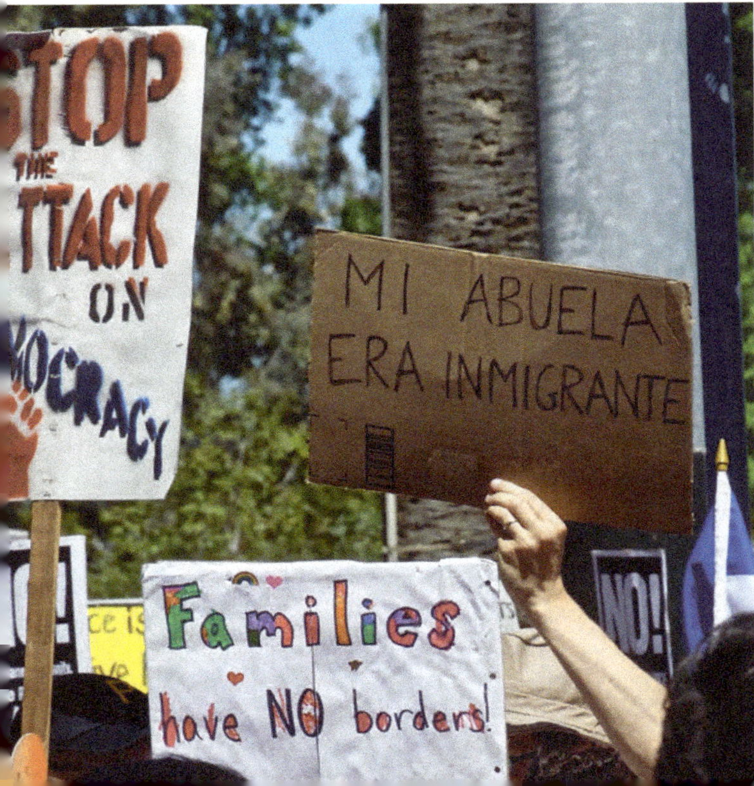

STOP
THE
ATTACK
ON
DEMOCRACY
MI ABUELA
ERA INMIGRANTE
NO!
Families
have NO borders!

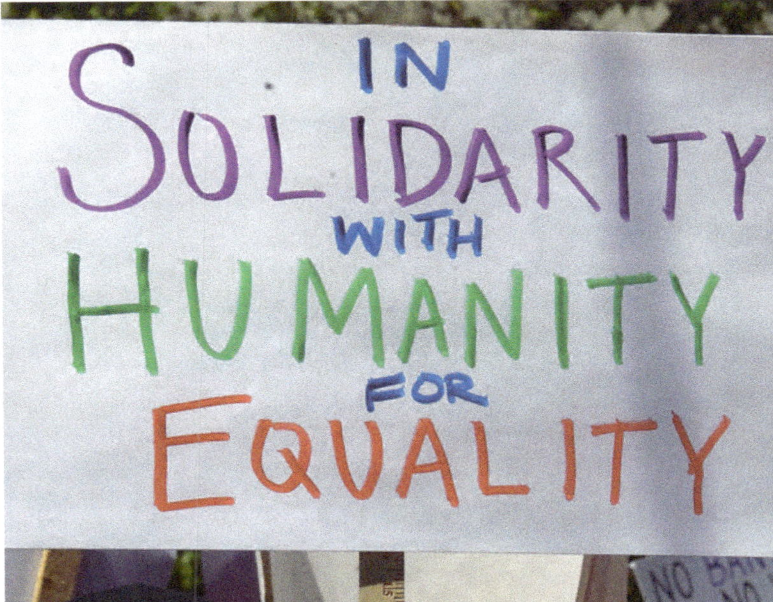

IN
SOLIDARITY
WITH
HUMANITY
FOR
EQUALITY
NO BA
NO B

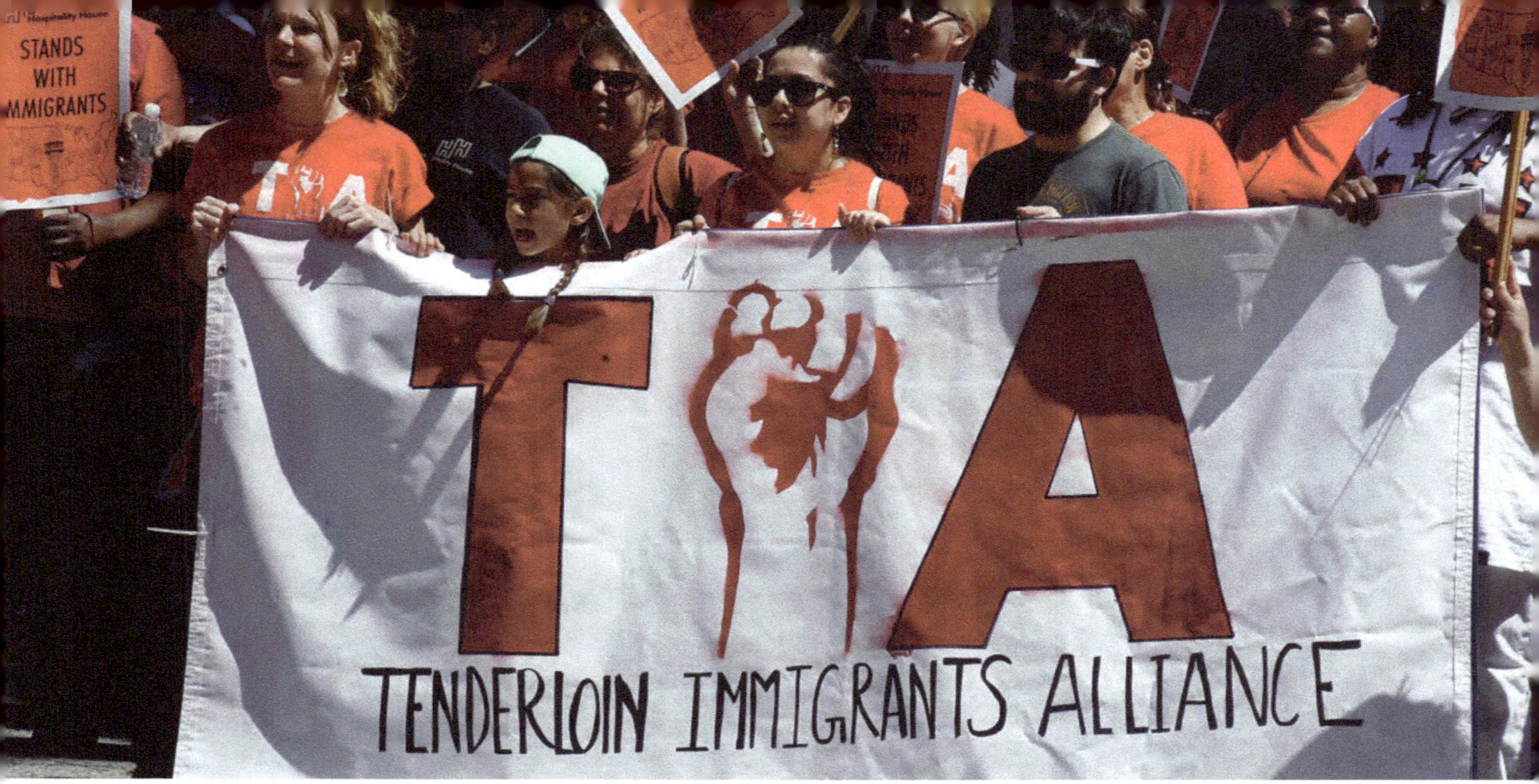

STANDS WITH IMMIGRANTS

TIA

TENDERLOIN IMMIGRANTS ALLIANCE

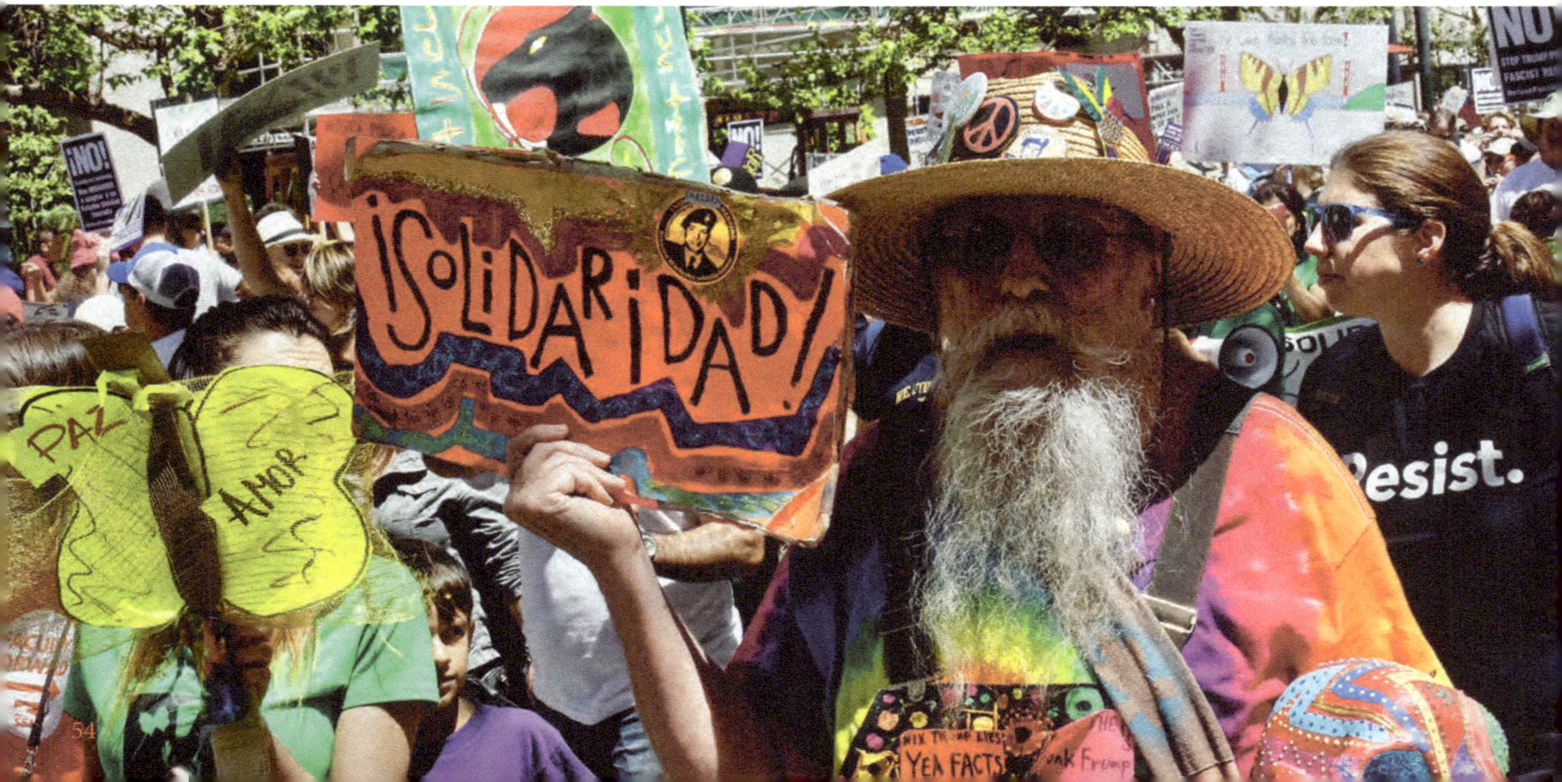

¡SOLIDARIDAD!

PAZ

AMOR

Resist.

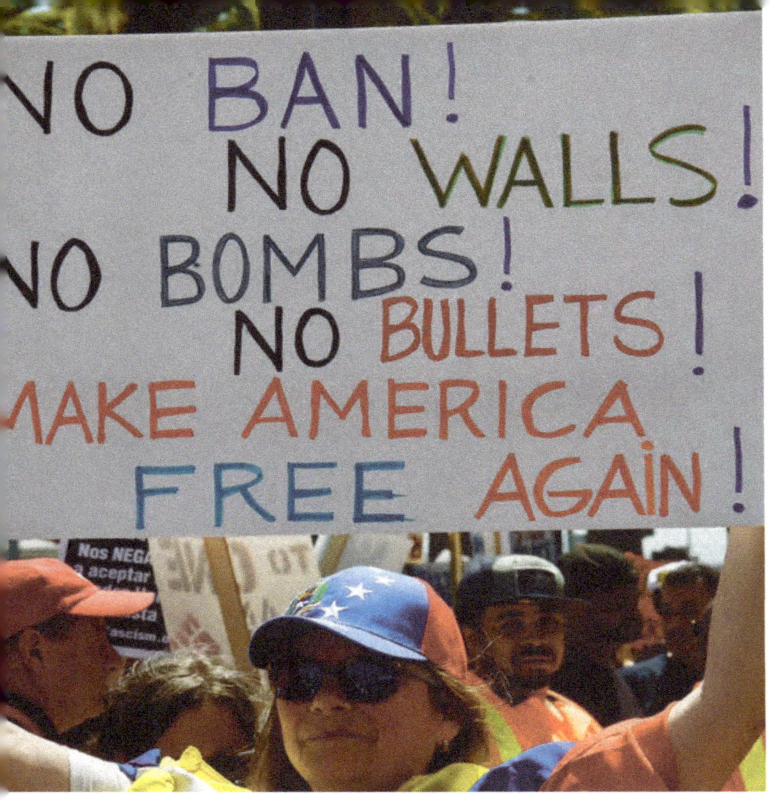

NO BAN!
NO WALLS!
NO BOMBS!
NO BULLETS!
MAKE AMERICA
FREE AGAIN!

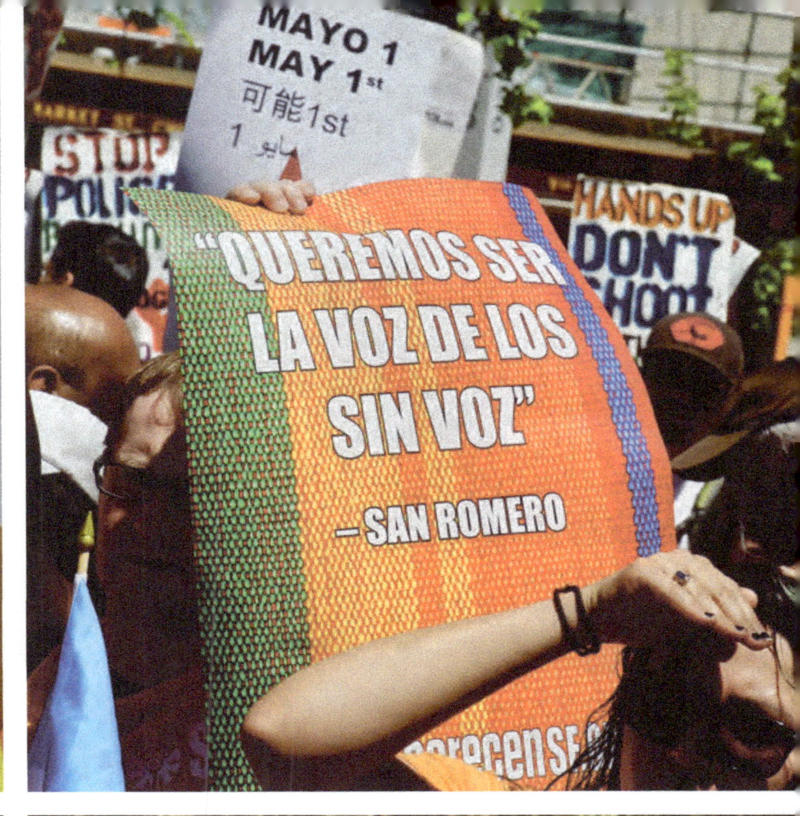

MAYO 1
MAY 1st
可能 1st
"QUEREMOS SER
LA VOZ DE LOS
SIN VOZ"
— SAN ROMERO
HANDS UP
DON'T
SHOOT

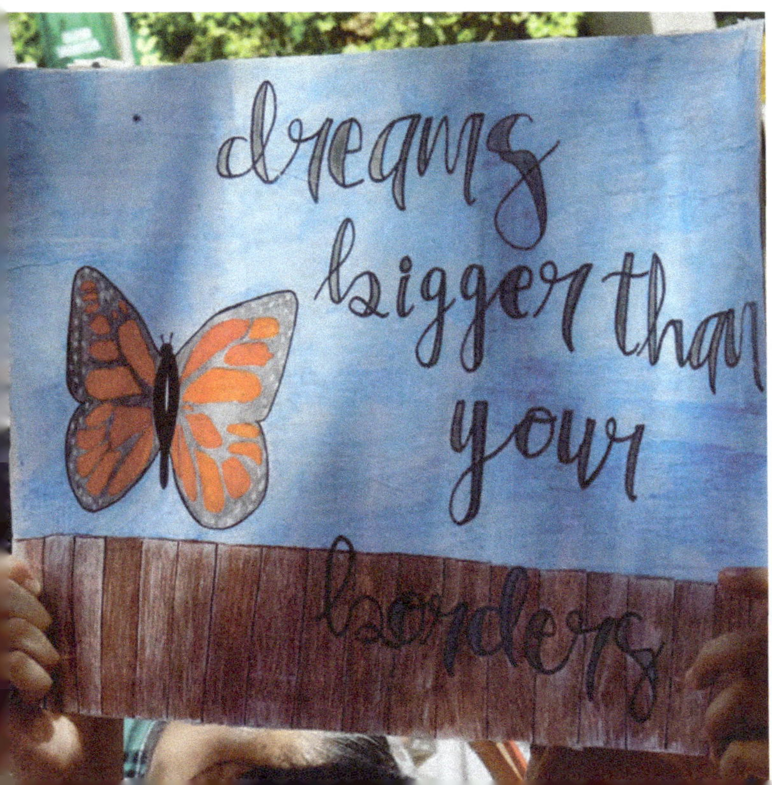

dreams
bigger than
your
borders

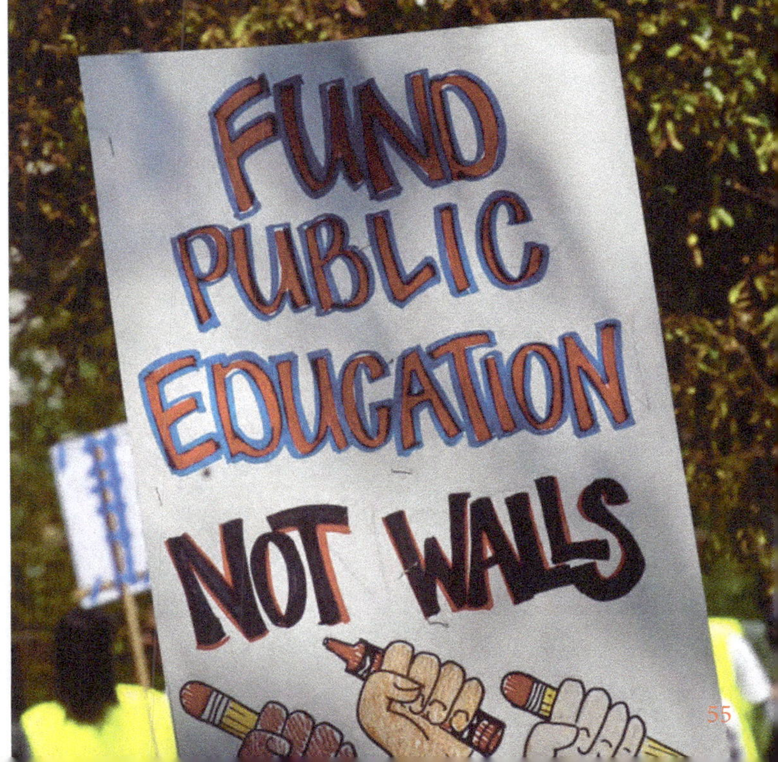

FUND
PUBLIC
EDUCATION
NOT WALLS

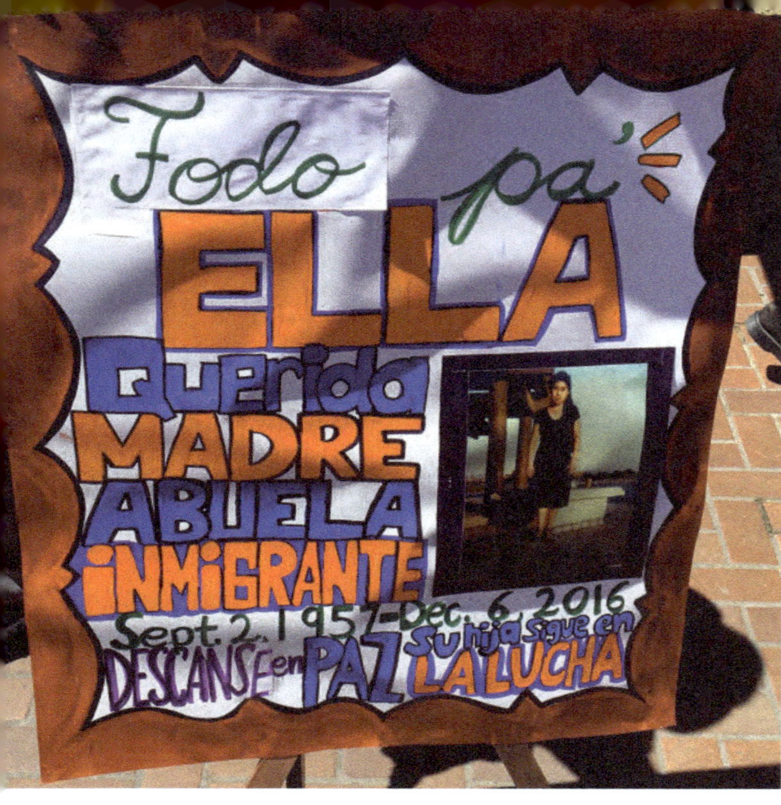
Todo pa'
ELLA
Querida
MADRE
ABUELA
INMIGRANTE
Sept. 2 1957 - Dec. 6 2016
DESCANSE en PAZ
Su hija sigue en LA LUCHA

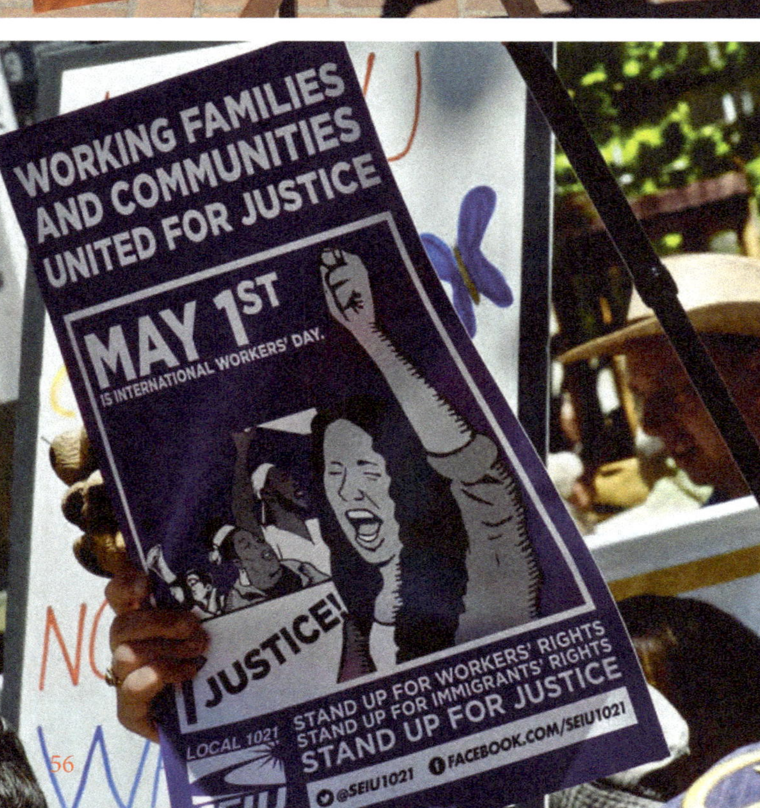
WORKING FAMILIES
AND COMMUNITIES
UNITED FOR JUSTICE
MAY 1ST
IS INTERNATIONAL WORKERS' DAY.
JUSTICE!
STAND UP FOR WORKERS' RIGHTS
STAND UP FOR IMMIGRANTS' RIGHTS
STAND UP FOR JUSTICE
LOCAL 1021
FACEBOOK.COM/SEIU1021
@SEIU1021

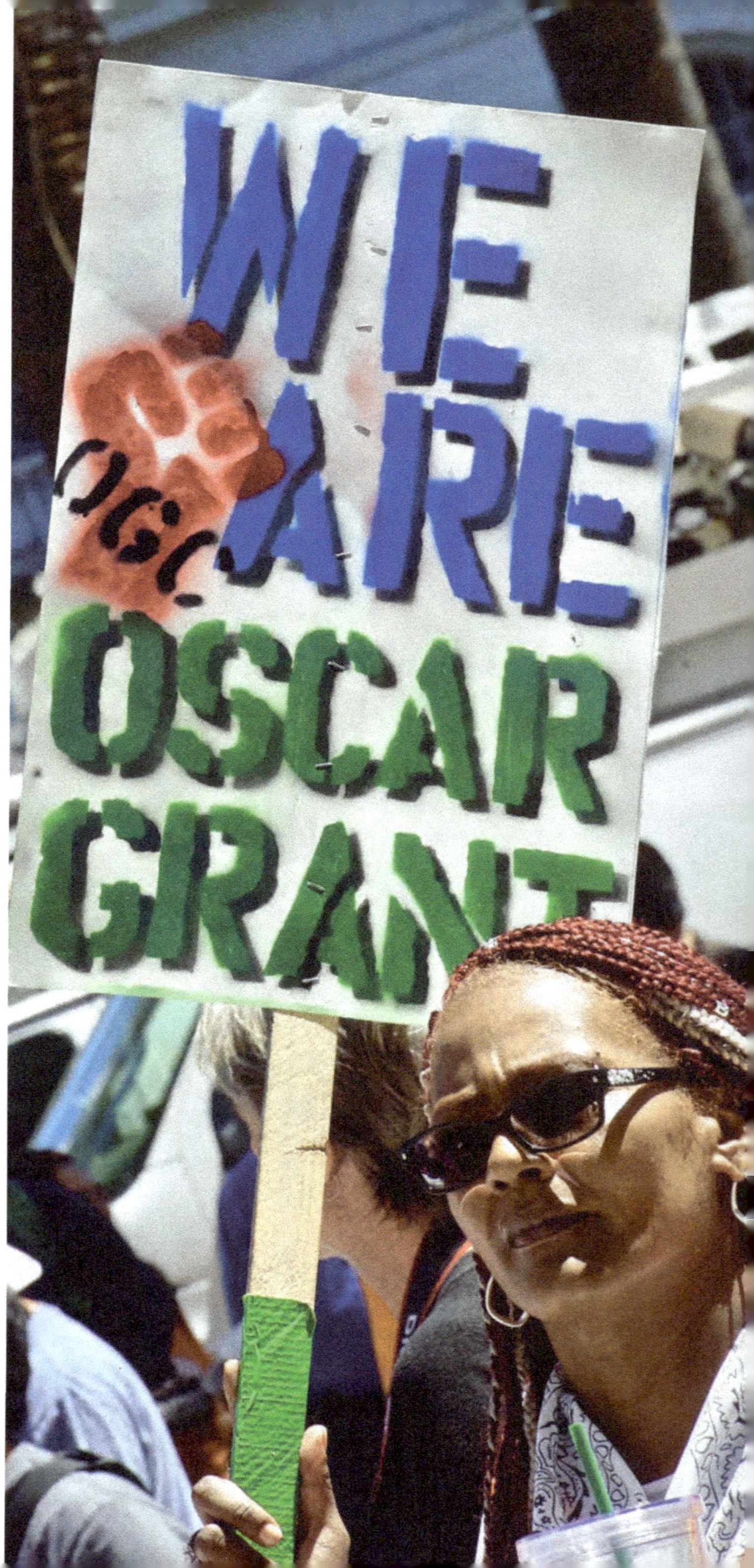

WE
ARE
OGC
OSCAR
GRANT

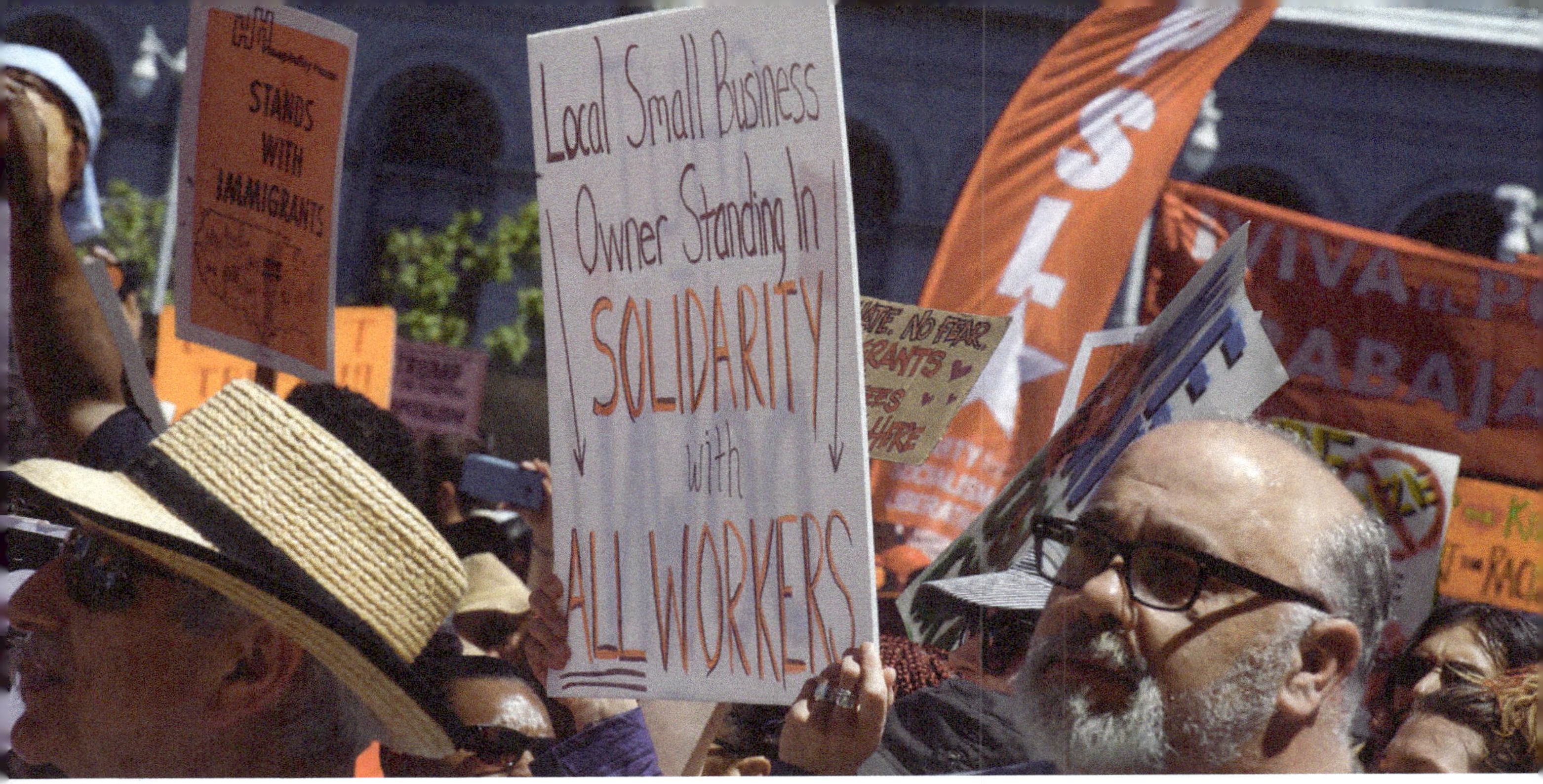

STANDS WITH IMMIGRANTS
Local Small Business Owner Standing In SOLIDARITY with ALL WORKERS
UNITE, NO FEAR
IMMIGRANTS
VIVA...
TRABAJA

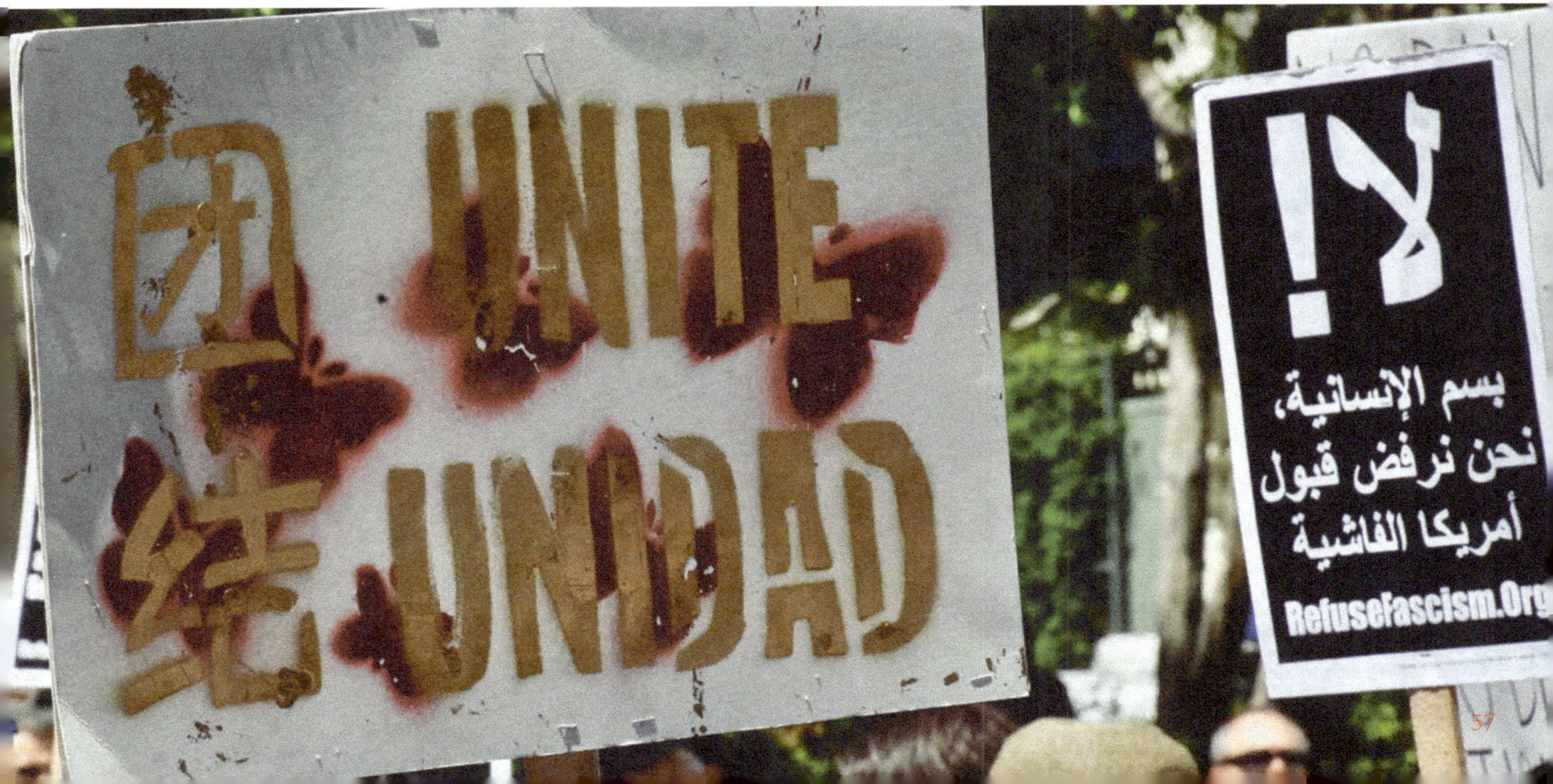

团结
UNITE
UNIDAD
لا!
بسم الإنسانية،
نحن نرفض قبول
أمريكا الفاشية
RefuseFascism.Org

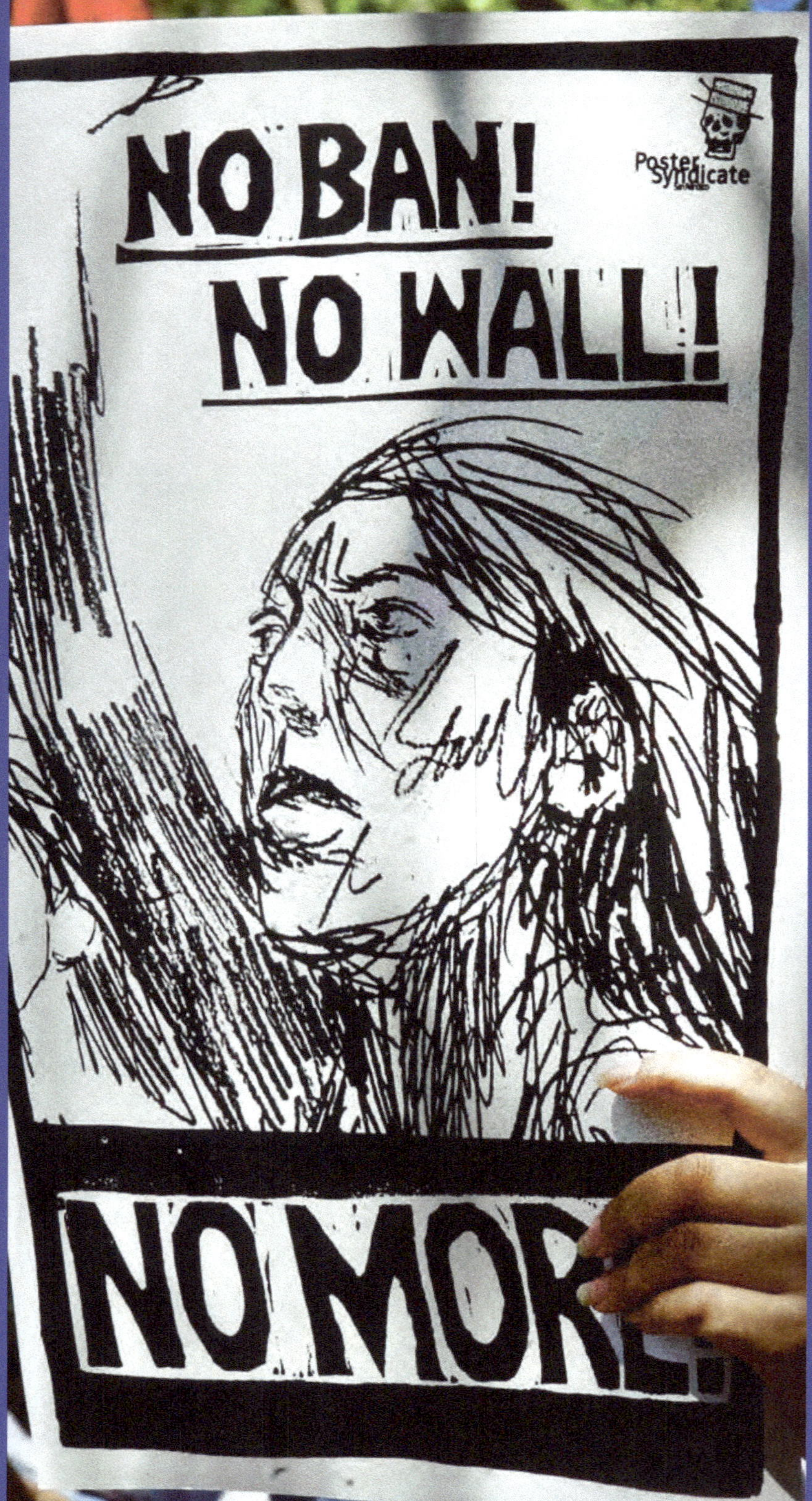

NO BAN!
NO WALL!
Poster Syndicate
NO MORE!

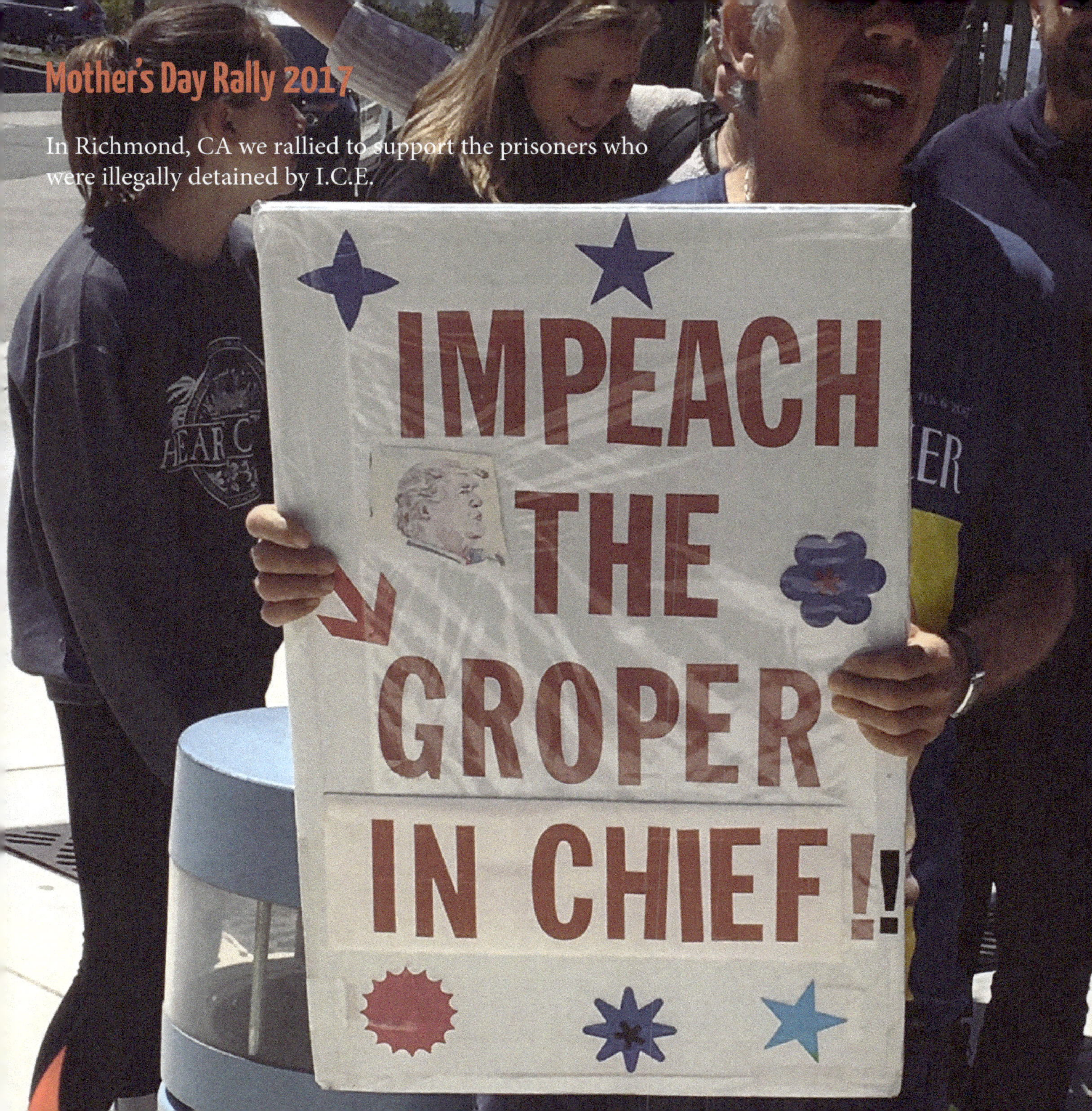

Mother's Day Rally 2017
In Richmond, CA we rallied to support the prisoners who were illegally detained by I.C.E.
IMPEACH THE GROPER IN CHIEF !!

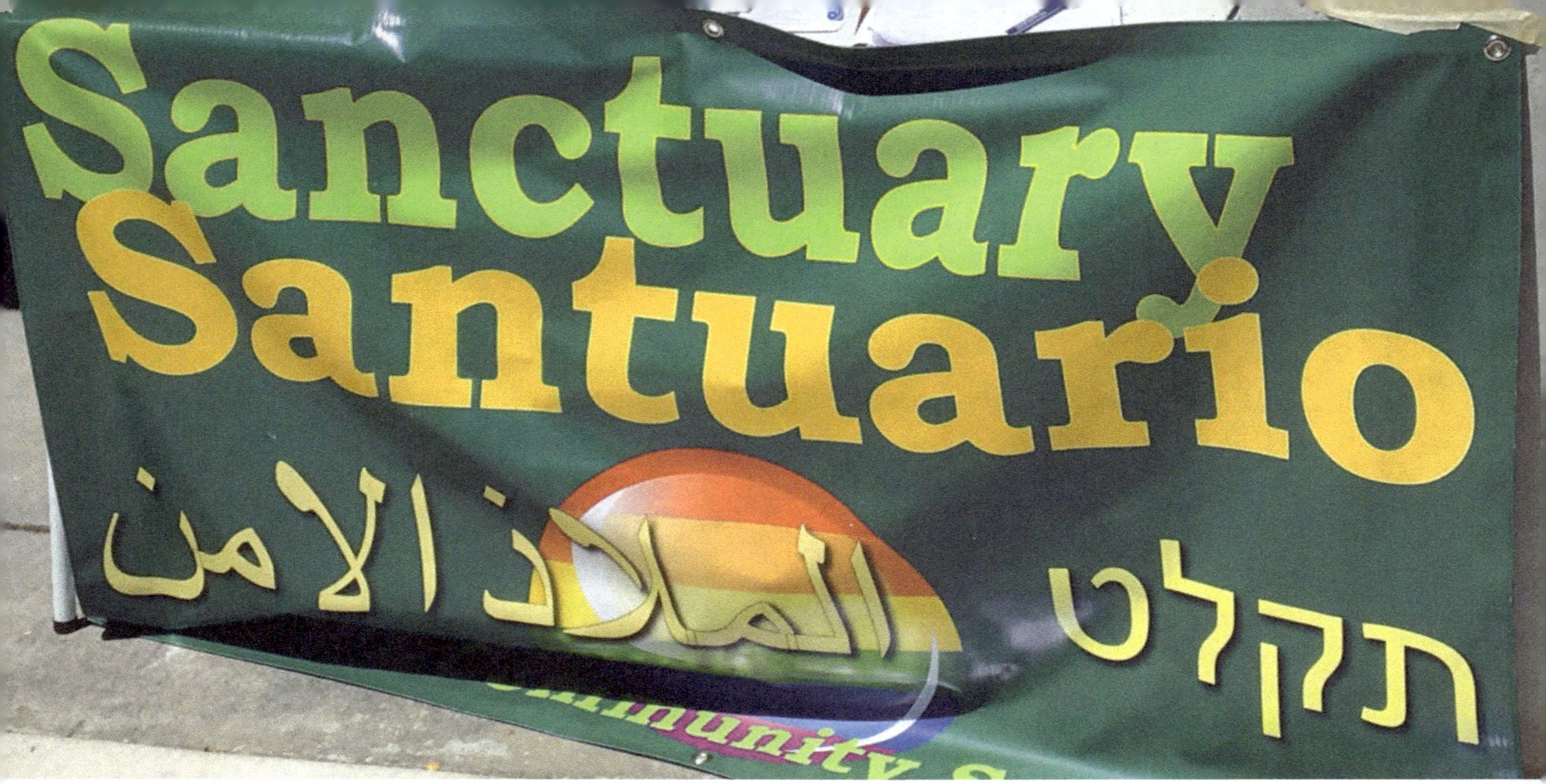

Sanctuary
Santuario
الملاذ الأمن
تקלט
Community S

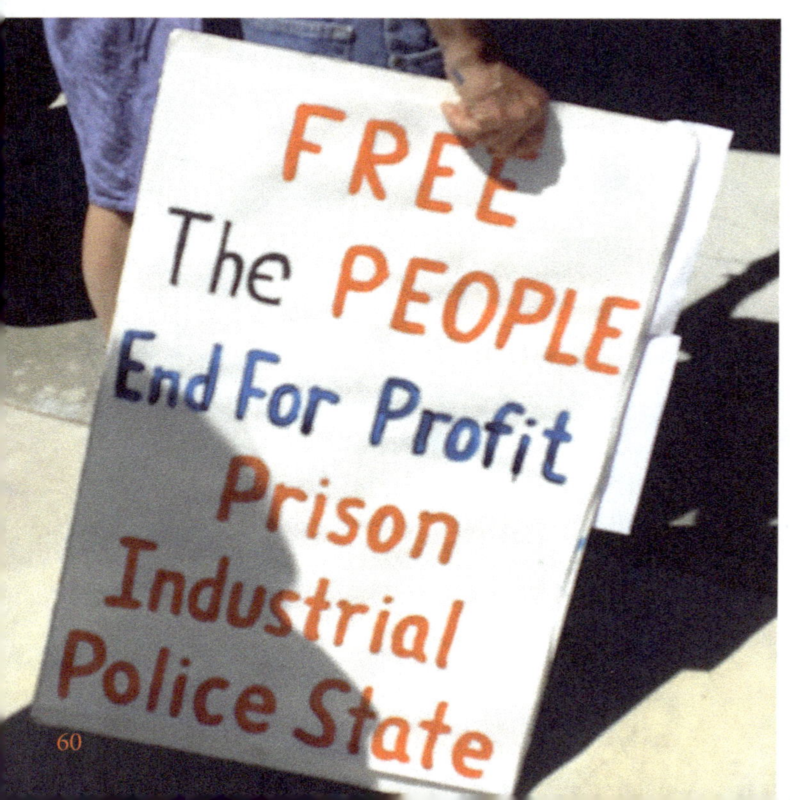

FREE
The PEOPLE
End For Profit
Prison
Industrial
Police State

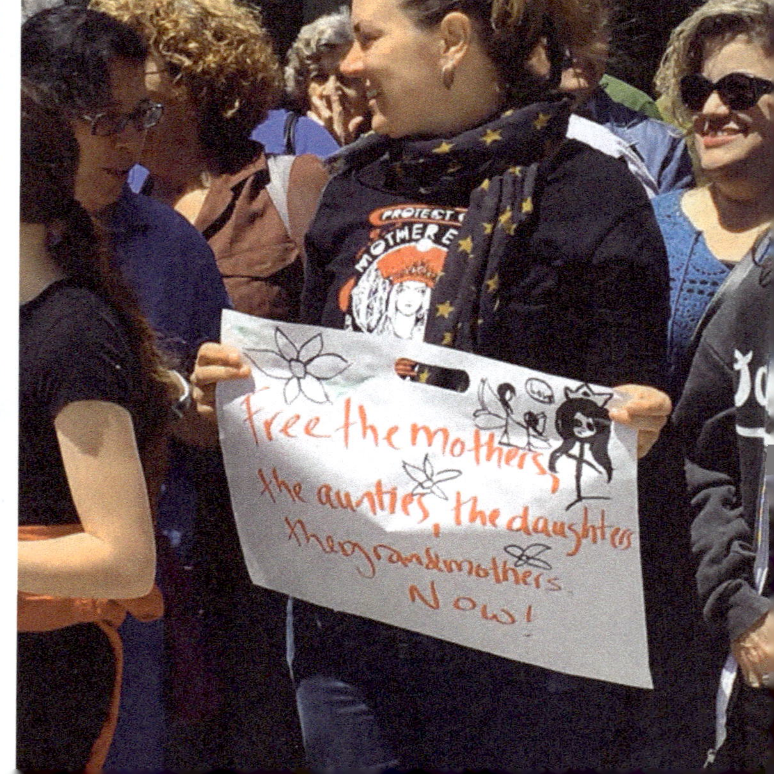

Free the mothers,
the aunties, the daughters
the grandmothers.
Now!

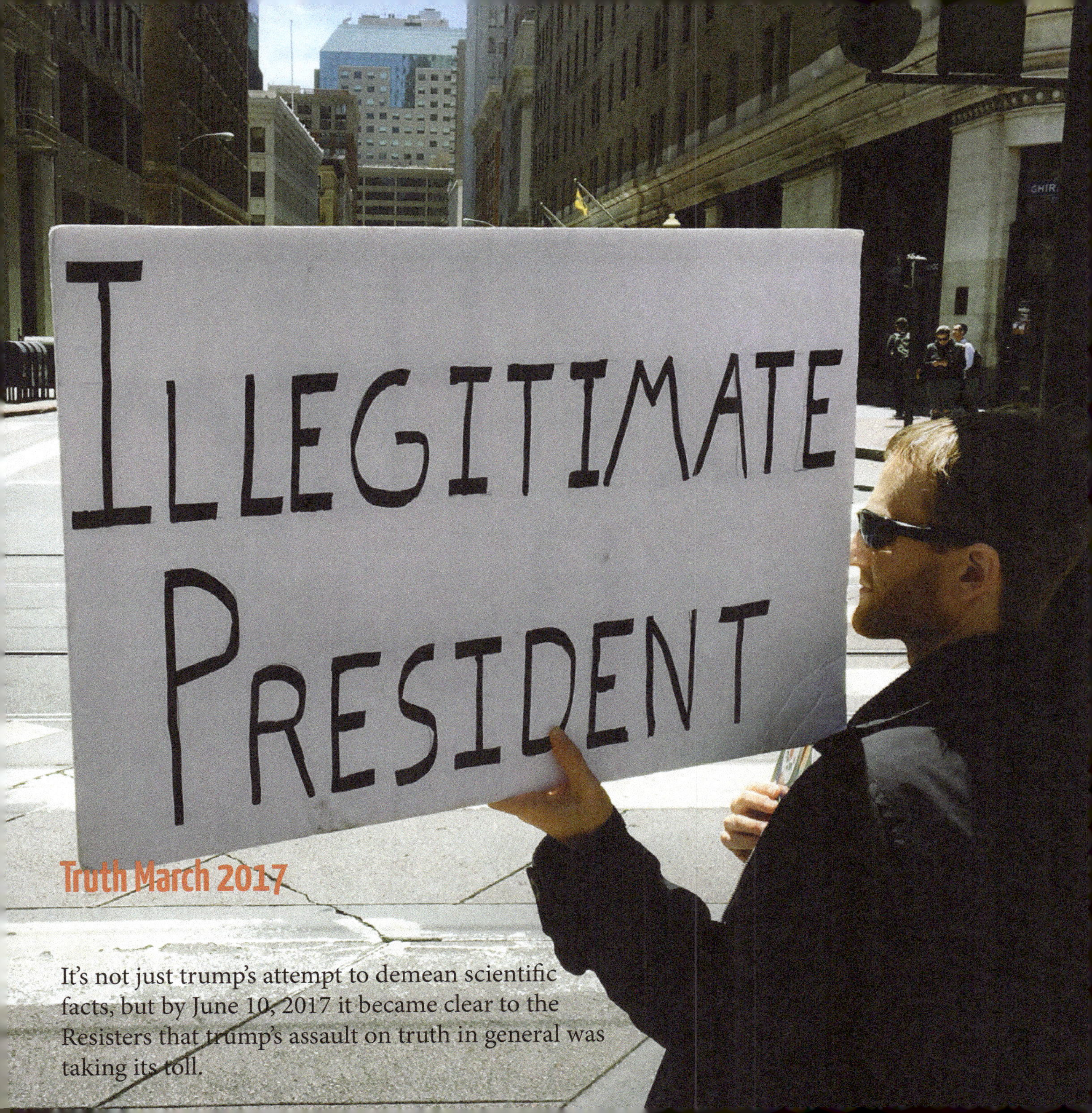

Truth March 2017

It's not just trump's attempt to demean scientific facts, but by June 10, 2017 it became clear to the Resisters that trump's assault on truth in general was taking its toll.

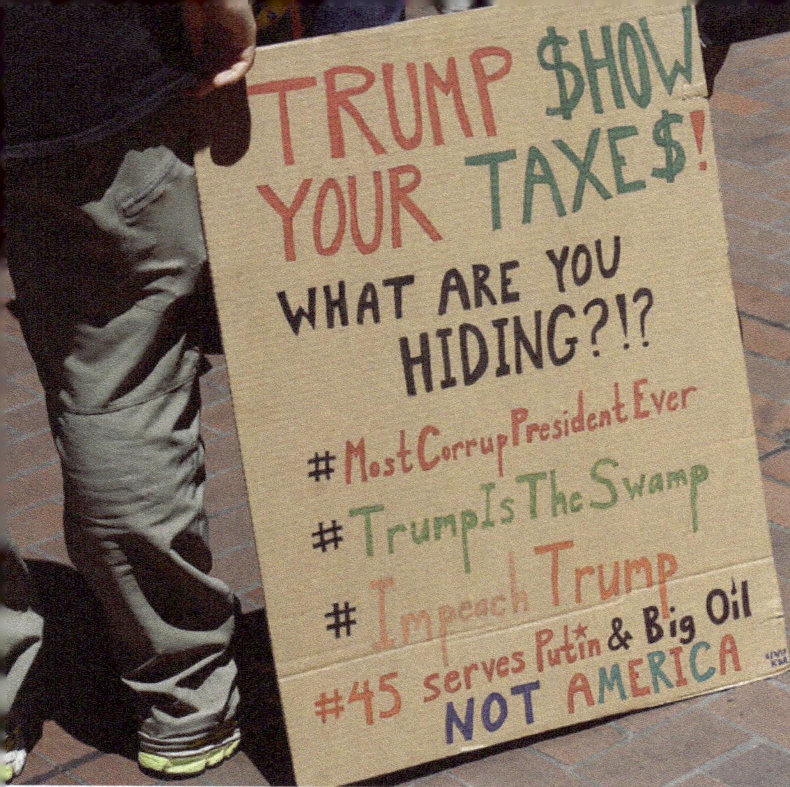
TRUMP $HOW YOUR TAXE$!
WHAT ARE YOU HIDING?!?
#MostCorrupPresidentEver
#TrumpIsTheSwamp
#ImpeachTrump
#45 serves Putin* & Big Oil
NOT AMERICA

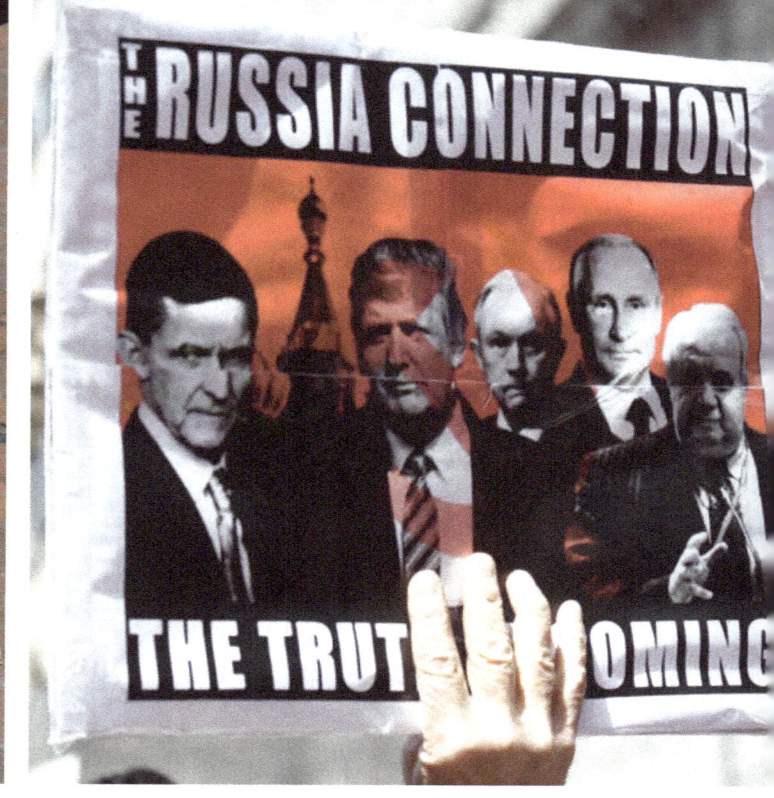
THE RUSSIA CONNECTION
THE TRUT OMING

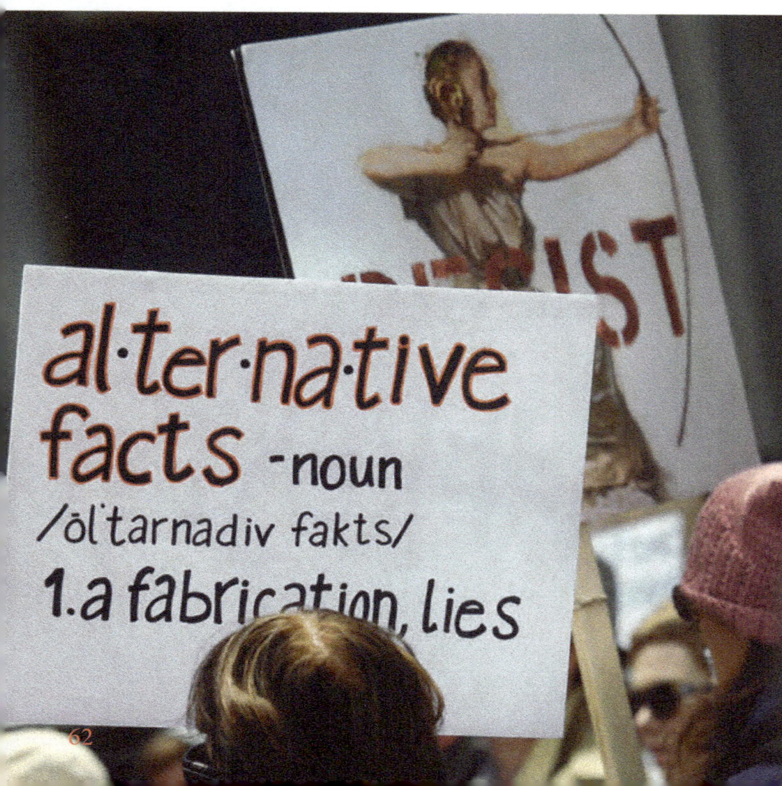
RESIST
alternative
facts -noun
/ȯl'tarnadiv fakts/
1.a fabrication, lies

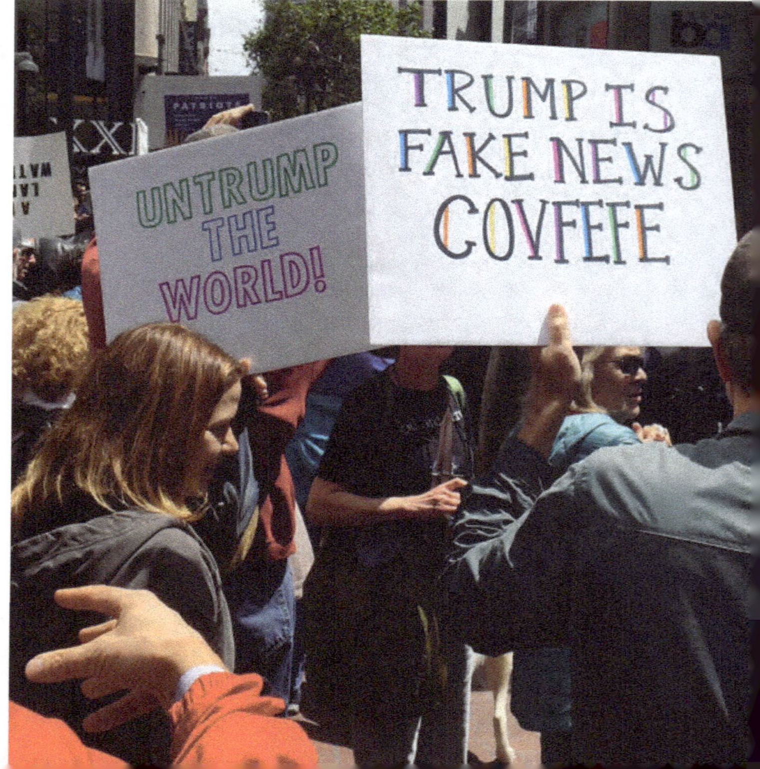
TRUMP IS FAKE NEWS COVFEFE
UNTRUMP THE WORLD!

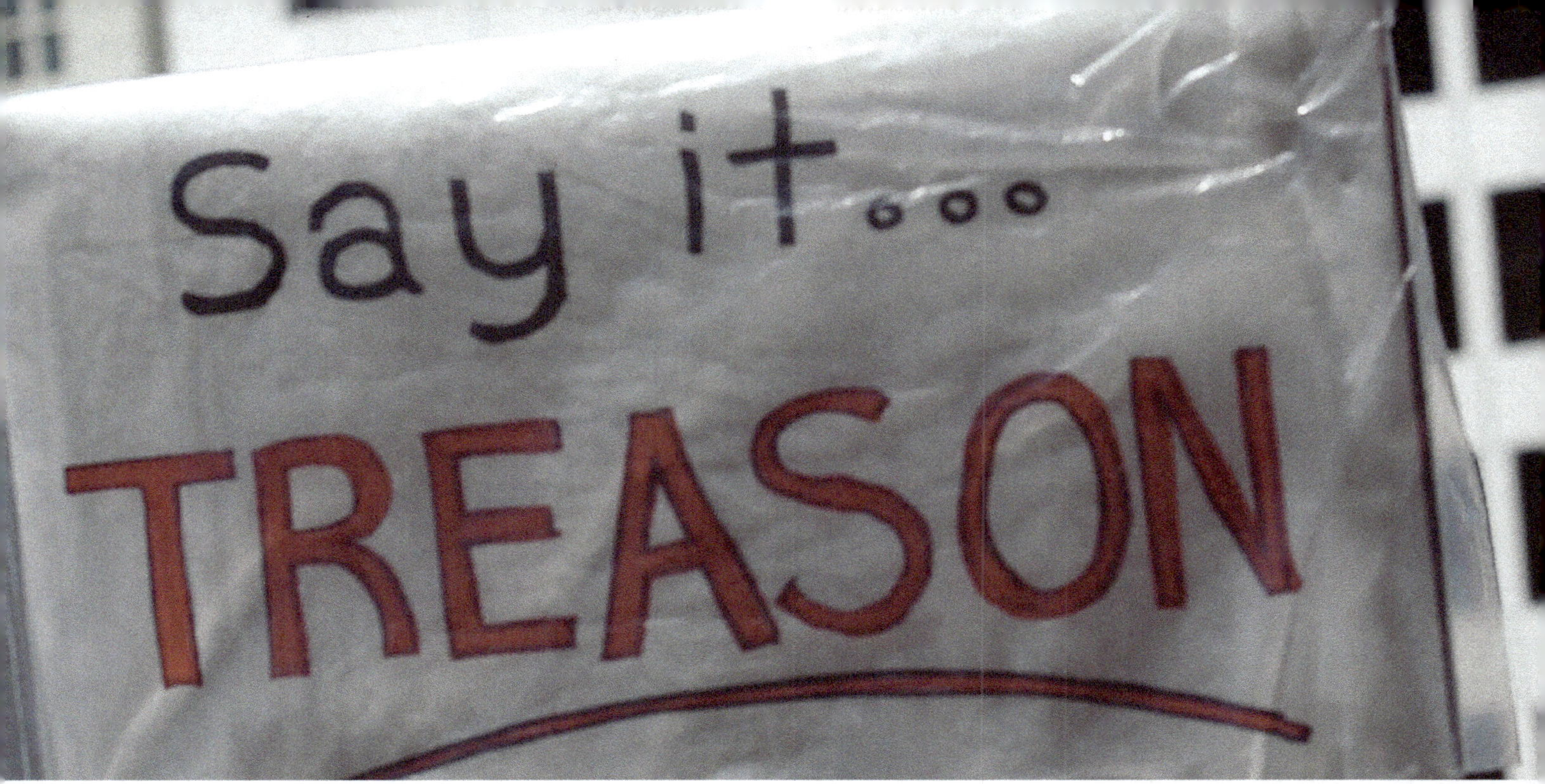

Say it...
TREASON

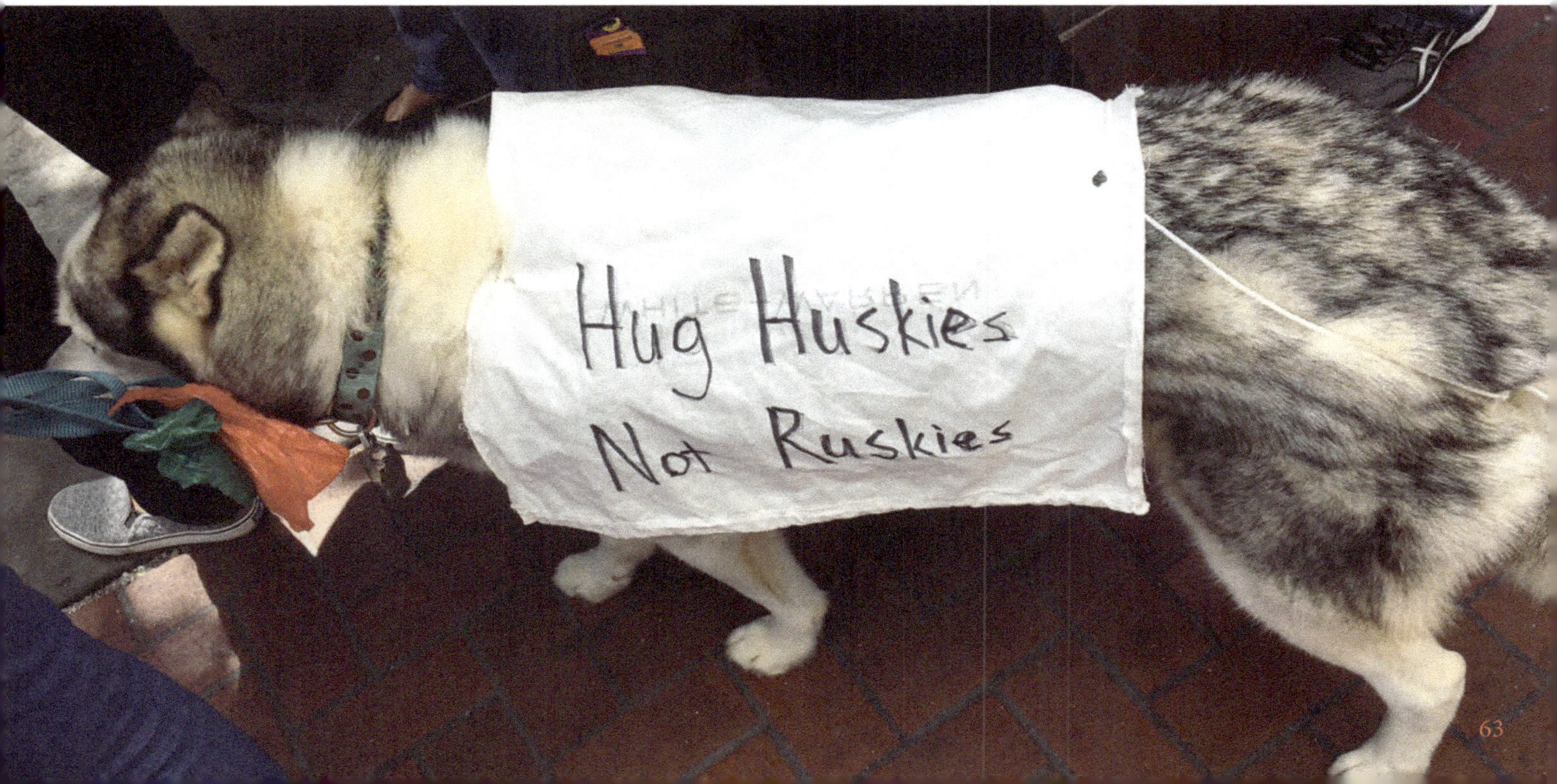

Hug Huskies
Not Ruskies

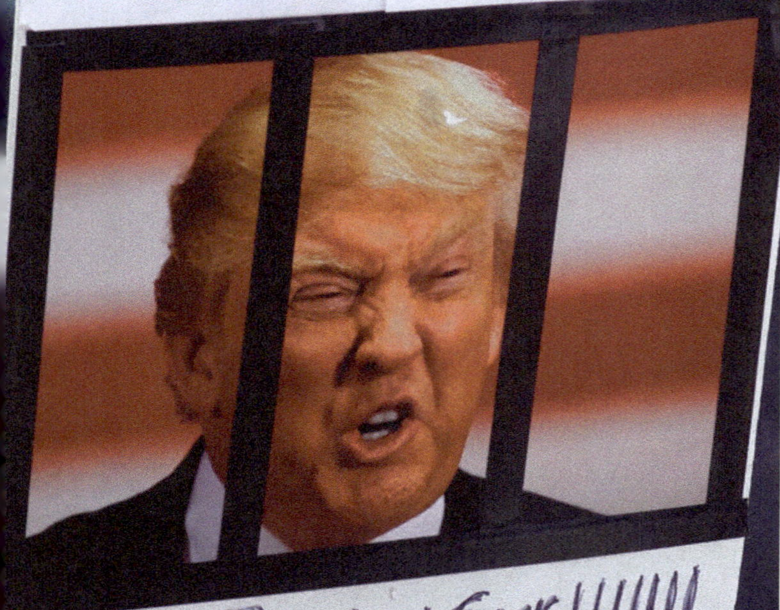
The Truth Shall
Set U.S. Free
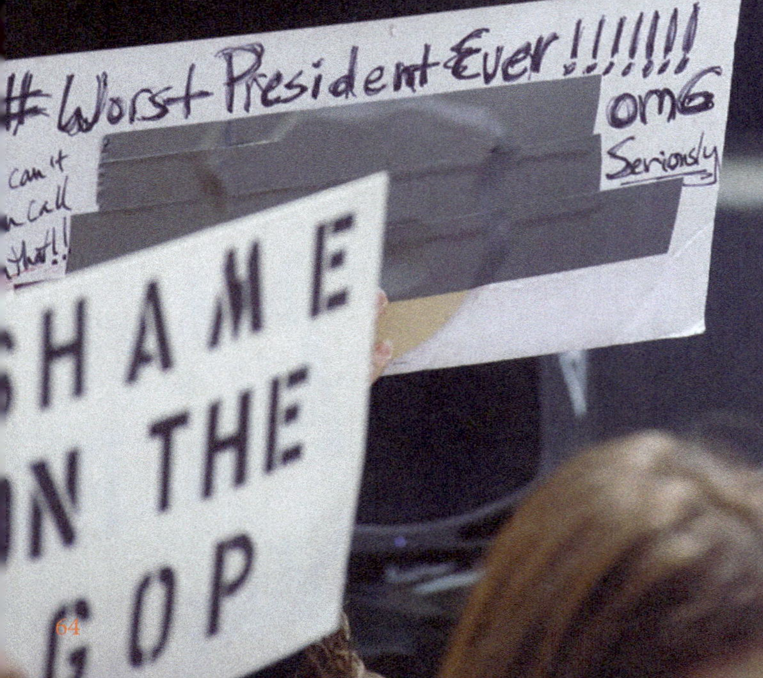
#WorstPresidentEver!!!!!!!
omg
Seriously
can't
call
that!!
SHAME
ON THE
GOP
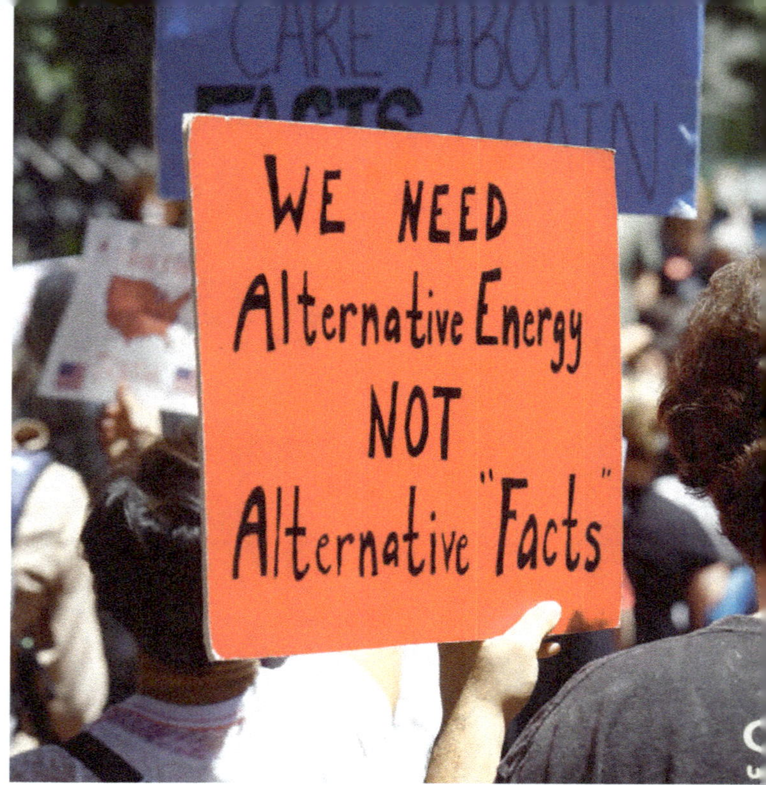
CARE ABOUT
FACTS AGAIN
WE NEED
Alternative Energy
NOT
Alternative "Facts"
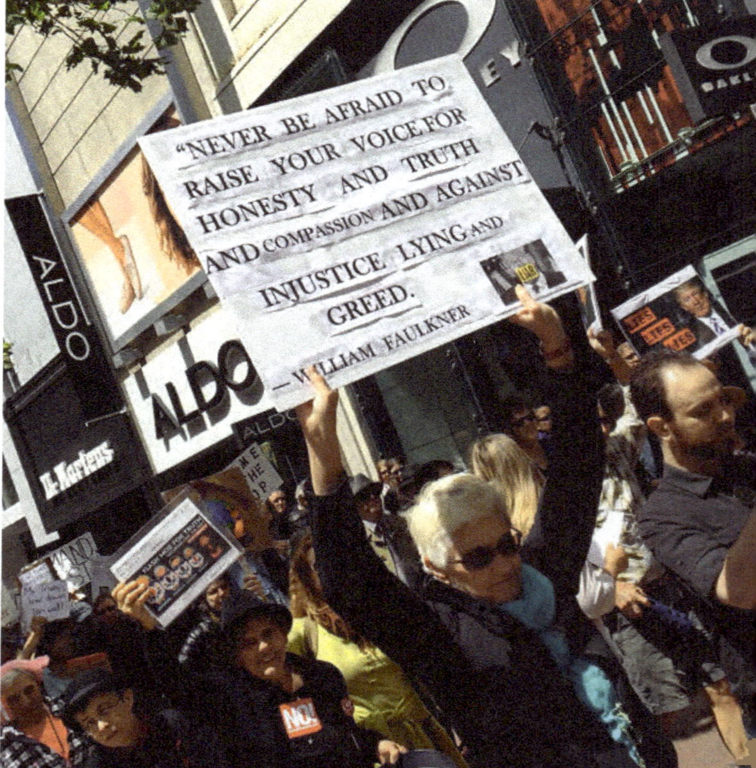
"NEVER BE AFRAID TO
RAISE YOUR VOICE FOR
HONESTY AND TRUTH
AND COMPASSION AND AGAINST
INJUSTICE, LYING AND
GREED.
—WILLIAM FAULKNER
ALDO
ALDO
Dr. Martens

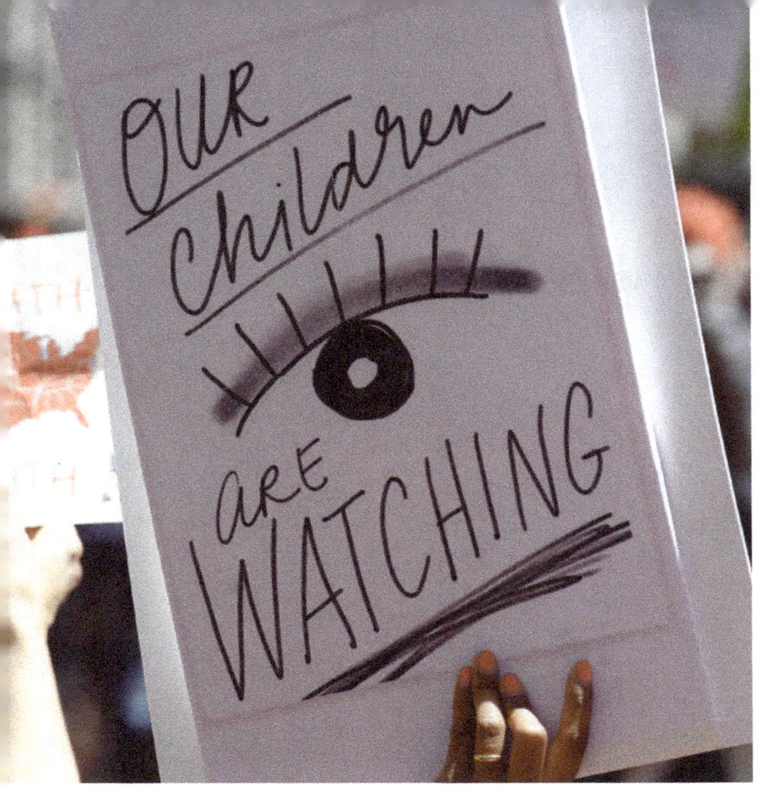

OUR children ARE WATCHING

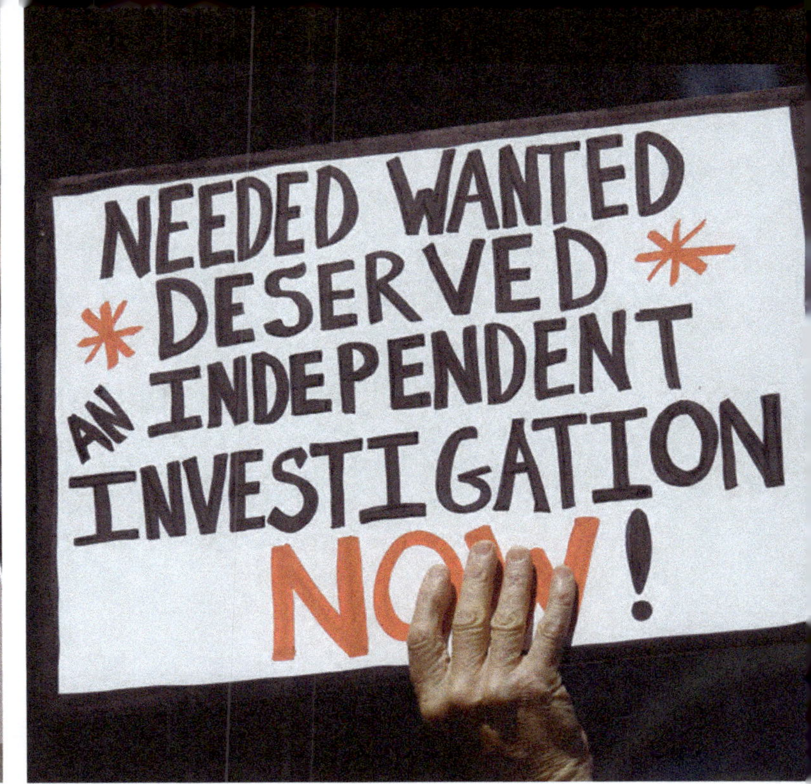

NEEDED WANTED
DESERVED
AN INDEPENDENT
INVESTIGATION
NOW !

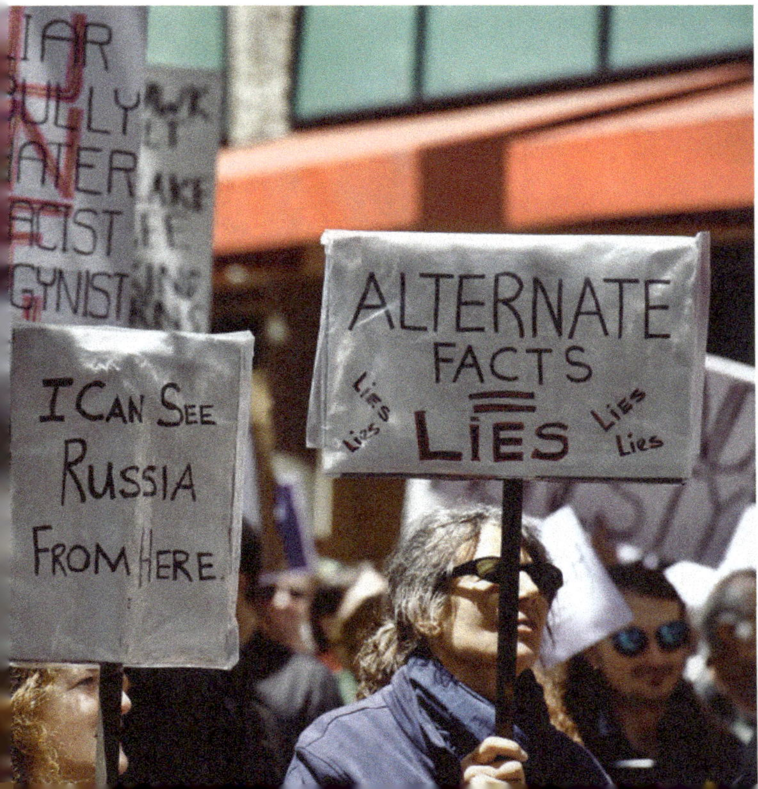

LIAR
BULLY
HATER
RACIST
MYSOGYNIST
I CAN SEE RUSSIA FROM HERE.
ALTERNATE FACTS
Lies Lies
LIES
Lies Lies

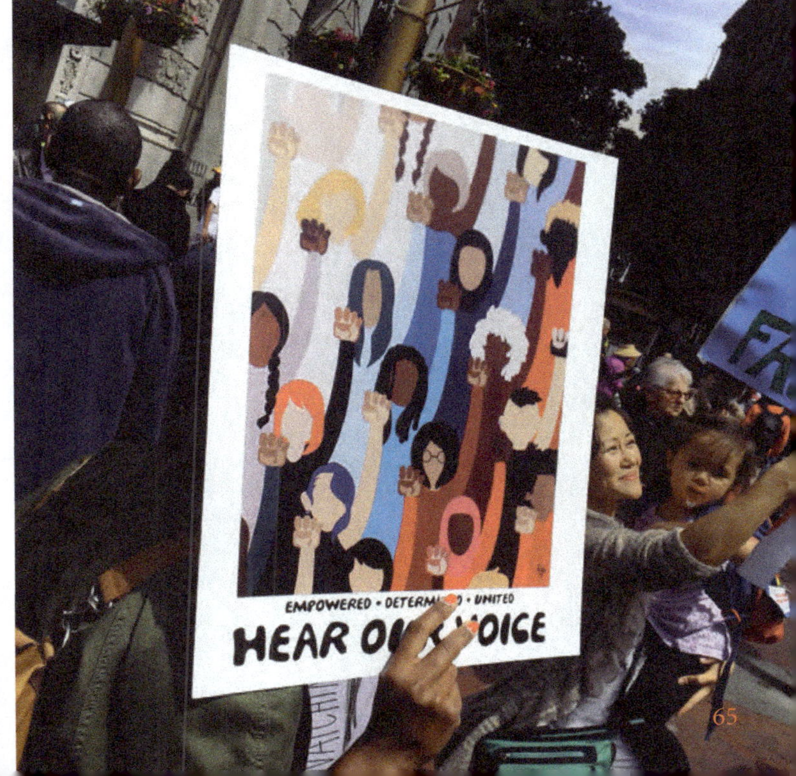

EMPOWERED · DETERMINED · UNITED
HEAR OUR VOICE

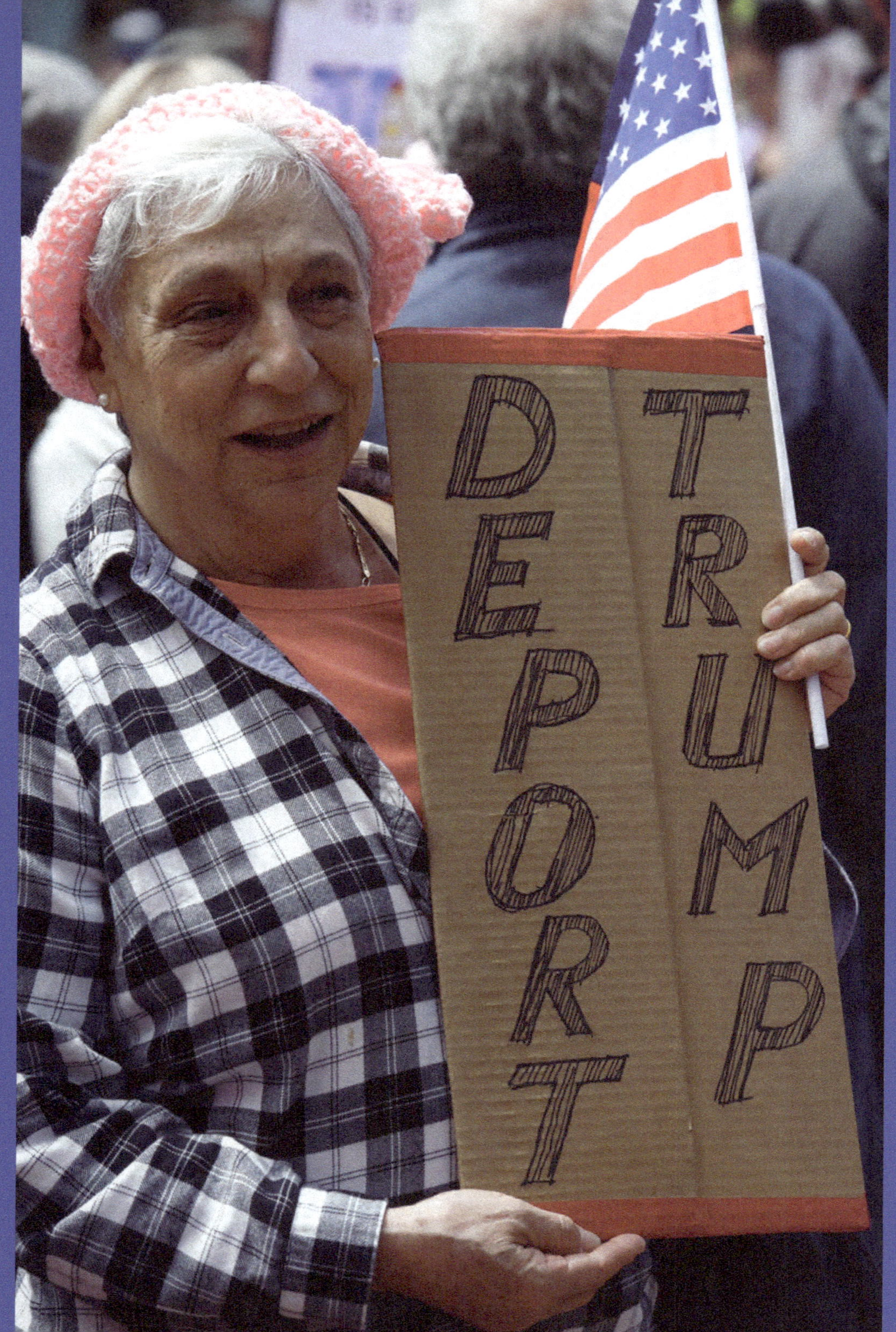

DEPORT
TRUMP

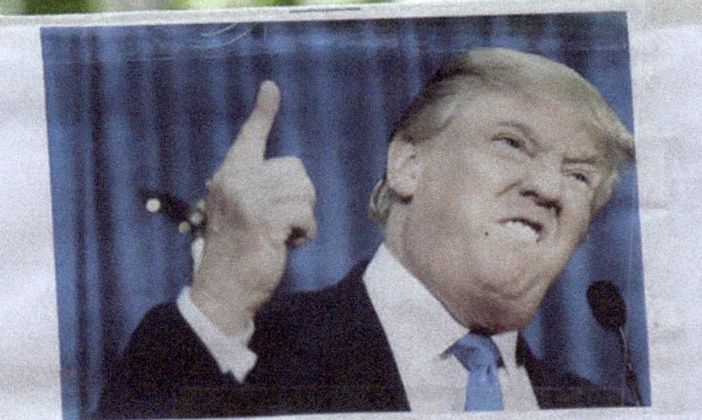

Your descriptor here _______________ (none are wrong)

You can fool some of the
people all of the time,
but you won't fool us, anytime!

MAKE AMERICA
CARE ABOUT
FACTS AGAIN

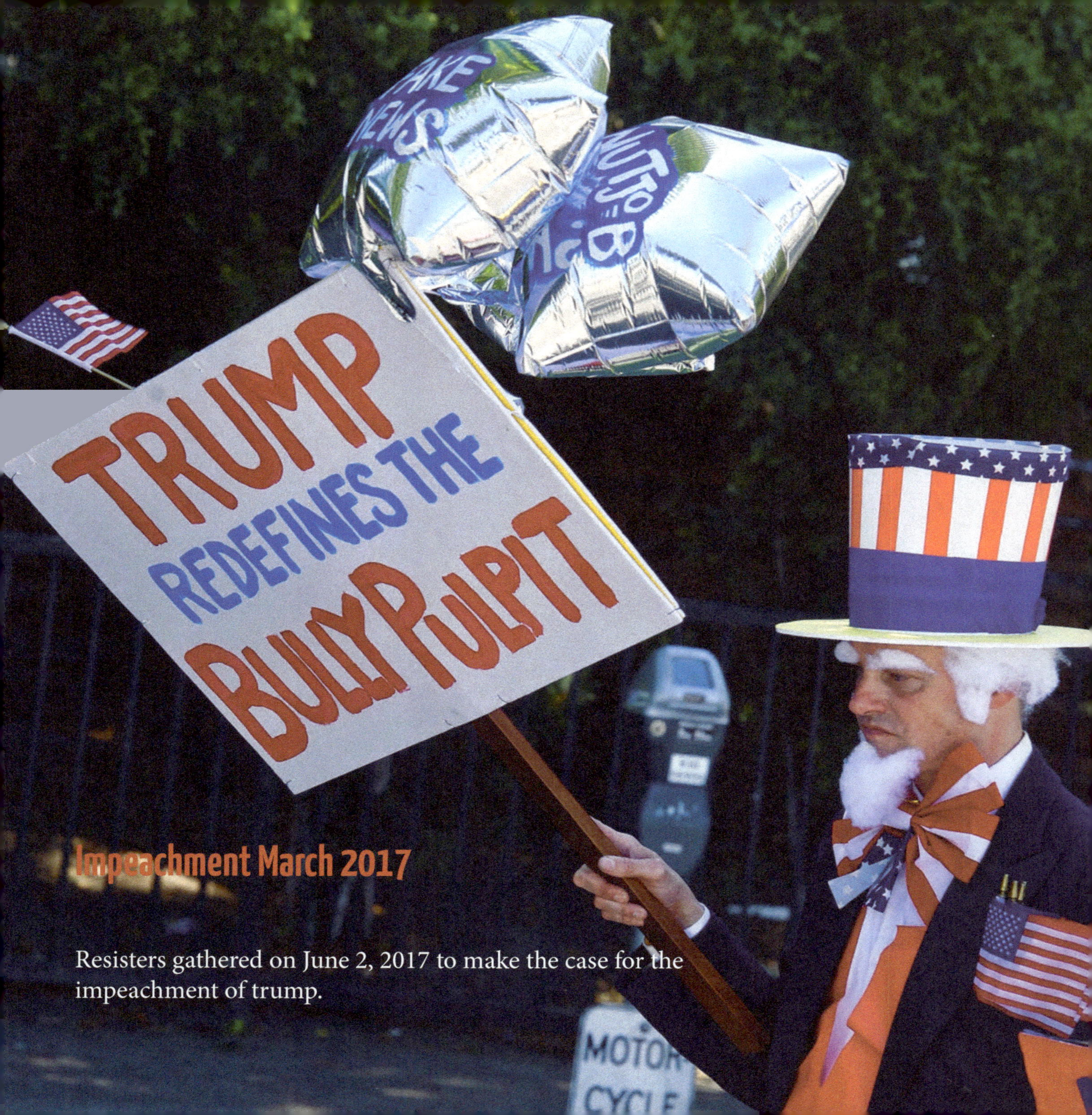

Impeachment March 2017

Resisters gathered on June 2, 2017 to make the case for the impeachment of trump.

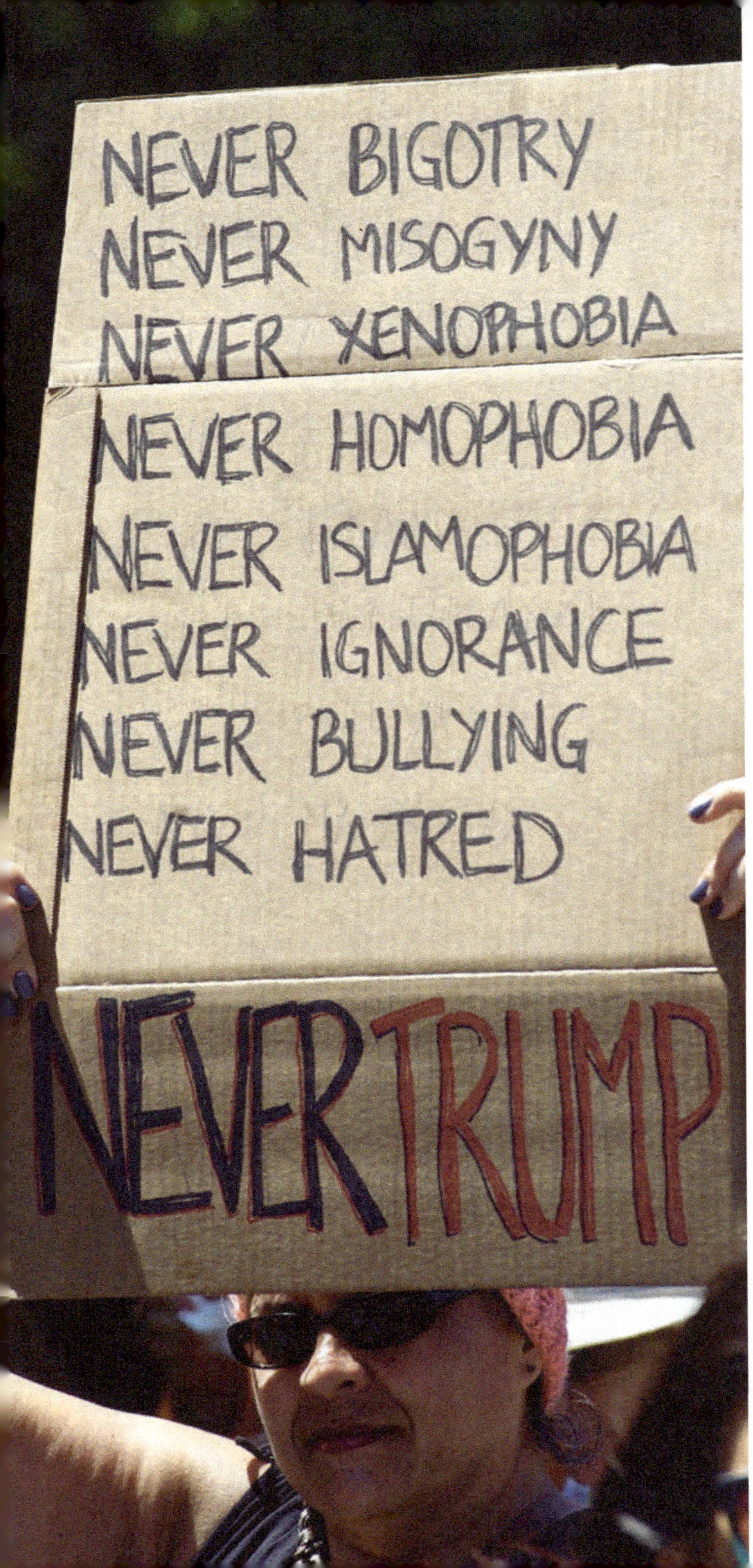

NEVER BIGOTRY
NEVER MISOGYNY
NEVER XENOPHOBIA
NEVER HOMOPHOBIA
NEVER ISLAMOPHOBIA
NEVER IGNORANCE
NEVER BULLYING
NEVER HATRED
NEVER TRUMP

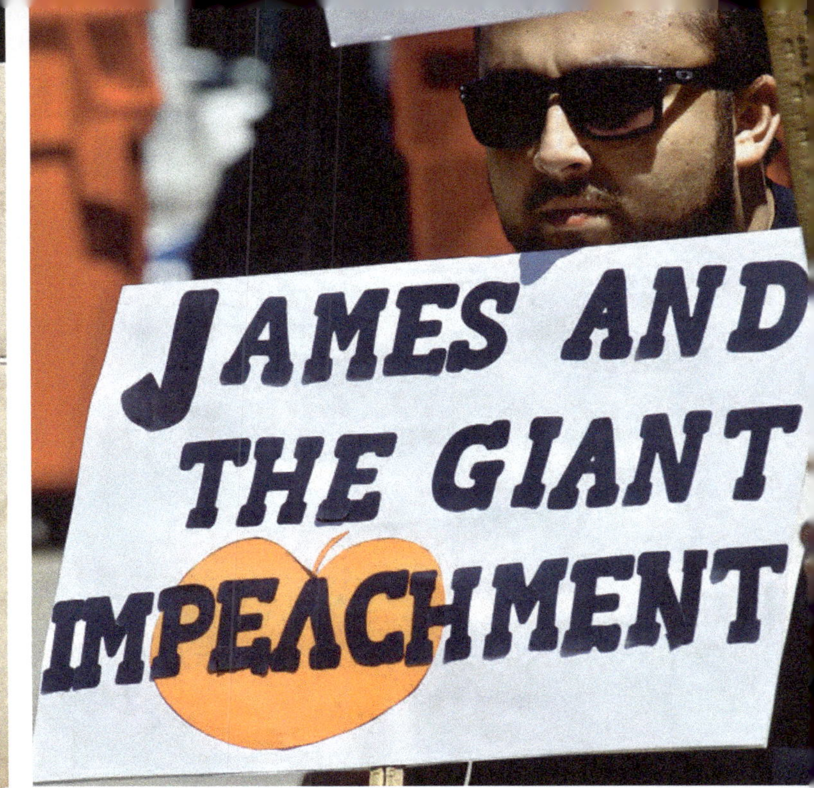

JAMES AND
THE GIANT
IMPEACHMENT

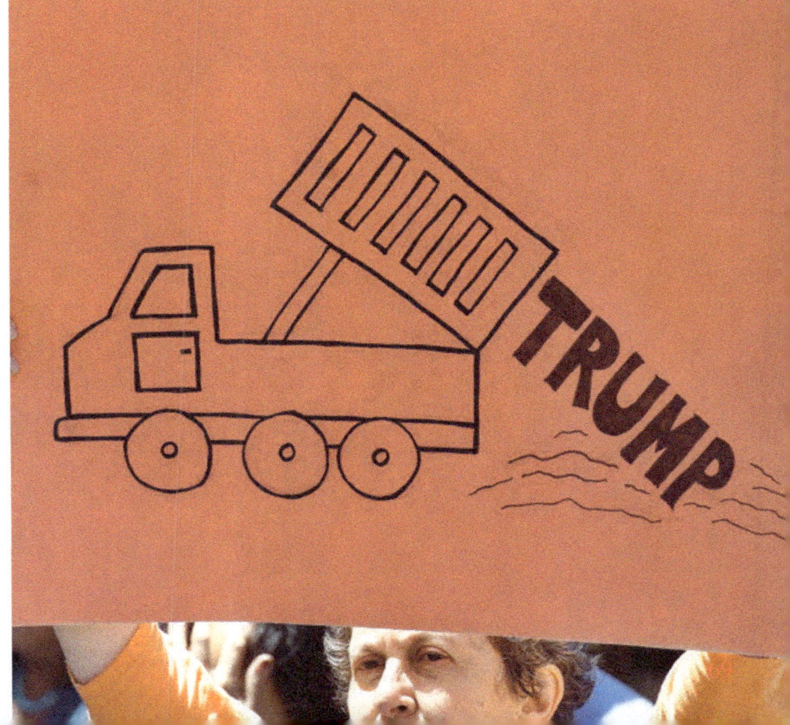

TRUMP

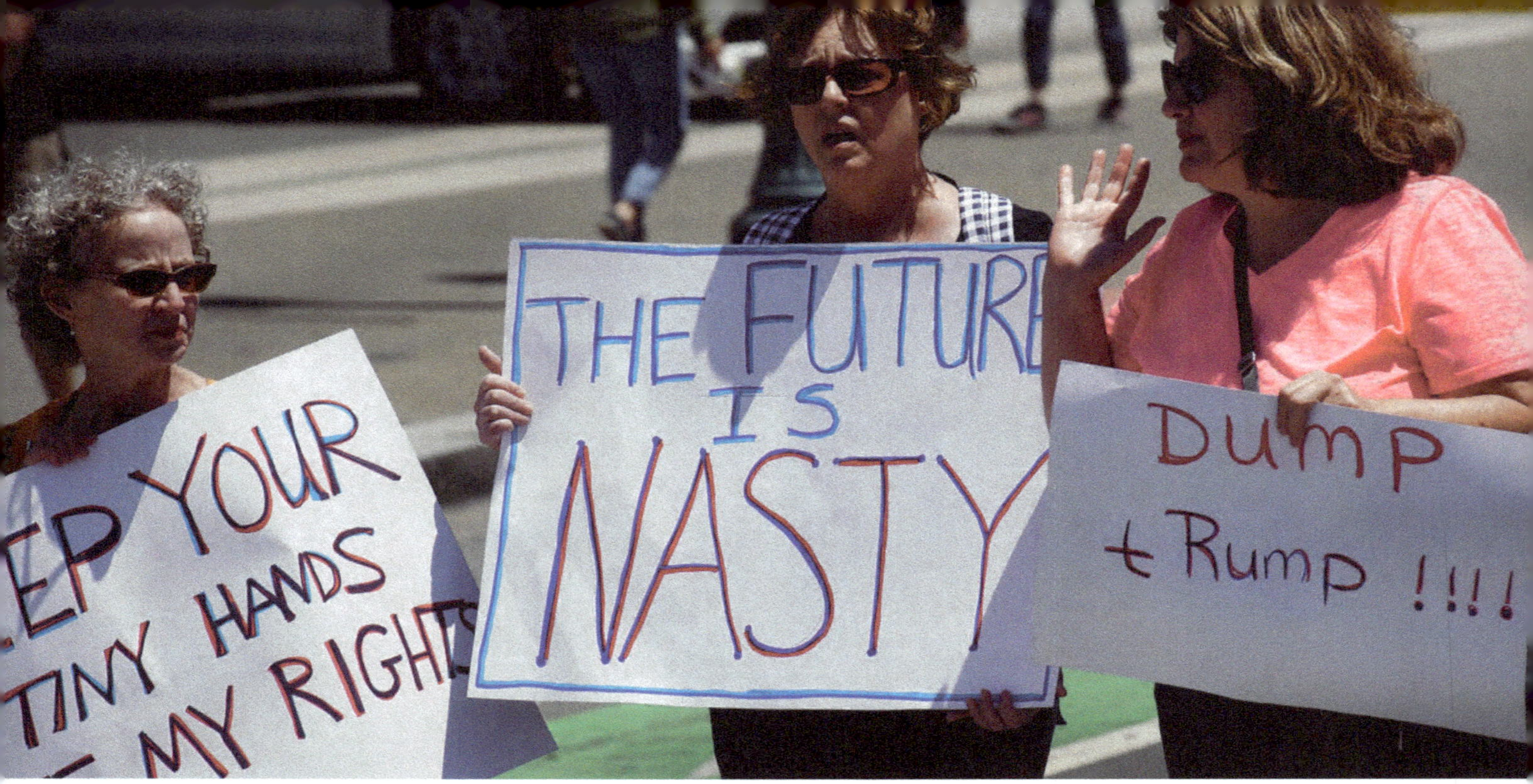

EP YOUR
TINY HANDS
F MY RIGHTS
THE FUTURE
IS
NASTY
DUMP
tRump !!!!

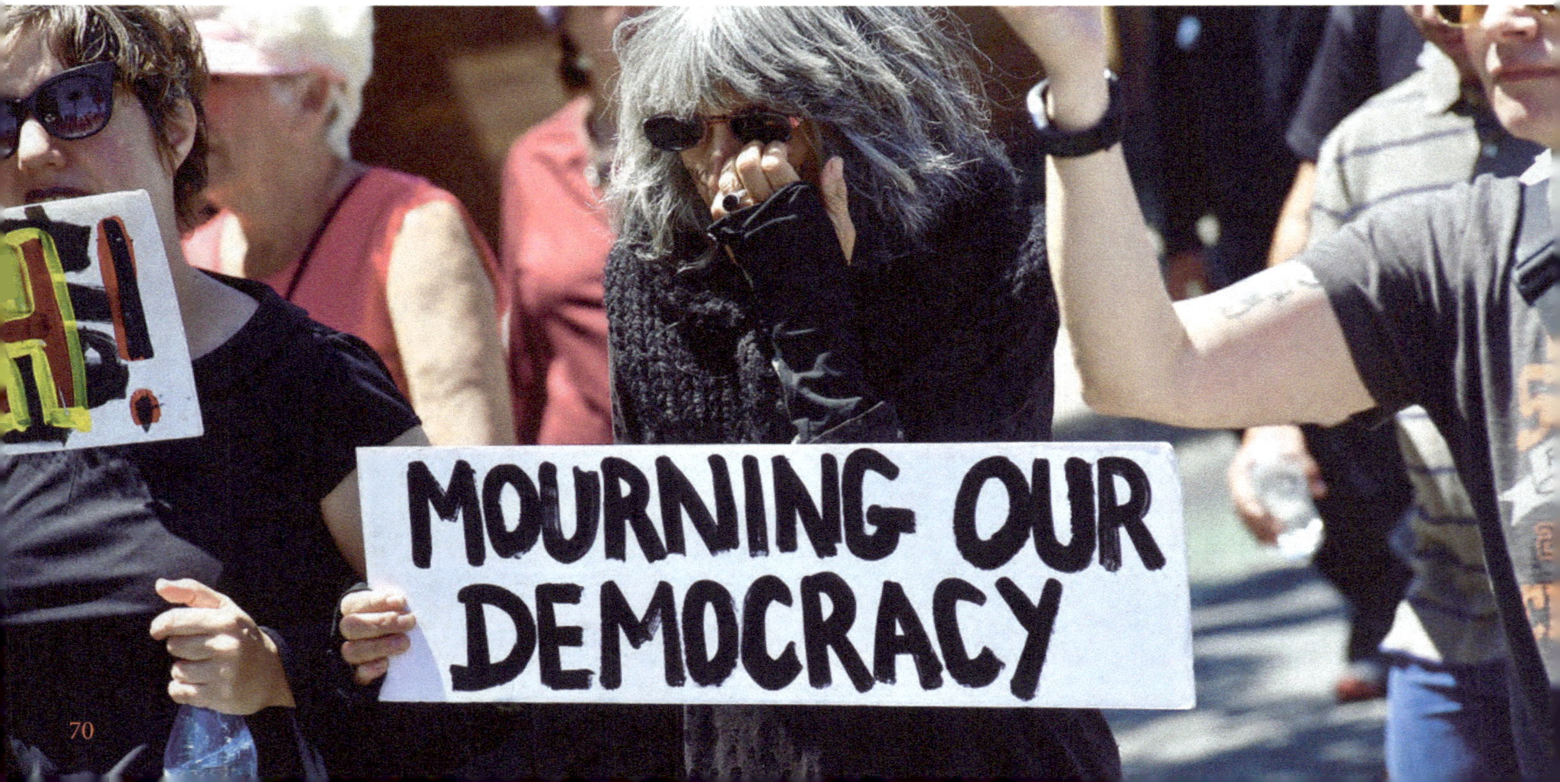

MOURNING OUR
DEMOCRACY

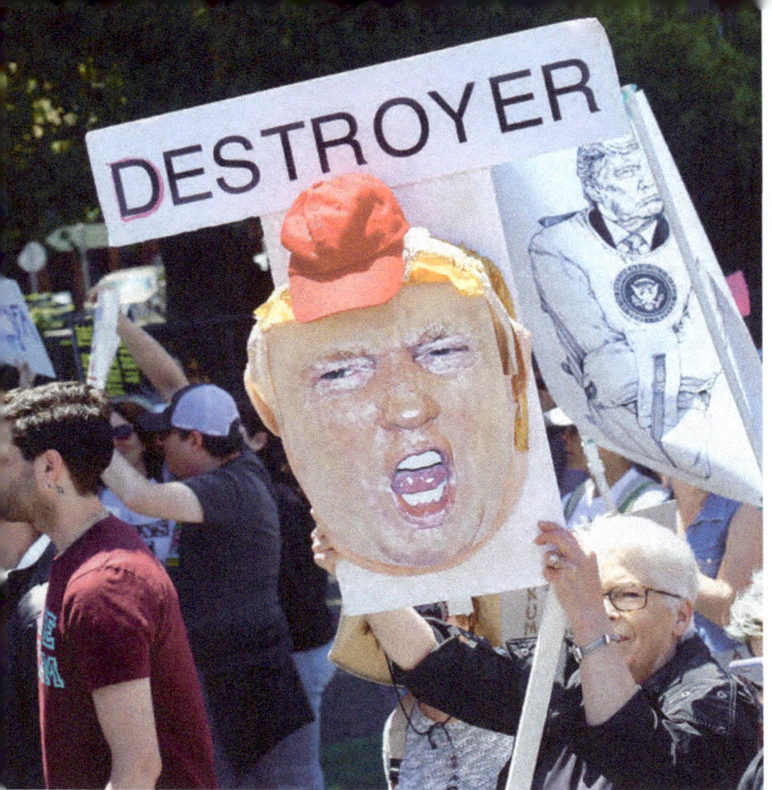
DESTROYER

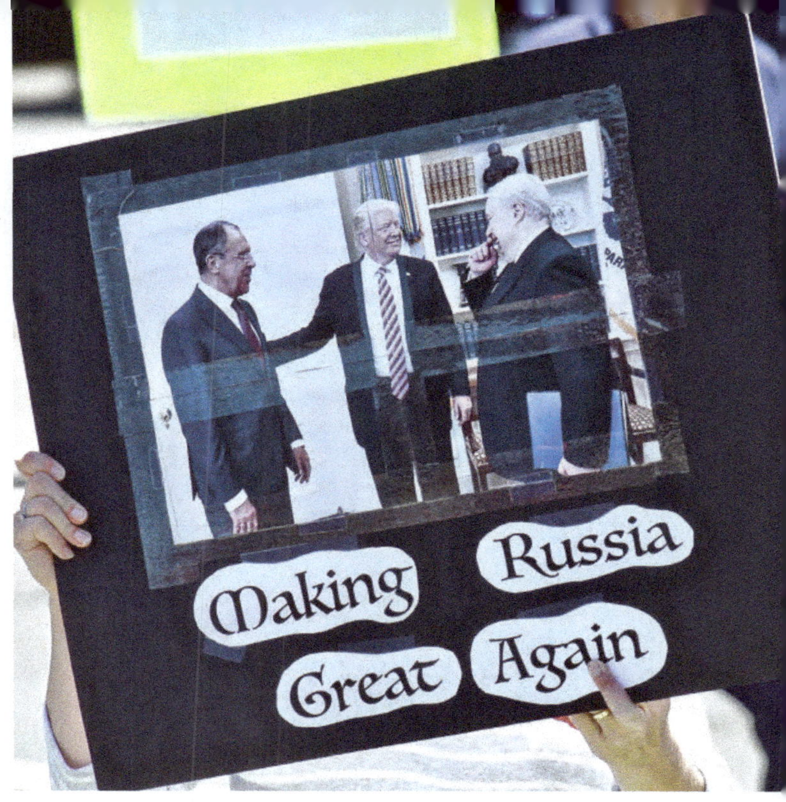
Making Russia Great Again

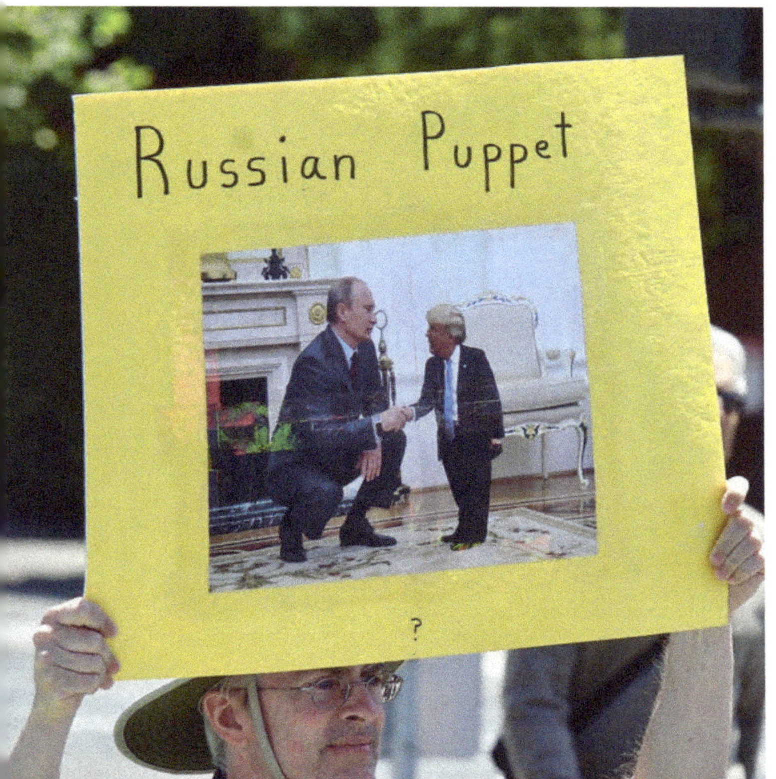
Russian Puppet
?

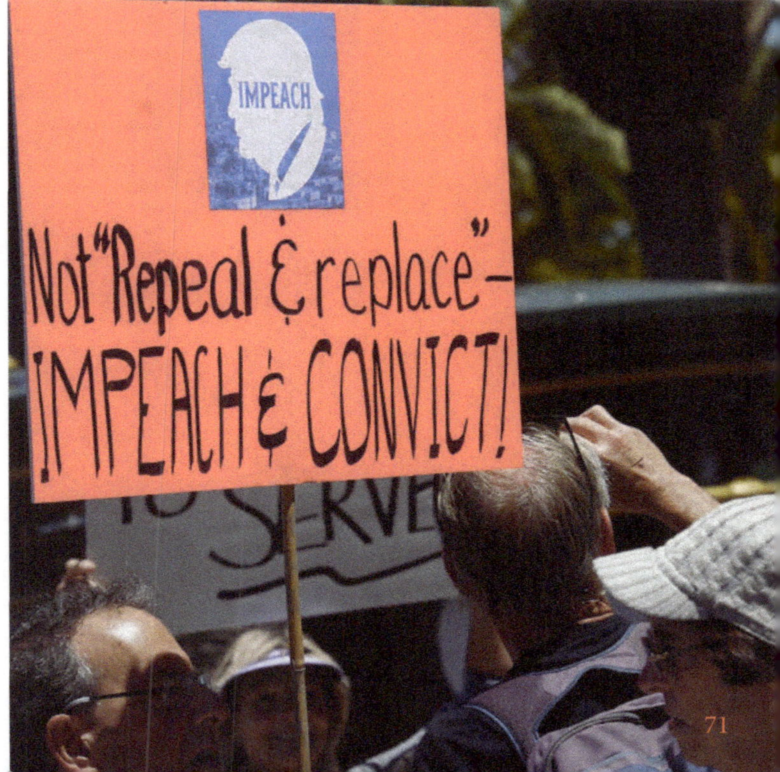
IMPEACH
Not "Repeal & replace"—
IMPEACH & CONVICT!
SERVE

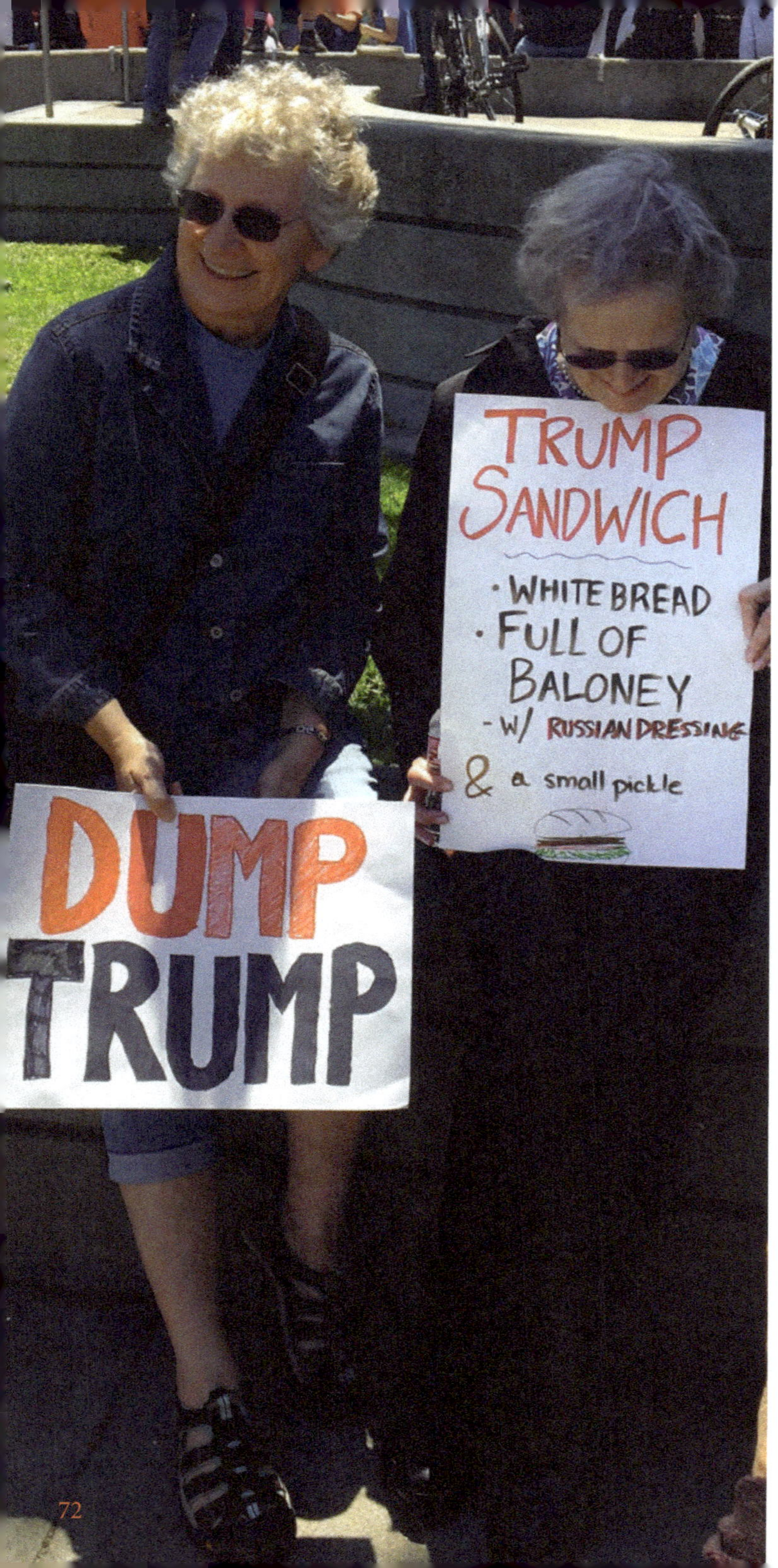

TRUMP
SANDWICH
• WHITE BREAD
• FULL OF
BALONEY
- W/ RUSSIAN DRESSING
& a small pickle

DUMP
TRUMP

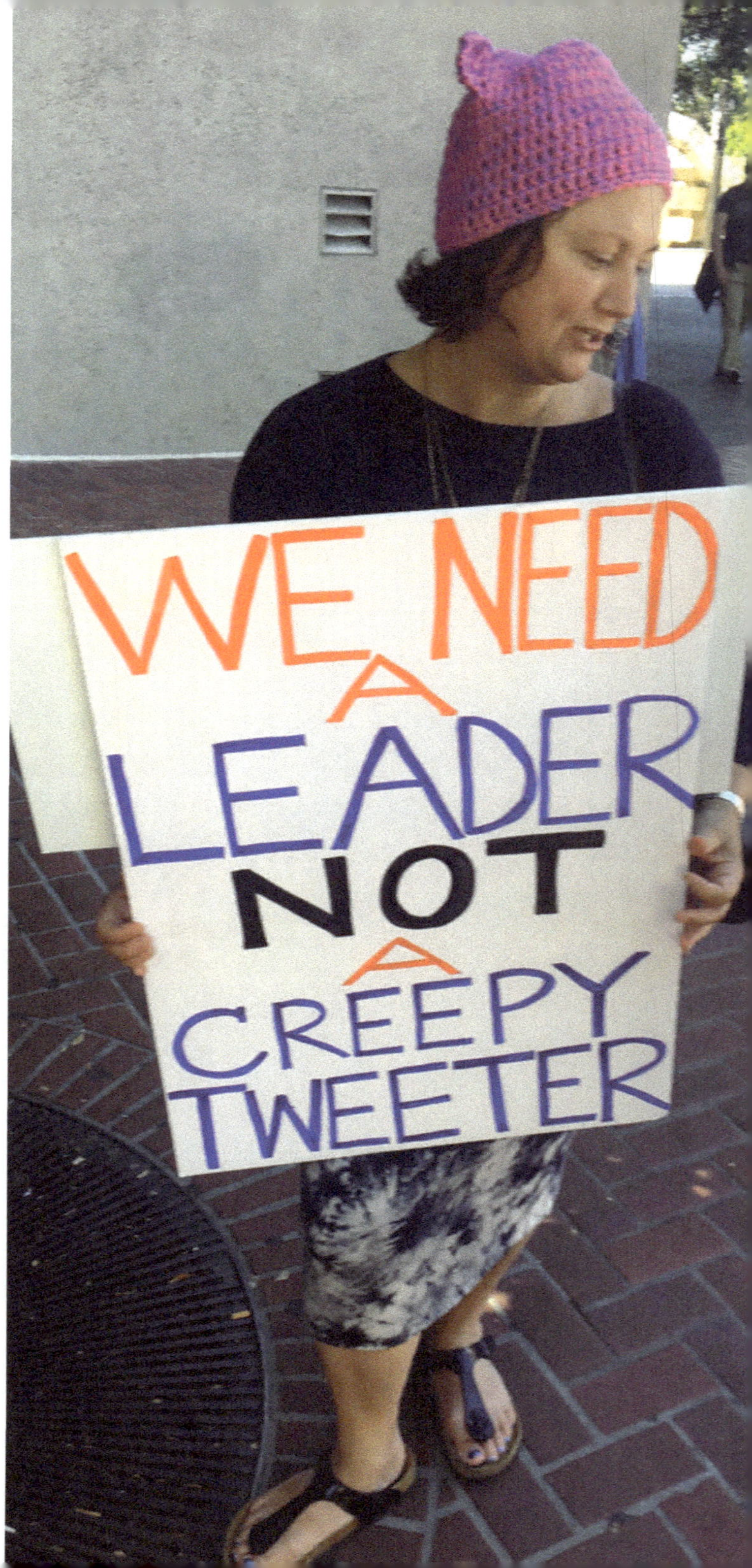

WE NEED
A
LEADER
NOT
A
CREEPY
TWEETER

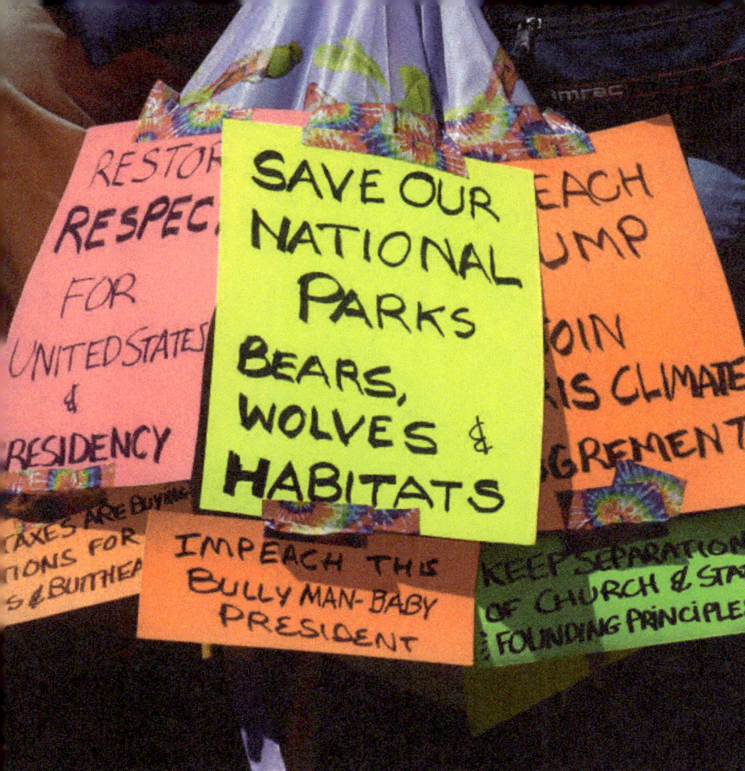
RESTORE
RESPECT
FOR
UNITED STATES
&
RESIDENCY
SAVE OUR
NATIONAL
PARKS
BEARS,
WOLVES &
HABITATS
IMPEACH
TRUMP
JOIN
THIS CLIMATE
AGREEMENT
IMPEACH THIS
BULLY MAN-BABY
PRESIDENT
KEEP SEPARATION
OF CHURCH & STATE
& FOUNDING PRINCIPLES

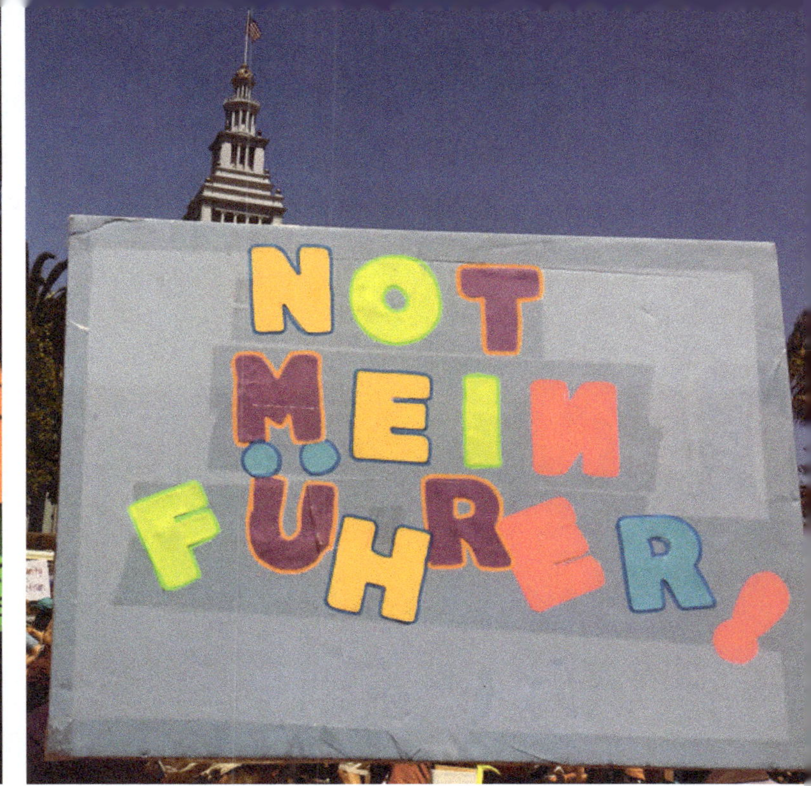
NOT
MEIN
FÜHRER!

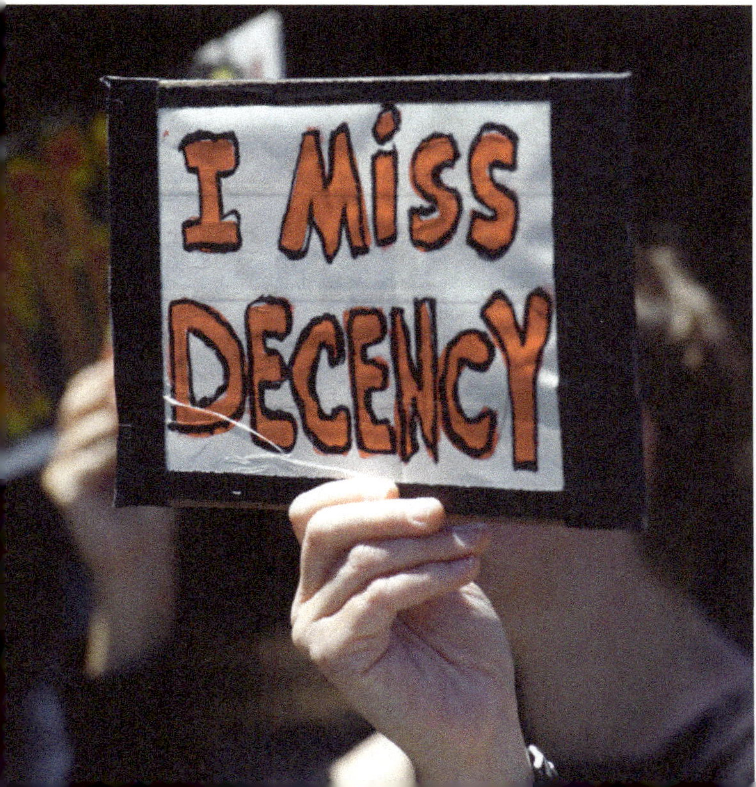
I MISS
DECENCY

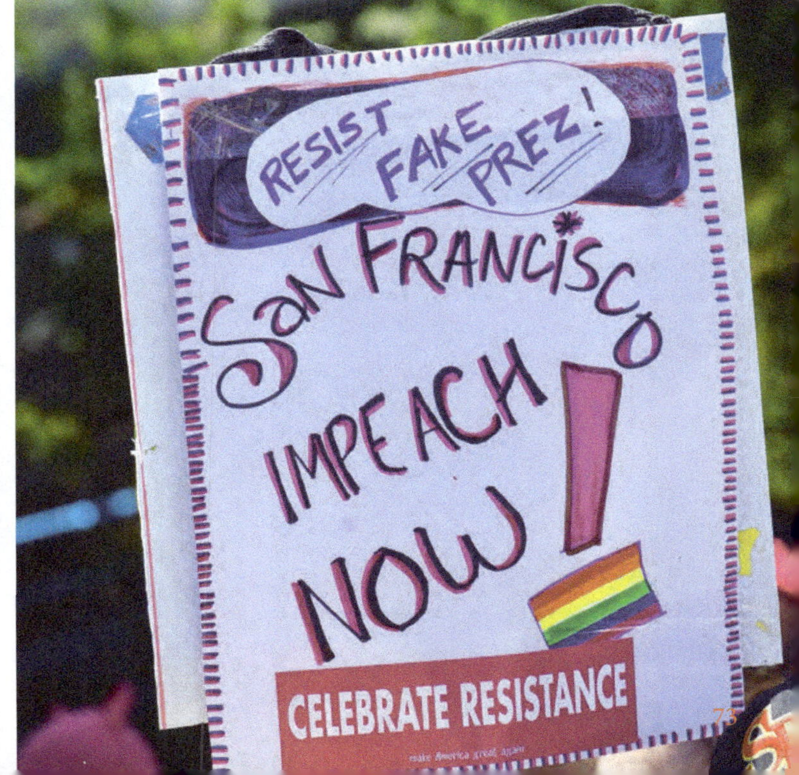
RESIST FAKE PREZ!
SAN FRANCISCO
IMPEACH
NOW
CELEBRATE RESISTANCE

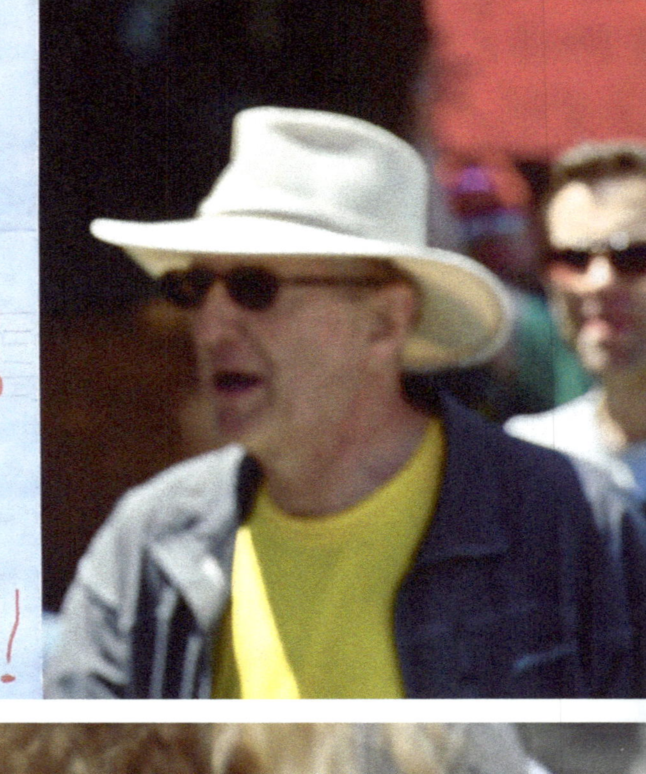
T R U M P
IS A
COCKWOMBLE
IMPEACH THE ENTIRE
ADMINISRATION NOW!!

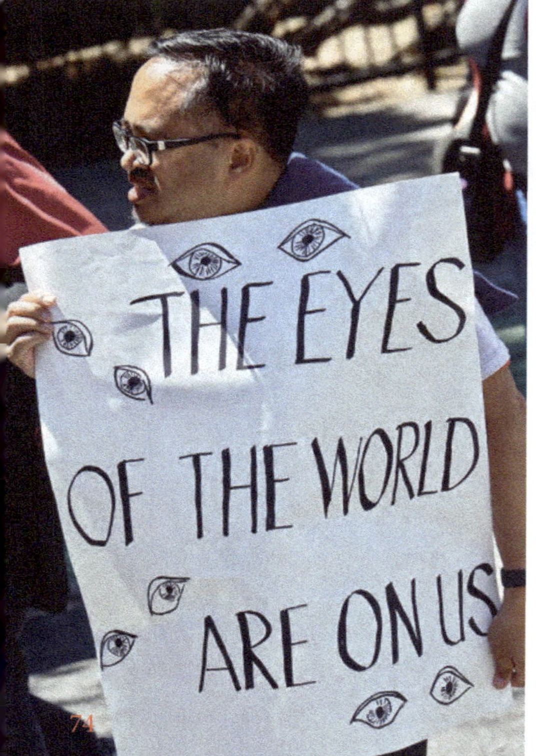
THE EYES
OF THE WORLD
ARE ON US

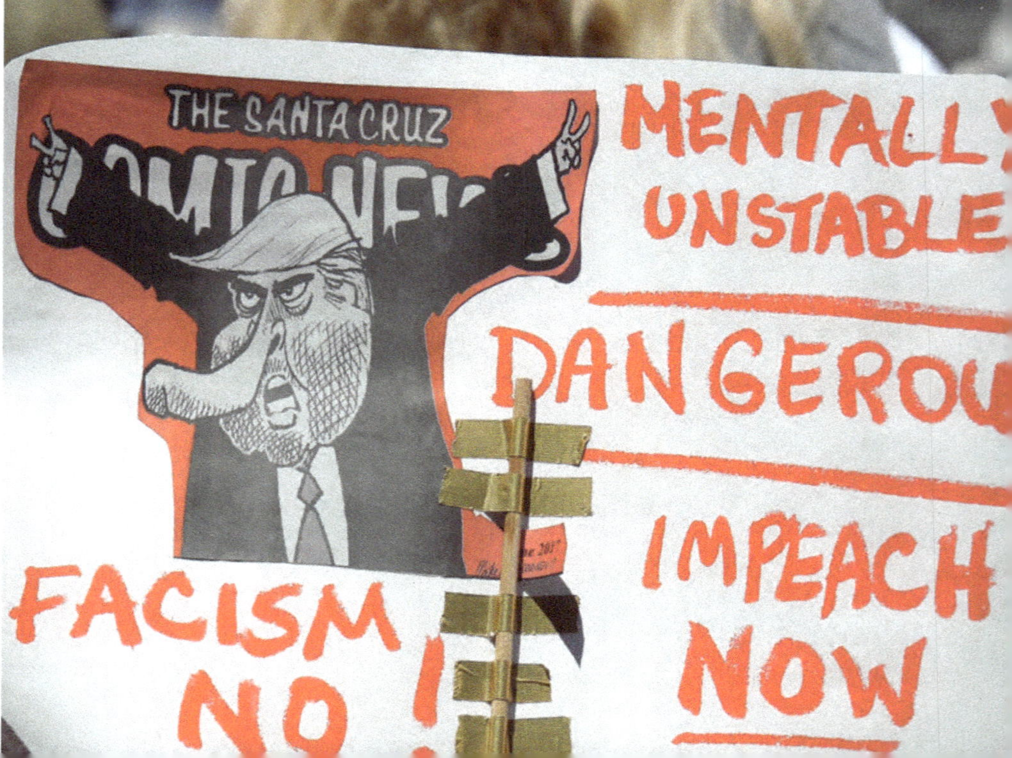
THE SANTA CRUZ
FACISM
NO!
MENTALLY
UNSTABLE
DANGEROU
IMPEACH
NOW

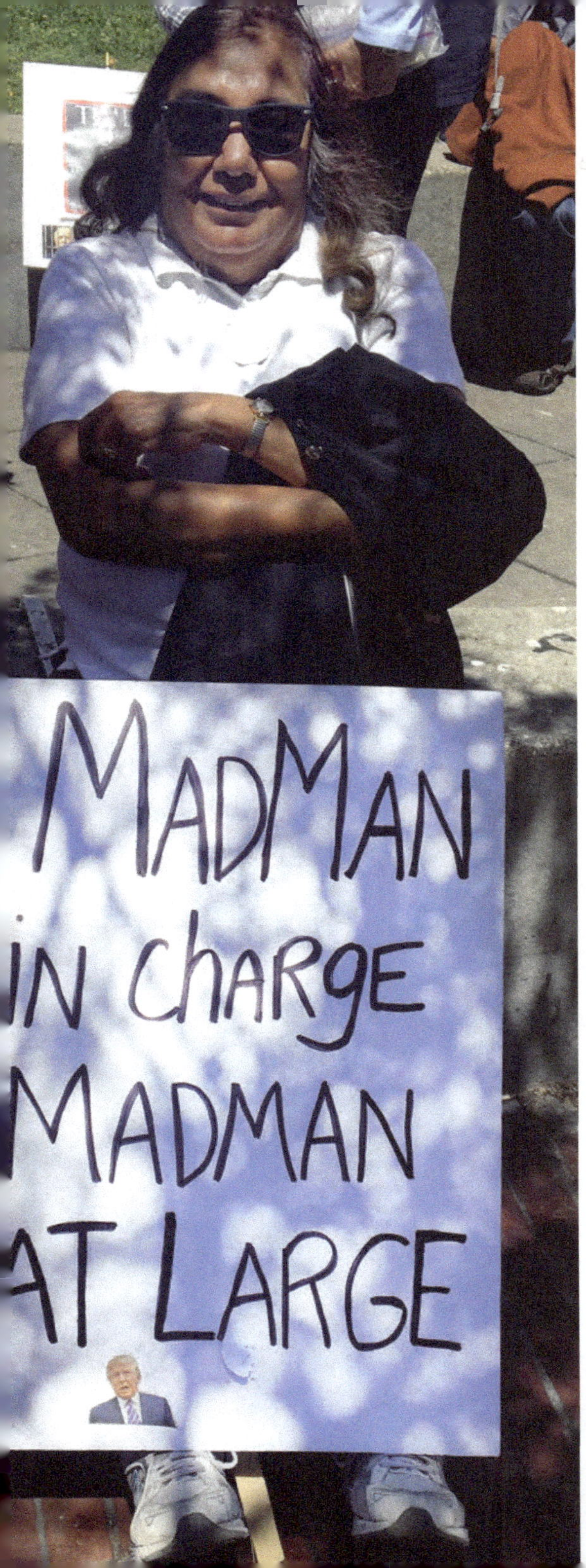

MADMAN
IN CHARGE
MADMAN
AT LARGE

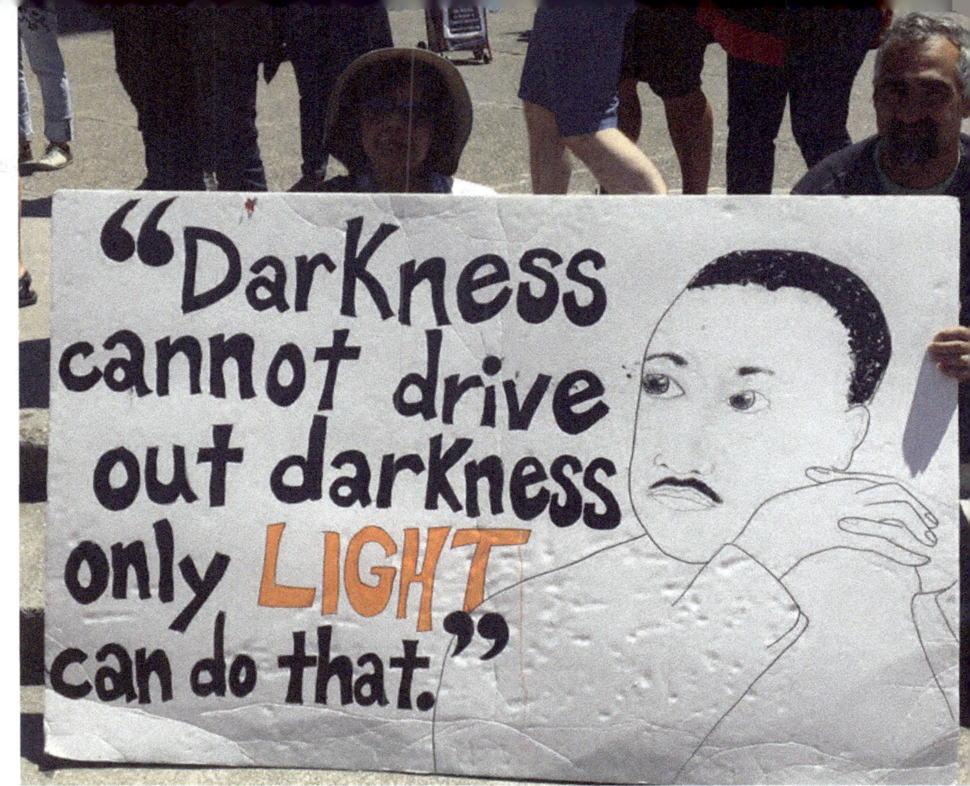
"Darkness
cannot drive
out darkness
only LIGHT
can do that."

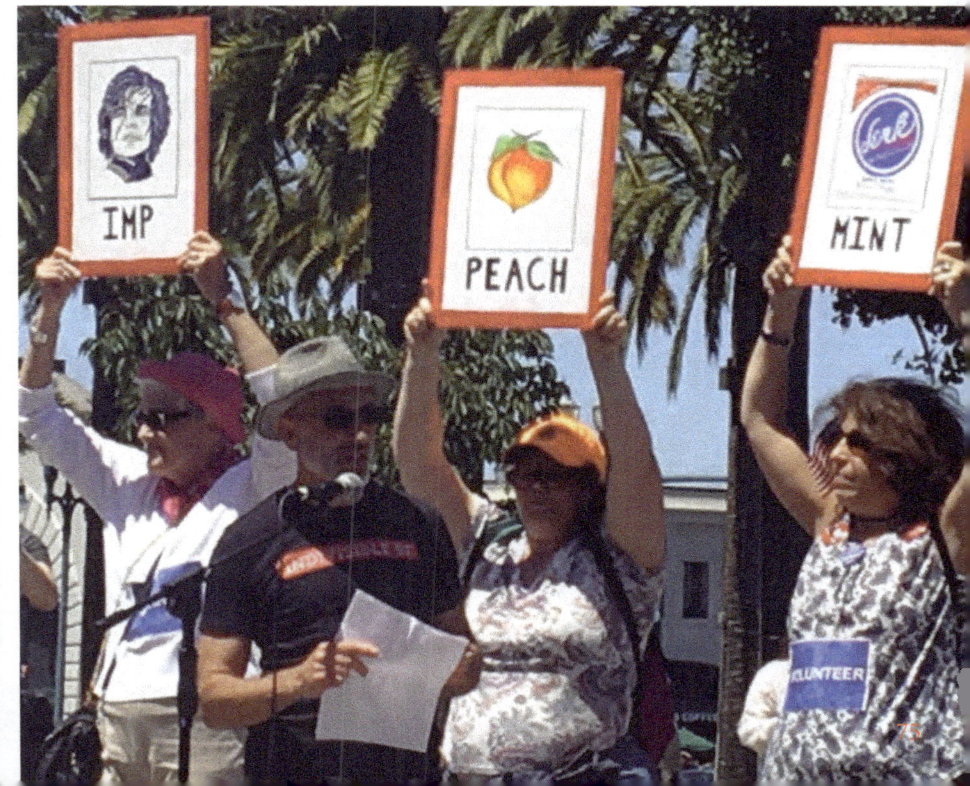
IMP
PEACH
MINT
VOLUNTEER

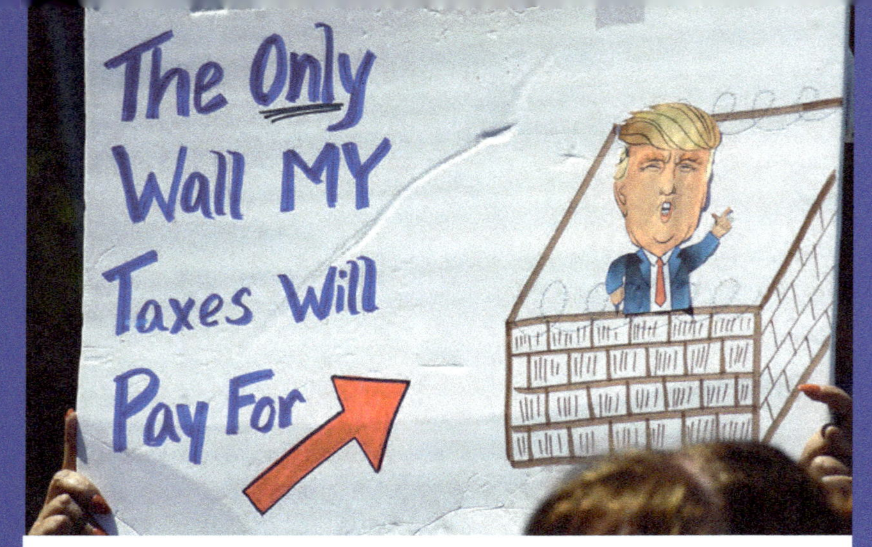
The Only
Wall MY
Taxes Will
Pay For

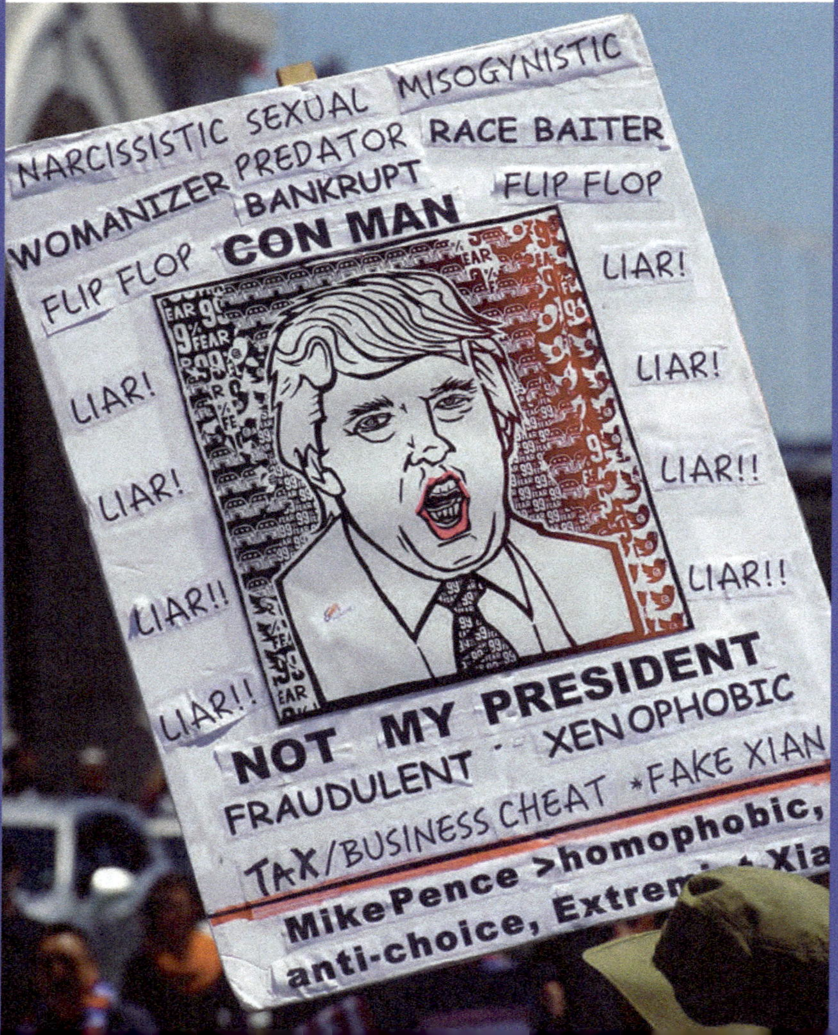

NARCISSISTIC SEXUAL MISOGYNISTIC
WOMANIZER PREDATOR RACE BAITER
BANKRUPT
FLIP FLOP CON MAN FLIP FLOP
LIAR! LIAR!
LIAR! LIAR!
LIAR!! LIAR!!
LIAR!! LIAR!!
LIAR!!
NOT MY PRESIDENT
FRAUDULENT XENOPHOBIC
TAX/BUSINESS CHEAT *FAKE XIAN
MikePence >homophobic,
anti-choice, Extremist Xia

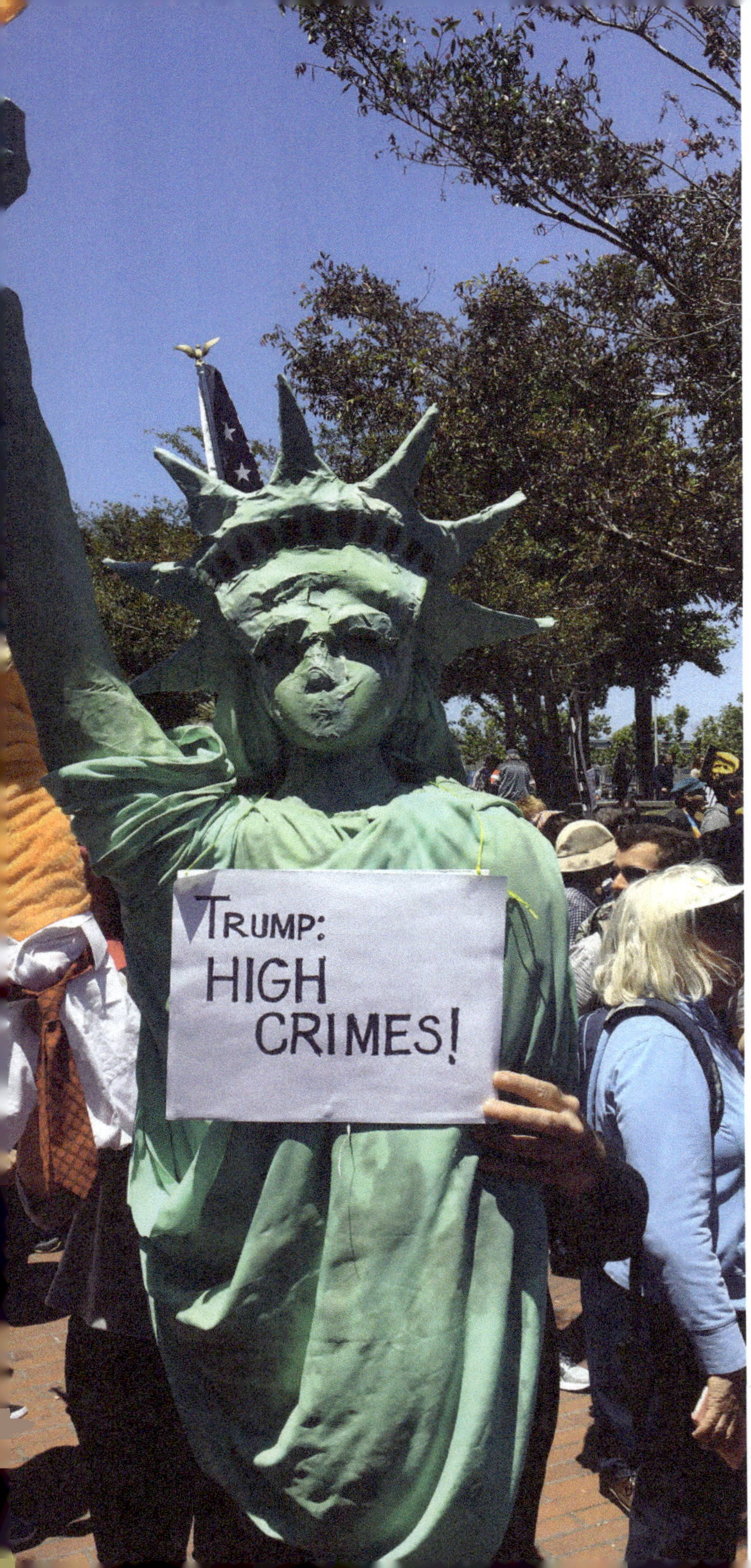

TRUMP:
HIGH
CRIMES!

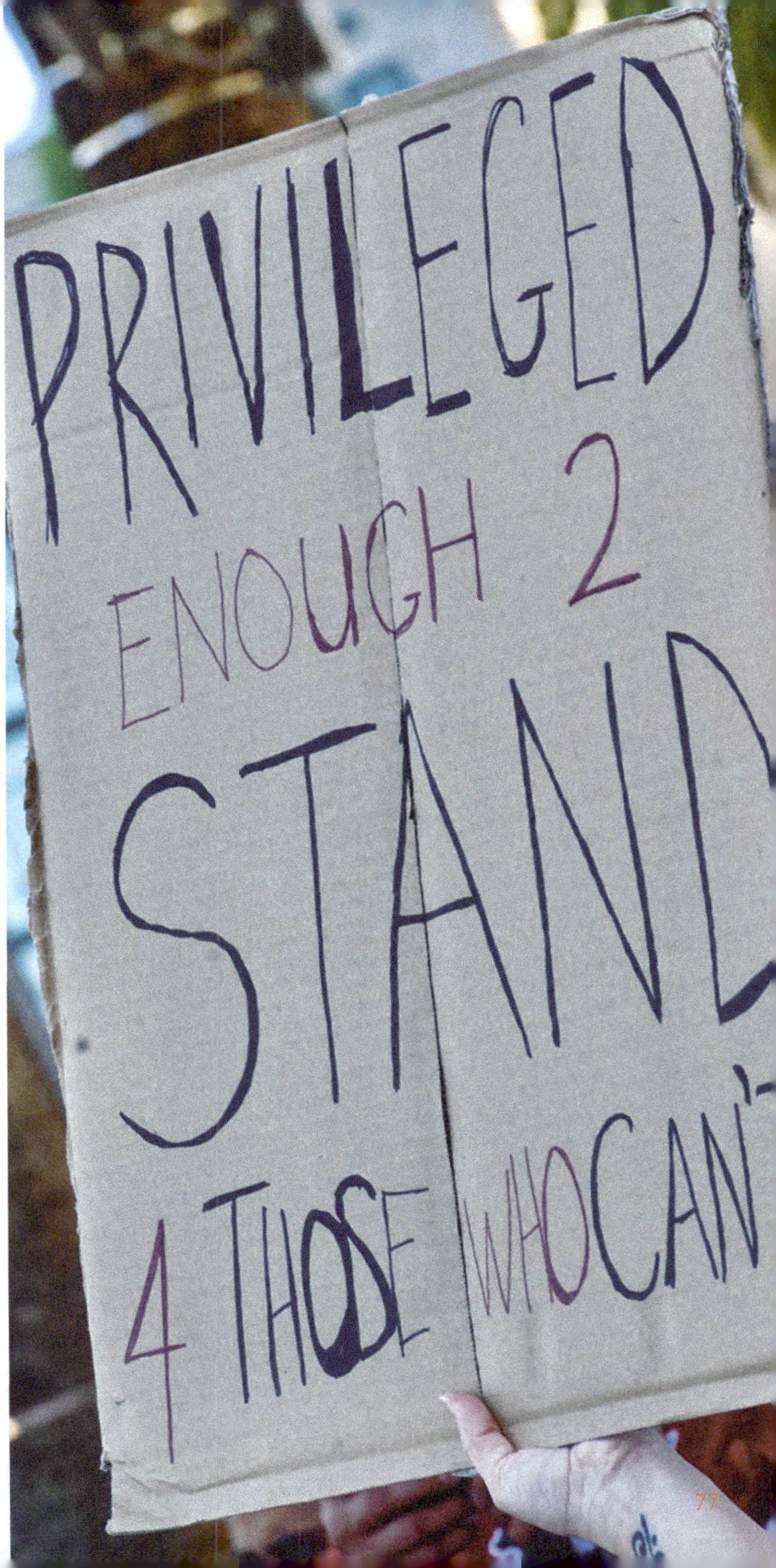

PRIVILEGED
ENOUGH 2
STAND
4 THOSE WHO CAN'T

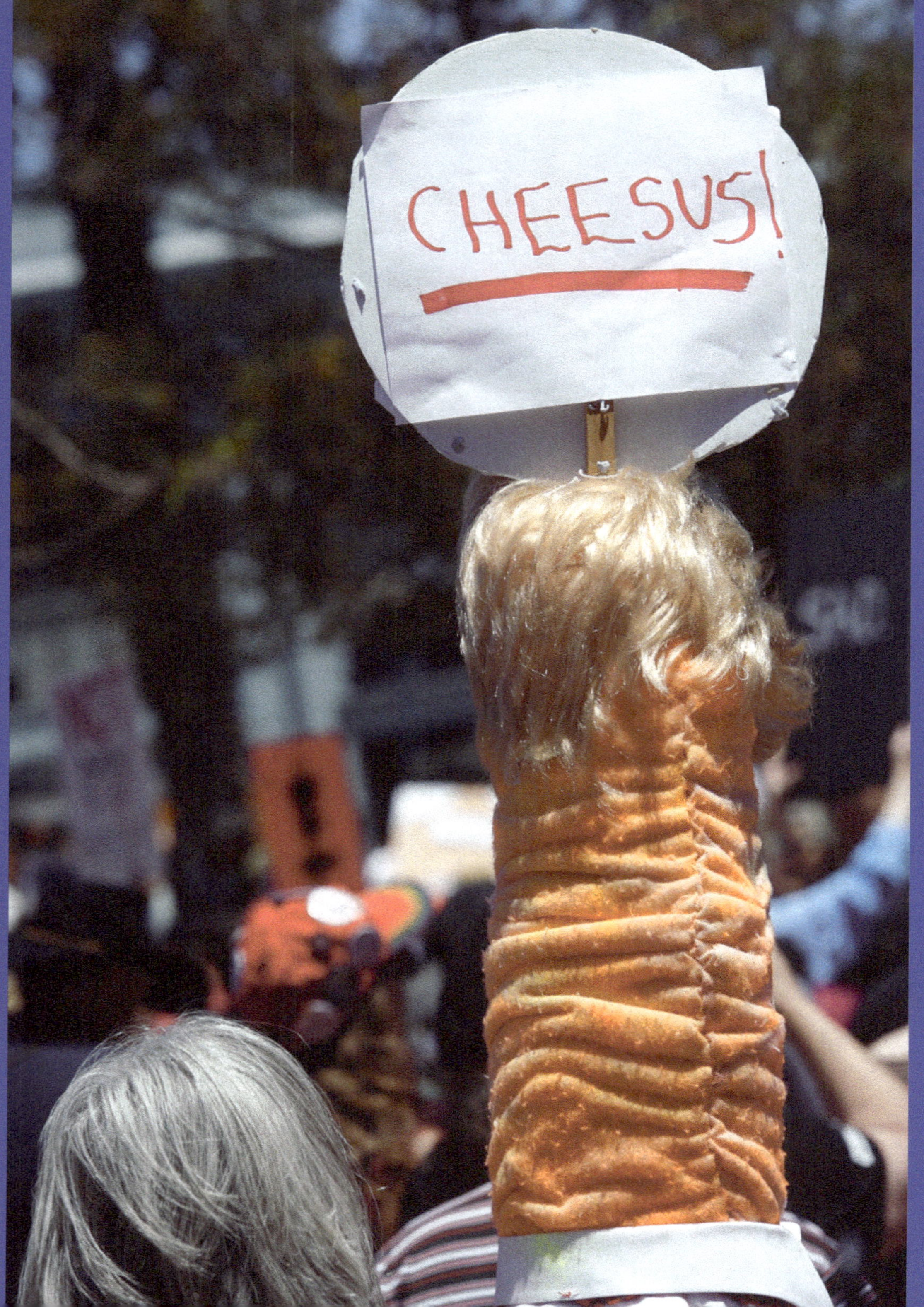
CHEESUS!

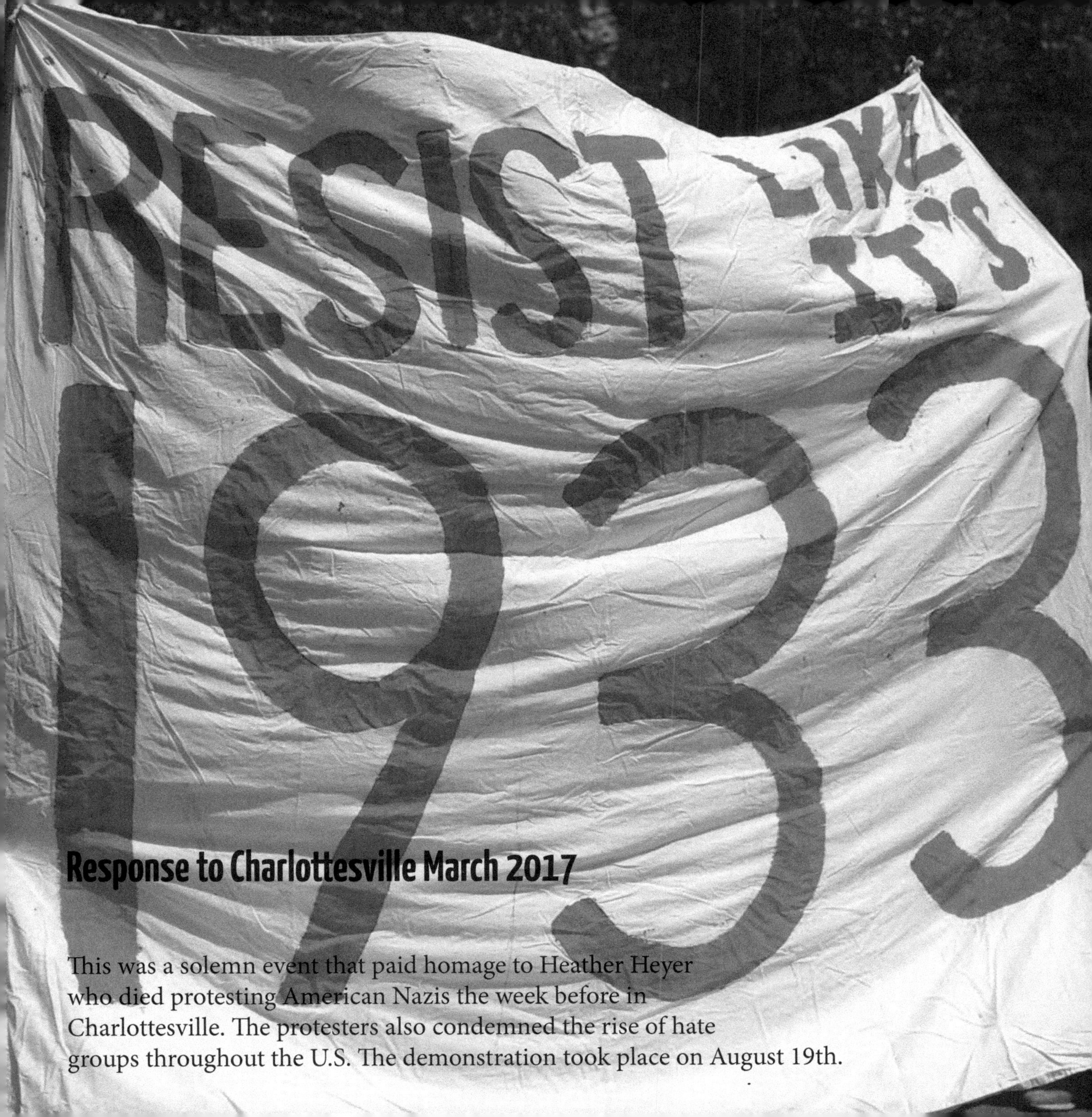

Response to Charlottesville March 2017

This was a solemn event that paid homage to Heather Heyer who died protesting American Nazis the week before in Charlottesville. The protesters also condemned the rise of hate groups throughout the U.S. The demonstration took place on August 19th.

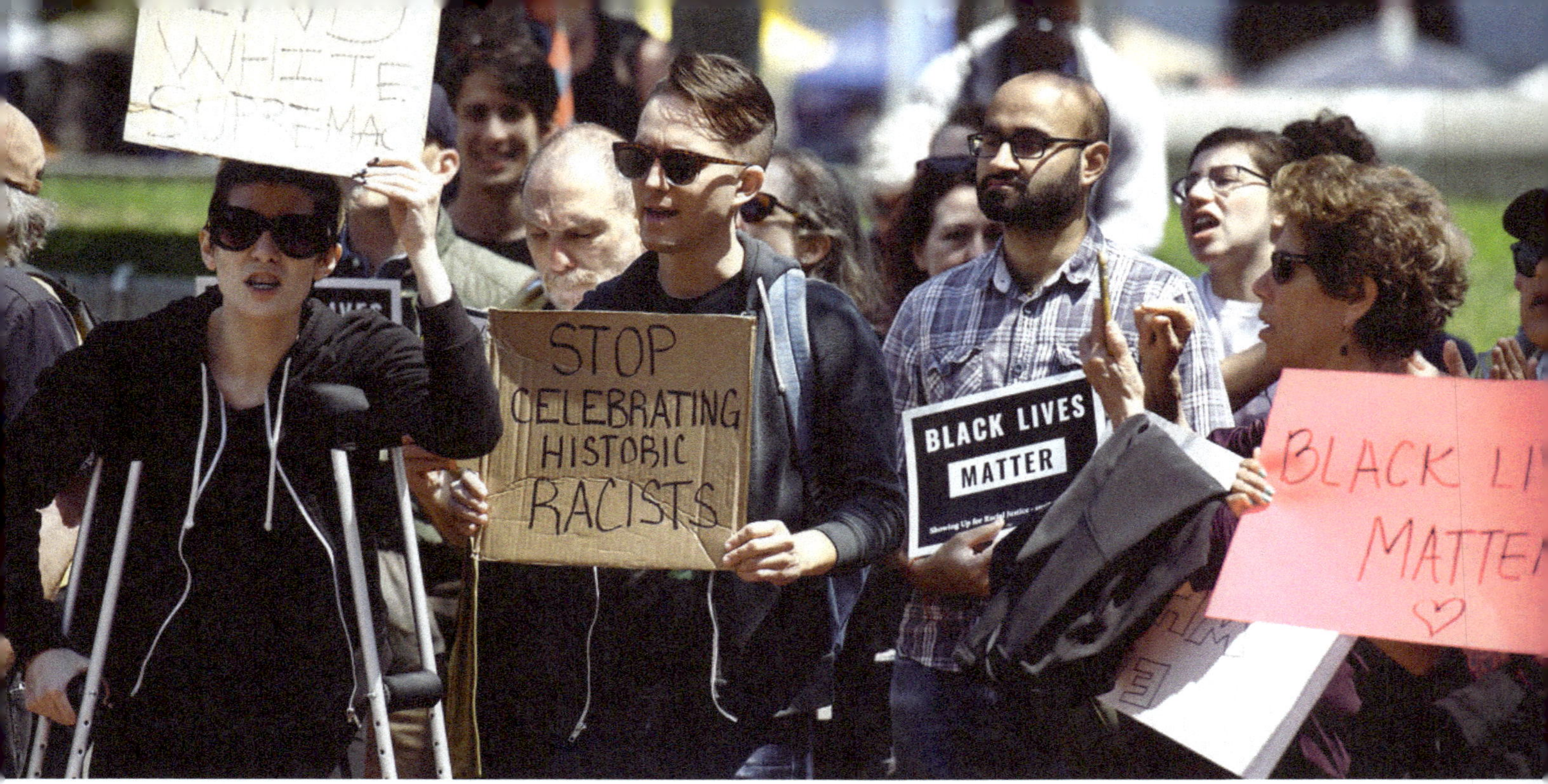

WHITE
SUPREMAC
STOP
CELEBRATING
HISTORIC
RACISTS
BLACK LIVES
MATTER
Showing Up for Racial Justice
BLACK LI
MATTE

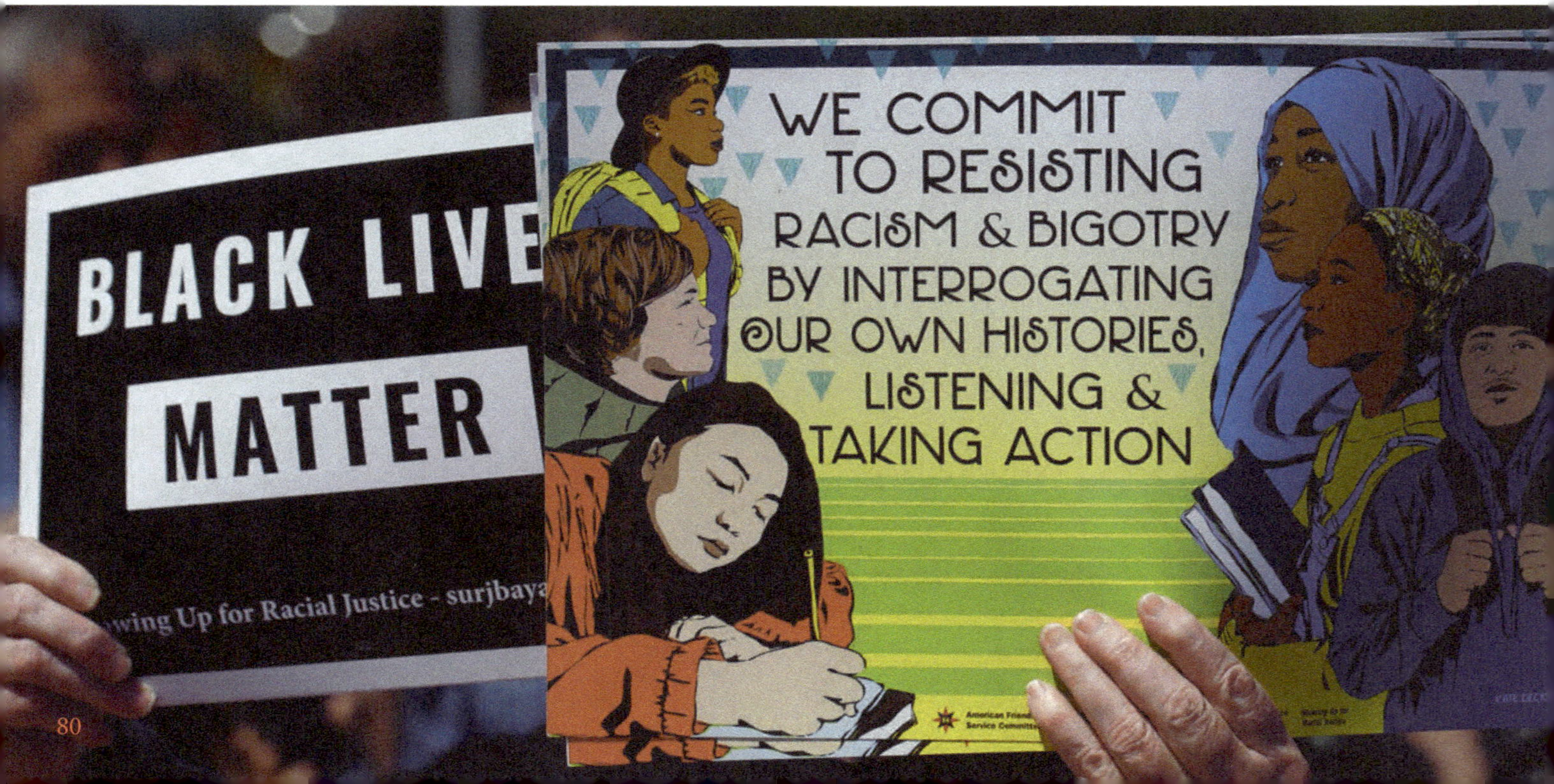

BLACK LIVE
MATTER
wing Up for Racial Justice - surjbaya
WE COMMIT
TO RESISTING
RACISM & BIGOTRY
BY INTERROGATING
OUR OWN HISTORIES,
LISTENING &
TAKING ACTION
American Friends
Service Committee

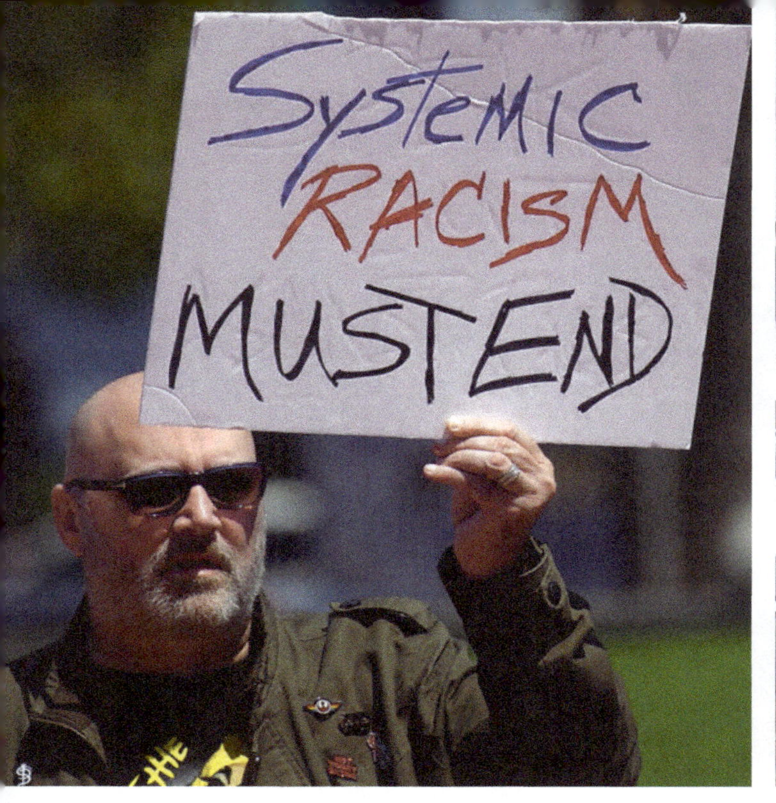

Systemic RACISM MUST END

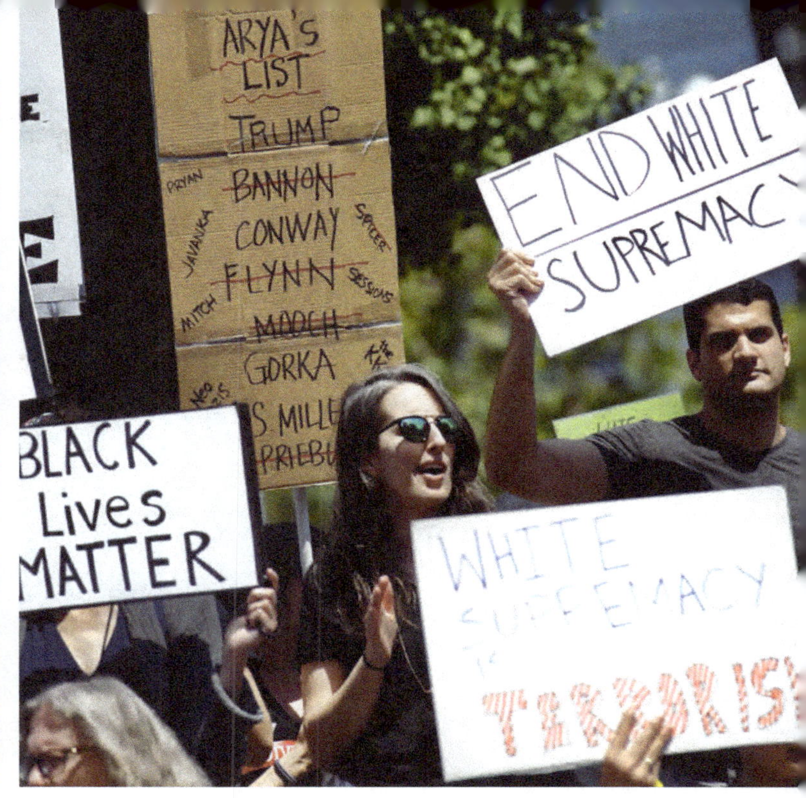

ARYA'S LIST
TRUMP
BANNON
CONWAY
FLYNN
MITCH
MOOCH
GORKA
S. MILLER
PRIEBU
BLACK Lives MATTER
END WHITE SUPREMACY
WHITE SUPREMACY IS TERRORISM

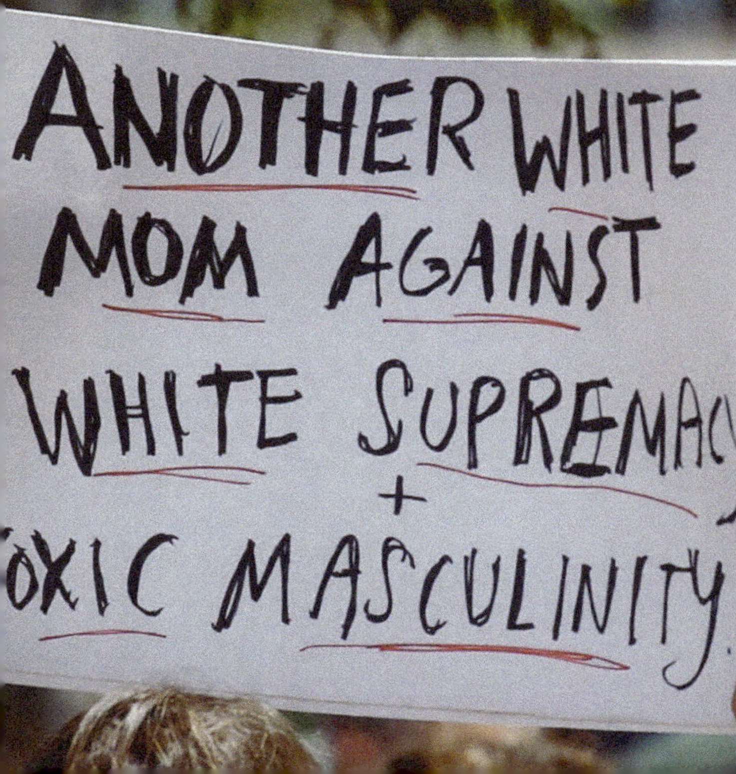

ANOTHER WHITE MOM AGAINST WHITE SUPREMACY + TOXIC MASCULINITY!

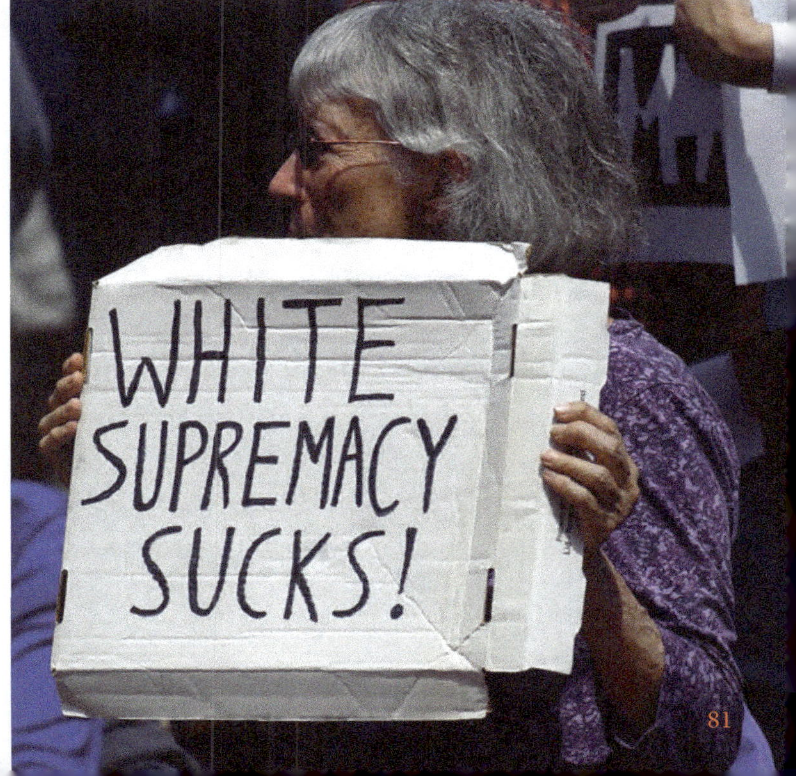

WHITE SUPREMACY SUCKS!

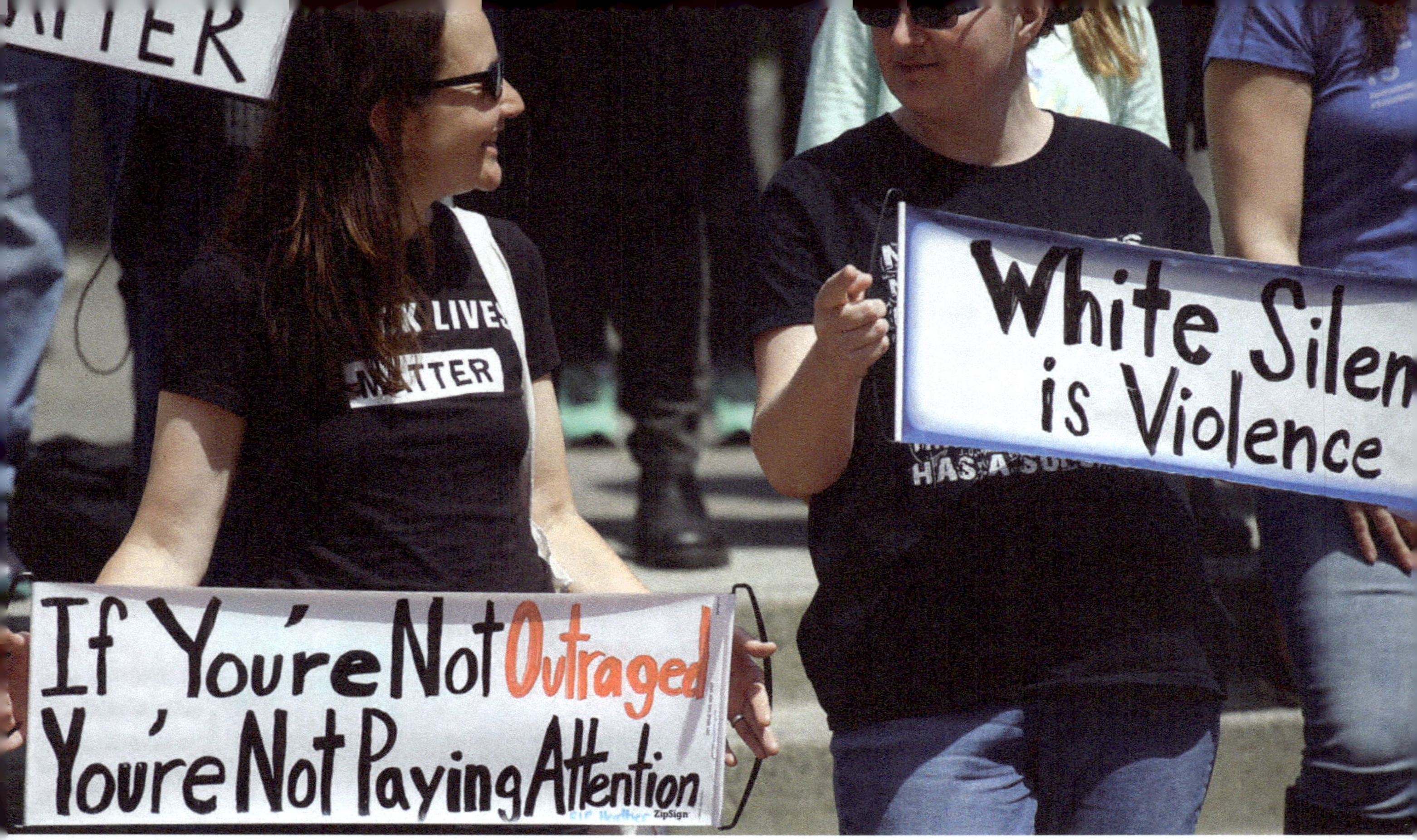

MATTER
LIVES
MATTER
White Silen
is Violence
HAS A SOL
If You're Not Outraged
You're Not Paying Attention
ZipSign
END
WHITE
SUPREMACY
END
WHITE
SILENCE
RISE
ABOVE
INJUSTICE
WE COMMIT
TO REBATING
RACISM & INJUSTICE
BY INTERROGATING
OUR OWN HISTORIES
LISTENING &

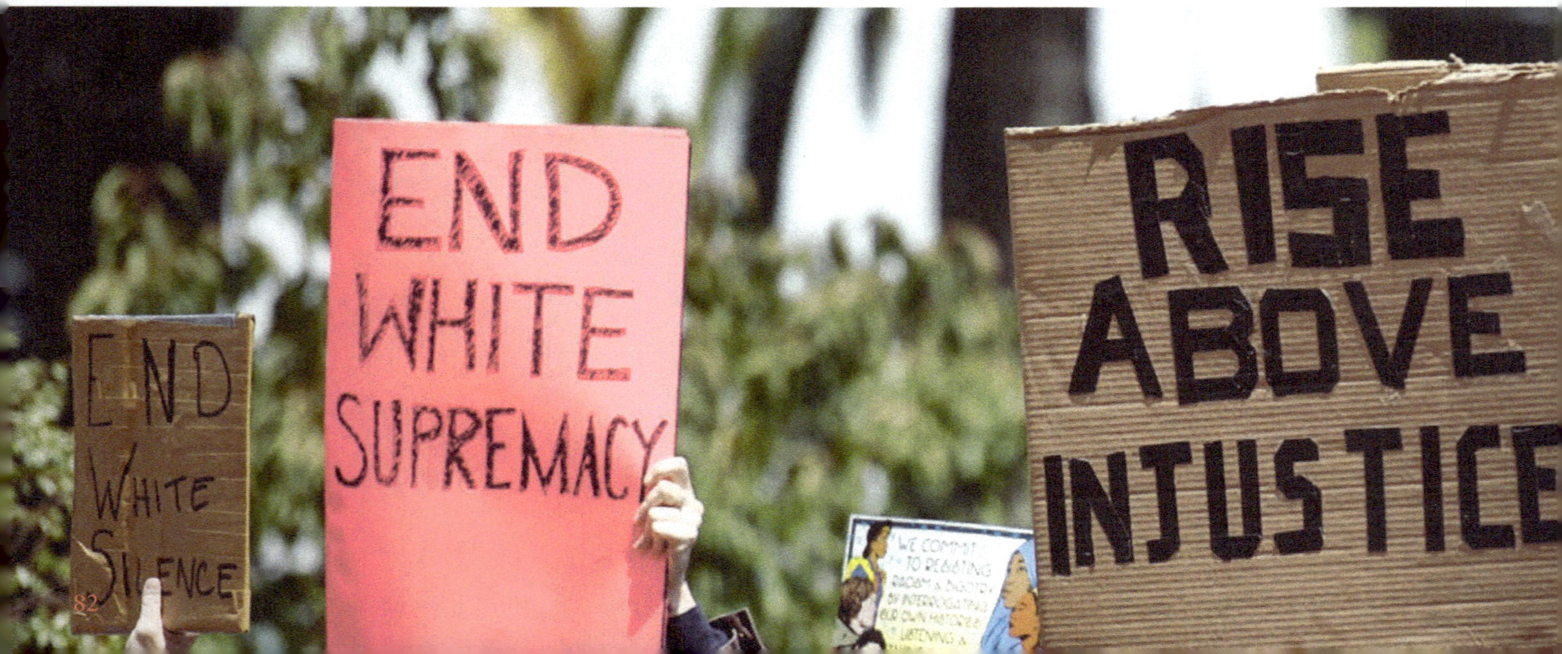

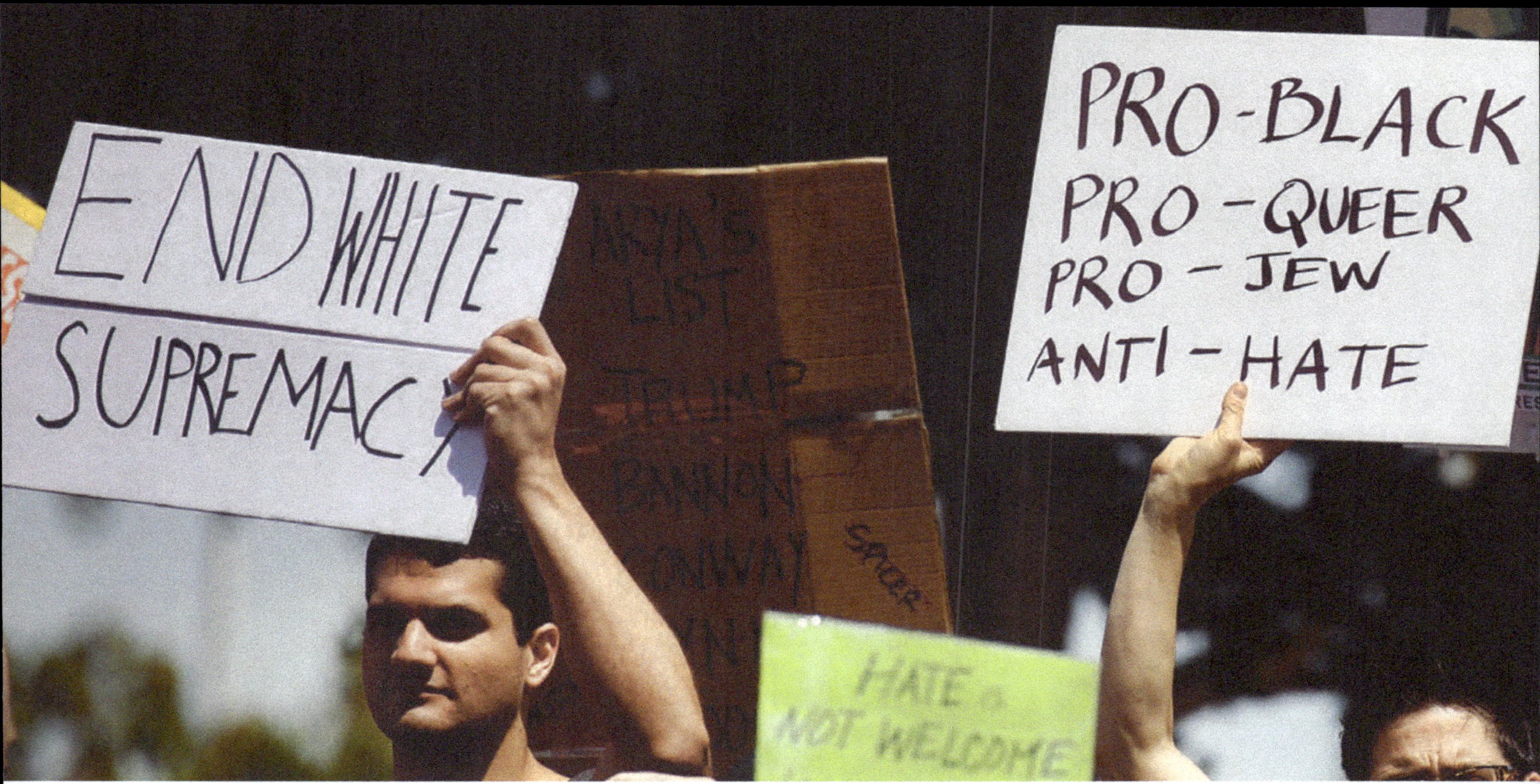

END WHITE
SUPREMACY
AYA'S
LIST
TRUMP
BANNON
CONWAY
PRO-BLACK
PRO-QUEER
PRO-JEW
ANTI-HATE
SPICER
HATE is
NOT WELCOME
RACISTS ≠ "FINE PEOPLE"

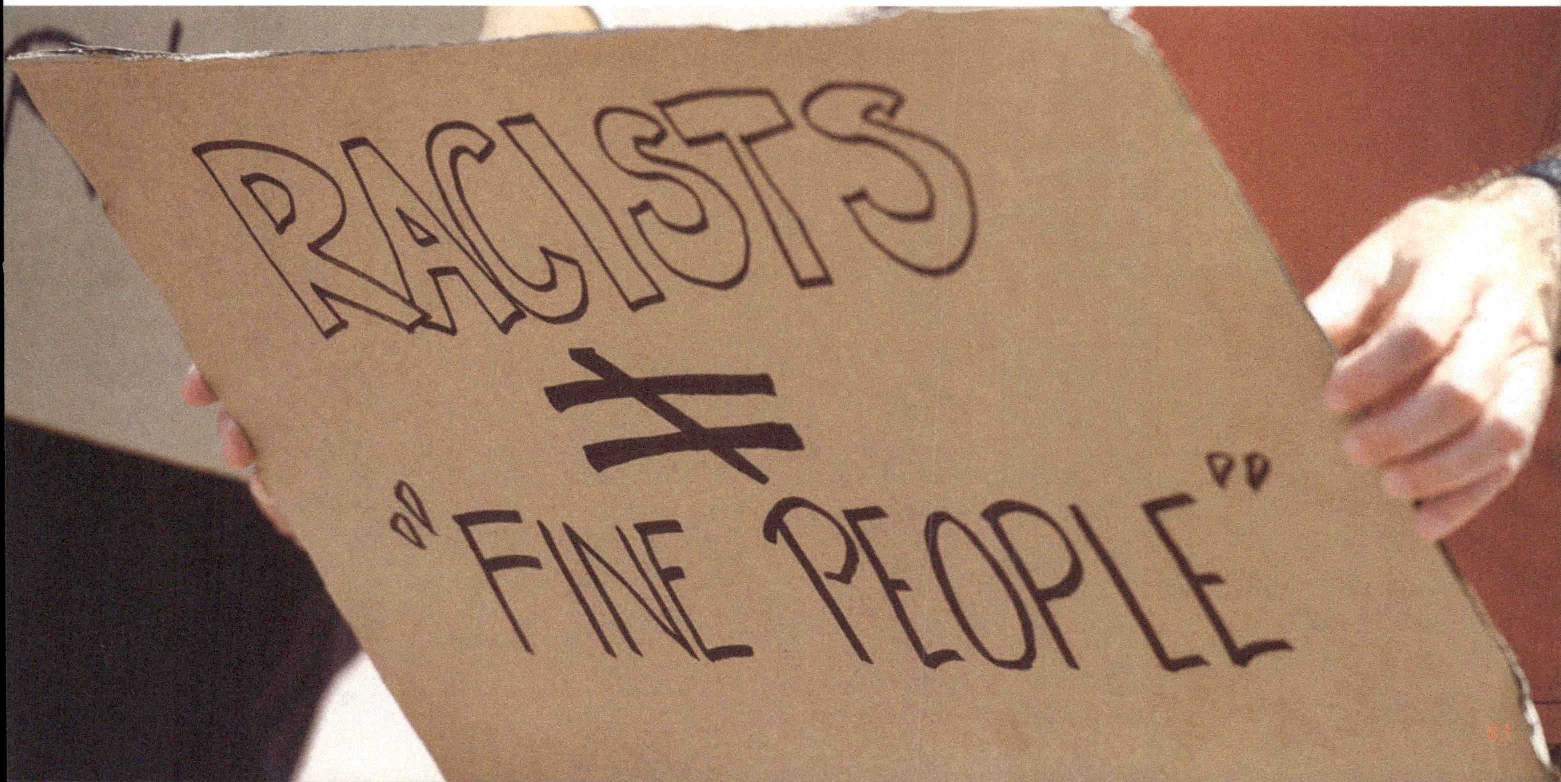

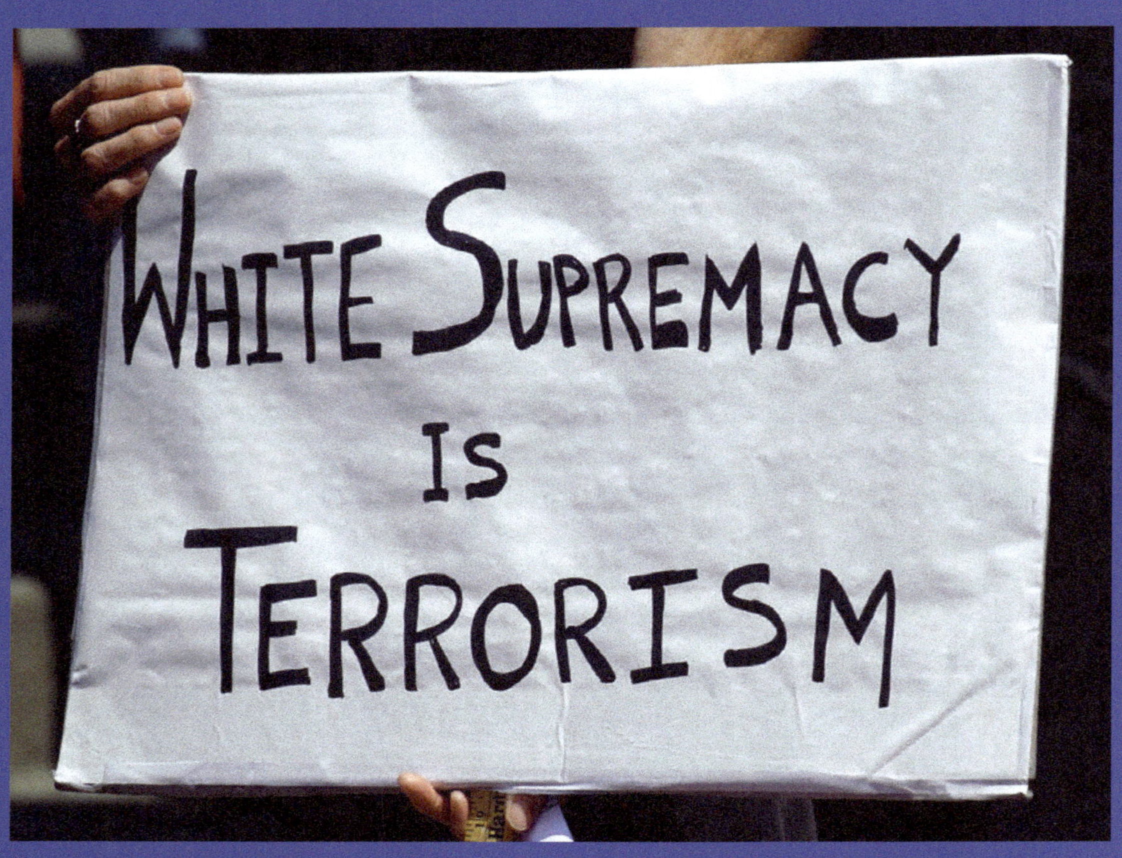
WHITE SUPREMACY
IS
TERRORISM

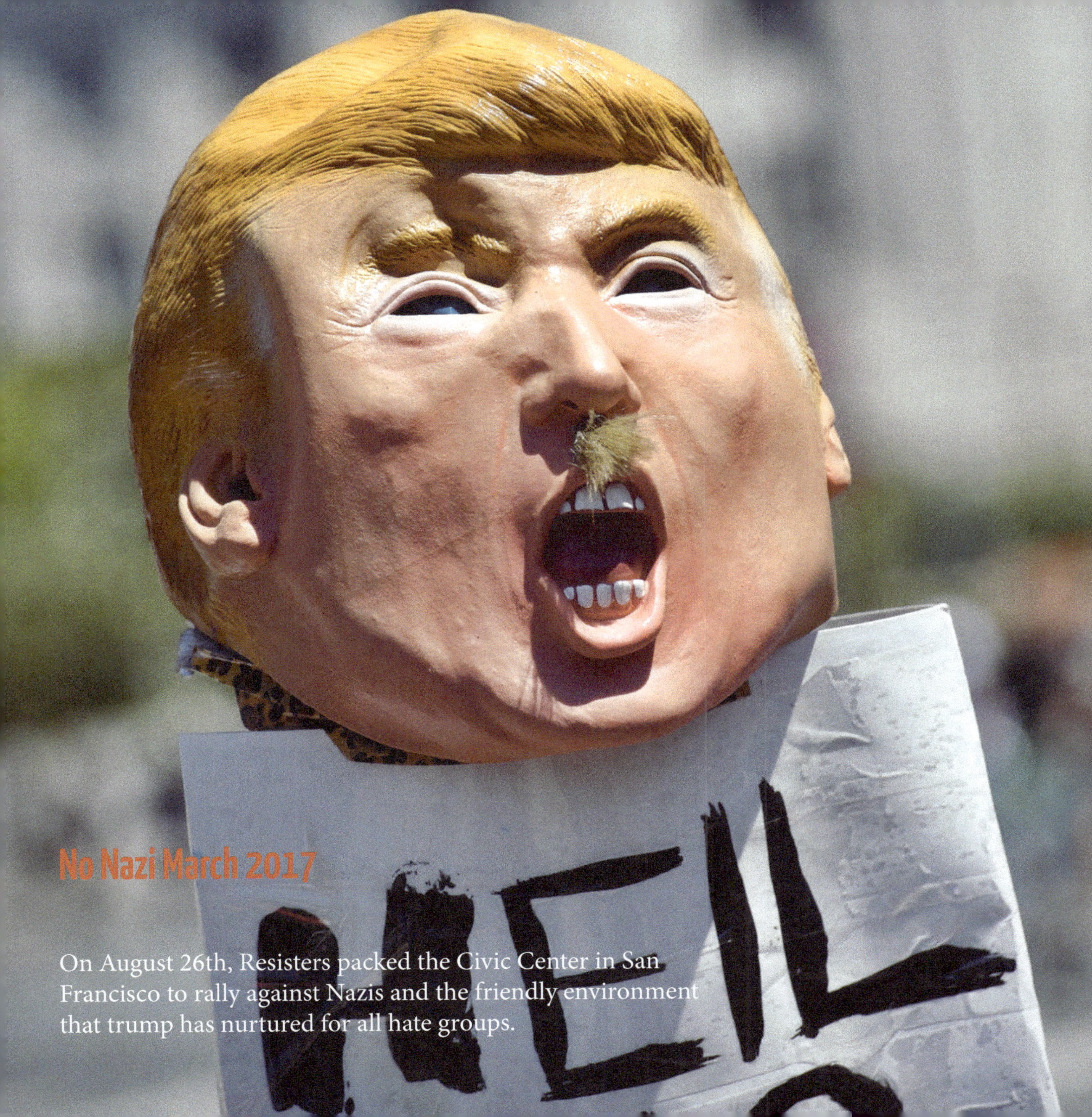

On August 26th, Resisters packed the Civic Center in San Francisco to rally against Nazis and the friendly environment that trump has nurtured for all hate groups.

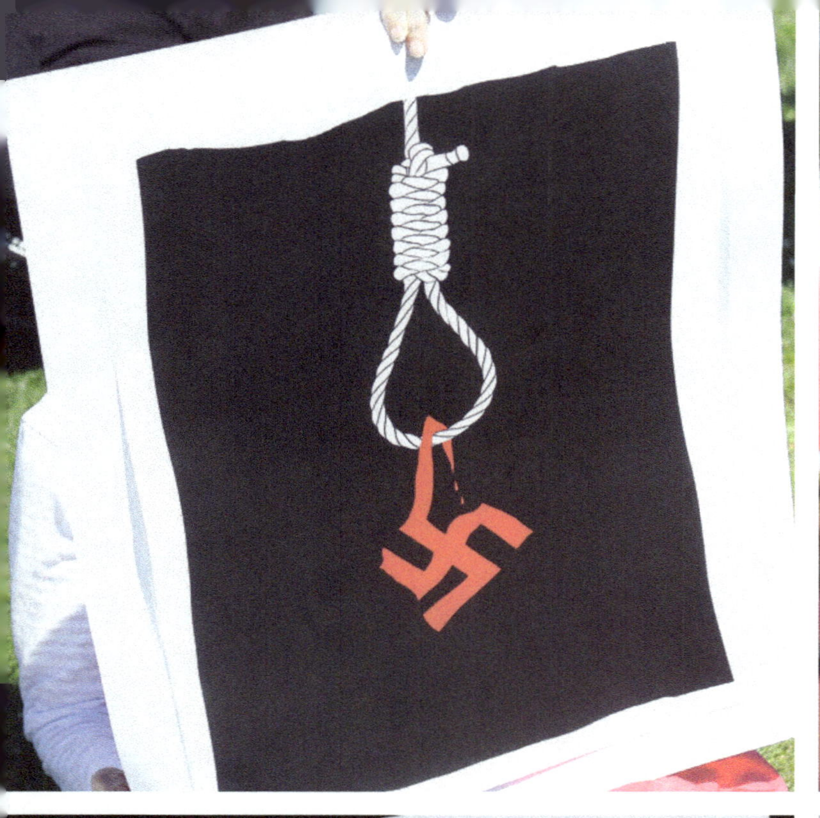
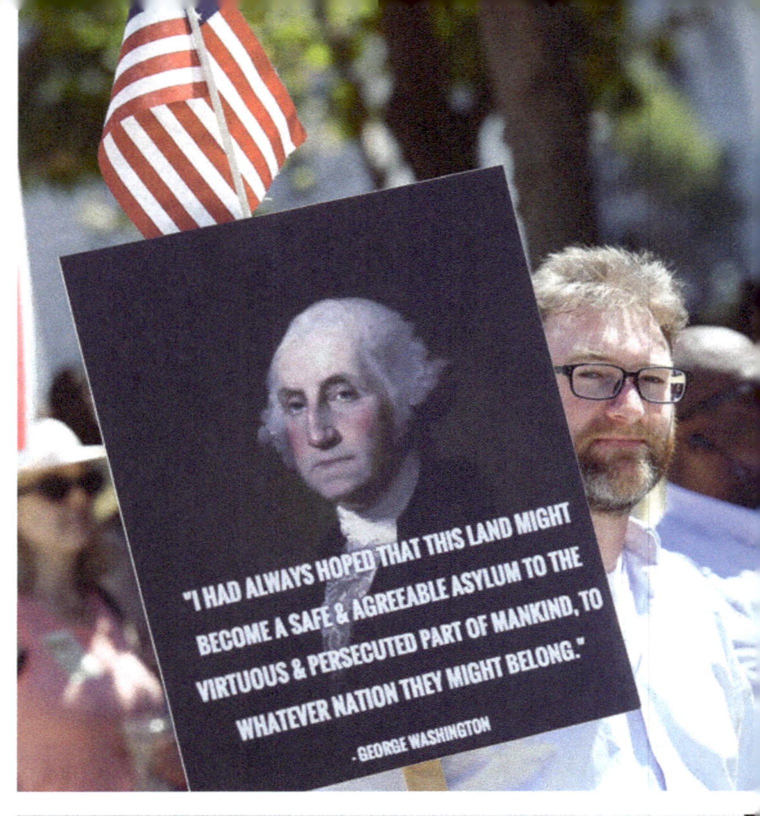

"I HAD ALWAYS HOPED THAT THIS LAND MIGHT BECOME A SAFE & AGREEABLE ASYLUM TO THE VIRTUOUS & PERSECUTED PART OF MANKIND, TO WHATEVER NATION THEY MIGHT BELONG."
- GEORGE WASHINGTON

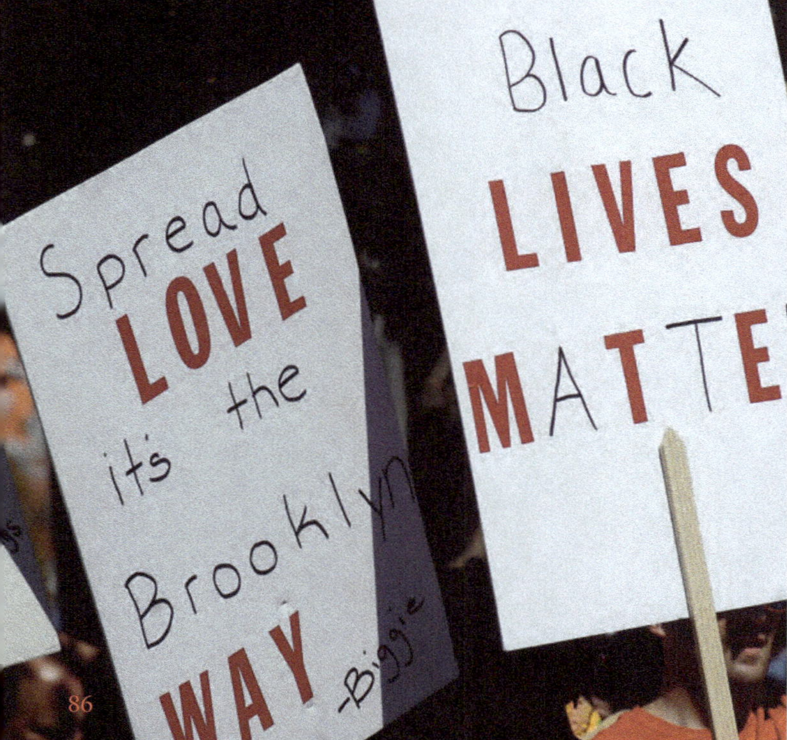

Spread LOVE it's the Brooklyn WAY
-Biggie
Black LIVES MATTER

"HATE IS TOO HEAVY a Burden to Bear"
MLK jr.

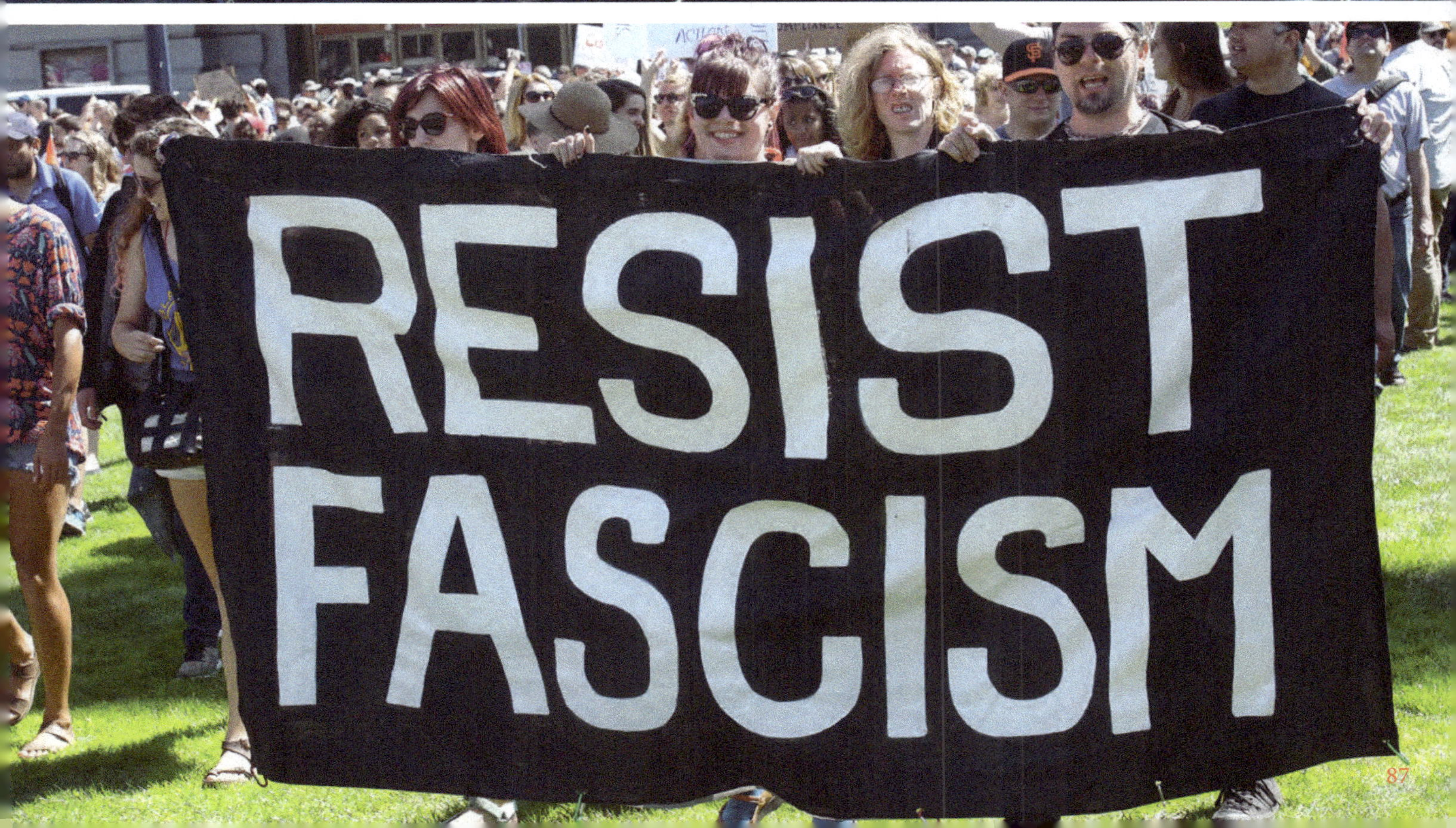
THOSE POOR FASCISTS:
FIRST THEY LOSE WW II,
AND THEN TRUMP
BEFRIENDS THEM.
RESIST
FASCISM

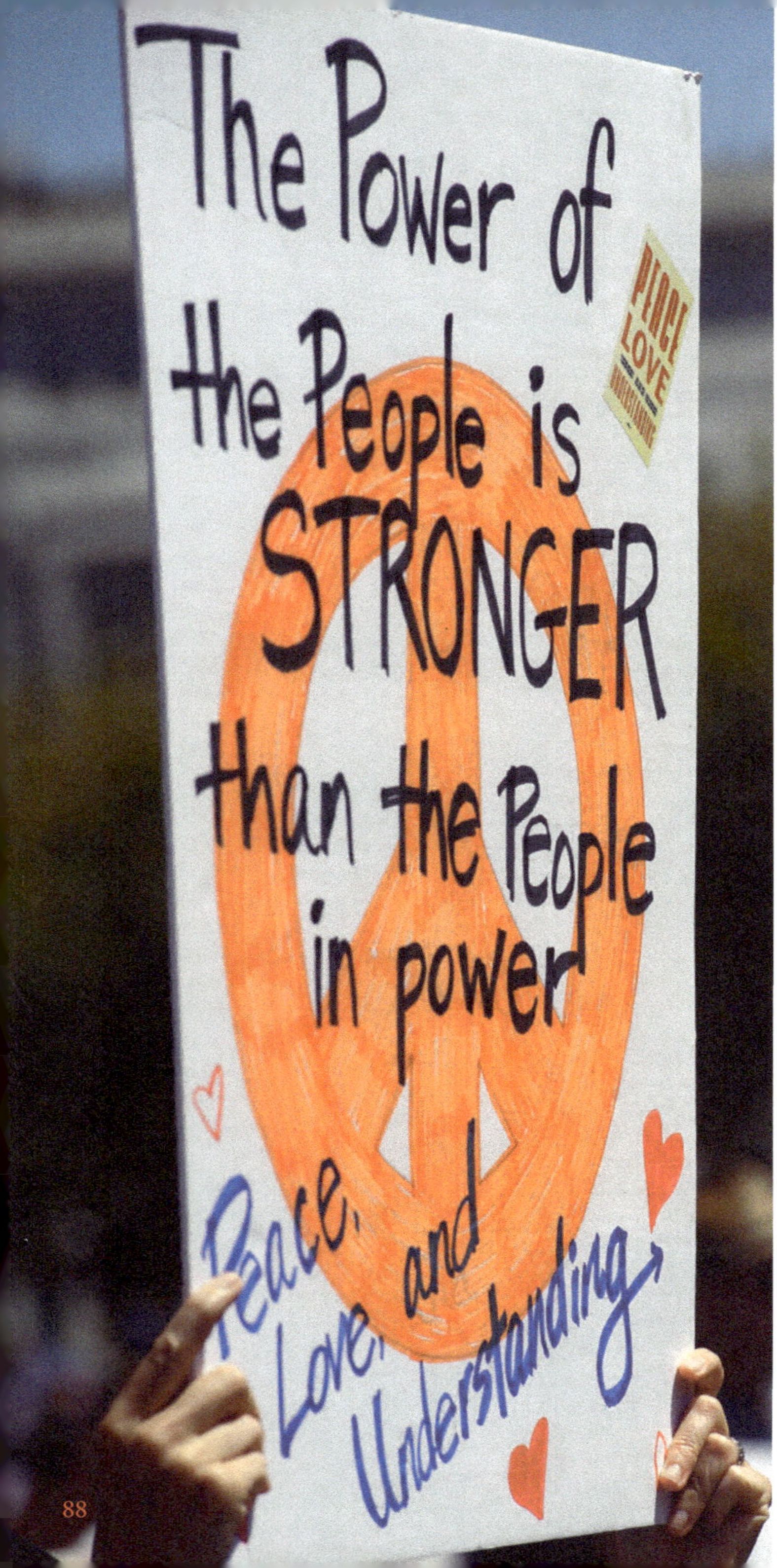

The Power of
the People is
STRONGER
than the People
in power
Peace,
Love, and
Understanding
PEACE
LOVE
AND
UNDERSTANDING

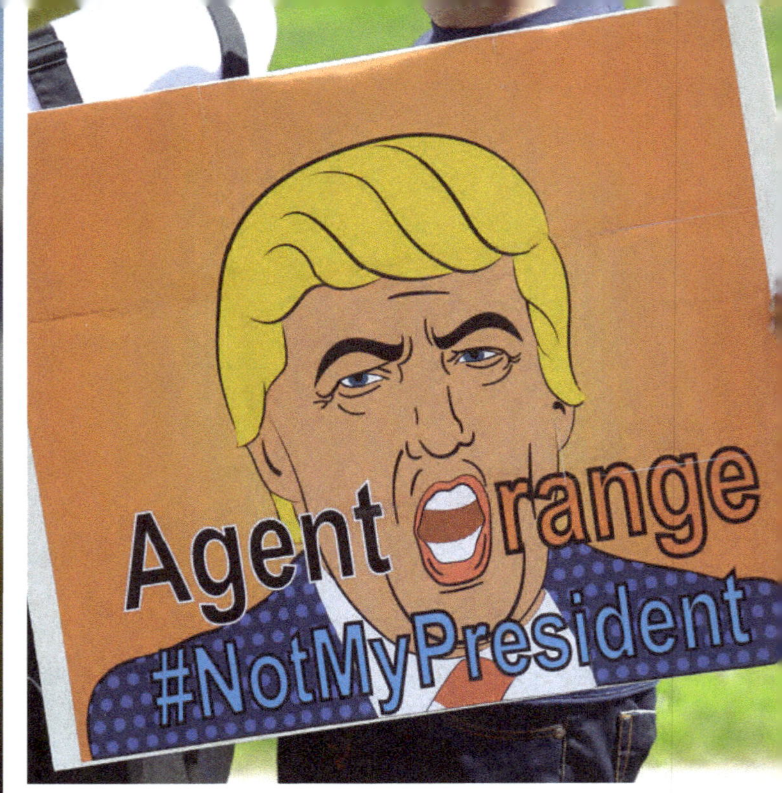
Agent orange
#NotMyPresident

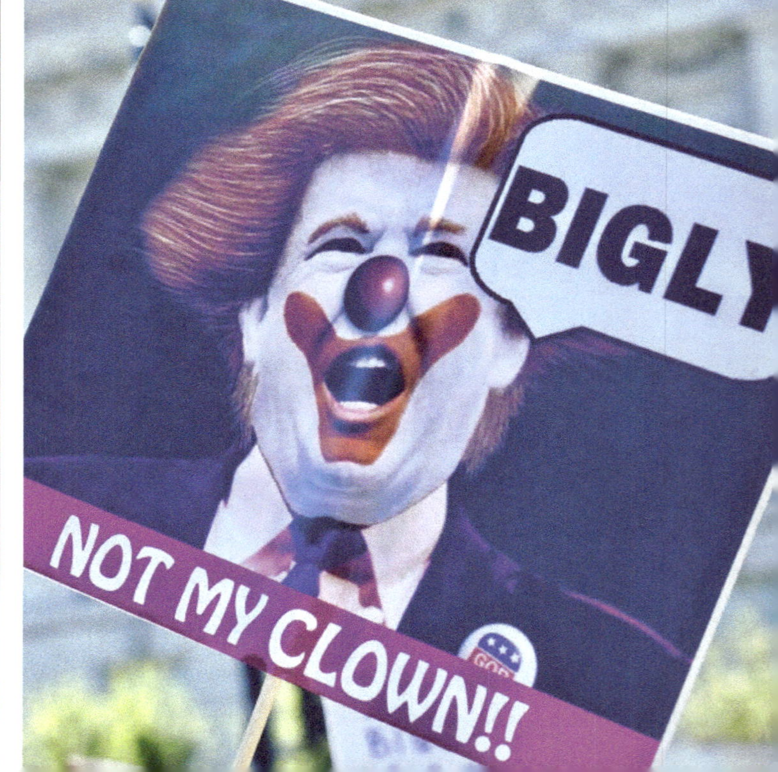
BIGLY
NOT MY CLOWN!!
GOP

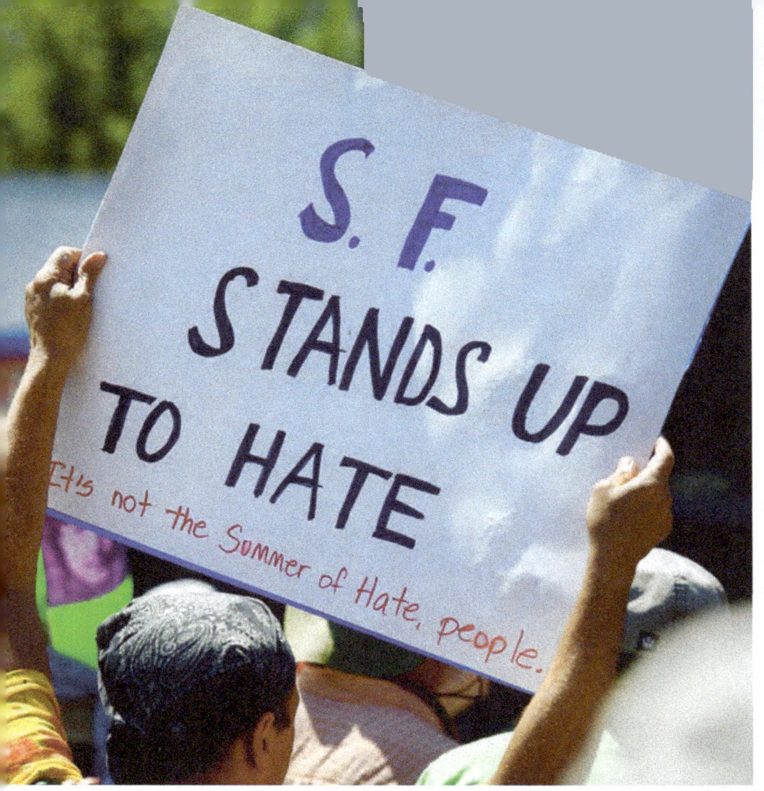

S.F.
STANDS UP
TO HATE
It's not the Summer of Hate, people.

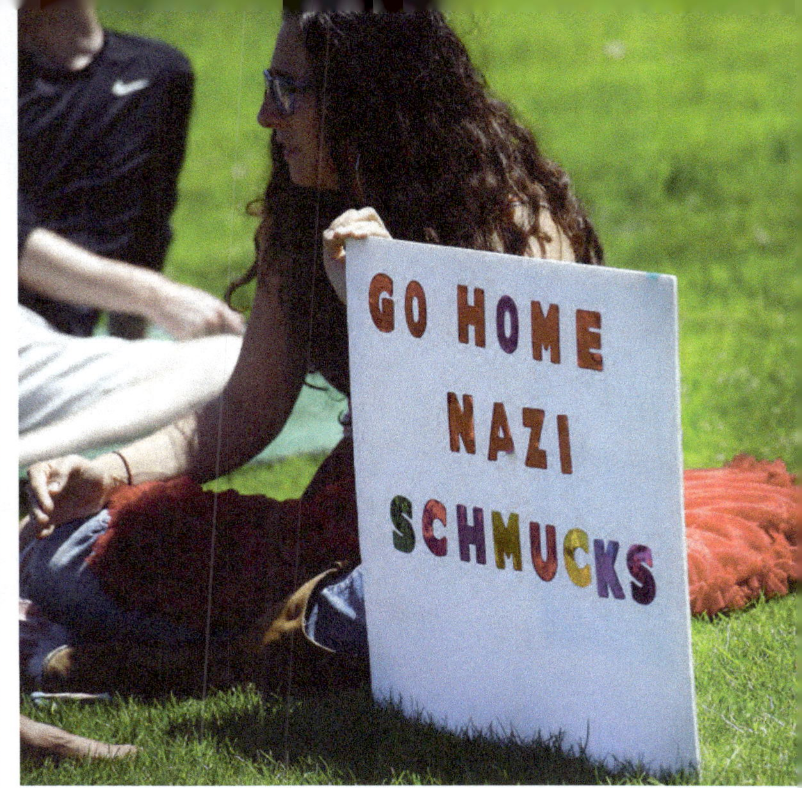

GO HOME
NAZI
SCHMUCKS

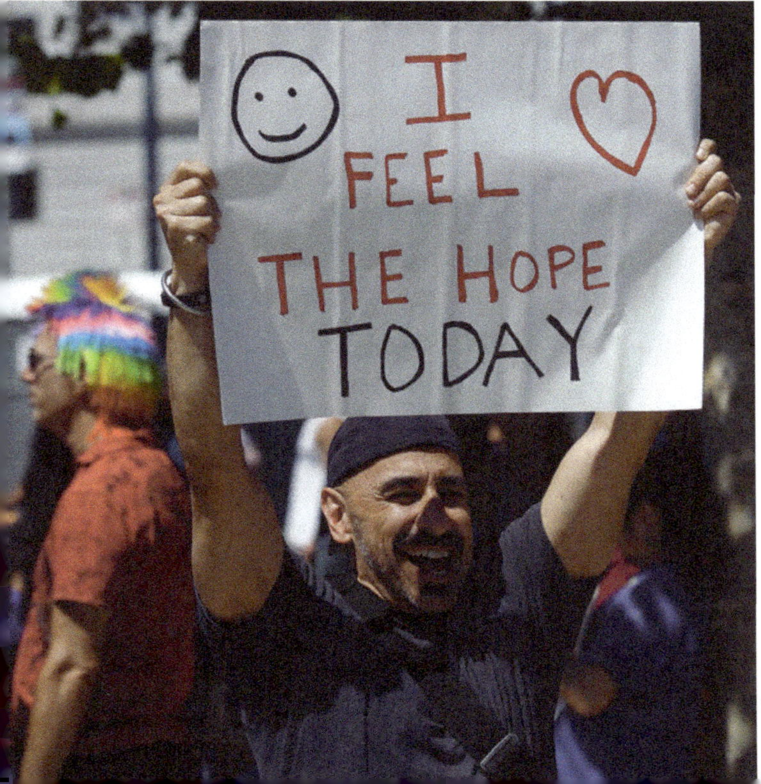

I
FEEL
THE HOPE
TODAY

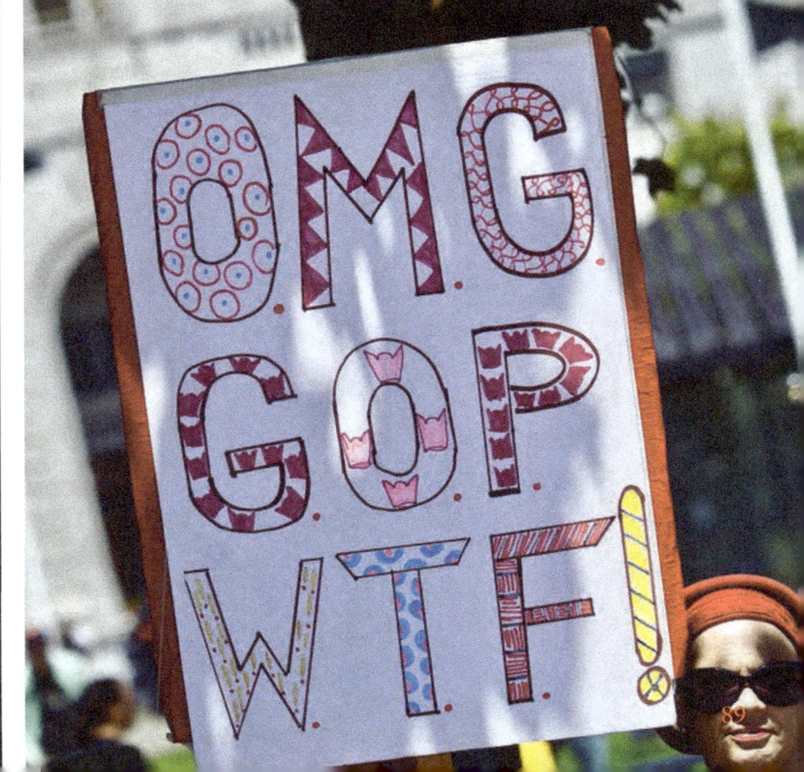

OMG
GOP
WTF!

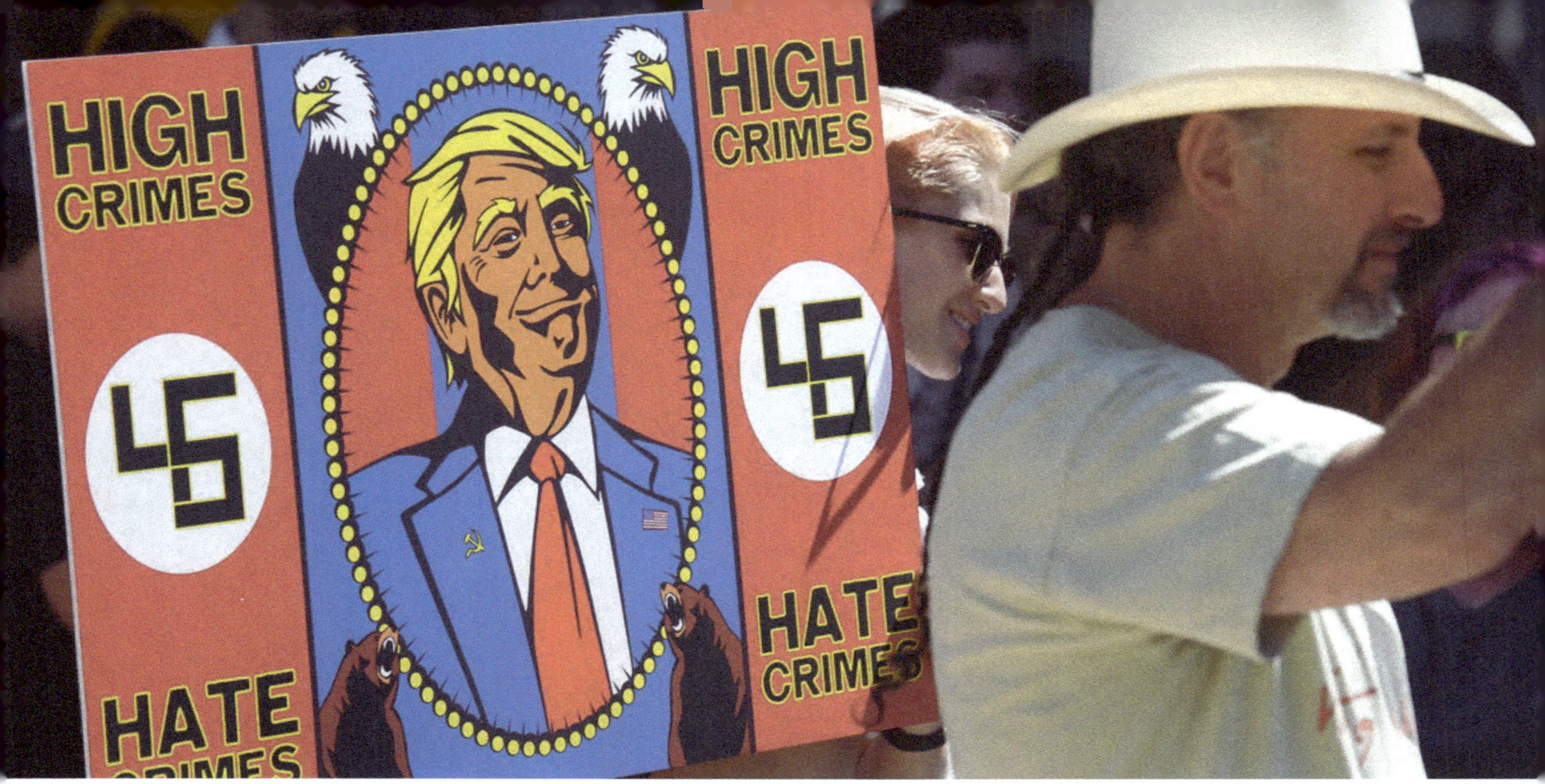

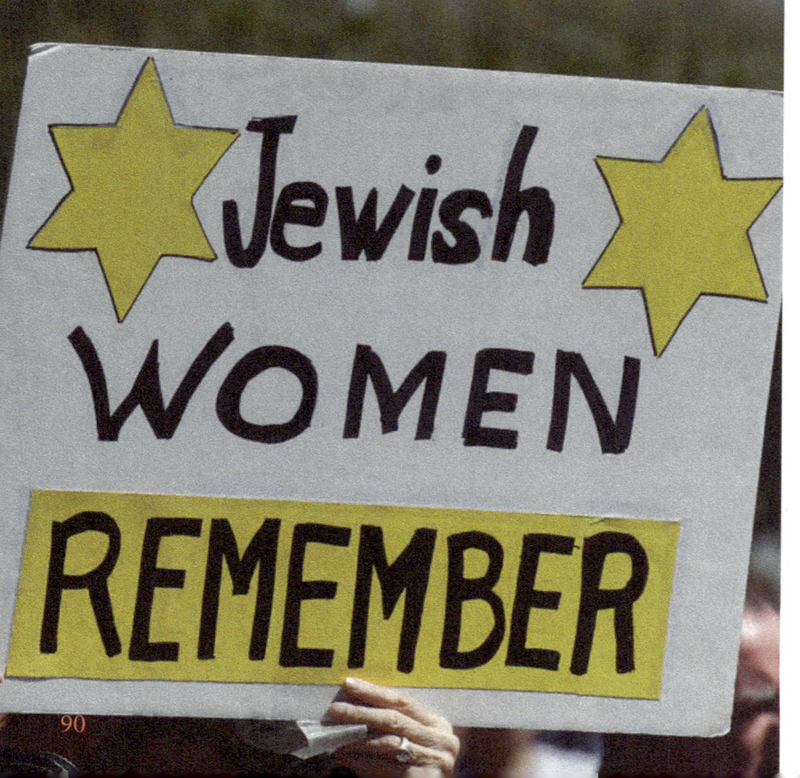
HIGH CRIMES
HIGH CRIMES
HATE CRIMES
HATE CRIMES
Jewish WOMEN REMEMBER
PEOPLE CLING TO HATE BECAUSE ONCE IS GON THEY WILL HAVE TO DEAL WITH PAIN 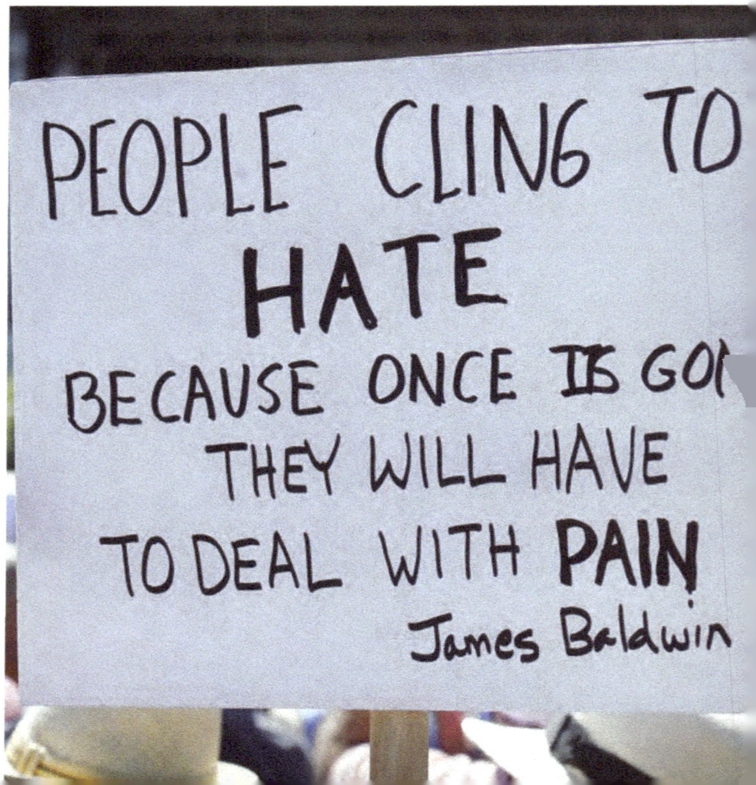
James Baldwin

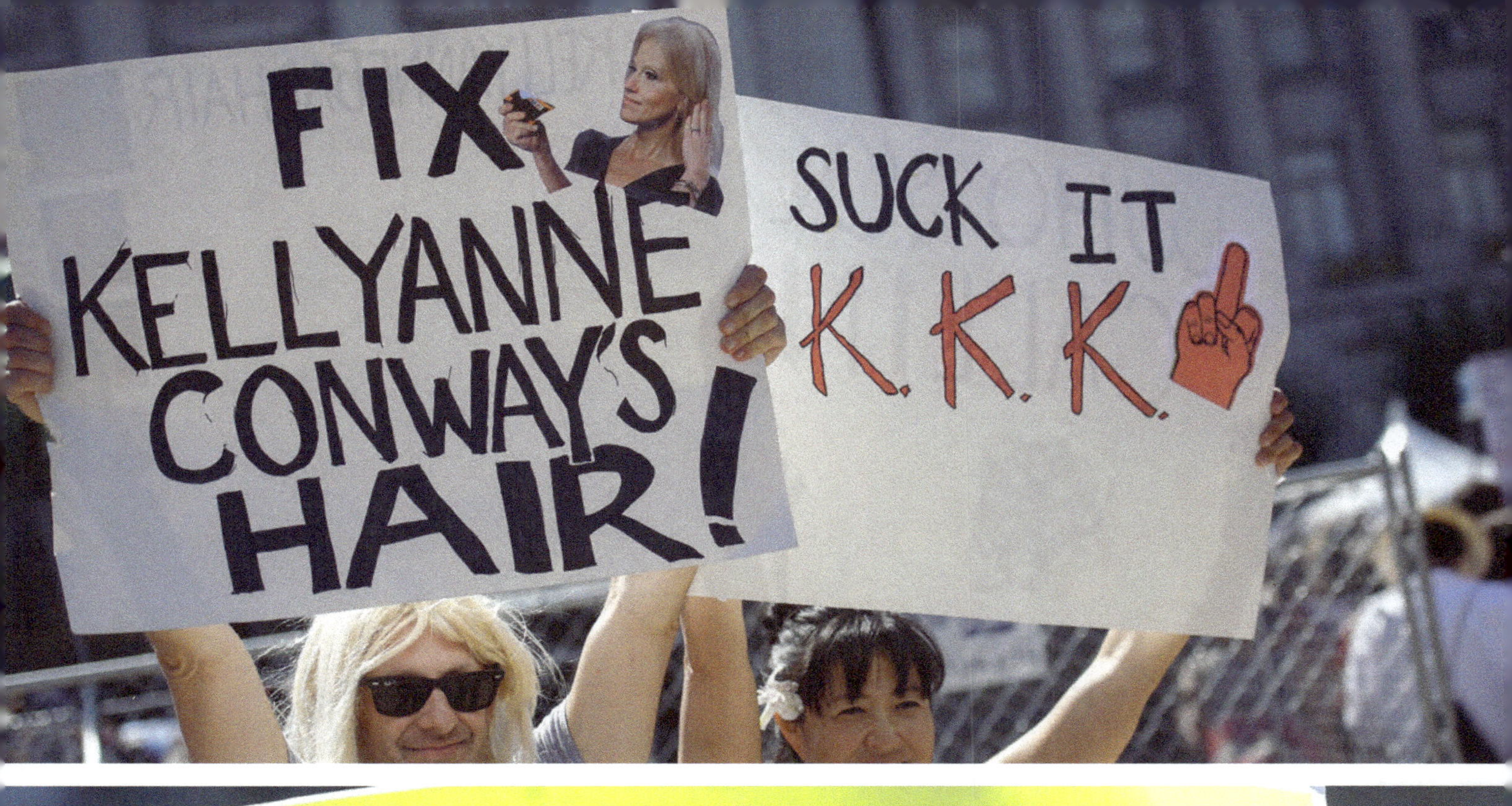

FIX KELLYANNE CONWAY'S HAIR!
SUCK IT K.K.K.

LITERALLY
NO ONE
likes you

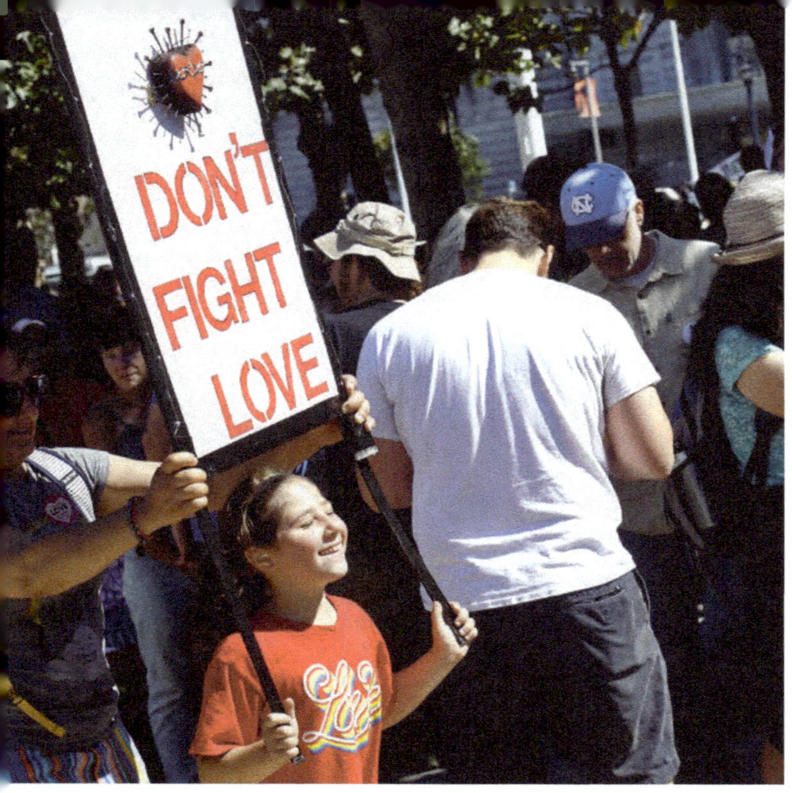

DON'T
FIGHT
LOVE

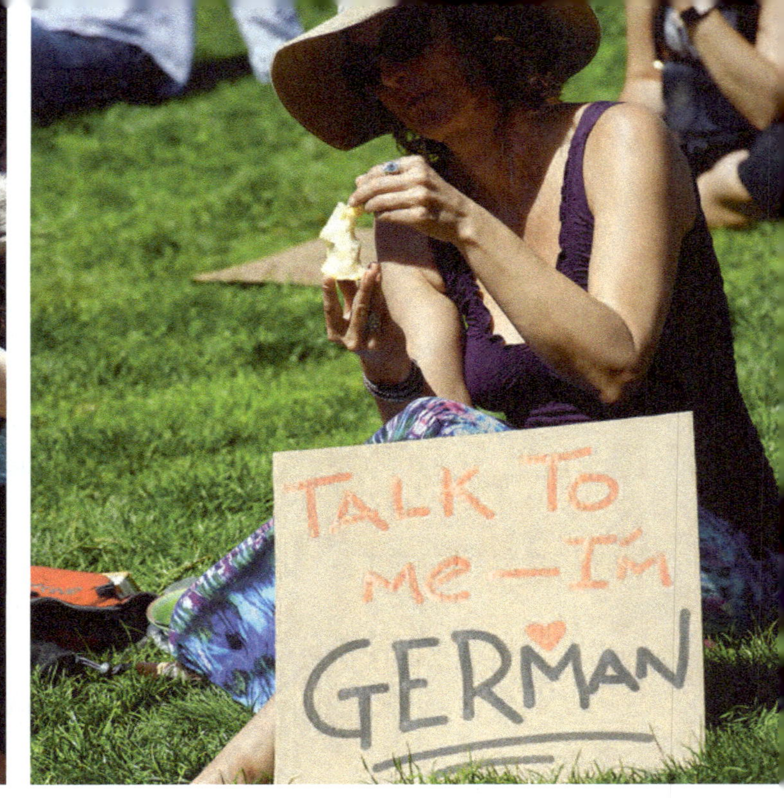

TALK TO
ME — I'M
GERMAN

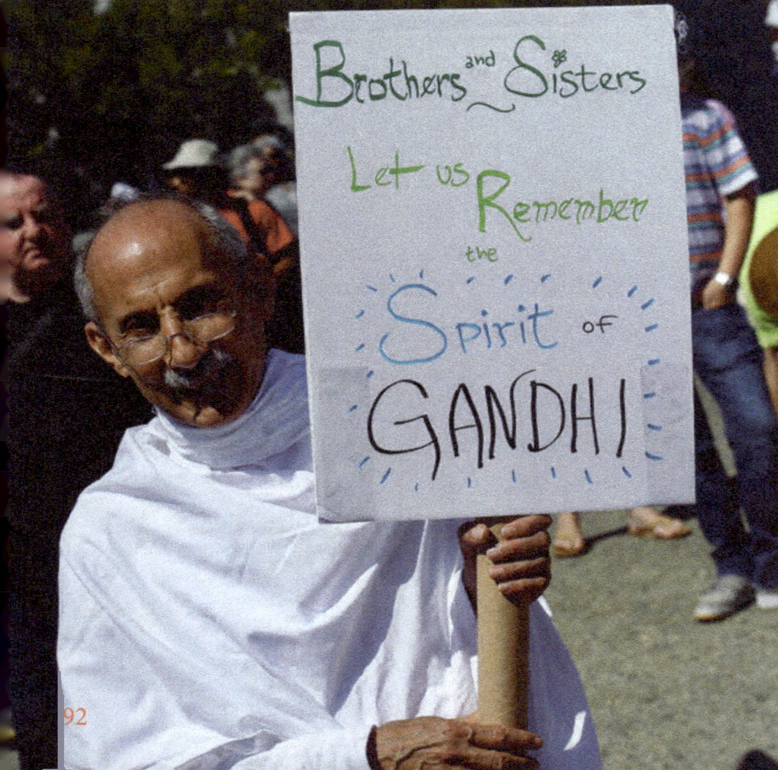

Brothers and Sisters
Let us Remember
the
Spirit of
GANDHI

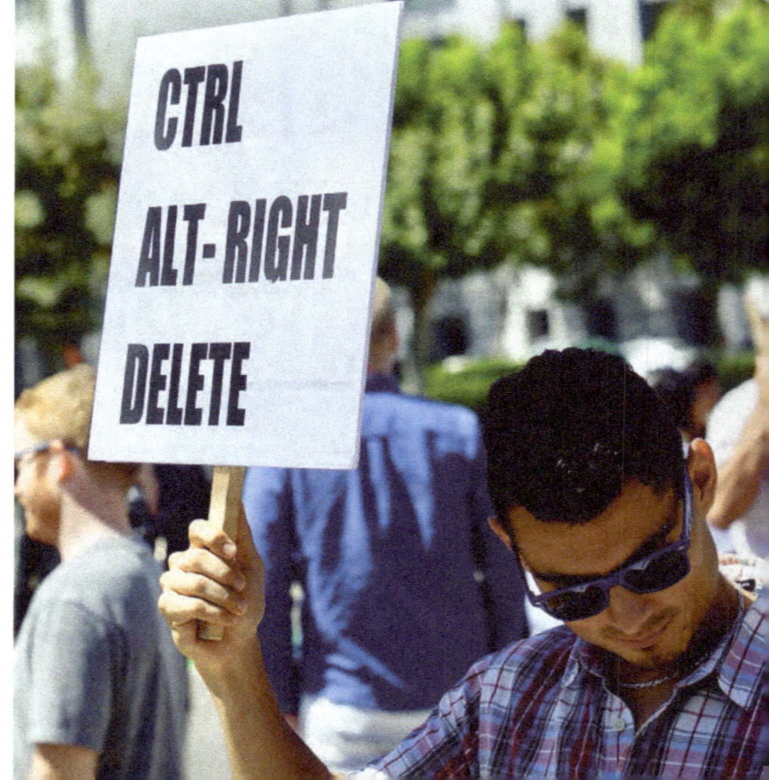

CTRL
ALT-RIGHT
DELETE

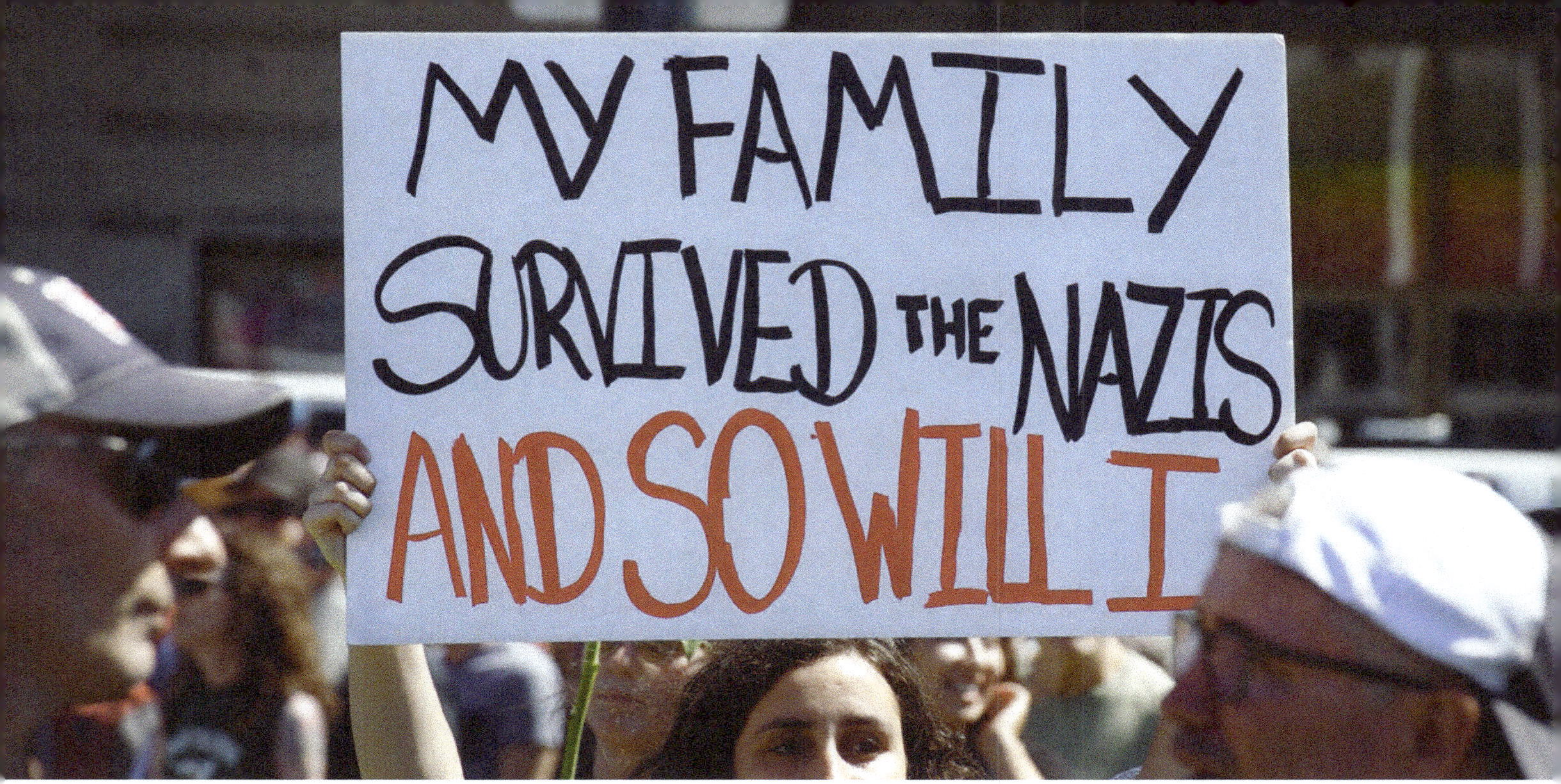

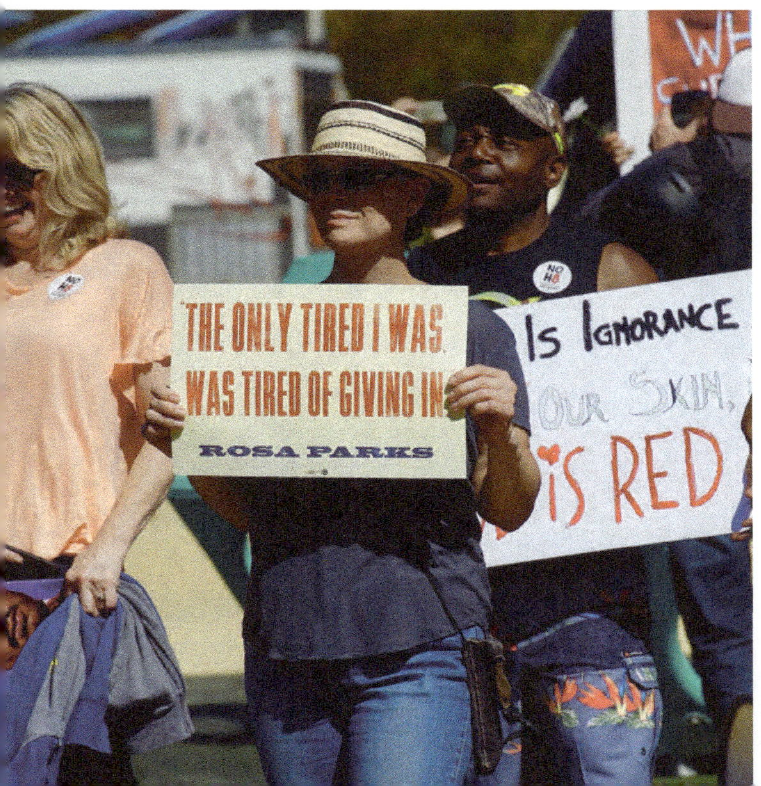

MY FAMILY SURVIVED THE NAZIS AND SO WILL I
THE ONLY TIRED I WAS, WAS TIRED OF GIVING IN
ROSA PARKS
Is Ignorance
OUR SKIN IS RED

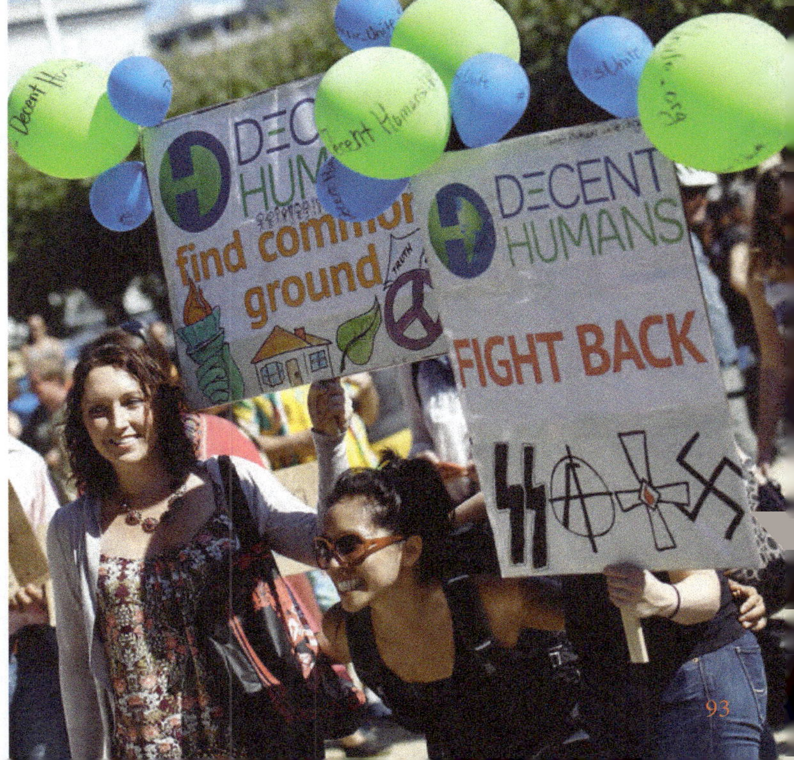

DECENT HUMANS
find common ground
DECENT HUMANS
FIGHT BACK

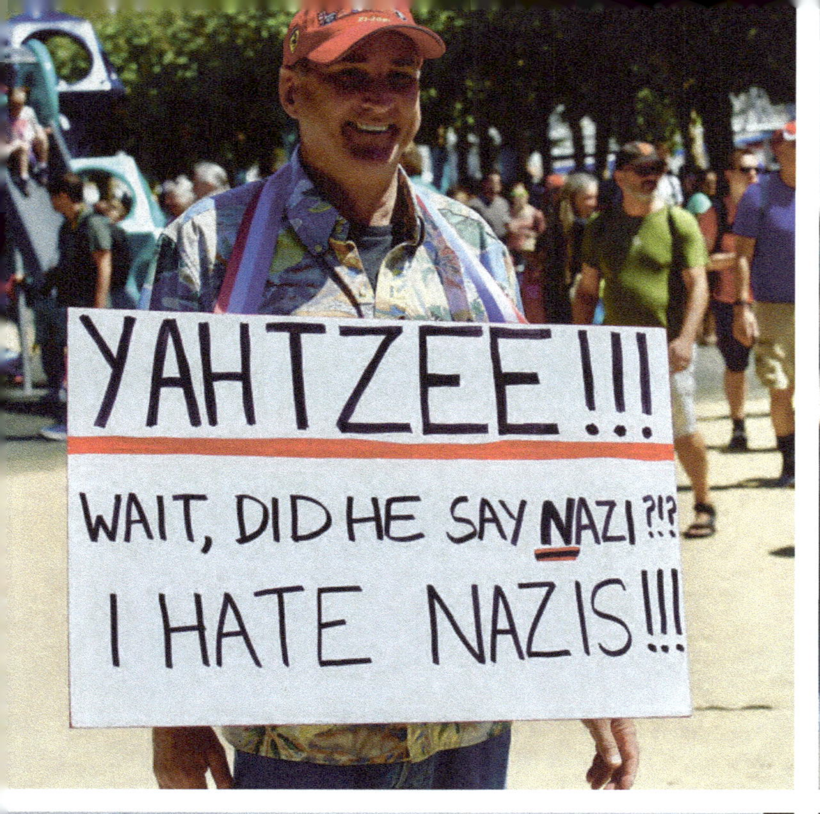

YAHTZEE!!!
WAIT, DID HE SAY NAZI?!?
I HATE NAZIS!!!

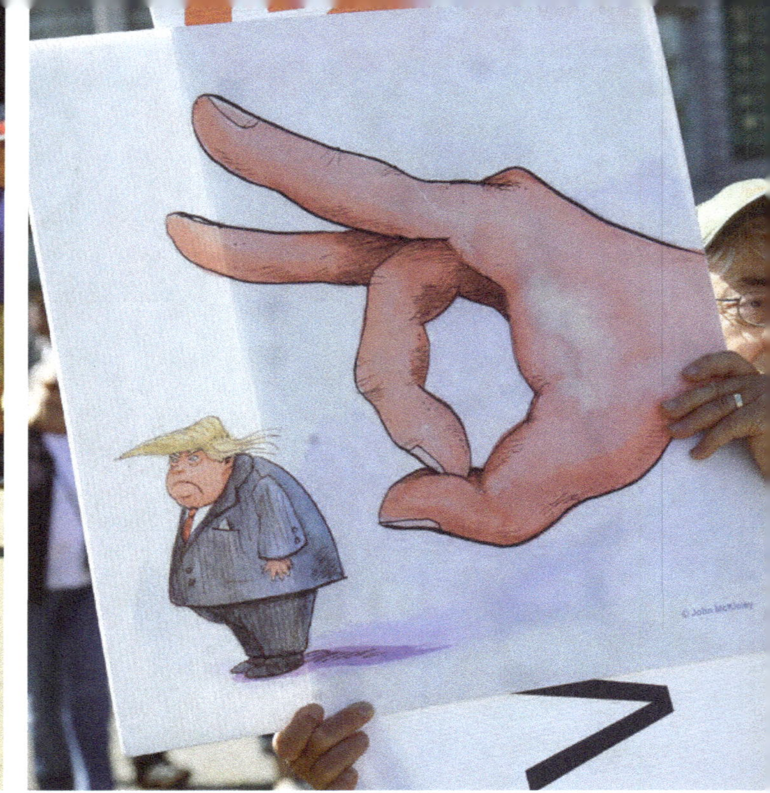

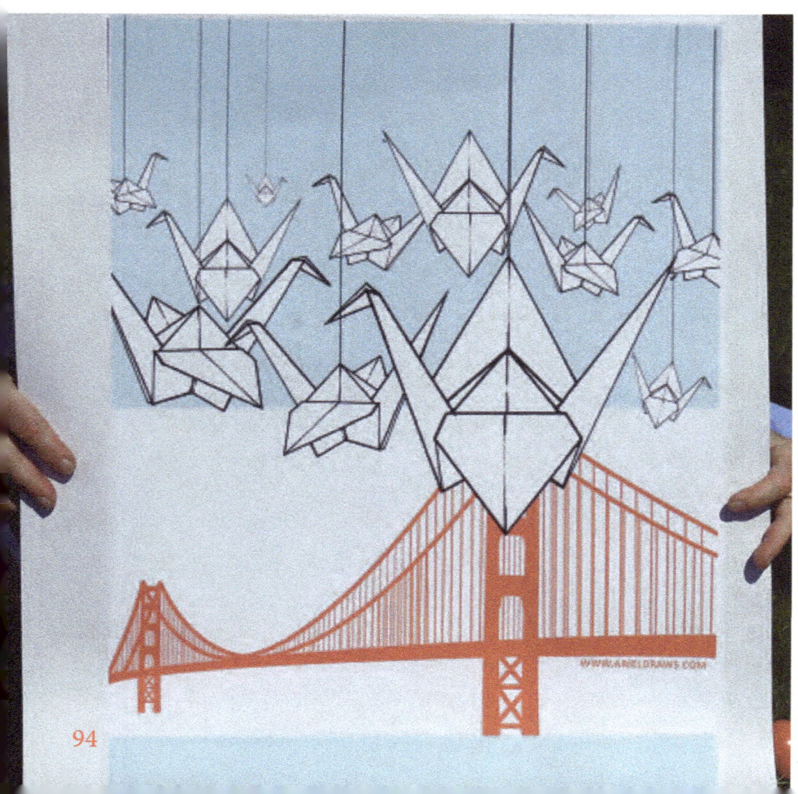

WWW.ARIELDRAWS.COM

94

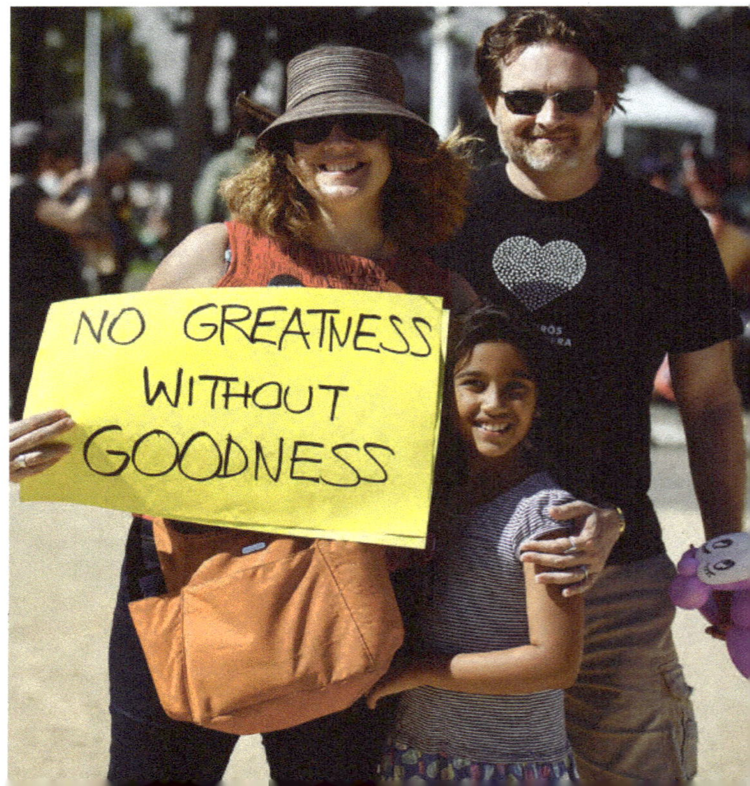

NO GREATNESS
WITHOUT
GOODNESS

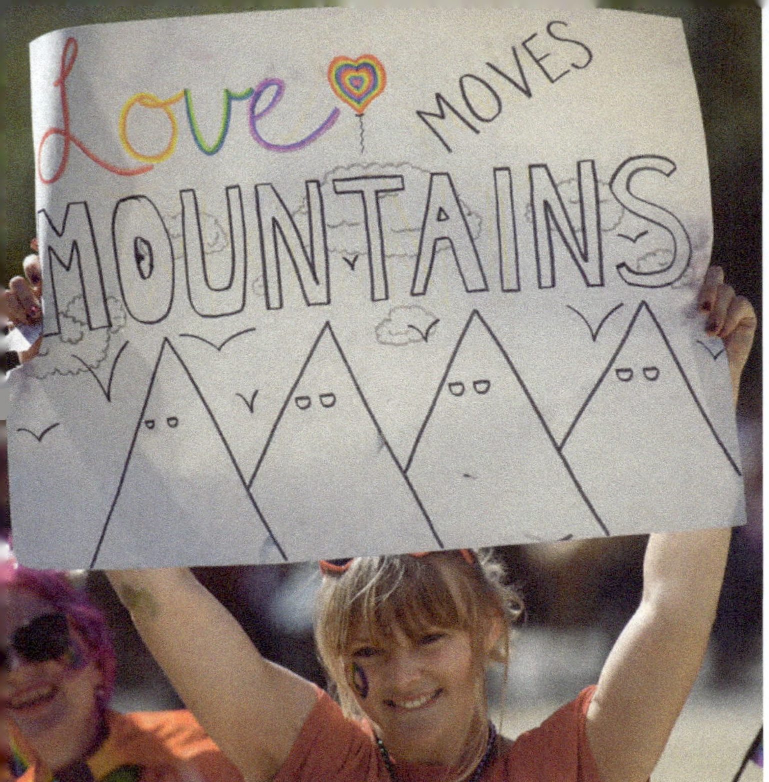

Love MOVES
MOUNTAINS

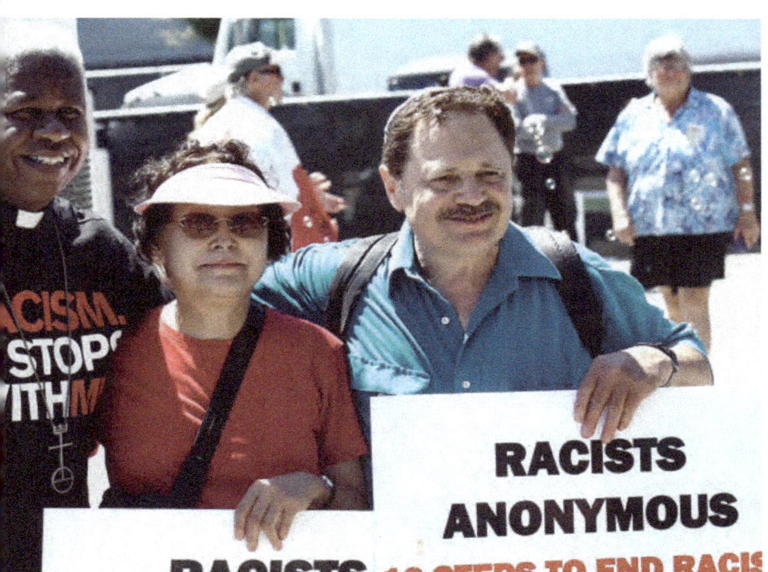

RACISM.
STOP
WITH M
RACISTS
ANONYMOUS
12 STEPS TO END RACIS
(Starting With Me)
RACISTS
ANONYMOU
12 STEPS TO END RA
(Starting With Me)

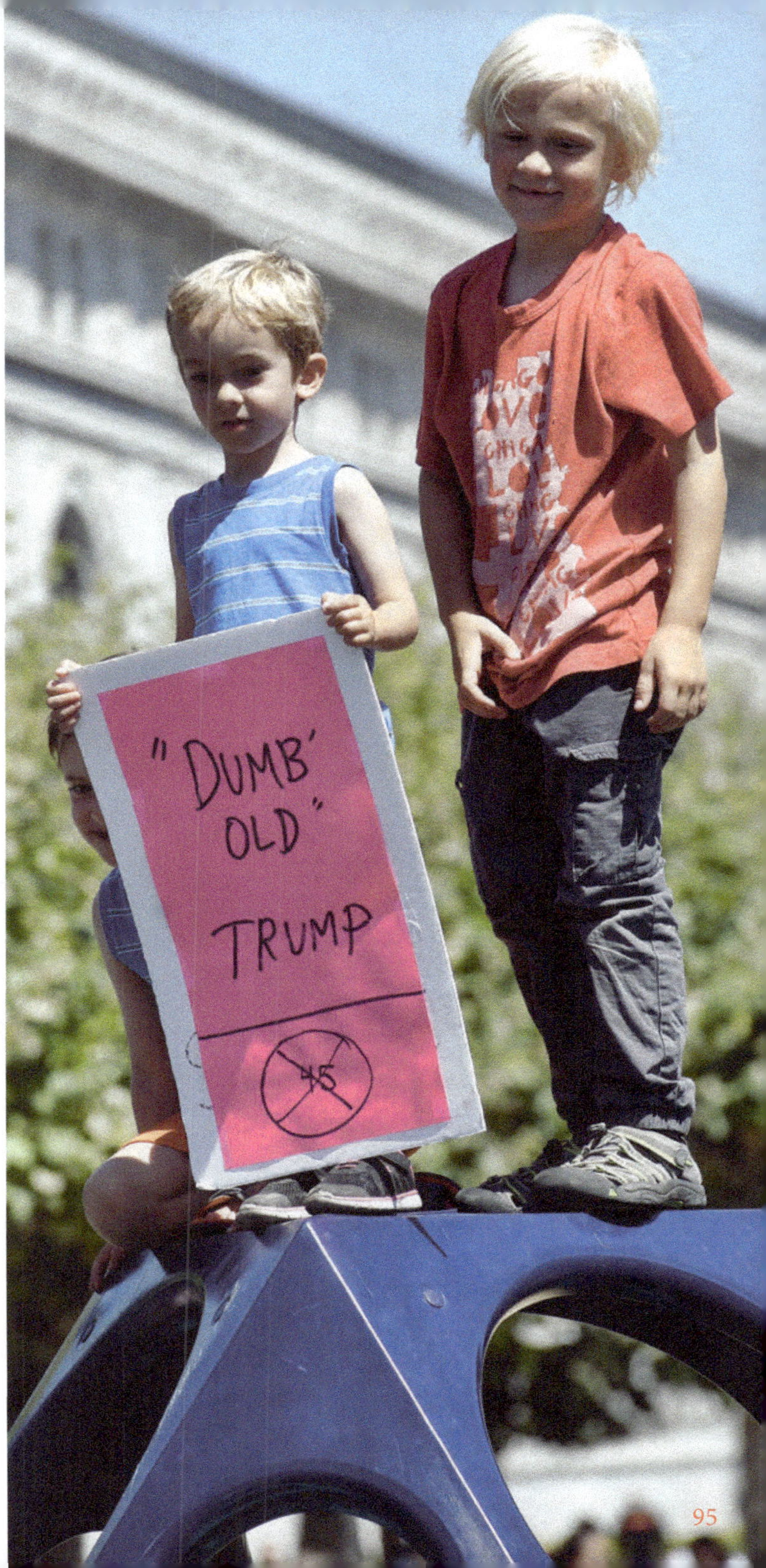

"DUMB"
OLD"
TRUMP

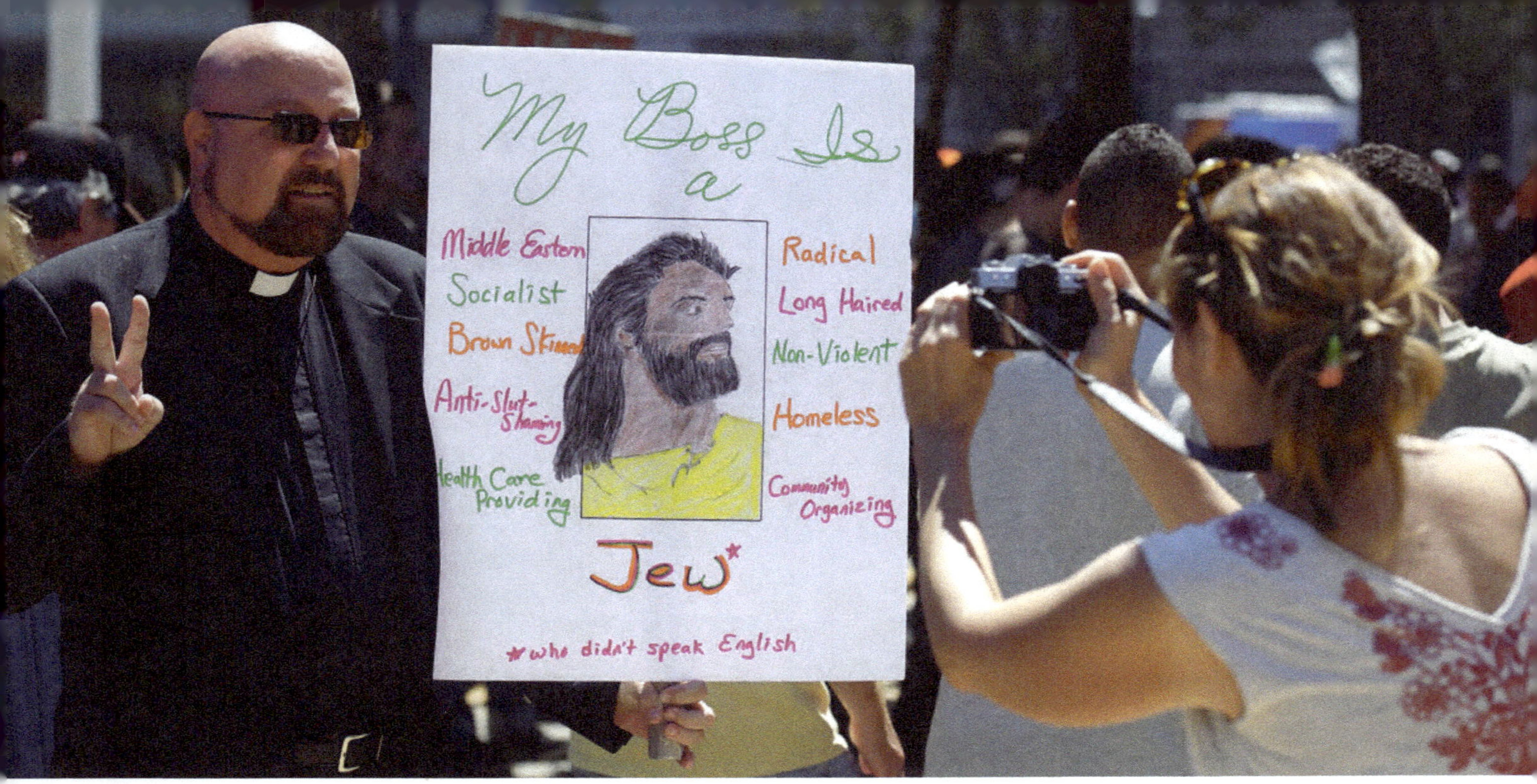

My Boss Is a

Middle Eastern
Socialist
Brown Skinned
Anti-Slut-Shaming
Health Care Providing

Radical
Long Haired
Non-Violent
Homeless
Community Organizing

Jew*

*who didn't speak English

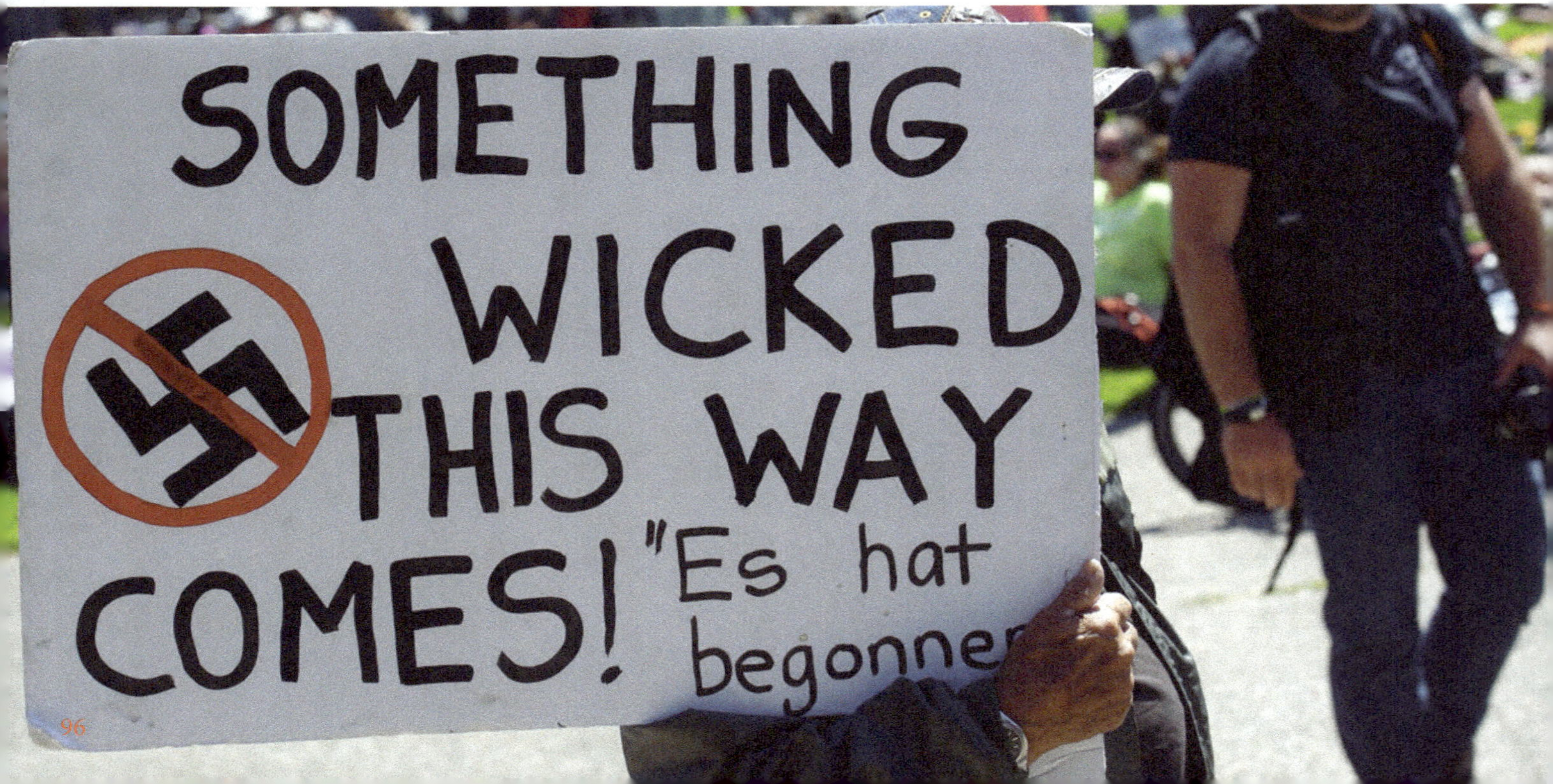

SOMETHING WICKED THIS WAY COMES! "Es hat begonnen"

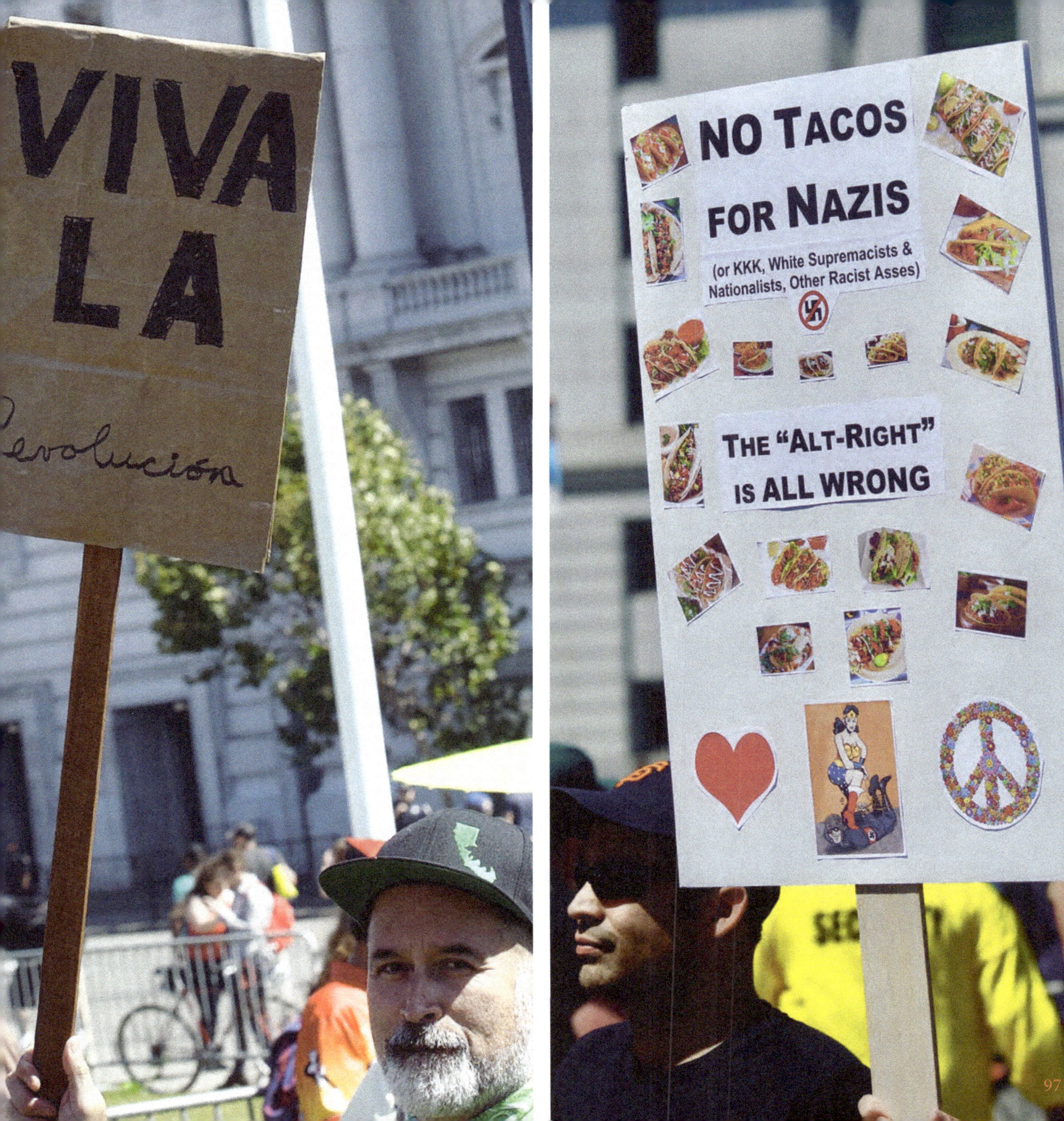

VIVA LA
Revolución

NO TACOS FOR NAZIS
(or KKK, White Supremacists &
Nationalists, Other Racist Asses)

THE "ALT-RIGHT" IS ALL WRONG

SEC

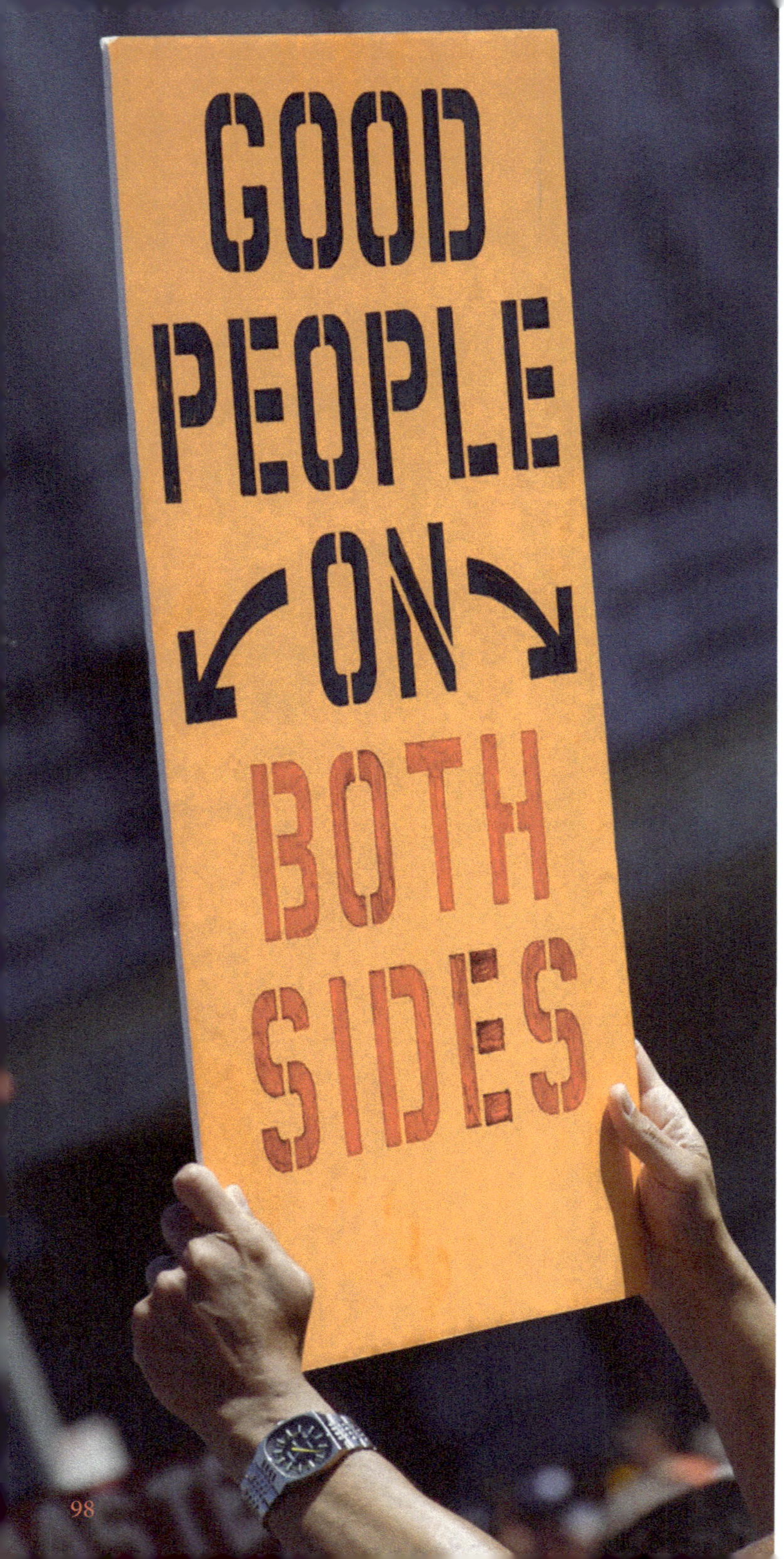

GOOD PEOPLE ON BOTH SIDES

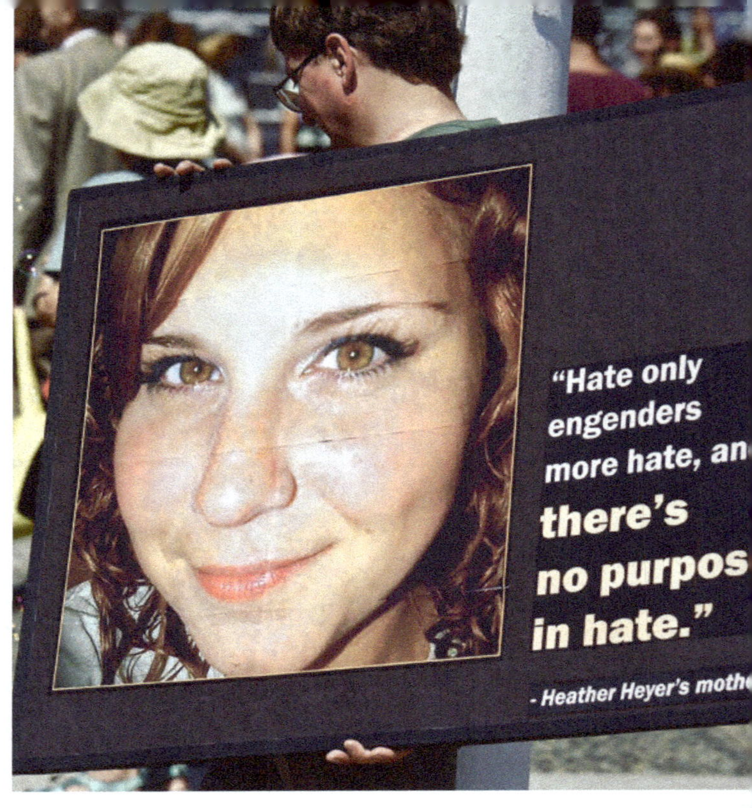

"Hate only engenders more hate, an there's no purpos in hate."
- Heather Heyer's mothe

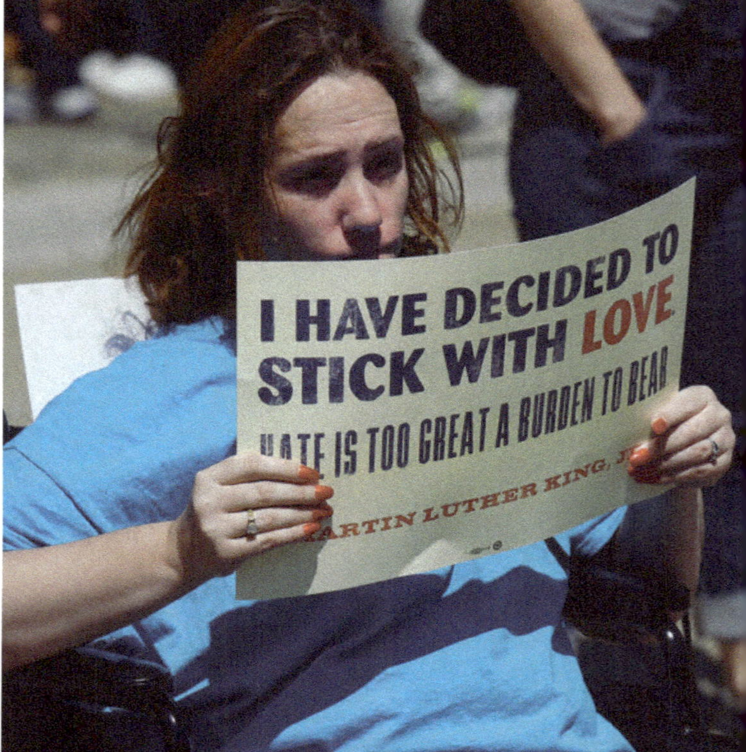

I HAVE DECIDED TO STICK WITH LOVE
HATE IS TOO GREAT A BURDEN TO BEAR
MARTIN LUTHER KING, JR.

WE MAY HAVE ALL COME ON DIFFERENT SHIPS, BUT WE'RE IN THE SAME BOAT NOW!

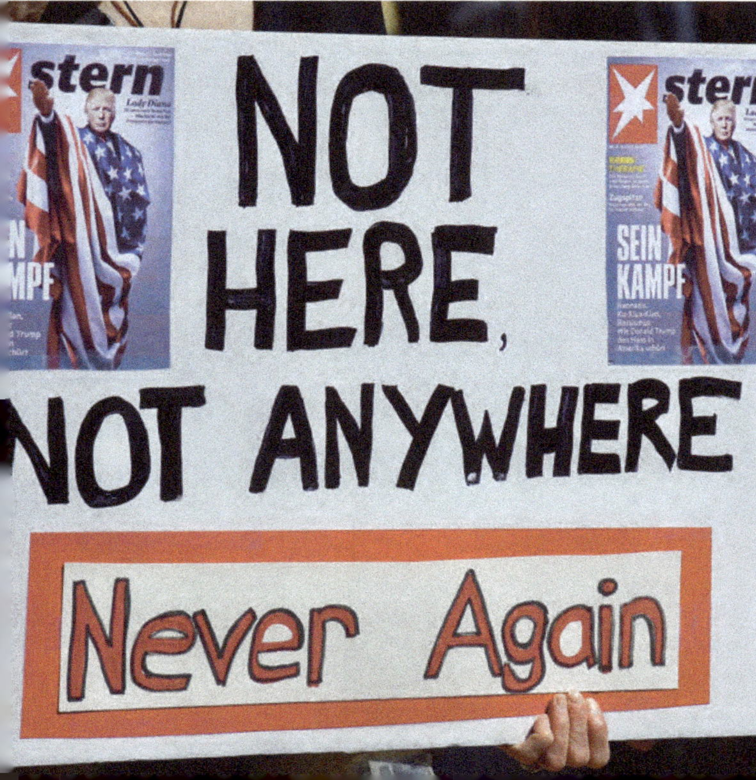
stern
stern
SEIN KAMPF
NOT HERE, NOT ANYWHERE
Never Again

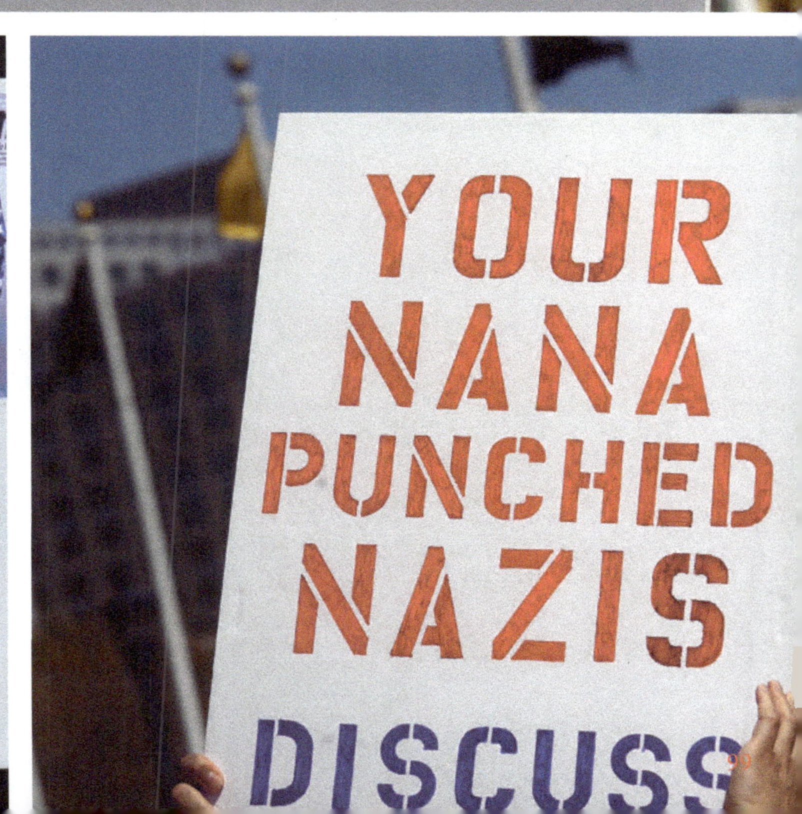
YOUR NANA PUNCHED NAZIS DISCUSS

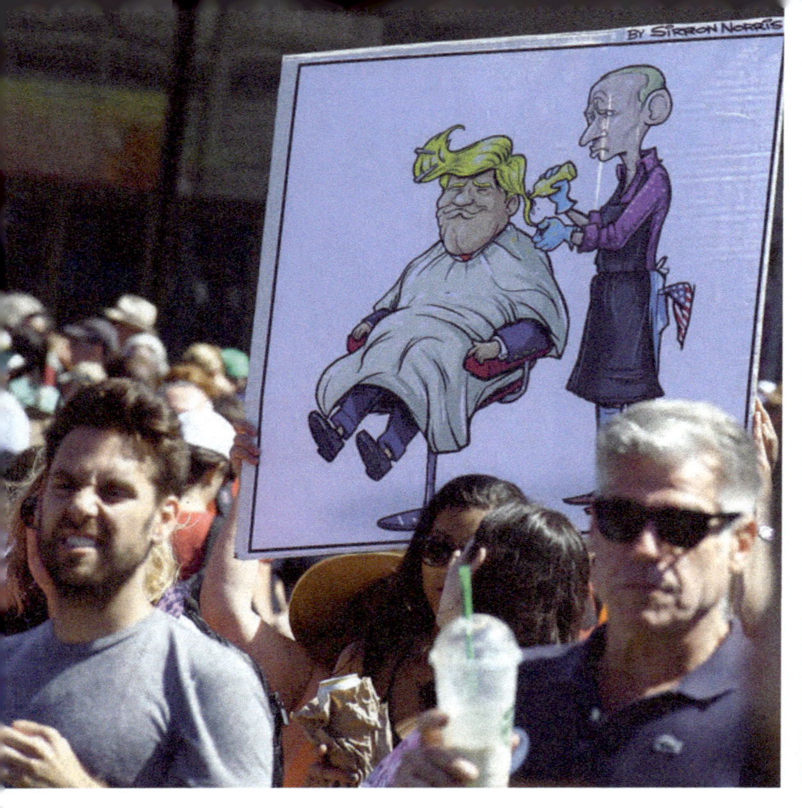

BY SIRRON NORRIS

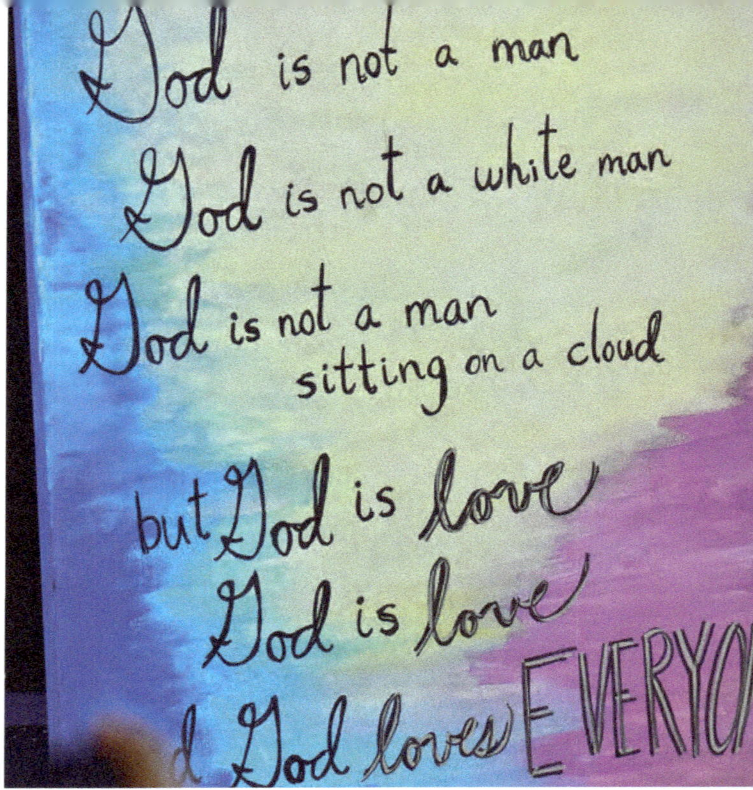

God is not a man
God is not a white man
God is not a man
sitting on a cloud
but God is love
God is love
d God loves EVERYO

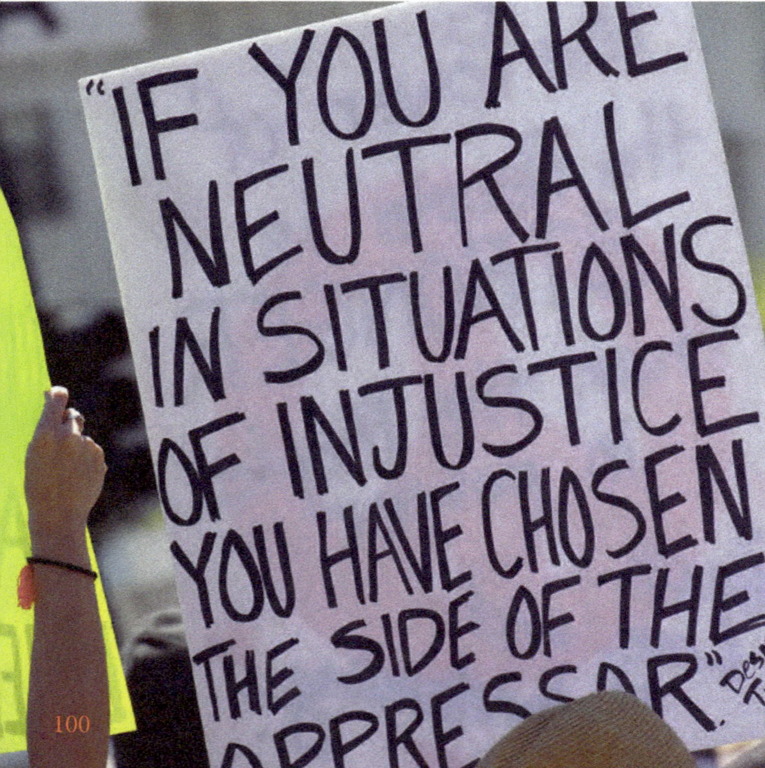

"IF YOU ARE
NEUTRAL
IN SITUATIONS
OF INJUSTICE
YOU HAVE CHOSEN
THE SIDE OF THE
OPPRESSOR"
Desm
Tu

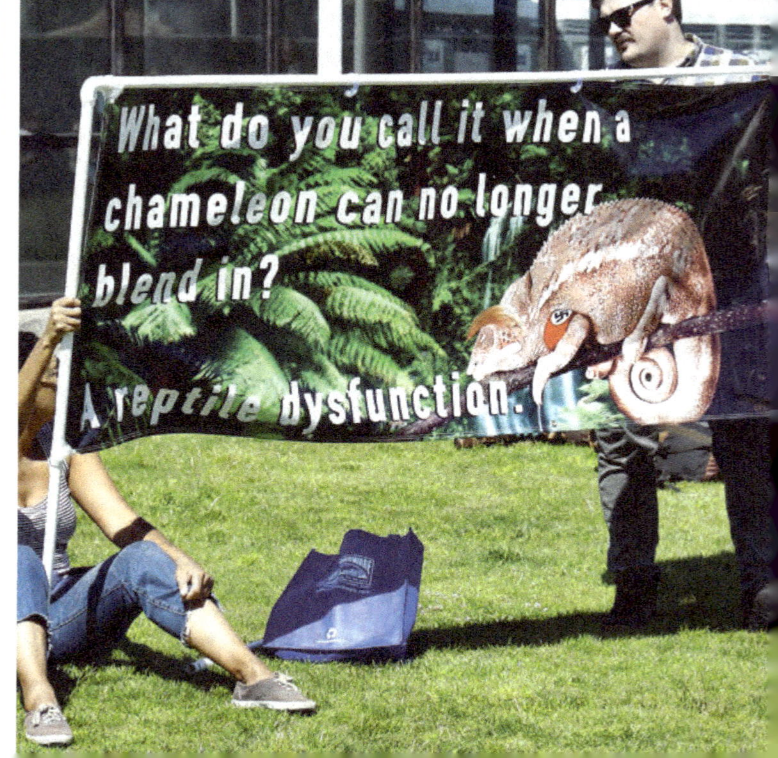

What do you call it when a
chameleon can no longer
blend in?
A reptile dysfunction.

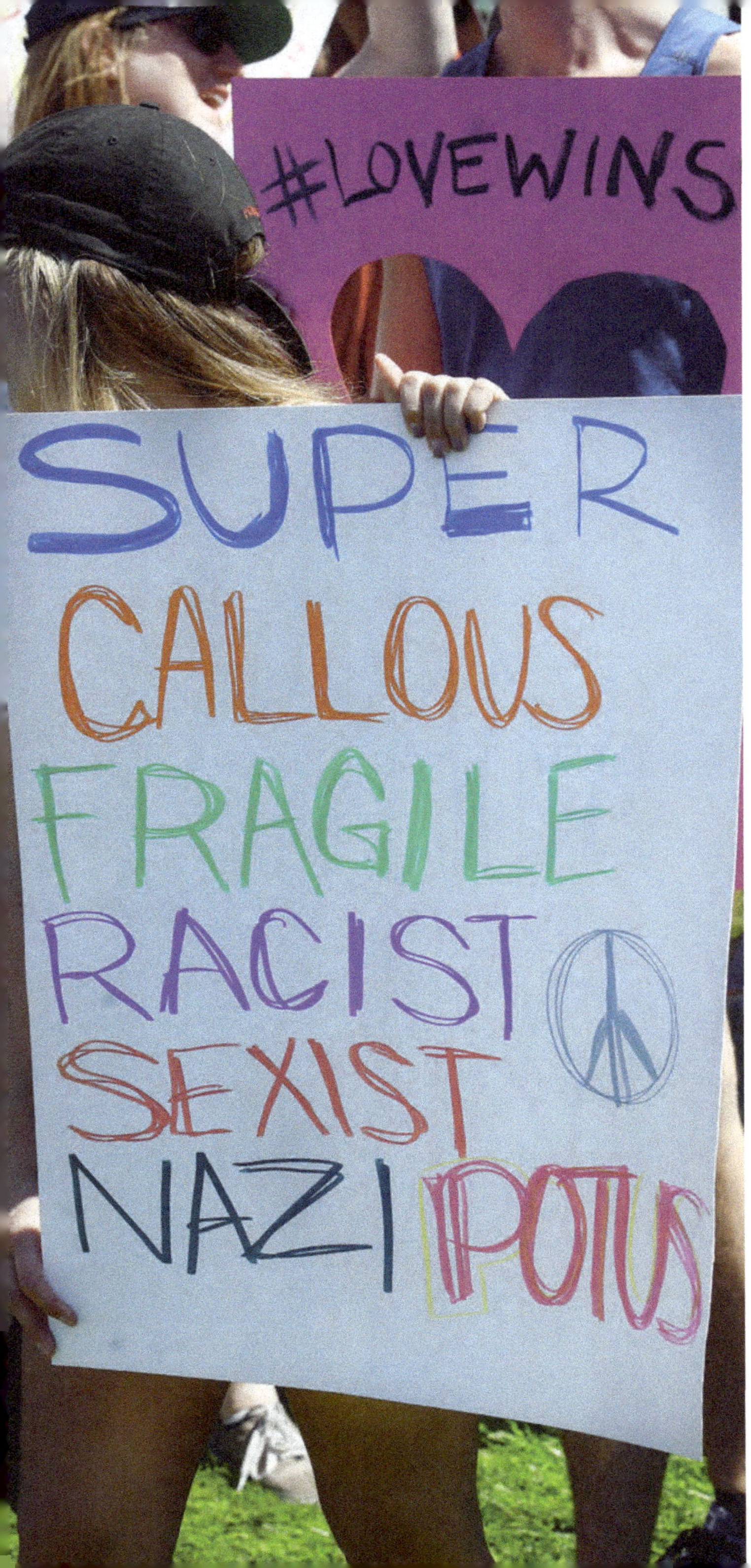

#LOVEWINS

SUPER
CALLOUS
FRAGILE
RACIST
SEXIST
NAZI POTUS

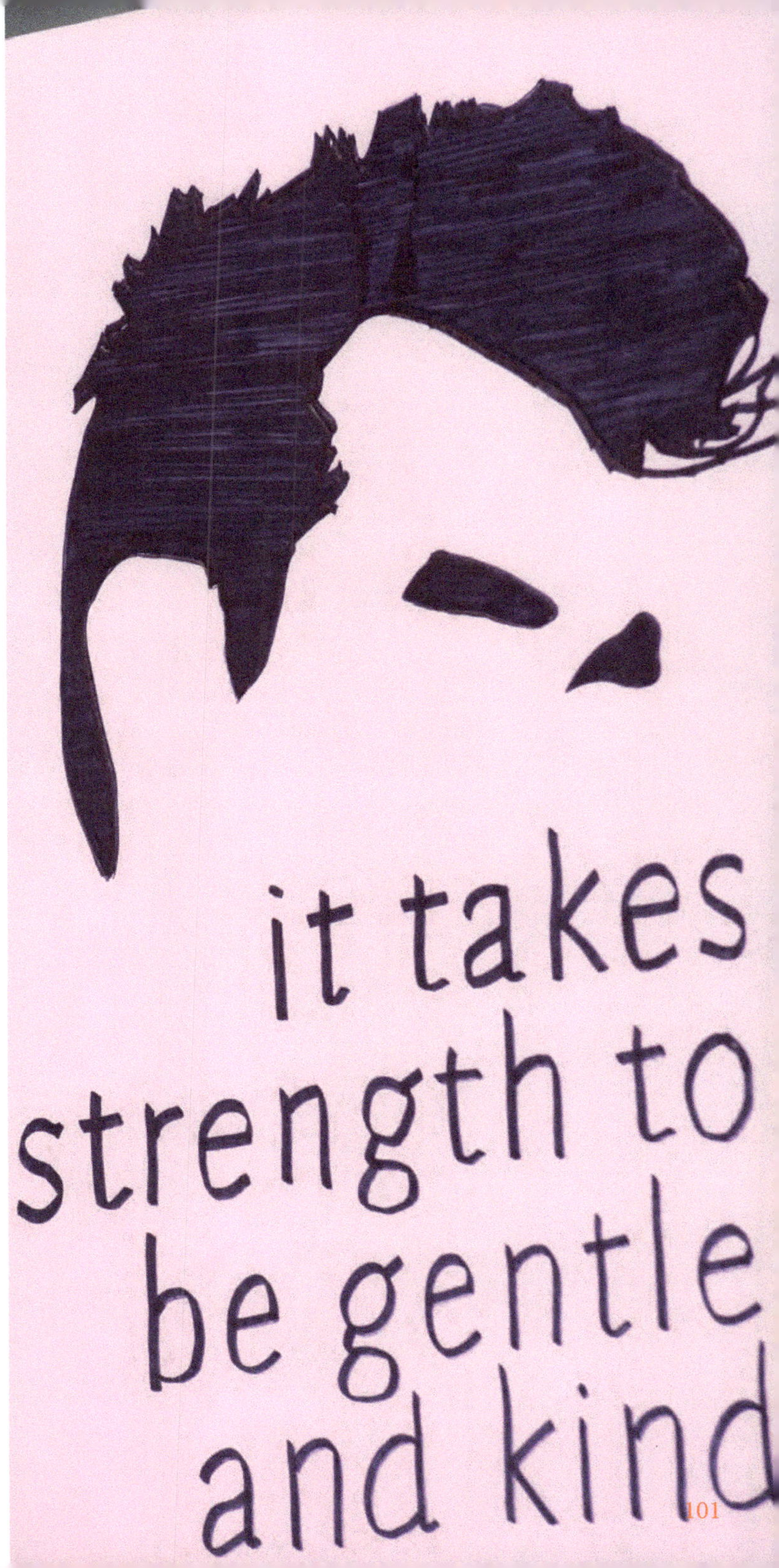

it takes
strength to
be gentle
and kind

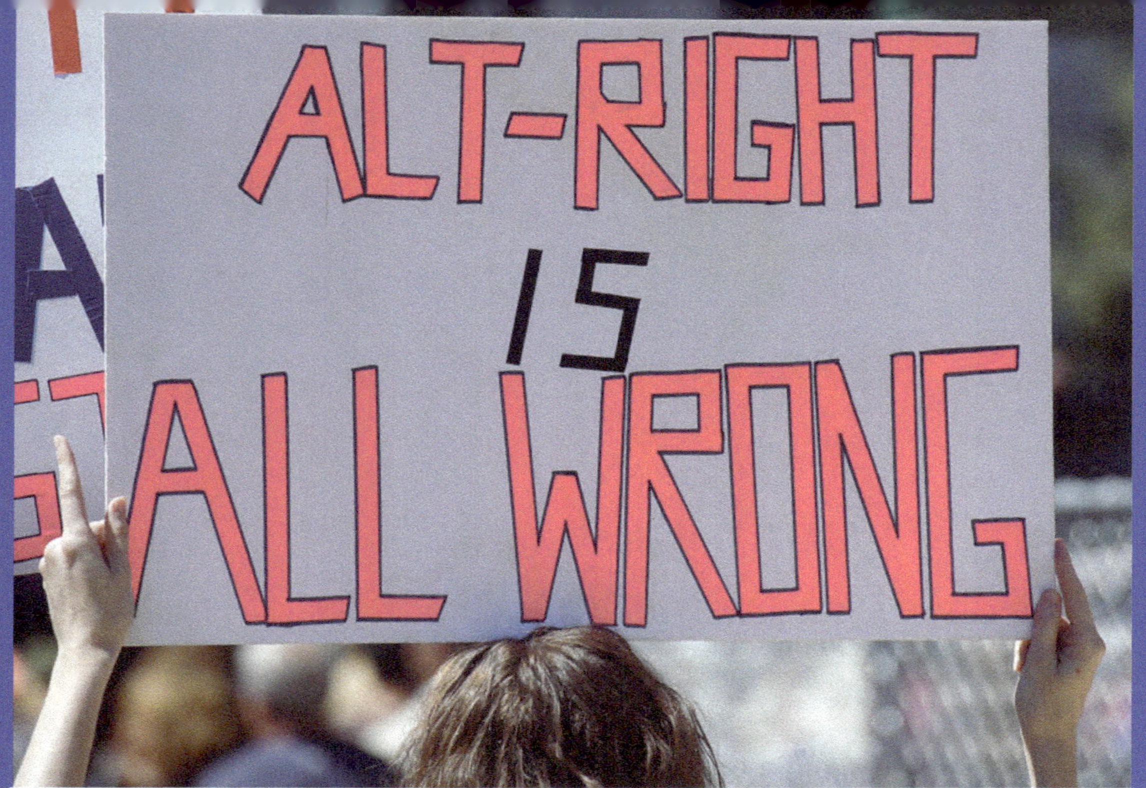
ALT-RIGHT
IS
ALL WRONG
ANTIFA
AND
PROUD

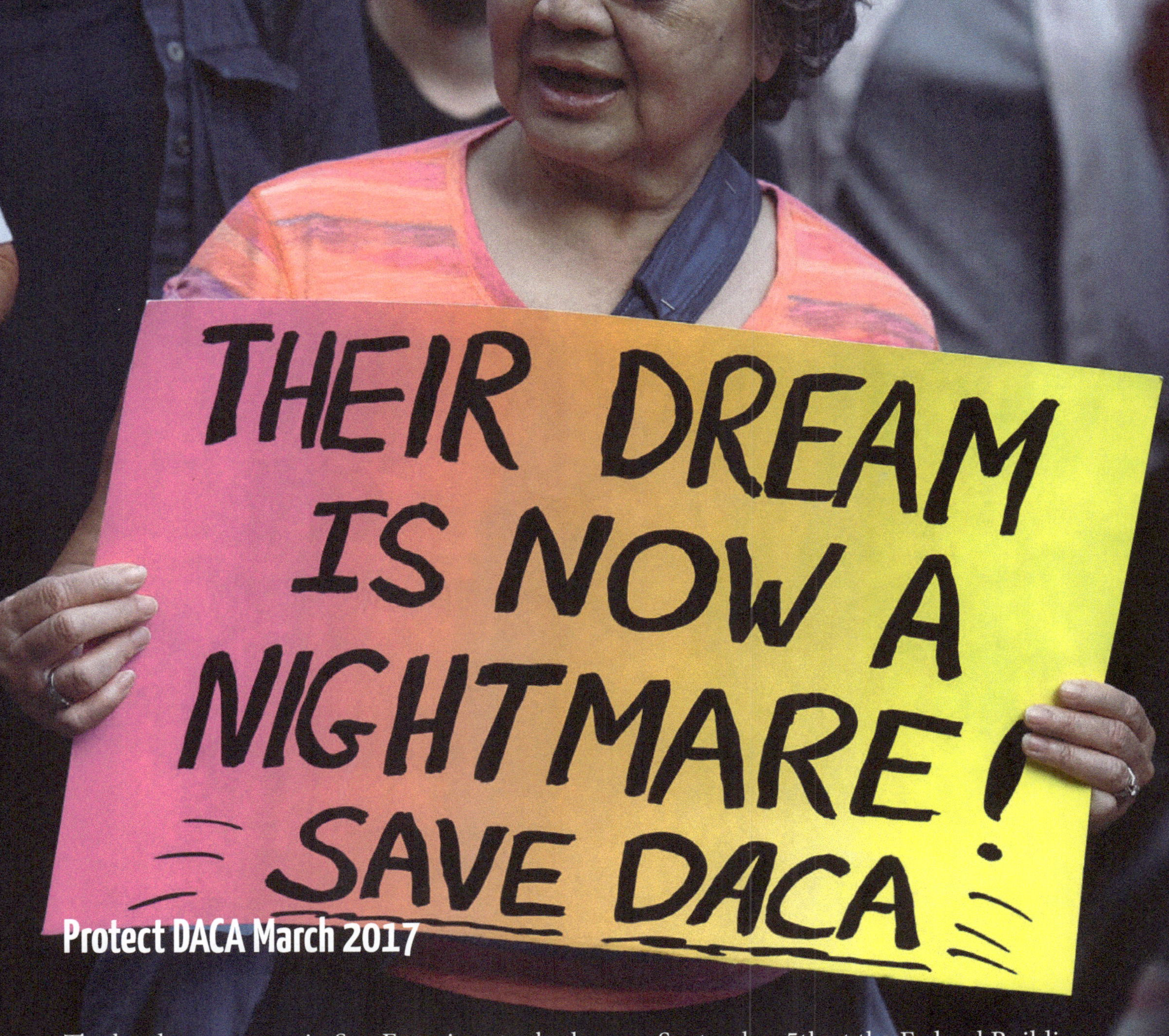

Protect DACA March 2017

The last large protest in San Francisco took place on September 5th at the Federal Building. Resisters offered support for the DACA students and condemned trump's position on DACA.

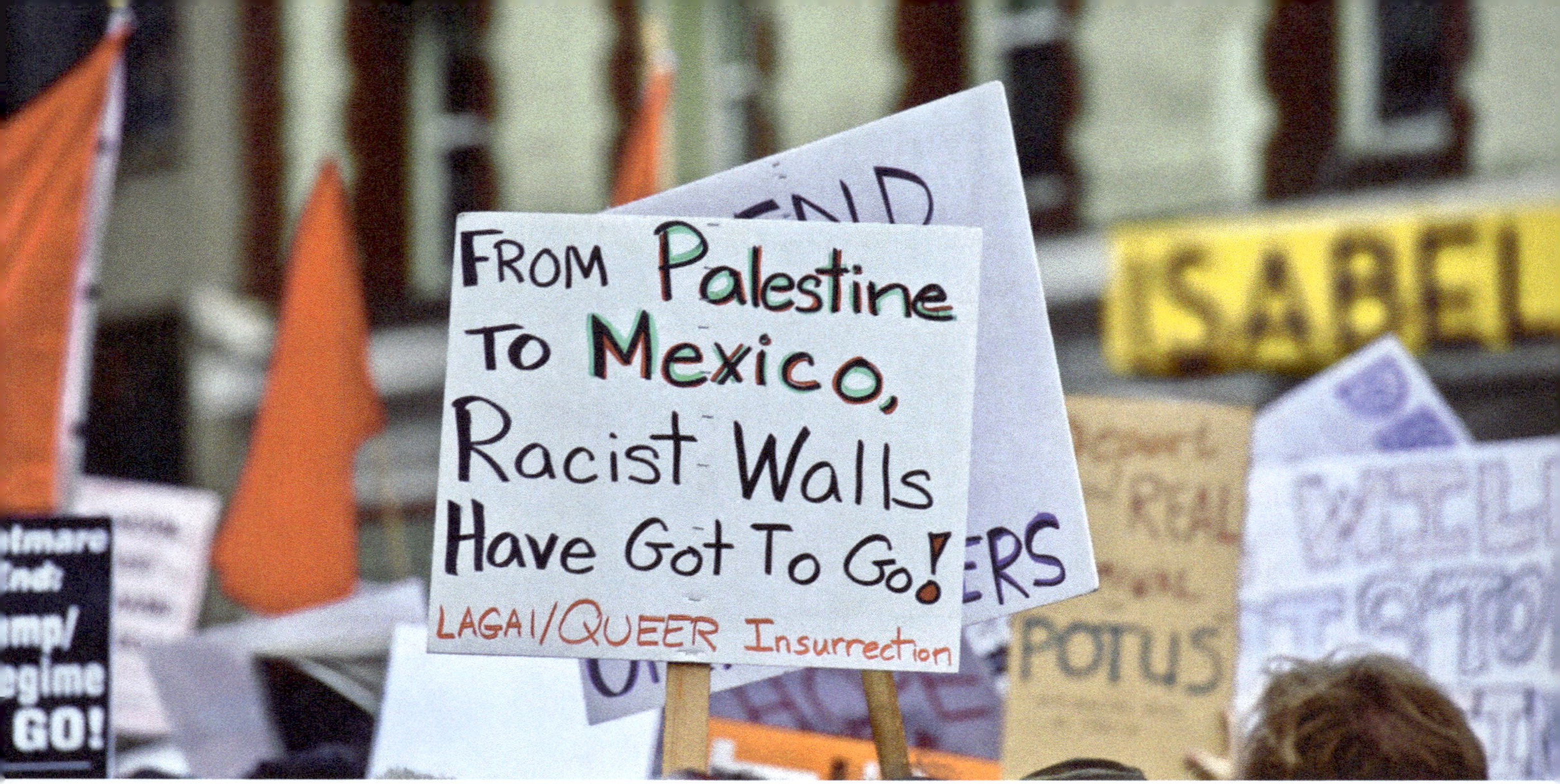

FROM Palestine TO Mexico, Racist Walls Have Got To Go!
LAGAI/QUEER Insurrection
ISABEL
REAL
POTUS

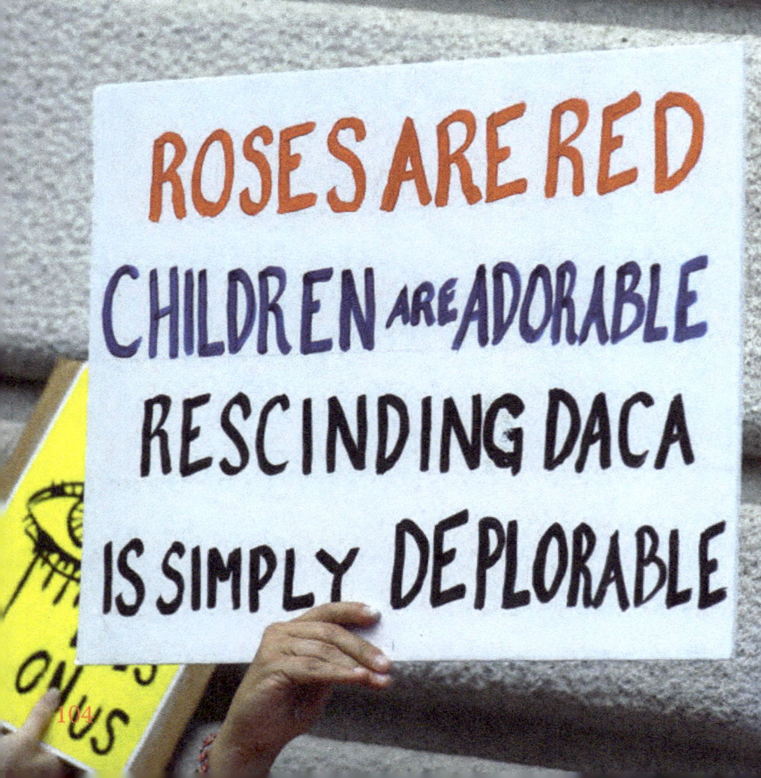

ROSES ARE RED
CHILDREN ARE ADORABLE
RESCINDING DACA
IS SIMPLY DEPLORABLE

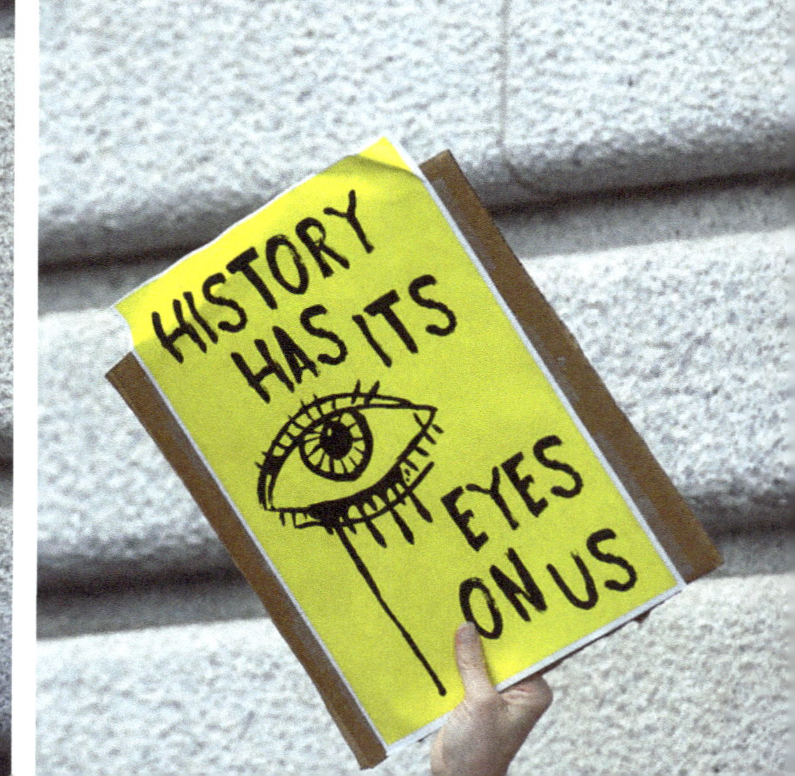

HISTORY HAS ITS
EYES ON US

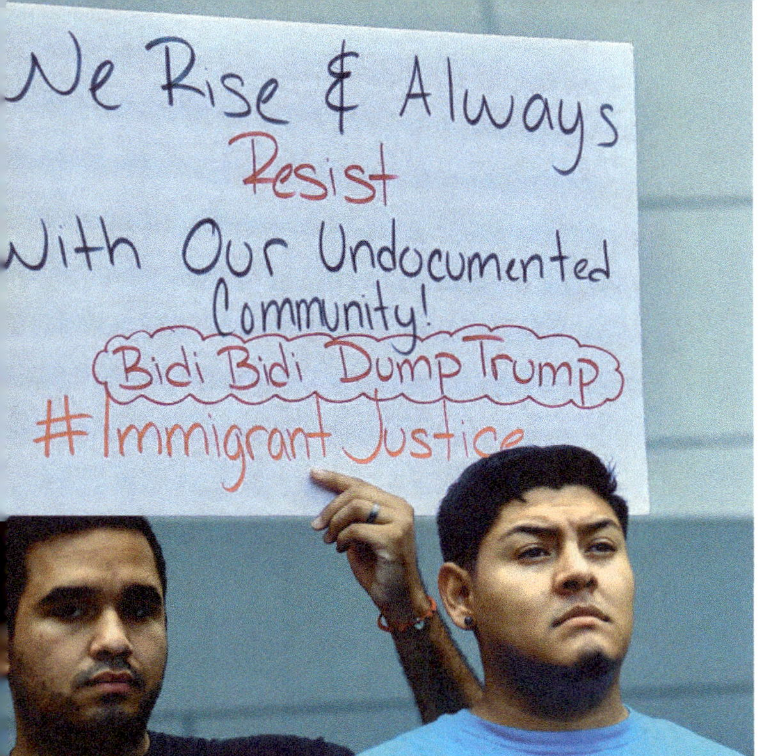
We Rise & Always Resist
With Our Undocumented Community!
Bidi Bidi Dump Trump
#ImmigrantJustice

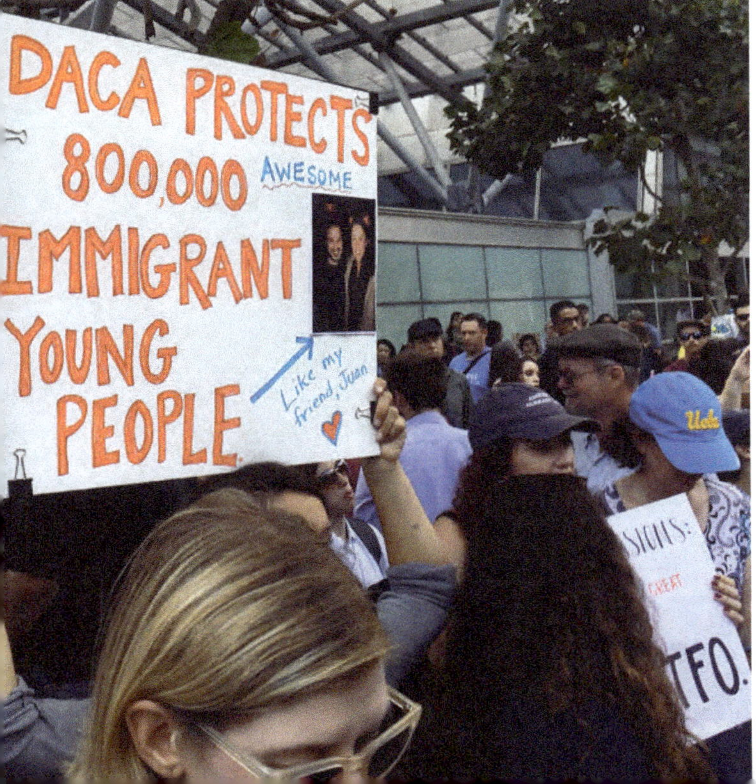
DACA PROTECTS 800,000 IMMIGRANT YOUNG PEOPLE
AWESOME
Like my friend, Juan

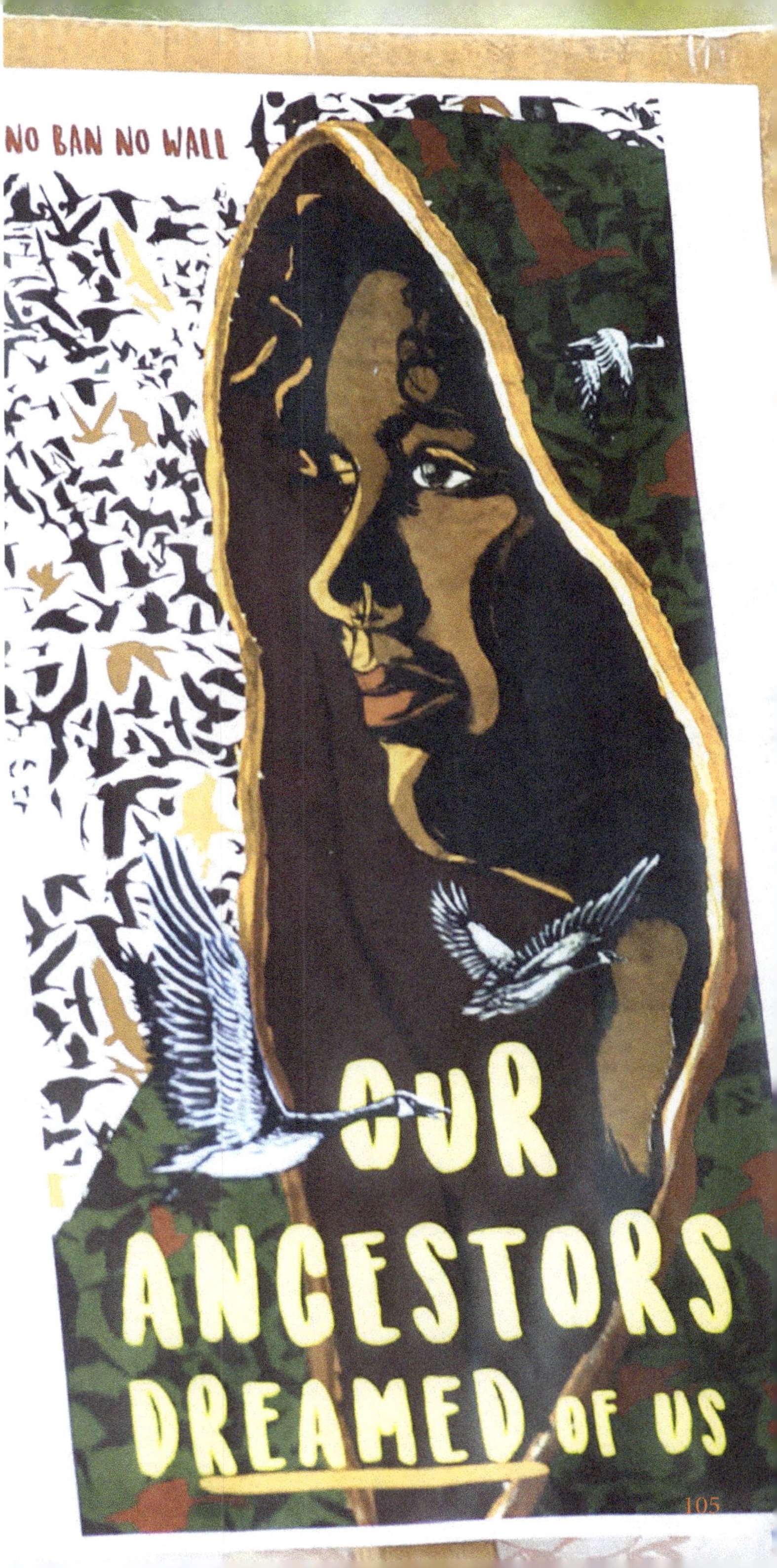

NO BAN NO WALL
OUR ANCESTORS DREAMED OF US

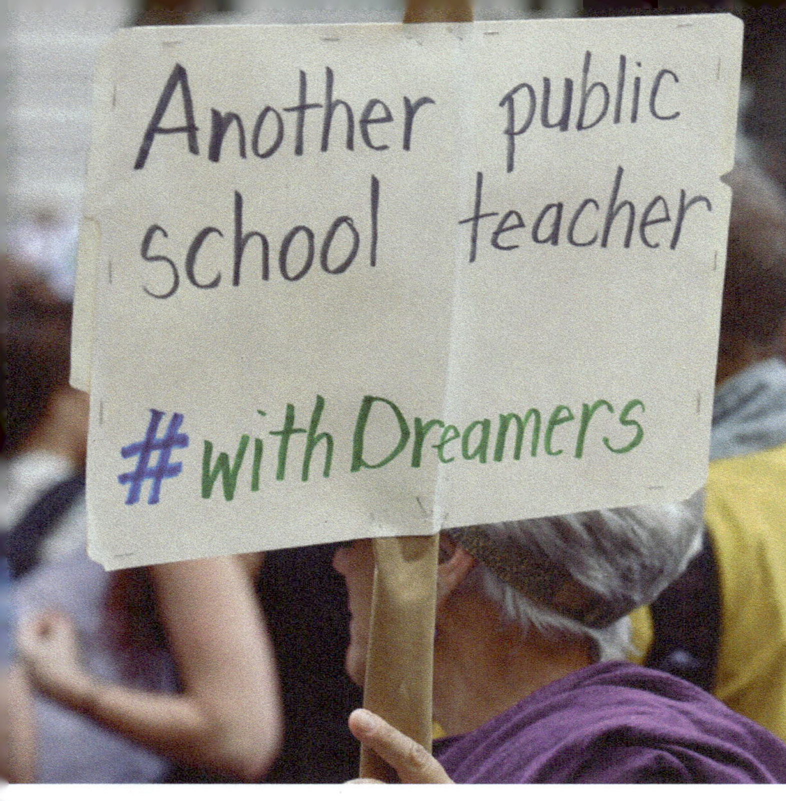
Another public
school teacher
#withDreamers

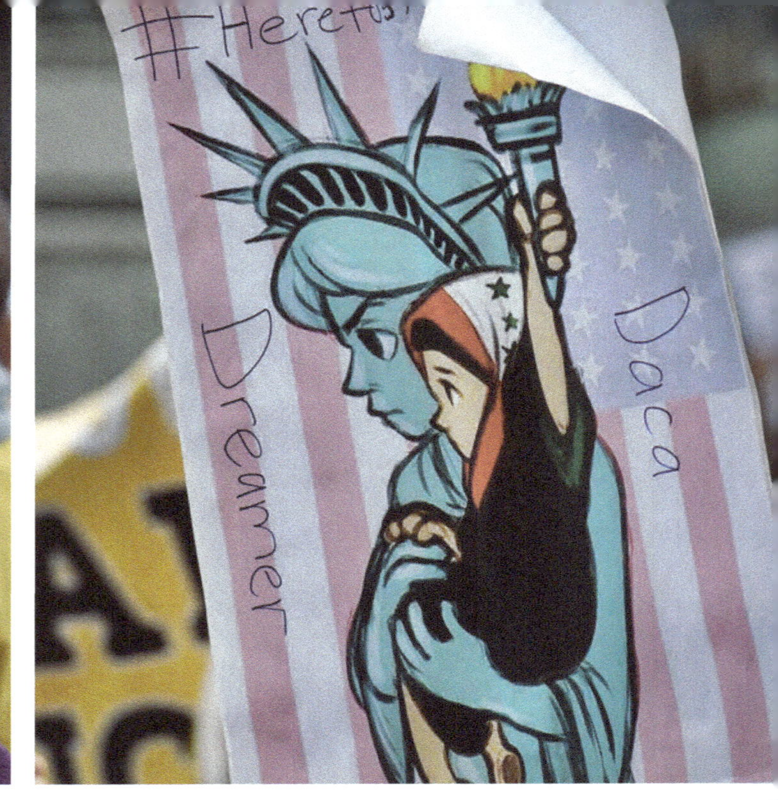
#Heretu
Dreamer
Daca

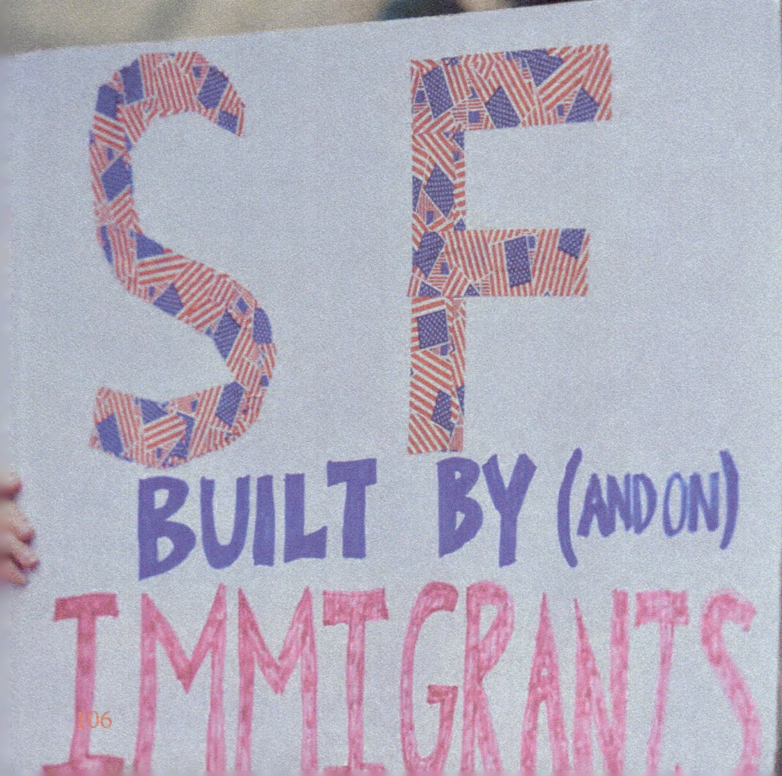
SF
BUILT BY (AND ON)
IMMIGRANTS

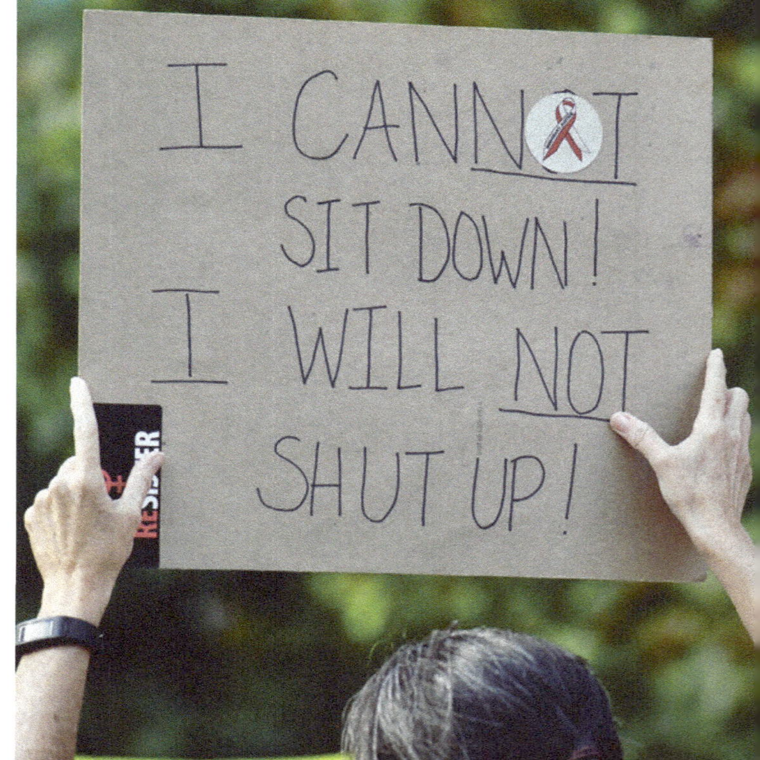
I CANNOT
SIT DOWN!
I WILL NOT
SHUT UP!

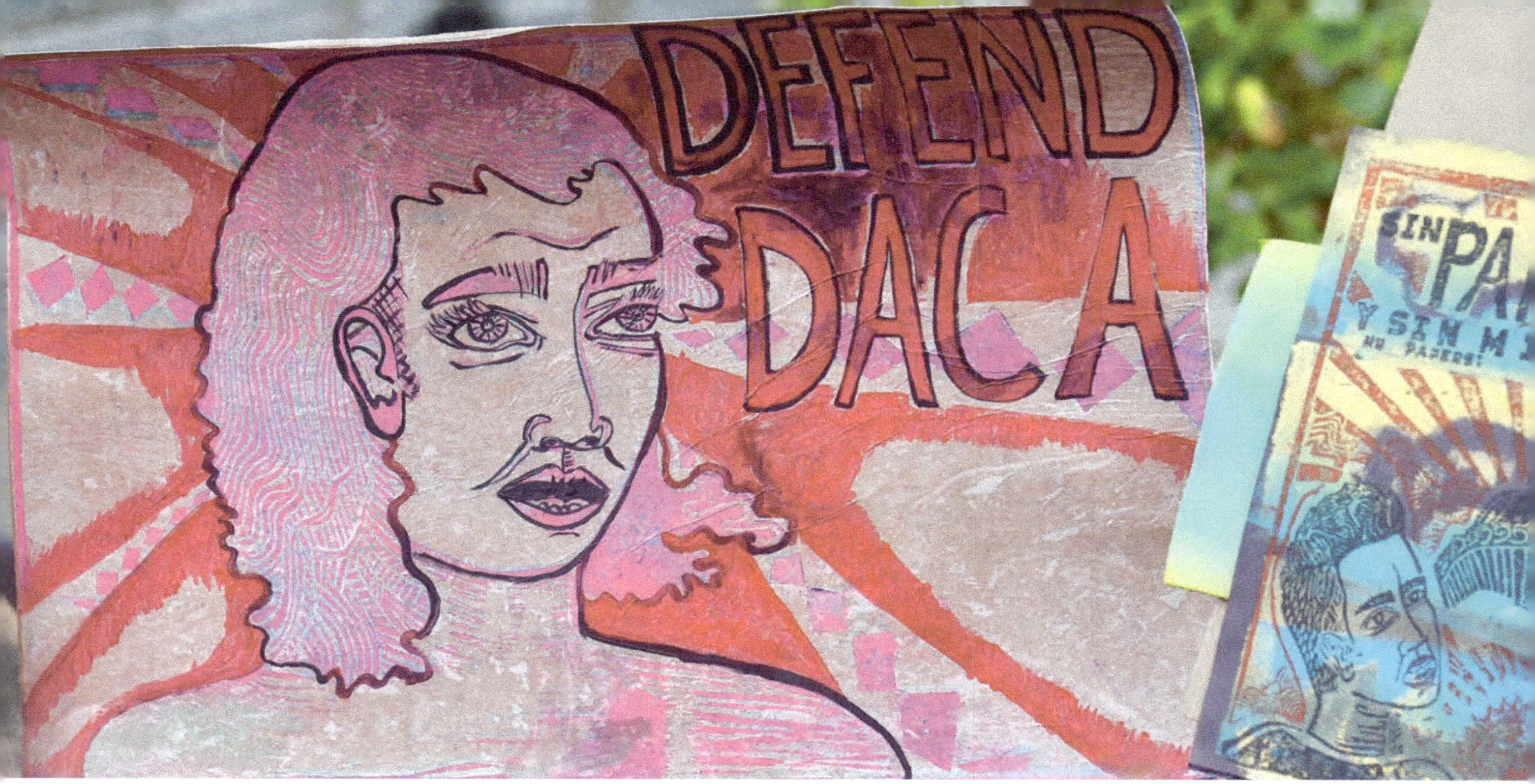

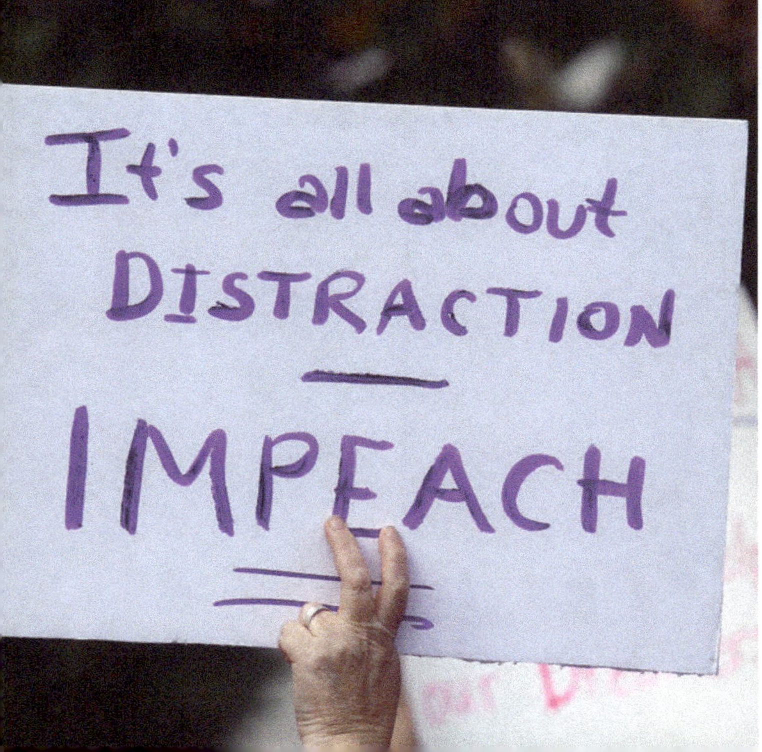
DEFEND
DACA
SIN PA
Y SIN MI
NO PAPERS!
It's all about
DISTRACTION
—
IMPEACH

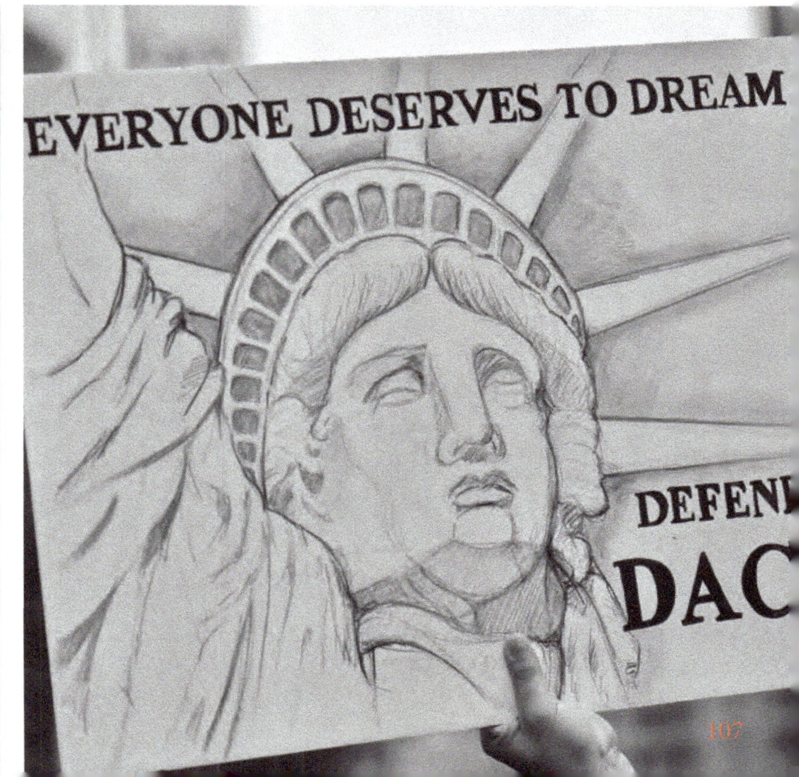
EVERYONE DESERVES TO DREAM
DEFEN
DAC

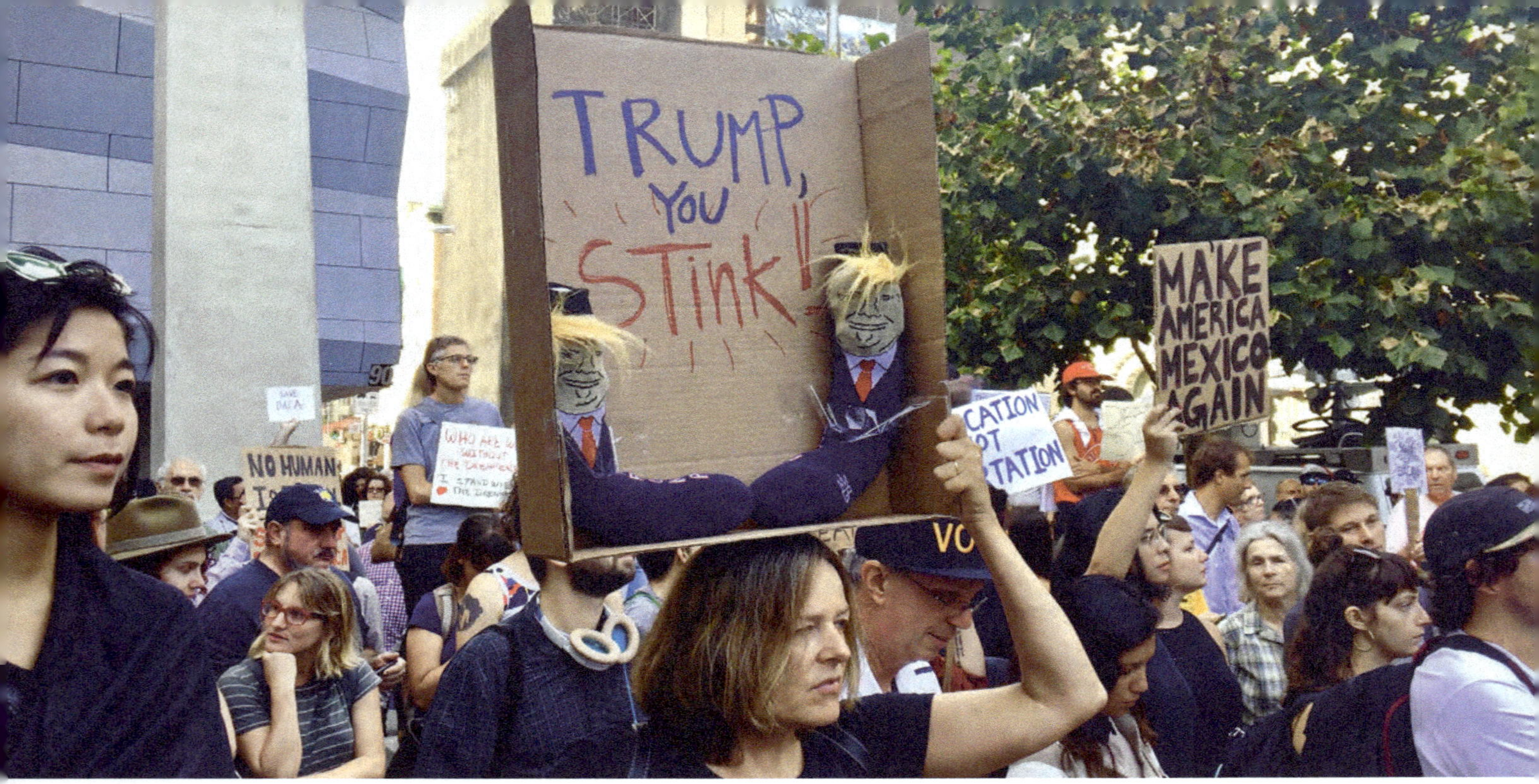

TRUMP, YOU STINK!
MAKE AMERICA MEXICO AGAIN
NO HUMAN
SAVE DACA
WHO ARE WE WITHOUT THE DREAMERS?
I STAND WITH THE DREAMERS
CATION NOT ATION
VO

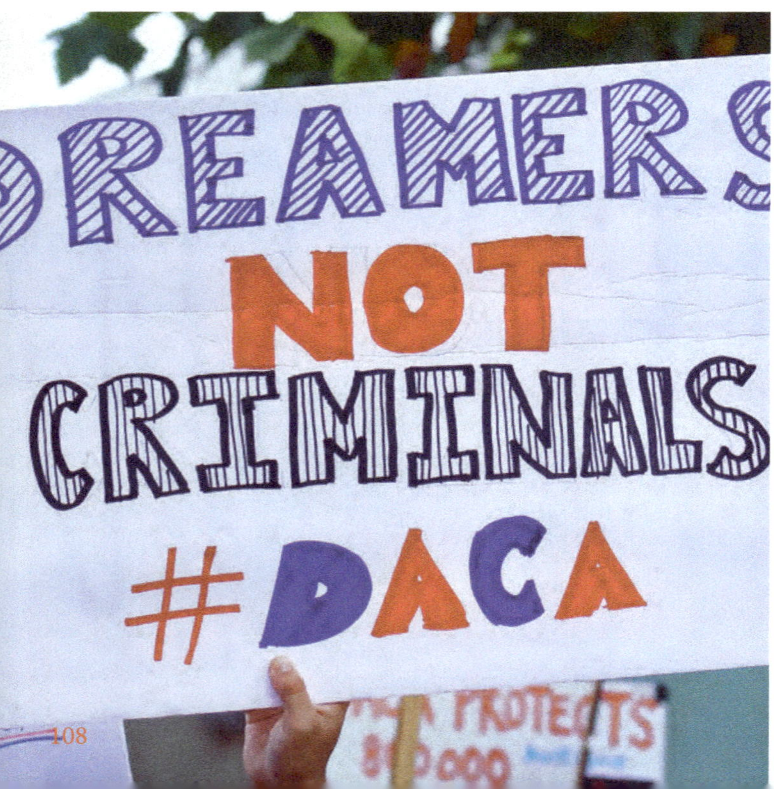
DREAMERS
NOT
CRIMINALS
#DACA
PROTECTS

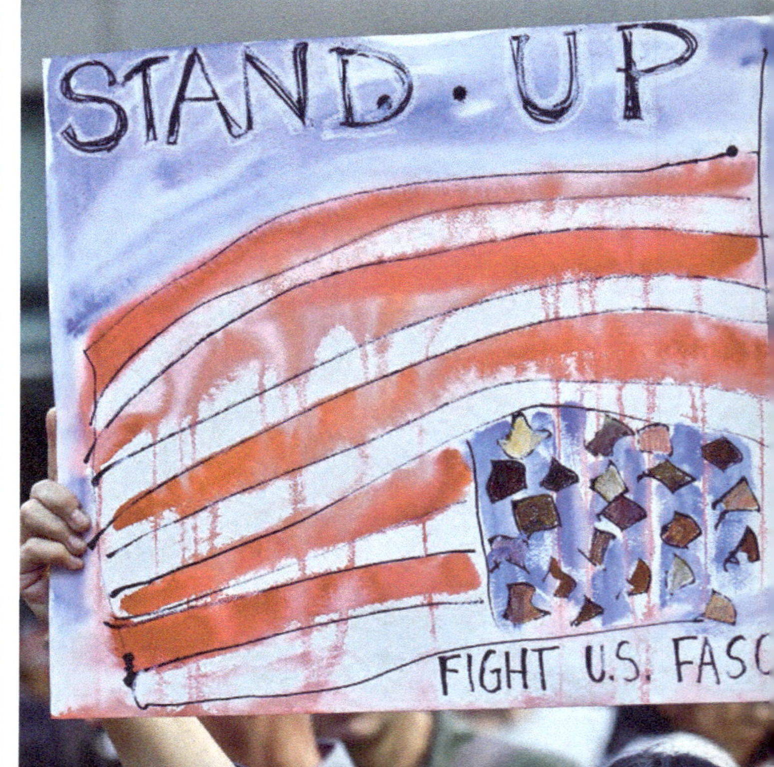
STAND · UP
FIGHT U.S. FASC

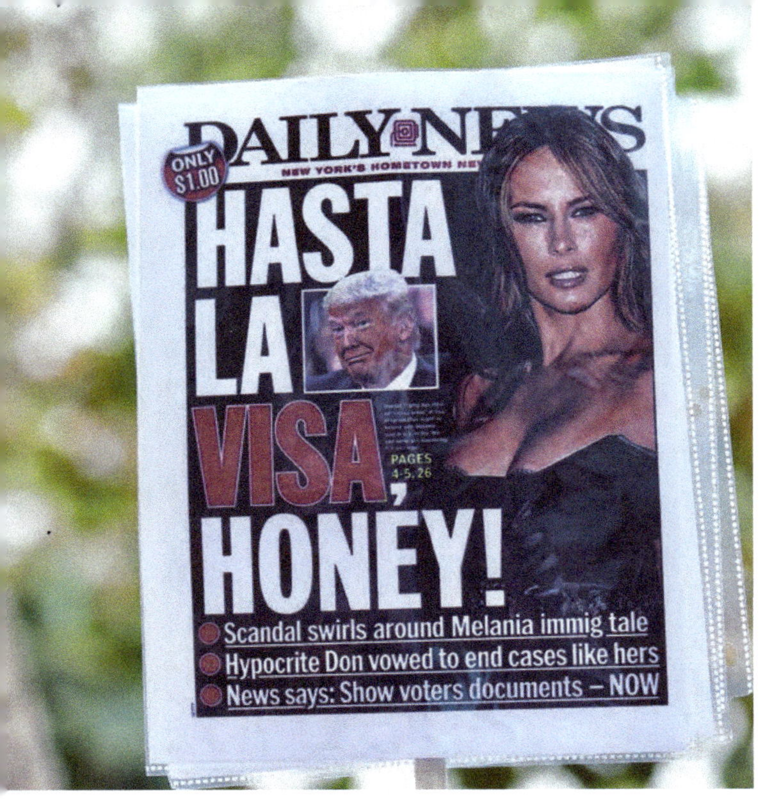
ONLY $1.00
DAILY NEWS
NEW YORK'S HOMETOWN NEWS
HASTA LA VISA, HONEY!
PAGES 4-5, 26
Scandal swirls around Melania immig tale
Hypocrite Don vowed to end cases like hers
News says: Show voters documents — NOW

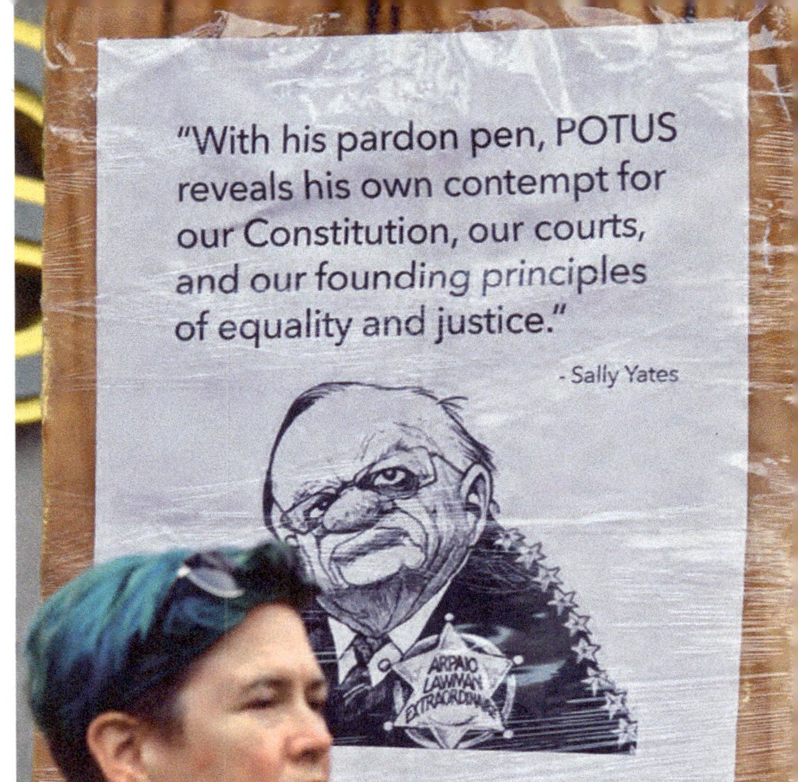
"With his pardon pen, POTUS reveals his own contempt for our Constitution, our courts, and our founding principles of equality and justice."
- Sally Yates
ARPAIO LAWMAN EXTRAORDINAIRE

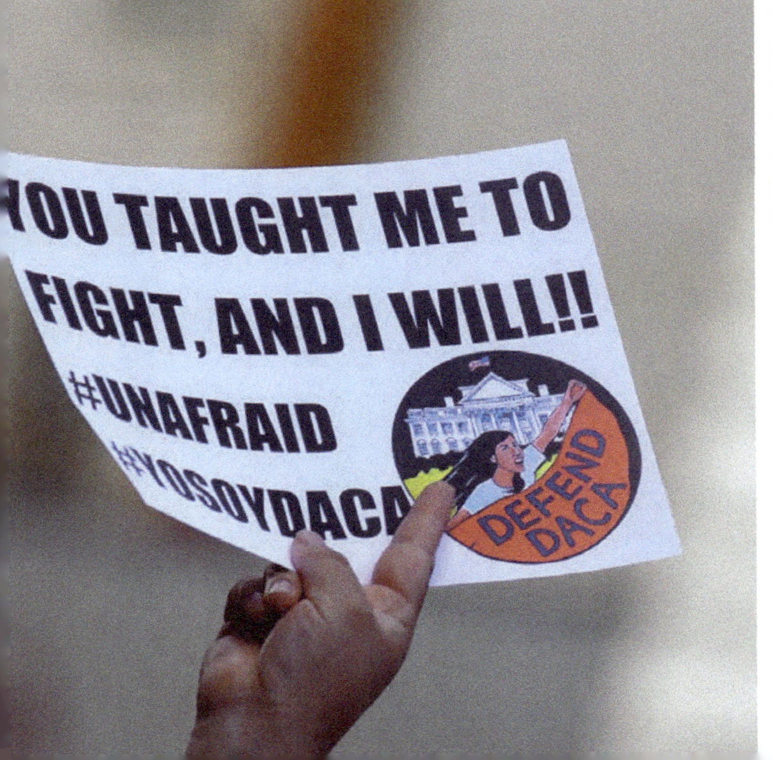
YOU TAUGHT ME TO FIGHT, AND I WILL!!
#UNAFRAID
#YOSOYDACA
DEFEND DACA

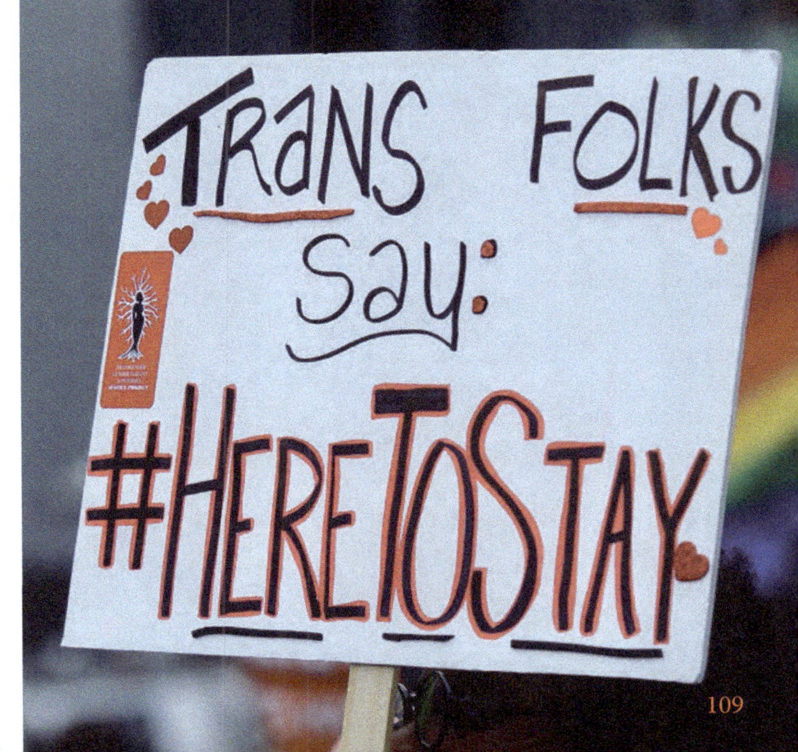
TRANS FOLKS SAY:
#HERETOSTAY

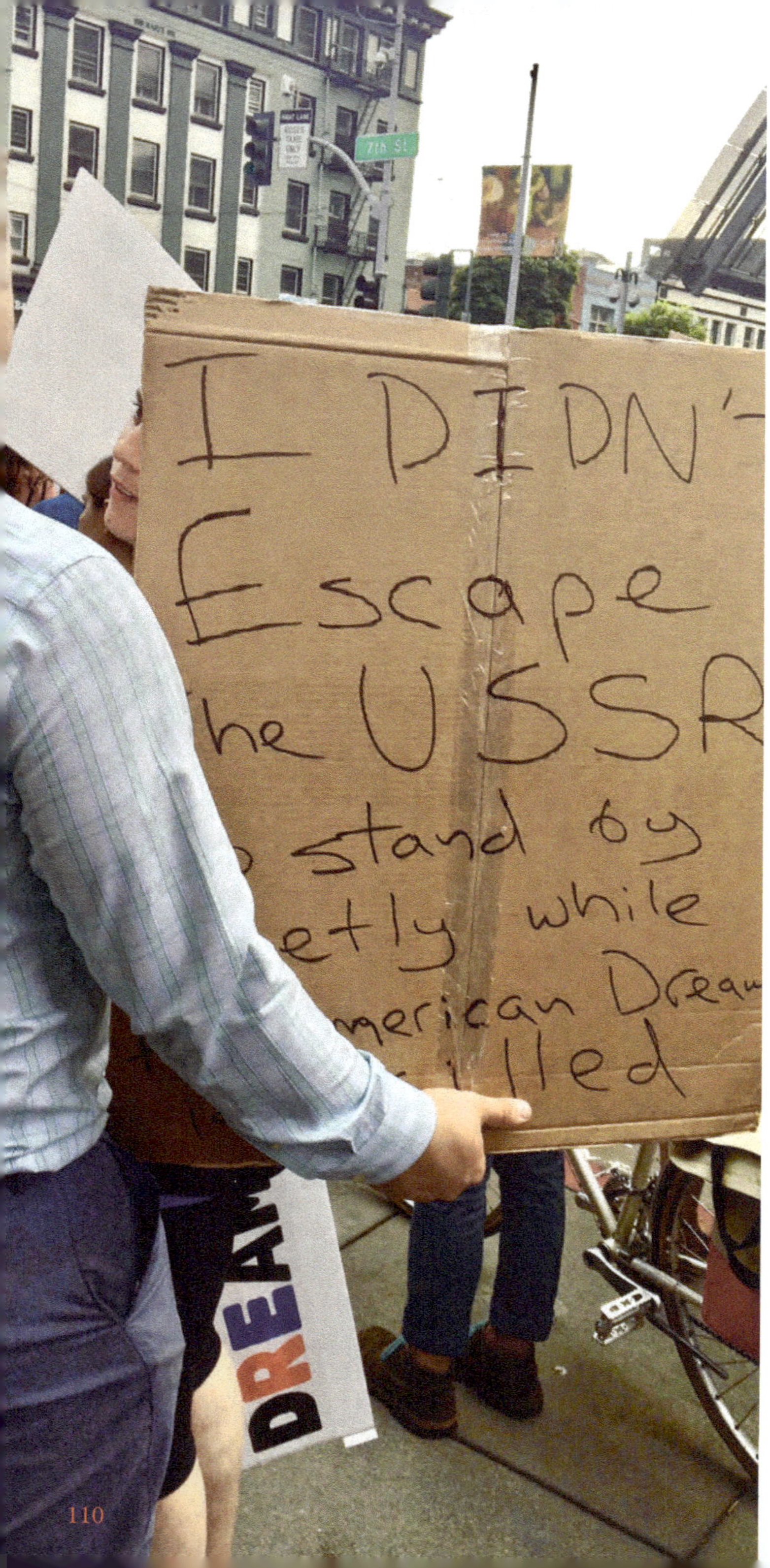

I DIDN'T
Escape
the USSR
to stand by
quietly while
American Dream
is killed

DREAM

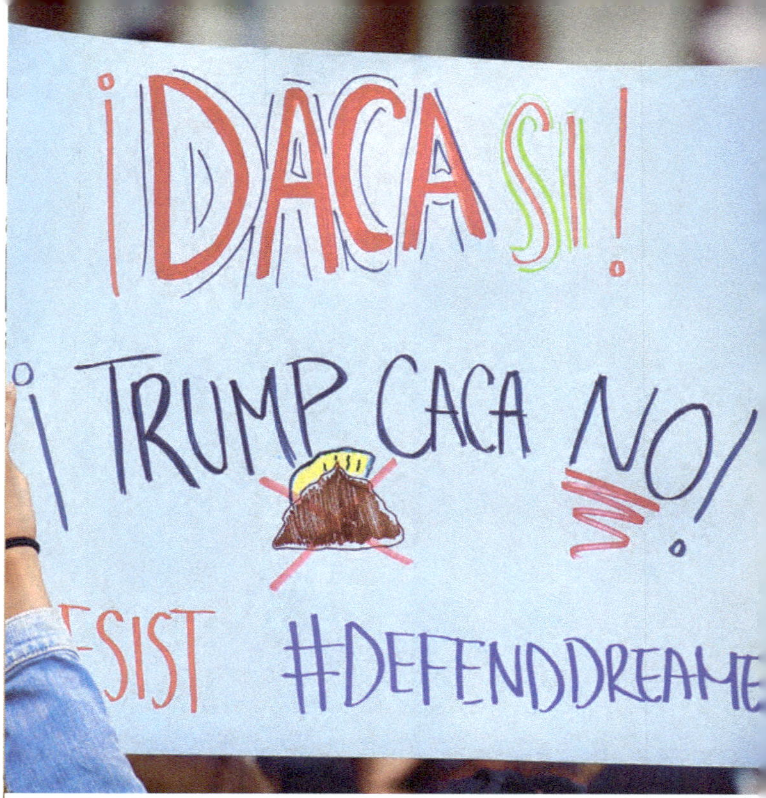

¡DACA SI!
¡TRUMP CACA NO!
RESIST #DEFENDDREAME

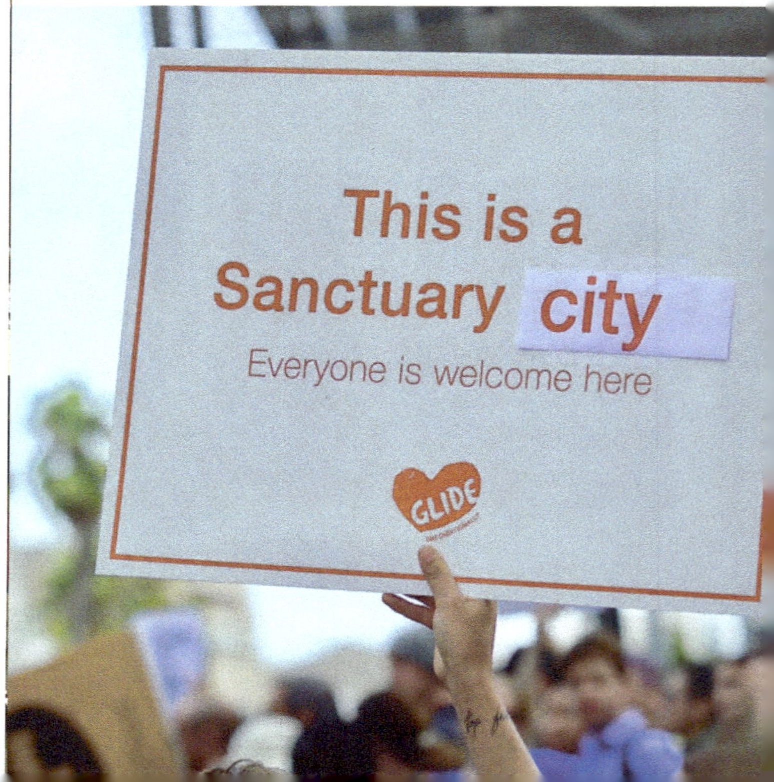

This is a
Sanctuary city
Everyone is welcome here
GLIDE

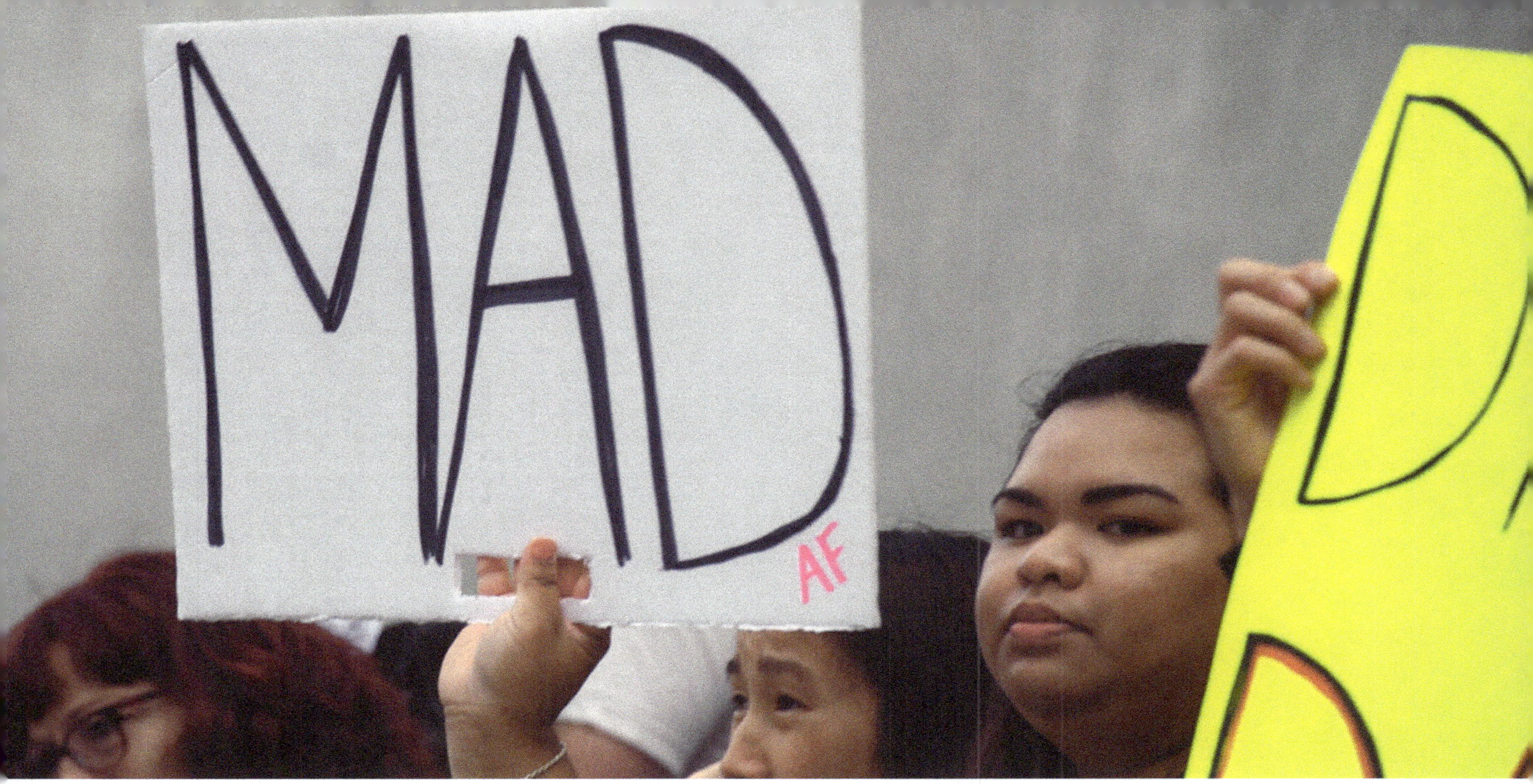

MAD
AF

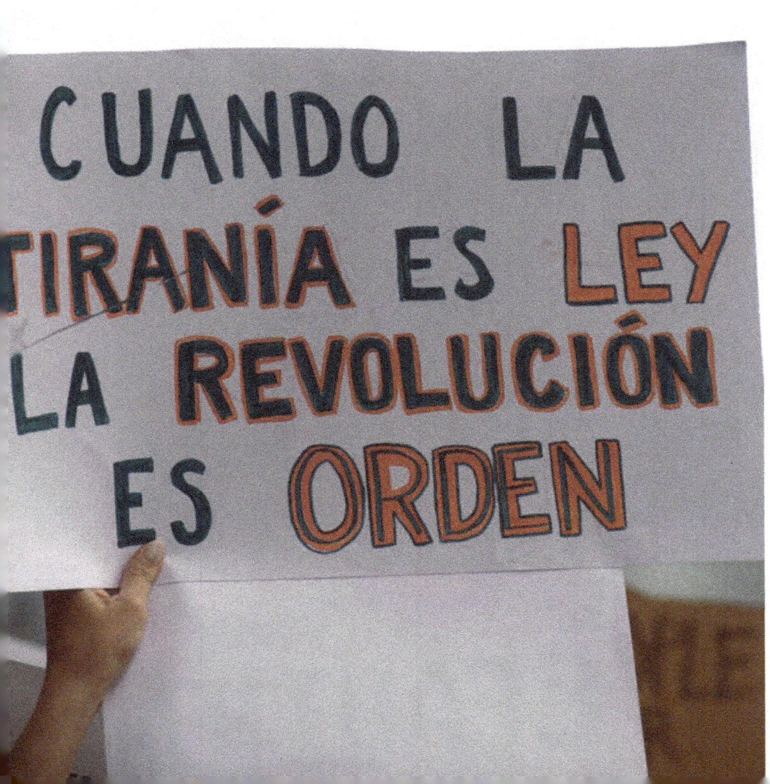

CUANDO LA
TIRANÍA ES LEY
LA REVOLUCIÓN
ES ORDEN

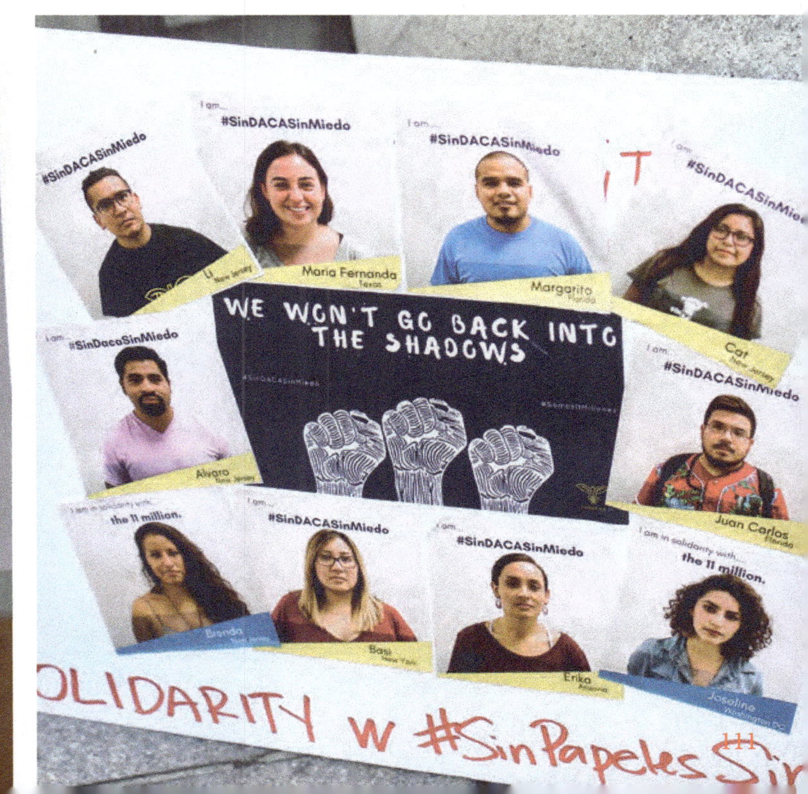

#SinDACASinMiedo
#SinDACASinMiedo
#SinDACASinMiedo
#SinDACASinMiedo
#SinDacaSinMiedo
#SinDACASinMiedo
Maria Fernanda
Texas
Margarito
Florida
Cat
New Jersey
Alvaro
New Jersey
Juan Carlos
Florida
the 11 million.
#SinDACASinMiedo
the 11 million.
Brenda
Baja
New York
Erika
Arizona
Josefina
WE WON'T GO BACK INTO
THE SHADOWS
SOLIDARITY W #SinPapeles Sin

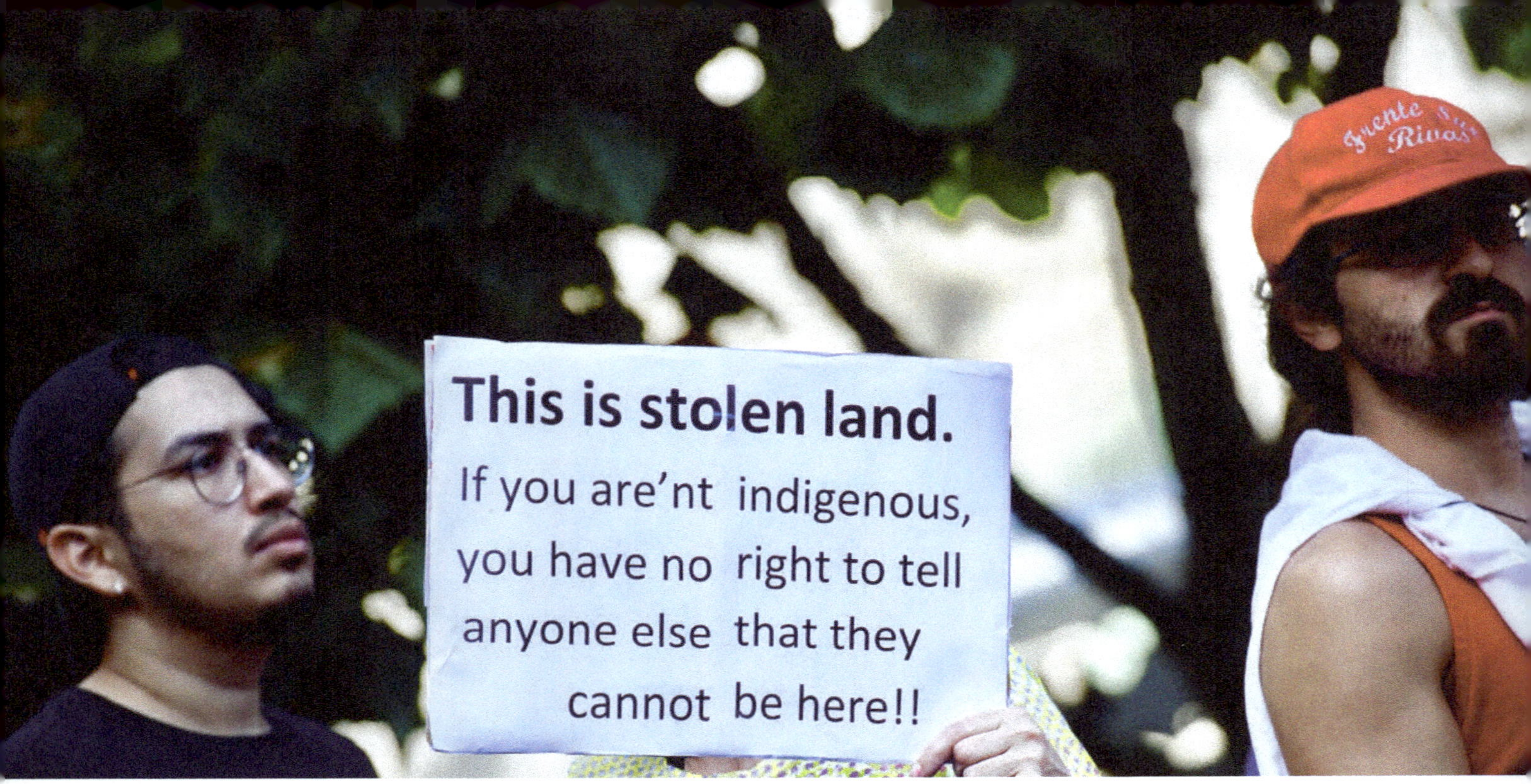

This is stolen land.
If you are'nt indigenous,
you have no right to tell
anyone else that they
cannot be here!!

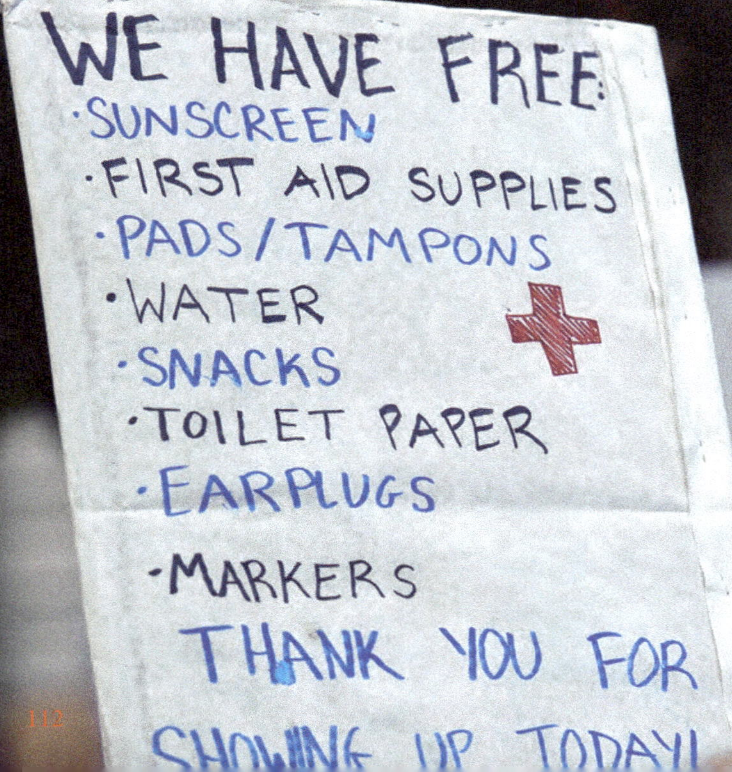

WE HAVE FREE:
·SUNSCREEN
·FIRST AID SUPPLIES
·PADS/TAMPONS
·WATER
·SNACKS
·TOILET PAPER
·EARPLUGS
·MARKERS
THANK YOU FOR
SHOWING UP TODAY!

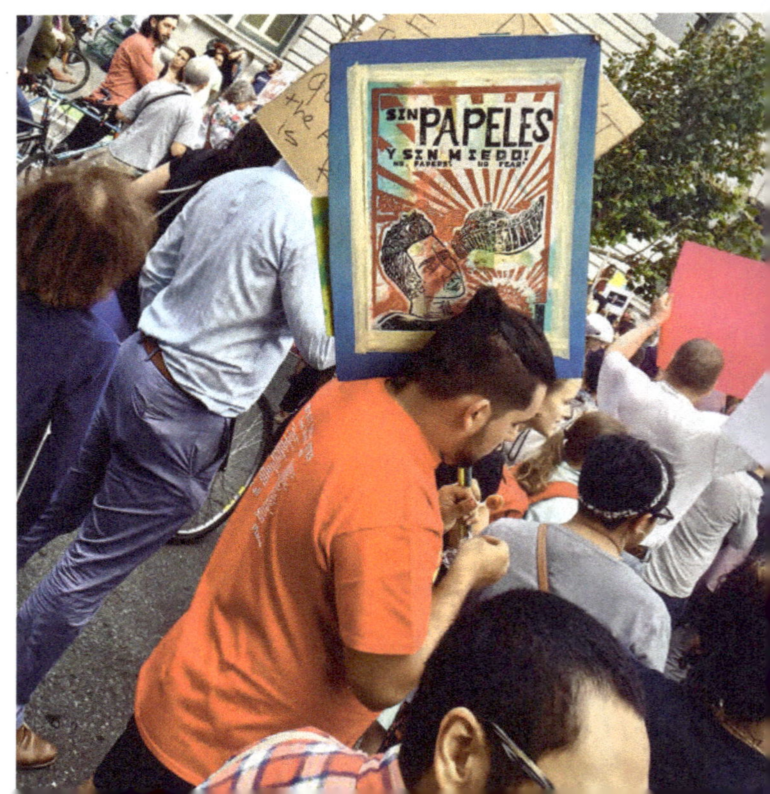

SIN PAPELES
Y SIN MIEDO!

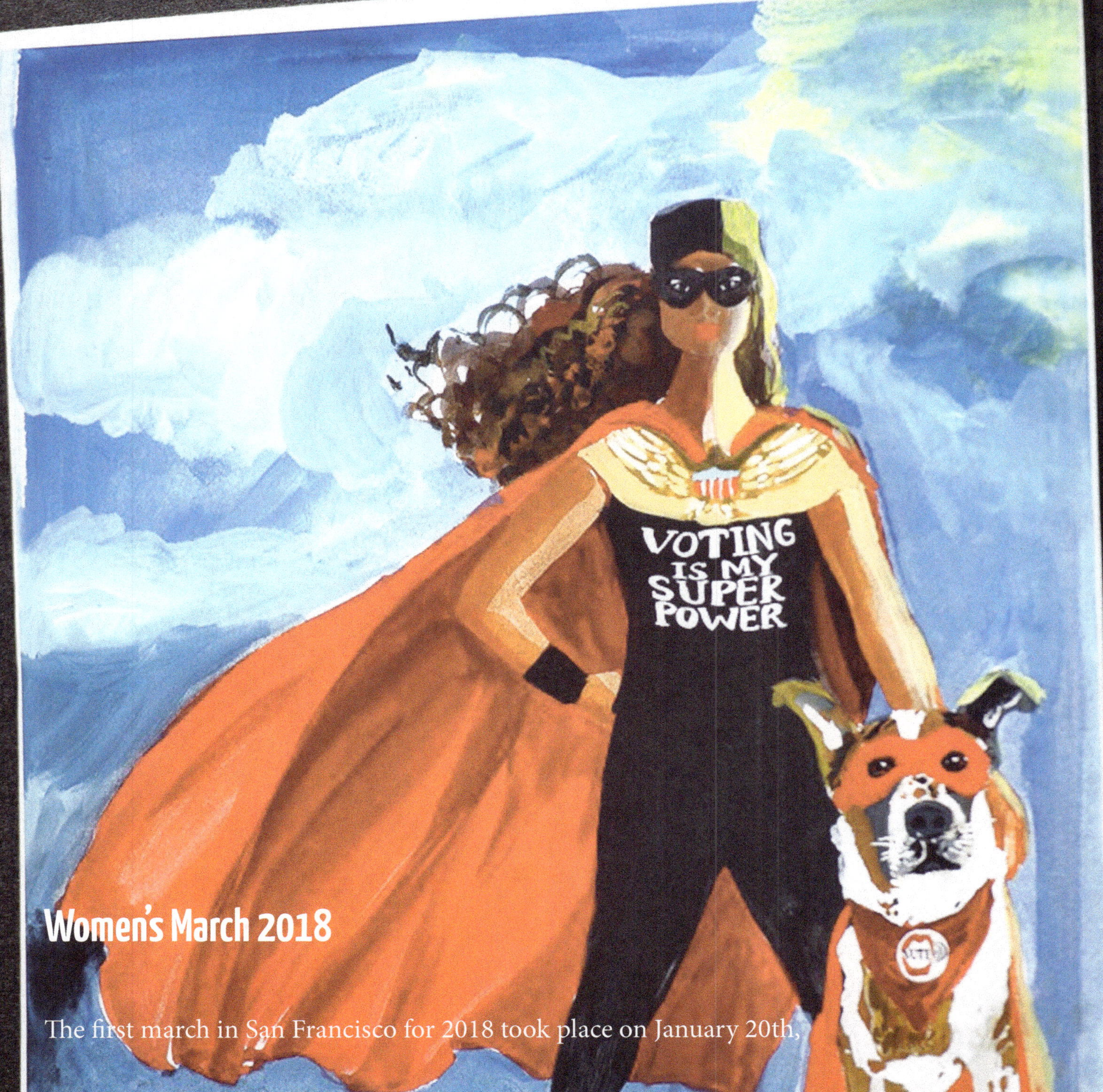

Women's March 2018

The first march in San Francisco for 2018 took place on January 20th,

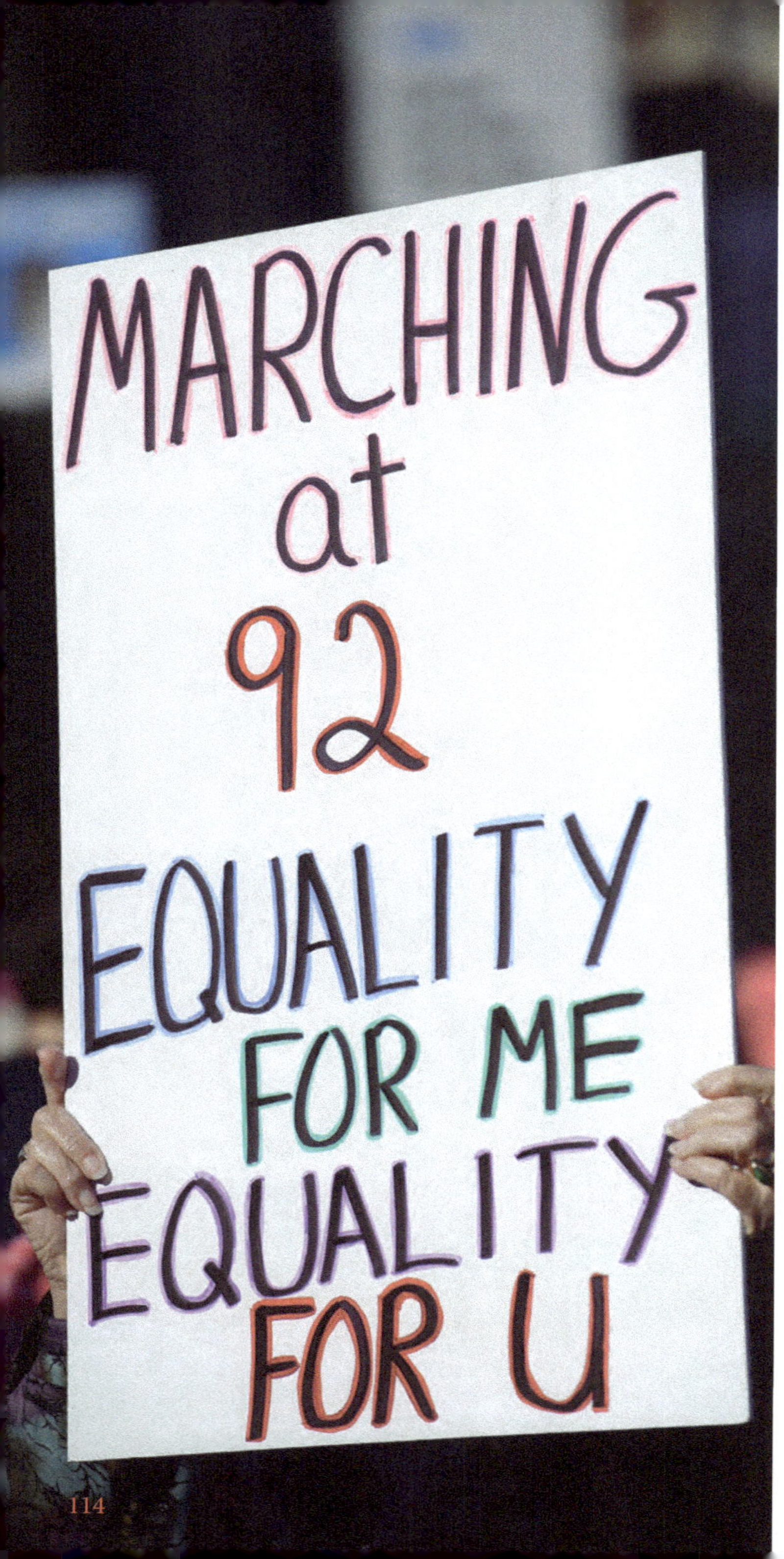

MARCHING
at
92
EQUALITY
FOR ME
EQUALITY
FOR U

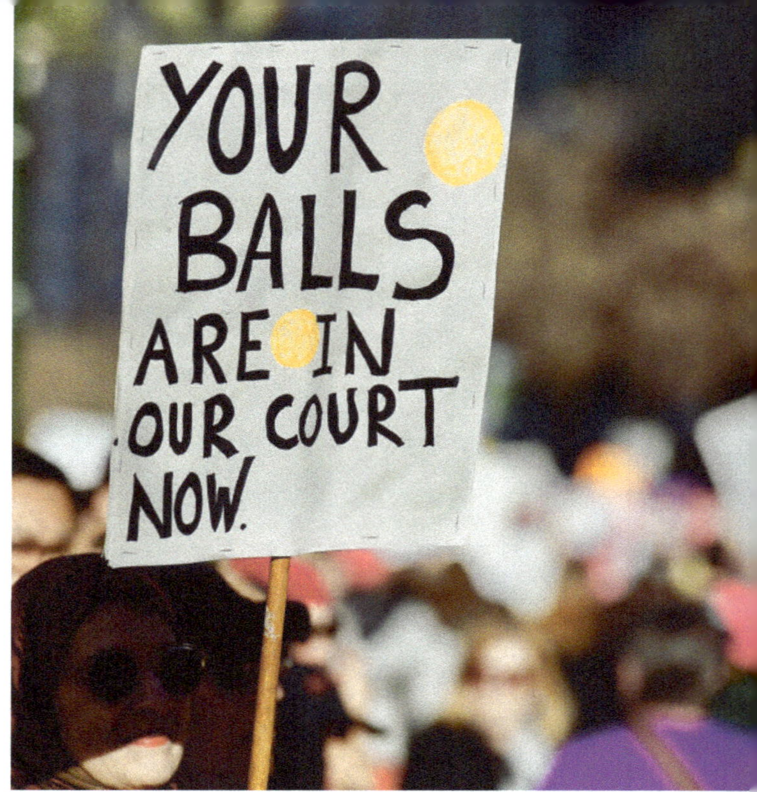
YOUR
BALLS
ARE IN
OUR COURT
NOW.

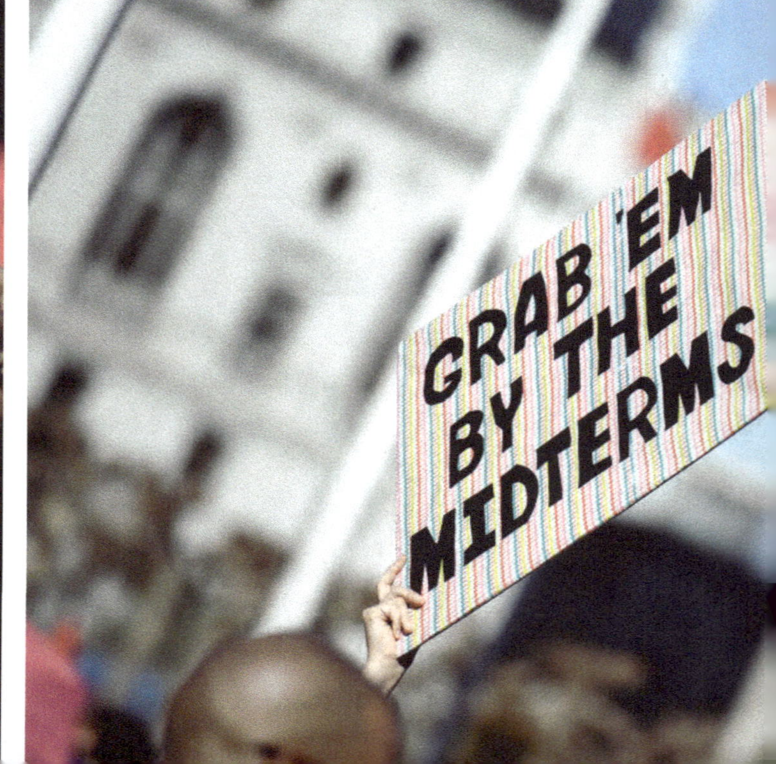
GRAB 'EM
BY THE
MIDTERMS

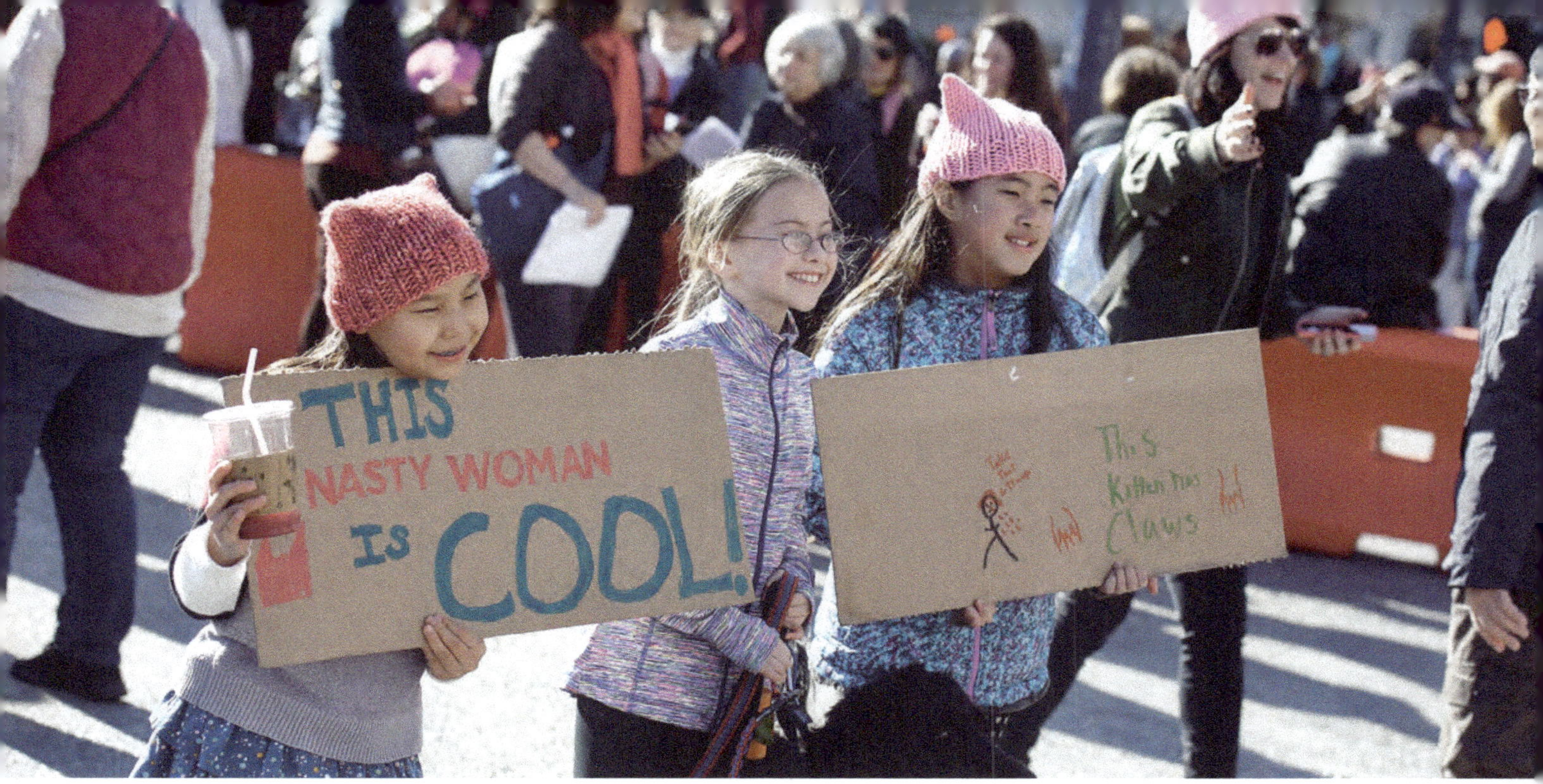

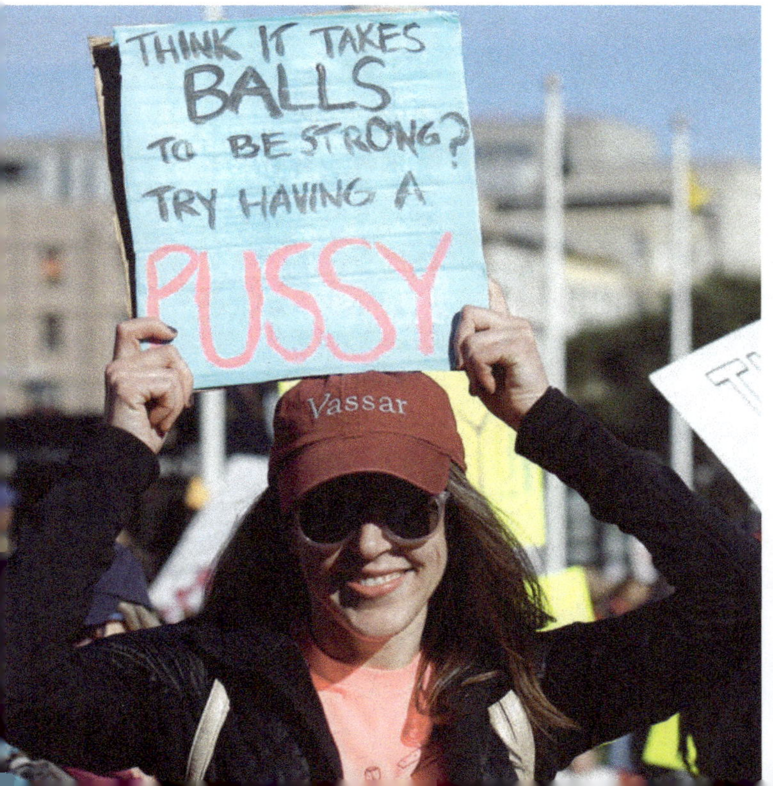
THINK IT TAKES
BALLS
TO BE STRONG?
TRY HAVING A
PUSSY
Vassar

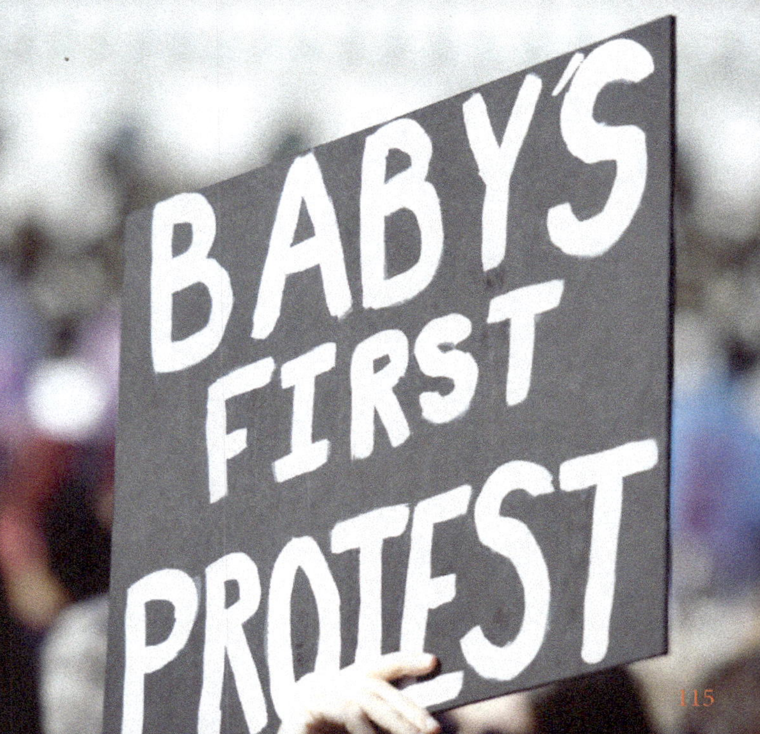
BABY'S
FIRST
PROTEST

THIS
NASTY WOMAN
IS COOL!

This
Kitten has
Claws

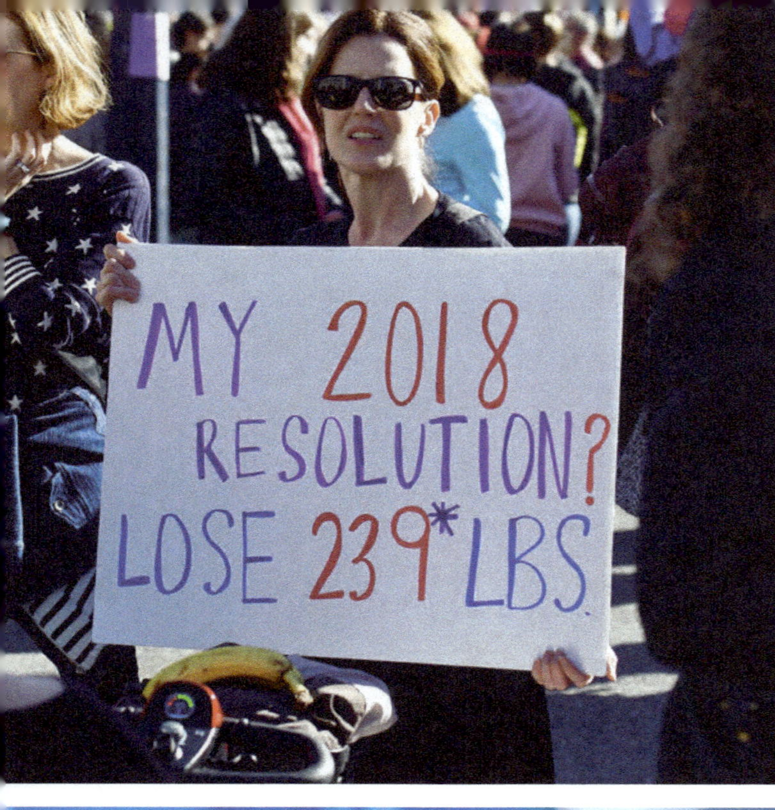
MY 2018 RESOLUTION?
LOSE 239* LBS.

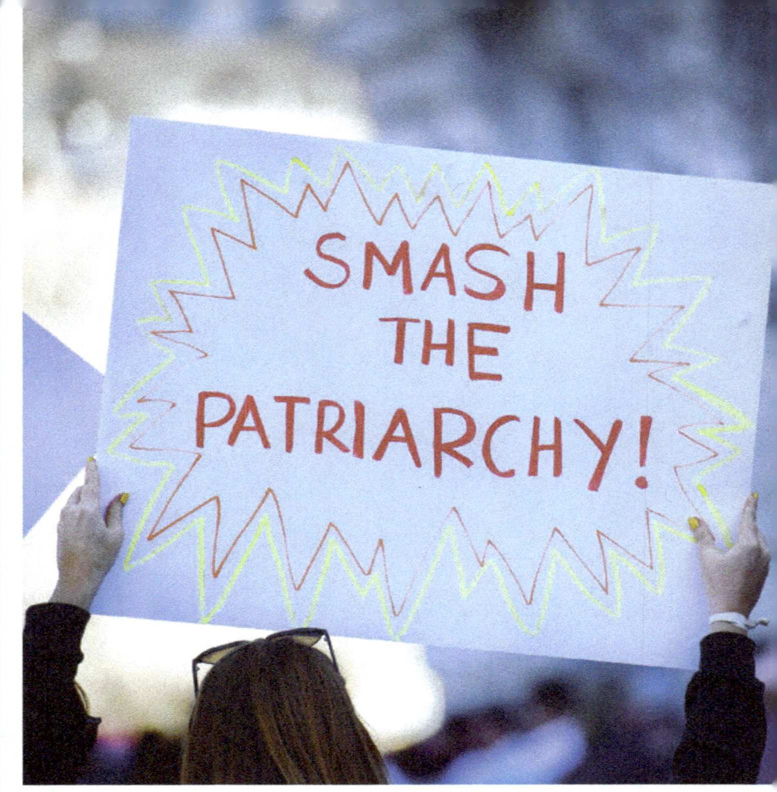
SMASH THE PATRIARCHY!

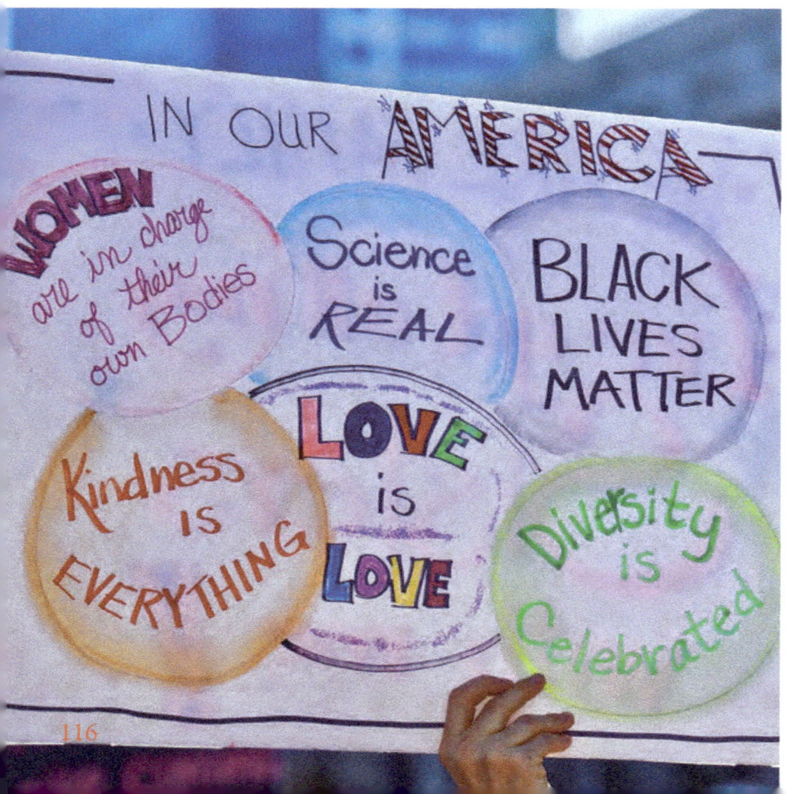
IN OUR AMERICA
WOMEN are in charge of their own Bodies
Science is REAL
BLACK LIVES MATTER
Kindness IS EVERYTHING
LOVE is LOVE
Diversity is Celebrated

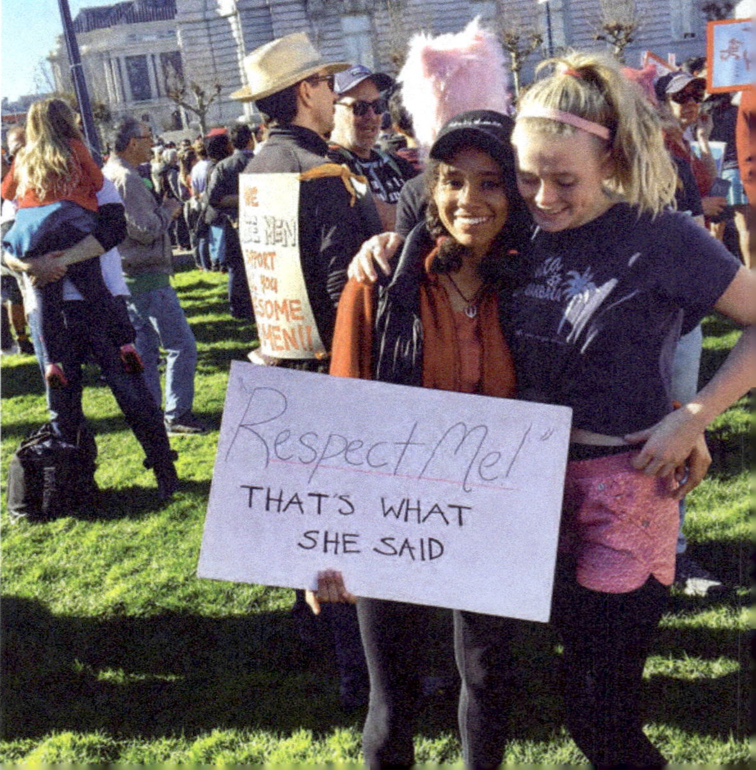
"Respect Me!"
THAT'S WHAT SHE SAID

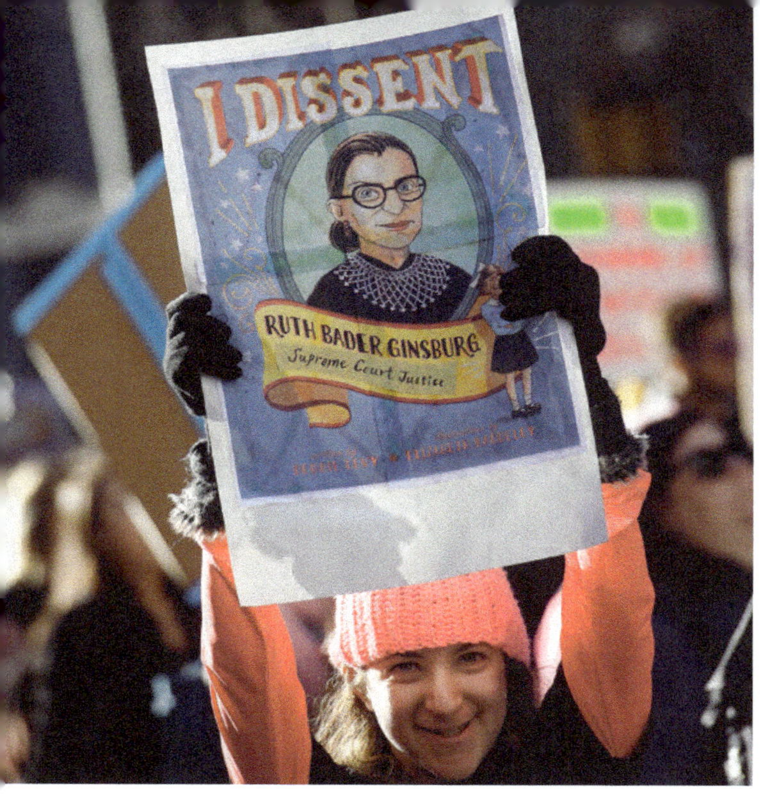
I DISSENT
RUTH BADER GINSBURG
Supreme Court Justice

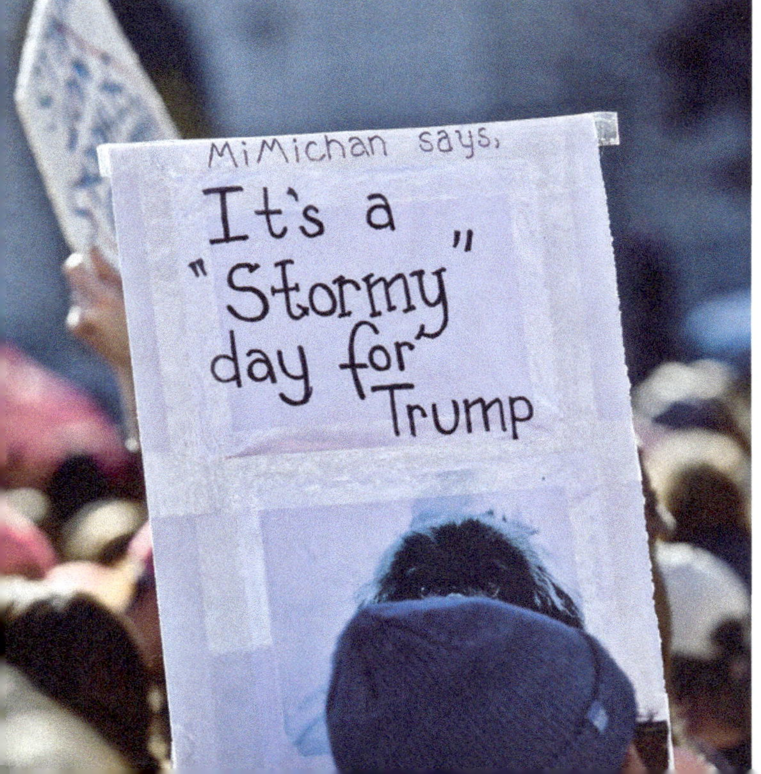
MiMichan says,
It's a "Stormy" day for Trump

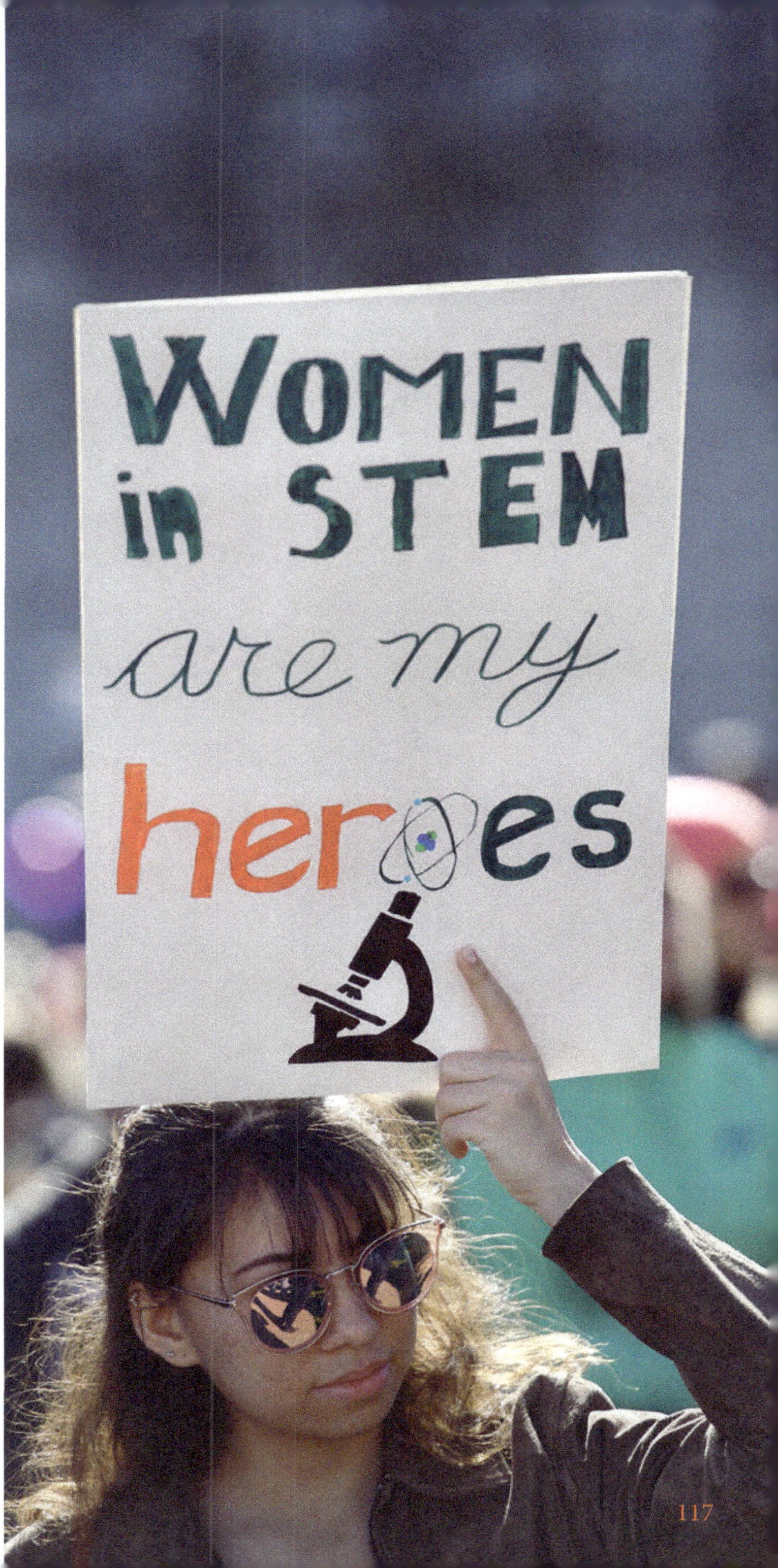

WOMEN in STEM are my heroes

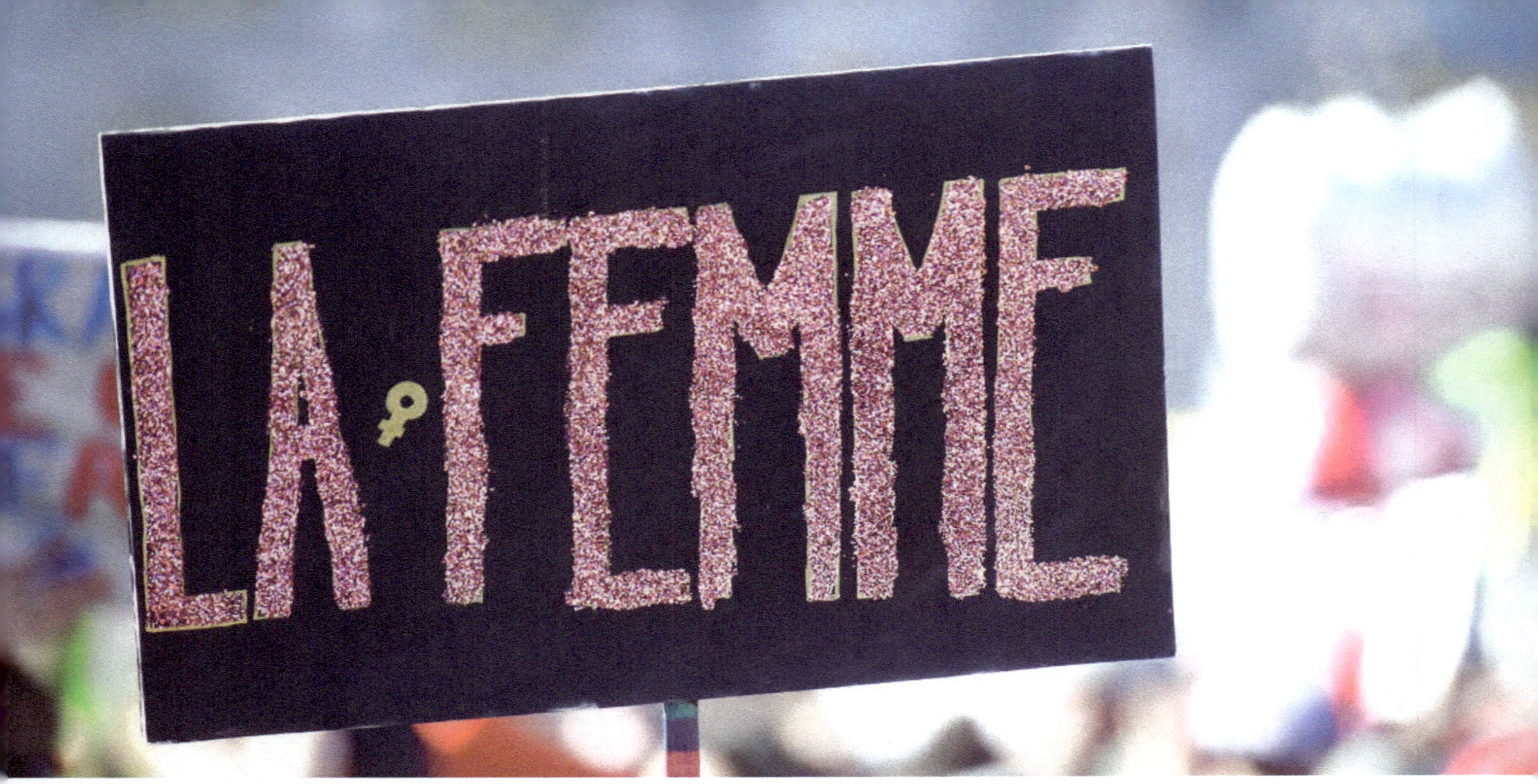

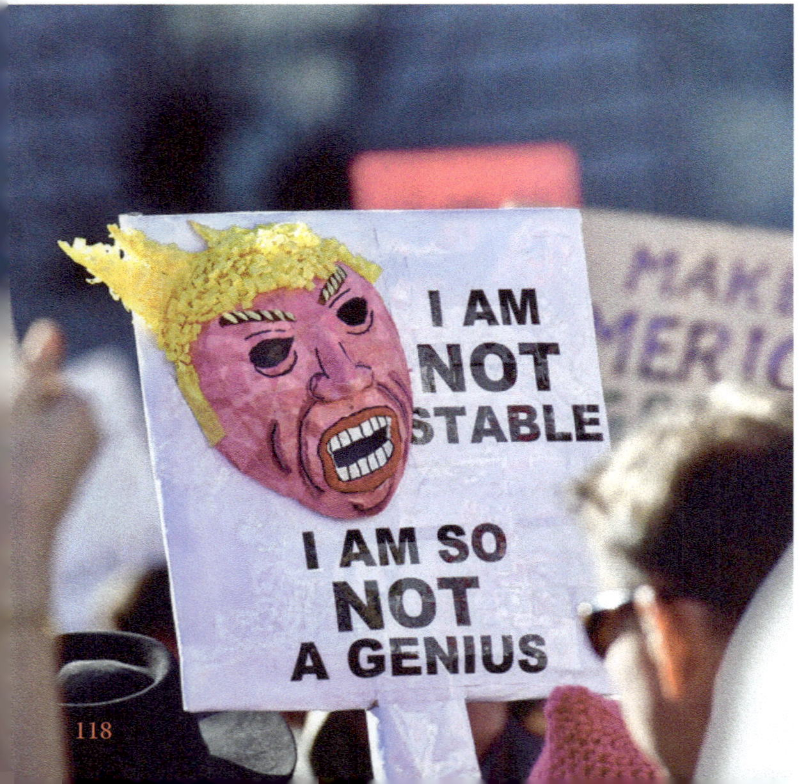
I AM
NOT
STABLE
I AM SO
NOT
A GENIUS

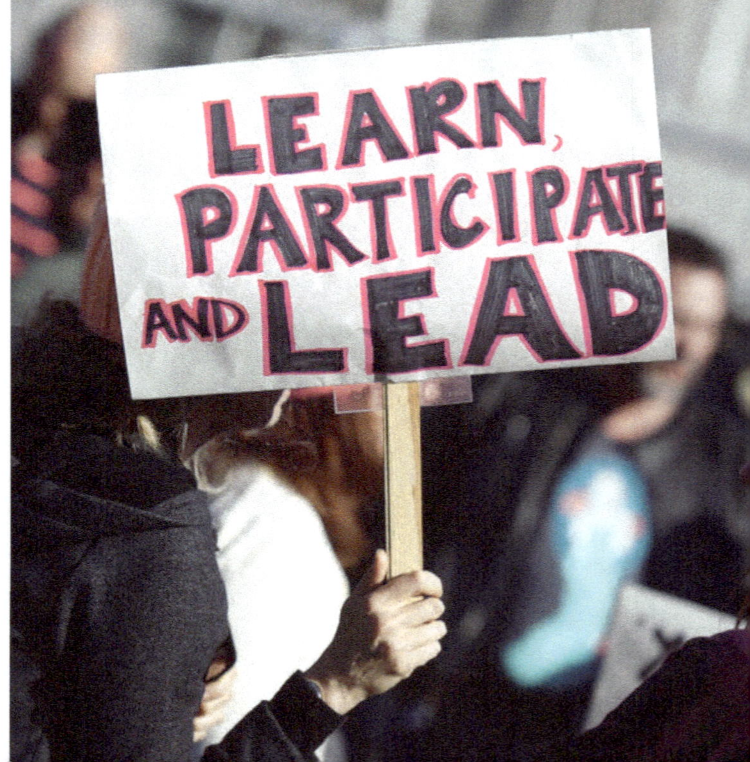
LEARN,
PARTICIPATE
AND LEAD

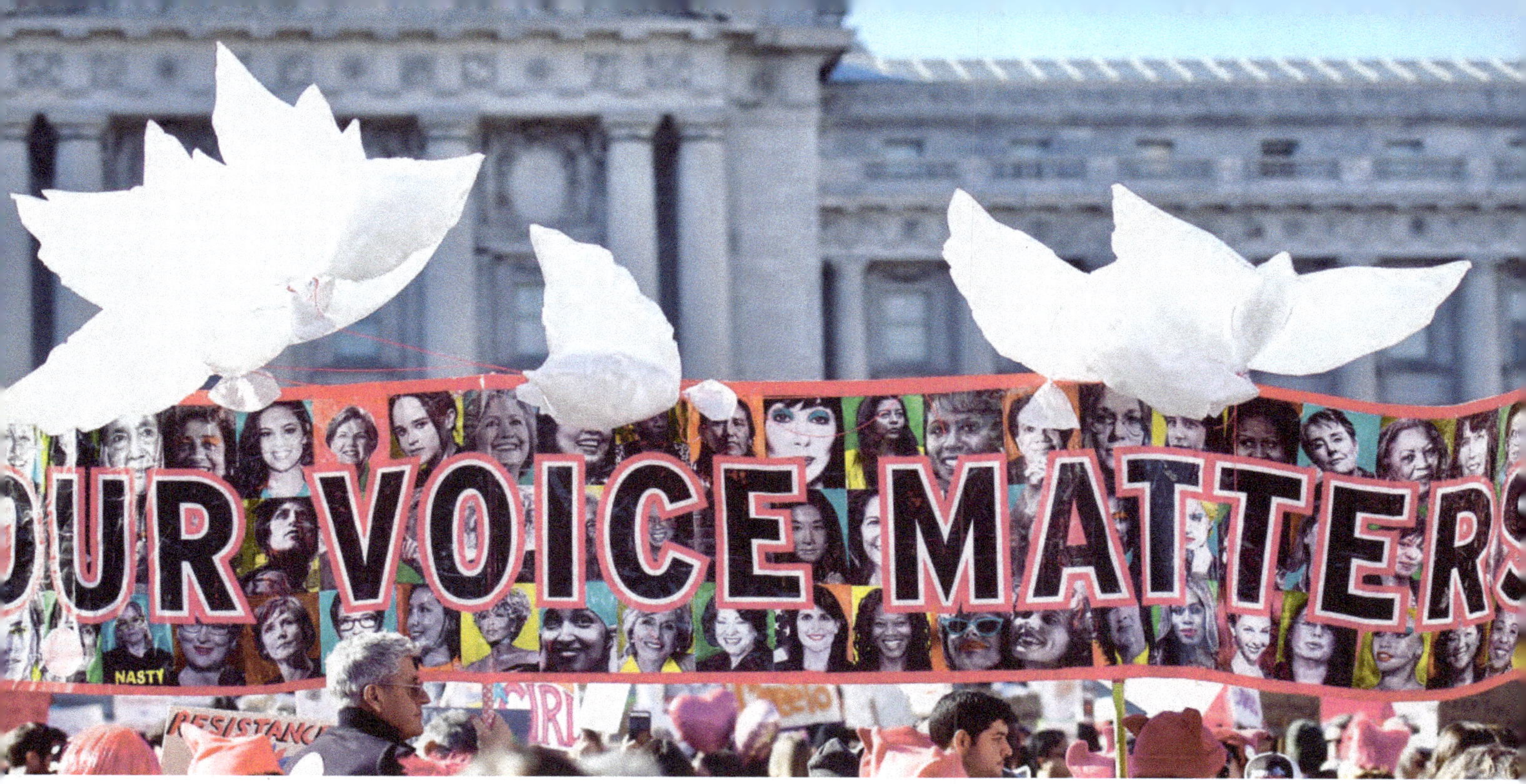

OUR VOICE MATTERS
NASTY
RESISTANCE

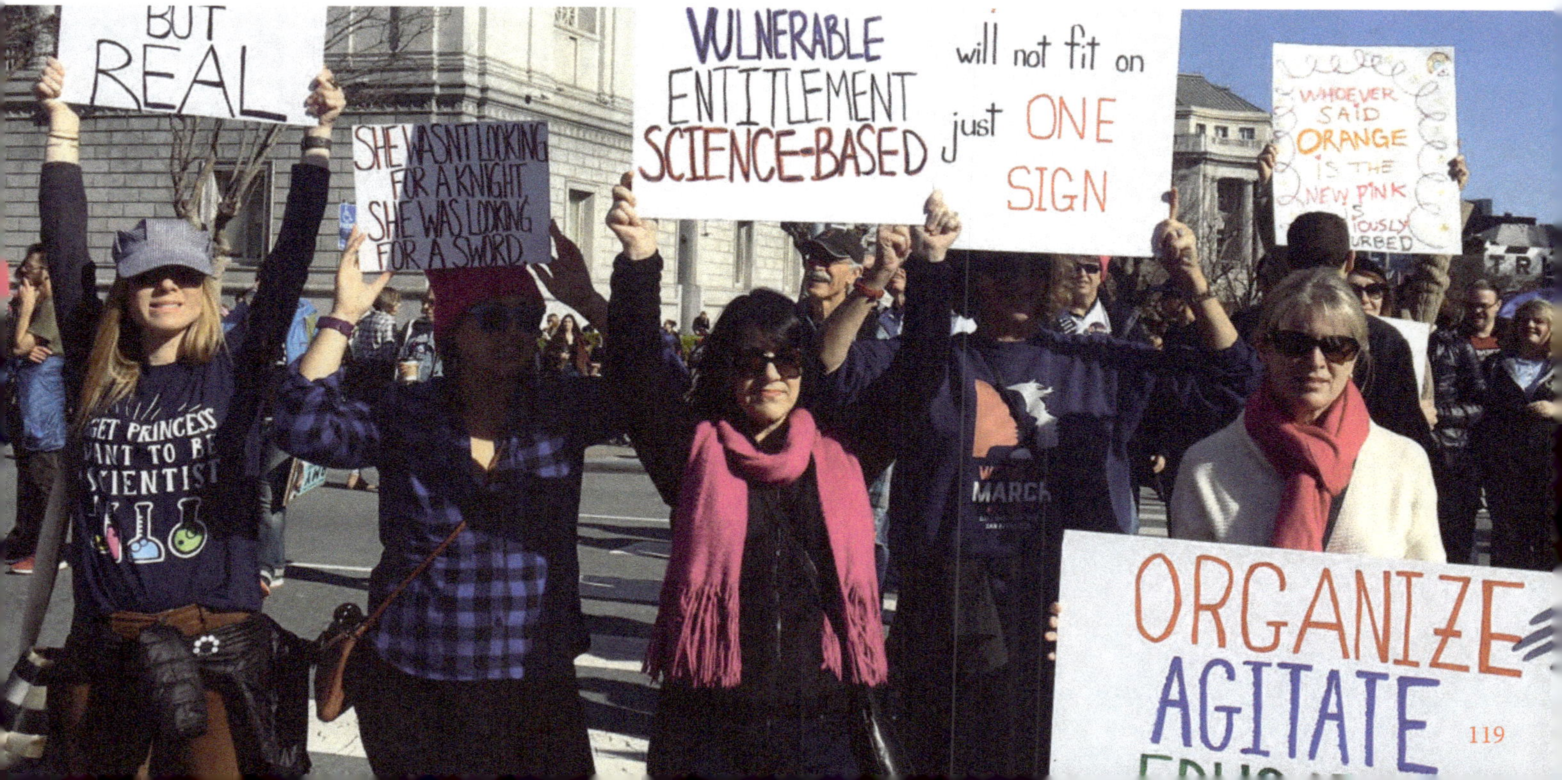

BUT REAL
SHE WASN'T LOOKING FOR A KNIGHT, SHE WAS LOOKING FOR A SWORD.
VULNERABLE ENTITLEMENT SCIENCE-BASED
will not fit on just ONE SIGN
WHOEVER SAID ORANGE IS THE NEW PINK
GET PRINCESS WANT TO BE SCIENTIST
MARCH
ORGANIZE AGITATE

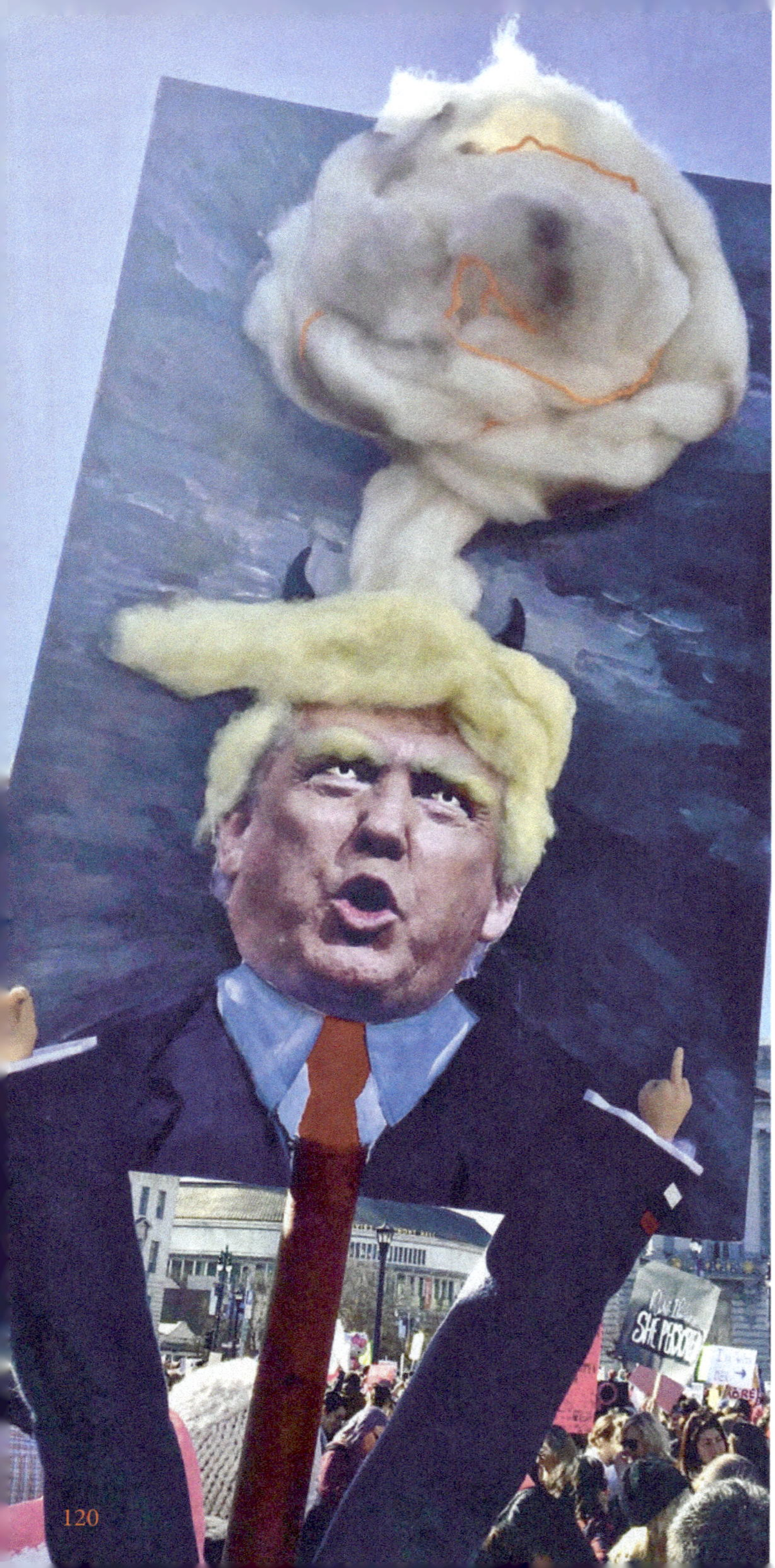

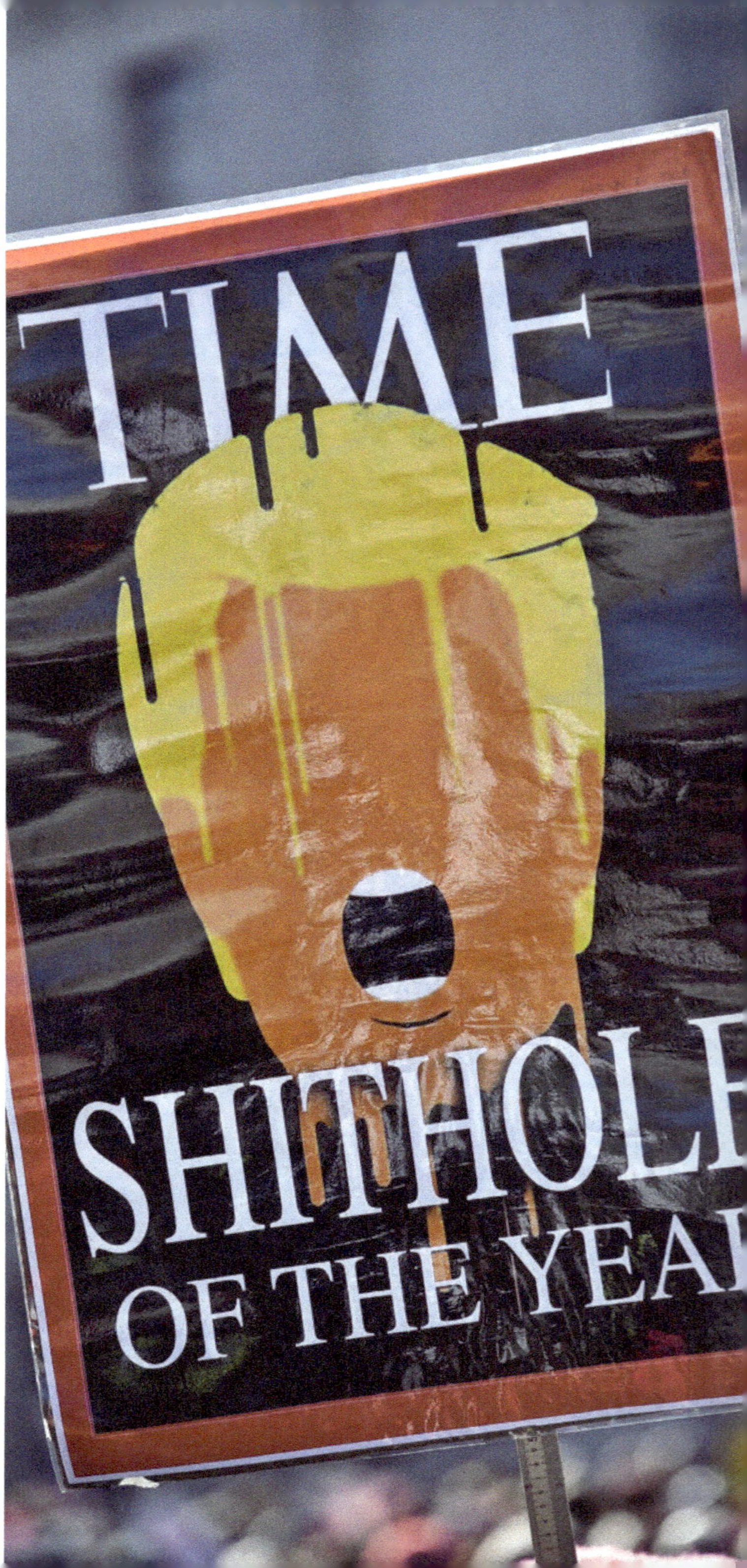

SHE PERSISTED

TIME
SHITHOLE
OF THE YEAR

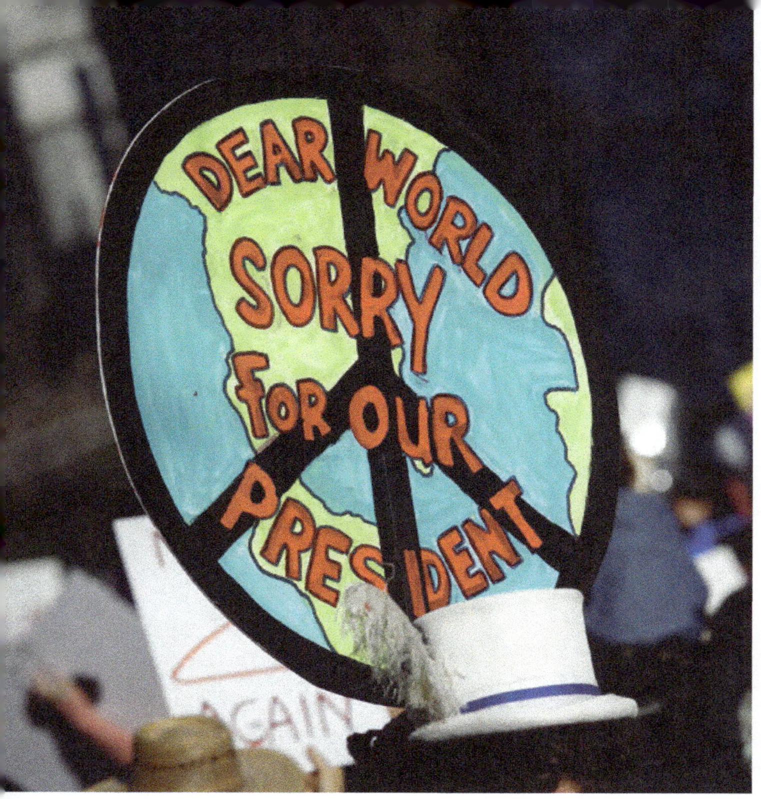

DEAR WORLD
SORRY
FOR OUR
PRESIDENT
AGAIN

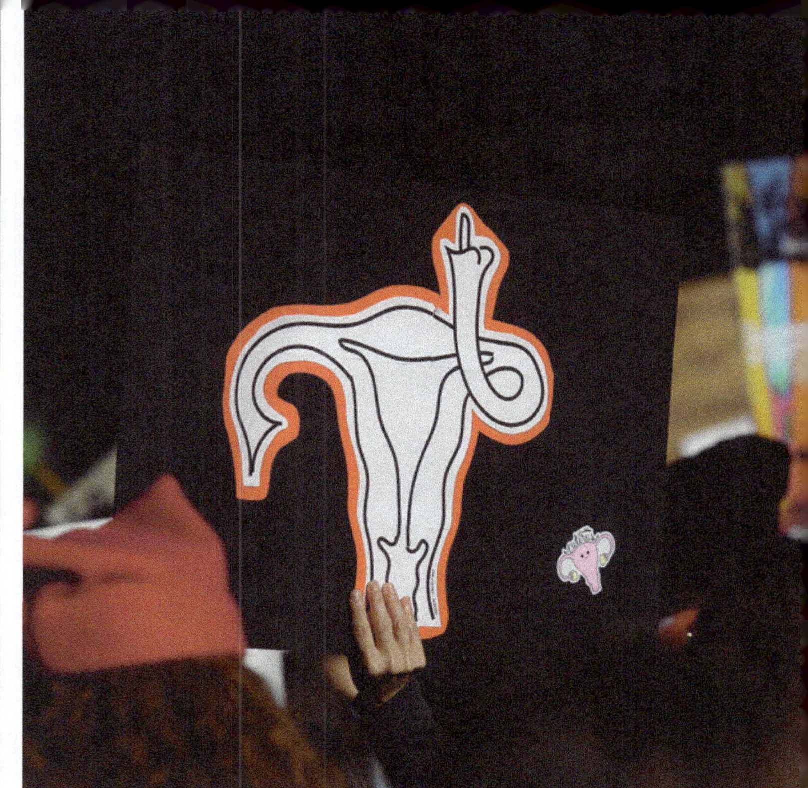

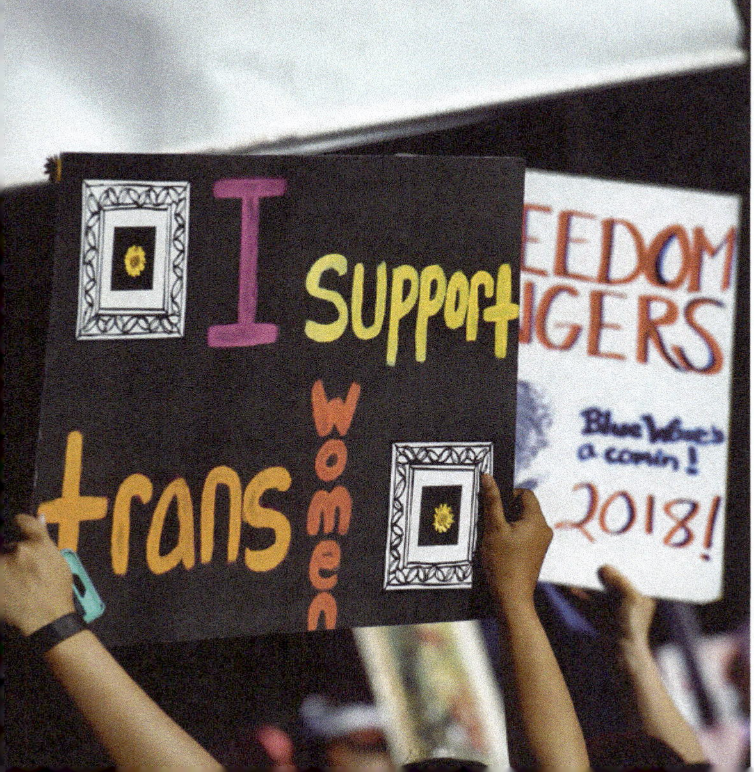

I support
trans women
EEDOM
IGERS
Blue Wave's
a comin!
2018!

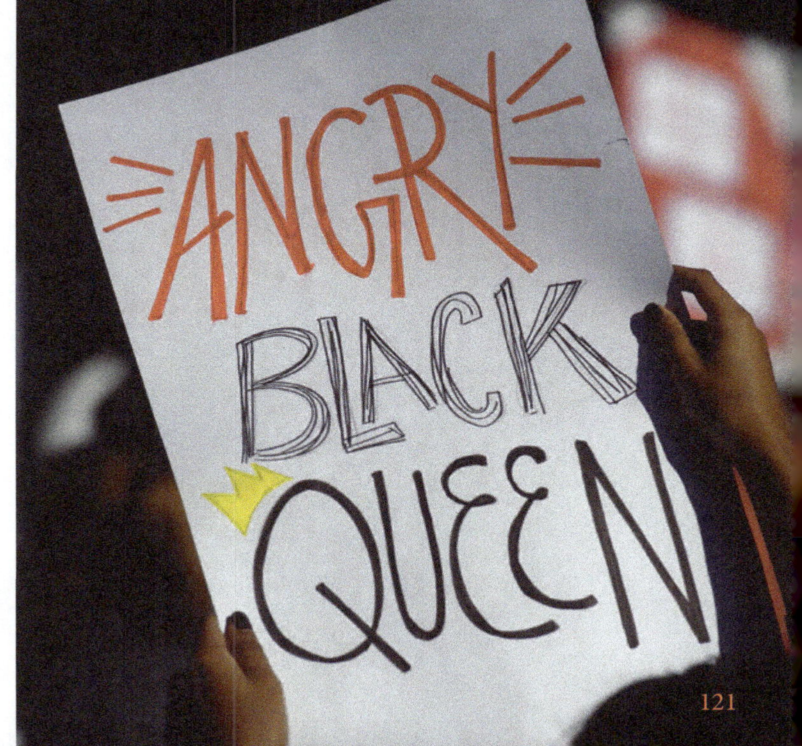

ANGRY
BLACK
QUEEN

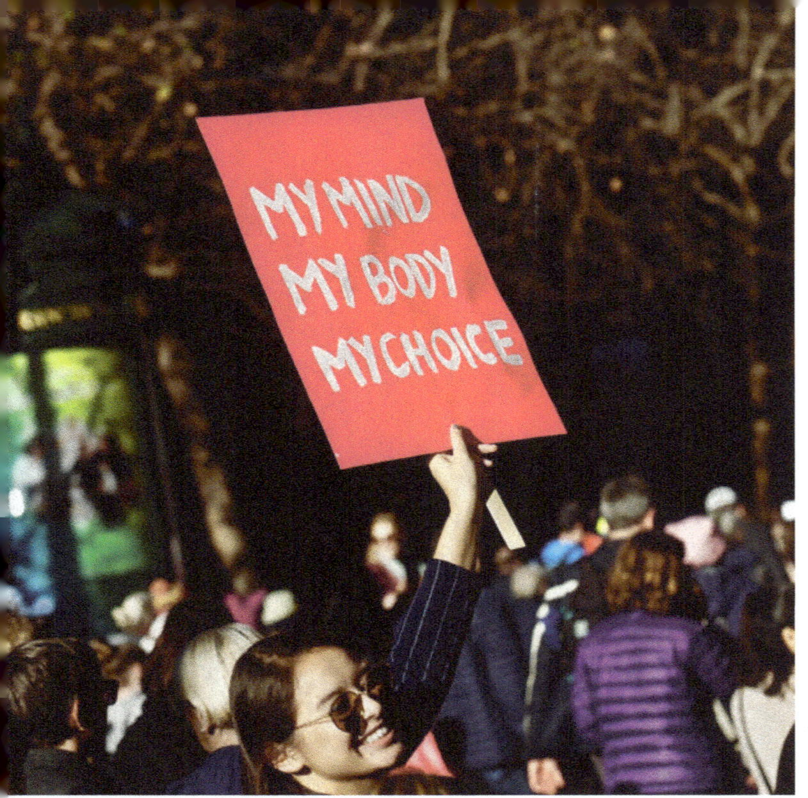
MY MIND
MY BODY
MY CHOICE

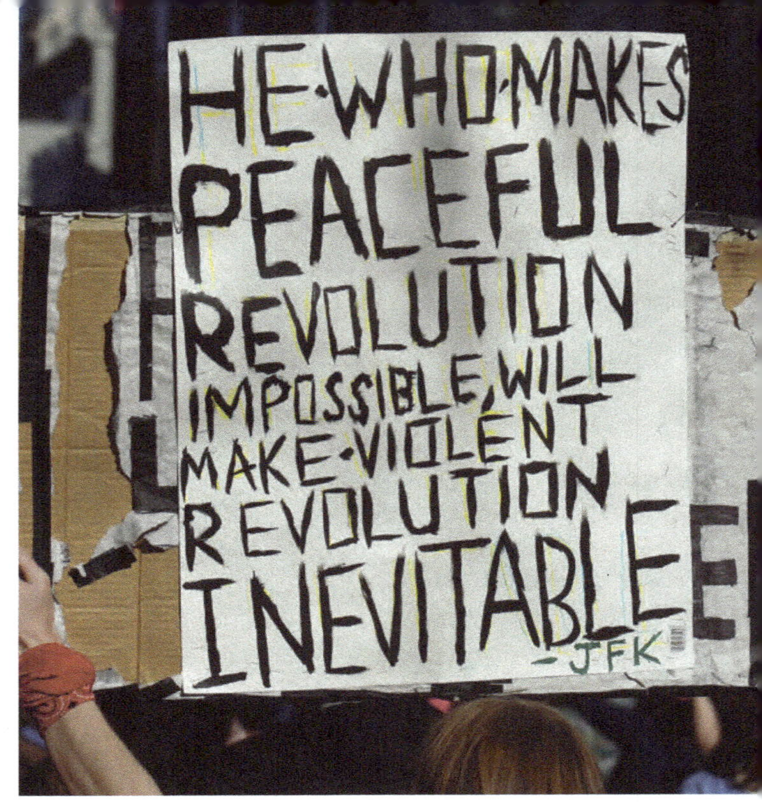
HE·WHO·MAKES
PEACEFUL
REVOLUTION
IMPOSSIBLE, WILL
MAKE·VIOLENT
REVOLUTION
INEVITABLE
-JFK

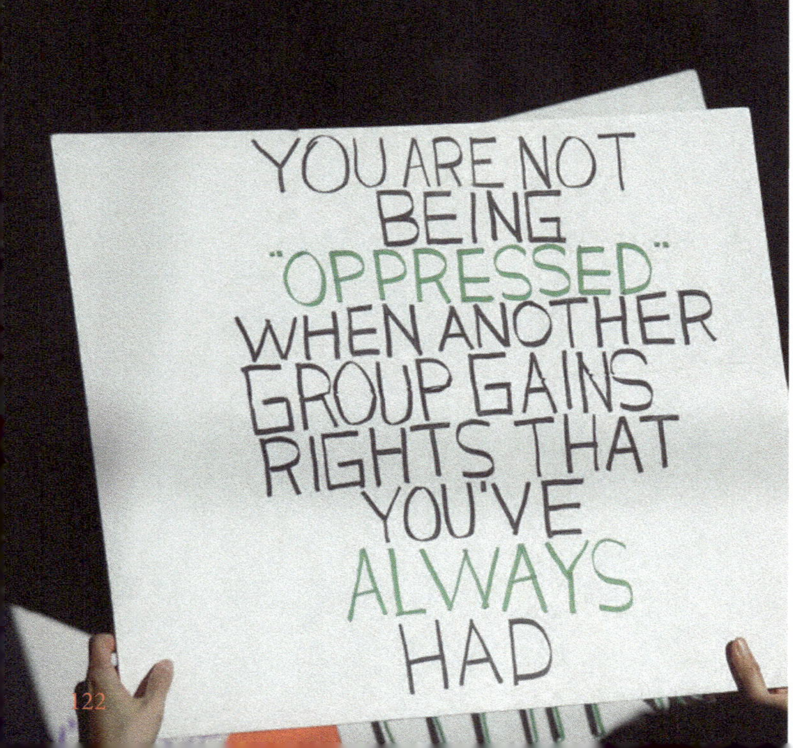
YOU ARE NOT
BEING
"OPPRESSED"
WHEN ANOTHER
GROUP GAINS
RIGHTS THAT
YOU'VE
ALWAYS
HAD

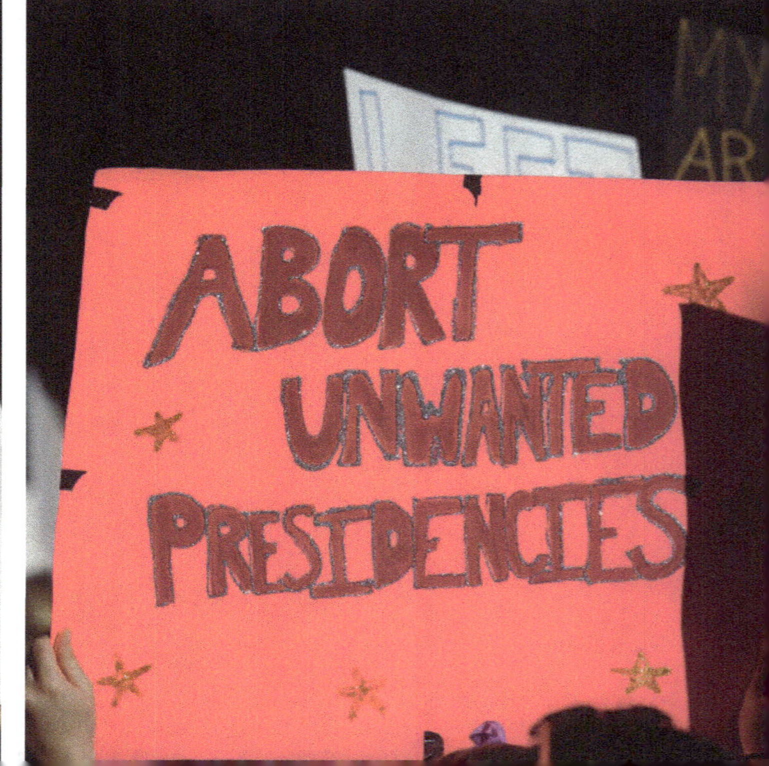
ABORT
UNWANTED
PRESIDENCIES

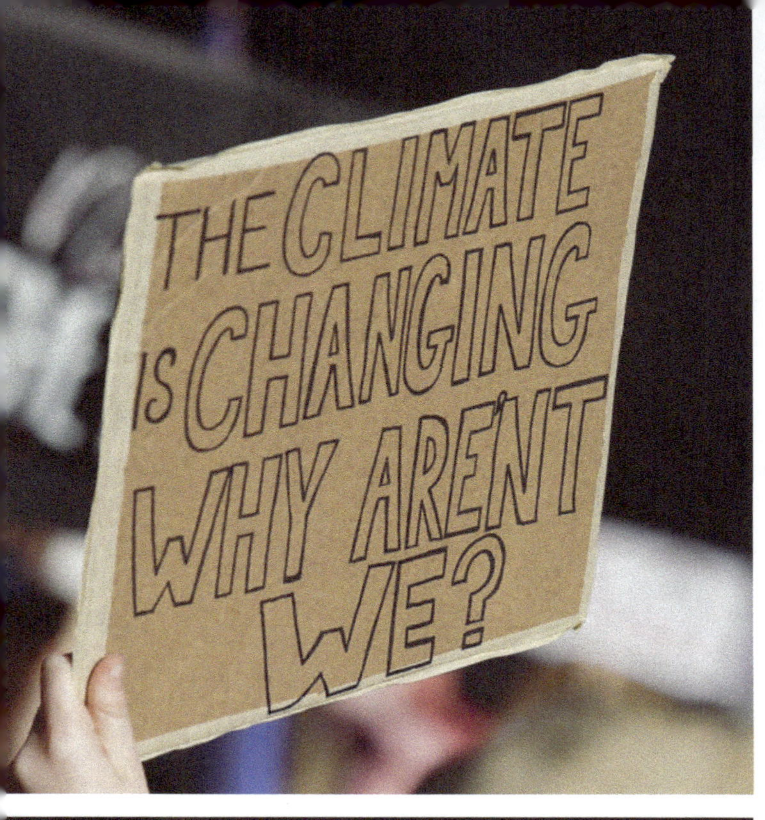

THE CLIMATE IS CHANGING WHY ARE'NT WE?

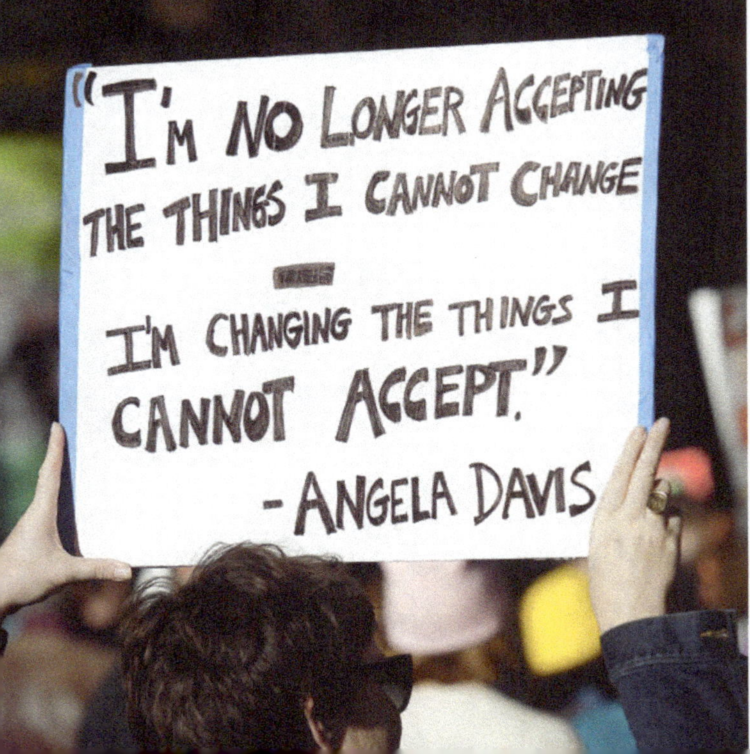

"I'M NO LONGER ACCEPTING
THE THINGS I CANNOT CHANGE
I'M CHANGING THE THINGS I
CANNOT ACCEPT."
- ANGELA DAVIS

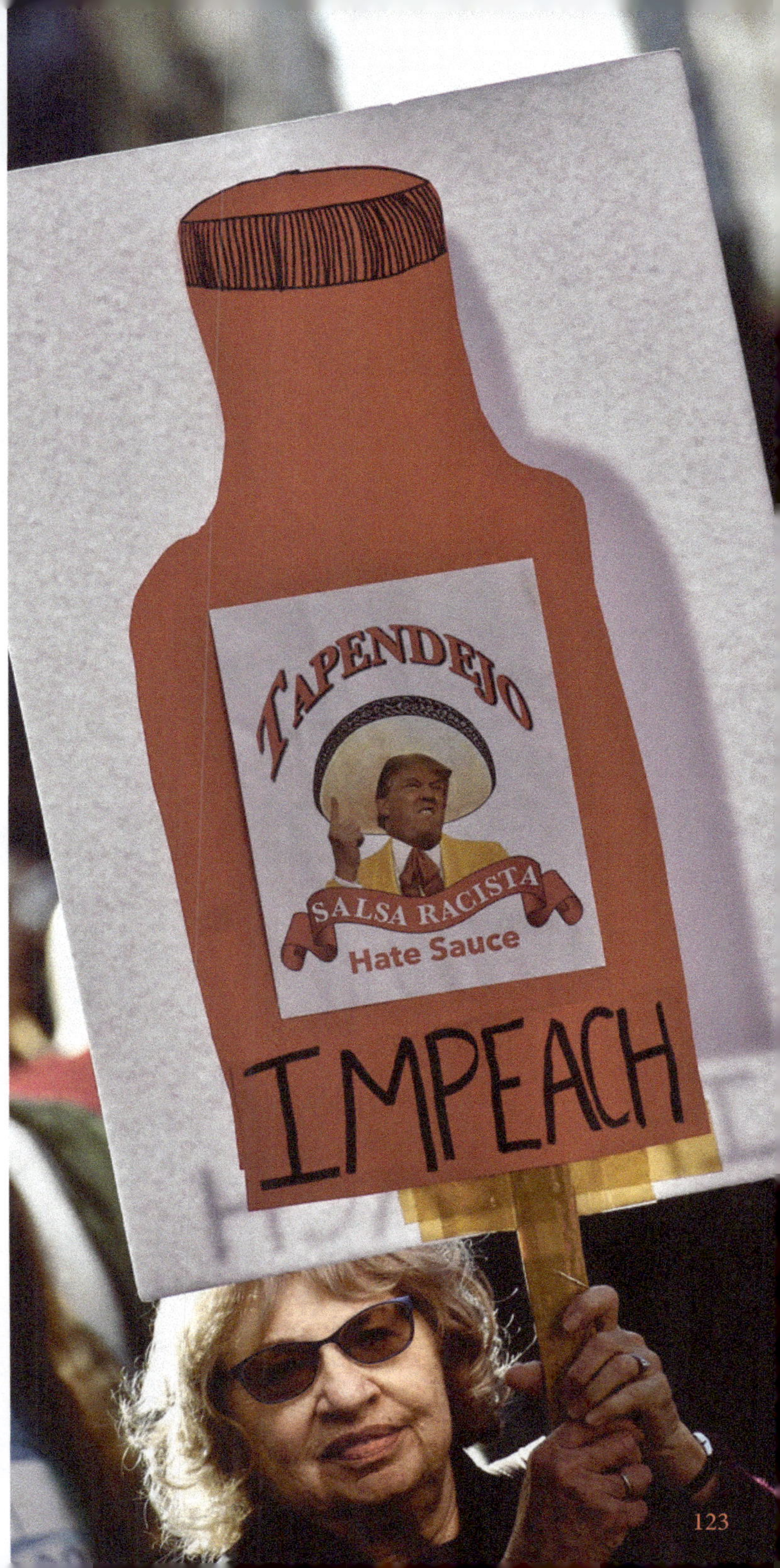

TAPENDEJO
SALSA RACISTA
Hate Sauce
IMPEACH

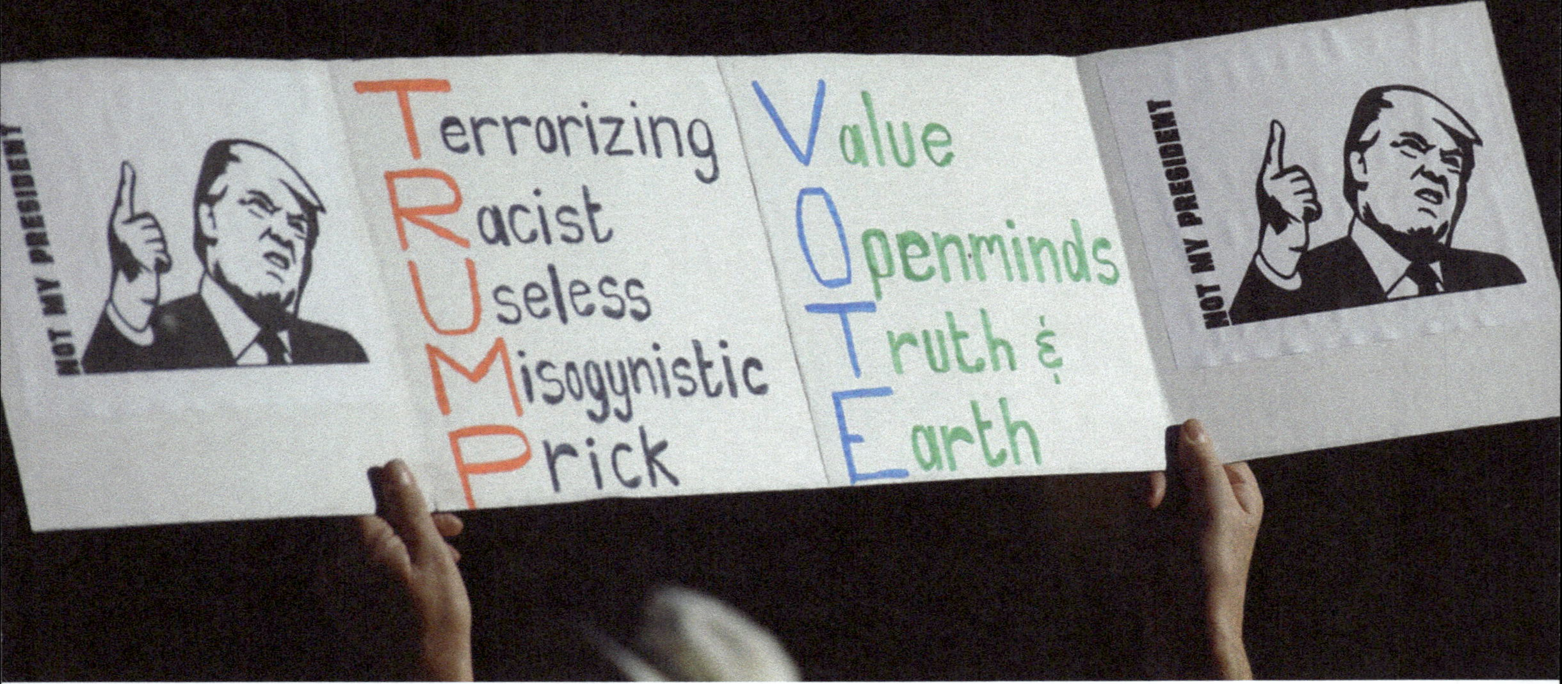

NOT MY PRESIDENT
Terrorizing
Racist
Useless
Misogynistic
Prick
Value
Openminds
Truth &
Earth
NOT MY PRESIDENT

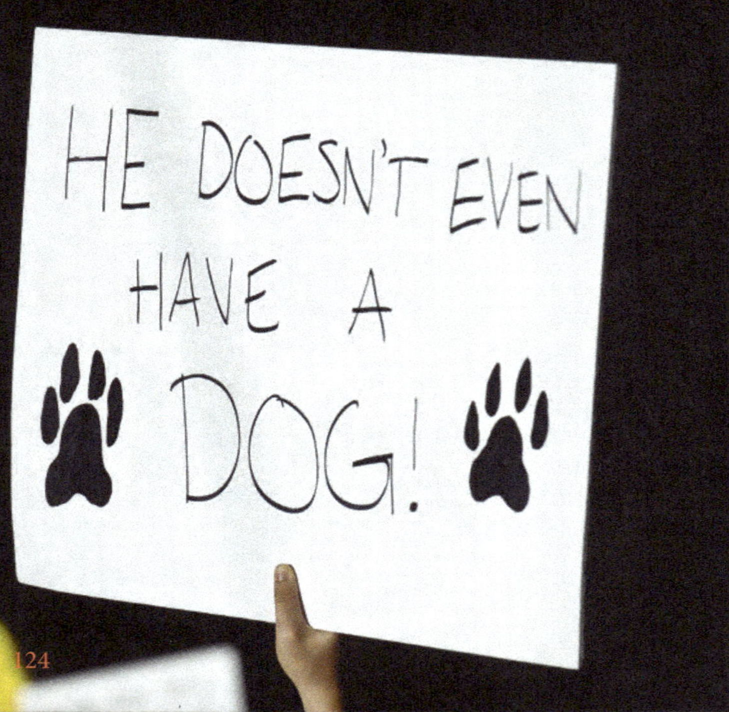

HE DOESN'T EVEN HAVE A DOG!

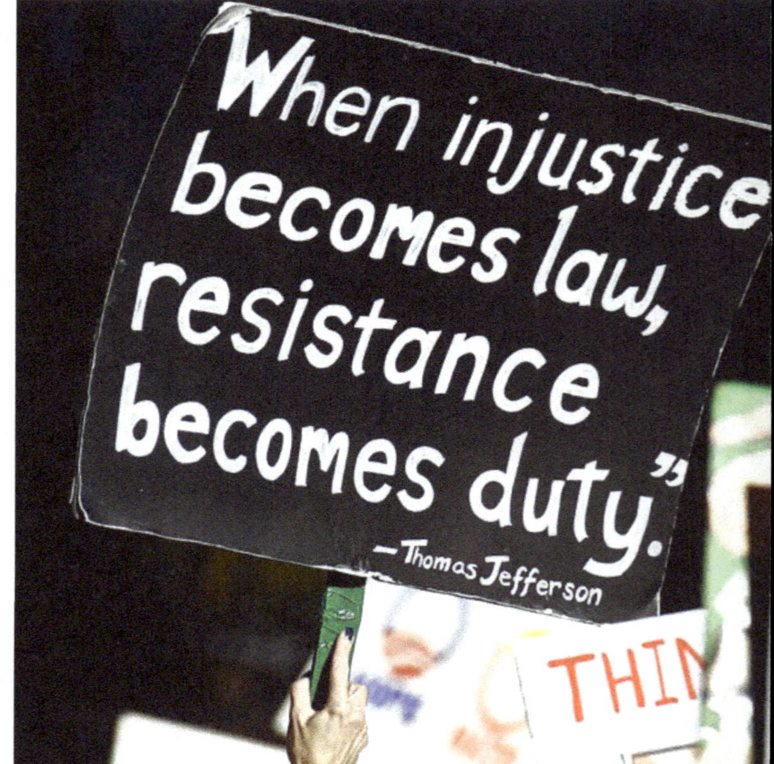

When injustice becomes law, resistance becomes duty."
-Thomas Jefferson
THIN

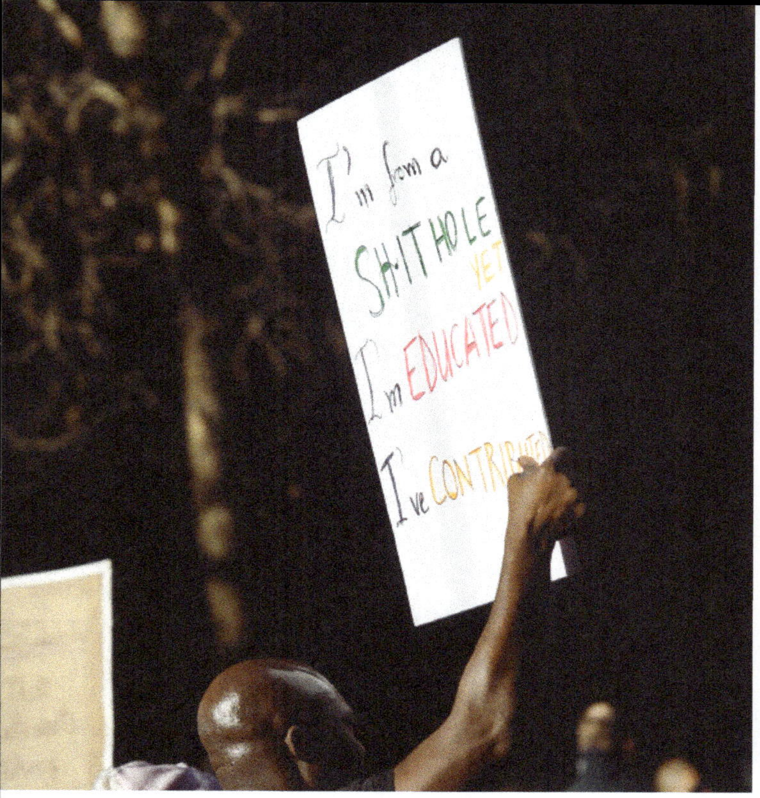

I'm from a
SHITHOLE
YET
I'm EDUCATED
I've CONTRIBUTED

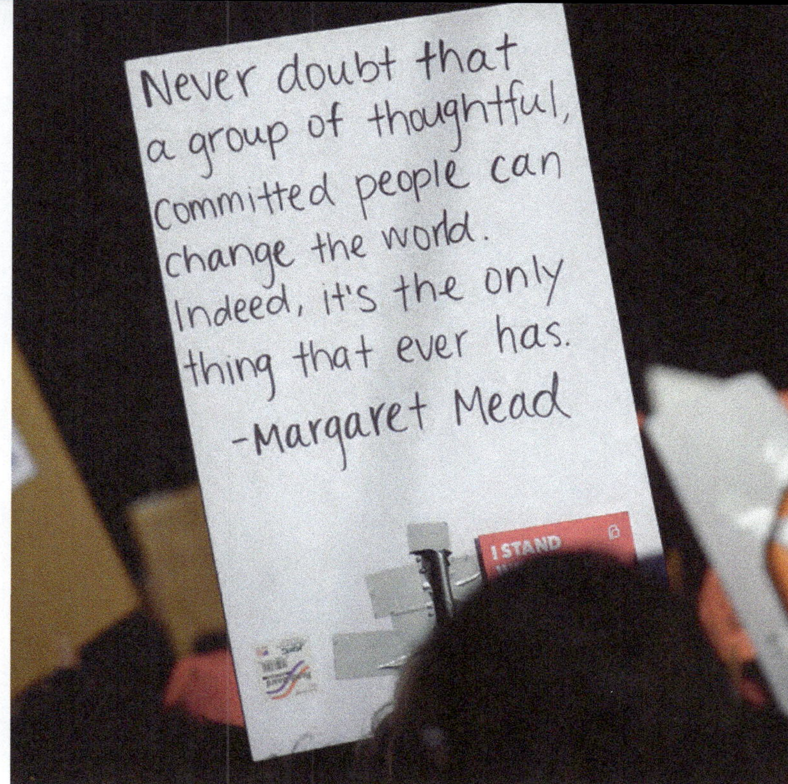

Never doubt that
a group of thoughtful,
committed people can
change the world.
Indeed, it's the only
thing that ever has.
-Margaret Mead
I STAND

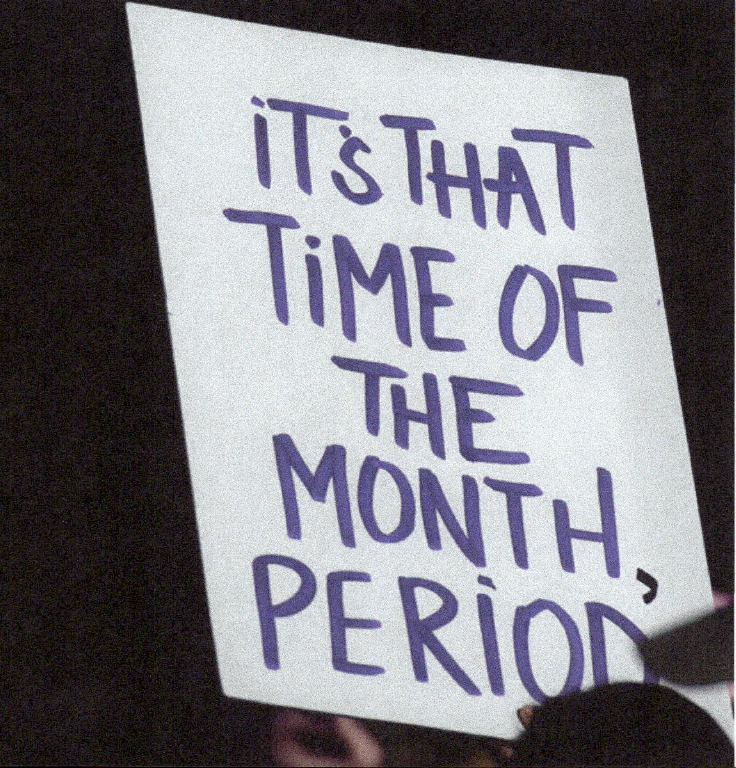

iTS THAT
TiME OF
THE
MONTH,
PERIOD

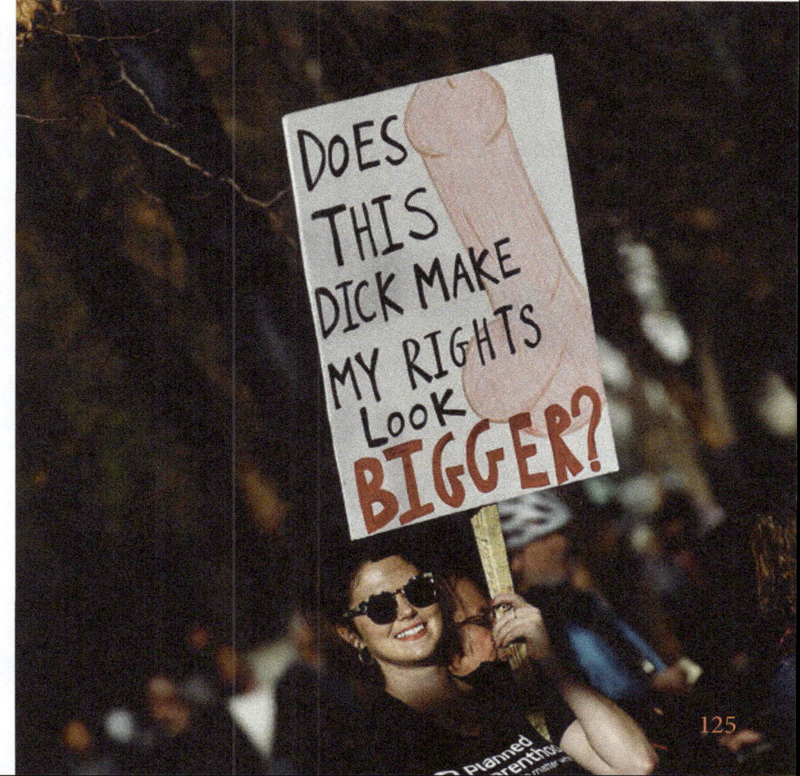

DOES
THIS
DICK MAKE
MY RIGHTS
LOOK
BIGGER?

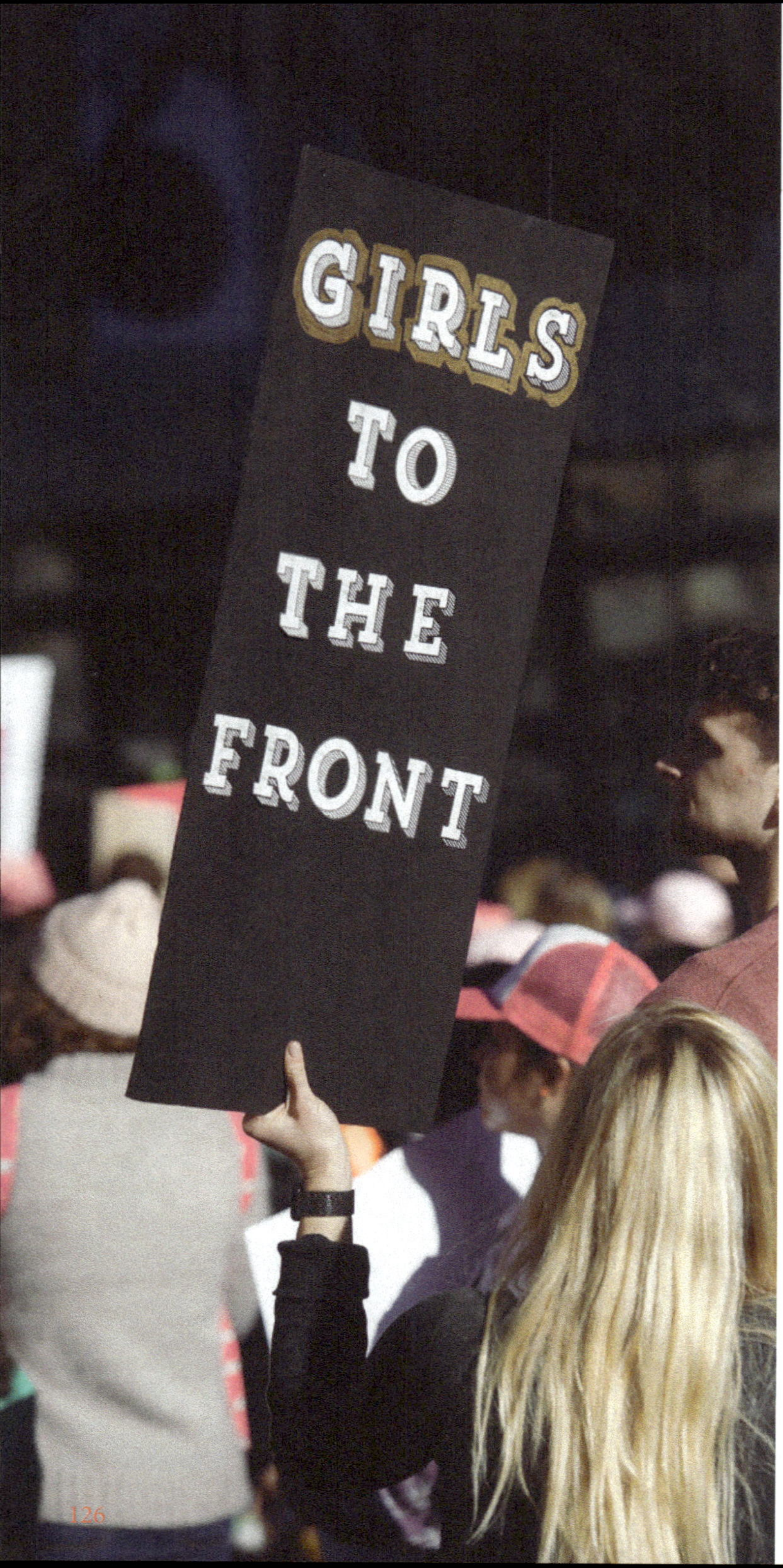

GIRLS
TO
THE
FRONT

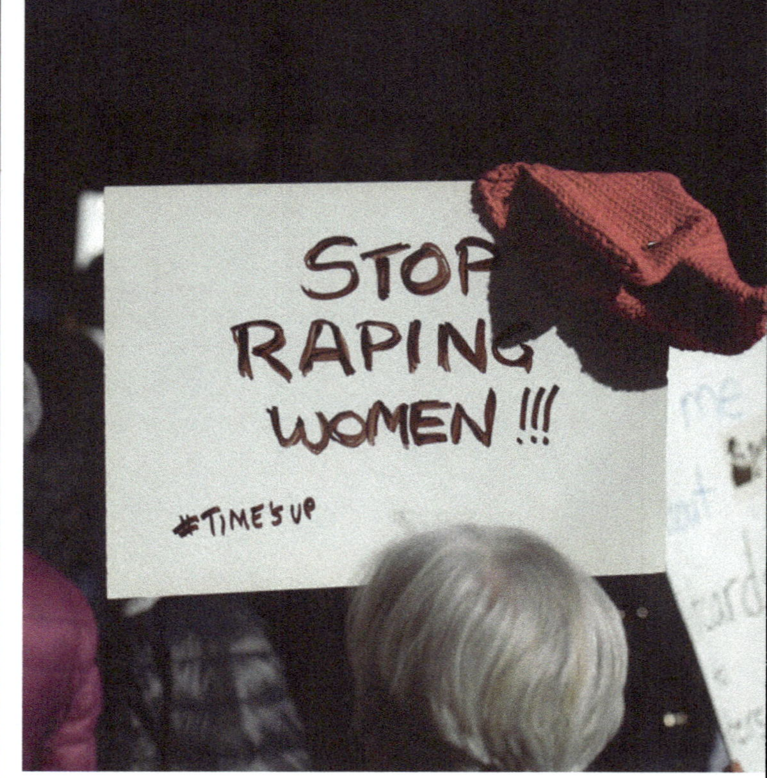

STOP
RAPING
WOMEN !!!
#TIME's UP

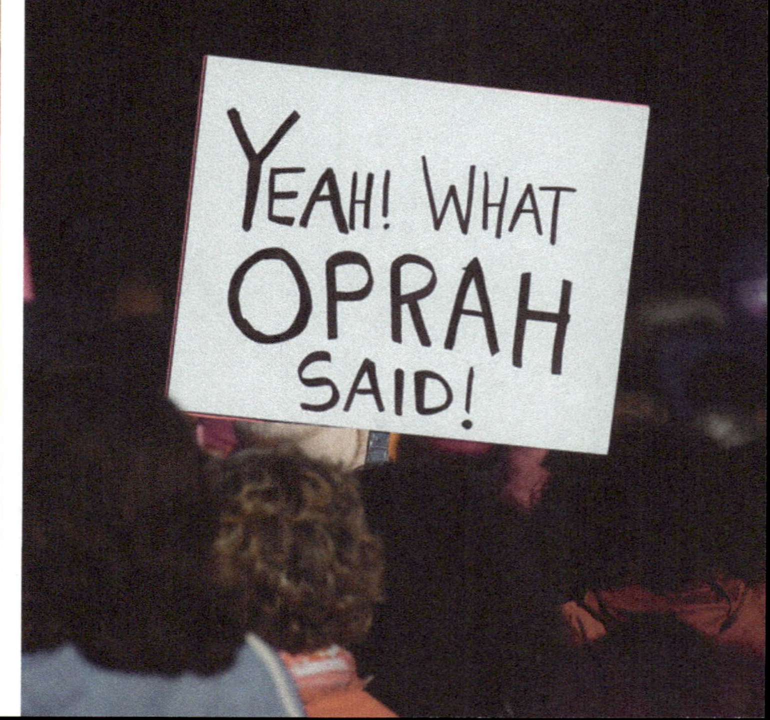

YEAH! WHAT
OPRAH
SAID!

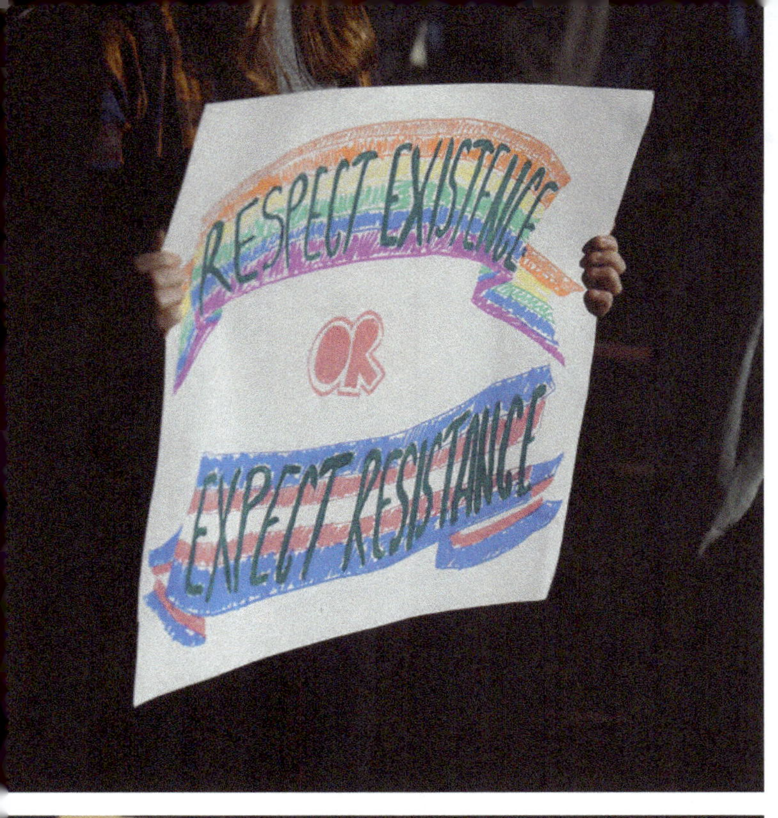

RESPECT EXISTENCE
OR
EXPECT RESISTANCE

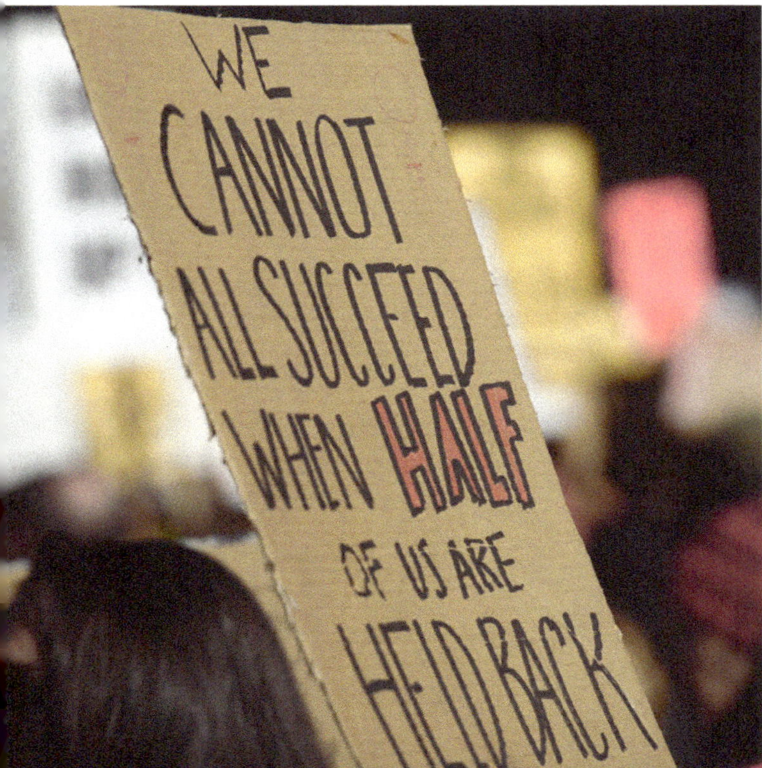

WE
CANNOT
ALL SUCCEED
WHEN HALF
OF US ARE
HELD BACK

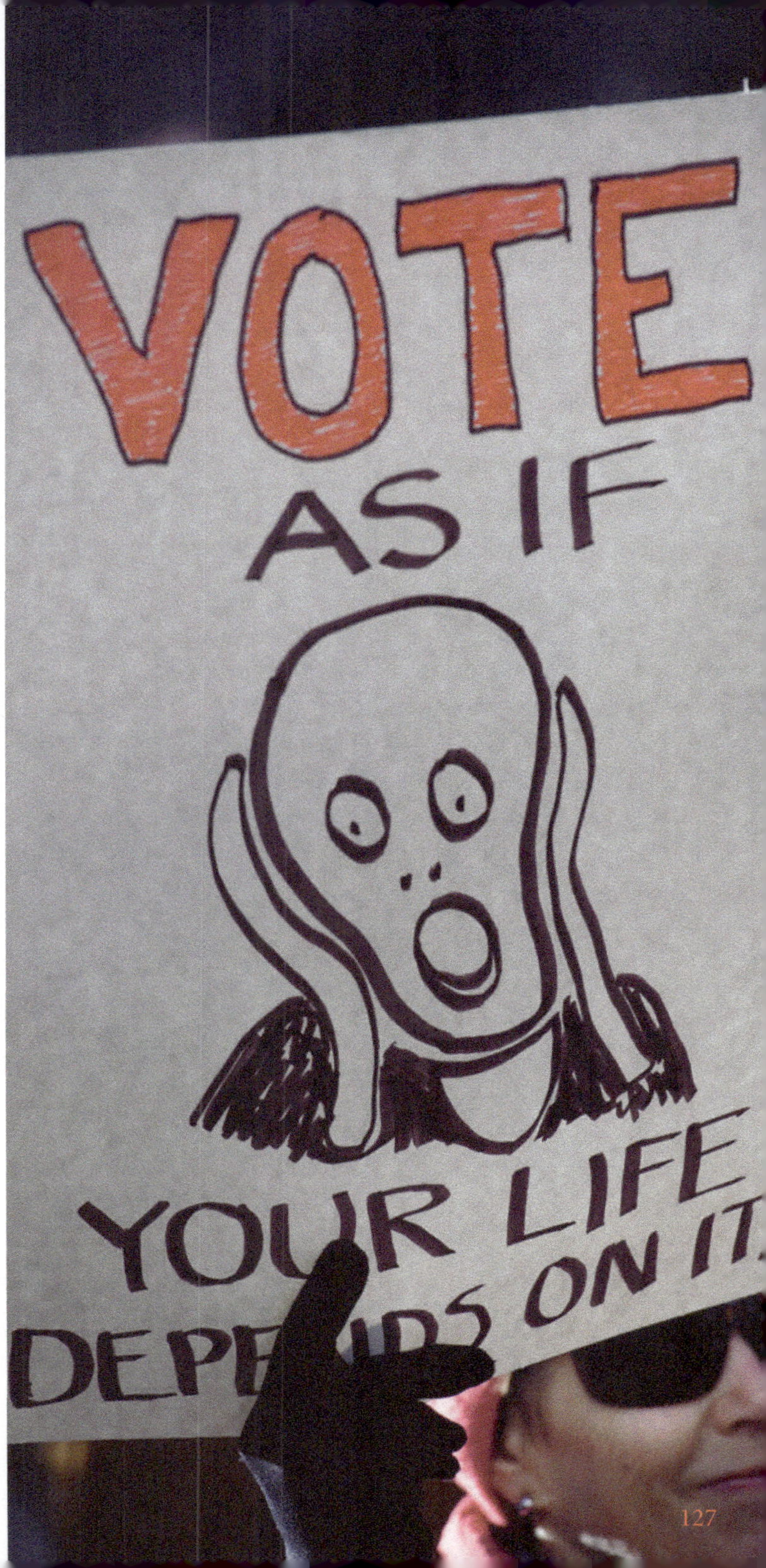

VOTE
AS IF
YOUR LIFE
DEPENDS ON IT.

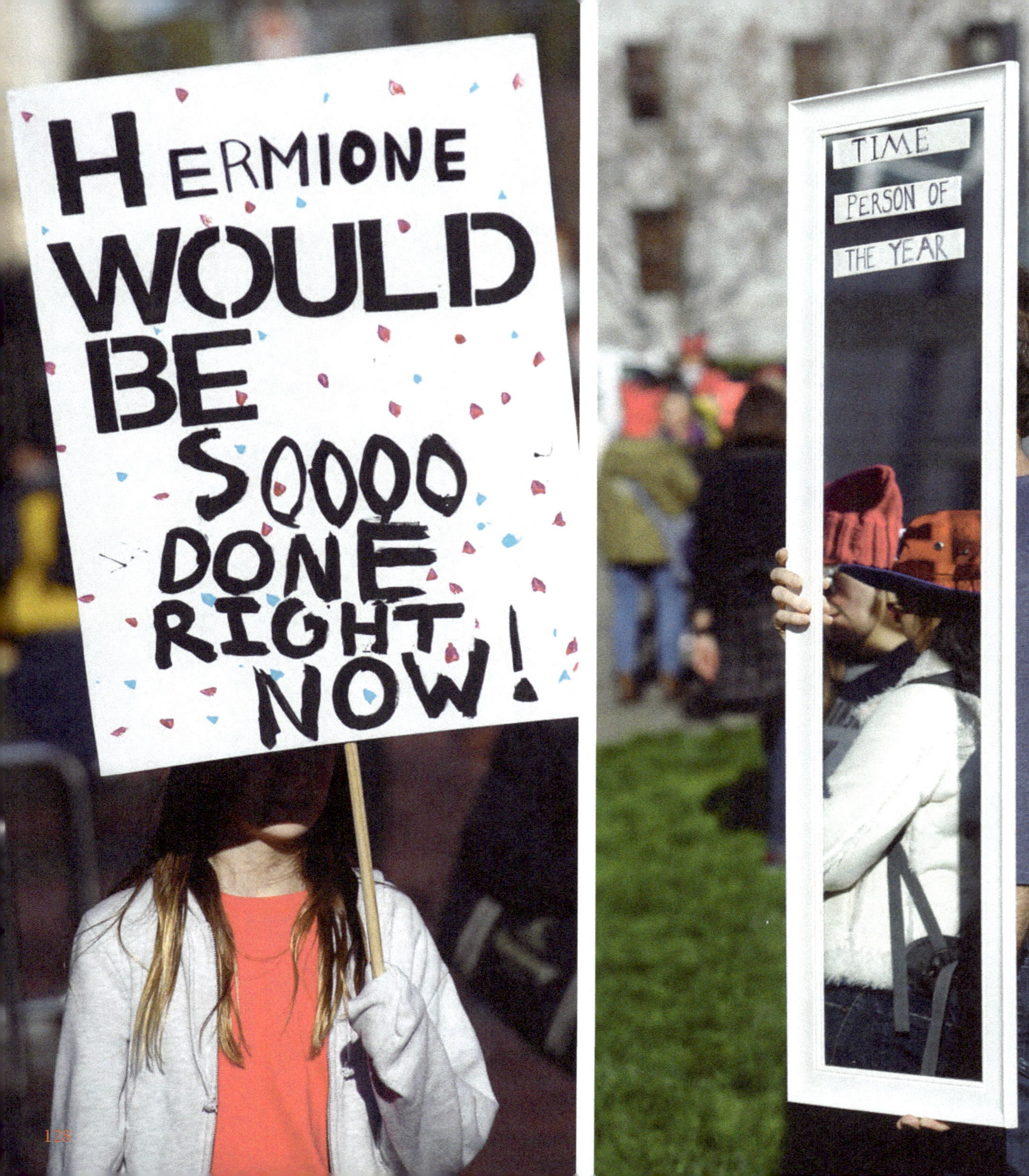
HERMIONE WOULD BE SOOOO DONE RIGHT NOW!
TIME
PERSON OF
THE YEAR

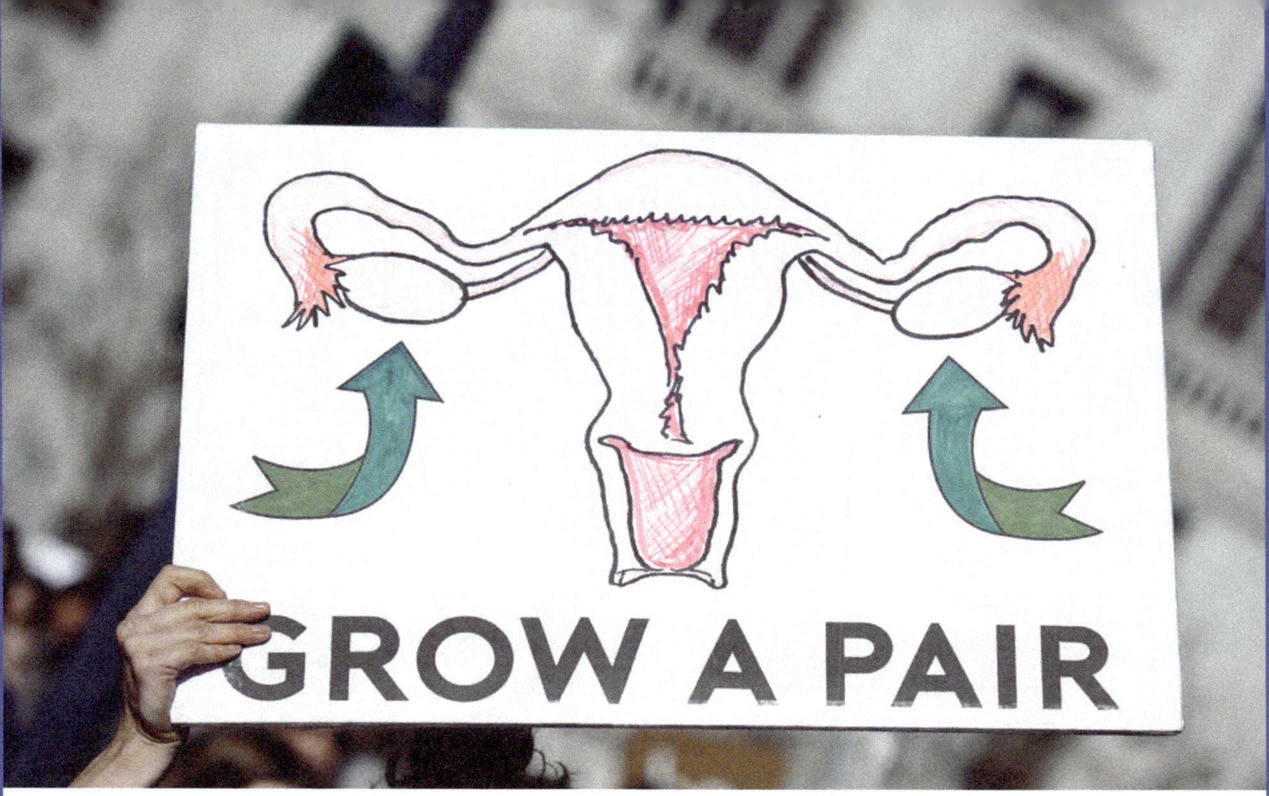

GROW A PAIR

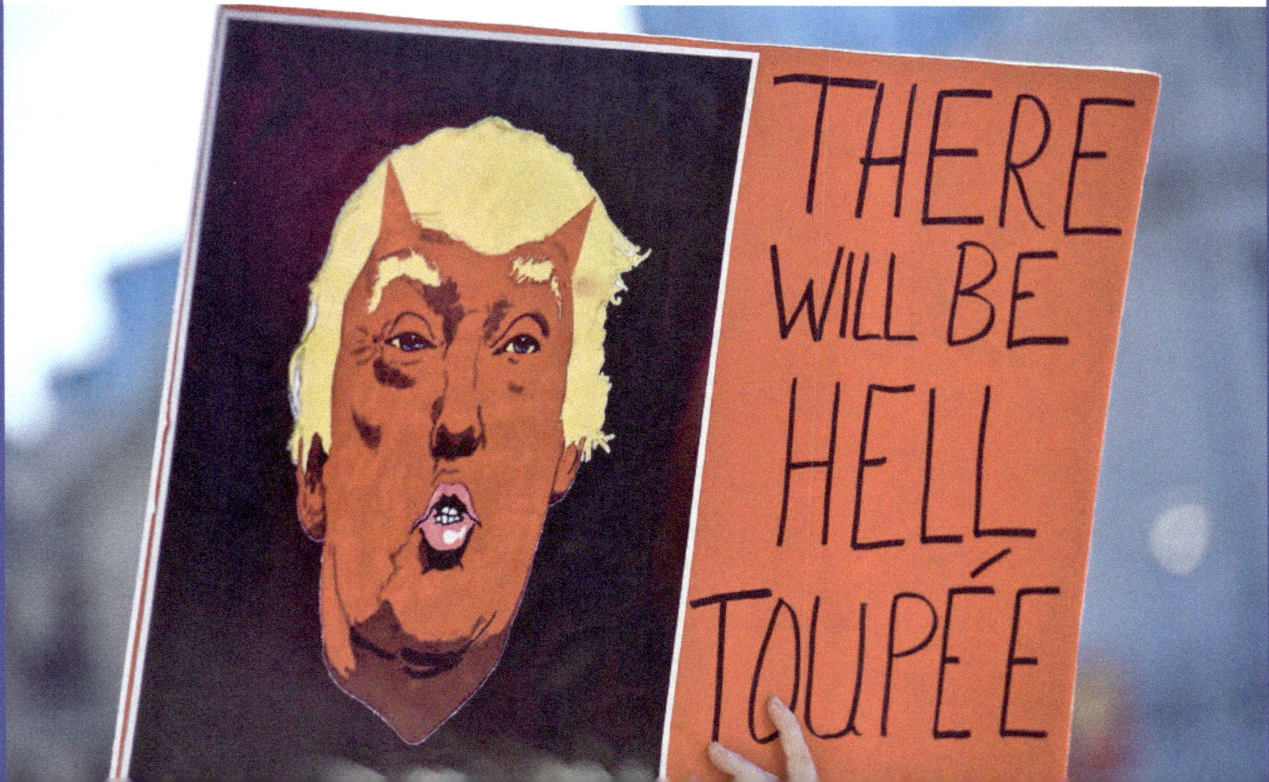

THERE
WILL BE
HELL
TOUPÉE

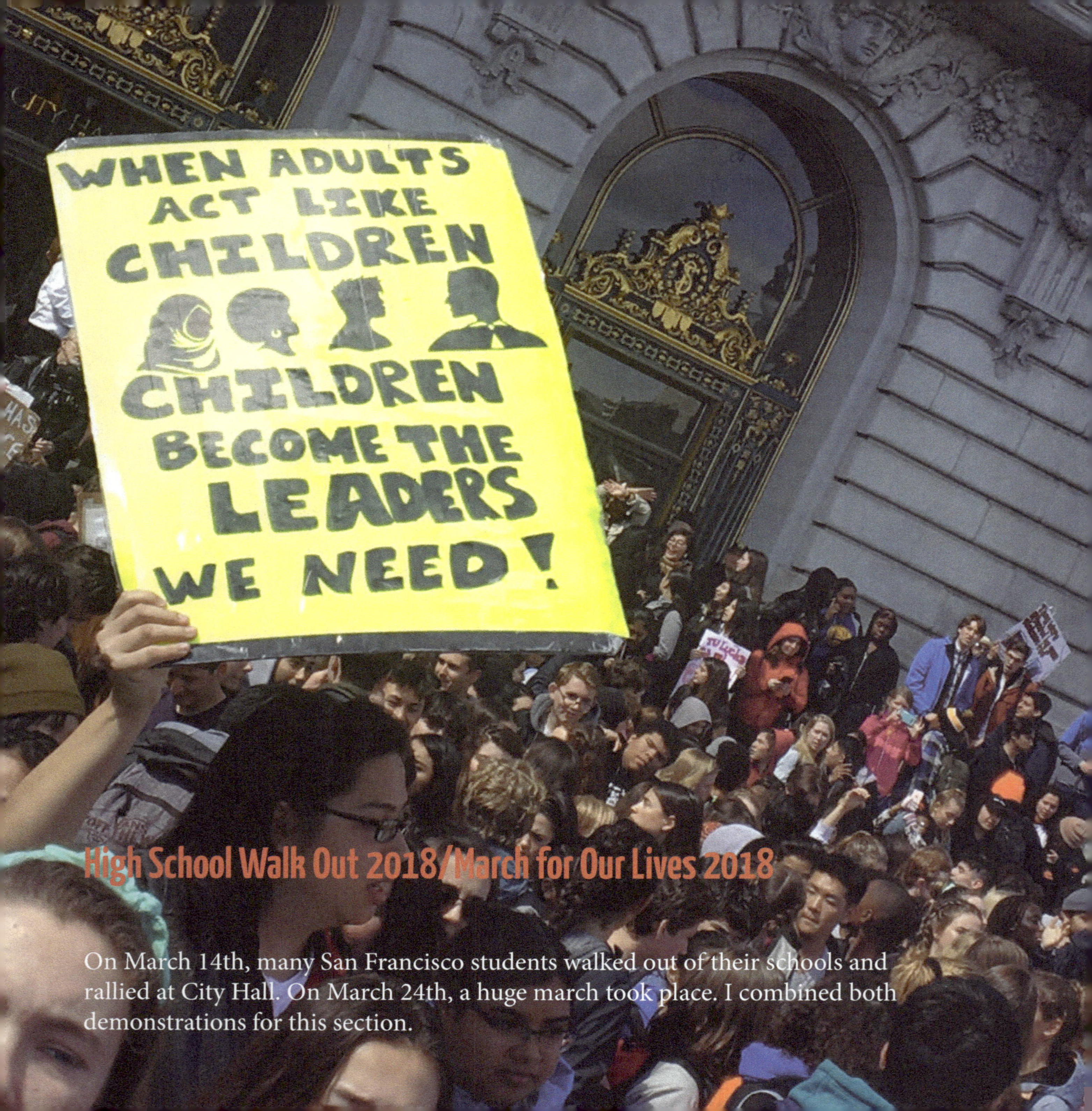

High School Walk Out 2018/March for Our Lives 2018

On March 14th, many San Francisco students walked out of their schools and rallied at City Hall. On March 24th, a huge march took place. I combined both demonstrations for this section.

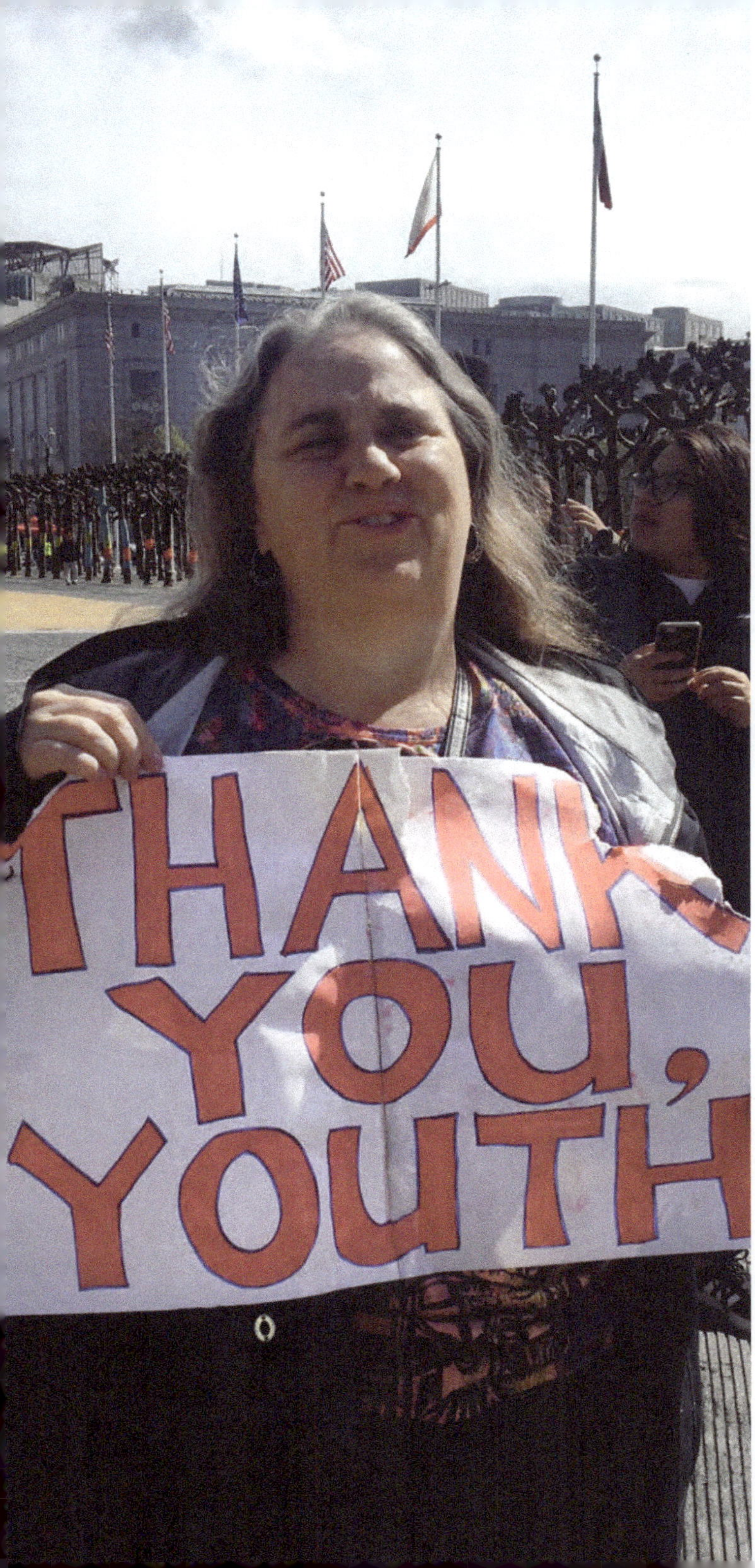

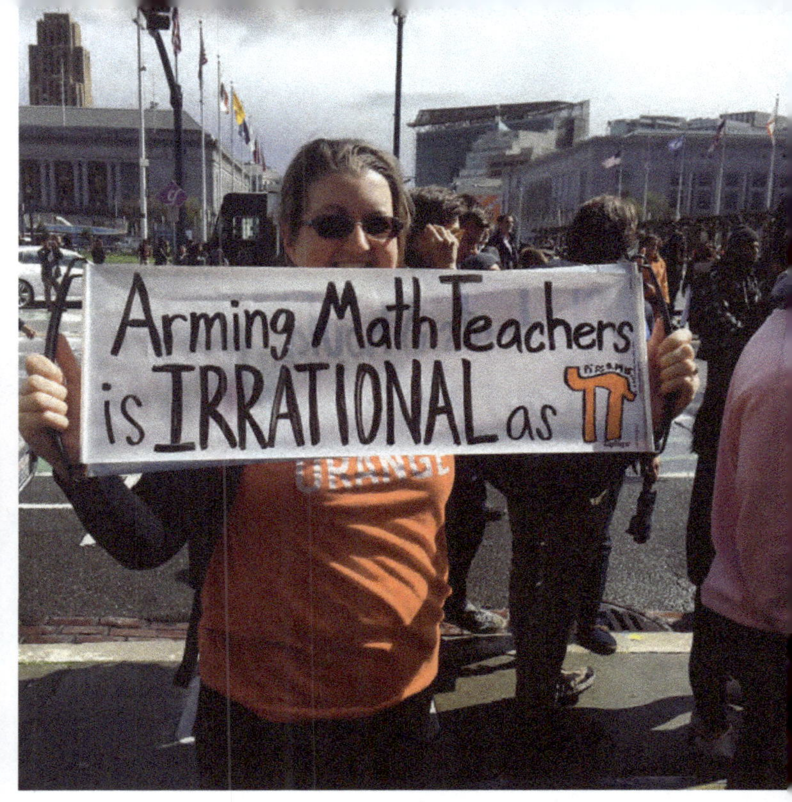
Arming Math Teachers
is IRRATIONAL as π

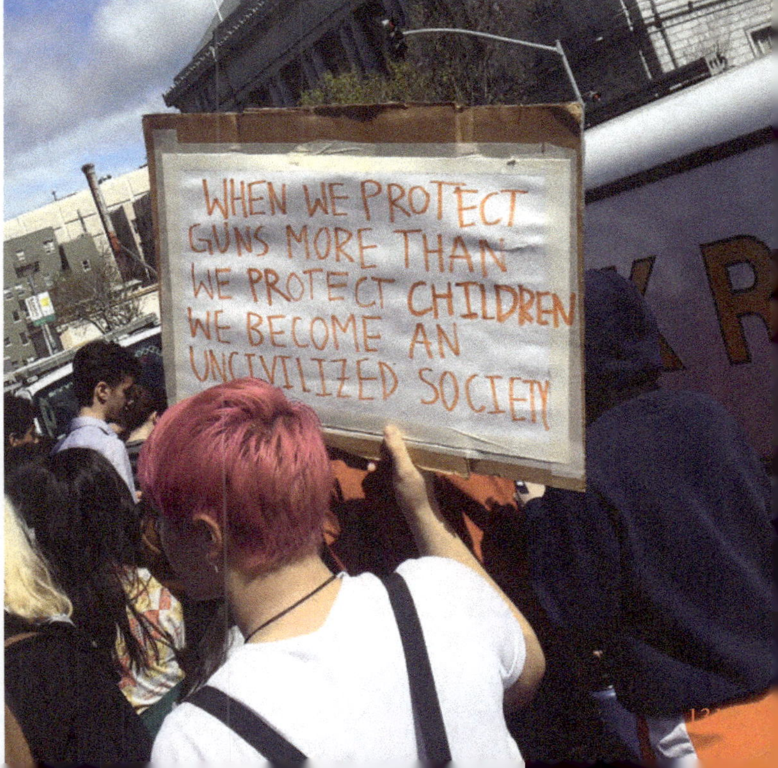
WHEN WE PROTECT
GUNS MORE THAN
WE PROTECT CHILDREN
WE BECOME AN
UNCIVILIZED SOCIETY

THANK
YOU,
YOUTH

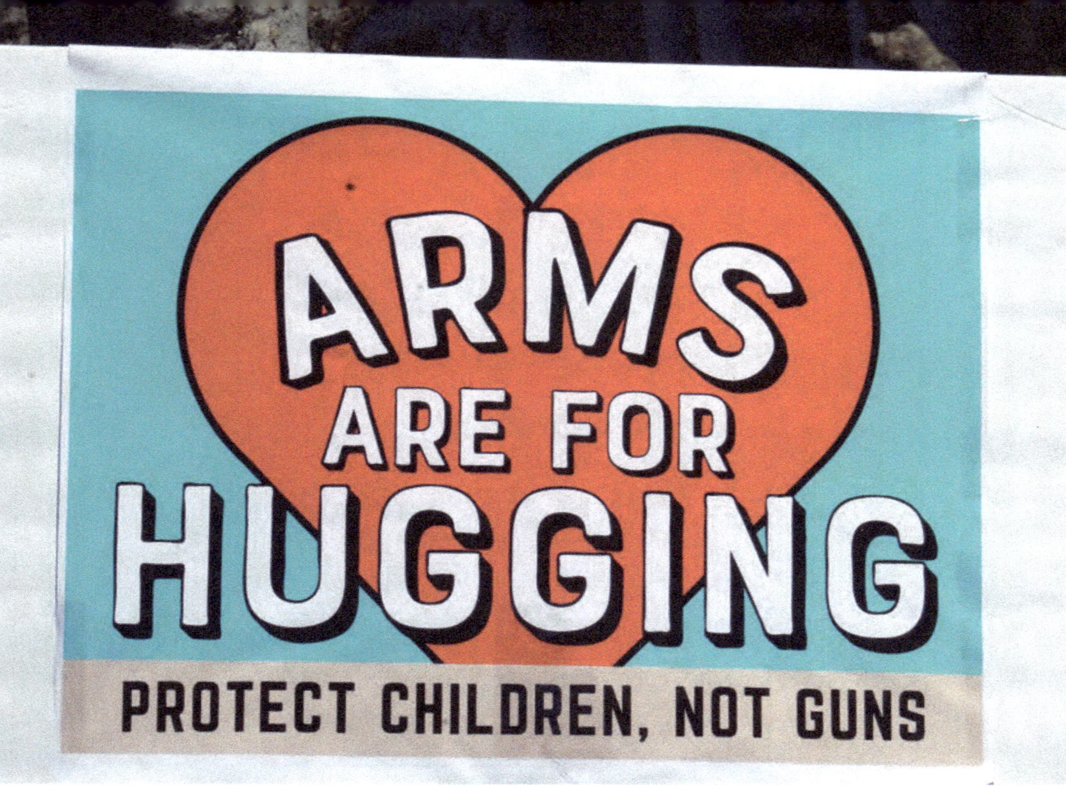

ARMS
ARE FOR
HUGGING
PROTECT CHILDREN, NOT GUNS

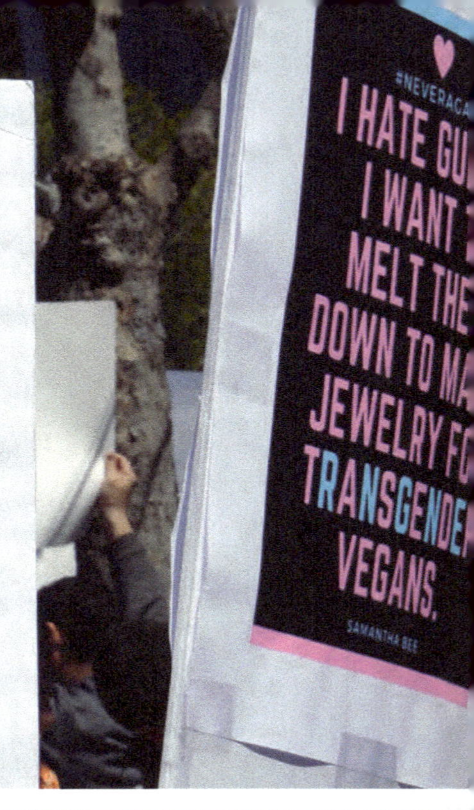

#NEVERAGA
I HATE GU
I WANT
MELT THE
DOWN TO MA
JEWELRY FO
TRANSGENDE
VEGANS.
SAMANTHA BEE

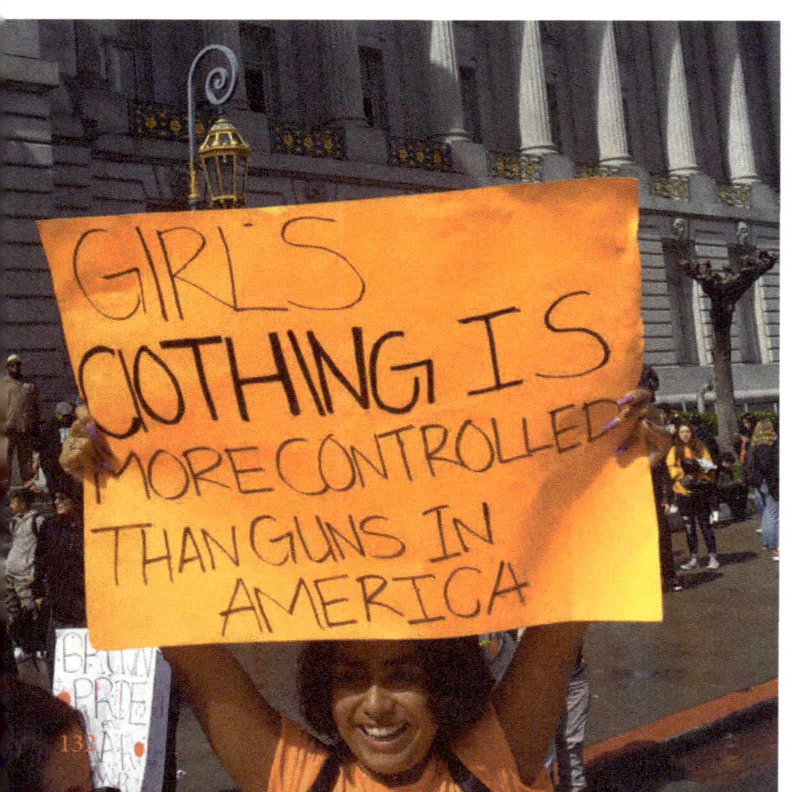

GIRL'S
CLOTHING IS
MORE CONTROLLED
THAN GUNS IN
AMERICA

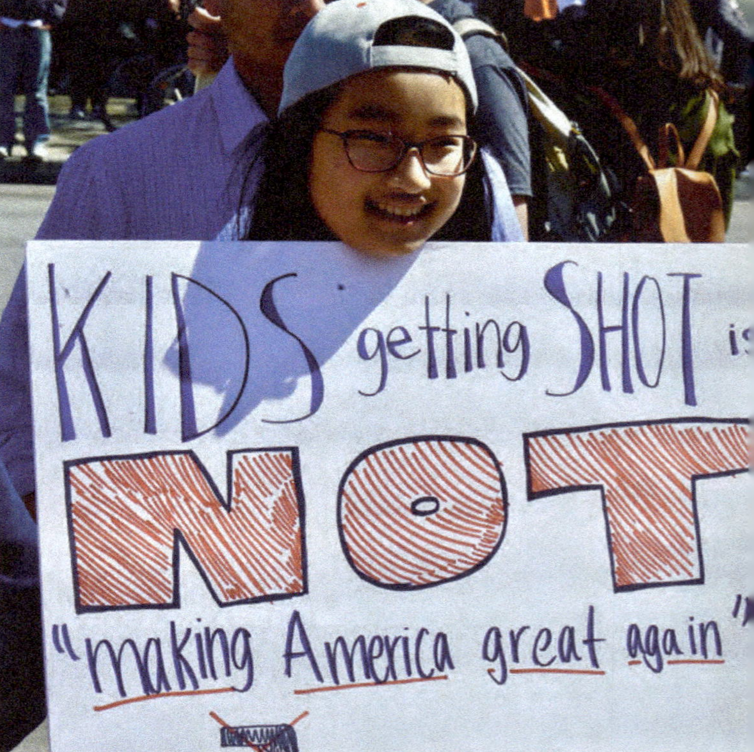

KIDS getting SHOT is
NOT
"making America great again"

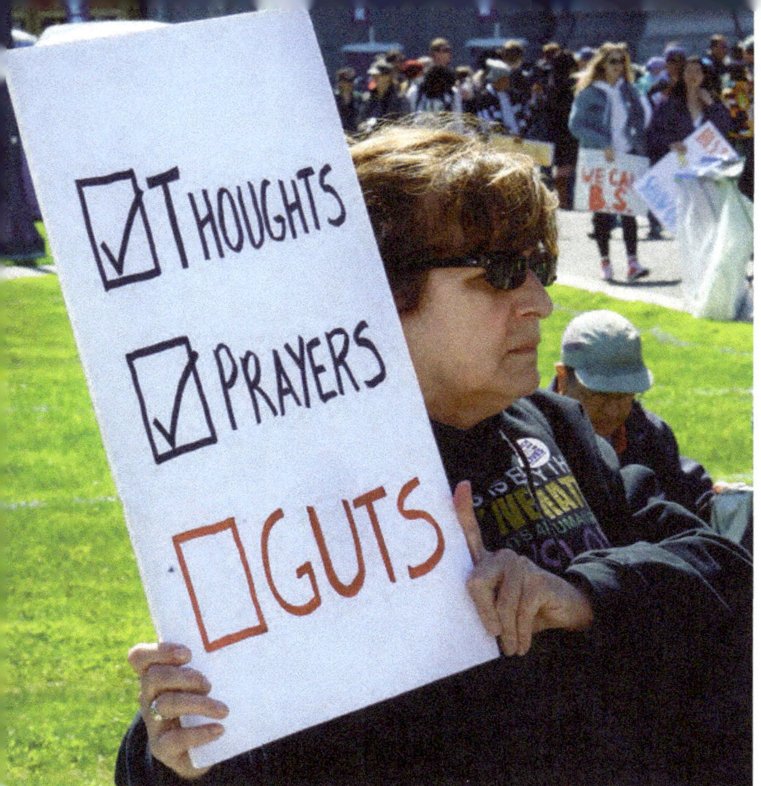

☑ Thoughts
☑ Prayers
☐ Guts

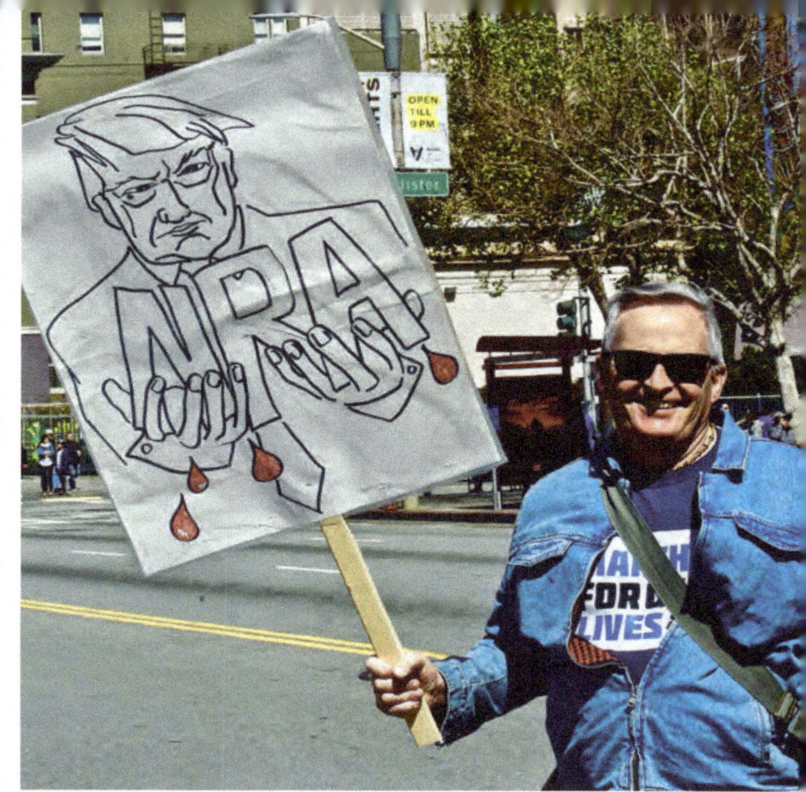

NRA

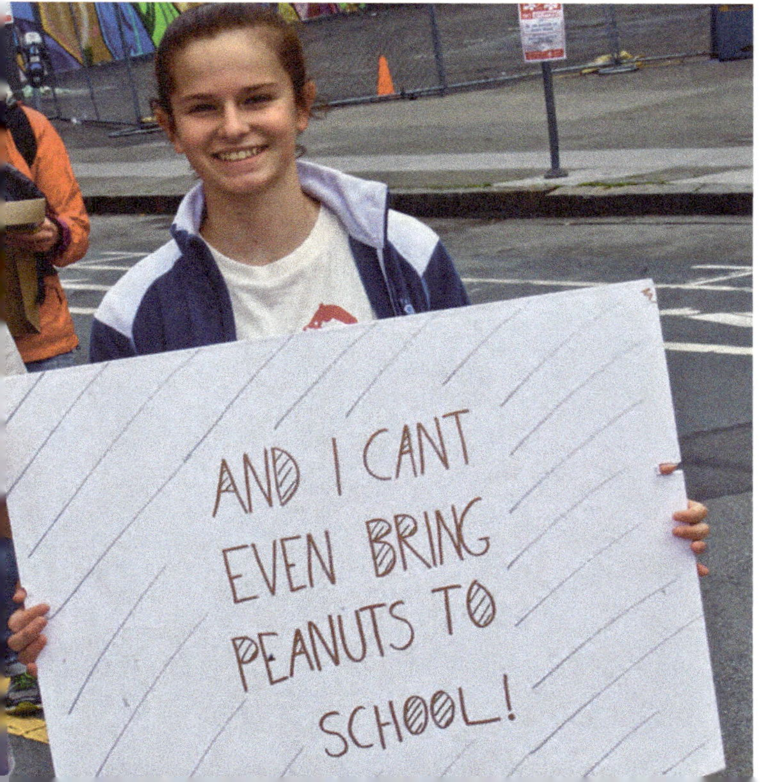

AND I CANT
EVEN BRING
PEANUTS TO
SCHOOL!

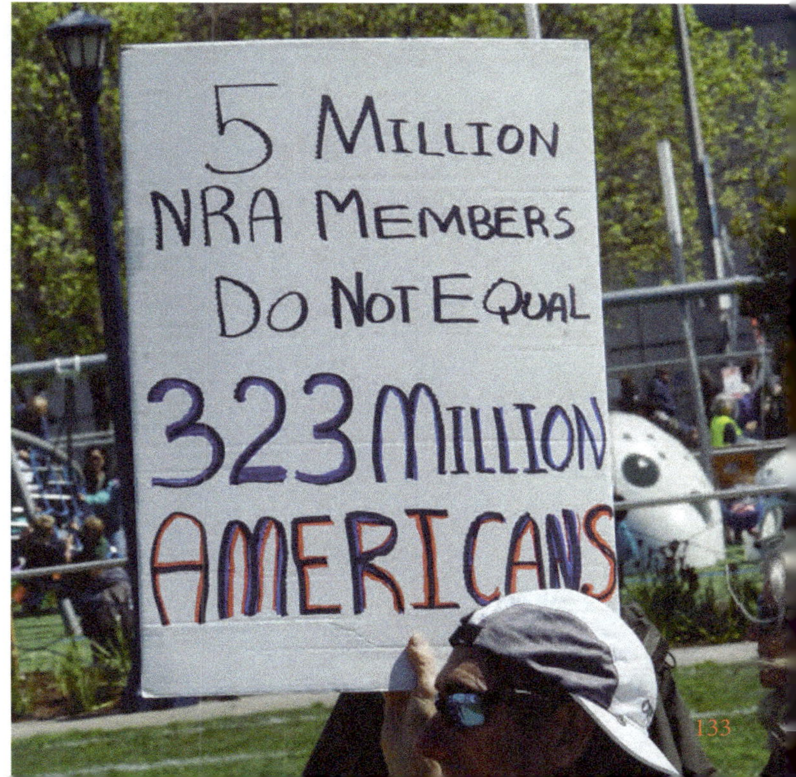

5 MILLION
NRA MEMBERS
DO NOT EQUAL
323 MILLION
AMERICANS

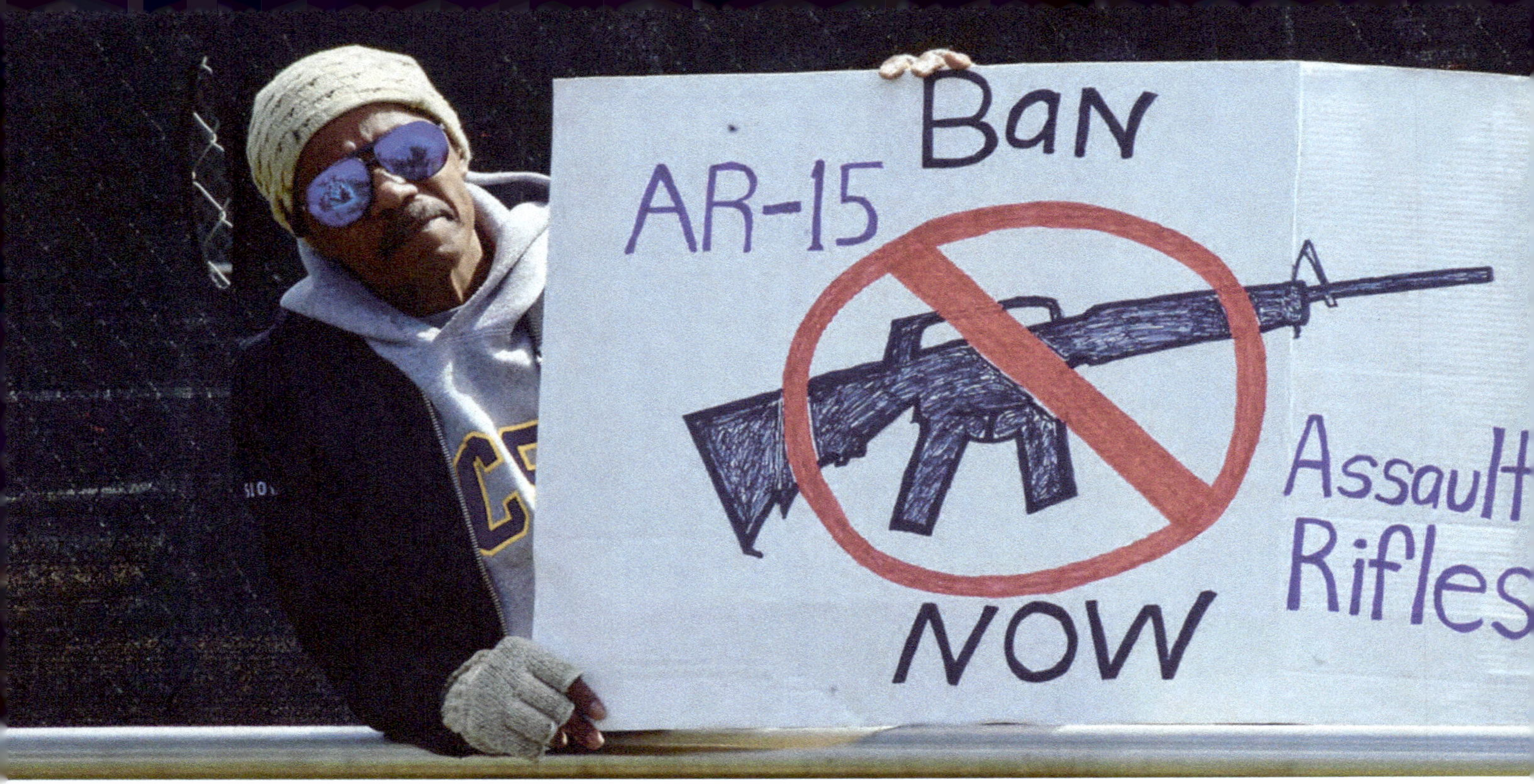

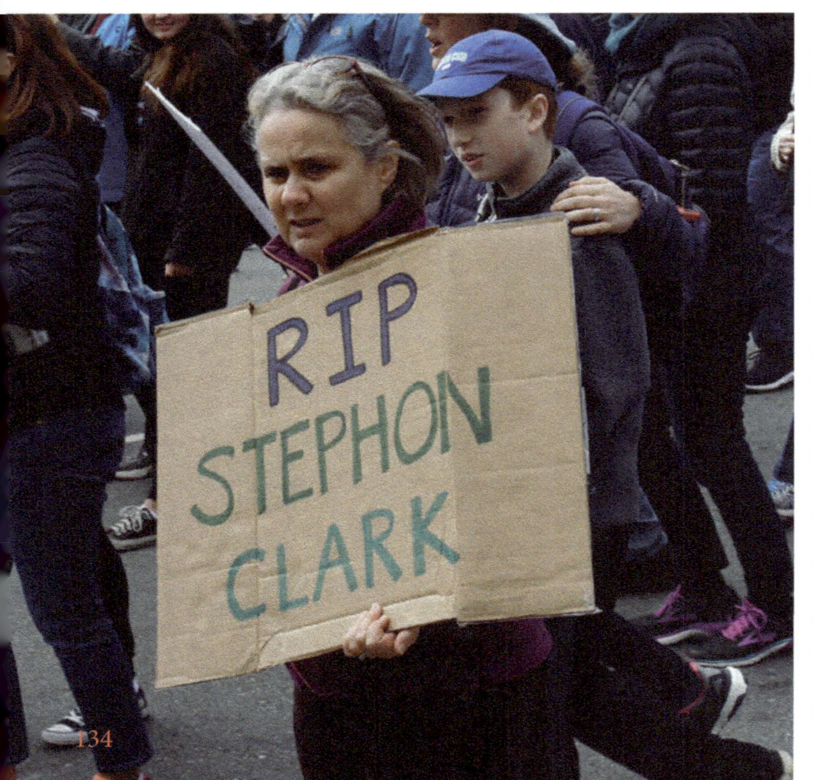

Ban
AR-15
Assault
Rifles
NOW
RIP
STEPHON
CLARK

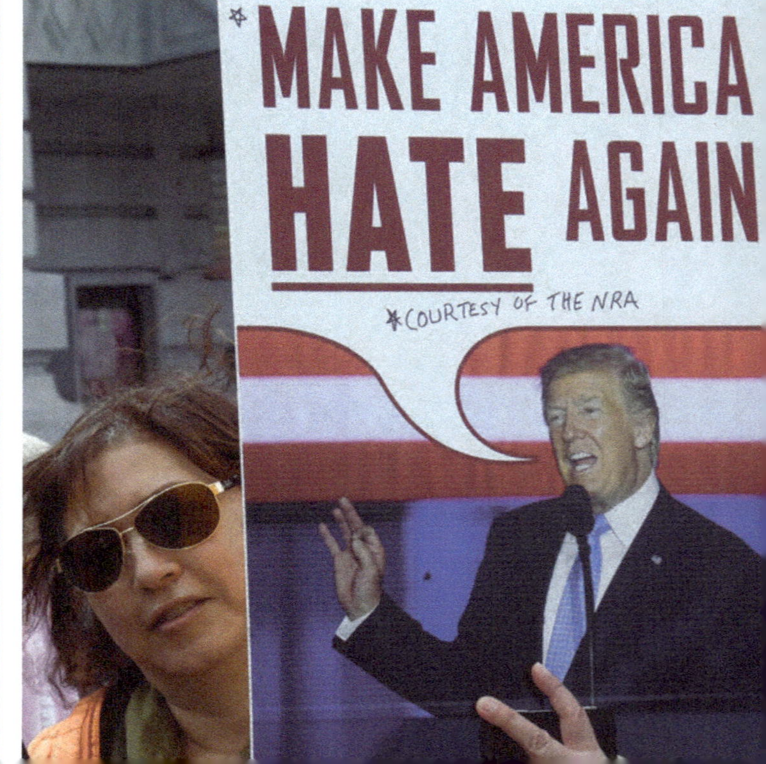

MAKE AMERICA
HATE AGAIN
#COURTESY OF THE NRA

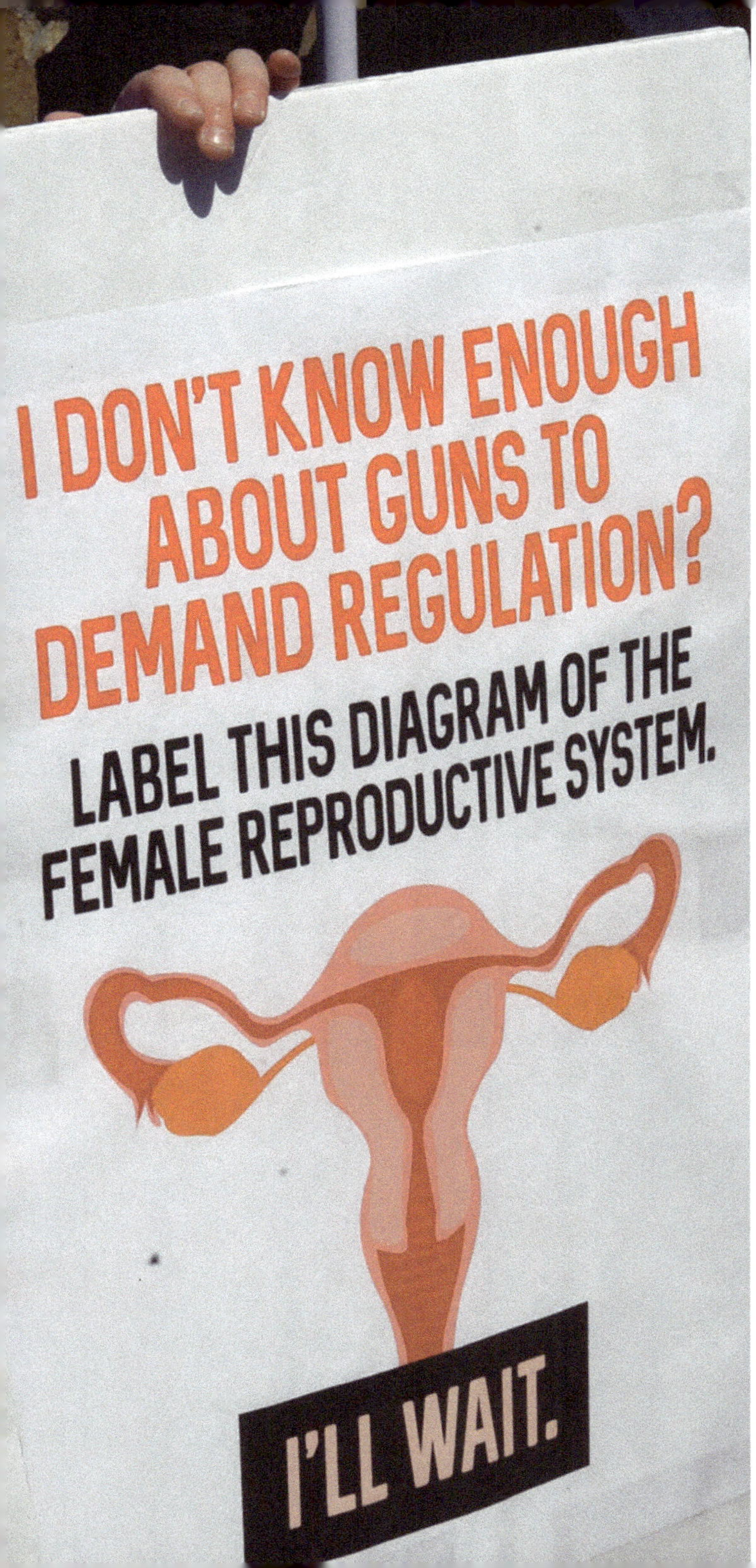

I DON'T KNOW ENOUGH
ABOUT GUNS TO
DEMAND REGULATION?
LABEL THIS DIAGRAM OF THE
FEMALE REPRODUCTIVE SYSTEM.
I'LL WAIT.

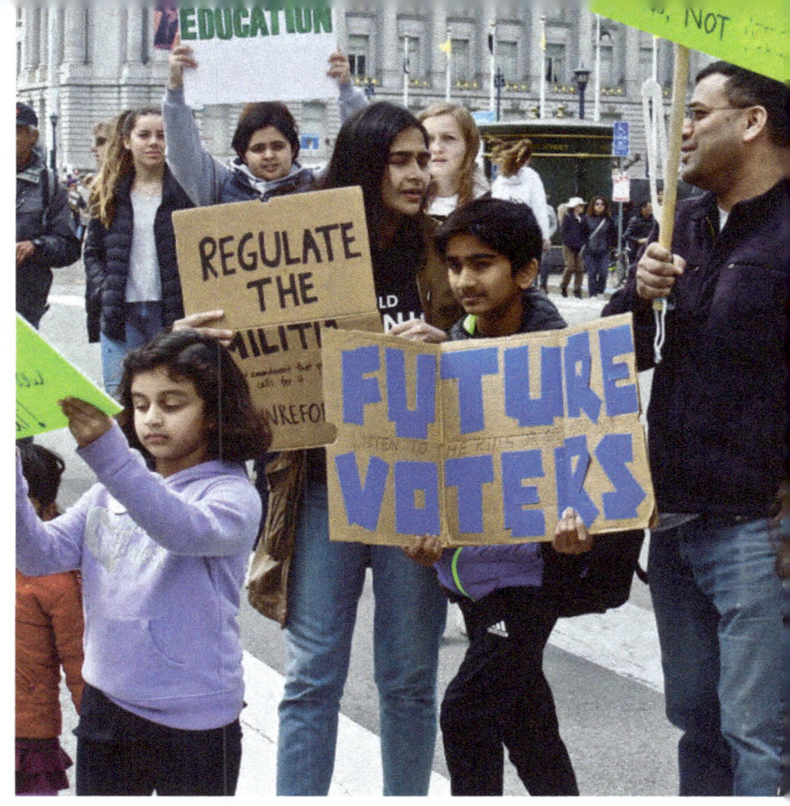
EDUCATION
REGULATE
THE
MILITIA
FUTURE
VOTERS

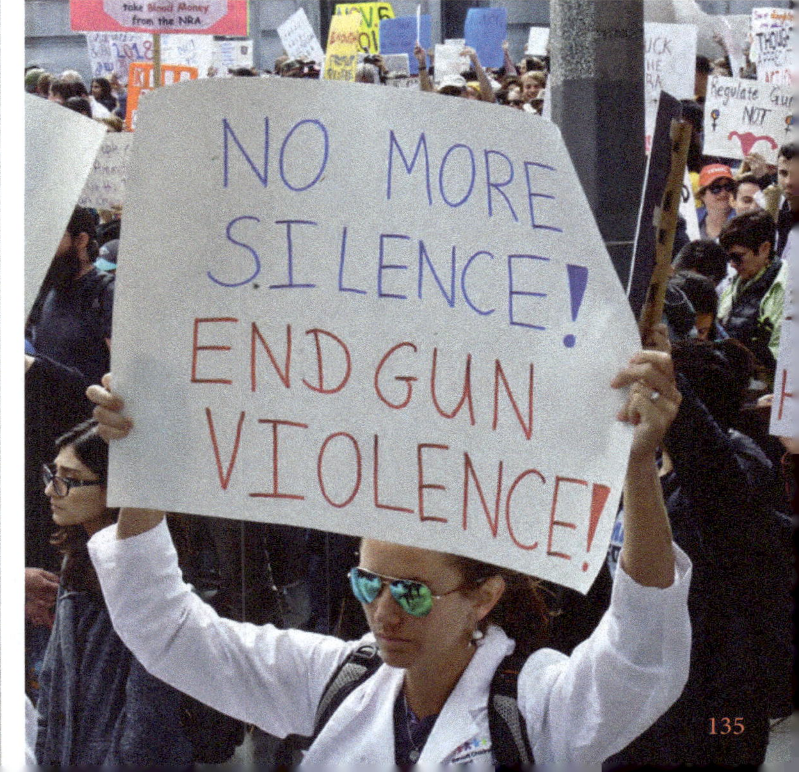
take Blood Money
from the NRA
NO MORE
SILENCE!
END GUN
VIOLENCE!

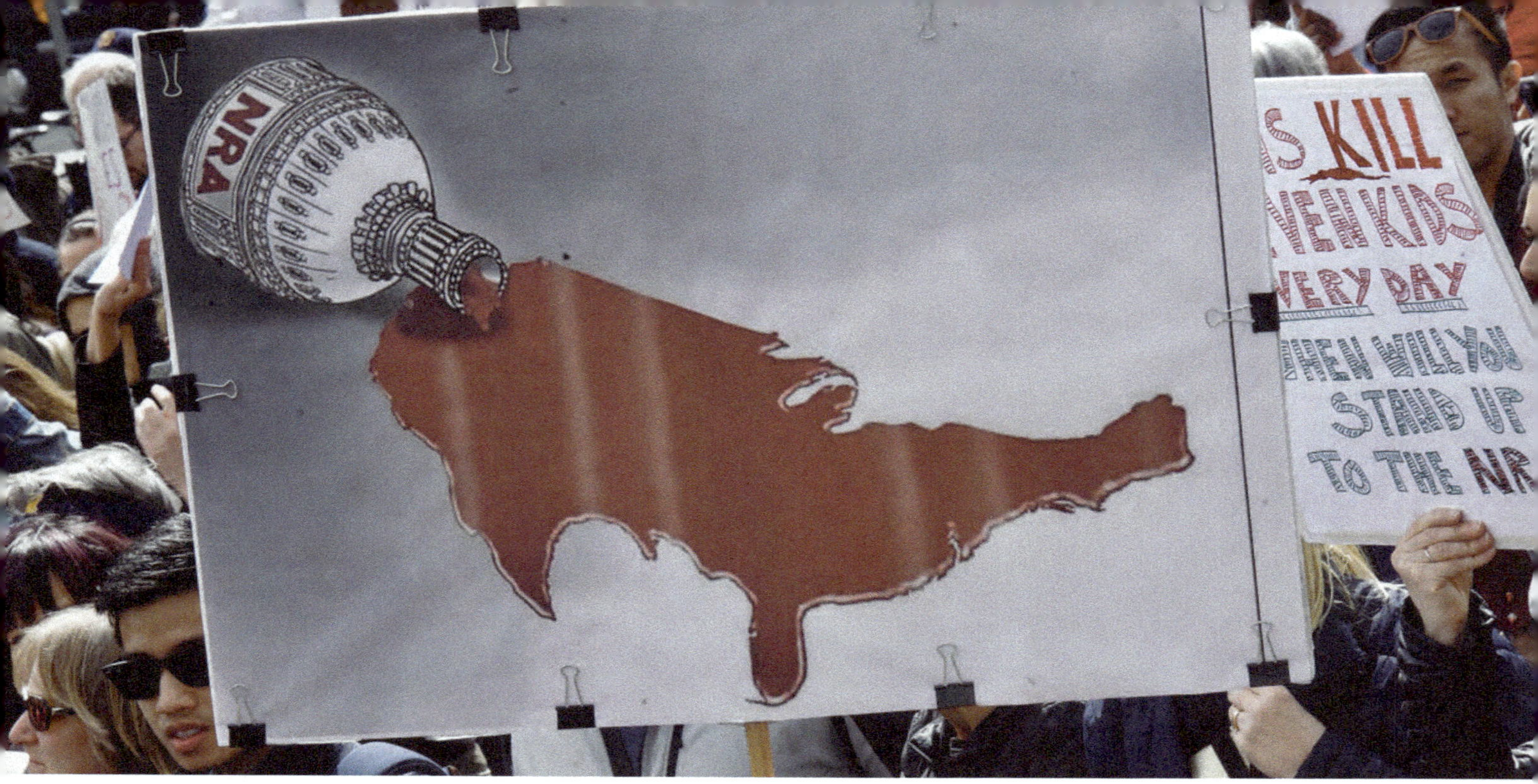

NRA

S KILL
EW KIDS
VERY DAY
HEN WILL YOU
STAND UP
TO THE NR

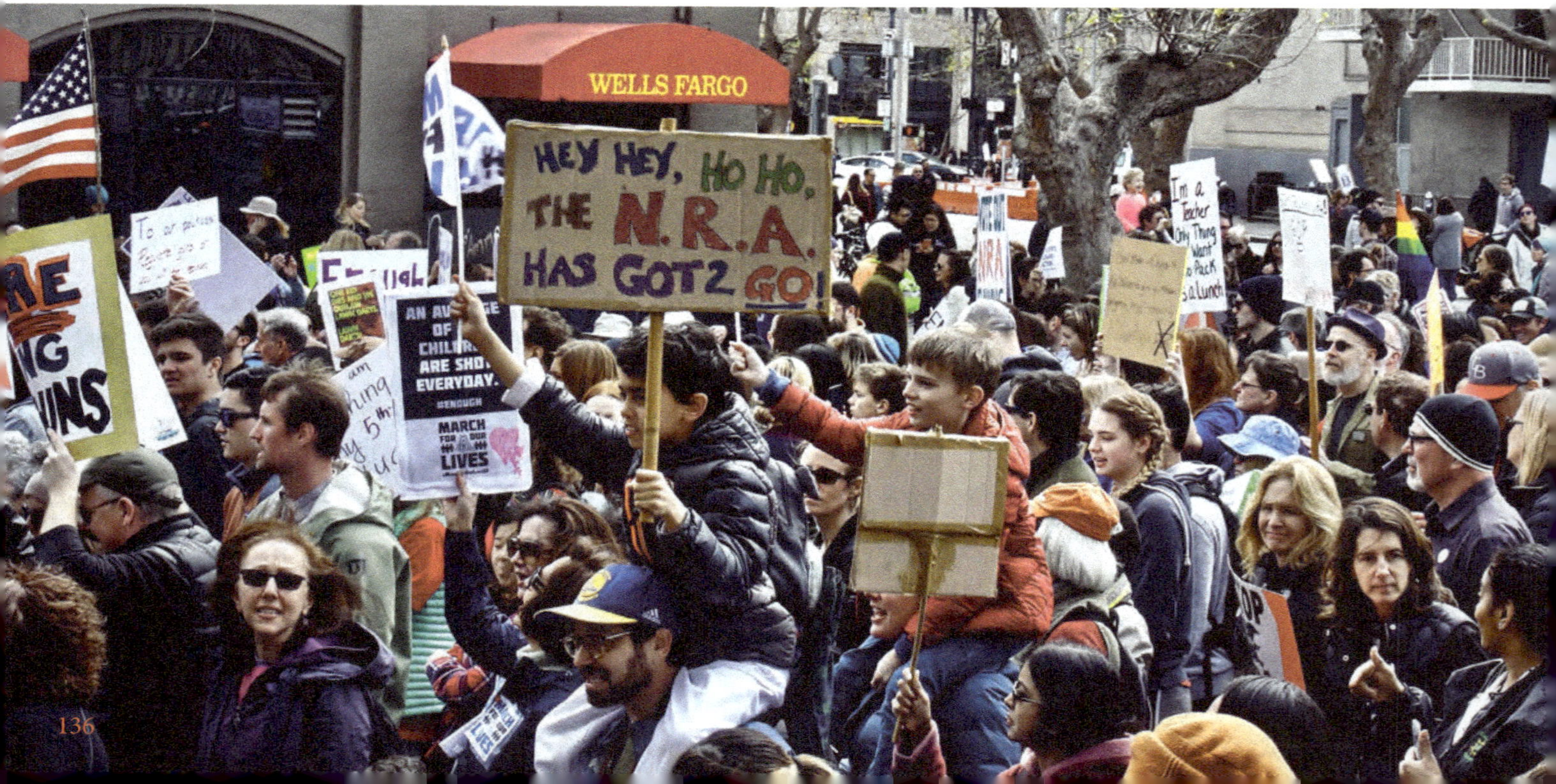

WELLS FARGO
HEY HEY, HO HO,
THE N.R.A.
HAS GOT 2 GO!
AN AVERAGE OF
CHILDREN ARE SHOT
EVERYDAY.
#ENOUGH
MARCH FOR OUR LIVES
I'm a Teacher

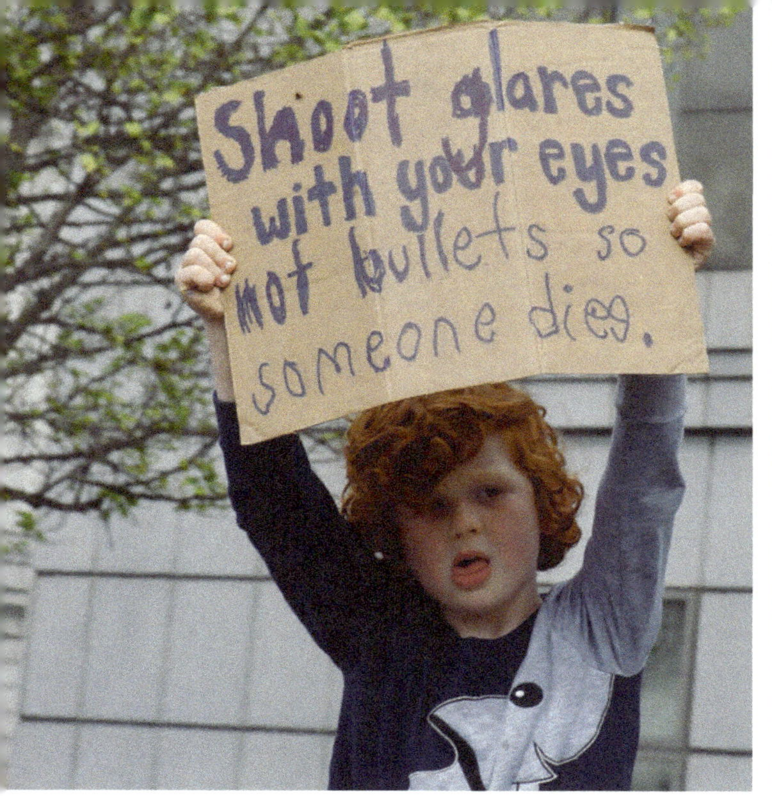
Shoot glares
with your eyes
not bullets so
someone dies.
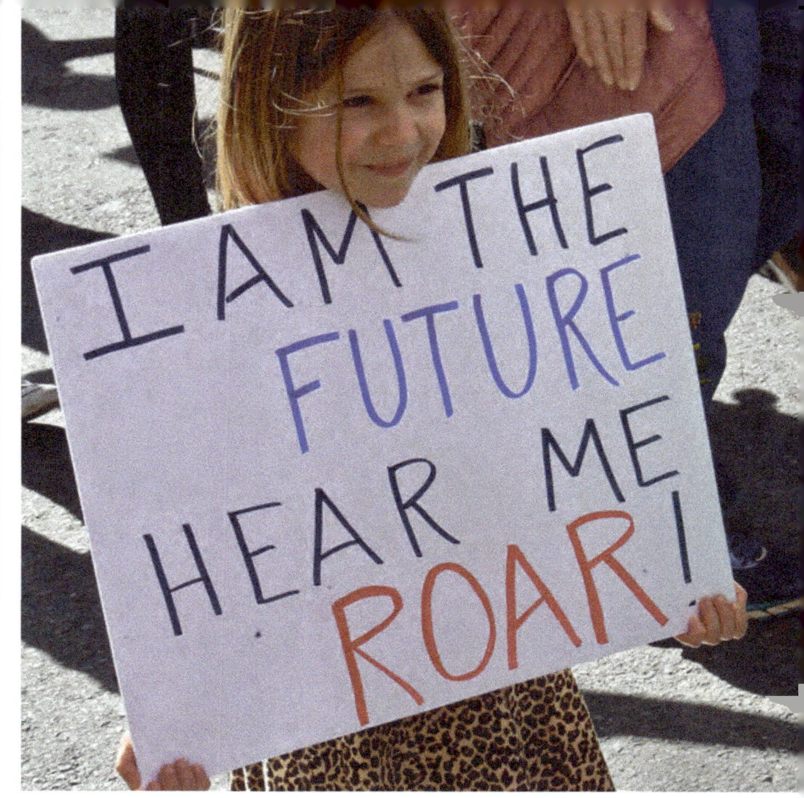
I AM THE
FUTURE
HEAR ME
ROAR!
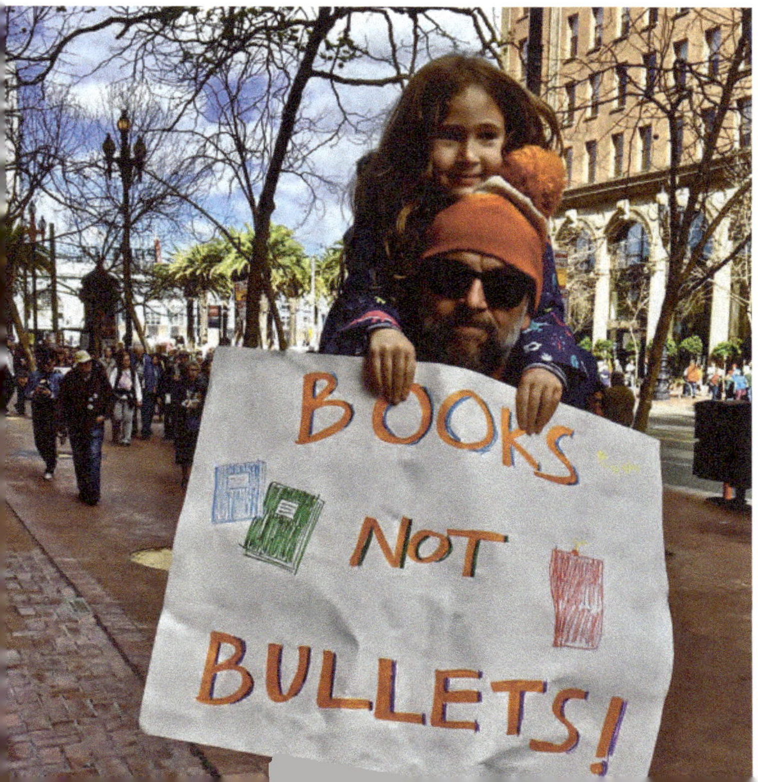
BOOKS
NOT
BULLETS!
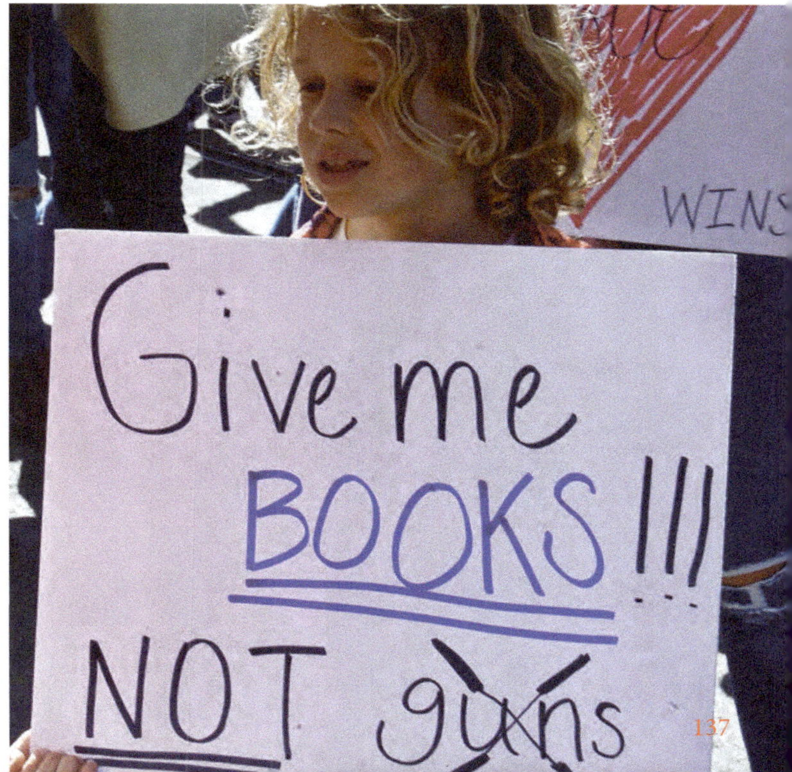
Give me
BOOKS !!!
NOT guns
WINS

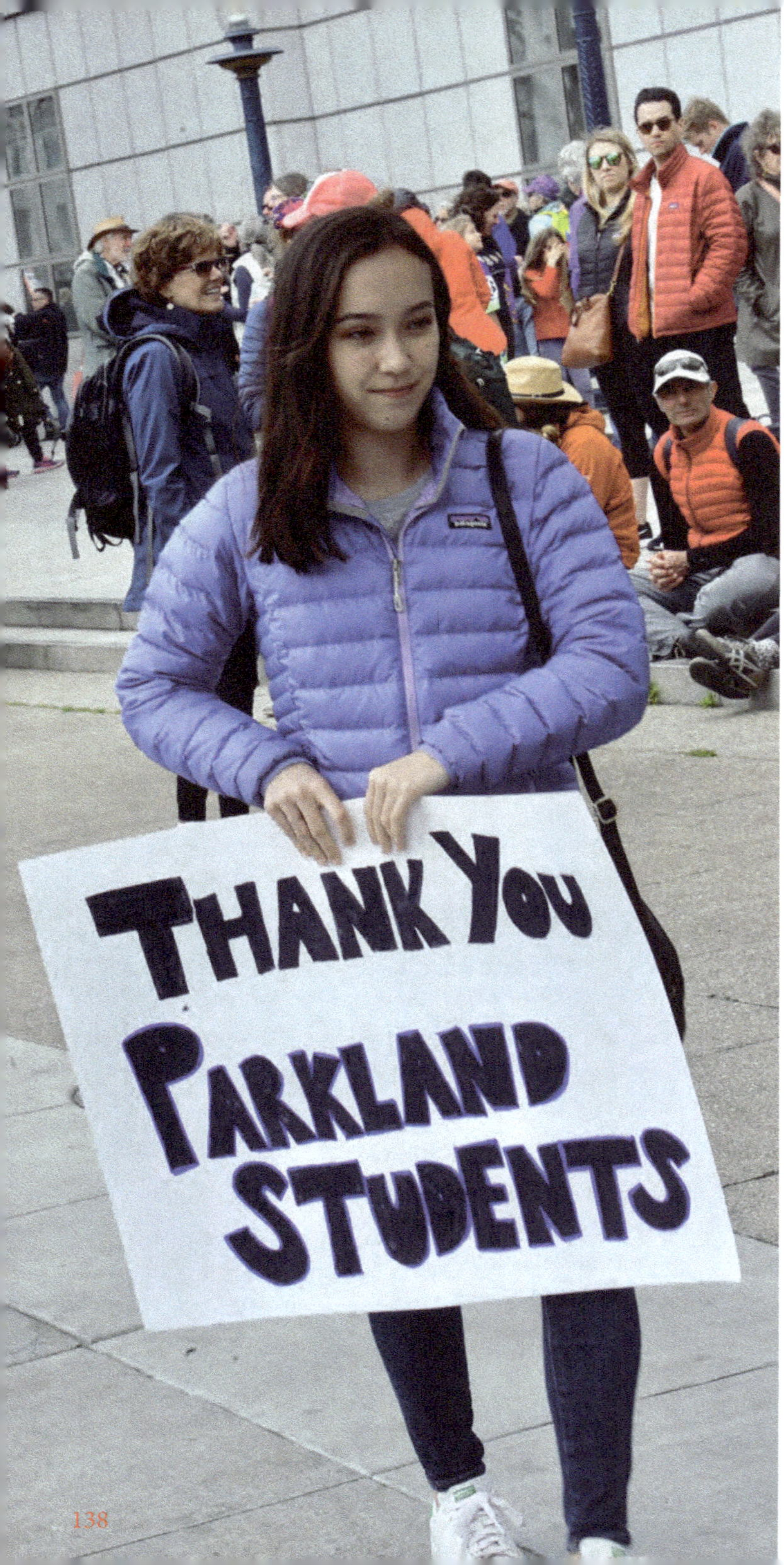

THANK YOU
PARKLAND
STUDENTS

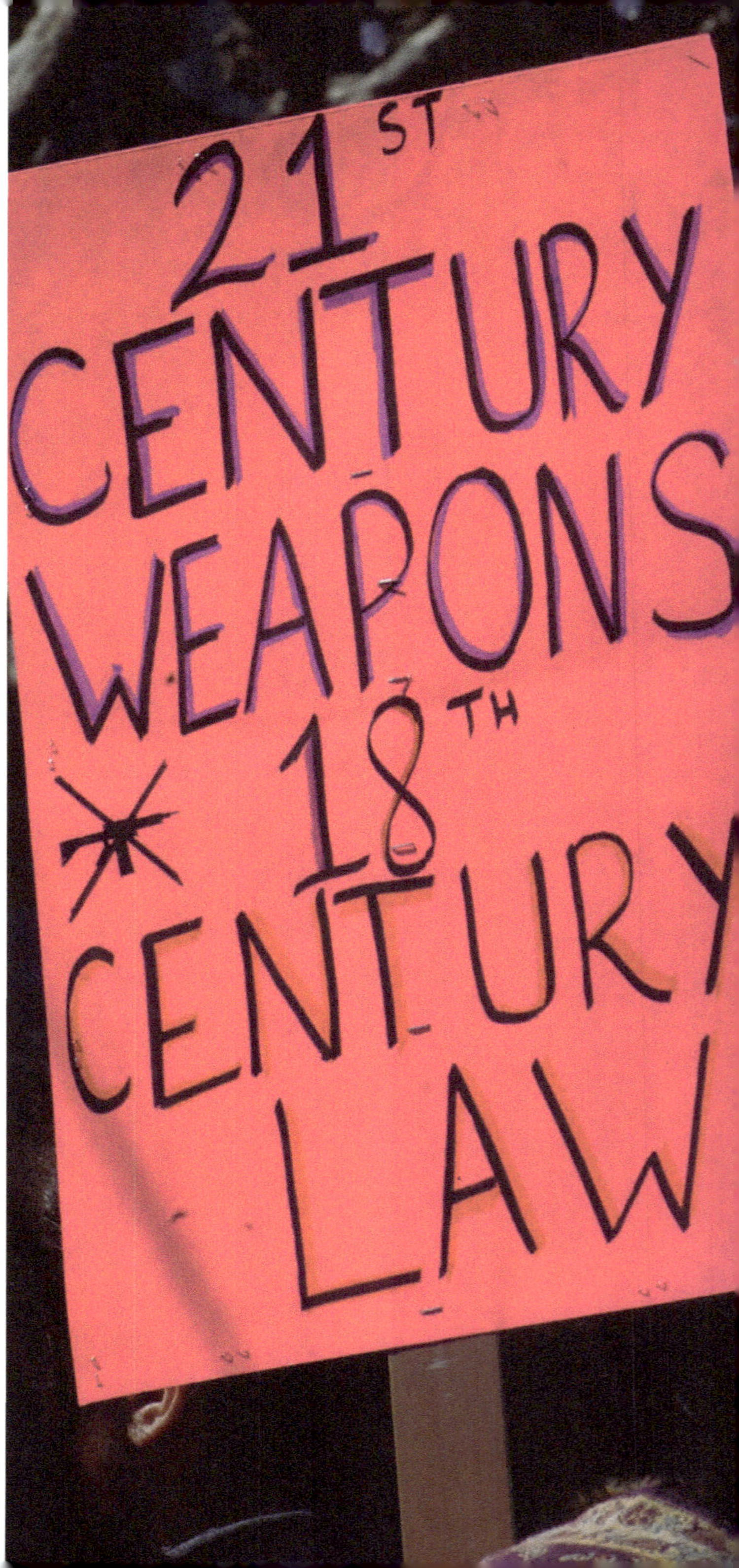

21ST
CENTURY
WEAPONS
* 18TH
CENTURY
LAW

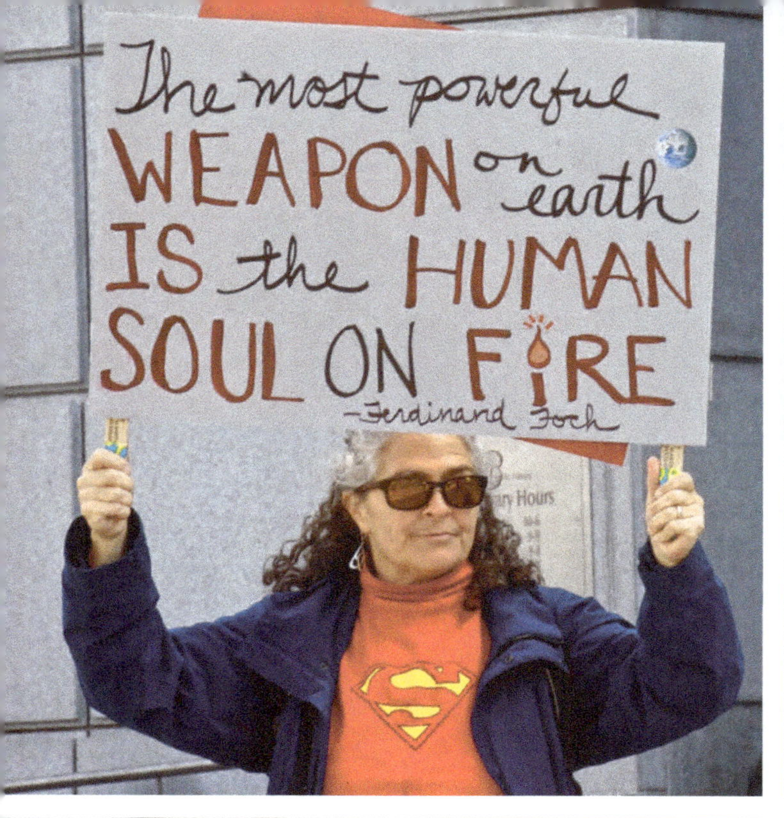
The most powerful
WEAPON on earth
IS the HUMAN
SOUL ON FIRE
—Ferdinand Foch

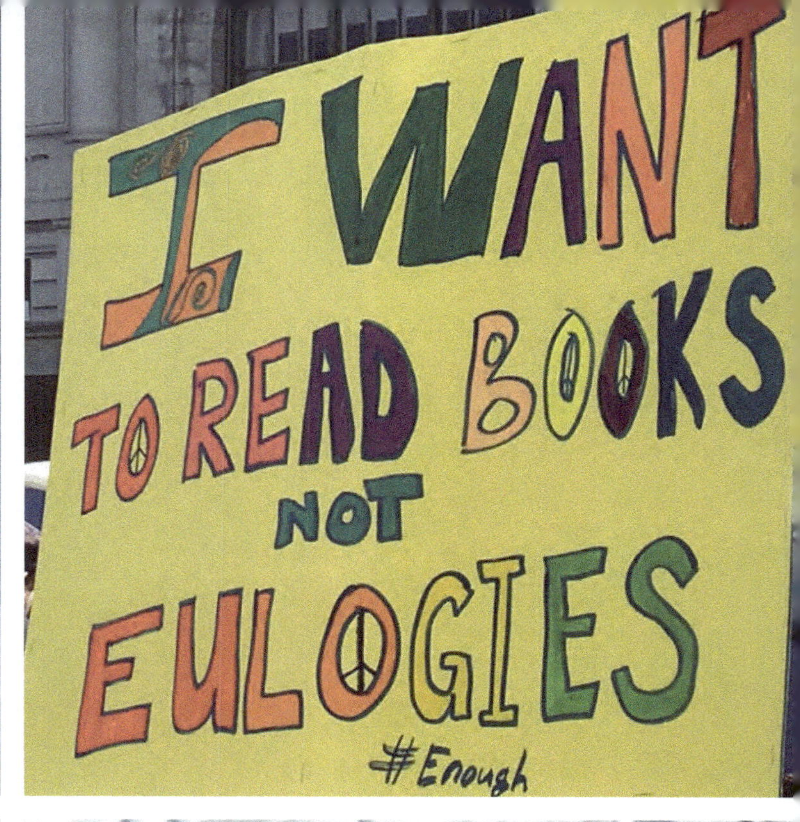
I WANT
TO READ BOOKS
NOT
EULOGIES
#Enough

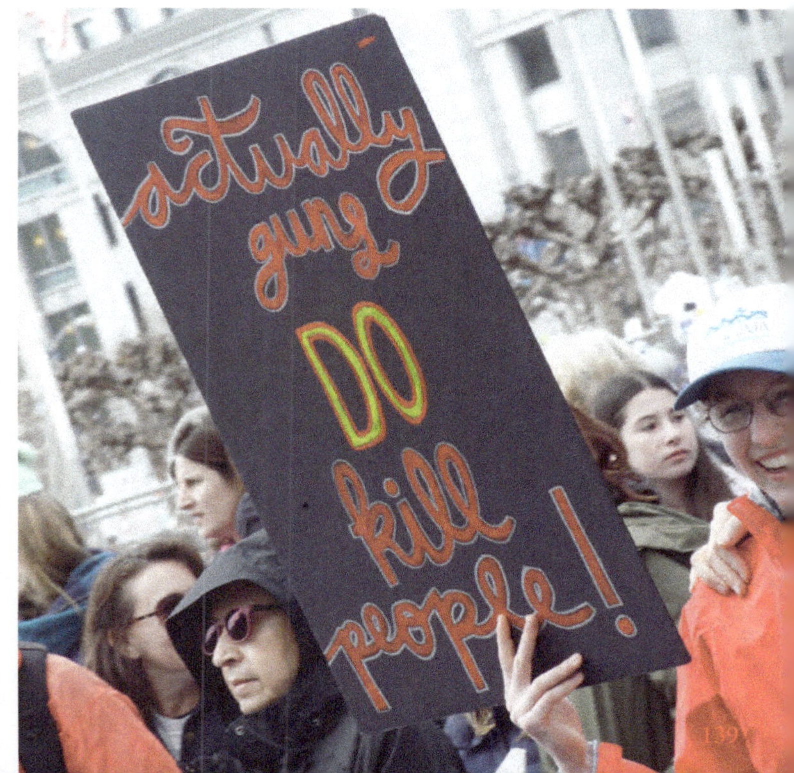
White
suppremacy
GROWS
'nice boy'
terrorists
actually guns
DO
kill
people!

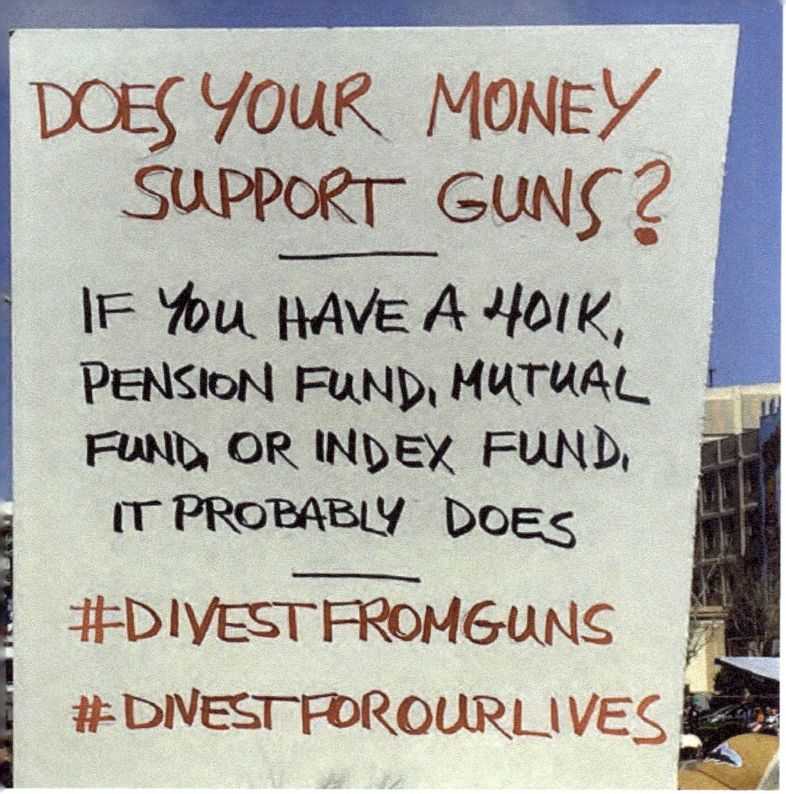

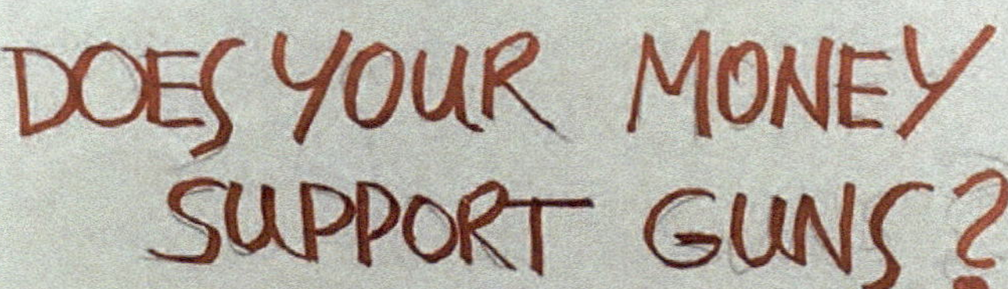

DOES YOUR MONEY SUPPORT GUNS?
IF YOU HAVE A 401K, PENSION FUND, MUTUAL FUND, OR INDEX FUND, IT PROBABLY DOES
#DIVESTFROMGUNS
#DIVESTFOROURLIVES

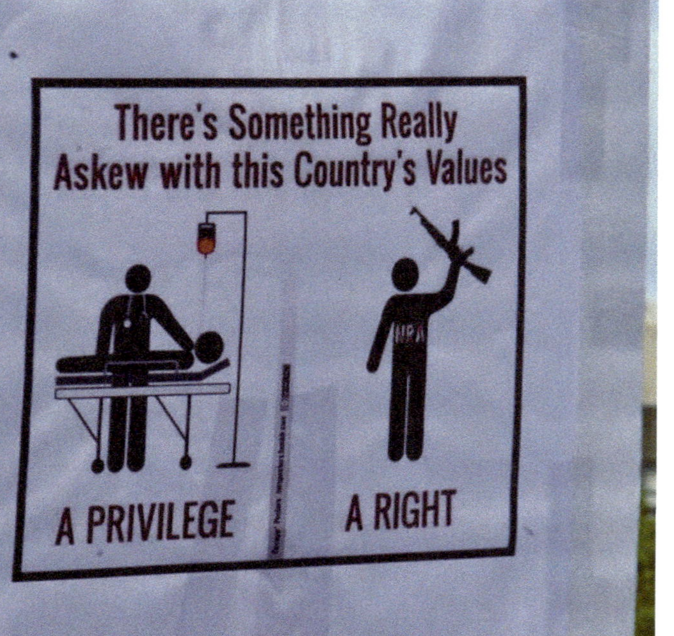

There's Something Really Askew with this Country's Values
A PRIVILEGE
A RIGHT

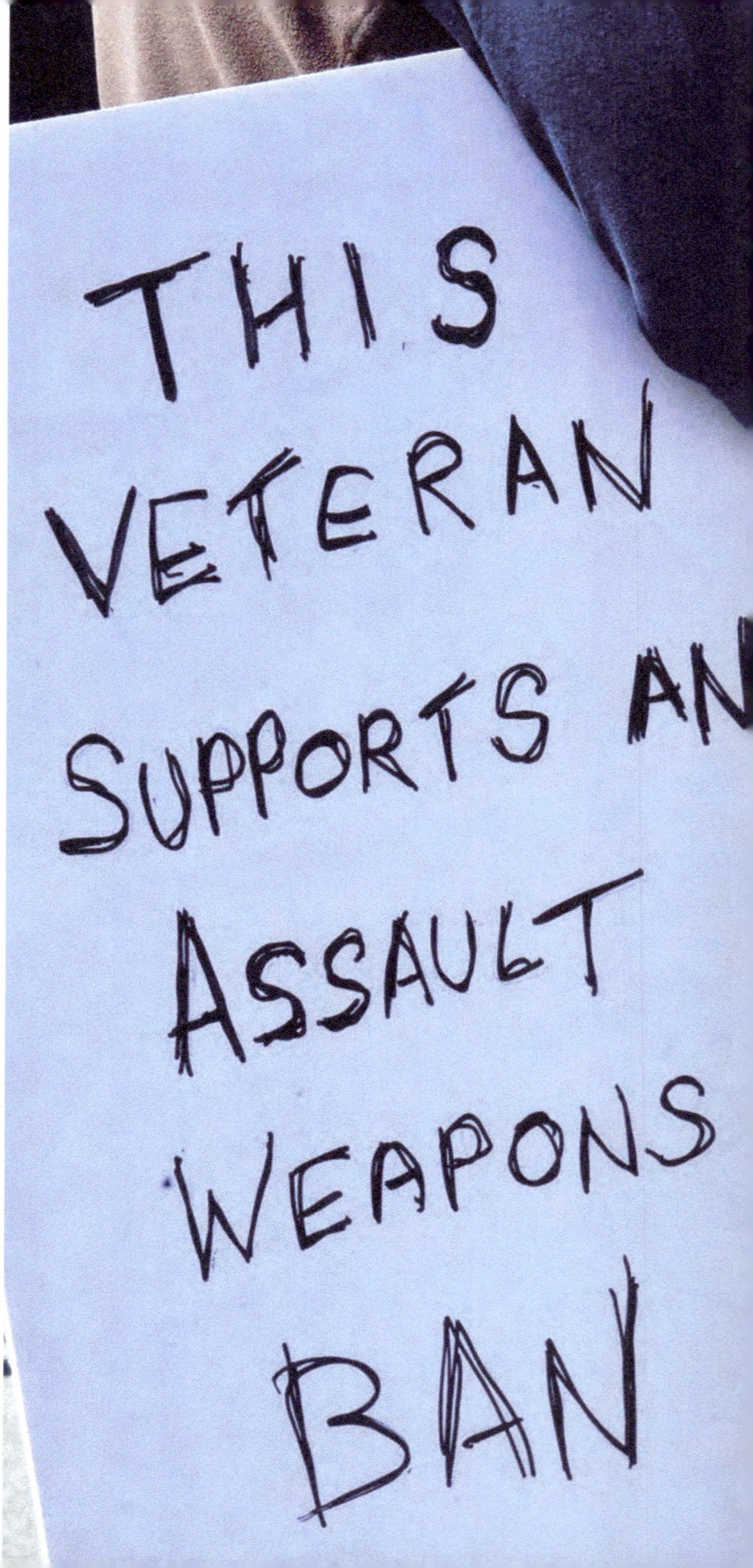

THIS VETERAN SUPPORTS AN ASSAULT WEAPONS BAN

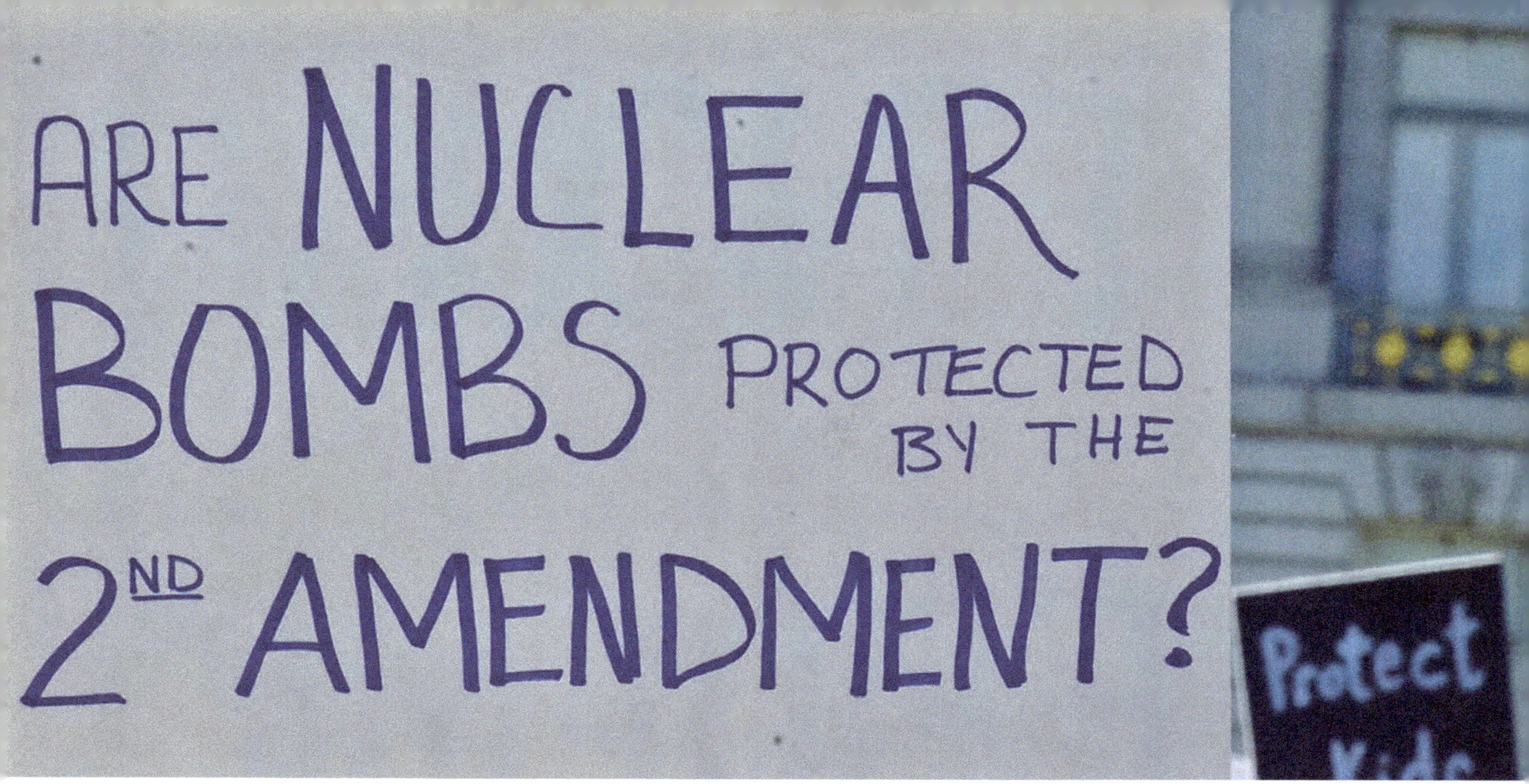

ARE NUCLEAR BOMBS PROTECTED BY THE 2ND AMENDMENT?
Protect Kids
LET US RESEARCH Gun Violence
like we can research any other epidemic
IF NOT US WHO? IF NOT NOW WHEN?
YOUR ELECTORAL
White Cou
AGAINS
un Violenc

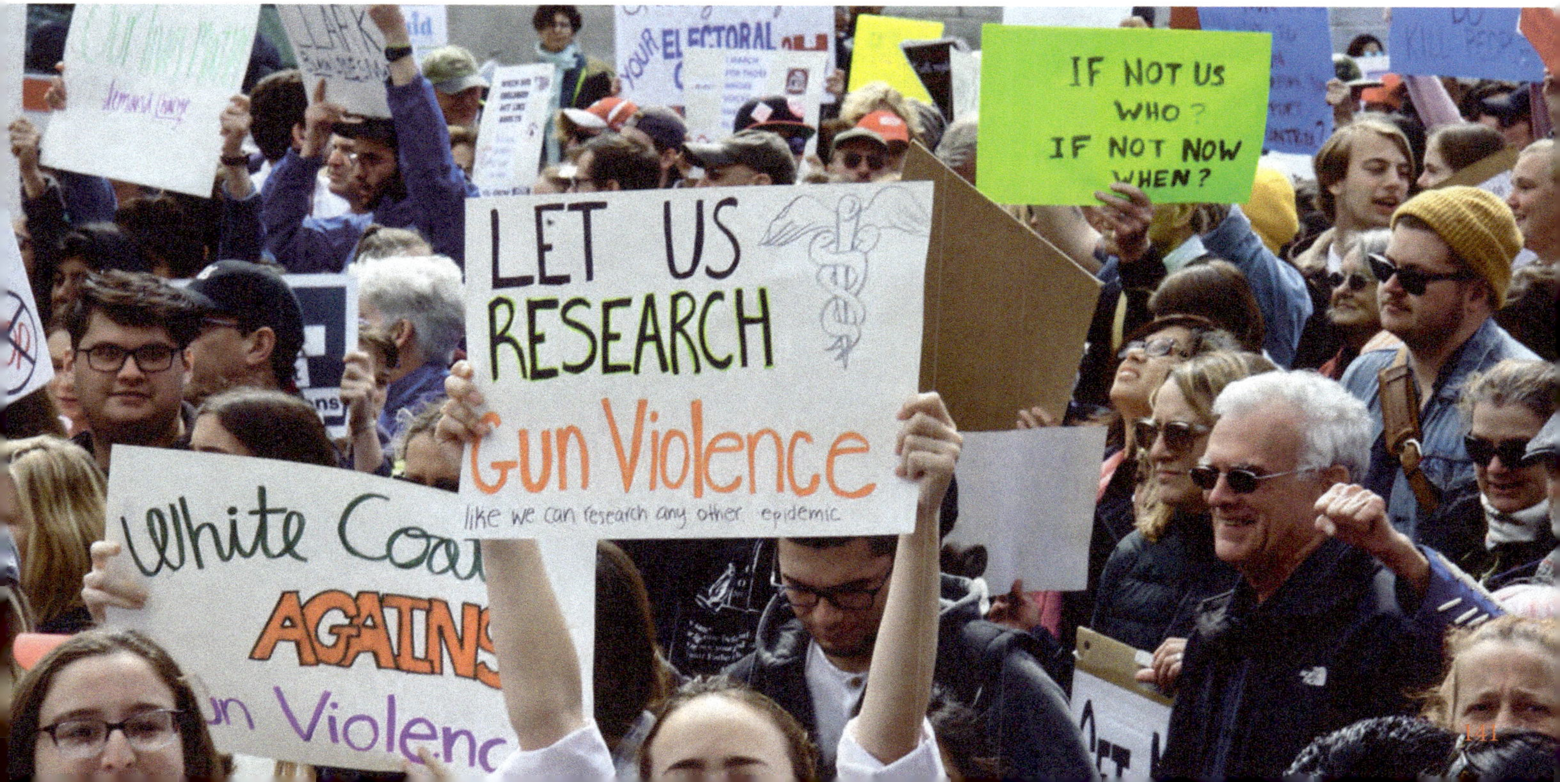

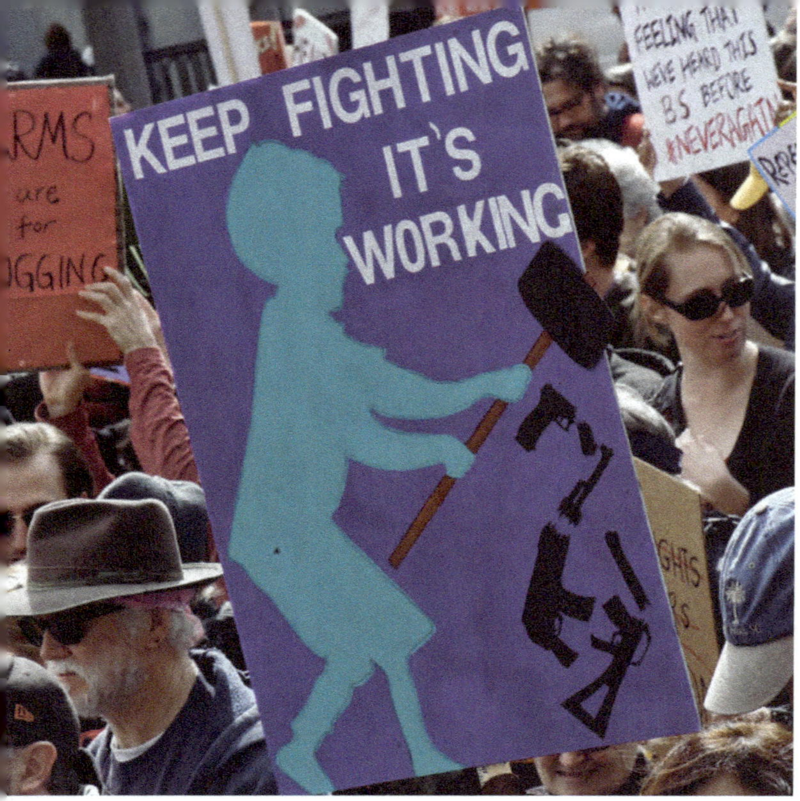

KEEP FIGHTING IT'S WORKING

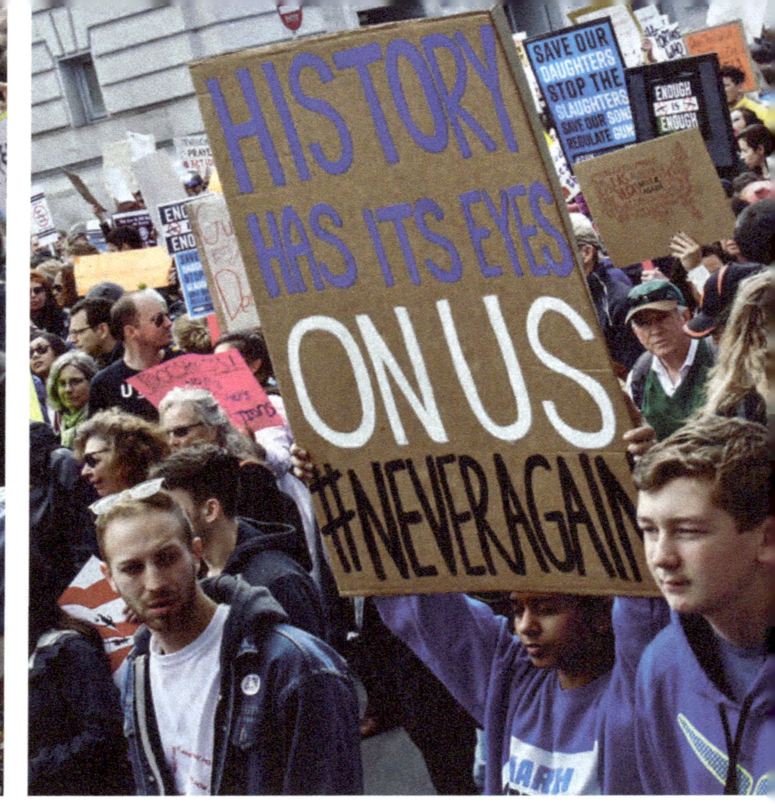

HISTORY HAS ITS EYES ON US
#NEVERAGAIN
SAVE OUR DAUGHTERS STOP THE SLAUGHTERS
ENOUGH IS ENOUGH

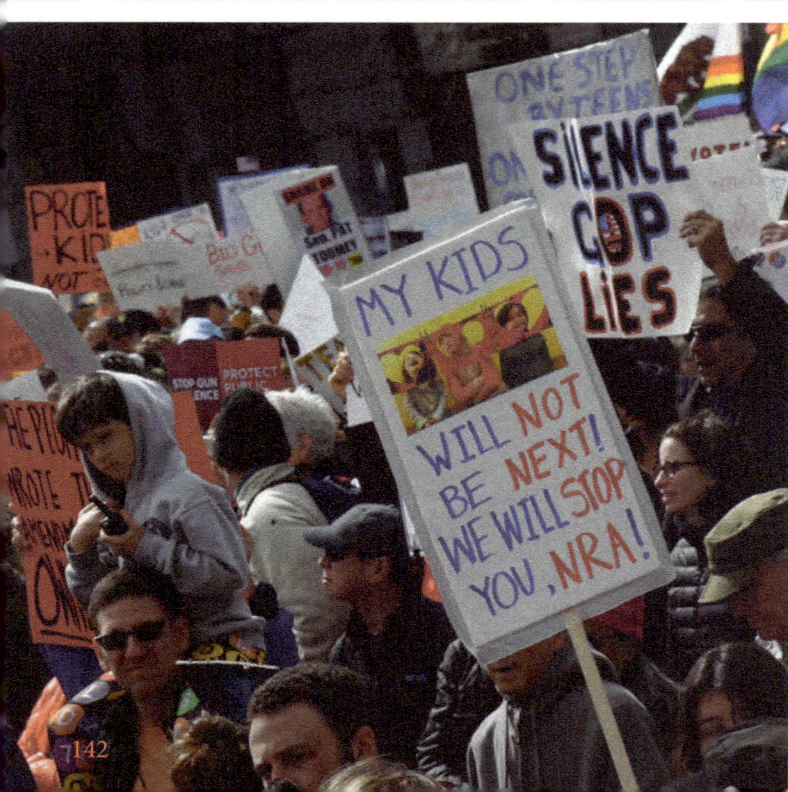

ONE STEP BY TEENS
SILENCE COP LIES
MY KIDS WILL NOT BE NEXT! WE WILL STOP YOU, NRA!
PROTECT KIDS

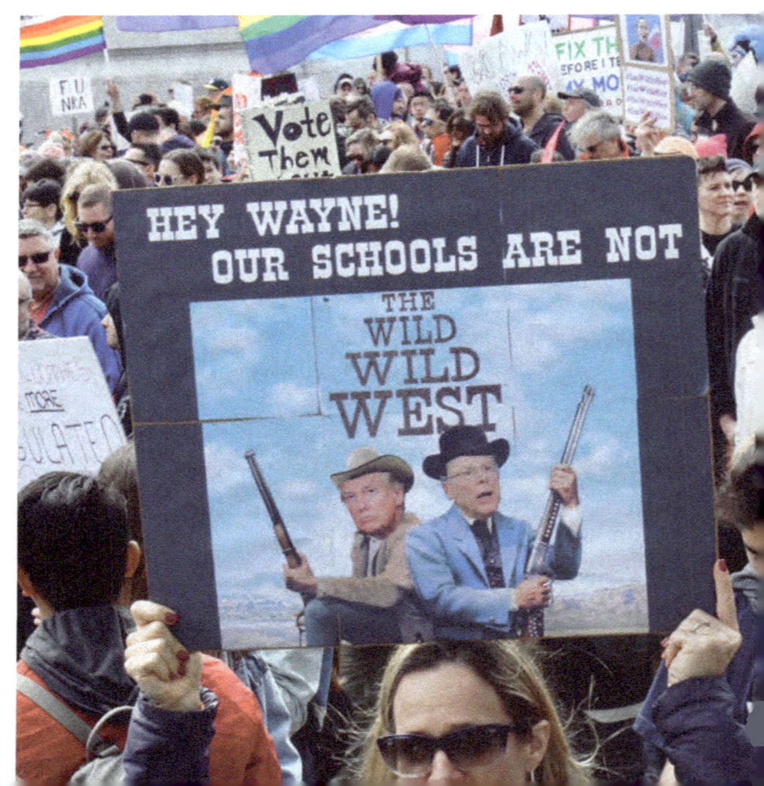

Vote Them Out
HEY WAYNE! OUR SCHOOLS ARE NOT
THE WILD WILD WEST
F U NRA

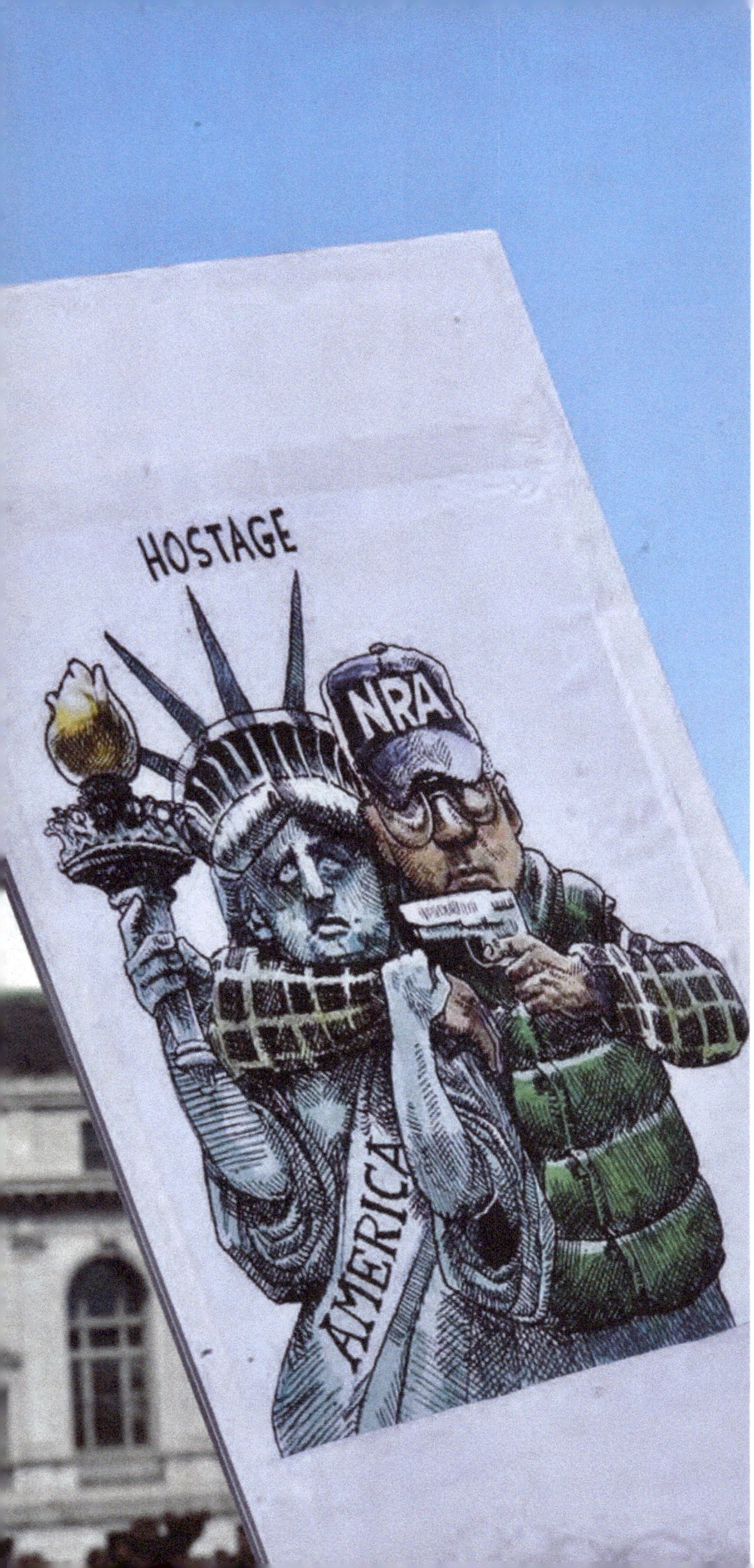

HOSTAGE
NRA
AMERICA

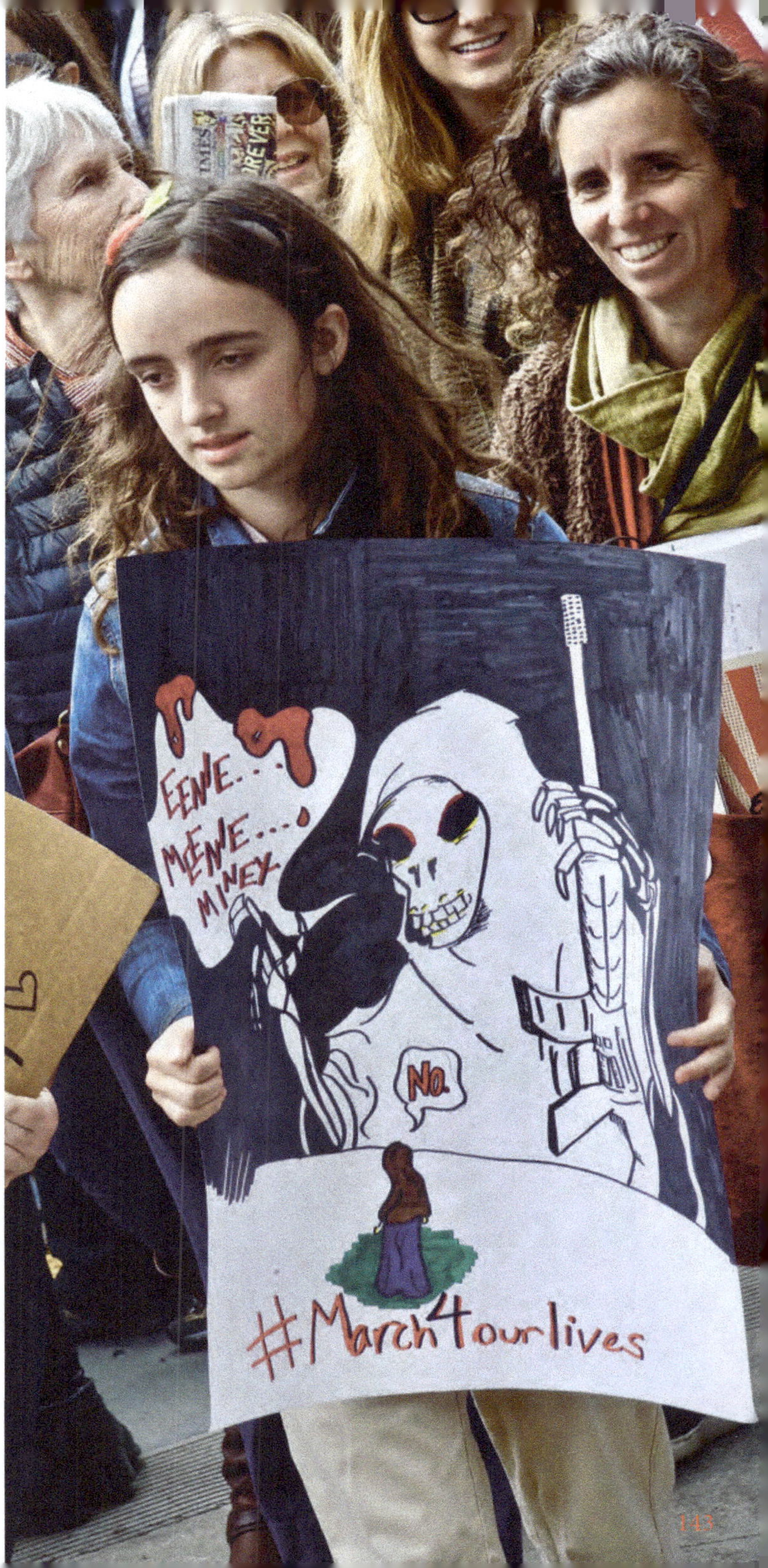

EENE...
MEENE...
MINEY
NO.
#March4ourlives

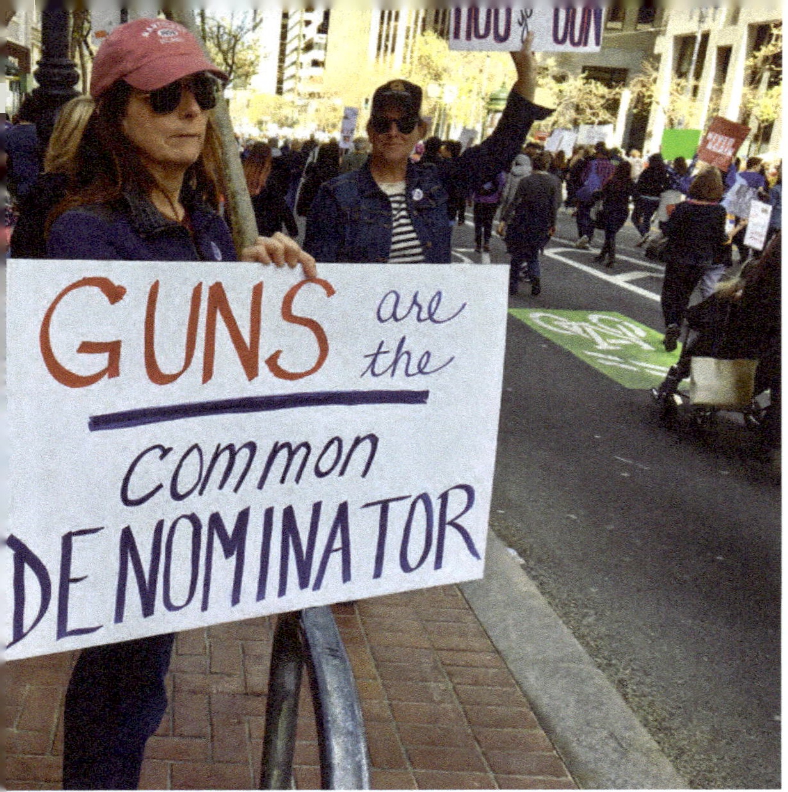
GUNS are the common DENOMINATOR

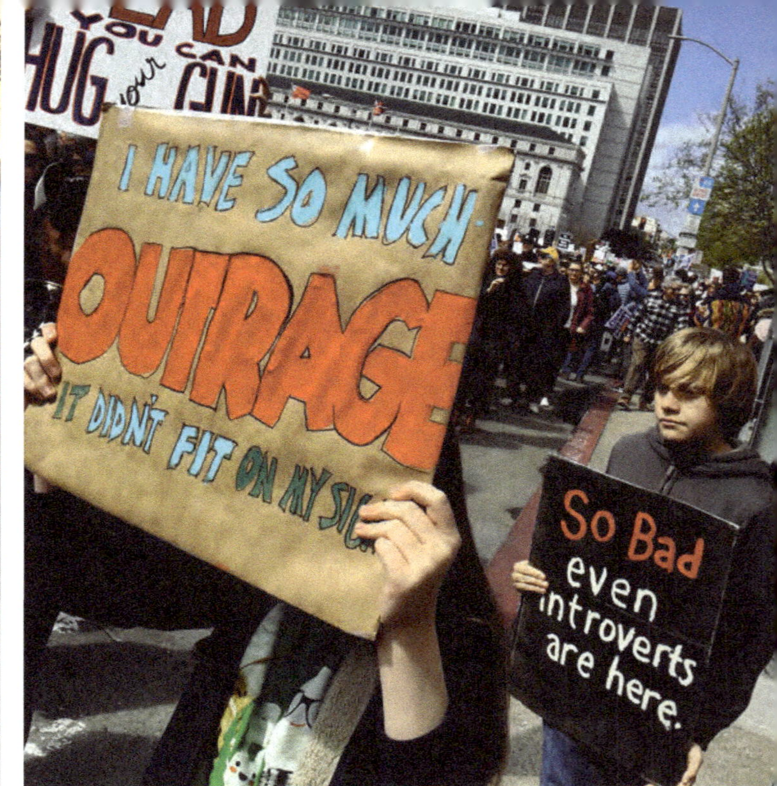
I HAVE SO MUCH
OUTRAGE
IT DIDN'T FIT ON MY SIGN
So Bad
even
introverts
are here.

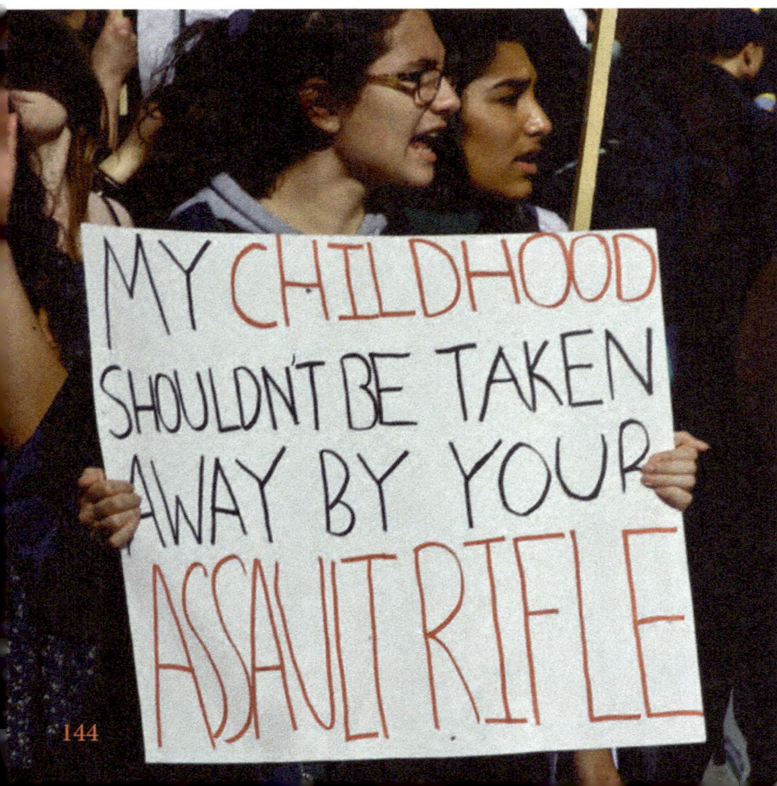
MY CHILDHOOD
SHOULDN'T BE TAKEN
AWAY BY YOUR
ASSAULT RIFLE

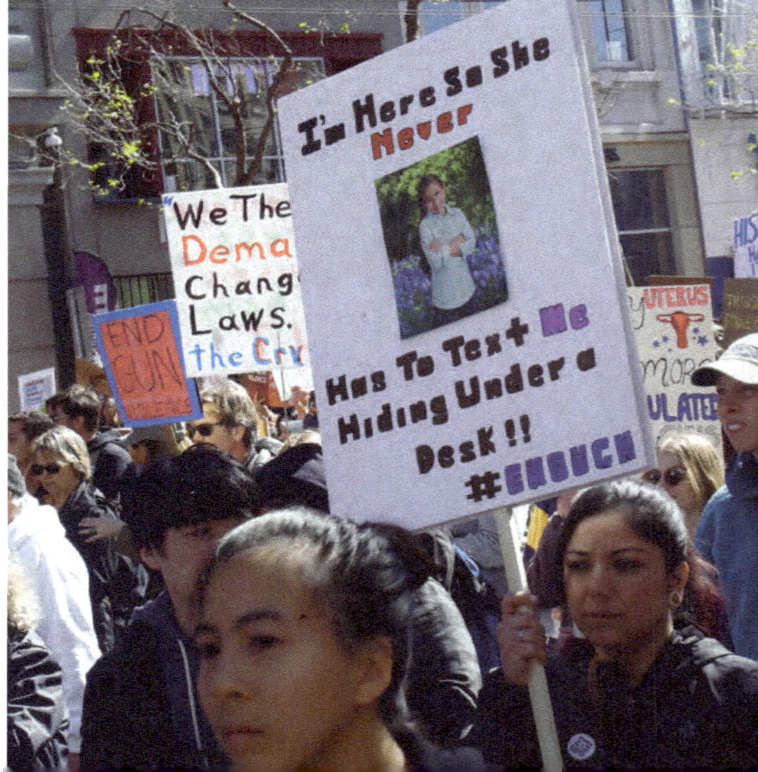
I'm Here So She
Never
Has To Text Me
Hiding Under a
Desk !!
#ENOUGH
We The
Dema
Chang
Laws.
the Cr
END
GUN
UTERUS

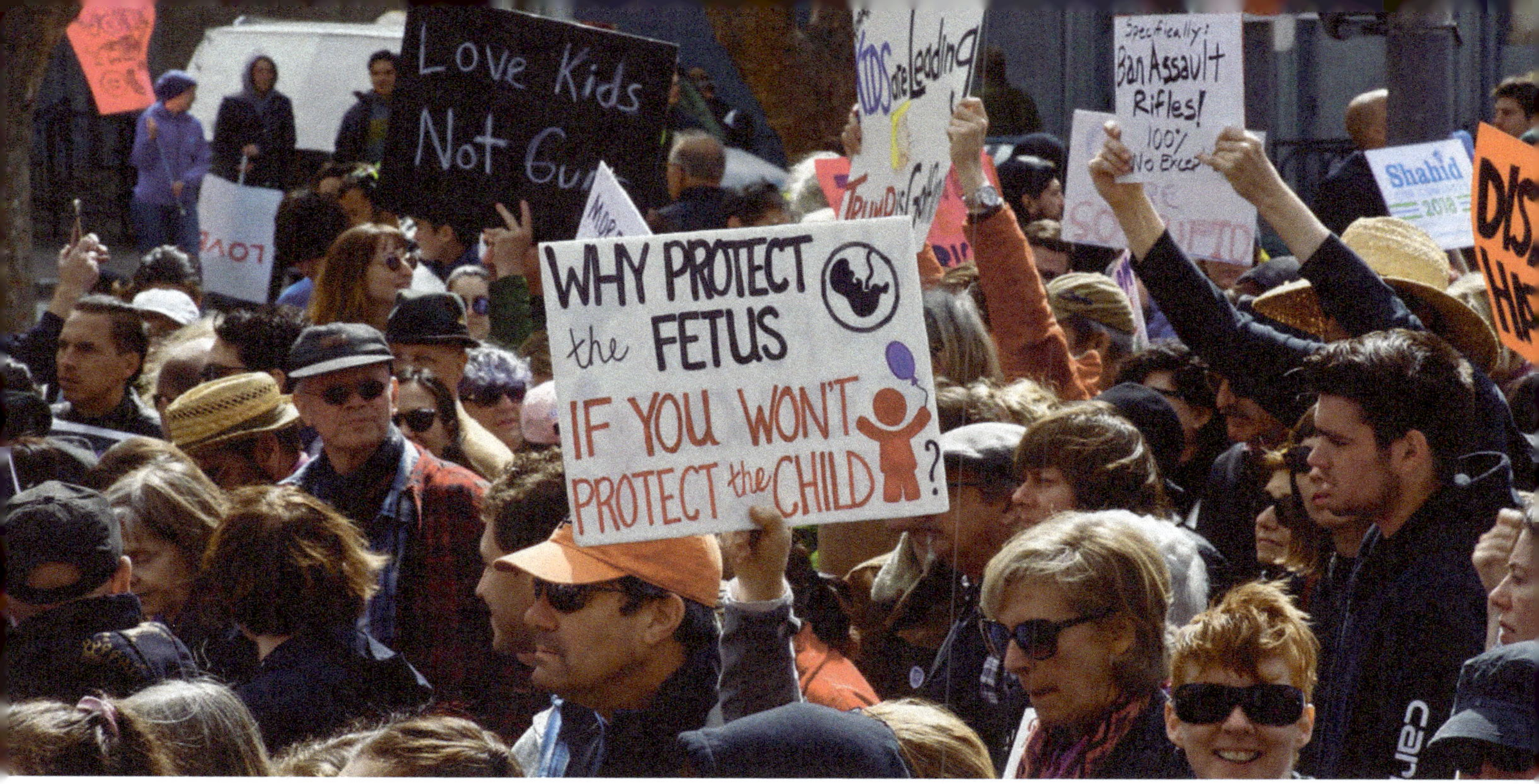

Love Kids Not Guns
KIDS are Leading
Specifically: Ban Assault Rifles! 100% No Excess
Shahid 2018
WHY PROTECT the FETUS IF YOU WON'T PROTECT the CHILD?

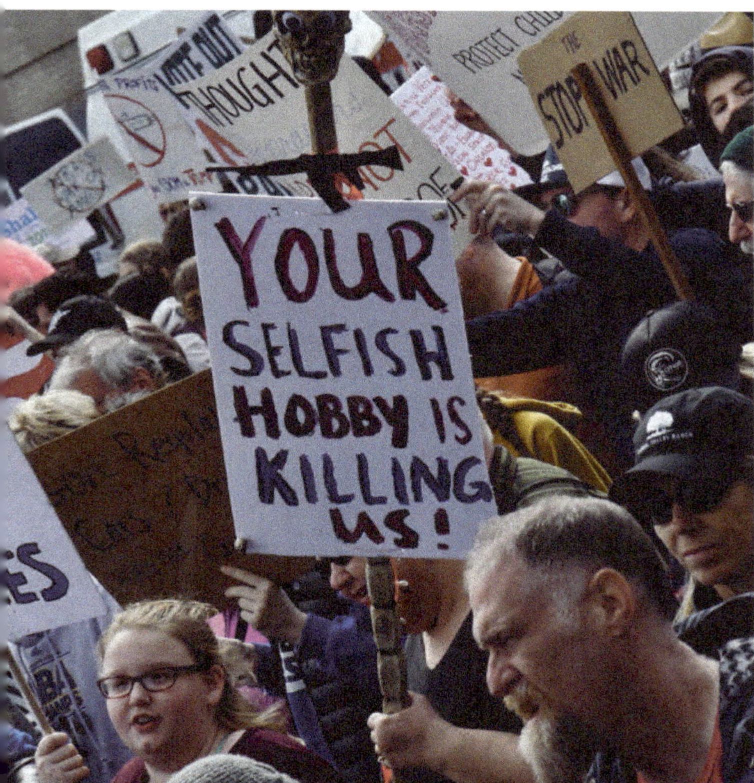

VOTE OUT THOUGHT
PROTECT CHILD
STOP WAR
YOUR SELFISH HOBBY IS KILLING US!

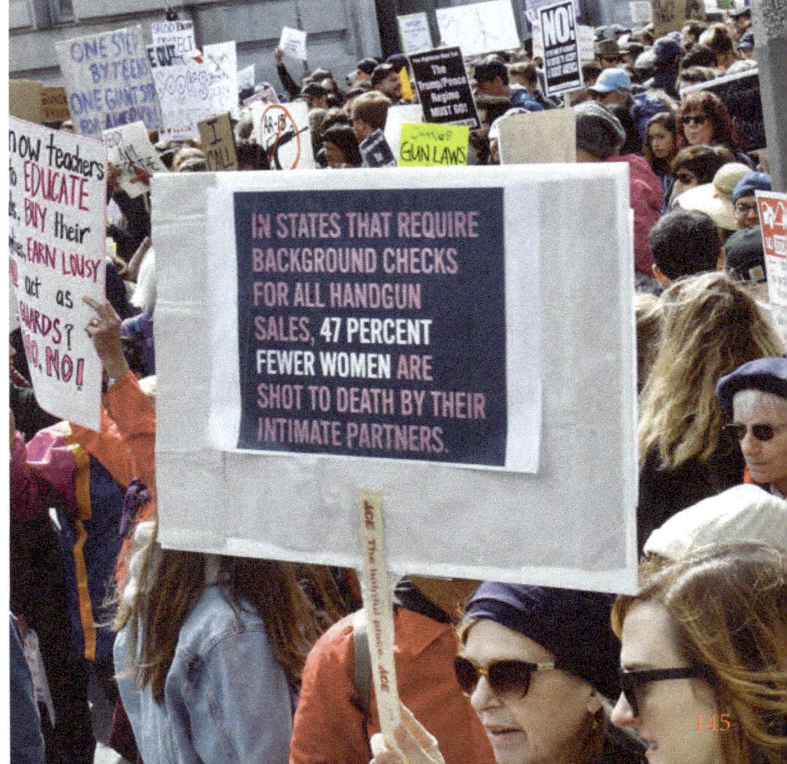

ONE STEP BY TEENS ONE GIANT LEAP
now teachers to EDUCATE Us. BUY their EARN LOUSY act as GUARDS? NO, NO!
The Trump/Pence Regime MUST GO!
NO!
GUN LAWS
IN STATES THAT REQUIRE BACKGROUND CHECKS FOR ALL HANDGUN SALES, 47 PERCENT FEWER WOMEN ARE SHOT TO DEATH BY THEIR INTIMATE PARTNERS.

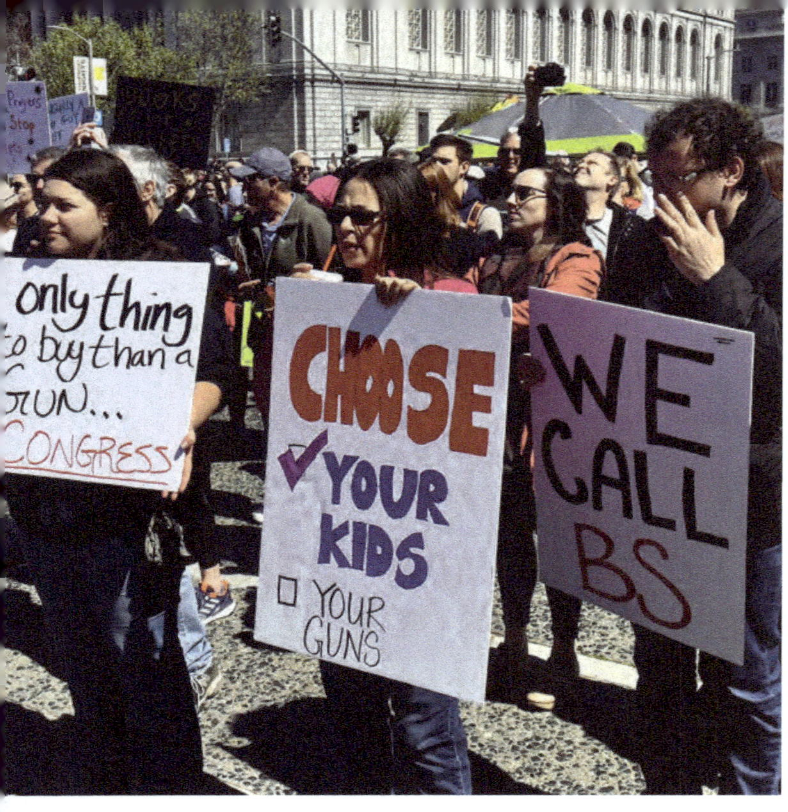
only thing
to buy than a
GUN...
CONGRESS
CHOOSE
YOUR
KIDS
YOUR
GUNS
WE
CALL
BS

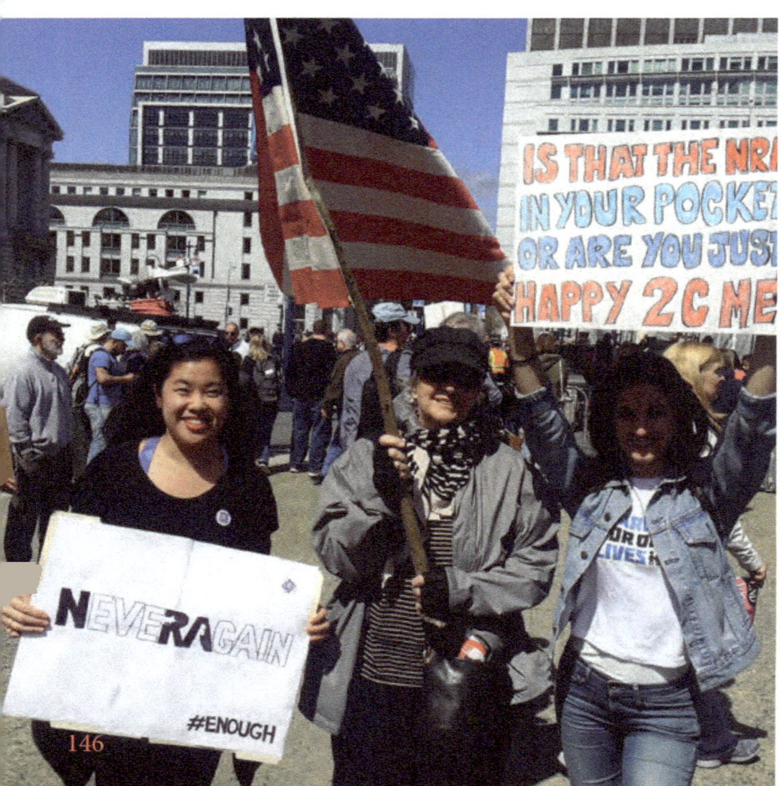
IS THAT THE NRA
IN YOUR POCKET
OR ARE YOU JUST
HAPPY 2 C ME
NEVER AGAIN
#ENOUGH

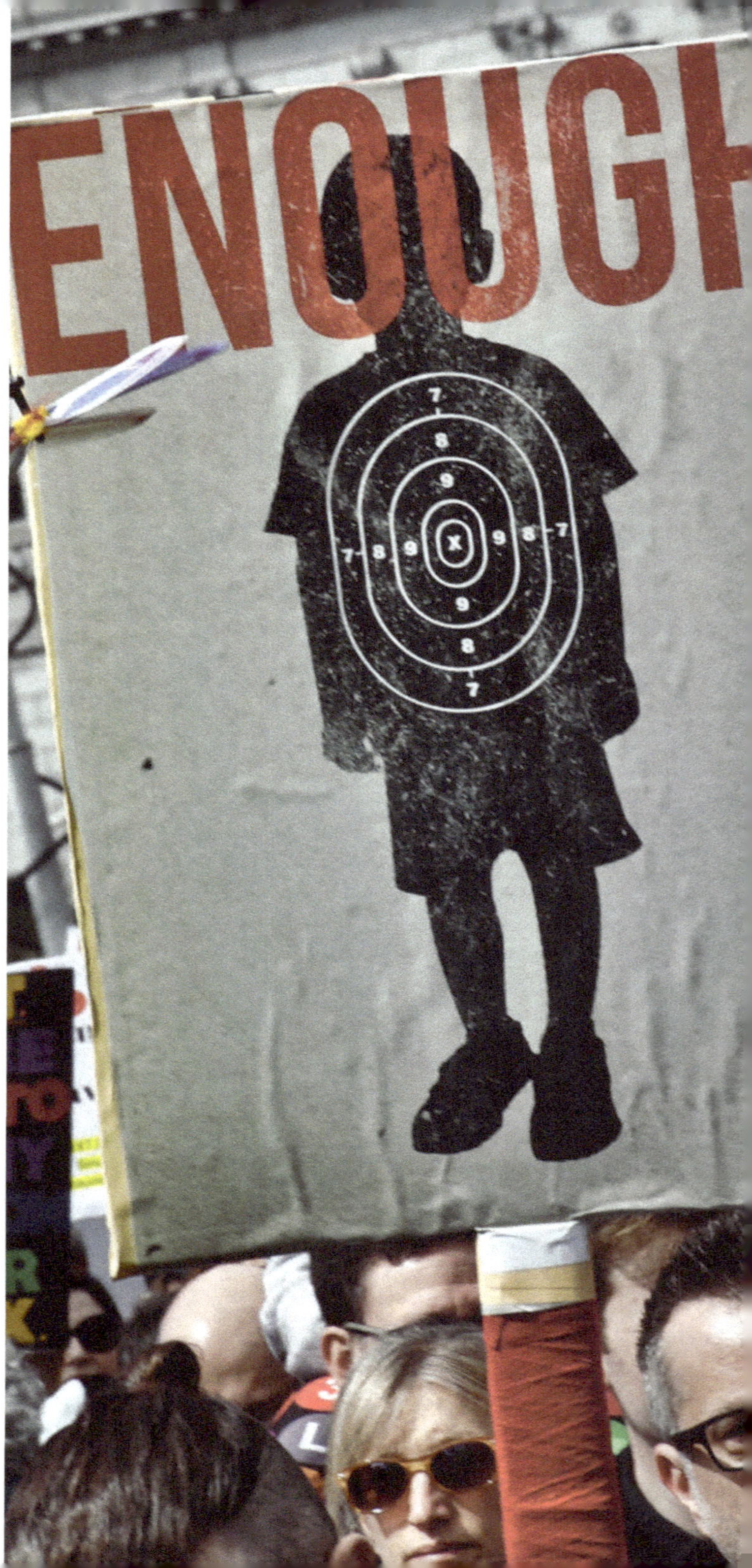

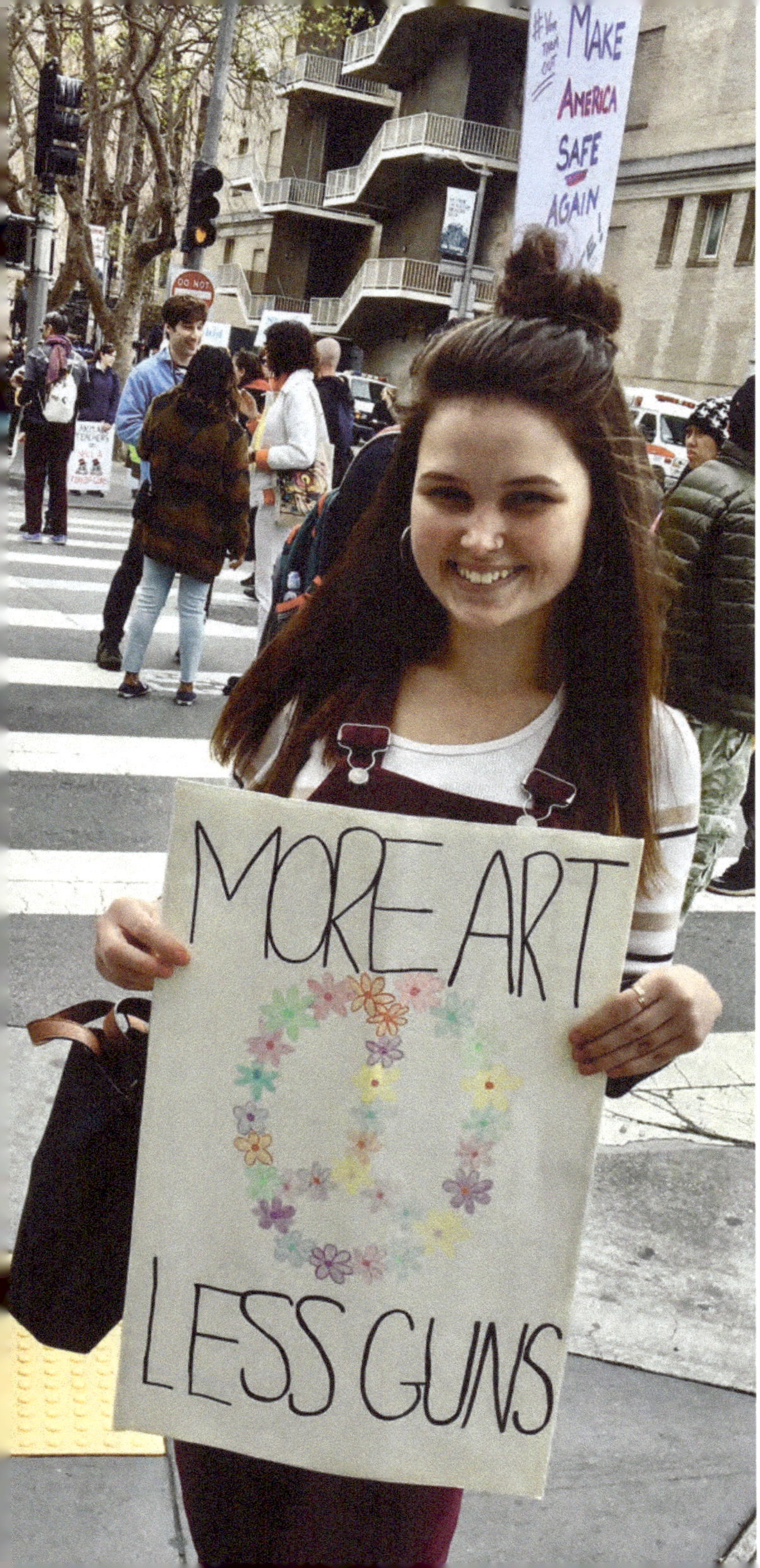

MAKE
AMERICA
SAFE
AGAIN
MORE ART
LESS GUNS
If lawn Darts 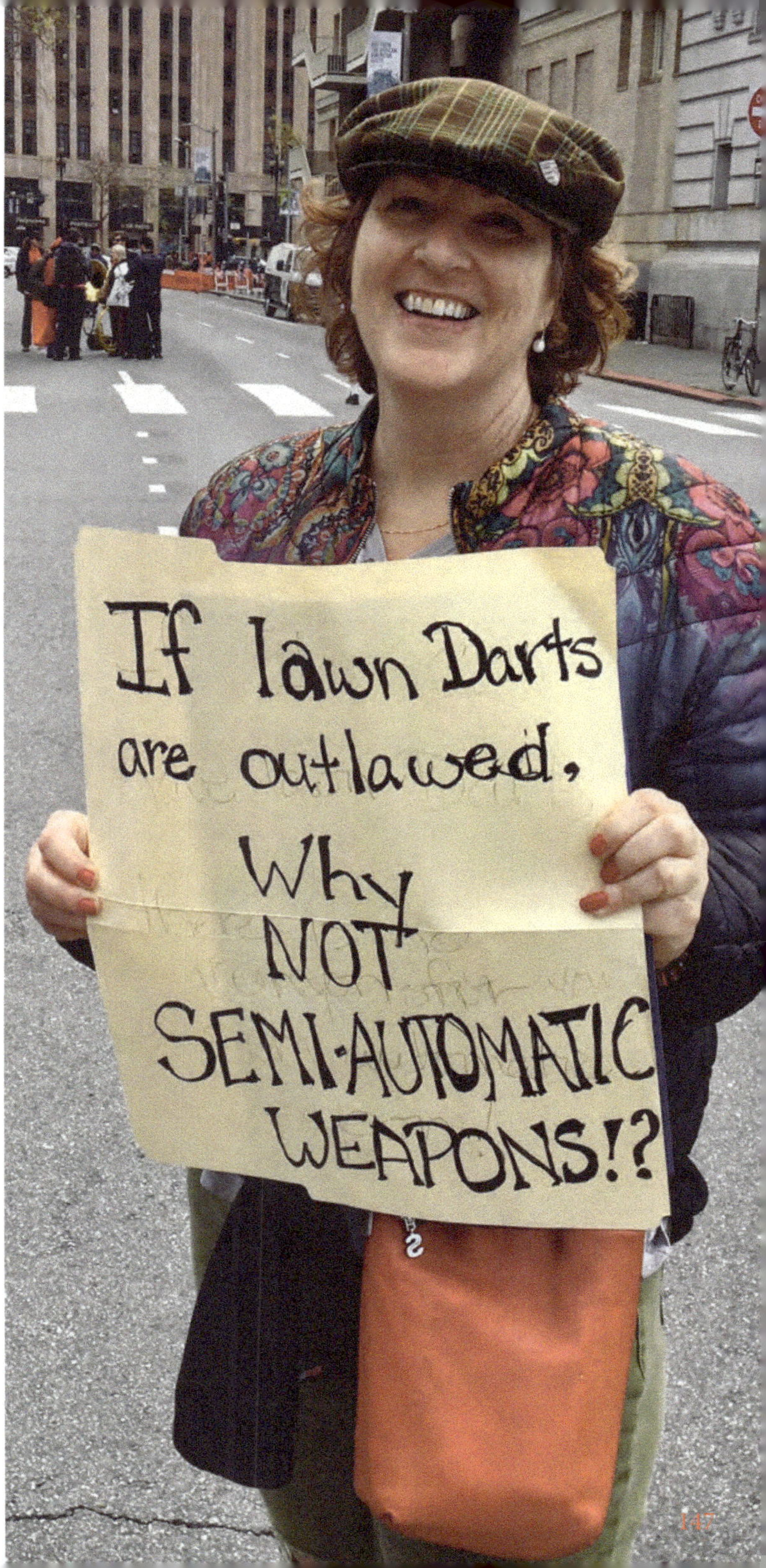
are outlawed,
Why
NOT
SEMI-AUTOMATIC
WEAPONS!?

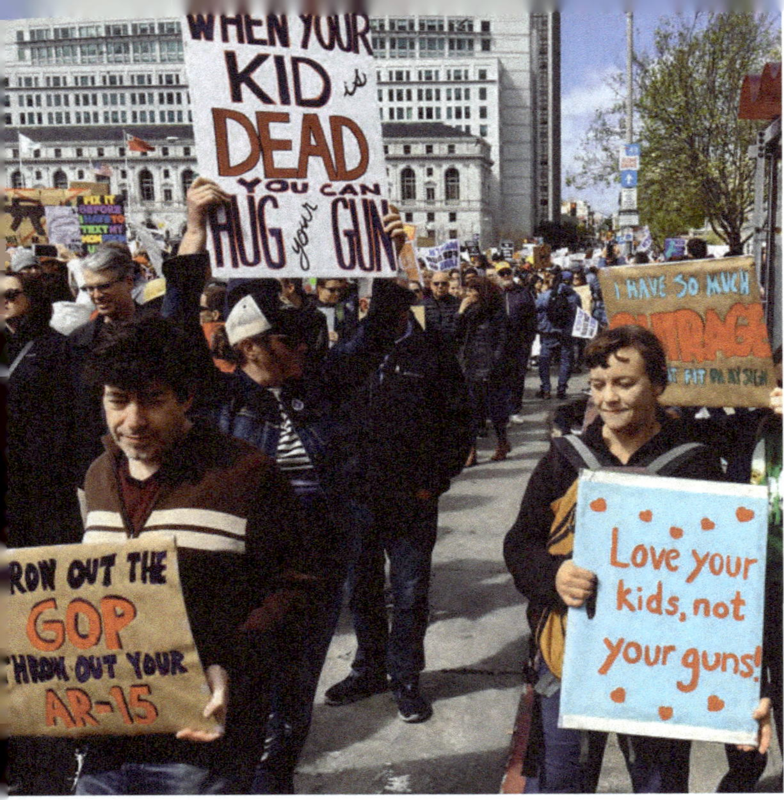

WHEN YOUR KID is DEAD YOU CAN HUG your GUN
I HAVE SO MUCH OUTRAGE
Love your kids, not your guns!
ROW OUT THE GOP THROW OUT YOUR AR-15

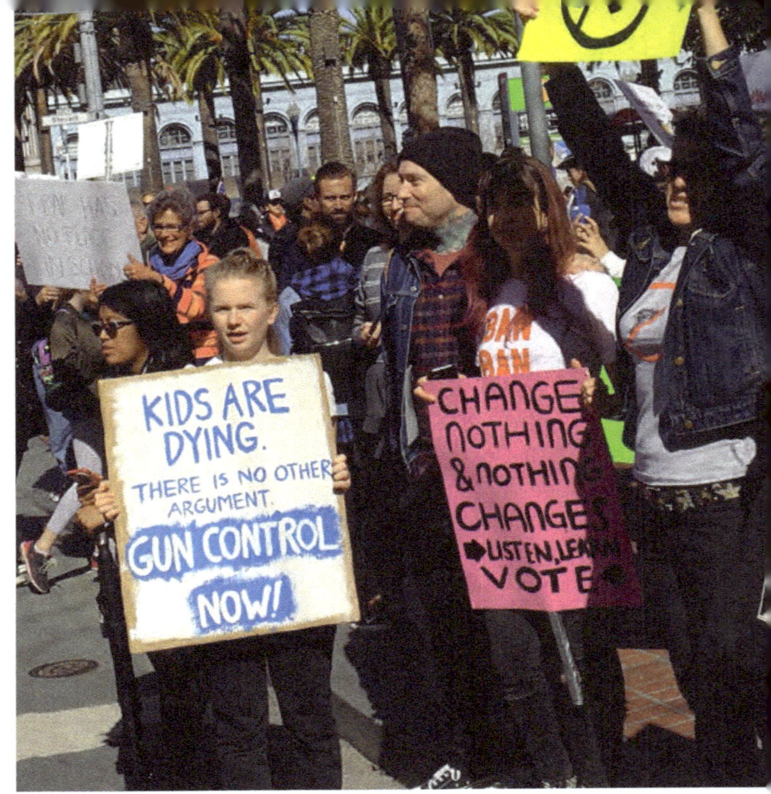

KIDS ARE DYING. THERE IS NO OTHER ARGUMENT. GUN CONTROL NOW!
CHANGE NOTHING & NOTHING CHANGES LISTEN, LEARN VOTE

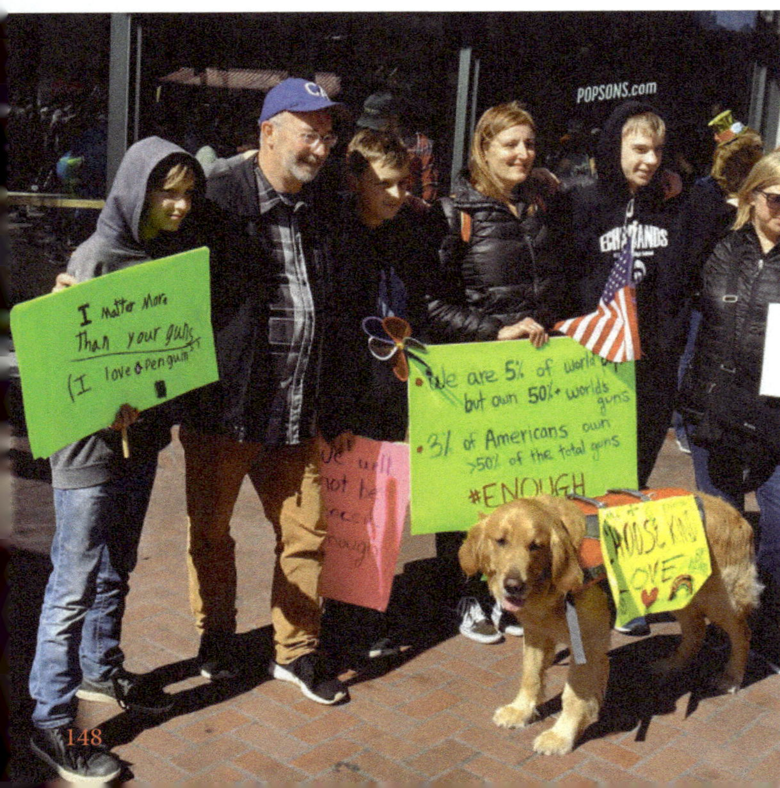

POPSONS.com
I Matter More Than your guns (I love open guns)
We are 5% of world but own 50%+ worlds guns
3% of Americans own >50% of the total guns
#ENOUGH

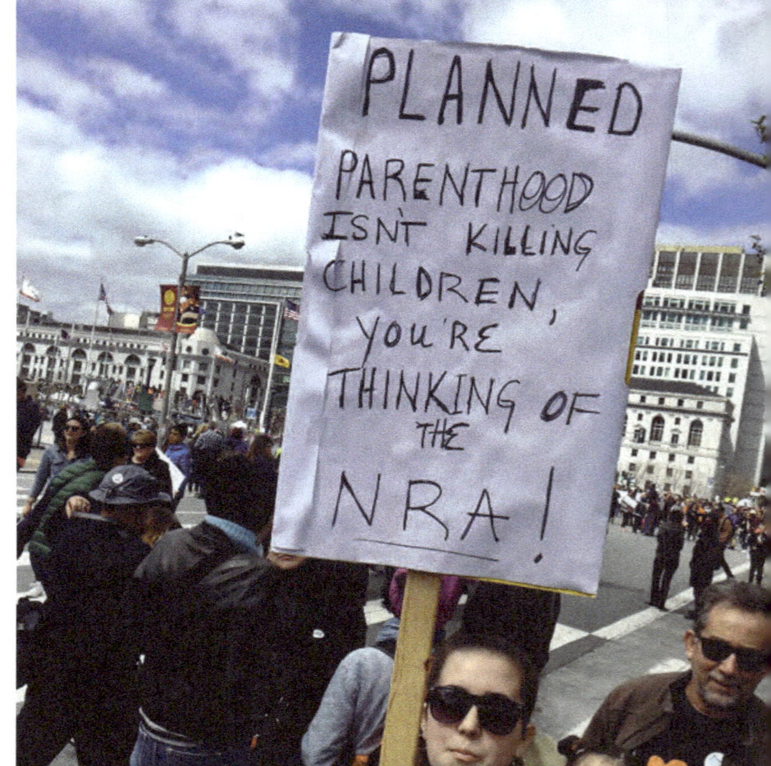

PLANNED PARENTHOOD ISN'T KILLING CHILDREN, YOU'RE THINKING OF THE NRA!

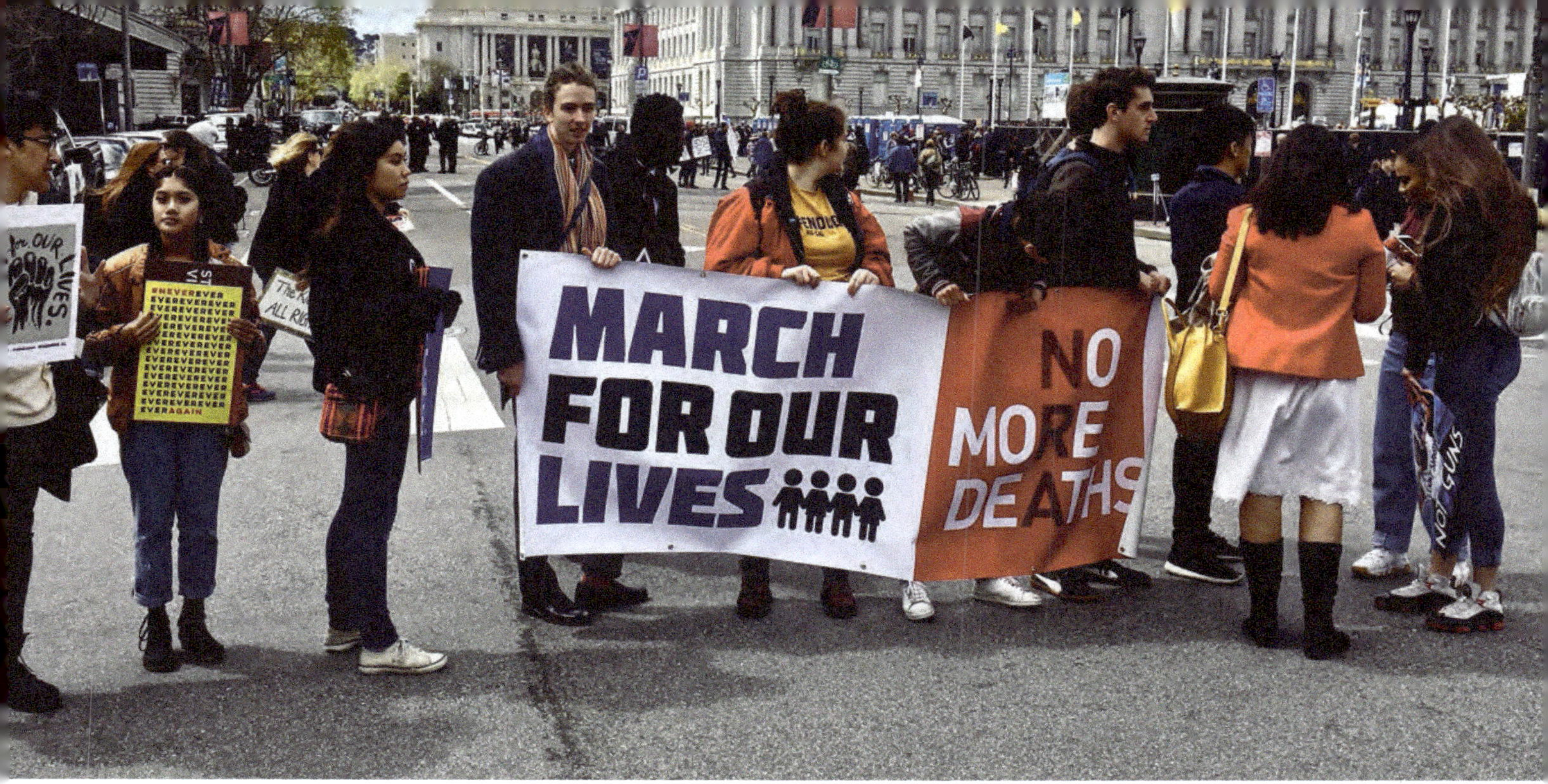

MARCH FOR OUR LIVES
NO MORE DEATHS

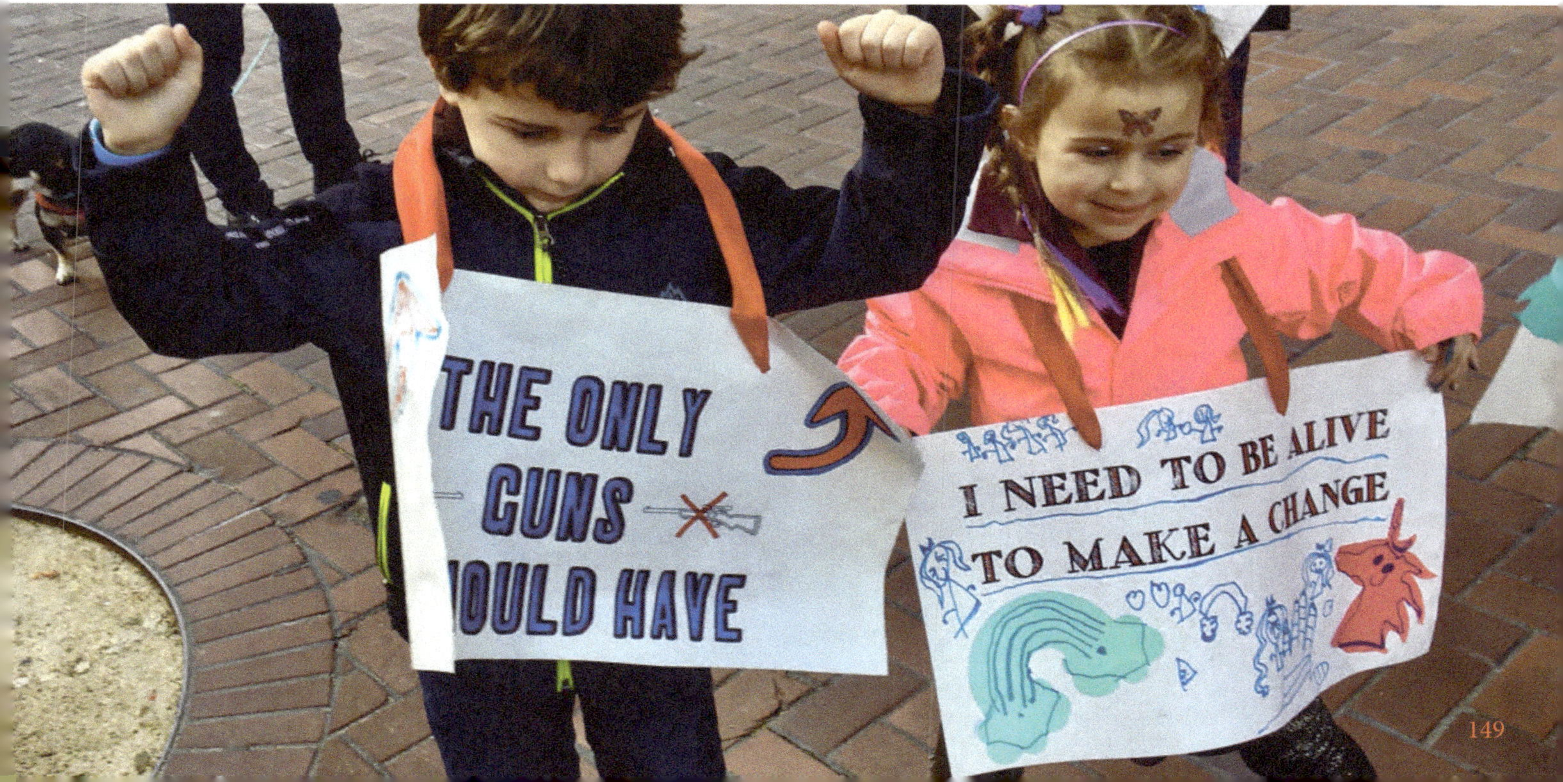

THE ONLY GUNS [SH]OULD HAVE
I NEED TO BE ALIVE TO MAKE A CHANGE

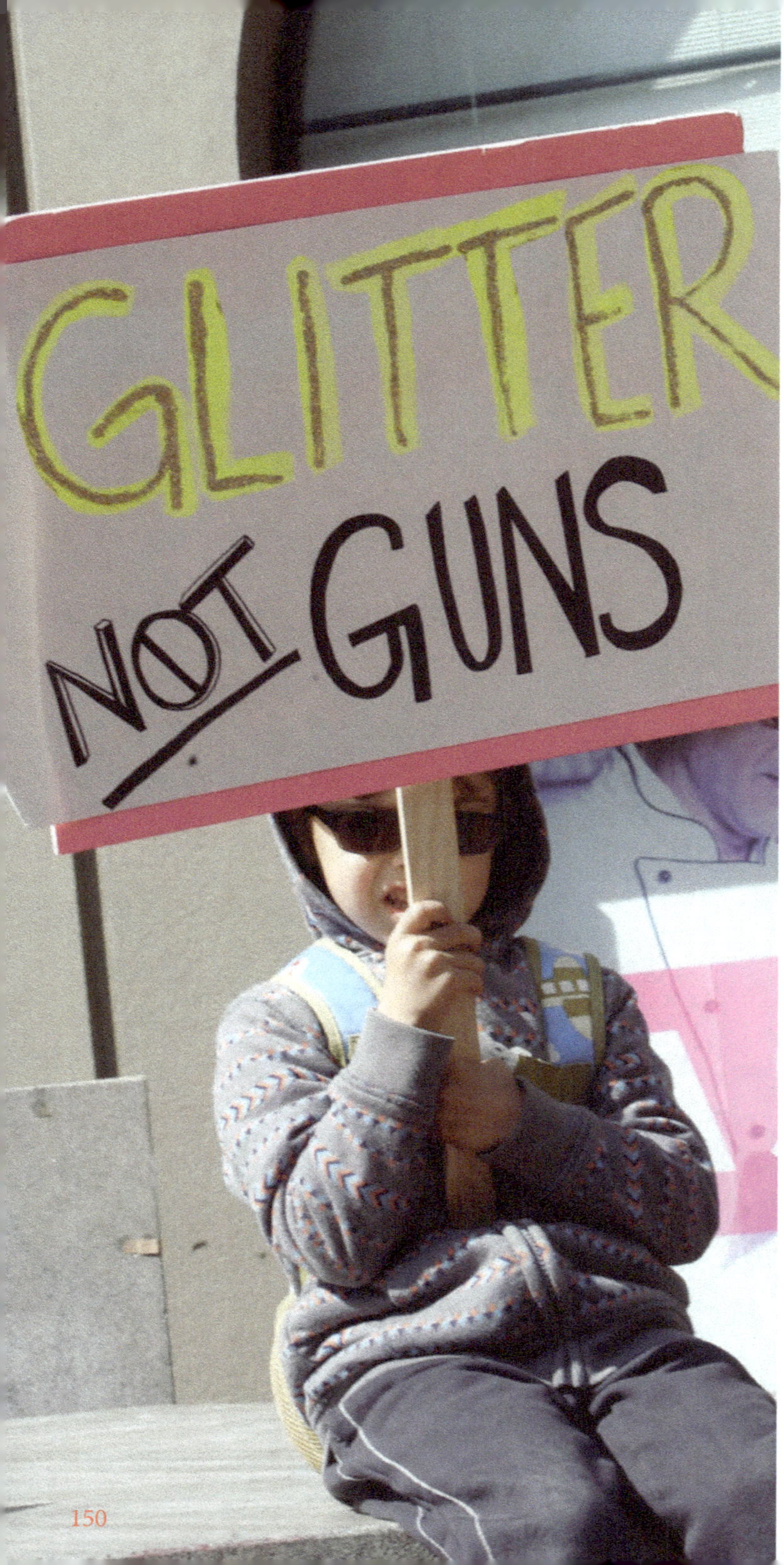

GLITTER
NOT GUNS

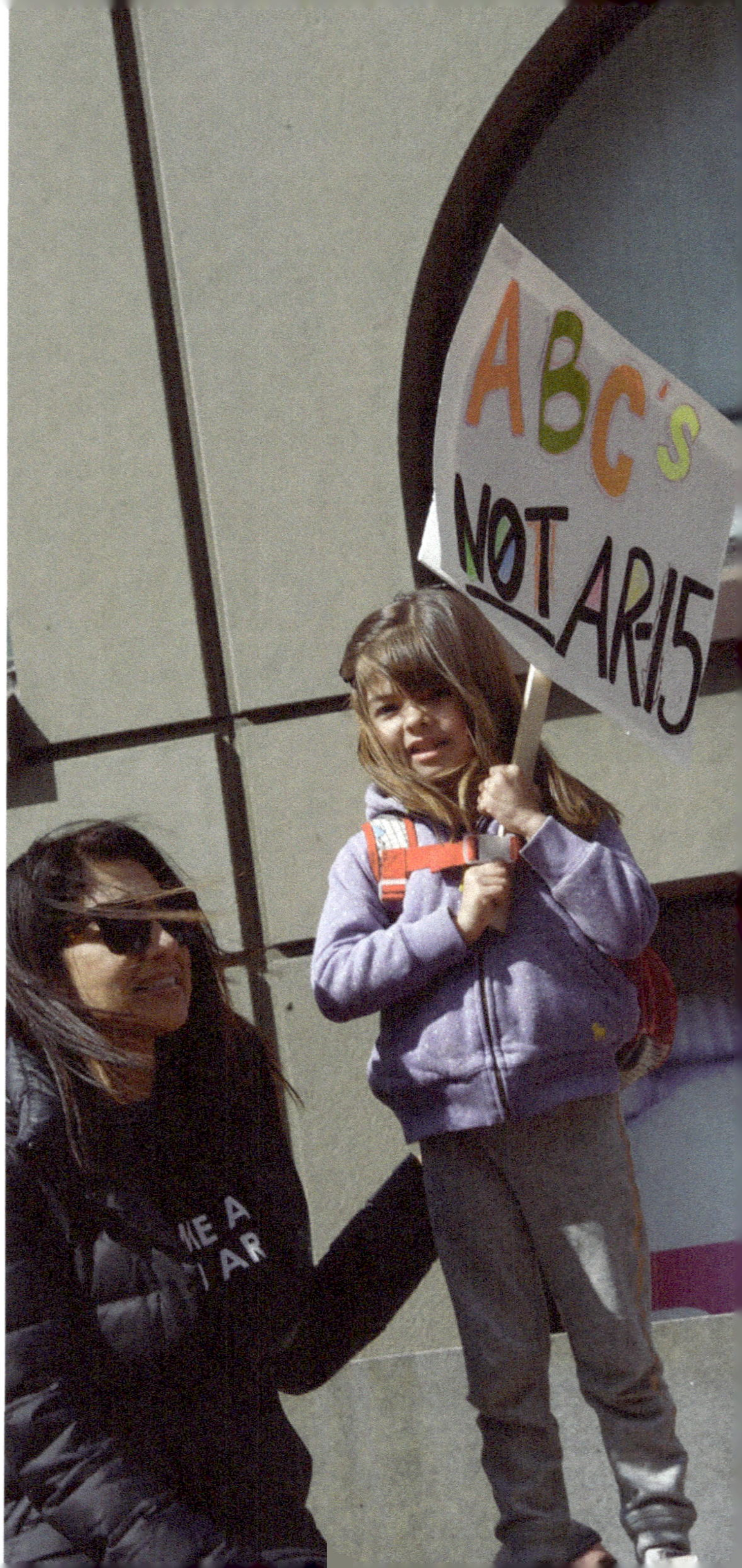

ABC's
NOT AR-15

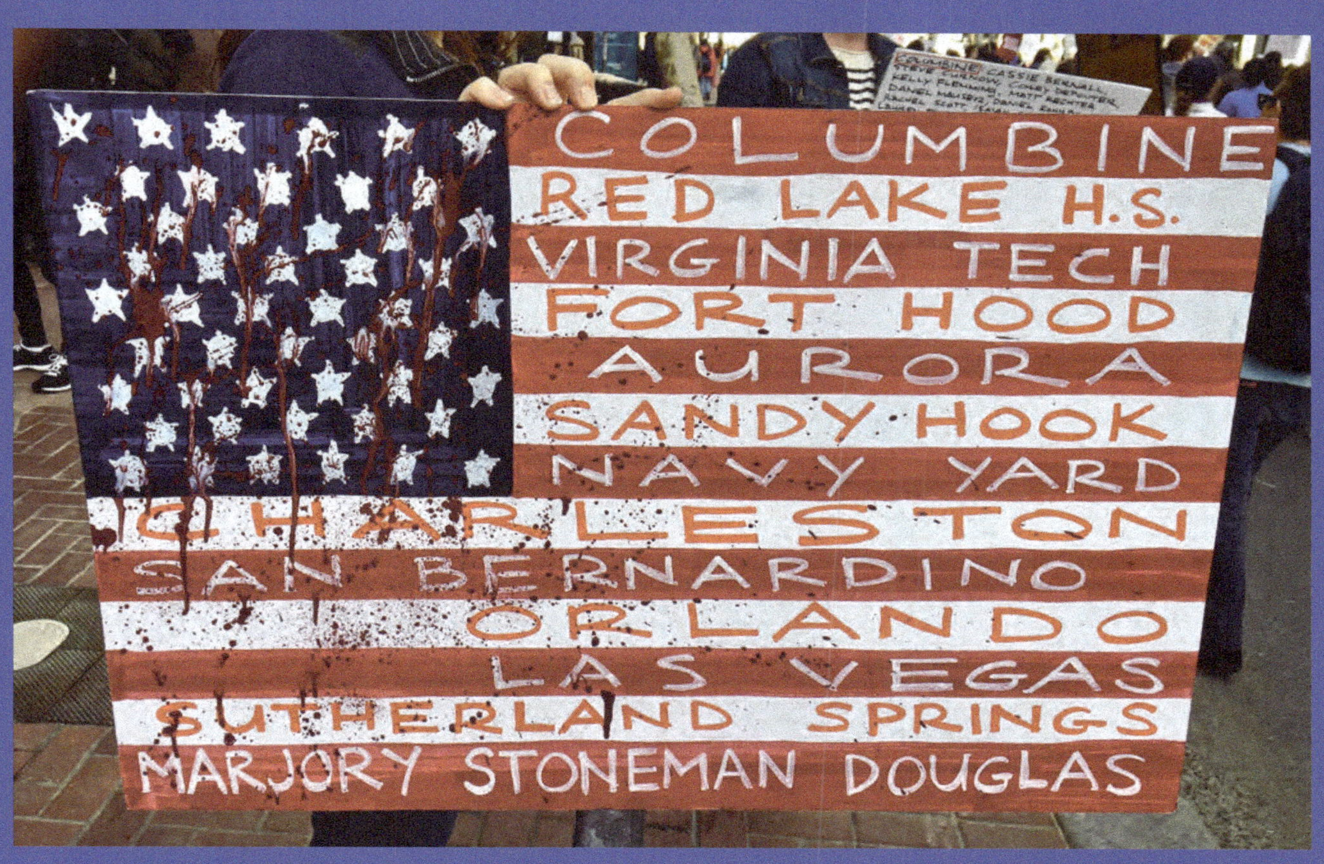
COLUMBINE
RED LAKE H.S.
VIRGINIA TECH
FORT HOOD
AURORA
SANDY HOOK
NAVY YARD
CHARLESTON
SAN BERNARDINO
ORLANDO
LAS VEGAS
SUTHERLAND SPRINGS
MARJORY STONEMAN DOUGLAS

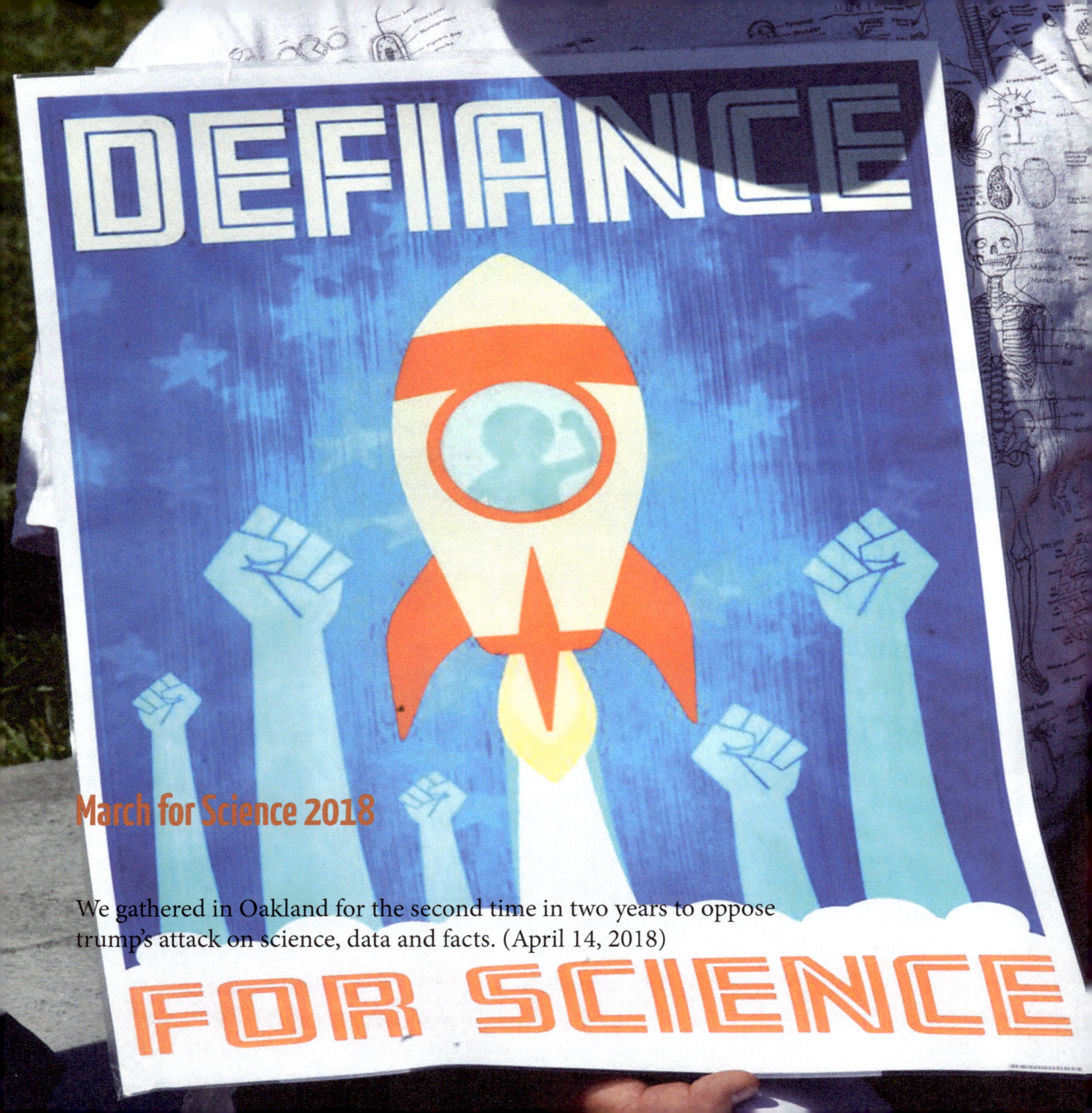

We gathered in Oakland for the second time in two years to oppose trump's attack on science, data and facts. (April 14, 2018)

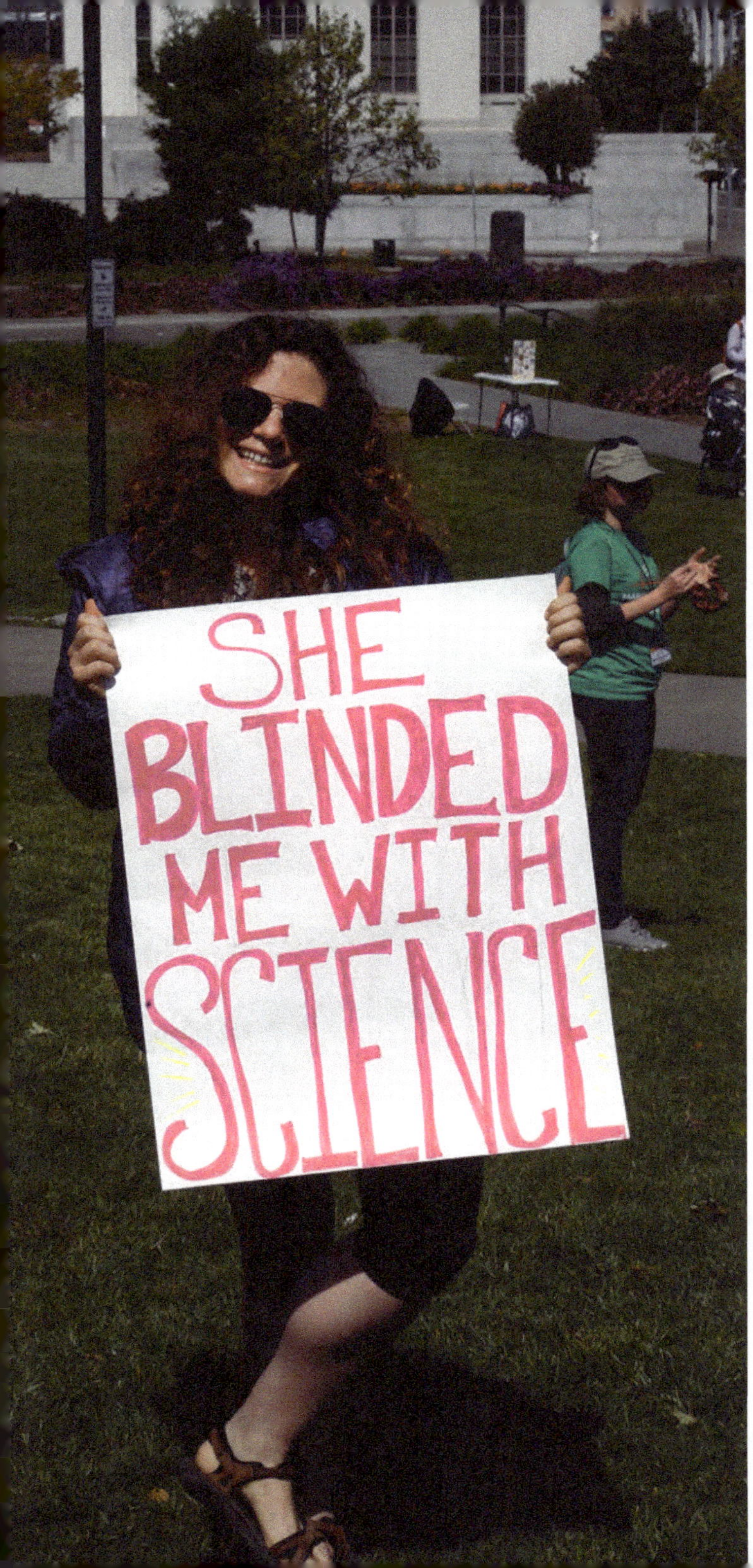

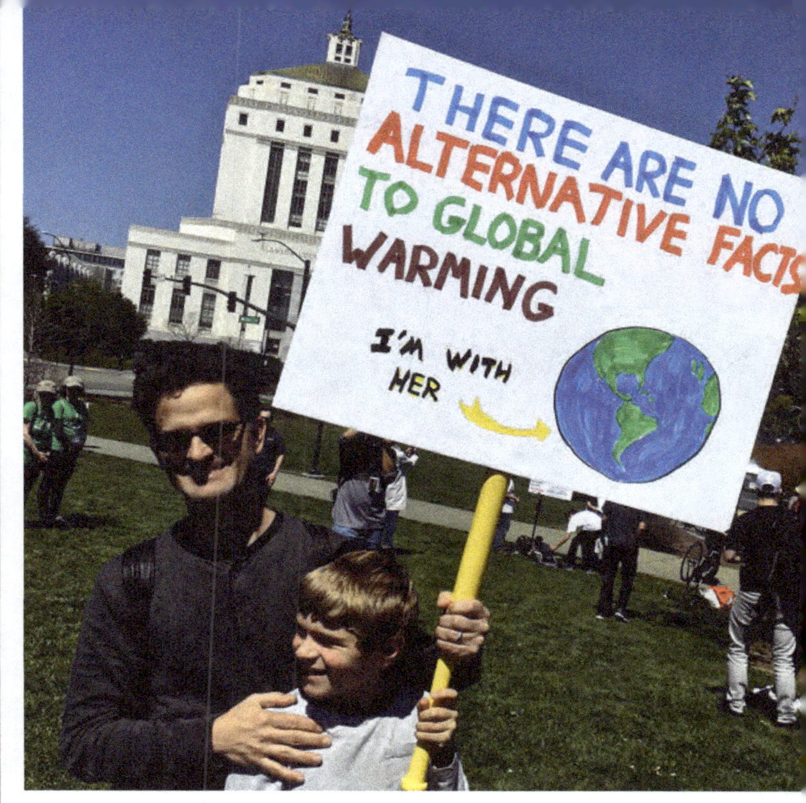

THERE ARE NO
ALTERNATIVE FACTS
TO GLOBAL
WARMING
I'M WITH
HER

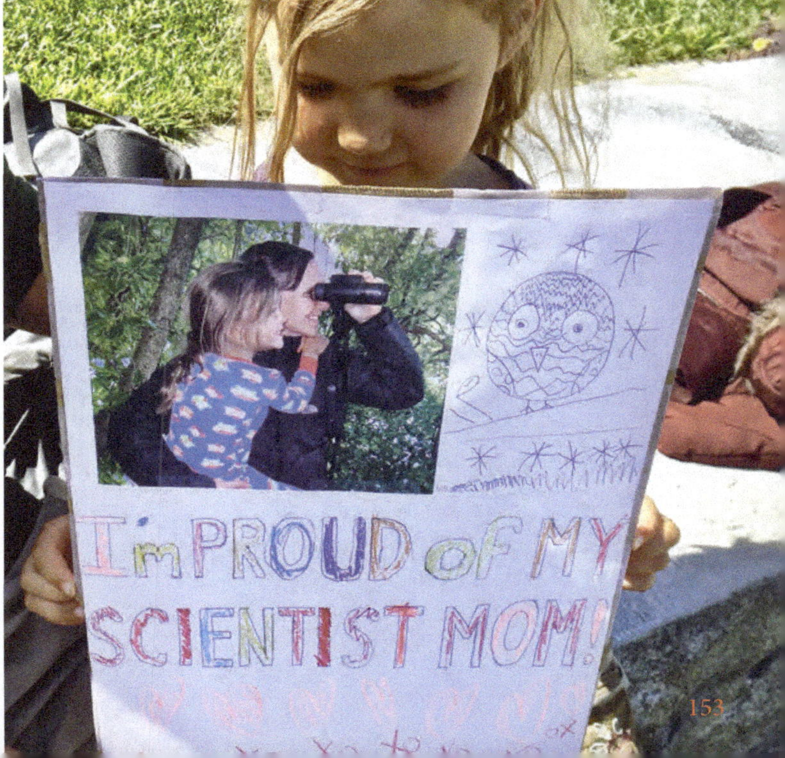

I'm PROUD of MY
SCIENTIST MOM!

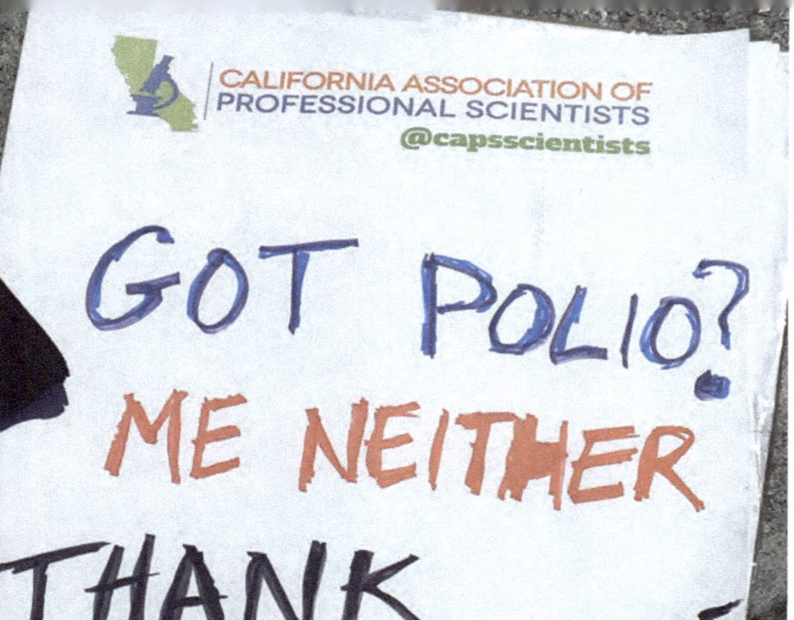
CALIFORNIA ASSOCIATION OF PROFESSIONAL SCIENTISTS
@capsscientists
GOT POLIO?
ME NEITHER
THANK SCIENCE

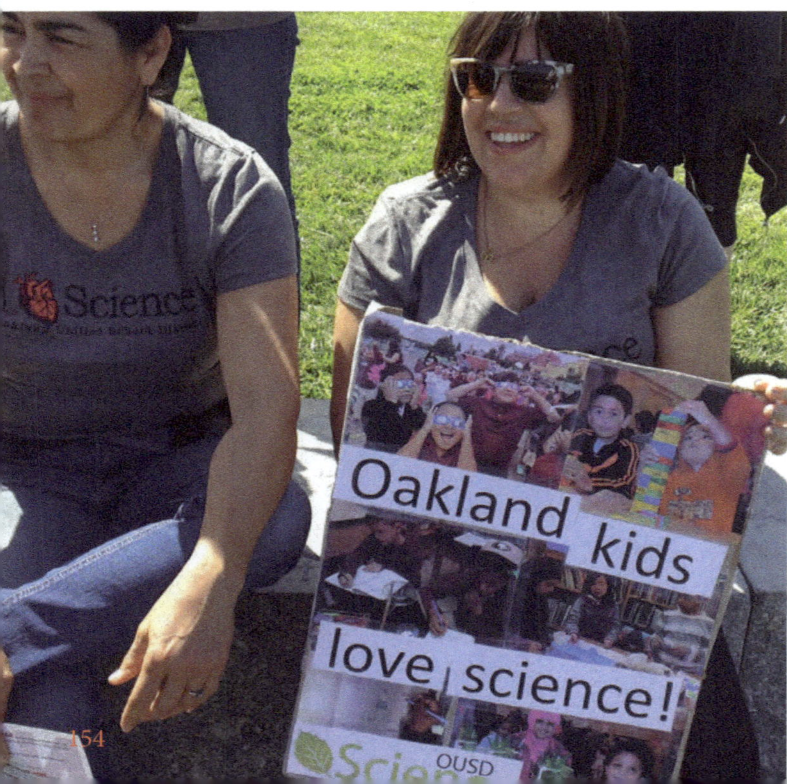
Science
Oakland kids
love science!
OUSD
Scien

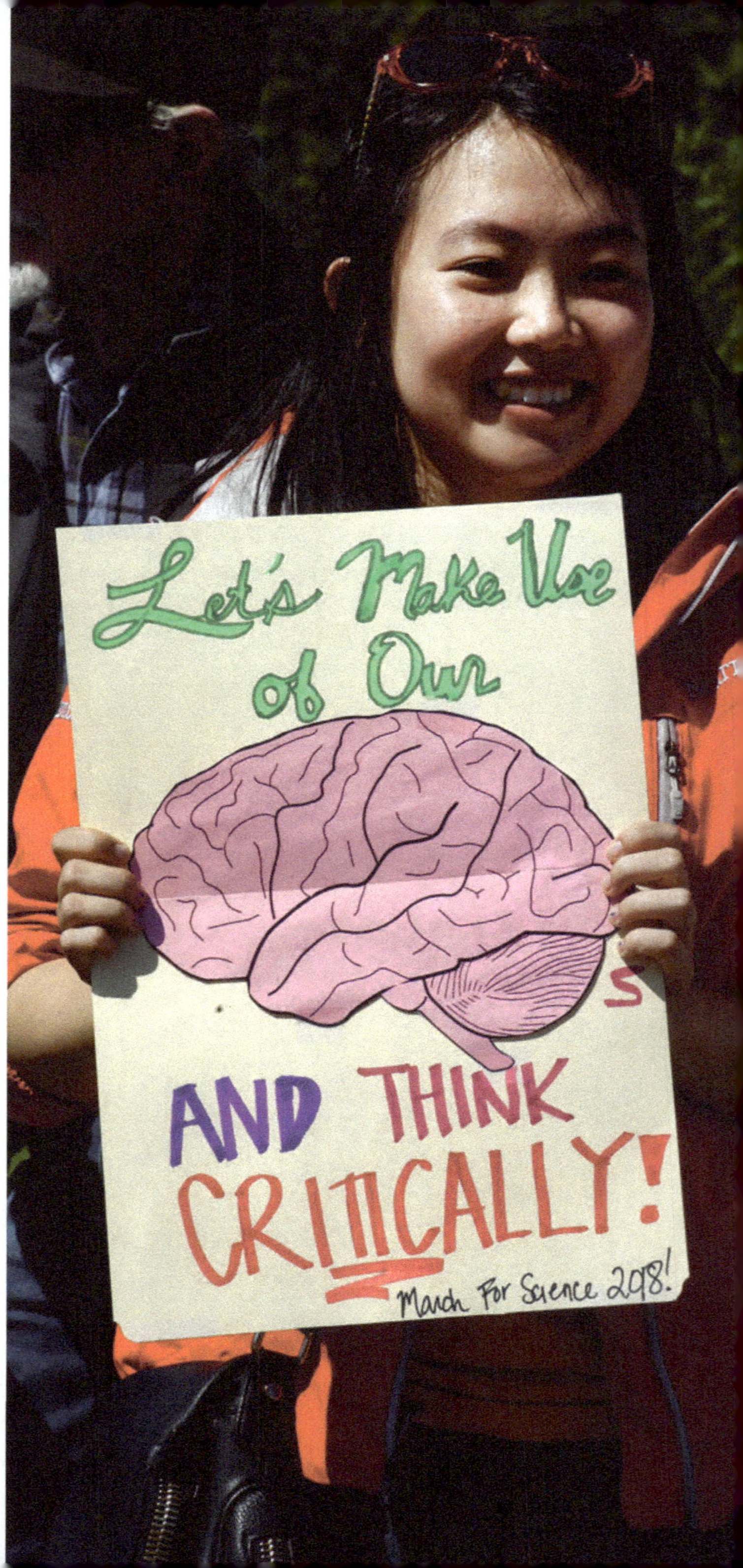

Let's Make Use of Our
AND THINK CRITICALLY!
March For Science 2018!

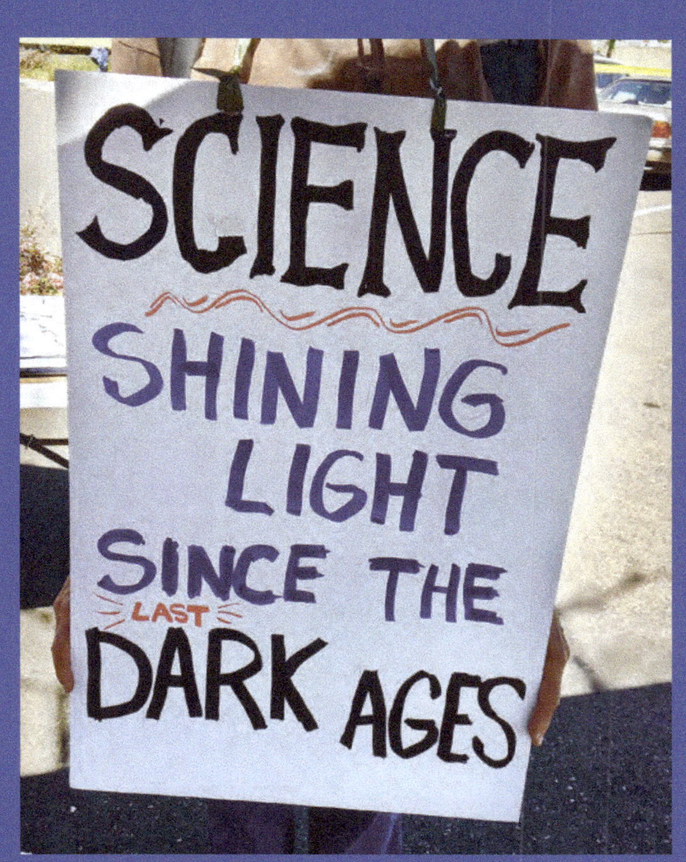
SCIENCE
SHINING
LIGHT
SINCE THE
LAST
DARK AGES

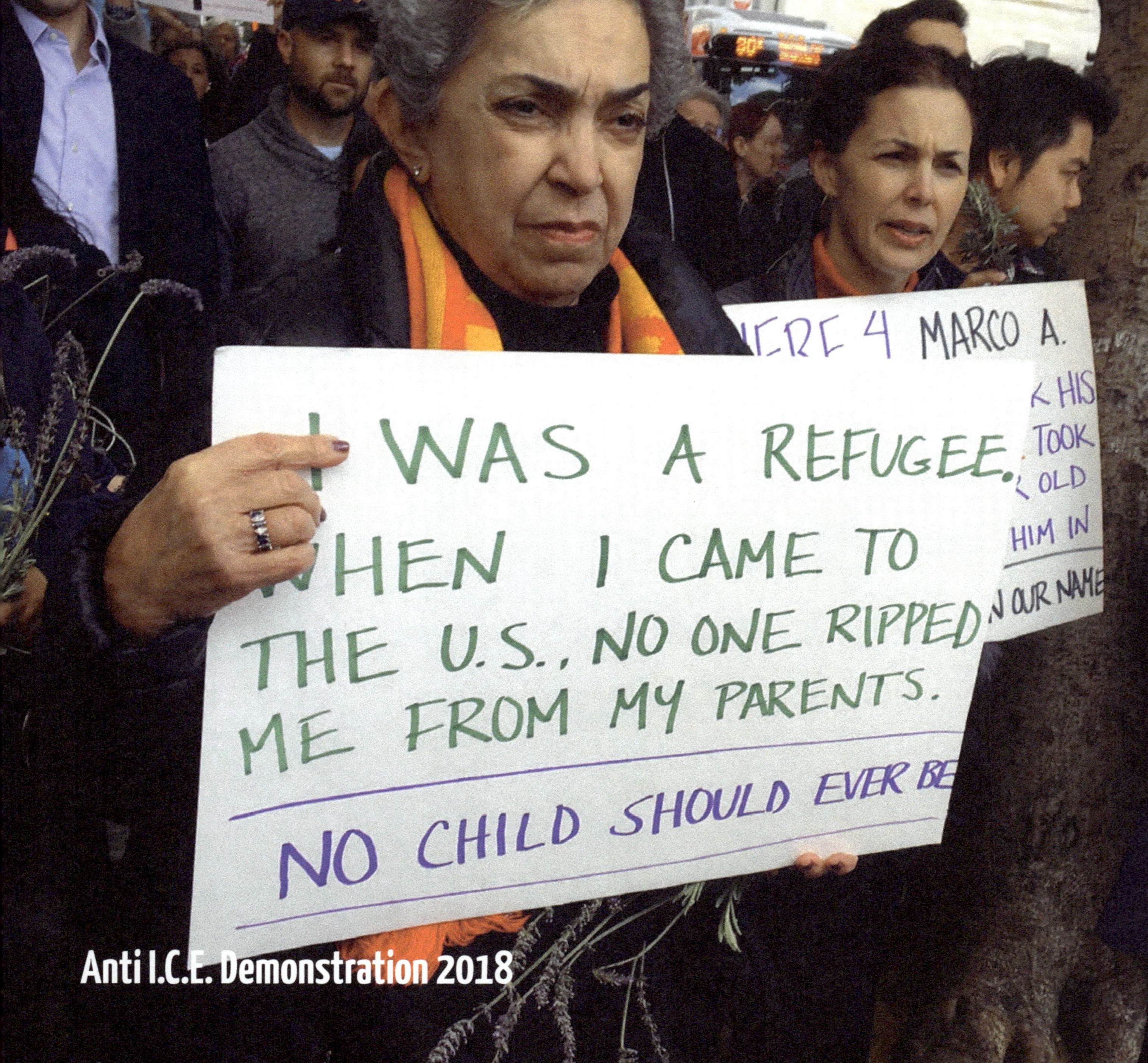

Anti I.C.E. Demonstration 2018

There was a spontaneous demonstration on June 15th in front of the I.C.E. offices in San Francisco. Demonstrators protested reports of jailed and caged children.

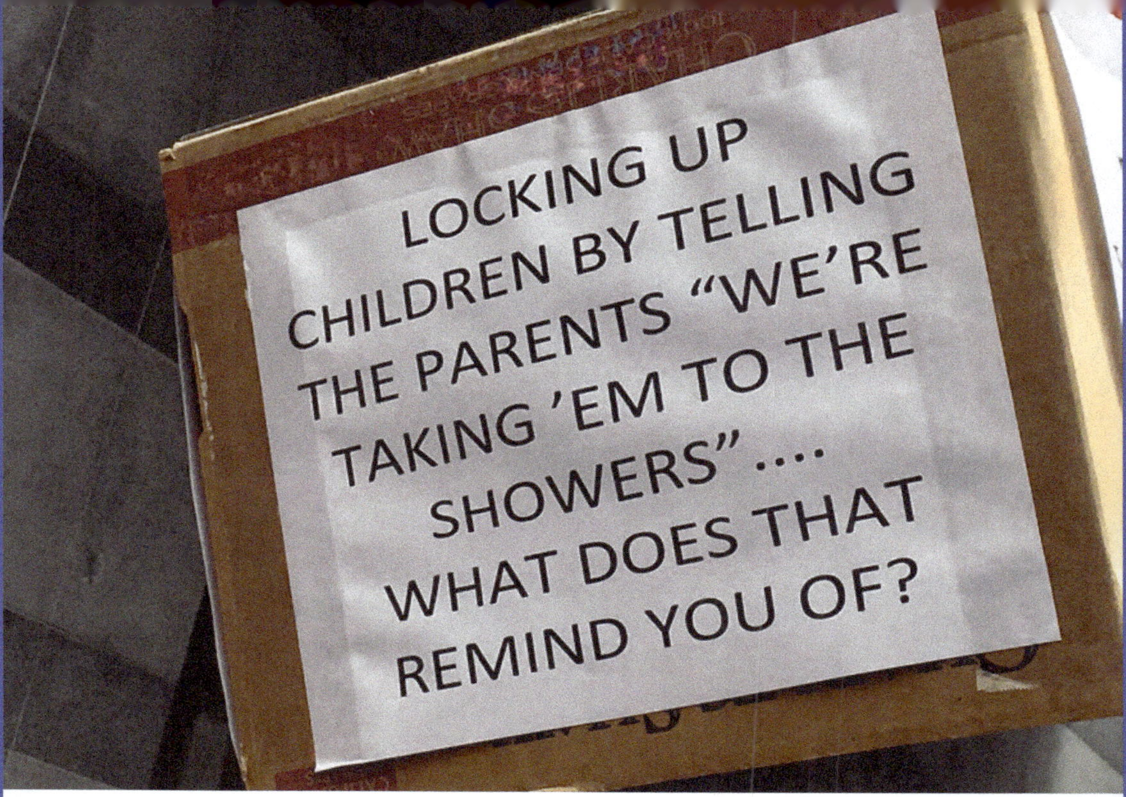

LOCKING UP
CHILDREN BY TELLING
THE PARENTS "WE'RE
TAKING 'EM TO THE
SHOWERS"....
WHAT DOES THAT
REMIND YOU OF?

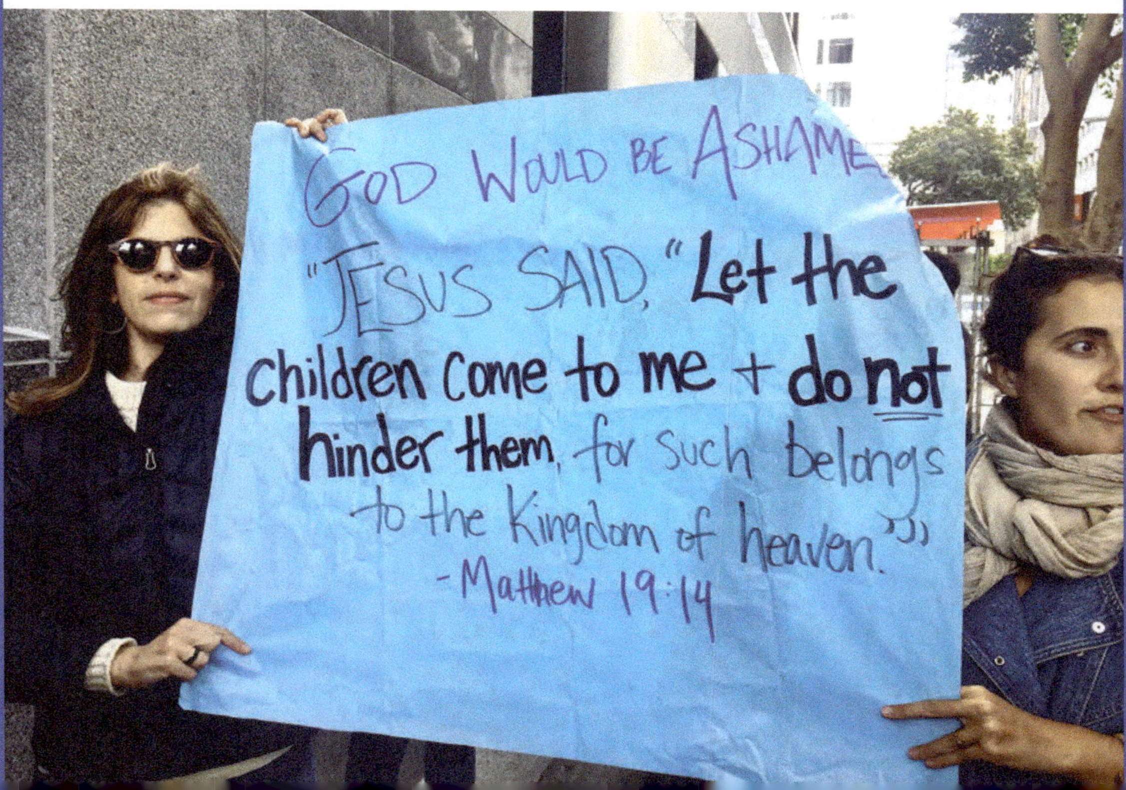

GOD WOULD BE ASHAMED
"JESUS SAID, "Let the
children come to me + do not
hinder them, for such belongs
to the kingdom of heaven."
- Matthew 19:14

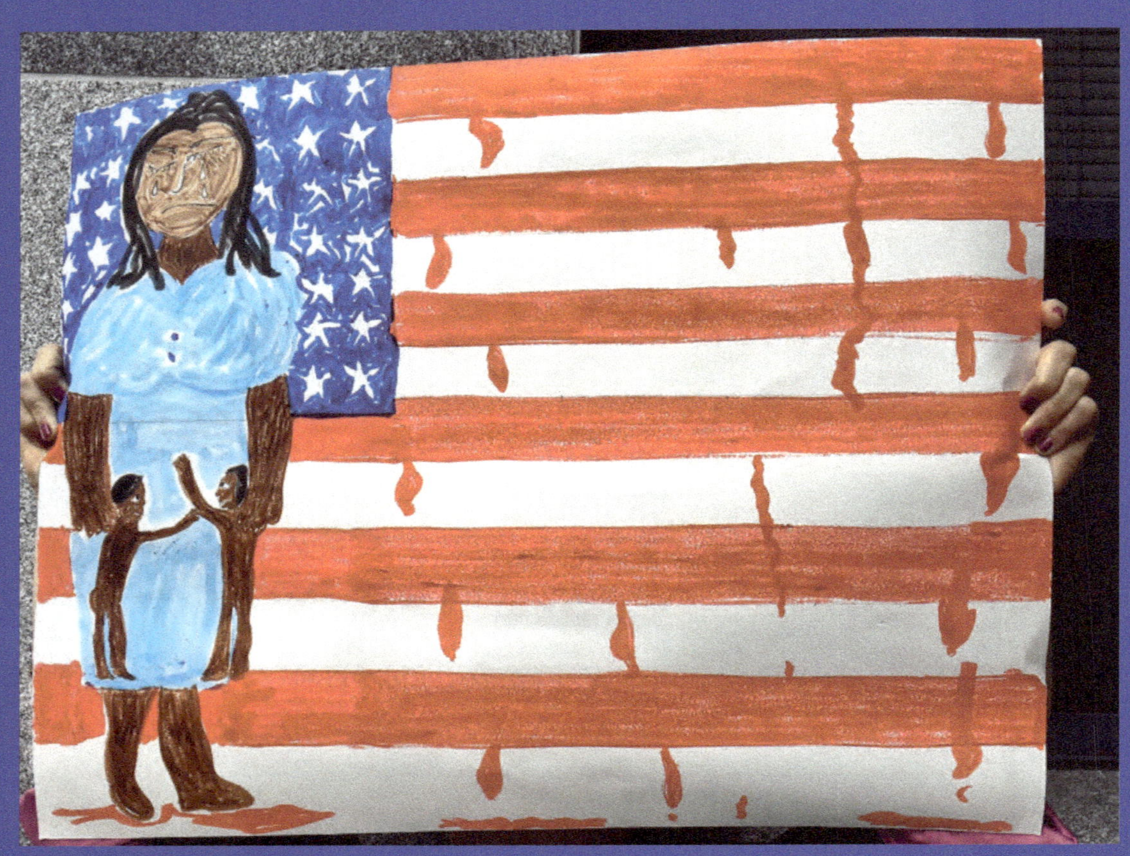

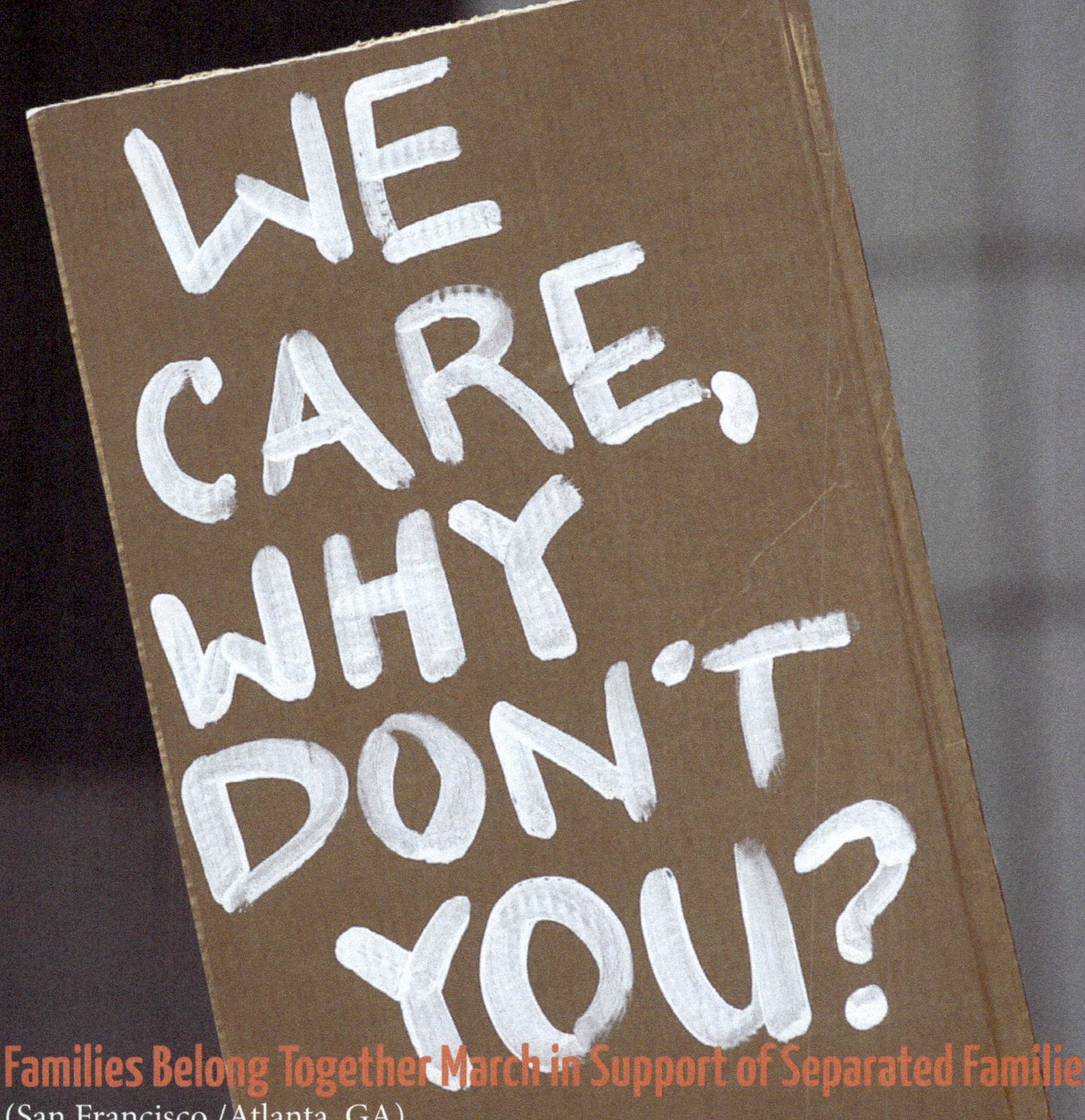

On June 30th, our daughter photographed the Resisters as they came out to express their outrage over trumps' hideously cruel order to imprison, deport, and separate immigrant families, some of them as young as 9 months old. My wife and I attended the march in Atlanta, GA.

HEY TRUMP
& SESSIONS !
You Are
DESCENDANTS
of
IMMIGRANTS

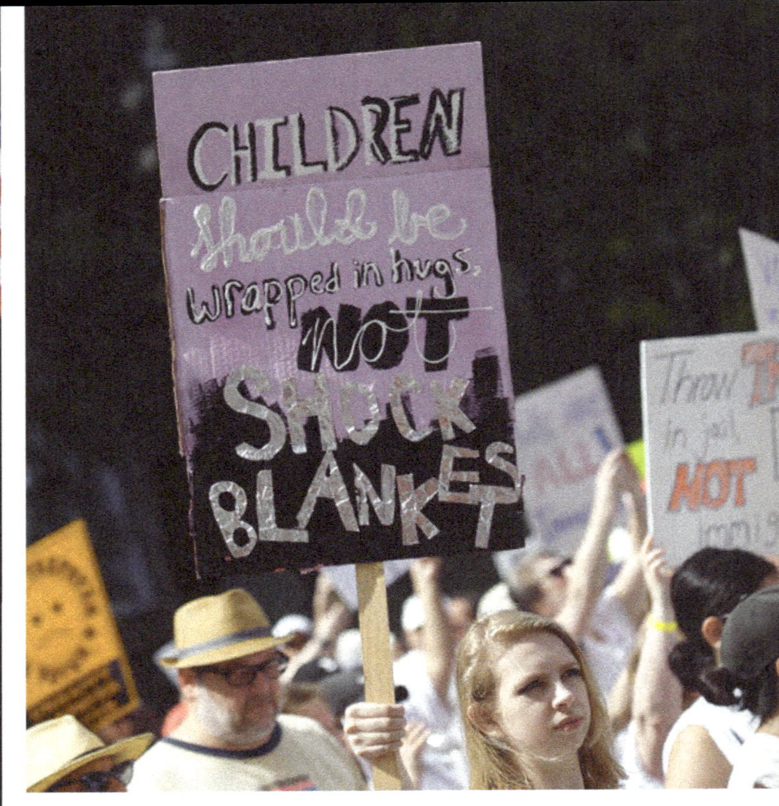

CHILDREN
should be
wrapped in hugs,
NOT
SHOCK
BLANKETS

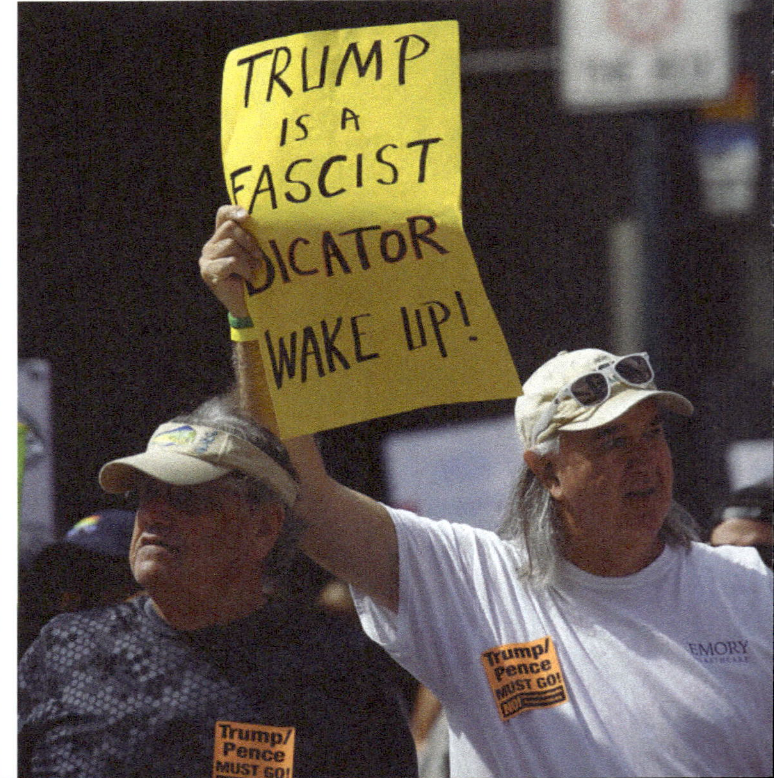

TRUMP
IS A
FASCIST
DICATOR
WAKE UP!
Trump/
Pence
MUST GO!
EMORY

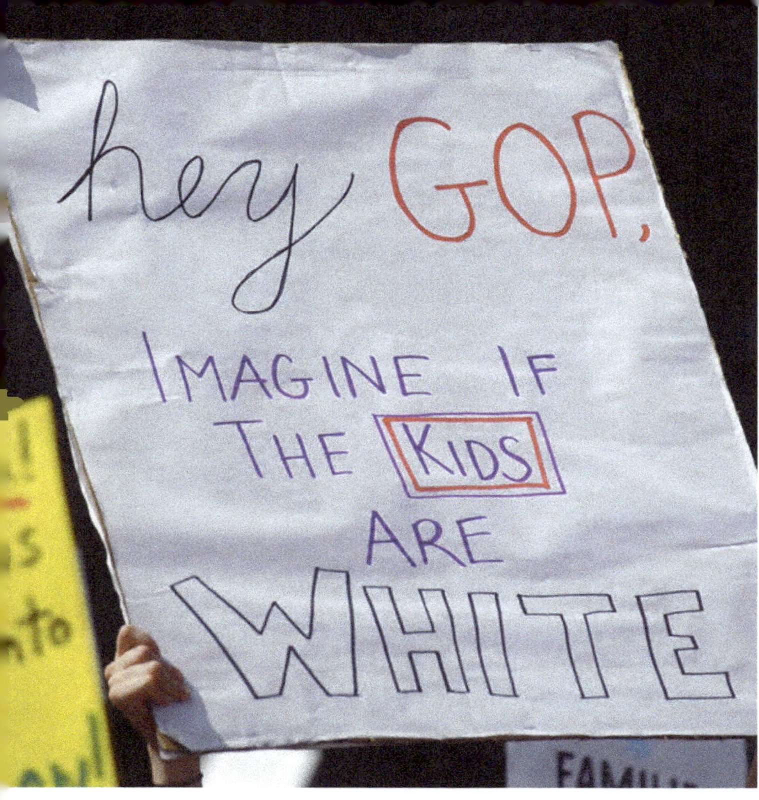
hey GOP,
IMAGINE IF THE KIDS ARE WHITE

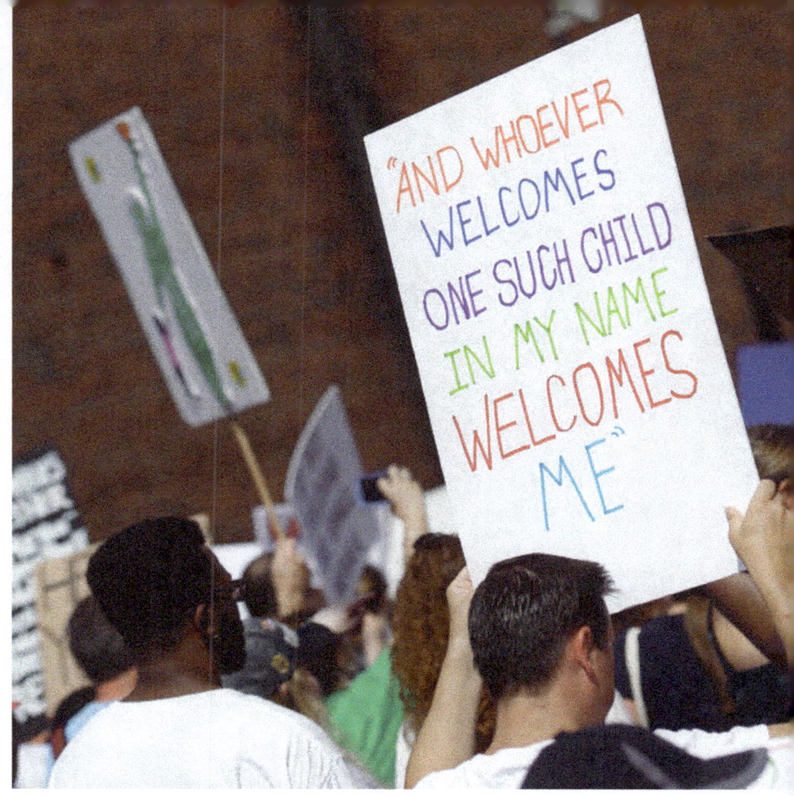
"AND WHOEVER WELCOMES ONE SUCH CHILD IN MY NAME WELCOMES ME"

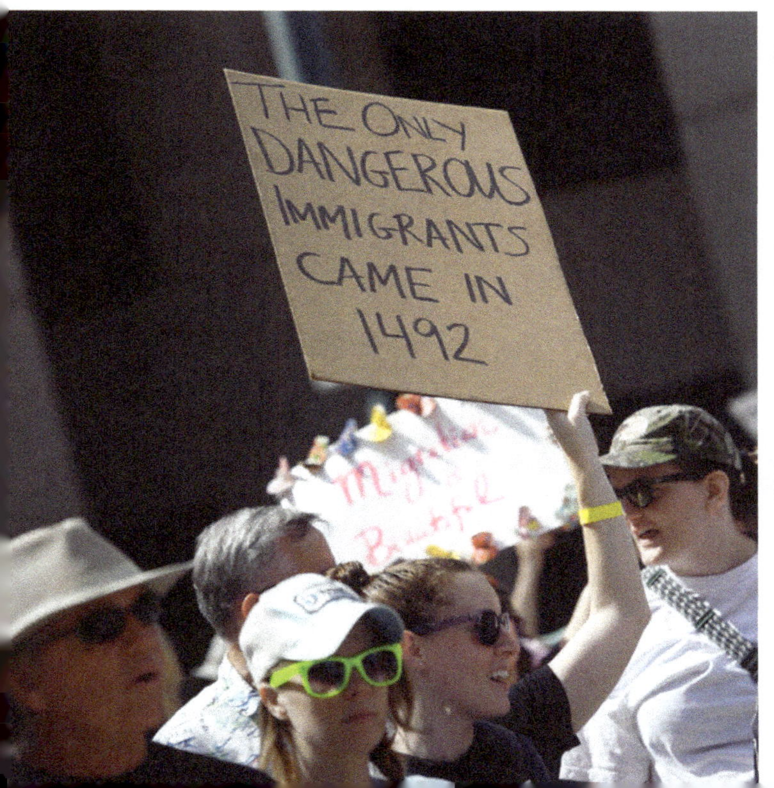
THE ONLY DANGEROUS IMMIGRANTS CAME IN 1492

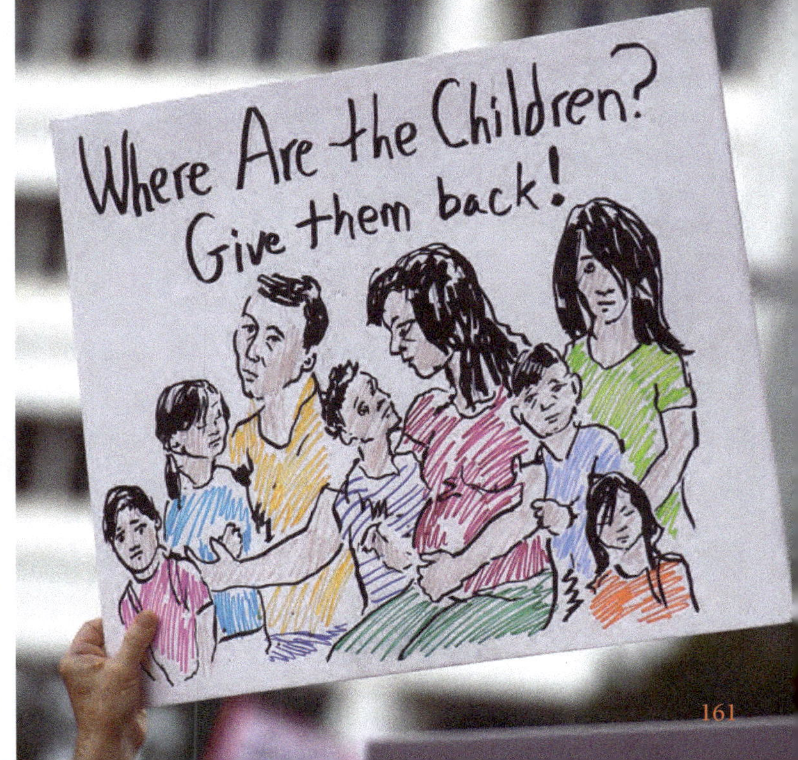
Where Are the Children? Give them back!

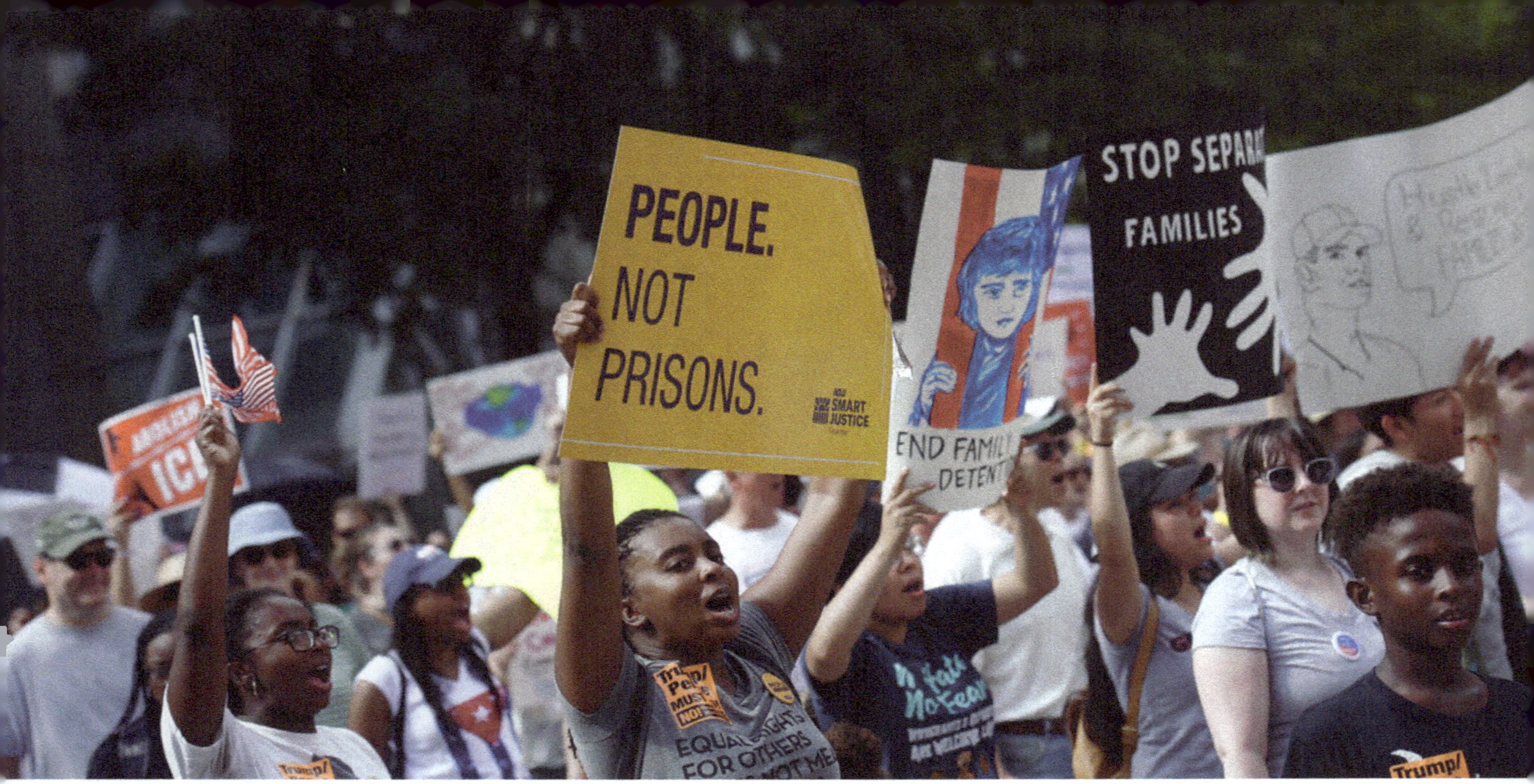

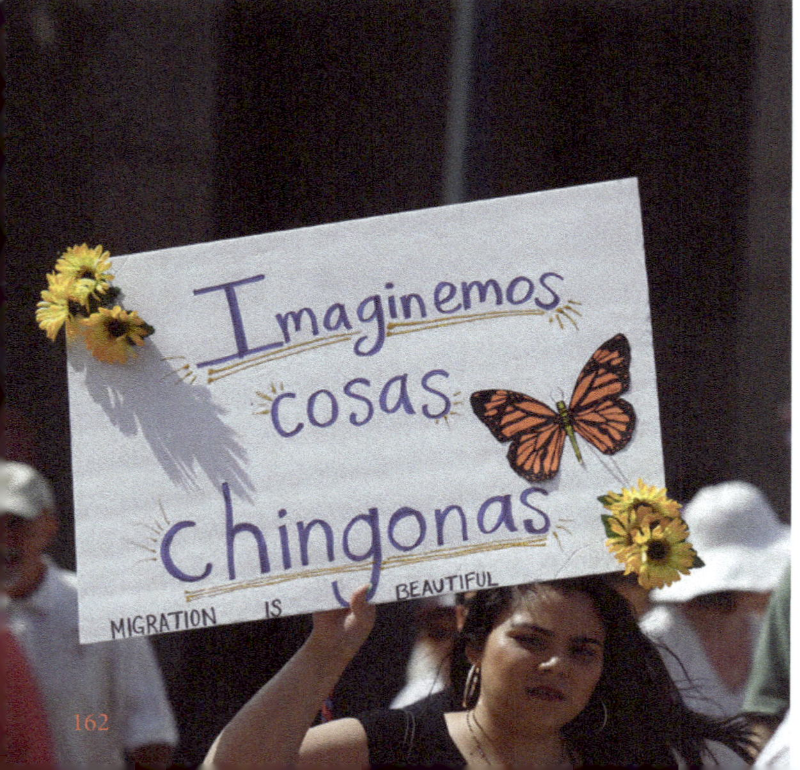
Imaginemos cosas chingonas
MIGRATION IS BEAUTIFUL

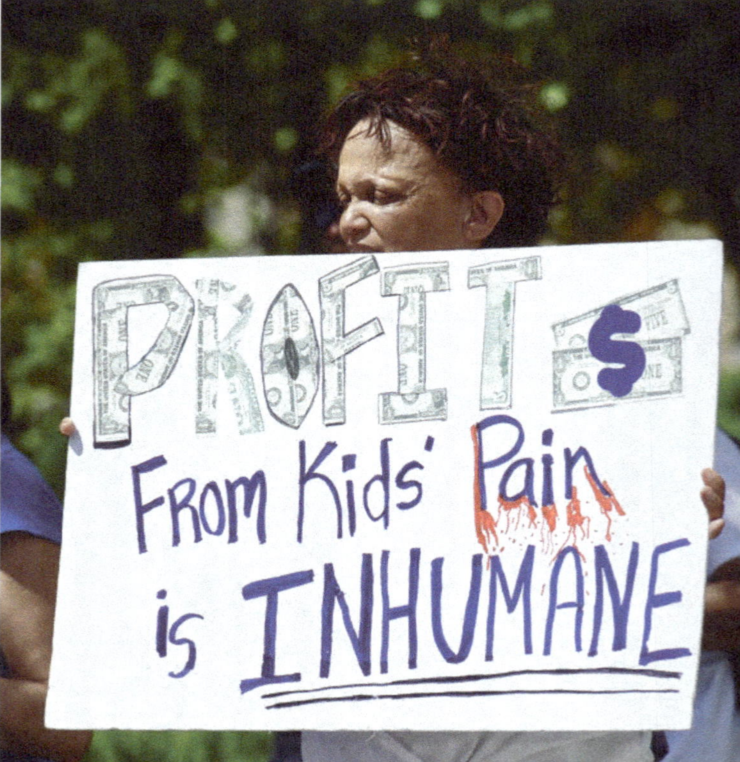
PROFIT$
From Kids' Pain
is INHUMANE

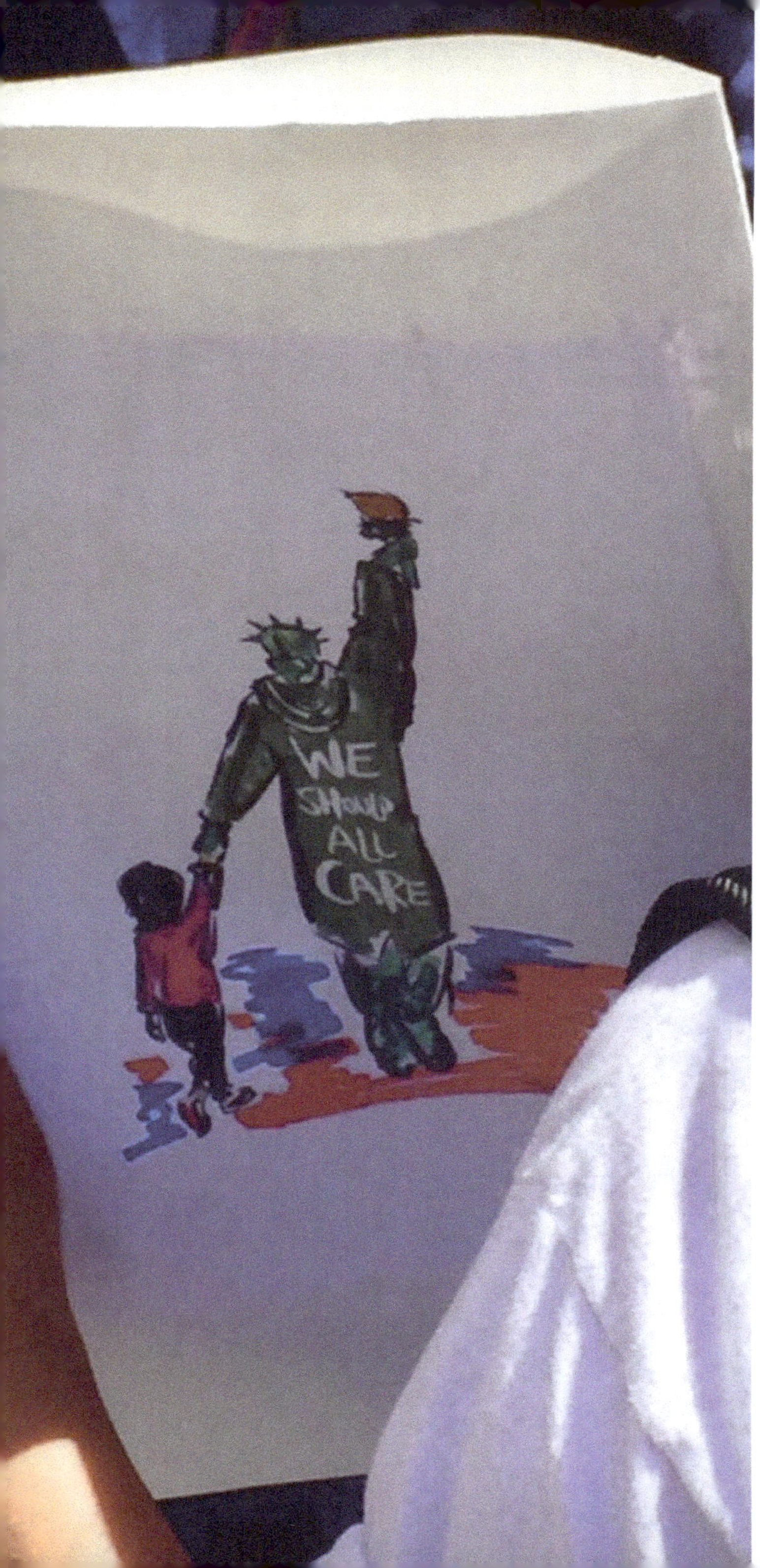

WE
SHOULD
ALL
CARE

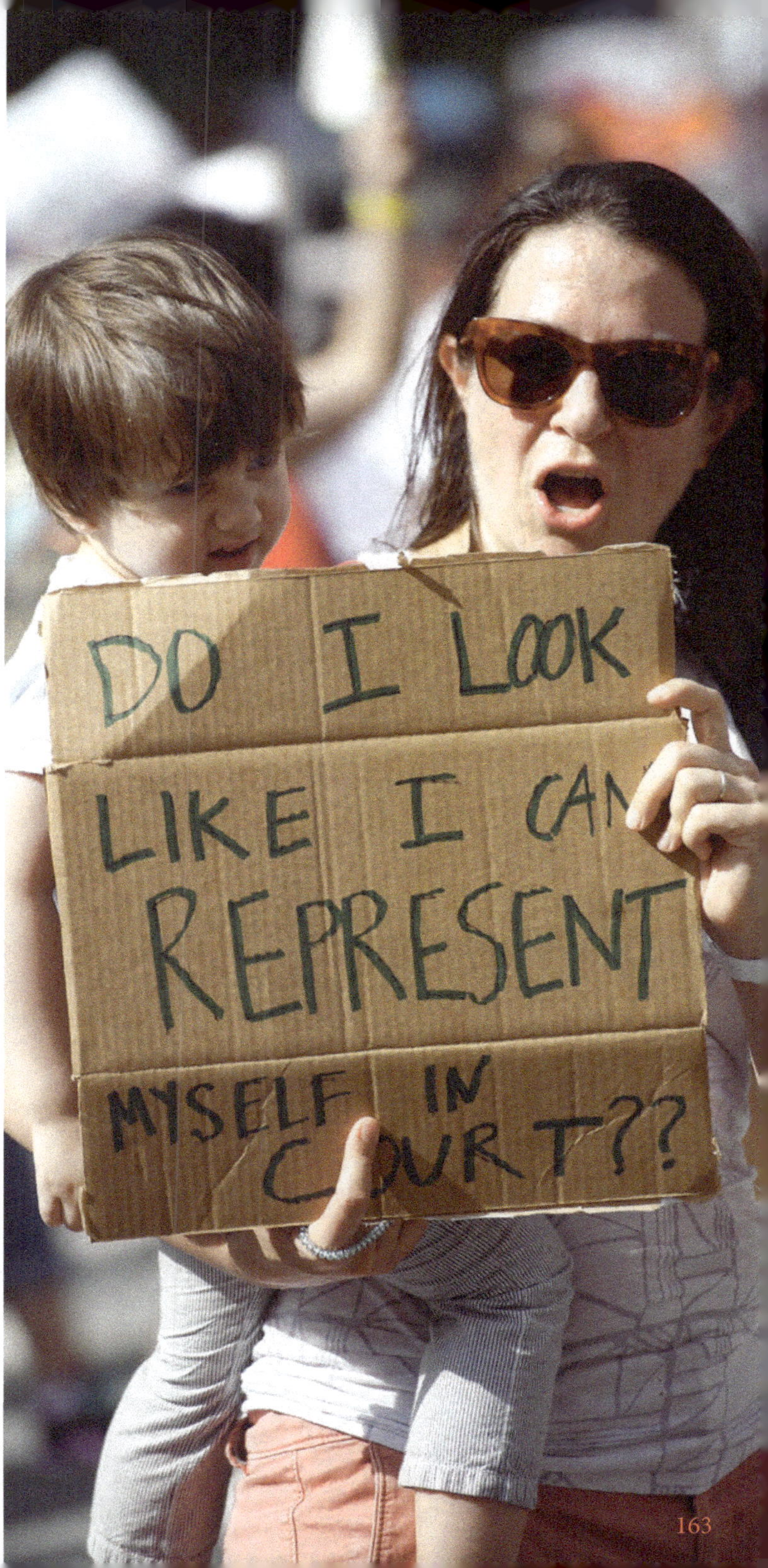

DO I LOOK
LIKE I CAN
REPRESENT
MYSELF IN
COURT??

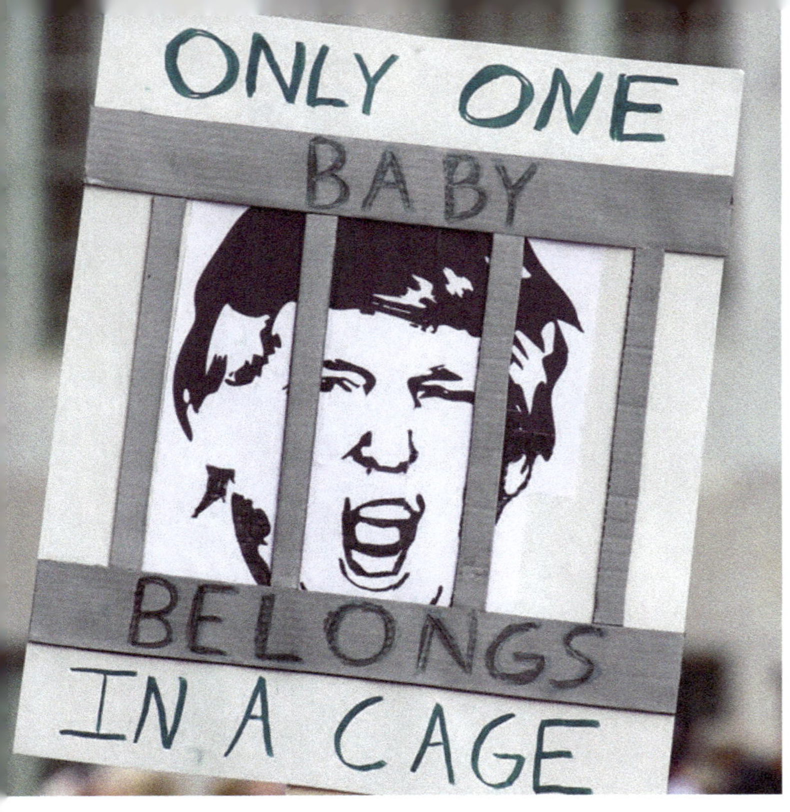

ONLY ONE
BABY
BELONGS
IN A CAGE

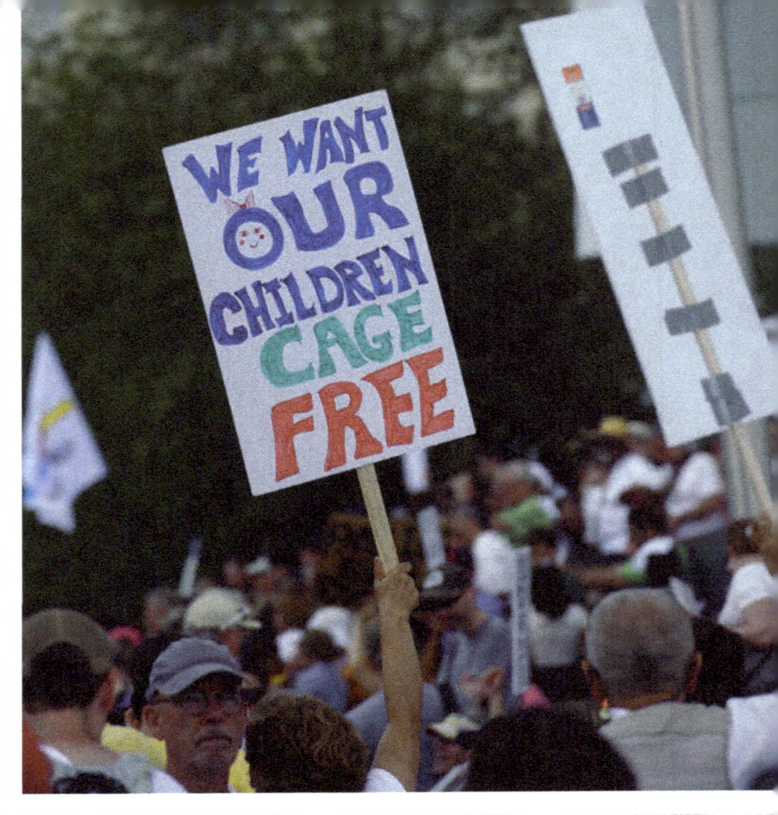

WE WANT
OUR
CHILDREN
CAGE
FREE

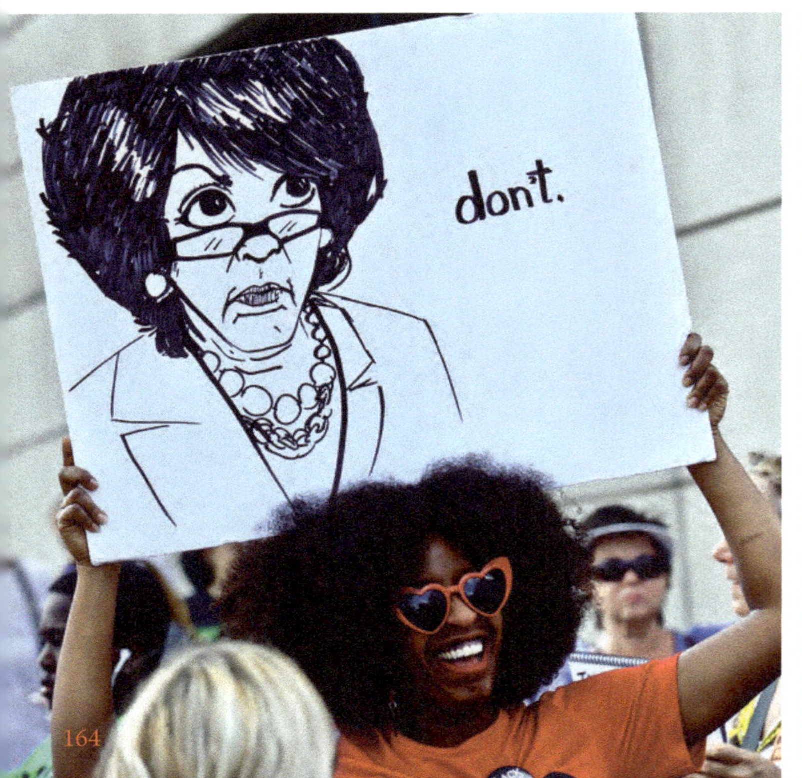

don't.

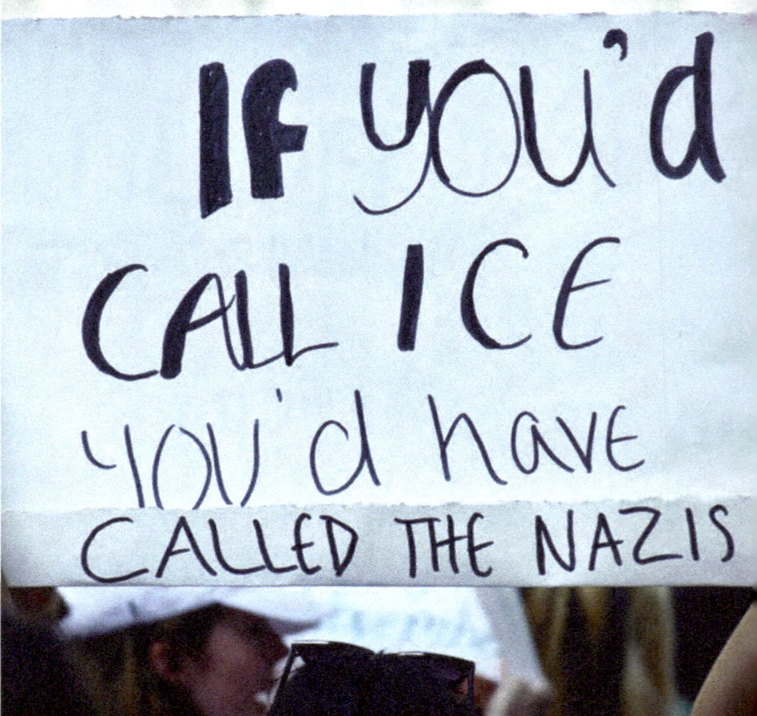

IF YOU'd
CALL ICE
YOU'd have
CALLED THE NAZIS

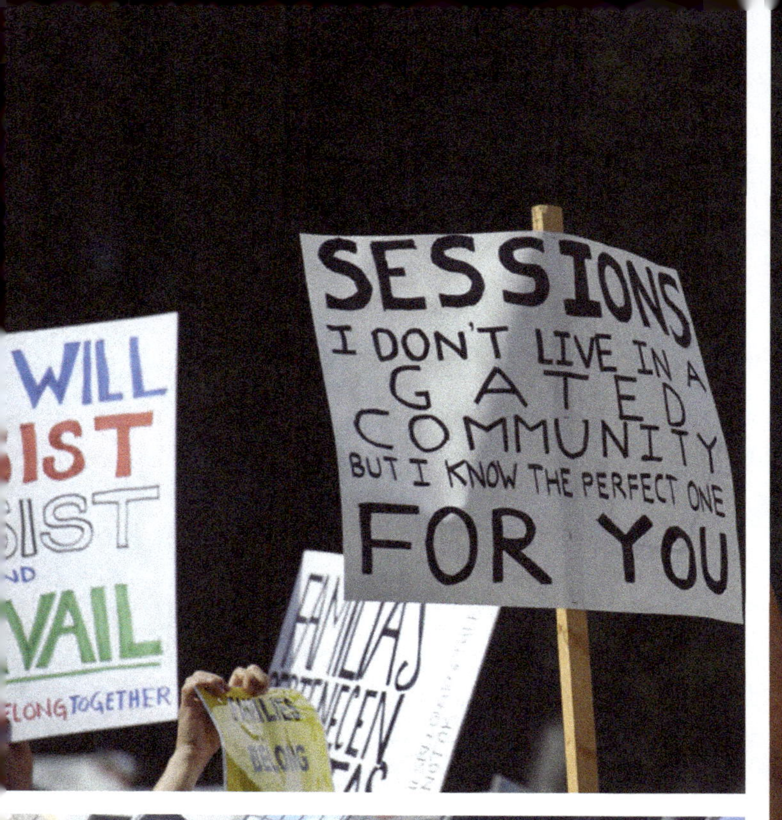
WILL
SIST
VAIL
BELONG TOGETHER
SESSIONS
I DON'T LIVE IN A
GATED
COMMUNITY
BUT I KNOW THE PERFECT ONE
FOR YOU
FAMILIAS
BELONG

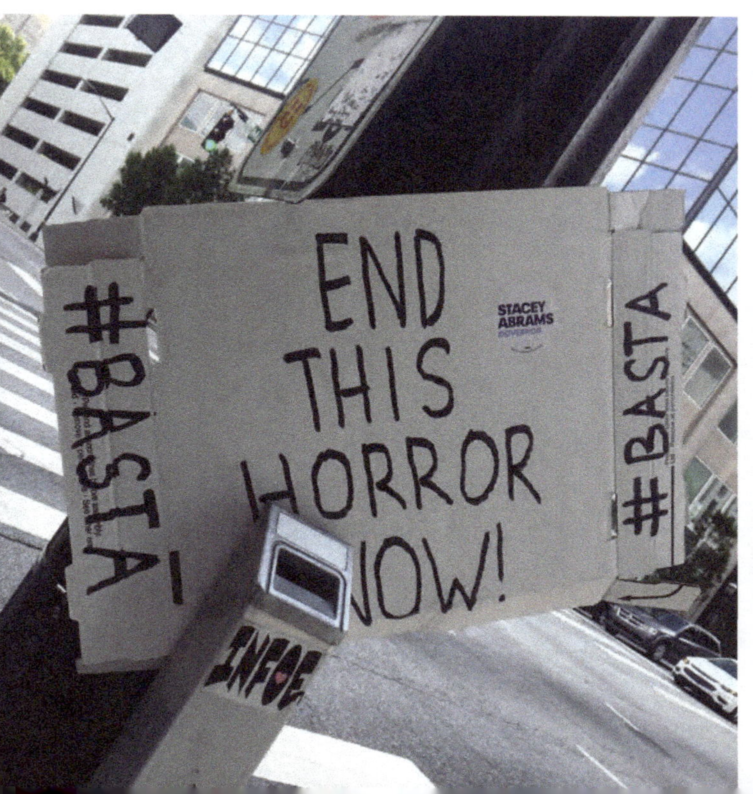
#BASTA
END
THIS
HORROR
NOW!
#BASTA
STACEY
ABRAMS
GOVERNOR

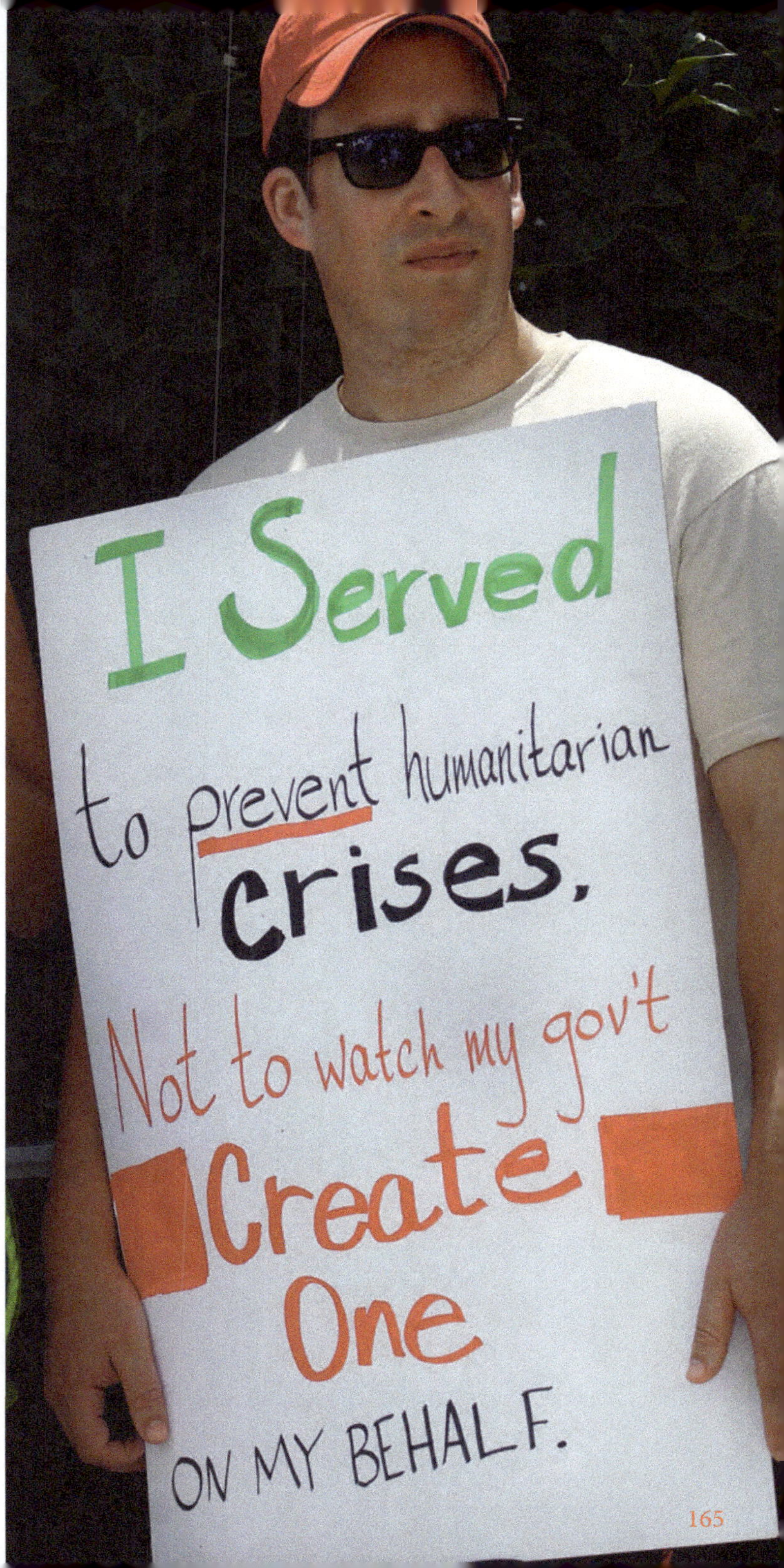

I Served
to prevent humanitarian
crises,
Not to watch my gov't
Create
One
ON MY BEHALF.

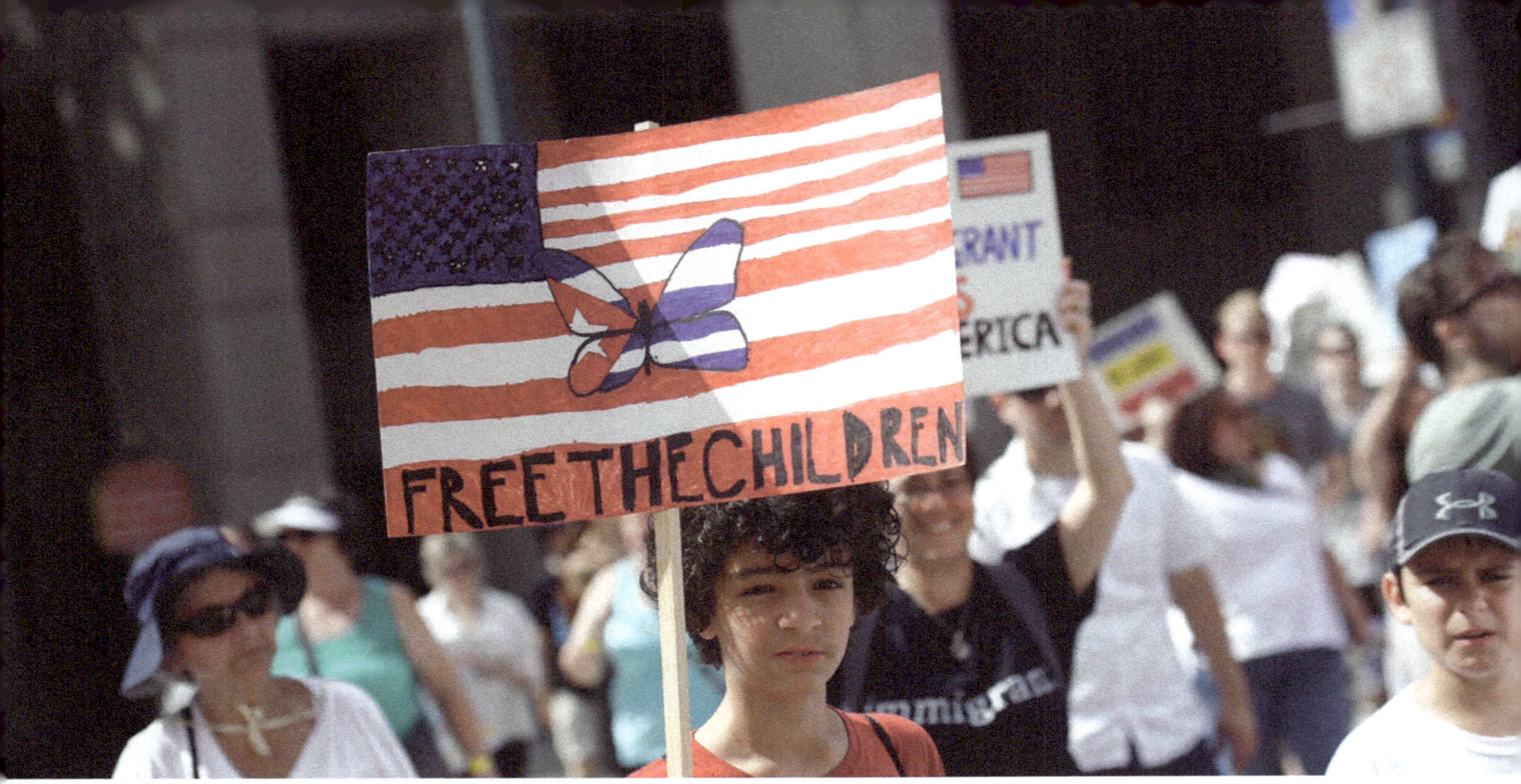

FREE THE CHILDREN
...WAIT! 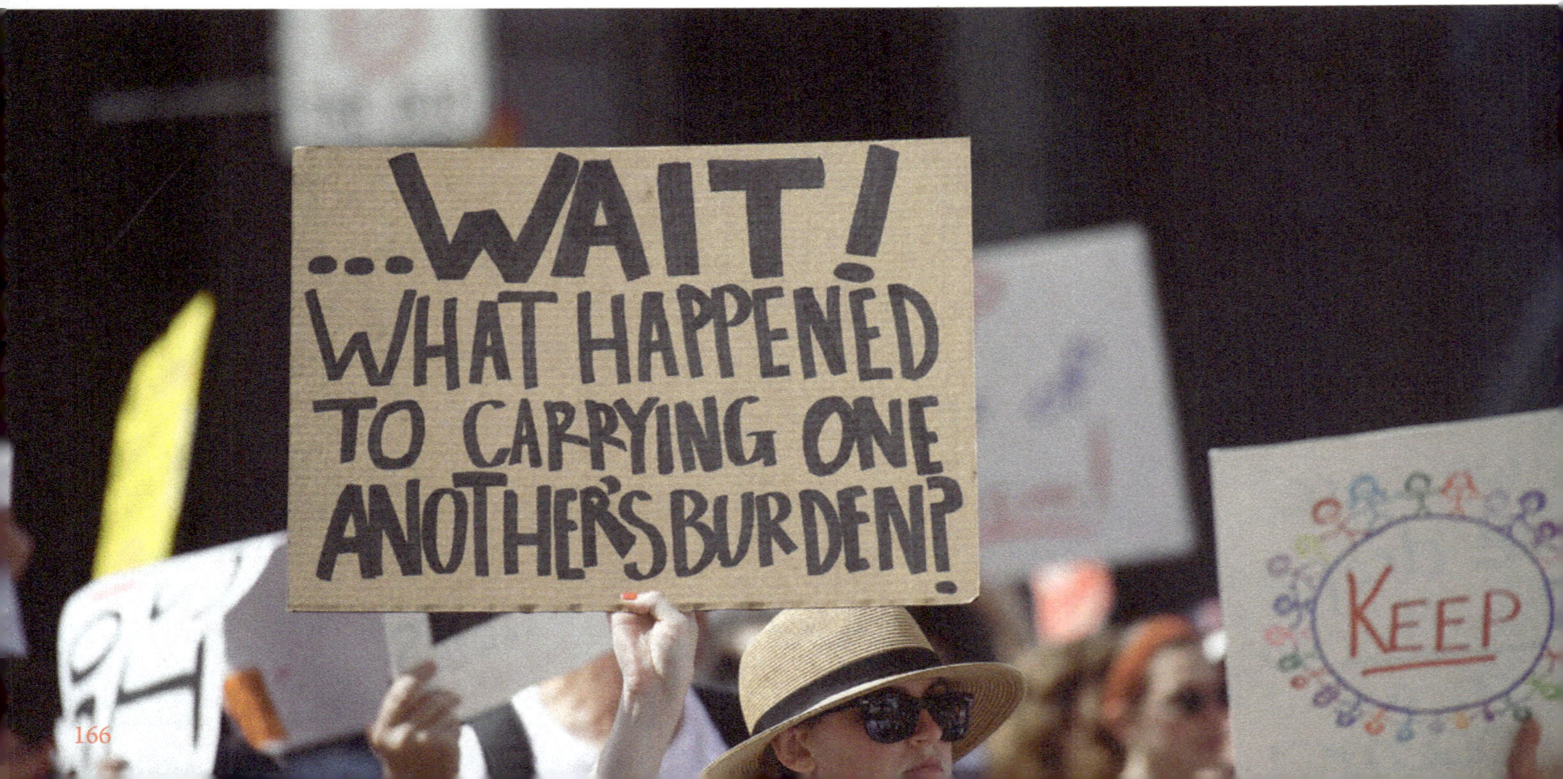
WHAT HAPPENED
TO CARRYING ONE
ANOTHER'S BURDEN?
KEEP

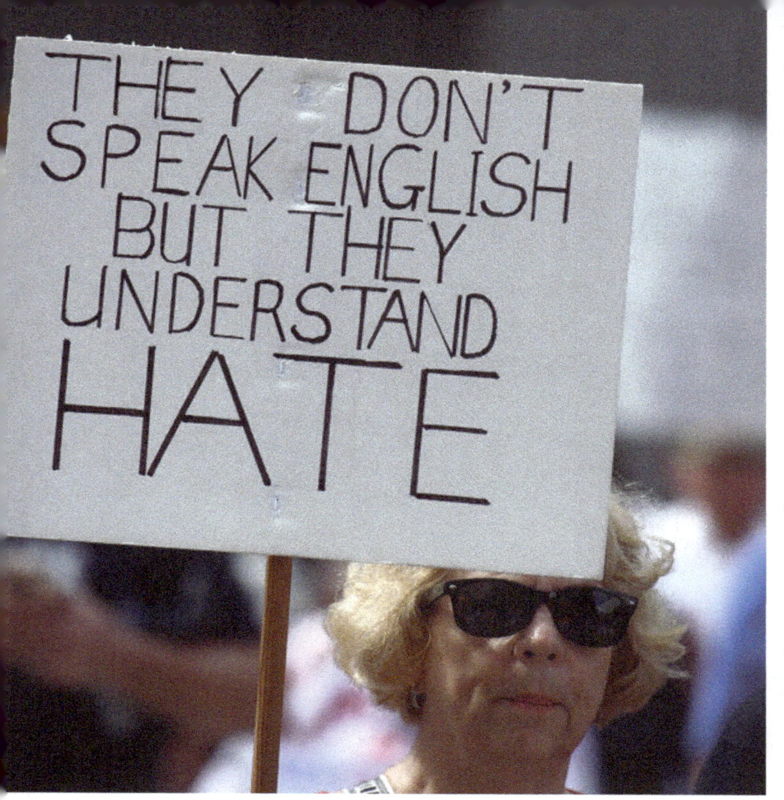

THEY DON'T SPEAK ENGLISH BUT THEY UNDERSTAND HATE

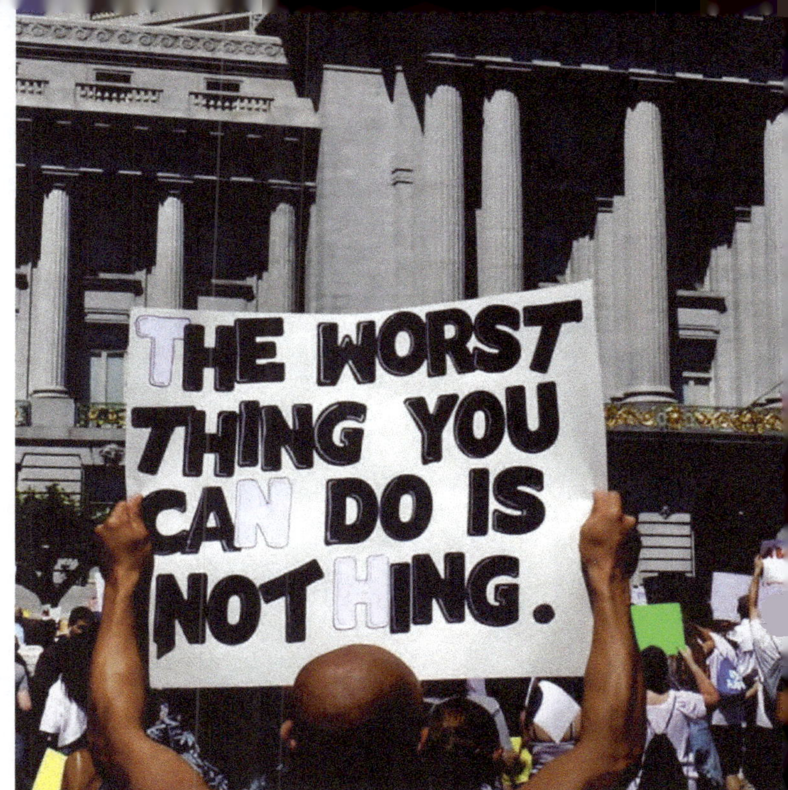

THE WORST THING YOU CAN DO IS NOTHING.

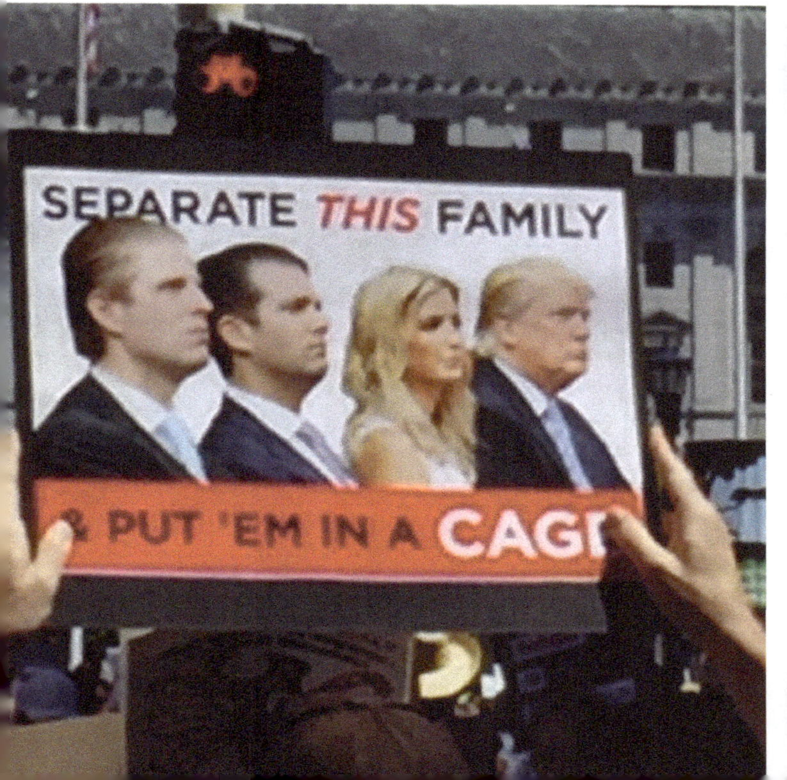

SEPARATE THIS FAMILY
& PUT 'EM IN A CAGE

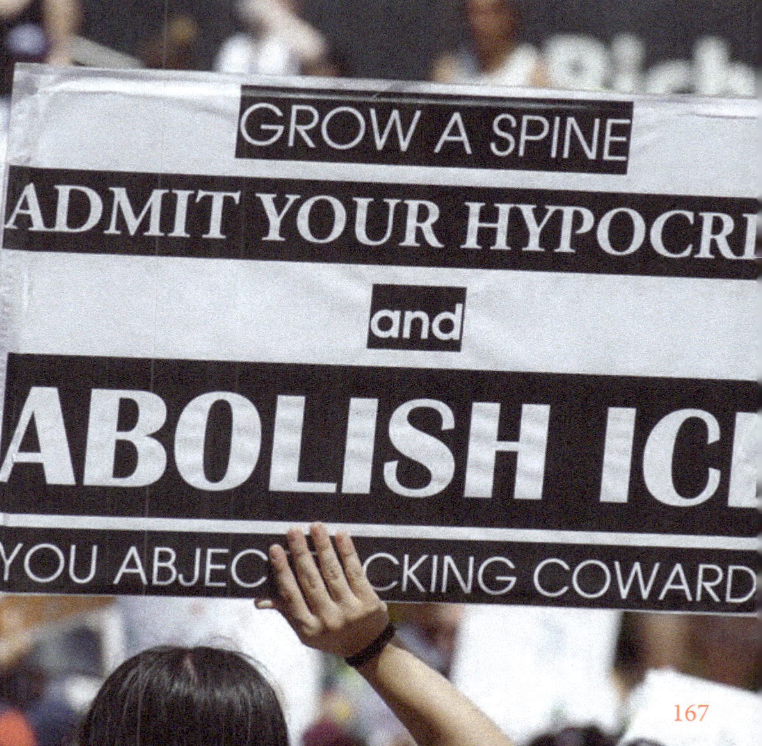

GROW A SPINE
ADMIT YOUR HYPOCRI
and
ABOLISH ICE
YOU ABJEC CKING COWARD

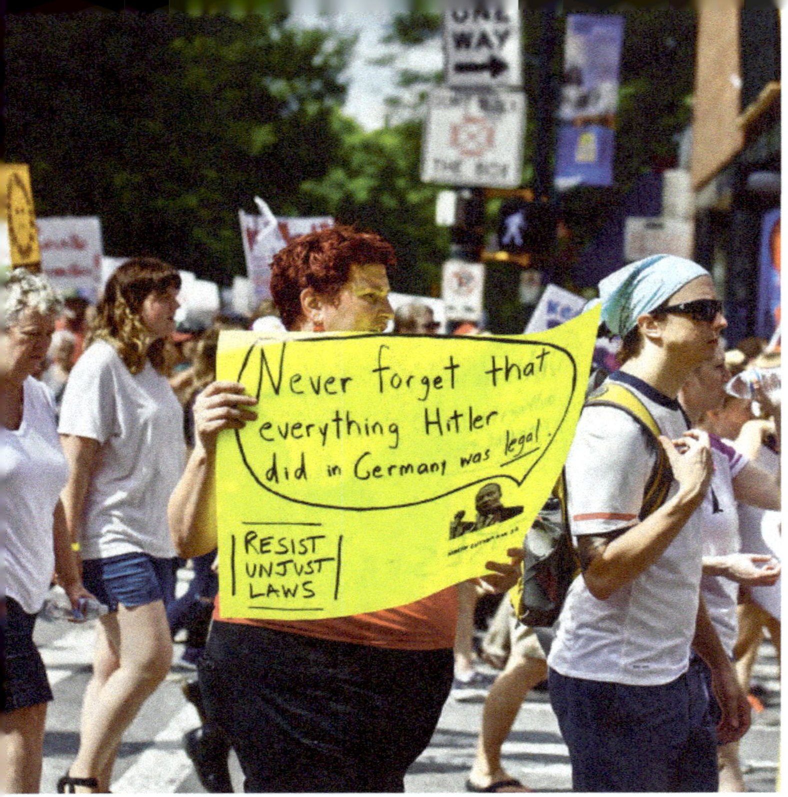
Never forget that everything Hitler did in Germany was legal.
RESIST UNJUST LAWS

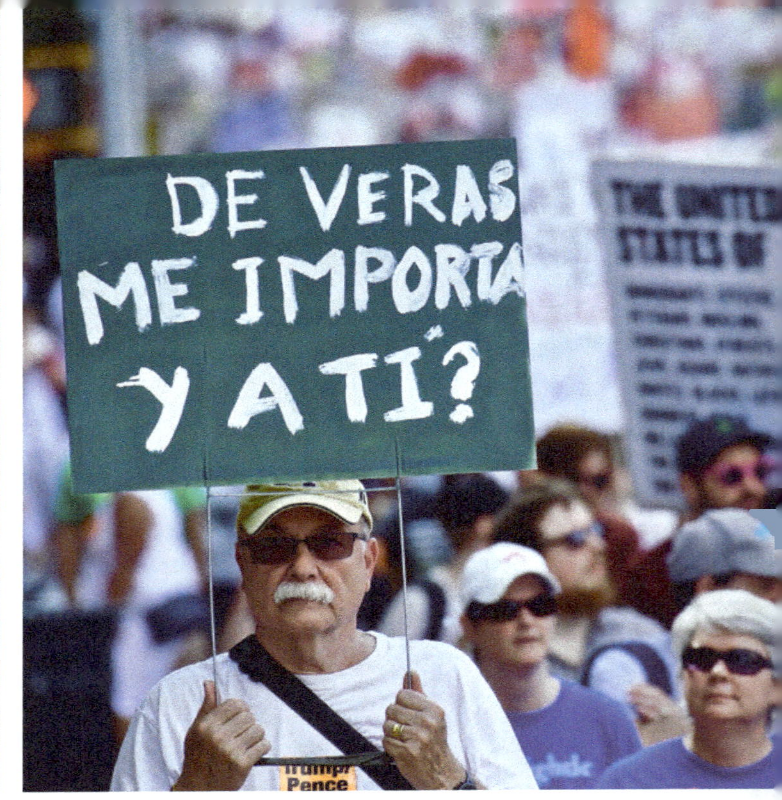
DE VERAS ME IMPORTA Y A TI?
THE UNITED STATES OF

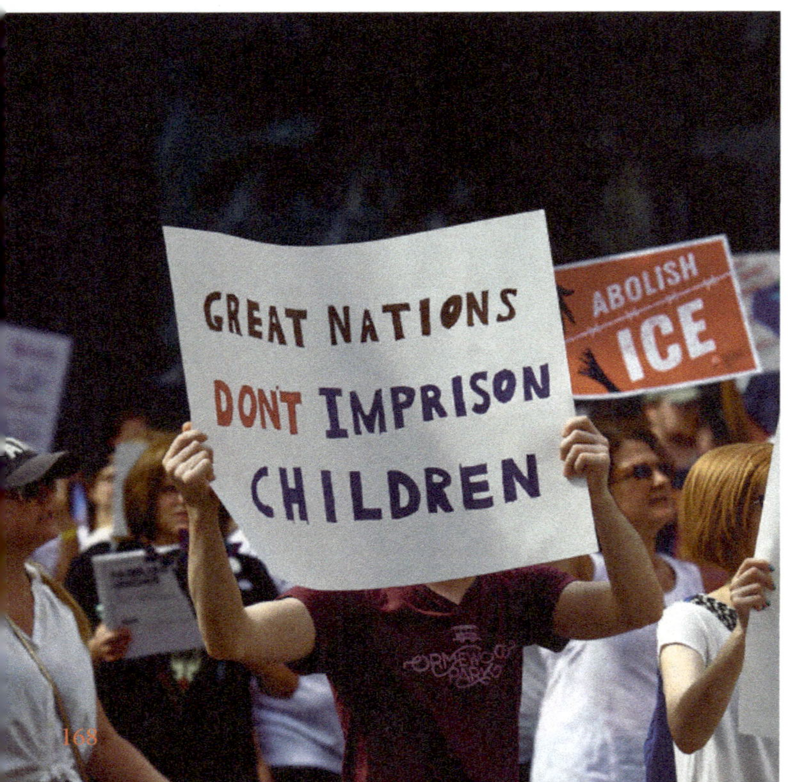
GREAT NATIONS DON'T IMPRISON CHILDREN
ABOLISH ICE

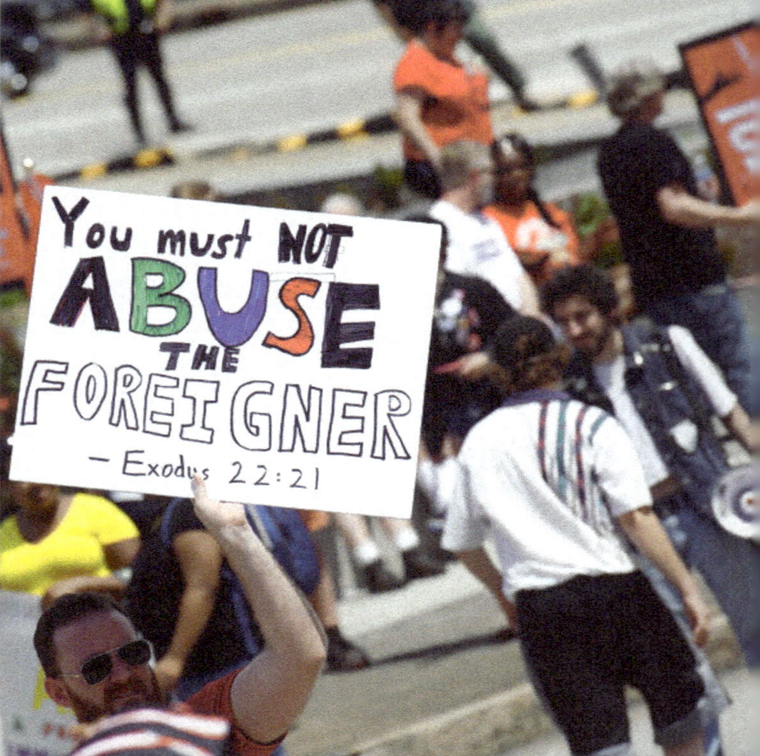
You must NOT ABUSE THE FOREIGNER
- Exodus 22:21

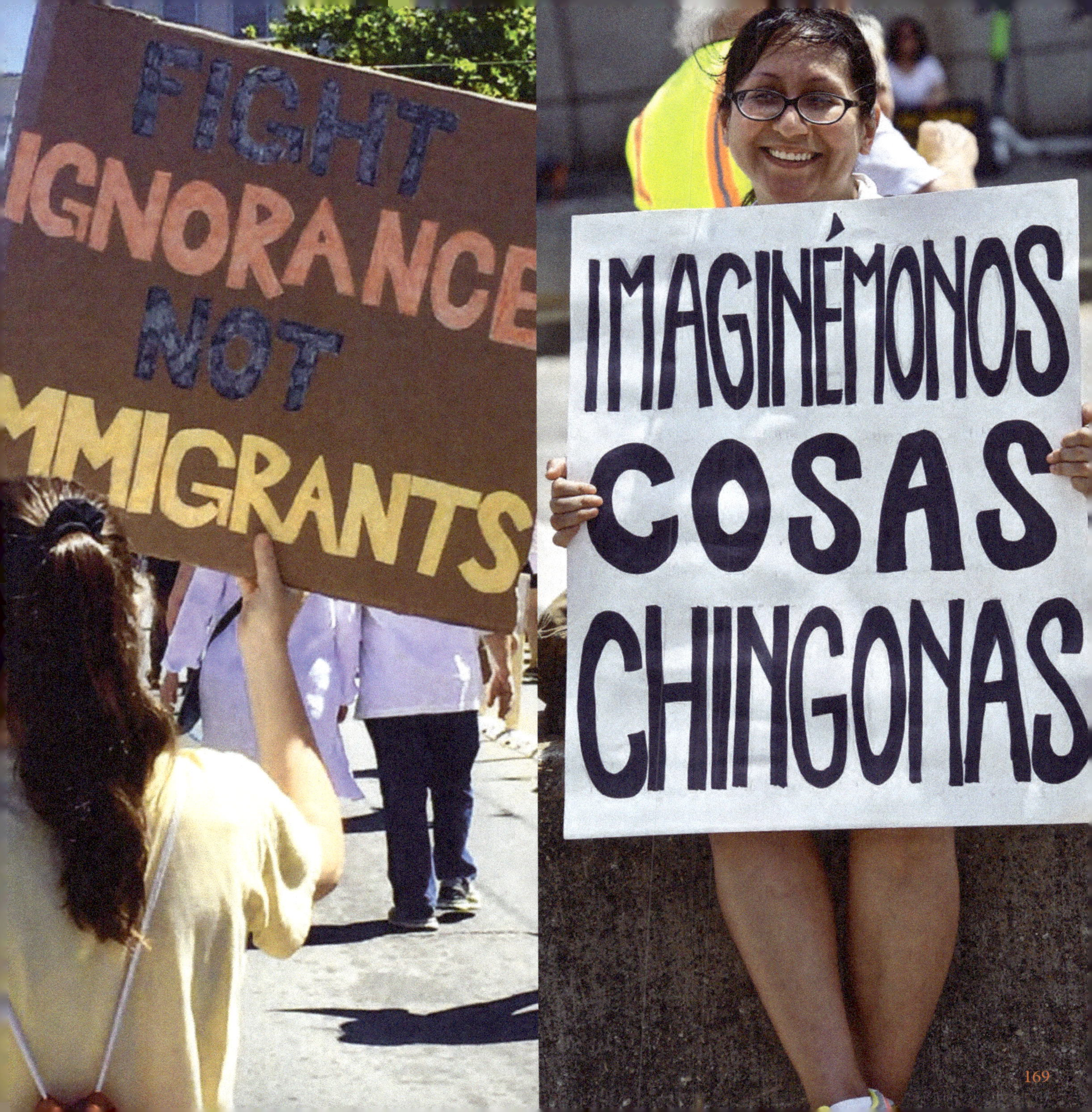

FIGHT
IGNORANCE
NOT
IMMIGRANTS
IMAGINÉMONOS
COSAS
CHINGONAS

Epilogue

I end *Love Letters to trump* with photographs of two beautiful children. For most people, children give us hope. However, I wonder what we have given them.

We as adults have used a tremendous amount of resources throughout our lives: natural, human and financial. What have we left them?

Will they figure out that some adults didn't leave them with much? Will they further discover that some adults have taken no responsibility to replenish what they've consumed or destroyed?

Embedded within each dying generation are builders and takers. On the preceding pages, they have been introduced to some of the builders.

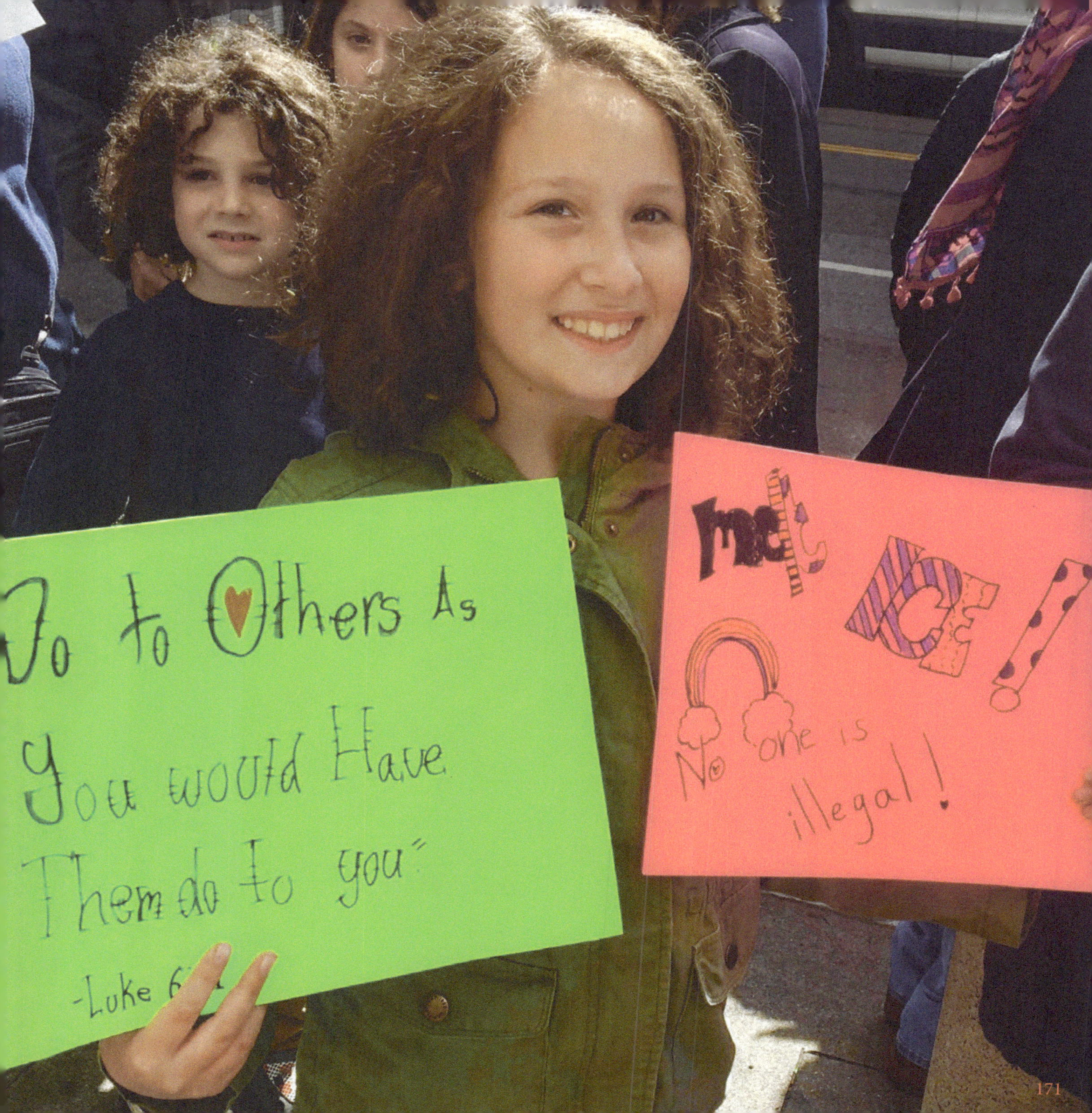

Do to Others As
You would Have
Them do to you."
-Luke 6:
melt ICE!!
No one is
illegal!

CPSIA information can be obtained
at www.ICGtesting.com
Printed in the USA
LVHW072303050119
602509LV00001B/4/P

9 780692 199206